The Nature of Insight

The Nature of Insight

edited by Robert J. Sternberg and Janet E. Davidson

A Bradford Book
The MIT Press
Cambridge, Massachusetts
London, England

This book was set in Trump Mediaeval by Asco Trade Typesetting Ltd., Hong Kong and was printed and bound in the United States of America.

Library of Congress Cataloging-in-Publication Data

The Nature of insight / edited by Robert J. Sternberg and Janet Davidson.
   p. cm.
"A Bradford book."
Includes bibliographical references and indexes.
ISBN 0-262-19345-0
1. Insight. 2. Problem solving. I. Sternberg, Robert J. II. Davidson, Janet E.
BF449.5.N38 1994
153.4—dc20   93-29646
                                                          CIP

Contents

Foreword

To assess progress in a field, it is often useful to compare current problems, issues, and conceptions with those advanced during the early stages of research. It is well known to all modern scientists interested in issues of human and animal learning that the seminal work of Donald O. Hebb (1949) on cell assemblies has proven to be an inspiration for computational modelers and has resulted in a revolution in our thinking about the problem of learning. What is less well known is that in the pages following his rather brief discussions of cell assemblies, Hebb went on to talk, at some length, about the construct of insight. He discussed the definitional problems with it, the debates that raged in the late 1940s, the flaws in those debates, the hopes that we might have of eventually understanding insight. He even provided a mechanism for insight. Hebb thought that insight is at the core of human and animal intelligence. Insight is the application of that intelligence to the particular situation at hand, and as such is central and fundamental to the organization of behavior. In Hebb's framework what distinguishes humans and higher primates from lower mammals, as well as adults from infants, is the complexity of organization, and it is this very complexity that allows for restructuring.

Hebb might be thought by some (perhaps by himself) to be the most hard-core of the associationists, and, as such, his views ought to be in opposition to those of the Gestalt psychologists of his day and indeed to those of some of the neo-Gestalt psychologists represented so liberally in this book. But, despite the seemingly dogmatic label, he was an astute and open minded scientist. The occurrence of the word "organization" in the title of his famous book, *Organization of Behavior*, was no accident. Organization, of course, goes beyond a simple-minded associationism such as was dominant at the time Hebb wrote his book. His emphasis on the difficult and complicated but nevertheless central issue of the role of insight in cognition speaks well of his need to address the real issues of higher human and animal cognition, rather than just those that might yield easily. In this foreword, then, in a manner that I hope is complementary to the historical overview given by Mayer on better-known insight researchers, I would like to take a look at the advances, issues, and insights on insight presented in this book in light of the views put forth by Hebb nearly fifty years ago.

EXISTENCE OF THE PHENOMENON

Because there seemed to be no agreed-upon mechanism that could explain insight, early researchers had divided into two camps: First, there were those whom Hebb called the learning theorists, who denied that the facts of insight were what they seemed. In opposition to the learning theorists were those whom he called the configurationists, who acknowledged the phenomenon of insight and sought evidence concerning both the phenomenon and mechanisms with which to explain it. A similar debate has raged in modem work. The persistent lack of a mechanism for insight, linked with the charge that the notion of insight is somehow supernatural, has shackled researchers who would explore this most important of cognitive processes. But natural phenomena of all sorts—lightning, tides, the very rising of the sun and the moon—have been attributed to divine intervention until the natural causes have come to be understood. We do not yet understand insight. But to say that we do not yet understand is quite different from saying that the phenomenon is caused by divine intervention or, perhaps worse, that there is no phenomenon. Interestingly, this volume sees some start of agreement concerning the existence of the phenomenon and as such we may hope that it heralds further progress toward the still elusive mechanism.

PHENOMENOLOGY

Hebb described insight as follows:

The task must be neither so easy that the animal solves the problem at once, thus not allowing one to analyze the solution; nor so hard that the animal fails to solve it except by rote learning in a long series of trials. With a problem of such borderline difficulty, the solution may appear out of a blue sky. There is a period first of fruitless effort in one direction, or perhaps a series of attempted solutions. Then suddenly there is a complete change in the direction of effort, and a cleancut solution of the task. This then is the first criterion of the occurrence of *insight*. The behavior cannot be described as a gradual accretion of learning; it is evident that something has happened in the animal at the moment of solution. (What happens is another matter.) (p. 160)

The advances in our understanding of the phenomenology of insight, given in this book, are underscored by the work of Csikszentmihalyi and Sawyer on social interactions and constraints as they impact upon insight, by Smith's careful descriptions of the insight and the incubation experiences as well as for his introduction of the concept of immanence (a feeling of having the answer but being unable to articulate it as yet) which promises to be of great importance, of Gruber's work—particularly the passages surrounding Darwin's "Malthusian moment," and of Ippolito and Tweney's idea that there is, between the perceptual and the symbolic, a particular form of consciously accessible representation that they call inception. Perhaps what Finke means by "preinventive forms" is the same as what Smith calls "immanence" and Ippolito and Tweney refer to as "inception." If there is such a level of representation it may be critical for insight problem solving, and certainly deserves research effort and exploration. Unfortunately, at this point, the existence of such an exciting stage or level of representation that presages insight is largely speculative, and hard data that point to its presence are badly needed.

Many of the authors in this book (including Gick and Lockhart in their chapter on affective components of insight) remark on the joy that is felt with creative insights and also on the appreciation for beauty that characterizes creative people. This aspect of the phenomenology of insight, until very recently, has been neglected as being too warm and soft for cool, hard Cognitive Science. But the emotional tone of the person solving problems, as Sternberg and Lubert would have it—their "attitude"—and the affective impact that solving, and trying to solve, has on such a person may prove to be essential in understanding the factors that permit, motivate, and select for creative endeavor. One must welcome this brave, fresh, and whole-hearted acknowledgment of the emotional aspects of insight as well as the attempts to delineate the role of emotion in the problem-solving process.

There is an increased emphasis, shown in the writings in this book, on trying to situate the processes of insight in the environment, rather than isolating them as general cognitive constructs. Thus, Gruber deals with specific insights of scientific creators. Dunbar, too, emphasizes social situations and conditions, rather than exclusively dwelling upon abstract cognitive variables. The chapters by Seifert, Meyer, N. Davidson, Patalano, and Yanif, and by Sternberg and Lubart both stress the opportunistic aspects of creative thought and creative thinkers. Csikszentmihalyi and Sawyer discuss the nature of interpersonal interactions, both actual and imagined, in the generation of creative ideas. Thus we see an expansion of the description of insight processes in this book. This specificity and the situatedness go well beyond the situations outlined by Hebb. What we lack is a deepened understanding of the cognitive mechanisms that are the underpinnings of these descriptions.

MECHANISM

Hebb (like many of the authors in this book) thought that insight involved a restructuring of thought—the elements of which he took to be conceptual rather than perceptual. In a manner that foreshadows the work of Dominowski, Hebb thought that insight was essential for extraction of meaning and for comprehension. He even proposed a rudimentary model of insight. He conceived of complex mental representations over which insight could work as being what he called phase sequences. They have many elementary parts that run off in some order (rather like a sequence of eye movements over a picture). As representations become more complex, the number of such elements becomes large; some of these elements can be considered to be central and necessary, whereas others are what he called fringe elements. The occurrence, in consciousness, of the fringe elements, when people or animals are thinking about a particular concept, is variable and depends on the conditions under which that thought is taking place. Two concepts may have fringe elements in common.

These are not shared because those concepts have occurred together in the past, that is, this commonality is not due to past learning or memory, but rather to some inherent similarity (conceptual similarity rather than merely perceptual similarity, as Hebb points out) between the two concepts. If the conditions are such that the relevant fringe elements common to both concepts emerge into consciousness, then the person can experience these fringe elements as a restructuring of those two concepts in their relation to one another. This constitutes an insight. According to Hebb, insights are the most common mode of adult learning, and depend on complex preexisting structures. Thus, they are unlike early (rote) learning and unlike perceptual learning, although, of course, the product of these earlier forms of learning and memory are essential to provide the elements on which the insights are based.

We do not know whether Hebb's idea of how restructuring comes about might be computationally and empirically plausible. To my knowledge, there has been no work on this fascinating aspect of Hebb's agenda, and few modern researchers even recognize that he mentioned the problem. And there is a decided paucity of alternative theoretical mechanisms for consideration. One, or rather two, of the most exciting attempts to delineate potential mechanisms for insight are put forth in this book by Simonton and by Perkins. Both of these researchers, in different ways, have postulated an emergence mechanism based on evolutionary theory. The exciting thing about this metaphor is that in it a new form or structure occurs spontaneously. This seems right for the phenomenology and for the extant data on insight. Qualitatively, then, this kind of model has the right feel for the emergence of concepts as a result of insight. One might add that it was also a creative act (which could be captured nicely by Hebb's model) for these researchers to perceive independently the connection between the apparently diverse fields of human problem solving and evolutionary biology. We do not yet know whether such ideas will prove fruitful for investigating insight, but at the least they provide a start.

One can imagine other possibilities for mechanisms that lie in an incipient form. There have been many advances in nonlinear dynamics, phase changes, chemistry, and other domains that may prove enormously fruitful as possible metaphors and mechanisms for human conceptual change by a process of insight. We have a pressing need, in this study of a most fascinating cognitive process, for explicit models based on coherent, and well-understood, physical principles. These models need to be delineated with a clear mapping between the concepts in those physical domains to the elements, representations, processes, systems, and conscious experiences in human problem solving so that the implications of the models may be apparent, and so that we may test the basic principles and assumptions of the various models against one another. One hopes that the data, the descriptive phenomenology, and the theoretical ideas presented in this book will stimulate many diverse creative frameworks that will provoke new experimental findings and which will contribute in a structurally coherent way to inform our understanding of insight.

Janet Metcalfe

REFERENCE

Hebb, D.O. (1949). *Organization of behavior.* New York: John Wiley & Son.

Preface

Suddenly one day, or so it seemed, we had the insight that the time had come for a book on the nature of insight. The problem of insight was certainly not new. A half century ago, Gestalt psychologists were interested in the nature of insight, and since then attention to this topic has waxed and waned. In recent years, after a long quiet period, there has been renewed interest, and we were eager to compile in one place new theories and discoveries and to bring them to a general audience. This volume on the nature of insight, therefore, began with the insight—correct or incorrect—that the field was ready for such a book, one that would summarize the current state of the field as well as herald developments to come.

Our goal in *The Nature of Insight* is to communicate to our readers a sense of what insight is, how it has been studied in the past, how it is being studied now, and how it might be studied in the future. To this end, we have included in this volume contributions that represent diverse points of view. They range equally widely in methodology, so that the reader will acquire a sense of the various approaches used to understand insight. Indeed, the book is divided into parts that correspond roughly to the various approaches, of which there are four. In one approach, subjects are presented with puzzle problems and asked to solve them. In a second approach, people are asked to invent something, usually within certain constraints governing how to design the invention. A third approach considers the insight processes of great thinkers in the context of their actual work rather than the laboratory. Finally, in a fourth approach, a metaphor is proposed and explained as a basis for understanding insight.

Part I comprises the introduction to the book. In Chapter 1, Richard Mayer provides a historical overview of the search for insight, reviewing the history of theory and research on this topic from the early part of the century to the present. In chapter 2, Roger Dominowski and Pamela Dallob review the contemporary state of the field, describing some of the problems and approaches currently being used to study insight. In their emphasis on puzzle problems, these authors provide a natural transition to part II.

Part II examines the puzzle-problem approach to insight, whereby subjects are presented with challenging verbal, spatial, and numerical problems that do not lend themselves to obvious solutions and are asked to figure out how the problems can be solved. In chapter 3, Colleen Seifert and her colleagues propose an opportunistic-assimilation view of insight, whereby people have insights when a stimulus from the environment helps them see an old problem in a new light. Janet Davidson, in chapter 4, combines a three-process view of insight (composed of selective encoding, selective comparison, and selective combination) with an approach that examines subjective feelings about insight. In chapter 5, Robert Weisberg suggests a taxonomy of types of puzzle problems and a means by which this taxonomy can be used to distinguish insight from noninsight problems. Mary Gick and Robert Lockhart propose, in chapter 6, that insight has both a cognitive and an affective component and that a full understanding of insight will arise only when we consider both of these. In chapter 7, Steven Smith presents a theory of fixation and insight, concentrating on how insight can occur when we remove mental blocks. In his chapter, Smith draws not only on puzzle problems but also on problems of design and invention, thus providing a natural transition to part III.

Part III considers the psychological phenomenon of insight in the context of people's generation of ideas as they create designs and inventions. In chapter 8, Ronald Finke presents a theory of creative cognition (which specifies generative processes, preinventive structures, preinventive properties, exploratory processes, and product constraints), shows its bearing on insight, and discusses the validity of the theory in terms of insights in inventive tasks. In their chapter (9), Matthew Isaak and Marcel Just describe three phases in inventive thinking (design-space limitation, design generation, and design analysis) and the relation between these three phases and insight. The authors use as examples some of the great inventive insights of the past, which set the stage for the fourth part of the book.

Part IV considers the great-minds approach to insight. Rather than looking at how everyday (lay) people solve problems presented to them in an experimental context, investigators using this approach explore, usually retrospectively, how some of the great minds of the past and present have generated insights in their work. In chapter 10, Mihaly Csikszentmihalyi and Keith Sawyer discuss what they refer to as the "social dimension of the solitary moment," whereby insightful discoveries are considered in the context of the field in which the discoveries are made and the domain of the symbolic systems of rules and procedures that operate within that field. Kevin Dunbar, in chapter 11, describes the role of analogies in insights, both in simulations of great discoveries and in actual discoveries as Dunbar observed them being made in scientists' laboratories. Next Howard Gruber considers, in chapter 12, the role of affective as well as cognitive processes in insight, much as did Gick and Lockhart, the primary difference being that Gruber focuses on great discoveries in the history of science rather than on puzzle-solving in the psychological laboratory. In chapter 13, Ippolito and Tweney discuss insight in the context of the discoveries of one of the great physicists of the nineteenth century, Michael Faraday. These authors emphasize the importance of mental models in insight, which serves as a natural bridge to the highly model-based approaches of part V.

The three chapters in part V have in common their use of an encompassing model or metaphor that serves as a basis for elucidating the nature of insight. Chapter 14, by Dean Simonton, draws on an evolutionary model and suggests that the processes of evolution—blind variation, selection, and retention—characterize insights much as they do evolution. In chapter 15, David Perkins also uses evolution as a model for insight and further suggests how the evolutionary process characterizing insight can be understood in terms of a spatial metaphor (which he calls a "Klondike space") that differs from the spatial metaphor characterizing noninsight processes (which he refers to as occurring in a "homing space"). Robert Sternberg and Todd Lubart, authors of chapter 16, use a different kind of model, one of investment (buying low and selling high), to characterize insight and its attendant antecedents and consequents.

The book ends with a brief epilogue, the goal of which is to summarize and integrate the various views of insight that have been proposed in the preceding chapters.

As always, many people have contributed to the realization of this book. First, we want to thank the authors who have worked with us and produced splendid chapters. Fiona Stevens, our acquisitions editor at MIT Press, was helpful to us in all phases of the book's development. Shannon Beeley at Yale University assisted in communications with authors, manuscript preparation, and communications with the MIT Press. Our joint work on insight was funded originally by the Spencer Foundation and was assisted later by contracts from the Army Research Institute and the Office of Naval Research. Our colleagues at Yale University, Carnegie-Mellon University, and Lewis & Clark College helped foster the interests that led eventually to the formulation of this book. Finally, we are grateful like to each other: Cross-continental collaborations are difficult to pursue and maintain, but we have managed through this book to appreciate each other's insights about insight.

Preparation of this book was supported under the Javits Act Program Grant No. R206R00001 as administered by the Office of Educational Research and Improvement, U.S. Department of Education. The findings and opinions expressed in this book do not reflect the positions or policies of the Office of Educational Research and Improvement or the U.S. Department of Education.

R.J.S.
J.E.D.

I Introduction

1 The Search for Insight: Grappling with Gestalt Psychology's Unanswered Questions

Richard E. Mayer

Creative thinking occurs when a problem solver invents a novel solution to a problem (Guilford, 1950). The term *insight* has been used to name the process by which a problem solver suddenly moves from a state of not knowing how to solve a problem to a state of knowing how to solve it (Mayer, 1992). Yet providing a name for this process does not substitute for providing an explanation. One of the central questions of the psychology of thinking that has persisted throughout this century concerns the nature of insight (Humphrey, 1963; Mandler & Mandler, 1964).

In the late 1930s, the Gestalt psychologist Max Wertheimer eloquently posed questions about the nature of insight that are still central to any complete theory of thinking:

Why is it that some people, when they are faced with problems, get clever ideas, make inventions and discoveries? What happens, what are the processes that lead to such solutions? (Luchins & Luchins, 1970, p. 1)

Wertheimer did not provide answers for these provocative questions (Luchins & Luchins, 1970), yet these unanswered questions of Gestalt psychology have been, and continue to be, a driving force in psychological research on problem solving. The goal of this chapter is to explore several paths that have been taken in the search for insight, including viewing insight as (1) completing a schema, (2) reorganizing visual information, (3) reformulating a problem, (4) overcoming a mental block, and (5) finding a problem analog.

OVERVIEW

Before exploring these five views of insight, it is useful to examine several key distinctions that are part of problem-solving theory. First, it is customary in problem-solving theory to distinguish between two phases in problem solving—problem representation and problem solution (Mayer, 1992). *Representation* occurs when a problem solver builds an internal mental representation of a problem that suggests a plan of solution; *solution* occurs when a problem solver carries out a solution plan. Modern research in cognitive psychology and cognitive science often has neglected the study of problem representation in favor of a focus on problem solution (Newell, 1985; Ohlsson, 1984a, 1984b), although there have been notable exceptions such as Kintsch and Greeno's (1985) study of how problem solvers represent arithmetic word problems. The search for insight requires a focus on problem representation—that is, on providing an account of how problem solvers understand and determine what to do when confronted with a problem.

A second distinction can be made between two types of problems: routine problems and nonroutine problems. *Routine problems* are those that problem solvers have already solved in the past and for which the problem solvers immediately recognize a ready-made solution procedure. For example, a long-division problem such as 552 divided by 12 is routine for most adults, because they know how to carry out the long-division procedure for this problem. *Nonroutine problems* are those that problem solvers have not previously solved and for which problem solvers do not possess a preexisting solution procedure. For example, the nine-dot problem is a nonroutine problem for people who have not seen it before: Given nine dots arranged as in the left panel of figure 1.1, draw four straight lines without lifting your pencil from the paper so that a line goes through each dot (Adams, 1974; Burnham & Davis, 1969). A solution is shown in the right panel of figure 1.1. The search for insight requires an account of how problem solvers invent solutions for nonroutine problems.

A third distinction involves reproductive versus productive thinking (Katona, 1940; Wertheimer, 1945/1959). In *reproductive thinking*, problem solvers apply solution procedures that they have used to solve identical or similar problems in the past. For example, if problem solvers have learned that area = height × base, they can use reproductive thinking to find the area of any rectangle for which the height and base are given. In *productive thinking*, problem solvers must invent a new way of solving a problem—that is, they must produce a novel solution. For exam-

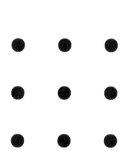
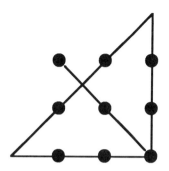

Problem: Draw four straight lines that connect the dots without lifting your pencil from the paper.

Solution: Draw the lines as shown.

Figure 1.1
The nine-dot problem and its solution.

ple, solving the nine-dot problem requires productive thinking. The search for insight involves an understanding of productive rather than reproductive thinking.

In summary, in the search for insight, researchers have limited their focus to representation rather than solution processes, to nonroutine rather than routine problems, and to productive rather than reproductive thinking. In line with these distinctions, Wertheimer (Luchins & Luchins, 1970, p. 9) foreshadowed the modern emphasis on situated cognition in authentic tasks:

Historically speaking, experimental psychologists have not started with creative situations of daily life in order to develop their theories of thinking.... Some psychologists, because of certain conceptions of what it means to be scientific, refused to use ordinary life activities. Instead, they created boring tasks that ordinary people would not call creative thinking.

Instead of dissecting the thinking processes for simple tasks, the Gestalt psychologists set as their goal the study of how people understand how to solve problems that require a creative solution.

SETTING THE STAGE FOR THE SEARCH FOR INSIGHT: INSIGHT AS NOTHING NEW

As the curtain opens on psychology's earliest experimental studies of creative thinking at the start of the twentieth century, the dominant cognitive theory is *associationism*, an approach borrowed from mental philosophy and dating back to the Greek philosophers (Humphrey, 1963; Mandler & Mandler, 1964; Mayer, 1992). According to this view, the mind consists of ideas (or elements) and associations (or links) between them. It follows that thinking is nothing more than moving from one idea to another via a chain of preestablished associations. For example, Aristotle proposed that mental associations will be formed between events or objects that occur in the same place or time (i.e., association by contiguity), that are similiar (i.e., association by similarity), or that are opposites (i.e., association by contrast), so that thinking of one will cause a person to think of the other.

In the seventeenth and eighteenth centuries, a group of mental philosophers led by Hobbes and Locke produced a revised version of associationism that included four psychological proposals involving atomism, mechanization, empiricism, and imagery (Mayer, 1992). The first of these proposals states that the elements of thinking are specific ideas and associations between them. Second, the process of thinking involves automatically moving from one idea to the next by following the strongest association. Third, the acquisition of ideas and associations comes from sensory experience. Fourth, the experience of thinking involves imagery (based on one of the five senses) because each idea represents a sensory experience.

The associationist view of mental life was appealing to many of the early psychologists interested in building a theory of learning and cognition. Accordingly, at the turn of the century, a prevailing view of insight was that it is nothing more than the exercise of stimulus-response associations—that is, finding a response that has been associated with the problem situation or similar situations in the past (Mayer, 1992; Thorndike, 1898). For example, each problem situation can be viewed as a stimulus with which many possible responses are associated; a problem solver will try the most strongly associated response first, the second most strongly associated response next, and so on, until hitting on a response that solves the problem. Thorndike (1898) referred to this process as "trial and error and accidental success," an account of problem solving that has no place for insight. Instead, the underlying mechanism is what Thorndike called the "law of effect," the idea that a successful response will become more strongly associated with the stimulus situation and an unsuccessful response will result in its connection to the stimulus being weakened. Later, Maltzman (1955) offered a behaviorist account intended to demystify the notion of insight: Insight is nothing more than switching to a new combination of responses associated with a problem situation or, in the jargon of the day, a new combination of habit strengths within a habit family hierarchy.

Although behaviorism has lost its grip on scientific psychology, there are still modern proponents of the nothing-new view of insight. Based on a series of studies in which past experience facilitated the solution of creativity problems (Weisberg, 1992; Weisberg & Alba, 1981a, 1981b, 1982; Weisberg & Suls, 1973), Weisberg (1986, p. 50) concluded that "there seems to be very little reason to believe that solutions to novel problems come about in flashes of insight, independently of past experience" and that "people create solutions to new problems by starting with what they know and later modifying it to meet the specific problem at hand." In contrast, some researchers argue that training in specific responses is less effective than learning about the general structural features of a problem (Dominowski, 1981; Ellen, 1982; Lung & Dominowski, 1985), and others offer new evidence for the existence of an "Aha!" experience in which a solution plan suddenly comes into consciousness (Kaplan & Simon, 1990; Metcalfe, 1986a, 1986b; Metcalfe & Wiebe, 1987).

Is there an alternative to the nothing-new view of insight, the idea that insight is nothing but following a chain of preestablished associations? The Gestalt psychologists and those they influenced argued for an alternative to associationist theories of thinking. For example, Katona (1940, p. 4–5) opined that "the main objection to the prevailing theory, which makes one kind of connection the basis of all learning, is not that it may be incorrect but that in the course of psychological research it has prevented an unbiased study of other kinds of learning." In the following sections, I explore a collection of five interrelated views of insight in the tradition of Gestalt psychology that offer a fundamental alternative to the associationist-inspired nothing-new account.

INSIGHT AS COMPLETING A SCHEMA

One of the earliest views of insight can be found in the landmark work of Otto Selz, who produced psychology's first nonassociationist theory of problem solving during the 1910s and 1920s (Frijda & De Groot, 1982; Humphrey, 1963). According to the insight-as-completing-a-schema view, creative problem solving involves figuring out how the givens and goal of a problem fit together within a coherent structure—that is, insight occurs when a problem solver fills in a gap in a structural complex. For example, when Benjamin Franklin wanted to bring electricity from lightning in the sky down to where he was standing on earth, he needed to imagine a coherent structure that contained lightning in the sky (i.e., the given) and electricity reaching him on earth (i.e., the goal). In thinking about how to complete this structure, Franklin's insight was to hold a wire attached to a kite that was flying into lightning. In this example, originally presented by Otto Selz, insight is needed to complete a partially developed schema (see Humphrey, 1963).

Otto Selz described this process as *schematic anticipation*, the idea that a novel solution to a problem arises when a problem solver sees how it fits as an integrated component into a larger system or complex. Accordingly, a problem is a coherent set of information with a gap, and problem solving involves figuring out how to fill the gap in a way that completes the structure (Humphrey, 1963). Following the methodology of the Wurzburg group (see Humphrey, 1963; Mandler & Mandler, 1964; Mayer, 1992), Selz asked subjects to think aloud as they solved a series of word-association problems such as determining a subordinate of tool (e.g., hammer) or a superordinate of newspaper (e.g., publication). For example, for the problem, "Newspaper—superordinate?" one subject produced the following protocol before stating the correct answer: "Read the thing and knew broadly what I had to do. When I let it sink in a little longer I became certain I knew exactly what to do. Then I went back to the first word, read it again and articulated the word internally, newspaper ..." (Selz, in Fridja & De Groot, 1982, p. 94) According to Selz's analysis of the resulting protocols such as this one, the problem is not always solved by blindly following a chain of associations from the given words to the solution word. Instead, the problem solver seeks to build a sort of integrated structure such as "Tool—is a superordinate of—_____," where the problem solver's job is to complete the complex in a way that maintains its structural integrity. Selz (in Frijda & De Groot, 1982, p. 53) noted: "It is not the intensity of association which systematically marks off successful movements from unsuccessful ones but the better fit with schematic anticipation of the operation to be executed."

The solution emerges "not through a senseless play of associations" (Selz, in Frijda & De Groot, 1982, p. 73) but rather "the initiatory event of a goal-directed cognitive operation must always be a schematic anticipation of the goal" (p. 43). When the solution to a problem is not immediately obvious, subjects attempt to build a structure: "New specific responses occur only as integrated members of a system ..." (Selz, in Frijda & De Groot, 1982, p. 47). In contrast to associationist theory's focus on specific responses, Selz noted that creative problem solving sometimes entails a search for a solution method that meets the requirements of the problem rather than a specific solution. In a review, Simon (1982, p. 155) states that "what is evoked by initial schematic anticipation is not a potential problem solution but a solving method."

Otto Selz deserves to be recognized as the "first psychologist to incorporate an explicitly nonassociationist doctrine into an experimentally induced psychology of thinking" (Humphrey, 1963, p. 149). Despite Selz's credentials as the author of psychology's first nonassociationist theory of thinking, his work is not widely cited among cognitive psychologists. Unfortunately, his books—originally published in German in 1913 as On the Laws of Ordered Thinking and in 1922 as On the Psychology of Productive Thinking and Error—were not generally available to English-speaking psychologists until recently (Frijda & De Groot, 1982). His isolation was also reinforced by the rise of Nazism in his native Germany, which put an early end to his promising career and, eventually, to his life.

Undeniably, Selz's writings are vague and his research methodologies are imprecise by modern standards. Yet his work foreshadowed not only the Gestalt revolution that was to follow but also the development of modern cognitive psychology. The schema-completion view with which Selz struggled continues to develop within current cognitive theory, including accounts of machine cognition. As in Selz's time, modern cognitive psychologists are working to understand the nature of schemas, including how they are constructed and used to support cognition (Mayer, 1992).

INSIGHT AS SUDDENLY REORGANIZING VISUAL INFORMATION

A second early view of insight corresponds with the Gestalt theory of perception (Kohler, 1929): Insight occurs when a problem solver literally looks at a problem situation in a new way—that is, when the visual information suddenly is reorganized in a way that satisfies the requirements of the goal. This view emphasizes the visual nature of insight: Just as perception involves building an organized structure from visual input, creative thinking often involves the reorganizing or restructuring of visual information. For example, in the geometrical problem on the left side of figure 1.2, the task is to determine the length of line x if the radius of the circle is r. The insight required to solve this problem, according to the Gestalt psychologist Wolfgang Kohler (1969, p. 146), is to re-

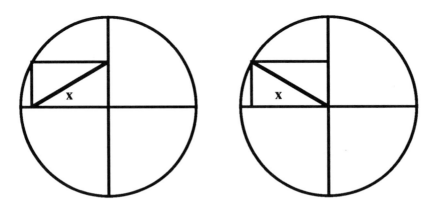

Problem: If the length of the radius is r, what is the length of line x?

Solution: The length of line x is r.

Figure 1.2
A geometrical problem and its solution.

alize that line x is one diagonal of a rectangle but it could be replaced by the other diagonal, as shown on the right side of figure 1.2. As soon as the problem solver modifies his or her way of looking at the material, the problem is solved because it can easily be seen that line x is the same length as the radius. Kohler (1969, p. 146) concludes that "the decisive step is what we may call a *restructuring* of the given material."

In his classic book, *The Mentality of Apes*, Wolfgang Kohler (1925) summarizes some of the first and most widely cited experiments on insight. In each study, a chimpanzee was confronted with a problem that required a creative solution. For example, in one study, a bunch of bananas is hanging overhead but far out of reach in a cage, and there are crates on the floor. The desired solution is to build a sort of ladder below the bananas by piling one crate on top of another. In another study, bananas are placed outside the cage beyond the reach of the chimp, and long sticks are inside the cage. The desired solution is to use a stick as a sort of rake that can pull the bananas closer to the cage so the chimp can reach them. An example is shown in Figure 1.3.

Problem: Three crates are on the floor and bananas are overhead out of reach. How can you reach the bananas?

Solution: Stack the crates as a ladder, climb up, and reach the bananas.

Figure 1.3
The banana problem and its solution.

Based on his observations, Kohler concluded that an associationist theory, the dominant theory of the day, could not explain many of the chimps' problem-solving behaviors. Associationist theory asserts that solutions come about by producing a response that has worked previously in the same situation or by producing responses by trial and error until accidentally hitting on responses that work. In contrast to associationist theory, Kohler (1925, p. 217) describes insightful problem solving as the production of behaviors (1) that represent "complete methods of solution" as "complete wholes" rather than individual responses, (2) that appear "quite suddenly" rather than being gradually reinforced, and (3) that were "never practiced formerly" rather than reproduced from prior experience.

As evidence, Kohler (1925, p. 217) describes "how two animals suddenly lift a box that stands too low and hold it high against the wall; how several of them endeavor to stand the box diagonally so as to make it reach higher; how Rana joins two sticks that are too small to make one that looks twice as long; how Sultan steers one stick with another from quite a distance right up to the objective and thus reaches it ..." As an alternative to the associationist view of thinking as following a chain of associations based on past experience, Kohler (1925, p. 267) provides examples of insight as a sort of visual reorganization of the presented materials: "The insight of the chimpanzee shows itself to be principally determined by his optical apprehension of the situation."

Admittedly, Kohler's research on problem solving in chimps can be criticized for its lack of methodological rigor as well as for a lack of close correspondence between theory and data. In addition, more rigorous research sometimes shows that animals solved problems mainly when they had previous experience with using objects in the problem (Birch, 1945). Yet Kohler's contribution to the search for insight rests largely in his provocative research questions about the role of sudden cognitive restructuring of visual information in problem solving. Interest in visual thinking is again in vogue in modern cognitive psychology (Finke, 1989; Kosslyn, 1980). In particular, the role of computer-assisted visualization and concrete representations that help people build mental models are the focus of ongoing research in scientific and mathematical problem solving (Mayer, 1989).

INSIGHT AS REFORMULATION A PROBLEM

A closely related view of insight can be derived from the work of the Gestalt psychologist Karl Duncker (1945), whose English-language publication, *On Problem Solving*, ranks as perhaps the single most important publication on insight. A motivating question for Duncker's work was: Where does insight come from? One of his proposed answers was that insight occurs when a problem solver mentally redefines and clarifies the problem, such as reformulating the givens or the goal. Duncker (1945, p. 9) proclaimed this view as follows: "What is really done in any solution of problems consists in formulating the problem more productively."

Duncker described two methods for reformulating a problem—suggestions from above and suggestions from below. A *suggestion from above* occurs when the problem solver redefines the goal; in these cases, the problem solver may seek to formulate the *functional value* of the goal—that is, the general purpose that needs to be satisfied. Duncker (1945, p. 8) observed that problem reformulations progress from the general to the specific: "The final form of an individual solution is, in general, not reached in a single step from the original setting of the problem; on the contrary, the principle, the functional value of the solution, typically arises first and the final form of the solution in question develops only as this principle becomes successively more and more concrete." According to this account, complex problem solving involves a succession of insights—that is, a succession of reformulations of the problem.

For example, Duncker's (1945, p. 1) most famous study involves the following radiation problem: "Given a human being with an inoperable stomach tumor and rays which destroy organic tissue at sufficient intensity, by what procedure can one free him of the tumor by these rays and at the same time avoid destroying the healthy tissue that surrounds it?" The picture on the left side of figure 1.4 accompanied the problem statement. When Duncker asked people to "think aloud" as they solved the problem, he found that they often tried to reformulate the goal in several ways. For example, reformulating the goal as "avoiding contact between rays and healthy tissue" suggested incorrect solutions such as sending the rays through the esophagus; reformulating

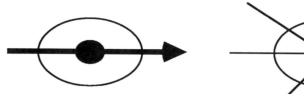

Problem: Given a human with an inoperable stomach tumor and rays that destroy the tissue at sufficient intensity, by what procedure can one free him of the tumor by these rays and at the same time avoid destroying the healthy tissue that surrounds it?

Solution: Focus many weak rays on the tumor as a lens.

Figure 1.4
The tumor problem and its solution.

the goal as "desensitize the healthy tissue" suggested incorrect solutions such as immunizing the healthy tissue with weak rays; and reformulating the goal as "lower the intensity of the rays on their way through the healthy tissue" suggested incorrect solutions such as turning the intensity of the ray from low to high as it begins to pass through the tumor and the correct solution of focusing several weak rays as a lens on the tumor. This solution is shown on the right side of figure 1.4. In this problem, a typical problem solver first thinks of one way of reformulating the goal, then derives some specific solutions, then thinks of another reformulated goal followed by some specific solutions, and so on.

Similarly, a *suggestion from below* occurs when a problem solver reformulates the given information in a new way. For example, Duncker (1945, p. 31) experimented with the following problem: "Why are all six-place numbers of the form 267267, 591591, 112112, divisible by 13?" To solve the problem, the problem solver must redefine the givens; rather than seeing the givens as "all six-place numbers of the form 267267, 591591, 112112," the problem solver can define the given information as "abcabc" and eventually as "abc × 1001." Having reformulated the givens, the problem solver must reformulate 1001 as a number that is divisible by 13, which leads to the conclusion that all numbers of the form abc × 1001 must also be divisible by 13.

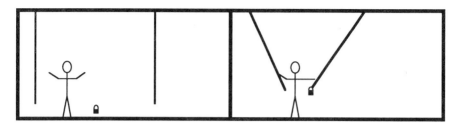

Problem: In a room with many objects on the floor, tie together two cords that are hanging from overhead but are too far apart to be grasped at once.

Solution: Tie a weight to the end of one cord and swing it as a pendulum; while holding the other cord, catch the pendulum on the upswing.

Figure 1.5
The two-string problem and its solution.

Duncker argues that the major difficulty in problem solving is to understand the problem givens and goal in a productive way. For example, he notes that "the real difficulty in the 13 problem is overcome as soon as the common divisor 1001 emerges" (Duncker, 1945, p. 34). This insight was greatly enhanced when the examples in the 13 problem changed from "276276, 591591, 112112" to "276276, 277277, 278278" or when the sentence "1001 is divisible by 13" is added. Thus, suggestions from below depend on the way the problem is presented.

Suggestions from below—ideas about how to reformulate the function of the given objects—can come from subtle aspects of the problem situation. According to research by Maier (1930, 1931, 1970), problem solvers sometimes need some sort of external hint, which Maier called *direction*. For example, in the two-string problem shown in figure 1.5, the problem solver is asked to tie together two cords that are hanging from overhead but are too far apart to be grasped at once. The solution is to tie a weight to the end of one of the cords and swing it like a pendulum; then, holding the other cord, catch the pendulum on the upswing so the two cords can be tied together. During the course of the problem, the experimenter walked by one of the cords, "accidentally" setting it into motion. Most of the subjects solved the problem shortly thereafter but were not aware of the hint. In this case, problem solvers needed to reformulate the hanging cord as a pendulum, a reformulation that was suggested by setting it into gentle motion. According to Duncker (1945, p. 16), "What Maier calls direction ... is nothing but the ... reformulation of the problem as it initiates the solution process."

Duncker provided empirical support for the idea that thinking often progresses through a series of qualitatively different phases rather than as a linear chain of associations. Thus, Duncker's findings can be taken as support for attempts to identify fundamental phases in thinking. For example, in his classic, *The Art of Thinking*, Wallas (1926) proposed a series of four definable phases in creative problem solving: (1) preparation, in which the problem solver begins to gather information about the problem; (2) incubation, in which the problem solver does not intentionally work on the problem; (3) illumination, in which the problem solver experiences insight into the problem solution; and (4) verification, in which the solution is tried and checked.

In summary, a key to insight is in looking at the givens or the goal in a new way. Duncker (1945, p. 11) concludes that "a solution has, so to speak, two roots, one which is sought and one which is given" and that "a solution arises from the claim made on that which is given by that which is sought." Duncker's words lack the objectivity required in modern cognitive theory, yet they seem to foreshadow the ongoing constructivist revolution (i.e., the idea that humans are sense makers who are actively trying to construct meaning in what they encounter) (Resnick, 1989). The roots of the current shift to viewing humans as information interpreters rather than information processors can be found in Duncker's theory of thinking as successive problem reformulation. Similarly, modern research suggests that expert problem solvers reason at a qualitative level before focusing on specific or quantitative solutions, whereas novices tend to focus too early on trying out specific or quantitative answers (Chi, Glaser, & Farr, 1988; Mayer, 1992). This finding is remarkably in line with Duncker's claim that successful problem solving begins at a general and functional level before it progresses to more specific and concrete solutions. The continued study of expert problem solving provides a modern avenue for the search for insight.

INSIGHT AS REMOVING MENTAL BLOCKS

Another early view, also found in Duncker's (1945) theory, addresses the question: What prevents people from inventing creative solutions to problems—that is, from reformulating a given or goal? The culprit, according to Gestalt theory, is the problem solver's reliance on inappropriate past experience. According to this view, insight occurs when a problem solver overcomes a mental block. Problem solving will be hindered, for example, when a problem solver can think of using an object only for its most common or habitual use in a problem that requires a novel use of the object. Duncker (1945) referred to this phenomenon as *functional fixedness*. For example, Duncker (1945, p. 85) argues that if a problem solver needs a stick to use as a tool to solve a problem, a branch of a tree is less likely to be used than an equivalent branch on the ground. When the branch is in a tree, its function of holding leaves may become fixed in the problem solver's mind, which blocks thinking of using the branch in a different way to solve a problem.

To investigate this phenomenon, Duncker devised a set of preutilization problems such as the box problem shown in figure 1.6: The goal is to mount three candles side by side at eye level on a door "for use in visual experiments" and the givens are three small pasteboard boxes containing small candles, tacks, and matches, respectively. The solution is to tack each box to the door so that each can serve as a platform for a candle. In this problem, the boxes are preutilized as containers, a situation that leads to functional fixedness. If the function of the boxes is seen as containment, then problem solvers will have difficulty in devising a new function for the boxes, namely, using them as platforms. In Duncker's experiments, most of the subjects were unable to solve the candle problem when the boxes contained candles, tacks, and matches; however, all the subjects eventually solved the problem if they were given empty boxes next to piles of candles, tacks, and matches.

Luchins (1942) provided another classic example of how previous experience can block creative problem solving. In his water-jar problems, such as the example in figure 1.7, the subject's task

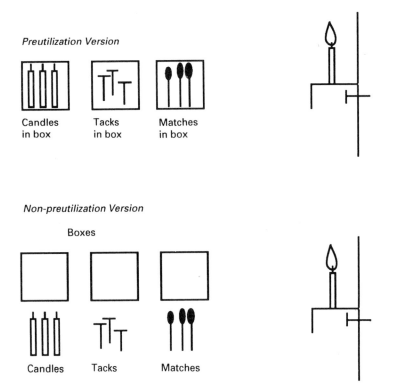

Preutilization Version

Candles
in box

Tacks
in box

Matches
in box

Non-preutilization Version

Boxes

Candles

Tacks

Matches

Problem: Given pasteboard boxes, candles, tacks, and matches, mount the candles at eye level on a door.

Solution: Tack each box to the door and use it as a platform for the candle.

Figure 1.6
The box problem and its solution.

is to "figure out on paper how to obtain a required volume of water given certain empty jars for measures" (Luchins, 1942, p. 2). After a practice problem, subjects were given a series of five problems (called *Einstellung problems*) all of which could be solved by one procedure—fill up the second jar and from it fill up the first jar and the third jar twice. For example, in problem 1, the task is to get 100 quarts using a 21-, 127-, and 3-quart jar; the solution is to fill the 127-quart jar and from it fill the 21-quart jar once and then the 3-quart jar twice, yielding 100 quarts left in the large jar. After receiving five problems that could be solved

An Einstellung Problem

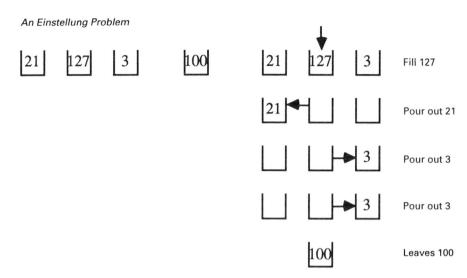

Problem: Given an unlimited supply of water and a 21-, 127-, and 3-quart jar, obtain exactly 100 quarts of water.

Solution: Fill the middle jar; from it fill the first jar and then twice fill the second jar.

A Critical Problem

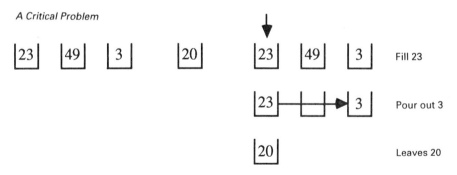

Problem: Given an unlimited supply of water and a 23-, 49-, and 3-quart jar, obtain exactly 20 quarts of water.

Solution: The shorter solution is to fill the first jar and from it fill the third jar (as shown). The longer solution is to fill the middle jar; from it fill the first jar and then twice fill the second jar (not shown).

Figure 1.7
Some water-jar problems and their solutions.

using this procedure, subjects received a series of similar-looking problems (called *critical problems*) that could be solved by a simpler procedure. For example, the first critical problem could be solved in a complex way $(49 - 23 - 3 - 3 = 20)$ or in a short way $(23 - 3 = 20)$. Subjects who solved the first five (Einstellung) problems tended to use the more complex procedure that they learned from previous problems when solving the critical problems. In contrast, subjects who did not have to solve the first five (Einstellung) problems solved the critical problems using the simpler procedure. Luchins (1945, p. 1) concluded that previous experience produced an "Einstellung" or "problem-solving set" that resulted in "mechanization in problem solving." In demonstrating the "blinding effect" of prior experience, Luchins (1945, p. vii) asked provocative questions such as, "What may be the real cause for the blinding effect? How are we to understand this phenomenon?"

In summary, insight involves overcoming the way one has learned to look at a certain situation so that one can look at it in a new way. In some cases, it seems that creative problem solving requires breaking down what Adams (1974, p. 11) calls "mental walls which block the problem-solver from correctly perceiving a problem or conceiving of its solution." Although Duncker's research on functional fixedness has been criticized justifiably on methodological grounds, it has been replicated under more rigorous conditions (Adamson, 1952).

The insight-as-removing-mental-blocks view continues to stimulate research, theory, and practice in the psychology of thinking. The teaching of problem solving has again become an educational goal (Chipman, Segal, & Glaser, 1985; Halpern, 1992; Segal, Chipman, & Glaser, 1985; Nickerson, Perkins, & Smith, 1985). For example, mathematics educators have examined methods for promoting the development of insight in students (Polya, 1965; Van Hiele, 1986). One effective technique for fostering creative thinking is a sort of cognitive apprenticeship in which a novice observes the problem-solving processes used by skilled problem solvers in a domain (Mayer, 1992). Thus, a potentially fruitful path for further research is to understand fully the nature of mental blocks and their amelioration.

INSIGHT AS FINDING A PROBLEM ANALOG

In contrast to research on mental blocks, in which past experience is viewed as a culprit, sometimes past experience can spark insight. In the Gestalt classic, *Productive Thinking*, Max Wertheimer (1945/1959) suggests that insight sometimes involves grasping the structural organization of one situation and applying that organization to a new problem. In thinking by analogy, a problem solver must focus on the structural organization of a situation rather than on the surface features.

For example, in the bridge problem, a child is given three blocks with which he or she can build a structure. Sitting at a table with a child, Wertheimer built a bridge with three blocks, as shown in the top panel of figure 1.8. According to Wertheimer, the structural relations in this situation involve two identical vertical

Original problem (performed by experimenter)

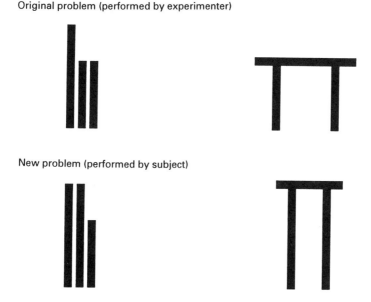

New problem (performed by subject)

Problem: Build a bridge with three blocks.   Solution: Make sure the horizontal block is perpendicular to the vertical blocks.

Figure 1.8
The bridge problem and its solution.

blocks and one different horizontal block that bridges the distance between them. Later, without saying a word, Wertheimer gave the child three different blocks and found (Wertheimer, 1959, p. 82): "It works, they build a bridge." Lastly, he gave the child three blocks like the original blocks except that one was short and two were long. The correct solution is shown at the bottom of figure 1.8. Wertheimer (1959, p. 82) summarizes the performance of a group of children:

Some ... place the short block vertically, the long one horizontally, holding it in this position, and appear anxious to find another small block. I do nothing. Then they begin to try to put the third block in a vertical position; it falls down.... After it falls down, they do it again, but most children, after about two trials, suddenly smile, and change the place and role of the blocks. Many of the children do this at once after a short pause, without any previous trials.

Wertheimer interprets these results as crucial for understanding the role of previous experience in problem solving. If students focused on the specific physical features of the original problem, they would be able to solve only identical or highly similar problems. In contrast, if students learned the structural relations in the original problem (e.g., that the horizontal block must be perpendicular to the two vertical blocks), they were then able to transfer what they learned to building a wide variety of bridges.

Wertheimer's parallelogram problem provides another example of the role of structural insight in transfer from one problem to another. First, Wertheimer (1945/1959) taught some students how to find the area of a parallelogram by measuring the height, measuring the base, and multiplying the height times the base, which he calls *senseless* or *arbitrary learning*. Other students learned by understanding the structural relationship between a parallelogram and a rectangle, such as realizing that a parallelogram becomes a rectangle when you cut off the triangle from one side and place it on the other side. The meaningful method of learning to solve the parallelogram is summarized on the top of figure 1.9. Students who learned by understanding were able to solve transfer problems, as shown on the bottom of figure 1.9, but senseless learners said, "We haven't had that yet" (Wertheimer, 1959, p. 15). Wertheimer concluded that only students

Original problem

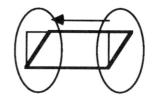

Problem: Find the area of a parallelogram (assuming you know how to find the area of a rectangle).

Solution: Cut off triangle on one side and move to the other side to turn it into a rectangle.

Transfer problems

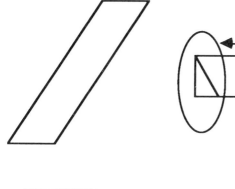

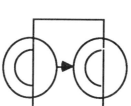

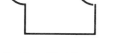

Problem: Find the area of these figures.

Solution: Notice that these figures can be reconstructed as rectangles.

Figure 1.9
Some area problems and their solution.

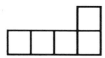

Problem: Given 16 matchsticks that form five
squares, move 3 sticks to form four squares.

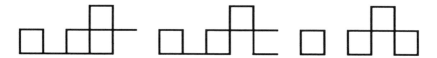

Solution: Move sticks as shown above.

Figure 1.10
A matchstick problem and its solution.

who learned by focusing on the structural qualities of the figure
were able to transpose that way of thinking to new problems.

A similar pattern of results was obtained by George Katona
(1940), using another geometrical puzzle called *matchstick problems*. Students learned to solve problems such as that shown in
figure 1.10 by a rote method or a meaningful method and then
were tested on solving similar matchstick problems. Students
who learned to solve the puzzles by discovering the underlying
structural principles—such as realizing that each stick could be
part of one or two squares—were better able to transfer what
they had learned to new problems than students who learned the
specific step-by-step moves—such as memorizing the moves
shown on the bottom of figure 1.10. Again, what is learned under
rote methods is a set of specific responses that does not transfer
well to new problems; in contrast, what is learned under meaningful methods is a structural principle—namely, the idea that
a stick can function as a side in two squares simultaneously—
which does transfer.

In short, insight involves grasping the structural relations of one
problem and applying them to the solution of a new problem. In
contrast to associationist theory, which emphasizes the role of
specific past experience, Wertheimer (1959, p. 61) claims that successful transfer from one problem to another depends on "not just

past experience but the nature and the structural fitting of past experience." He (1959, p. 65) argues against the idea that transfer involves applying specific solutions from past problem solving to new problems: "Past experience ... is ambiguous in itself; so long as it is taken in piecemeal, blind terms, it is not the magic key to solve all problems." Wertheimer (1959, p. 69) concludes: "The crucial question is not whether past experience, but what kind of past experience plays a role—blind connections or structural grasp." Finally, he attempted to clarify the role of past experience (Wertheimer, 1959, p. 62):

In short, the role of past experience is of high importance, but what matters is what one has gained from experience—blind, ununderstood connections, or insight into structural inner relatedness. What matters is how and what one recalls, how one applies what is recalled, whether blindly, in a piecemeal way, or in accordance with the structural requirements of the situation.

Wertheimer's examples, though tantalizing, are hardly acceptable by modern standards of scientific rigor. However, the study of analogical thinking, originating in the first half of the twentieth century, is a surprisingly contemporary topic (Mayer, 1992), and the search for transfer is again a popular issue in cognitive psychology (Detterman & Sternberg, 1992; Singley & Anderson, 1989). For example, modern cognitive psychologists have investigated the conditions under which problem solvers abstract the structural organization from previous problems so that it can be applied to new problems (Gick & Holyoak, 1980, 1983) and the role of mental models in thinking (Gentner & Stevens, 1983). Echoing Wertheimer's distinction between arbitrary connections and structural relations, modern cognitive theory distinguishes between surface similarity and structural similarity between problems (Gentner, 1983). Research on thinking by analogy represents a promising avenue for future research (Vosniadou & Ortony, 1989).

ADVANCING THE SEARCH FOR INSIGHT

In this review, I have abstracted five views of insight from the Gestalt and pre-Gestalt literature on problem solving, all of which are still highly relevant today. It is presumptuous, of course, to abstract a list of themes from the vast Gestalt literature (Henle, 1961), and I do so to stimulate further discussion rather than to draw conclusions. This list is not intended to be exhaustive. For example, the view of insight as a mental trait—the idea that certain types of people are more likely to have creative insights than others—was not a major theme in Gestalt theory but has become an interesting avenue of research on creativity (Guilford, 1950; Sternberg, 1988). Furthermore, some Gestalt themes such as a physiological basis for cognition also are not included in the list (Lewin, 1936). The five views are not assumed to be independent but rather seem to fit together into a collection of related ideas.

Gestalt theory has been criticized for its lack of methodological rigor and theoretical clarity (Dellarosa, 1988; Ohlsson, 1984a, 1984b; Weisberg, 1986). In addition to these shortcomings, the Gestalt psychologists and their predecessors failed to provide a coherent theoretical account of human cognition. Yet it would be wrong to dismiss the Gestaltists' search for insight as a fruitless venture without relevance to modern cognitive psychology. These researchers left us with some questions and the beginnings of some answers. They challenged us to invent an alternative to the atomistic approach of classical associationism.

Sometimes the Gestaltists are accused of being soft scientists, whereas contemporary psychologists consider themselves workers in a hard science. An alternative way to frame the distinction is that the Gestalt psychologists work on *hard* questions, whereas modern cognitive psychologists sometimes prefer *easy* ones.[1] Given the increase in research tools, including computer technology, and the increase in basic knowledge since the heyday of Gestalt psychology in the 1930s and 1940s, it may be time to return to some of the great unanswered questions of Gestalt psychology: What is insight? Where does it come from? How can we foster it?

Can we invent a fundamentally new unit of thought that goes beyond the association—an idea born in mental philosophy and applied to psychological theory throughout the first half of this century (Humphrey, 1963; Mandler & Mandler, 1964)—and beyond the cognitive process—a product of the cognitive revolution of the second half of this century (Miller, Galanter & Pribram, 1960)? The yearning for a new kind of theory is apparent, for example, in cognitive psychology's current interest in metacognition, the control and coordination of cognitive processes. Can we address the hard questions about creative thinking and meaningful learning rather than the more clearly defined questions about procedure execution and knowledge acquisition?

The issue here is not whether the Gestalt theory of insight is correct or incorrect. If this were our major concern, we could dismiss Gestalt psychology on the grounds that both the research questions and the tentative answers are too vague even to be called right or wrong. That decision would be a mistake, in my opinion. Instead, the real challenge is to reformulate and clarify in a more productive way the questions we have inherited from the Gestalt psychologists. Modern cognitive psychologists continue to grapple directly with questions about insight (Davidson, 1986; Davidson & Sternberg, 1984; Kaplan & Simon, 1990; Lockhart, Lamon & Gick, 1988; Metcalfe, 1986a, 1986b; Metcalfe & Wiebe, 1987; Montgomery, 1988; Wertheimer, 1985). Without using the term *insight*, they also continue to search along each of the five original paths I have described in this review of Gestalt theory. These paths have opened onto some of the most exciting avenues of contemporary research in cognition, including the study of schemas, mental models, expertise, teaching of problem solving, and analogical thinking.

The classic conflict between associationist and Gestalt conceptions of mental life is still alive, though rarely framed in these terms. For example, the resurgence of interest in analogical reasoning and expert problem solving provides a modern battleground for the conflict. On one side, the associationist view seems to be vindicated by the finding that analogical transfer—solving a new problem by using a previously solved problem—depends on experience in solving specifically related problems. However, remnants of the Gestalt view can be found in the proposal that analogical problem solving is not an automatic process in which trial-and-error application of past experience results in creative solutions; instead, within the tradition of insightful thinking, the problem solver must strategically control processes such as abstracting a general principle or structure from specific problems or recognizing that a new and old problem share the same underlying structure. Similarly, the associationist approach seems consistent with the currently popular idea that expert problem solving, in domains ranging from chess playing to medical reasoning, depends on domain-specific knowledge. Yet in the tradition of Gestalt theory, it can be pointed out that experts not only possess relevant knowledge but also know how to use it. Although the term *insight* may not be used, experts differ from novices in the way they represent problems, with experts focusing on the underlying structure or principles and novices focusing on the surface characteristics. Clearly, prior knowledge plays a role in both analogical reasoning and expert problem solving; however, the key to creative problem solving continues to be the process by which a person understands the underlying structure of a problem, a process that the Gestalt psychologists called *insight.*

My hope, in writing this review of early views of insight, is that an exploration of where the field's questions have come from will foster a better understanding of where to look for their answers. For example, the search for insight leads to the process of problem understanding rather than procedure execution, to nonroutine rather than routine problems, and to productive rather than reproductive thinking. Like Kohler (1969, p. 151), I hope that "we do not refer to funny or mysterious notions when we use such words as understanding and insight." In short, a crucial task facing cognitive psychology is to develop a scientifically acceptable account of how creative thinking happens; a review of the classic conceptions of insight is a good place to start.

NOTE

1. This distinction is based on a personal communication from David Berliner.

REFERENCES

Adams, J.L. (1974). *Conceptual blockbusting.* New York: Freeman.

Adamson, R.E. (1952). Functional fixedness as related to problem solving: A repetition of three experiments. *Journal of Experimental Psychology, 44,* 288–291.

Birch, H. (1945). The relation of previous experience to insightful problem solving. *Journal of Comparative Psychology, 38,* 367–383.

Burnham, C.A., & Davis, K.G. (1969). The 9-dot problem: Beyond perceptual organization. *Psychonomic Science, 17,* 321–323.

Chi, M.T.H., Glaser, R., & Farr, M.J. (Eds.). (1988). *The nature of expertise.* Hillsdale, NJ: Erlbaum.

Chipman, S.F., Segal, J.W., & Glaser, R. (Eds.). (1985). *Thinking and learning skills: Vol. 2. Research and open questions.* Hillsdale, NJ: Erlbaum.

Davidson, J.E. (1986). The role of insight in giftedness. In R.J. Sternberg & J.E. Davidson (Eds.), *Conceptions of giftedness.* Cambridge, England: Cambridge University Press.

Davidson, J.E., & Sternberg, R.J. (1984). The role of insight in intellectual giftedness. *Gifted Child Quarterly, 28,* 58–64.

Dellarosa, D. (1988). A history of thinking. In R.J. Sternberg & E.E. Smith (Eds.), *The psychology of human thought* (pp. 1–18). Cambridge, England: Cambridge University Press.

Detterman, D.K., & Sternberg, R.J. (Eds). (1992). *Transfer on trial: Intelligence, cognition, and construction.* Norwood, NJ: Ablex.

Dominowski, R.L. (1981). Comment on "An examination of the alleged role of 'fixation' in the solution of 'insight' problems." *Journal of Experimental Psychology: General, 110,* 199–203.

Duncker, K. (1945). On problem solving. *Psychological Monographs, 68*(5), whole no. 270.

Ellen, P. (1982). Direction, past experience, and hints in creative problem solving: Reply to Weisberg and Alba. *Journal of Experimental Psychology: General, 111,* 316–325.

Finke, R.A. (1989). *Principles of mental imagery.* Cambridge, MA: MIT Press.

Frijda, N.H., & de Groot, A.D. (Eds.). (1982). *Otto Selz: His contribution to psychology.* The Hague: Mouton.

Gentner, D. (1983). Structure mapping: A theoretical framework. *Cognitive Science, 7,* 155–170.

Gentner, D., & Stevens, A.L. (Eds.). (1983). *Mental models.* Hillsdale, NJ: Erlbaum.

Gick, M.L., & Holyoak, K.J. (1980). Analogical problem solving. *Cognitive Psychology, 12,* 306–355.

Gick, M.L., & Holyoak, K.J. (1983). Schema induction and anological transfer. *Cognitive Psychology, 15,* 1–38.

Guilford, J.P. (1950). Creativity. *American Psychologist, 5,* 444–454.

Halpern, D.F. (Ed.). (1992). *Enhancing thinking skills in the sciences and mathematics.* Hillsdale, NJ: Erlbaum.

Henle, M. (Ed.). (1961). *Documents of Gestalt psychology.* Berkeley: University of California Press.

Humphrey, G. (1963). *Thinking: An introduction to its experimental psychology.* New York: Wiley.

Kaplan, C.A., & Simon, H.A. (1990). In search of insight. *Cognitive Psychology, 22,* 374–419.

Katona, G. (1940). *Organizing and memorizing: Studies in the psychology of learning and teaching.* New York: Columbia University Press.

Kintsch, W., & Greeno, J.G. (1985). Understanding and solving word arithmetic problems. *Psychological Review, 92,* 109–129.

Kohler, W. (1925). *The mentality of apes.* New York: Liveright.

Kohler, W. (1929). *Gestalt psychology.* New York: Liveright.

Kohler, W. (1969). *The task of Gestalt psychology.* Princeton, NJ: Princeton University Press.

Kosslyn, S.M. (1980). *Image and mind.* Cambridge, MA: Harvard University Press.

Lewin, K. (1936). *Principles of topological psychology.* New York: McGraw-Hill.

Lockhart, R.S., Lamon, M., & Gick, M.L. (1988). Conceptual transfer in simple insight problems. *Memory & Cognition, 16,* 36–44.

Luchins, A.S. (1942). Mechanization in problem solving: The effect of einstellung. *Psychological Monographs, 54*(6), whole no. 248.

Luchins, A.S., & Luchins, E.H. (1970). *Wertheimer's seminars revisited: Problem solving and thinking* (Vol. 1–3). Albany, NY: State University of New York.

Lung, C., & Dominowski, R.L. (1985). Effects of strategy instructions and practice on nine dot problem solving. *Journal of Experimental Psychology: Learning, Memory, and Cognition, 11,* 804–811.

Maier, N.R.F. (1930). Reasoning in humans: I. On direction. *Journal of Comparative Psychology, 10,* 115–143.

Maier, N.R.F. (1931). Reasoning in humans: II. The solution of a problem and its appearance in consciousness. *Journal of Comparative Psychology, 12,* 181–194.

Maier, N.R.F. (1970). *Problem solving and creativity.* Belmont, CA: Brooks/Cole.

Maltzman, I. (1955). Thinking: From a behaviorist point of view. *Psychological Review, 62,* 275–286.

Mandler, J.M., & Mandler, G.S. (1964). *Thinking: From association to Gestalt.* New York: Wiley.

Mayer, R.E. (1989). Models for understanding. *Review of Educational Research, 59,* 43–64.

Mayer, R.E. (1992). *Thinking, problem solving, cognition* (2nd ed). New York: Freeman.

Metcalfe, J. (1986a). Feeling of knowing in memory and problem solving. *Journal of Experimental Psychology: Learning, Memory, and Cognition, 12,* 288–294.

Metcalfe, J. (1986b). Premonitions of insight predict impending error. *Journal of Experimental Psychology: Learning, Memory, and Cognition, 12,* 623–634.

Metcalfe, J., & Wiebe, D. (1987). Intuition in insight and nonsight problem solving. *Memory & Cognition, 15,* 238–246.

Miller, G.A., Galanter, E., & Pribram, K.H. (1960). *Plans and the structure of behavior.* New York: Holt, Rinehart & Winston.

Montgomery, H. (1988). Mental models and problem solving: Three challenges to a theory of restructuring and insight. *Scandinavian Journal of Psychology, 29,* 85–94.

Newell, A. (1985). Duncker on thinking: An inquiry into progress in cognition. In S. Koch & D. Leary (Eds.), *A century of psychology as science.* New York: McGraw-Hill.

Nickerson, R.S., Perkins, D.N., & Smith, E.E. (1985). *The teaching of thinking.* Hillsdale, NJ: Erlbaum.

Ohlsson, S. (1984a). Restructuring revisited: I. A summary and critique of the Gestalt theory of problem solving. *Scandinavian Journal of Psychology, 25,* 67–78.

Ohlsson, S. (1984b). Restructuring revisited: II. An information processing theory of restructuring and insight. *Scandinavian Journal of Psychology, 25,* 117–129.

Polya, G. (1965). *Mathematical discovery: Vol. 2. On understanding, learning, and teaching problem solving.* New York: Wiley.

Resnick, L.B. (1989). Introduction. In L.B. Resnick (Ed.), *Knowing, learning, and instruction: Essays in honor of Robert Glaser* (pp. 1–24). Hillsdale, NJ: Erlbaum.

Segal, J.W., Chipman, S.F., & Glaser, R. (Eds.). (1985). *Thinking and learning skills: Vol. 1. Relating instruction to research.* Hillsdale, NJ: Erlbaum.

Simon, H.A. (1982). Otto Selz and information-processing psychology. In N.H. Frijda & A.D. De Groot (Eds.), *Otto Selz: His contribution to psychology* (pp. 147–163). The Hague: Mouton.

Singley, M.K., & Anderson, J.R. (1989). *The transfer of cognitive skill.* Cambridge, MA: Harvard University Press.

Sternberg, R.J. (Ed.). (1988). *The nature of creativity: Contemporary psychological perspectives.* Cambridge, England: Cambridge University Press.

Thorndike, E.L. (1898). Animal intelligence: An experimental study of the associative processes in animals. *Psychological Monographs, 2*(8).

Van Hiele, P.M. (1986). *Structure and insight: A theory of mathematics education.* Orlando, FL: Academic Press.

Vosniadou, S., & Ortony, A. (Eds.). (1989). *Similarity and analogical reasoning.* Cambridge, England: Cambridge University Press.

Wallas, G. (1926). *The art of thought.* New York: Harcourt Brace Jovanovich.

Weisberg, R.W. (1986). *Creativity: Genius and other myths.* New York: Freeman.

Weisberg, R.W. (1992). Metacognition and insight during problem solving: Comment on Metcalfe. *Journal of Experimental Psychology: Learning, Memory, and Cognition, 18,* 426–431.

Weisberg, R.W., & Alba, J.W. (1981a). An examination of the alleged role of "fixation" in the solution of several "insight" problems. *Journal of Experimental Psychology: General, 110,* 169–192.

Weisberg, R.W., & Alba, J.W. (1981b). Gestalt theory, insight and past experience: Reply to Dominowski. *Journal of Experimental Psychology: General, 110,* 193–198.

Weisberg, R.W., & Alba, J.W. (1982). Problem solving is not like perception: More on Gestalt theory. *Journal of Experimental Psychology: General, 111,* 326–330.

Weisberg, R.W., & Suls, J. (1973). An information-processing model of Duncker's candle problem. *Cognitive Psychology, 4,* 255–276.

Wertheimer, M. (1959). *Productive thinking.* Chicago: University of Chicago Press. (Original work published 1945)

Wertheimer, M. (1985). A Gestalt perspective on computer simulations of cognitive processes. *Computers in Human Behavior, 1,* 19–33.

2 Insight and Problem Solving

Roger L. Dominowski and Pamela Dallob

What is insight? What role does it play in problem solving? These are interesting and worthwhile questions, but their answers are difficult and burdened by controversy. For example, some psychologists consider *insight* to be a meaningless term, in which case insight cannot possibly have an important role in problem solving. This chapter is based on the contrary belief that insight is a useful concept.

We will begin by drawing some distinctions between problem solving and memory retrieval and between reproductive and productive thinking. Insight will be characterized as a form of understanding (of a problem and its solution) that can result from restructuring, a change in a person's perception of a problem situation. Several kinds of insight problems will be discussed. We will describe the influence of the structure of a problem situation and the sometimes negative effects of prior learning on problem solving. Methods for identifying insightful behavior will be reviewed. Finally, we will consider whether memory for problem solutions has special properties and whether insightful problem solving can be taught.

CHARACTERISTICS OF PROBLEM SOLVING

What is a problem? In ordinary usage, a problem is a difficult or perplexing situation, a puzzle. Somewhat more formally, a problem exists when there is a goal to be achieved but the means of attaining the goal are not clear or one's initial attempt fails to attain the desired goal. In most formulations, the key ingredient of a problem is the need to discover the appropriate response to the situation, to overcome some minimum difficulty in attaining the goal. For a simple example, let us suppose John Doe goes out to the garage one morning to start the car (to go to work, or to the store, etc.). He puts the key in the ignition and turns it and the engine starts. Ordinarily, we would not say that John had just solved a problem (for John, this behavior is routine; for someone unfamiliar with starting a car, the situation would, of course, be different). However, if John had turned the key and the engine had not started, or the key had not fit into the ignition, or John could not find the key or get the garage door open, then we would readily admit that he faced a problem. Furthermore, we would credit him with problem solving even if he then achieved his goal rather easily.

Relation to Memory

Some theorists argue that problem solving is just a kind of re-membering. In contrast, we want to distinguish between problem solving and memory. Let's first consider what it means to remem-ber something. Skipping over a number of theoretical complex-ities (which will be left to memory theorists) and focusing on recall, we would say—in modern parlance—that remembering involves retrieving information from some memory. Psychology commonly distinguishes between short-term and long-term mem-ory so that the desired information might be retrieved from a re-cently activated and still active short-term memory or from a more-or-less inactive (until the retrieval was attempted) long-term memory. The classic example of short-term retrieval is re-membering (dialing or writing down) an unfamiliar telephone number that one has just looked up in a directory and perhaps kept in mind by rehearsal. Long-term remembering concerns retrieval of information acquired at some earlier time (with the interval between acquisition and retrieval *not* filled by active re-hearsal of the material). There are countless examples of long-term memory—remembering the name of a friend you haven't seen for weeks, or the way home, or how to ride a bicycle, or what you had for breakfast today, and so on.

If we were to ask someone, "What's the capital of the United States of America?" and the person immediately responded, "Washington, DC," that person has just remembered, but has he or she solved a problem? The inclination is to say no. If, however, the person had tried to remember but failed (at least initially), then we might say that a problem is involved.

The above characterizations of problem solving and remembering carry an important implication: that problem solving and remembering are different. Some psychologists would object to this implication because they argue that memory retrieval is the core of problem solving (e.g., Weisberg & Alba, 1981). In contrast, distinguishing between problem solving and remembering is at the core of arguments that insight is an important component of problem solving.

It is an interesting aspect of human memory that when people are unable to remember an item initially, they nonetheless can predict quite accurately whether they will eventually remember it. Metcalfe (1986) used this fact to devise a comparison of problem solving with memory. She theorized that if problem solving is like remembering, then people should, after brief exposure to a problem, be able to predict whether they will solve the problem when given more time. Her results did not support this theory: Whereas people were able to predict their later remembering with reasonable accuracy, they were unable to predict problem-solving success. This finding supports a distinction between memory and problem solving. In her study, Metcalfe deliberately used problems typically labeled *insight problems* (to be described shortly). Consequently, her results imply a difference between memory and insightful problem solving; because other problems were not included, we do not know how they would compare to memory.

Reproductive and Productive Thinking

Early efforts to study insight (e.g., Kohler, 1925; Maier, 1940; Wertheimer 1945/1982) employed different situations and varying language, but they may reasonably be summarized as follows. Given a goal-oriented situation, there are two very different ways in which an organism might behave. In one, the organism readily produces the behavior needed to attain the goal (we might say the organism knows what to do), and the episode comes to an end. Maier called this *reproductive thinking*; it represents, approximately, the no-problem case from our earlier discussion.

In the second instance, prior learning is not sufficient for success. Past experience can get in the way; something new and different must be done to achieve the goal. Such *productive thinking* is argued (sometimes) to involve insight (e.g., Maier, 1940).

The distinction being drawn must be carefully examined. If an individual readily achieves the goal, it is reasonable to conclude that the cues present in the situation elicited the appropriate, previously acquired behavior. It does *not* follow, however, that taking a relatively long time to solve or failing to solve a problem means that some completely different process is involved.

Slow solutions and failures might occur for a number of reasons. A person may fail to produce a solution because information necessary to solve the problem was never learned, just as a person may apparently fail to remember something because he or she never knew the material in the first place. We also know that the likelihood and speed of remembering something is affected by the retrieval cues that are presented. For example, suppose a person is given the task of producing a particular person's name. Compare these sets of cues (all of which fit the same answer):

• He died in 1980.
• He was a film director who died in 1980.
• He directed the films "Psycho" and "The Birds."
• He directed the films "Psycho" and "The Birds," and often was called The Master of Suspense; his initials are AH and his first name is Alfred.

Given to someone who has never heard of Alfred Hitchcock, none of these cue sets will be effective in eliciting his name. If the person has some relevant knowledge, the cue sets should differ markedly in effectiveness. In an analogous fashion, the behavior of a person who fails to solve a problem or who solves slowly might be explained in terms of the effectiveness of the cues present in the problem situation. From this perspective, the same principles account for ordinary remembering, readily produced (so-called no-problem) solutions, slow solutions, and no solutions.

Problem solving often requires people to do something more than produce a single idea. When learning to do something, the change from knowing nothing to maximum efficiency ordinarily takes time and practice. In earlier phases of learning, execution can be erratic and slow and sometimes may fail. A related idea is that more complex acts, those having more components, are likely to be slower and more error-prone. Research on problem solving has demonstrated that tasks requiring more to be done to reach a solution yield more failures and slower solutions. For example, increasing the number of disks in a disk-transfer problem produces a disproportionately sharp increase in unnecessary moves (Gagne & Smith, 1962). Matching problems require people to use relational information in sentences (e.g., "The accountant drives a green car." "Bob lives next to the doctor.") to work out the matches among individuals, cars, occupations, and so forth. Increasing the number of required matches from 10 to 20 yields a modest increase in difficulty, but a further increase to 25 or more matches results in a very large number of failures to solve the problem (Polich & Schwartz, 1974). The central point is that variation in solution speed or likelihood can reflect the complexity of the required solution procedure or the degree to which the procedure has been mastered.

A focus on retrieval cues, complexity of solutions, and degree of learning represents an alternative (a competitor) to what the Gestalt psychologists stressed in discussing productive thinking and insight. From the Gestalt perspective, not all instances of problem solving involve productive thinking; rather, productive thinking and insight apply only to certain kinds of problem solving. The focus is on doing something new and on overcoming the constraints of past experience. Insight is associated with the change in meaning that sometimes occurs.

THE NATURE OF INSIGHT

The concept of insight is closely related to understanding and comprehension. To gain insight is to understand (something) more fully, to move from a state of relative confusion to one of comprehension. There are numerous everyday examples of such changes, as in "getting" a joke or reading some material that seems murky but then becomes clear. The difference between "I don't understand" and "I see!" is what is intended. The occurrence of insight is associated with the "Aha!" experience, with the proverbial light bulb going on over one's head. To summarize its major characteristics, insight is: (1) a form of understanding of a problem and its solution; (2) the product of a process of restructuring; (3) dependent on the features of the problem situation; and (4) only one determinant of success in problem solving.

Understanding

There is more than one way to describe understanding. Emphasis can be given to its external or internal aspects (see Greeno, 1977). On some occasions, we come to understand something new or unfamiliar by relating it to something that we already know, thus making external connections. The use of analogies is a prime example of this form of understanding. Suppose that, in trying to explain some mechanism, we tell the listener that "it operates like a pair of hot and cold water faucets." The attempt is to map the person's knowledge of faucets onto the new mechanism, thus enabling understanding.

The internal aspect of understanding concerns the relations existing among the components of an entity—that is, how the parts are related to make up the whole. A simple example is comprehending a sentence: Knowing the meanings of the individual words is not sufficient; one must relate the words properly to one another to grasp the meaning of the sentence. Organizational charts, wiring diagrams, and the like are other examples emphasizing internal connectedness.

In the case of problem solving, the relations among the problem elements and the solution are of central importance. Many problems, such as games and puzzles, have few, if any, connections with other aspects of our knowledge. Nonetheless, there can be huge differences in understanding such problems. Compare, for example, the assessment of the relations among the pieces in a chess game by a novice versus a master player. The master has far greater understanding of the structure of chess. The notion of insight seems to be most closely related to the internal features of understanding. That is, the emphasis in discussions of insight is on grasping the structure (the relations) of a problem.

Product or Process?

Insight is a particular knowledge state that is attained. It is not itself a process. There have been objections to the postulation of a mysterious process of insight that somehow produces solutions to problems (e.g., Weisberg, 1992; Weisberg & Alba, 1981). Objections to mysterious processes are appropriate, but they seem misdirected in this case (see Dominowski, 1981).

Kohler (1925) studied problem solving in apes, observing them in situations where they had to do something novel to obtain a desired object (e.g., a banana, an orange). The fruit was hung from the ceiling, too high to be grasped by jumping but readily obtained if the animal would move a box to a place under the fruit and climb onto the box to reach for it. In other tests, the fruit was placed outside the bars of the cage, too far to be reached directly but retrievable if a stick, or tree branch, or even two short sticks that had to be joined together were used effectively to extend the ape's reach. To summarize a number of reported observations, the prototypical behavior pattern involved the ape's repeated and vain direct attempts to get the banana, jumping or reaching and stretching without success. Solution-irrelevant behaviors also occurred (e.g., banging the cage, moaning) as well as general activity. At some point, a change would occur—other actions would cease, and the animal would proceed to use the implement to obtain the fruit. For the change to happen, it was important that the ape had the implement and the objective simultaneously in the visual field. Here is part of Kohler's (1925, p. 32) description of the behavior of a female chimpanzee named Nueva:

Thus, between lamentations and entreaties, some time passes, until— about seven minutes after the fruit has been exhibited to her—she suddenly casts a look at the stick, ceases her moaning, seizes the stick, stretches it out of the cage, and succeeds, though somewhat clumsily, in drawing the bananas within arm's reach.

In a later discussion of insight, Kohler (1947, pp. 341–342) made these remarks:

The direct awareness of determination ... may also be called *insight*. When I once used this expression in a description of the intelligent behavior of apes, an unfortunate misunderstanding was, it seems, not entirely prevented.... Apparently, some readers interpreted this formulation as though it referred to a mysterious mental agent or faculty which was made responsible for the apes' behavior. Actually, nothing of this sort was intended ... the concept is used in a strictly descriptive fashion.

Maier (1940) contrasted "habitual directions," which lead to reproducing previously learned solutions, with "new directions," which give rise to new combinations of old experiences. The new combinations produce the meaning changes that constitute *insight*. Maier's account clearly makes insight "a consequence rather than a cause in problem solving" (p. 51).

Situational Influence

The Gestalt psychologists' interest in insight stemmed from their interest in intelligent behavior, which they considered to be effective goal-oriented behavior in relatively novel situations. They were concerned with how people did new things and with what prevented people from solving problems for which, it would appear, they possessed all the requisite knowledge. They did *not*, as is sometimes implied, consider past experience to be irrelevant to problem solving. As noted earlier, prior learning was considered an adequate account of reproductive problem solving. They did claim that past experience was *insufficient* to explain instances of productive problem solving or failures to think productively. Kohler (1925) noted that apes with prior experience playing with sticks tended to use sticks more readily to retrieve goal objects. Nonetheless, referring to such experience was not enough to explain completely the apes' behavior in the problem situation and was certainly inadequate for explaining problem solving by apes without such experience. Ellen and Pate (1986) present an interesting discussion of learning "versus" insight.

Gestalt accounts of problem solving stress the features of the current (problem) situation, especially the structural relations existing among situational components. They are concerned with the problem solver's interpretation of the situation, particularly with problems requiring a change in interpretation for a solution to be reached. Information-processing theories employ the concept of a *problem representation*, which is similar in meaning to the Gestalt use of *interpretation.* In rough terms, to represent a problem (to oneself) is to interpret the problem. Problem representations usually are discussed as rather static entities, whereas Gestalt accounts characterize interpretations as involving structural forces and dynamic changes. This difference may be more rhetorical than substantive; it does seem, however, that the Gestalt psychologists were more interested in changes in representation (interpretation).

Some information-processing theorists also used the term *insight* (e.g., Newell, Shaw & Simon, 1958) but not in the same way as did the Gestalt psychologists. In Newell and colleagues' formulation, insight is essentially a parameter of behavior. Characterizing problem solving as a search process (in a conceptual "problem space"), they suggested that a problem solver exhibits "insight" to the extent that a solution is found while minimizing the amount of search. This use of the term *insight* is neither common nor controversial. Rather, it is the Gestalt notion of insight as a particular knowledge state arising from an appropriate (re)interpretation of the problem situation that is the focus of attention and argument.

Insight Problems

Many writers have discussed so-called insight problems, implying that there exists a fairly well-defined class of such problems. It is important to realize, however, that the term *insight problem* is applied to tasks having different characteristics. Precisely how the differences might influence findings is not known, but the fact of the differences is worth keeping in mind. In addition, we must try hard to avoid closing off theoretical issues; that is, describing insight problems as "those solved via insight" just will not do. We need to identify the task features while leaving open the interesting questions. We would expect tasks that might involve insight to have certain features—to require something new or nonobvious to be done and to be difficult enough so that the initial solution attempt is seldom successful. These features would at least provide a situation relevant to the claims made about insight, and indeed tasks labeled *insight problems* usually have these characteristics.

One type of insight problem is the *object-use problem*, similar to the tasks Kohler (1925) set for the chimpanzees. In studies of human problem solving, object-use problems typically involve multiple objects and require that one object be used in a relatively novel manner to achieve the goal (which itself might be arbitrary). An example is the two-string problem: Imagine a large, bare room in which two strings hang from the ceiling. The goal is to tie the two strings together, but they are too far apart to allow the person to grasp one string, walk over, and reach the other string. Any of a number of objects might be in the room and available for use. The task is to find a way to use some object to achieve the goal.

How the goal is attained depends on the objects provided and the precise instructions or criteria used for the task. An important point needs to be made. Suppose an available object is a piece (or ball) of string, sufficient to allow the problem solver to tie it to one string, walk to the other string, and pull the first one over so the two target strings can be tied. Such behavior would achieve the goal, but it is irrelevant to any claims regarding insight: The problem is solved by "doing the obvious," using an object in its usual function.

The task is relevant to insight issues when some object must be used in a *novel* fashion to reach a solution. For this reason, attention has focused on the pendulum solution, which involves tying some appropriate object (e.g., a screwdriver) to the end of one string and causing that string to swing back and forth. One then simply walks to the other string and waits for the first string to swing close enough to grasp. The form of the solution is original (having the string come to the person) and the object is used in a relatively unusual fashion. These two solutions to the problem illustrate Maier's (1940) distinction between habitual and new directions; insight is proposed to be relevant only to solutions involving new directions.

Object-use problems have been presented with actual objects in real environments or in paper-and-pencil (or computer-screen) versions. It does not seem that manipulating the objects has any effect on performance (Jacobs & Dominowski, 1981), which suggests that the problems are primarily perceptual and mental tasks rather than perceptual-motor tasks.

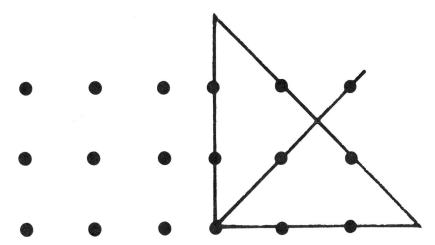

Figure 2.1
(Left) The nine-dot problem, in which a person is instructed to connect all the dots using only four straight lines without lifting the pencil from the page or retracing any lines. (Right) Solution to the nine-dot problem.

Another type of insight problem might be labeled a *spatial insight problem*. A frequently used example of this type is the nine-dot problem, illustrated in figure 2.1. There are no objects involved, although there is required activity (drawing lines), and spatial relations among problem elements are relevant. The Gestalt analysis of such problems is that difficulty arises because people make an incorrect assumption (adopt an inappropriate interpretation)—namely, that lines should begin and end on dots (i.e., that lines should be confined to the area defined by the dots). The problem cannot be solved with this constraint. Solving this type of problem may require doing something novel but not in the same sense as when an object is used in an unusual manner. These problems do require doing something nonobvious. Indeed, the nine-dot problem is difficult for college students who are given no hints about the solution.

Another type of insight problem is the *verbal insight problem*, which is loosely defined. Although the tasks are presented in verbal form, their content might refer to spatial or numerical concepts as well as verbal meanings. It is reasonable to suspect that as the content changes, different sorts of abilities might affect performance. Such effects would have no theoretical connection to insight phenomena but could make data interpretation less clear. Furthermore, two subtypes of verbal insight problems have been used, usually with no recognition of the distinction. For want of better terms, let these be called *wrong-answer* versus *no-answer* problems. In the first case, people typically give an answer to the problem, often rather quickly, but the answer is wrong. In the second case, failure to solve usually involves giving no answer, even after a number of minutes.

The following is an example of the wrong-answer subtype: "A man bought a horse for $60 and sold it for $70. Then he bought it back again for $80 and sold it for $90. How much money did he make in the horse-trading business?" The most typical error is to say $10 (e.g., Maier & Casselman, 1970), but $20 is correct.

In contrast, failures to solve the following problem usually involve no answer: "A gardener is told to plant four trees so that each one is exactly the same distance from each of the others. How would you arrange the trees?" The answer is to arrange them in a three-dimensional equilateral pyramid with three trees forming an equilateral triangle on the ground and the fourth centered and raised above them the correct distance (an appropriate pyramidal hill would perhaps need to be found or built).

These subtypes of problems ordinarily are not distinguished but rather are thrown together and discussed collectively, implying that common processes apply to them all. Do the differences pointed to here affect results and interpretation? We do not yet know; it would seem plausible that the dynamics of problem solving might not be the same in all instances, which suggests that caution is appropriate until relevant information is obtained.

KEY CONCEPTS

Gestalt treatments of problem solving emphasize behavior in situations requiring relatively novel means of attaining goals. Insight is associated with understanding problem structure. Two concerns stem from this emphasis: What prevents the attainment of insight, and how is insight eventually achieved?

Fixation

When the structure of a situation is understood properly, appropriate behavior should be exhibited. In short, attaining insight should lead to solutions to problems (some qualifications will be given later). Of course, one could correctly comprehend a situation on initial exposure to it and know what to do, a perhaps sophisticated version of "no problem"—expert behavior, essentially. The Gestalt psychologists were especially concerned with situations where in an individual misinterprets the situation or fails to see the true structure. The person is described as "fixated" on an inappropriate interpretation of the problem. Such fixation is an obstacle to solution and must be overcome. There is a difference between saying "A person has a wrong interpretation" and "A person is fixated on a wrong interpretation." The latter connotes force, obsession, not just mere possession. The Gestalt psychologists used *fixation* deliberately because they believed that an inappropriate representation was a force directing problem-solving efforts and providing resistance to a new interpretation.

Fixation has proved to be a troublesome concept (see Dominowski, 1981; Weisberg & Alba, 1981). There have been attempts to deal with some implications related to the notion of fixation, although it is not clear how much of the "extra meaning" has been tapped. Consider the following: Suppose it is worse to have an incorrectly structured problem interpretation than to have no, or a very weakly structured, representation. If so, then presenting a problem in a way that encourages wrong representations should impair finding the solution.

There are many research findings demonstrating that the way a problem is presented affects performance. Arranging the presentation to suggest a wrong approach retards solutions (see Bourne, Dominowski, Loftus & Healy, 1986, for a summary), but do these findings require the fixation concept? It seems reasonable to explain such findings in terms of cuing; the cues in the situation promote the retrieval of certain information in long-term memory, and retrieving incorrect material will delay a solution. What is not clear is whether forcelike notions are needed.

A very interesting attempt to study fixation phenomena concerned the solution of scrambled-word problems called *anagrams*, strings of letters that can be rearranged to form words (e.g., *htcik* [solution: *thick*]). The essential point is that any anagram is, by definition, incorrectly ordered. A special type of anagram can be presented by using letter sets from which two words can be made; one word is used as the anagram whereas the other serves as the solution (e.g., *worth* [solution: *throw*]). Both ordinary non-sense anagrams and word anagrams are wrongly ordered and need to be rearranged; the interesting difference is that word anagrams are highly structured. The contrast does not, in principle, concern cuing a better or worse approach; both kinds of anagrams mislead equally if the problems are constructed properly. The question is whether organization hinders rearrangement. The answer appears to be yes (Ekstrand & Dominowski, 1968), providing some support for the ideas underlying fixation.

If it is assumed that the greater structure of a word anagram leads to a more organized but still incorrect representation of the problem, then the results imply that adopting a wrong but more structured interpretation impairs finding a solution. This interpretation is not based solely on using word anagrams. Dominowski (1969) had people practice pronouncing nonsense anagrams (without telling them that words could be made from the letter strings) before giving them the anagrams to solve. Pronunciation practice increased organization (smoothing the encoding) without adding meaning, and this practice made the anagrams harder to solve.

Another approach to fixation involves giving hints at different points in problem solving. The idea is that, if wrong interpretations are forces that must be overcome, then giving a hint to a person who is already pursuing a wrong direction should be less helpful than giving the hint at the very beginning of the problem, before a representation has been constructed. There has been very little research on this topic, but the available evidence does *not* show that the timing of a hint affects its usefulness (Dominowski & Jenrick, 1972; Maier & Burke, 1967). This implication of the fixation concept has not been supported. The force connotations remain elusive. It has been suggested that fixation be considered merely a temporary blockage of retrieval of information needed for solution (Smith & Blankenship, 1991).

A different approach to studying fixation was employed in a study using wrong-answer verbal insight problems. These are tasks for which people typically give incorrect solutions when they fail to solve, rather than offering no solution. For example, having been told that the area covered by water lilies in a lake doubles every 24 hours and that the entire lake is covered in 60 days, when asked how long it takes to cover half the lake, people tend to respond "30 days" (59 days is correct). In this study (Dallob & Dominowski, 1992), the attempt was made to contrast an explanation of these wrong solutions in terms of fixation with an explanation based on inadequate monitoring of solution attempts.

In either case, it is accepted that people offer incorrect solutions because of inaccurate interpretations of the problem. The force connotation of fixation implies that people are trapped by these wrong interpretations, that it will be difficult to change them. An alternative account is that having thought of wrong solutions (which are typically encouraged by a quick, shallow reading of the problem), people give them as solutions because they fail to check adequately the accuracy of the solution; they only weakly monitor their own problem-solving efforts.

These two accounts make different predictions for what should happen if people are told that their answers are wrong. If people are truly fixated on their inaccurate representations, telling them that their answers are wrong should not help them find a different, correct answer. If, however, people gave wrong answers due to "sloppiness" (weak monitoring), error feedback should lead them to reconsider the problem features, note the inadequacy of their first answers, and find the correct solution. Dallob and Dominowski (1992) concluded that approximately one-third of wrong answers could be attributed to inadequate monitoring because error feedback led to correct answers approximately one-third of the time. In the remaining cases, being told an answer was wrong did not help. Although these feedback failures do not uniquely establish fixation as the explanation for the wrong answers, they are consistent with what should happen if people were fixated on their wrong representations.

Functional Fixedness

One emphasis in Gestalt work on problem solving was that prior experience or familiarity could increase the difficulty of a problem requiring something new or nonobvious to be done. In effect, habitual directions can get in the way of finding new directions. This point has been demonstrated many times in the phenomenon of *functional fixedness*, which concerns the solution of object-use problems. The essential idea is that emphasizing the ordinary use of a critical object will make it more difficult for a person to think of using that object in a novel manner. Functional fixedness can be viewed as a special case of fixation—that is, fixation on the ordinary retarding attainment of the novel.

Two procedures have been used to study functional fixedness, with the emphasis on an object's usual function coming either from an experience occurring immediately prior to the problem situation or from the way in which the problem is presented. We will consider both cases.

The pendulum solution to the two-string problem can be achieved with any small object of appropriate weight. In studies of functional fixedness, small electrical switches and relays have been used; either can be used as the pendulum weight. To attempt to induce functional fixedness, some subjects would use the switch (or the relay) to complete an electrical circuit just prior to being given the two-string problem, with both objects available. The consistent finding was that using an object in its usual function decreased the chances of its being used in an unusual way to solve the two-string problem (e.g., DiVesta & Walls, 1967; Duncker, 1945). If the switch (relay) were used to complete the electrical circuit, then the relay (switch) would be used as a pendulum weight.

It is important to note the specific nature of this phenomenon—that is, *unusual* use of an object does *not* diminish its subsequent use in its ordinary function (Van de Geer, 1957). Prior use of an object in several nonstandard functions (e.g., using a switch to hold pins in place) does not have a clear effect on its use to solve the two-string problem (DiVesta & Walls, 1967). Hence, it is not the case that any prior use affects any subsequent use; rather, prior standard or ordinary use inhibits subsequent novel use. It is also worth noting that functional fixedness has been shown with other objects and tasks. For example, requiring people to use some paper clips in the usual way (clipping papers together) resulted in

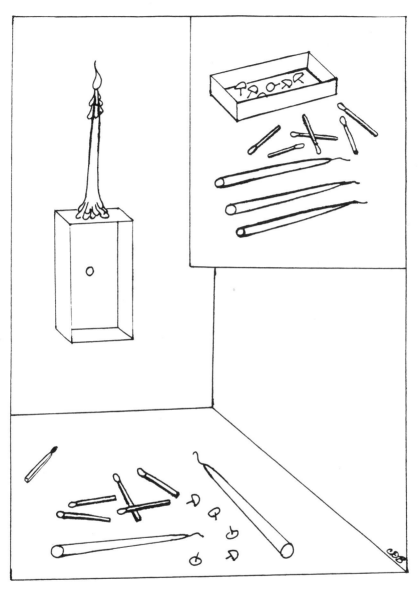

Figure 2.2
The box-candle problem, the objective of which is to attach a candle to the wall so that it will not drip wax on the table. Shown are the materials provided and (upper left) the solution.

those people taking longer to think of using a different paper clip as a hook from which to suspend a light object (Adamson, 1952).

The perceptual version of functional fixedness involves presenting a problem so that the ordinary use of a critical object is emphasized. Research has employed the box-candle problem (figure 2.2), the solution to which requires the person to tack the box to a soft (e.g., cork) wall and thus use the box as a platform for the candle. The critical manipulation is whether the box is holding the tacks, stressing its usual function, or is empty when the problem materials are presented. This problem is easily solved when the box is empty but very difficult when the box is filled (e.g., Adamson, 1952). The box-filled presentation leads people to not notice the box as a separate, usable object; drawing their attention to the box aids solution (Glucksberg & Weisberg, 1966). Similar effects have been obtained in other situations. For example, needing a piece of string to tie sticks together, people readily used a string hanging by itself on a nail on the wall but, if the string were holding up a sign or mirror, many people failed to use it (Scheerer, 1963). The effects of such perceptual influences tend to be very strong, lending support to force connotations for this form of fixation.

Restructuring

The process of arriving at a new understanding of a problem situation was called *restructuring* by the Gestalt psychologists. Changing from one representation of a problem to a very different representation is restructuring. Wertheimer (1945/1982) provides a compelling example in the case of the two boys playing badminton. The older boy was a more skilled player than the younger. Consequently, when they played the usual games, the outcome was predictable and one-sided. The younger boy lost interest in playing, so the older boy faced a problem. He wanted to play badminton, but his friend did not; both were unhappy.

At this point, Wertheimer (1945/1982, p. 172) asks the reader, "What do you suggest?" and reports some of the answers he received. These include offering candy, playing a different game, shaming the younger boy into playing, and not playing to full ability. These are contrasted with the boy's eventual solution (after considerable pondering): to change the game from one of competition to one of cooperation. The older boy proposed that they try to keep the bird in play as long as possible, counting the number of consecutive hits, and starting with easy shots and making them harder as their success increased. The proposal was happily accepted, and the revised game was on.

Restructuring need not be involved in all instances of problem solving. For example, an initial failure to solve might be due to failure to retrieve a needed item from long-term memory; should retrieval later succeed, the solution would be achieved without a change in representation of the entire problem situation. Alternatively, one could have the appropriate problem representation but still be unable to execute the necessary solution steps. Such behavior was called a "good error" by Duncker (1945): The person is proceeding in the appropriate direction but has not yet found the specific means of achieving the goal.

In a review of restructuring, Ohlsson (1984) concluded that restructuring clearly occurs in problem solving as well as in other situations (e.g., in the changes from one to another perception of ambiguous figures), but he had concerns about some ideas related to restructuring. For example, a change in representation is sometimes an improvement, sometimes not; there is no clear basis for predicting when each type of change will occur. Alternatively, it has been suggested that restructuring is more likely with deeper analysis of the problem and the goal; testing this idea requires an independent measure of depth of analysis, which does not currently exist. Although Ohlsson accepted the fact of restructuring, he was not sure how useful the concept might be for explaining problem solving.

Metcalfe's (1986) contrast between memory and (insightful) problem solving was based on restructuring. Recall that she used insight problems predicted to involve restructuring. Their solution presumably stems from a complete change in representation of the problem, a change that could not be predicted from the initial representation. For this reason, people were expected to be unable to predict accurately which problems they would solve. In contrast, people can predict memory because they have partial information about target items on the basis of initial retrieval attempts. The representational change involved in restructuring would prevent useful partial information from being available prior to the change.

Suddenness of Solution

Restructuring is proposed to result in an abrupt transition from one problem representation to a different representation. If the new representation is appropriate and leads quickly to a solution, then the solution should appear suddenly and disconnected from preceding solution attempts rather than as a natural extension of prior efforts. The sudden change in behavior was stressed in Kohler's (1925) studies of apes, and most writers have incorporated suddenness in their characterizations of insightful solutions. Metcalfe and Wiebe (1987) contrasted this solution process with an incremental solution process by studying people's judgments of "warmth" (nearness to solution) during problem solving. If a solution is reached by gradual accrual of information, with successive attempts generally more similar to the solution, then problem solvers' warmth ratings should increase prior to solution. In contrast, for solutions produced by a radical restructuring of problem interpretation, no gradual increase in warmth should occur prior to finding the solution. Rather it would be expected that perceptions of nearness to solution would stay steady and "cold" until the solution itself occurs.

Warmth ratings were obtained at regular intervals while people worked on a number of problems. The insight problems were a mixture of verbal and spatial problems, as described earlier. The noninsight problems represented tasks designated by previous researchers as multistep or incremental problems. The results showed different patterns of warmth ratings for the two types of problems: gradual increases in warmth for the noninsight problem but essentially flat warmth ratings for the insight problems prior to solution. Despite some objections (Weisberg, 1992), the essential results seem to stand. Problems differ in their patterns of warmth ratings prior to solution and, for some, the pattern fits expectations based on the concept of restructuring.

A caution seems in order regarding suddenness of solution in relation to restructuring and insight. The Gestalt psychologists did not propose that insightful solutions were fast solutions;

rather restructuring (and solution) could occur at any point in problem solving. Indeed, it was sometimes suggested that restructuring was more likely with extended effort (see Ohlsson, 1984). Nor did they propose that, once the appropriate problem interpretation had been attained, the complete solution would occur suddenly. Kohler (1925) reported, for example, that an ape, having suddenly switched to a deliberate attempt to use a stick to retrieve fruit outside the cage, might handle the stick clumsily and take some time to get the fruit. It should be clear that the time between correct representation and final solution will depend on what needs to be done to execute the solution. For instance, the nine-dot problem is said to depend on the critical insight of extending lines beyond the dots. Yet extending lines is not itself the final solution; one must still identify the correct extended lines and their order to execute the complete solution (Lung & Dominowski, 1985). Attaining insight is not necessarily the only solution component. When there is little to do to execute a solution, as in many verbal insight problems, then sudden solutions do occur (Metcalfe & Wiebe, 1987).

RELATED ISSUES

Many issues have been raised by distinguishing between different kinds of problem solving and by focusing on solutions involving restructuring and insight. Some of those issues concern the very nature of insight and the criteria for making distinctions among types of problem solving, as already discussed. In this section, we will consider two additional interesting issues related to insight that are of potential theoretical and practical importance.

Memory for Solutions

One implication of solving a problem with insight is that the solution should be well remembered. This prediction follows from the idea that, in attaining insight, one grasps the relations among problem components and the solution. In other words, the solution becomes bound to the problem structure. If this is so, when the problem is encountered again, the solution should occur, and rather readily (Scheerer, 1963). Kohler's (1925) studies of apes include multiple references to efficient solutions when problems were repeated. It was not necessarily the case that the solution was produced immediately, although there were dramatic changes from first to second solutions (for example, from 2 hours to a minute or so).

This expectation of excellent memory for insightful solutions can be contrasted with ordinary memory phenomena, wherein it is commonplace to expect (and observe) forgetting over time. It is surprising that for many years there was no research on solution memory. In 1981, Weisberg and Alba reported that, in distinct contrast to the insight prediction, only 65 percent of their subjects solved the nine-dot problem when it was presented a second time after a 1-week interval. They concluded that solution memory showed ordinary forgetting and thus required no special explanatory constructs. In fact, Weisberg and Alba's subjects had failed to solve the nine-dot problem on first presentation and had been shown the solution. The question is whether this mattered. Gestalt theory held that it did matter; Wertheimer (1945/1982) had argued that providing a solution was unlikely to produce the restructuring necessary for real understanding.

Nearly concurrently with Weisberg and Alba's work, researchers in verbal memory began studying the *generation effect*, finding that people remembered words they had generated better than words that had been shown to them (Jacoby, 1978). These studies typically used simple verbal puzzles, such as presenting the word av__d with the instruction to find the opposite of *pursue*. Control subjects were given the word (e.g., *avoid*), whereas generating subjects were required to complete the target word. It can be seen that these were minimal problems, at best.

Two aspects of work on the generation effect are particularly relevant to our discussion. First, generating subjects typically showed far less than 100 percent retention (although better than that of control subjects). Second, retention for generating subjects was the same whether or not they succeeded in producing the correct solution on the initial presentation (Slamecka & Fevreiski, 1983). The explanation was that the generation effect will occur only for items already represented in memory and stems from greater activation of material related to the target item. Both successful and unsuccessful generation attempts were proposed to activate such information, the only difference being whether the target item itself had been reached. The implication was that Weisberg and Alba's findings (1981) accurately depicted solution memory.

Subsequent research has proved this implication to be incorrect—that is, the retention findings are different when tasks that are more clearly problems are employed. In one study (Dominowski & Buyer, 1985), people attempted a number of problems (including the nine-dot problem and several other insight problems); if they failed to solve within the time limit, they nonetheless were shown the solution. When the problems were presented again one week later, two clear findings emerged: (1) People who had initially solved a problem showed near-perfect memory for the solution. (2) Those who had generated the solution initially performed much better than people who had been shown the solution after failing to produce it. The results were in strong agreement with insight predictions and supported the notion that understanding problem structure (required for solving initially) results in excellent solution memory and the idea that providing solutions lacks necessary restructuring.

Another study showed that even generating a solution could be relatively ineffective if the problem solver was not required to comprehend all problem relations (Buyer & Dominowski, 1989). In the first session, people were given number riddles relating specific numbers to common phrases (e.g., "24 = hours in a day"). Those in the read-only control condition were shown the complete items and asked to rate them for familiarity. Two generation conditions were employed. In the difficult generation condition, people were given the number and had to produce the phrase when given only the first letters of the key words (e.g., "24 = h in a d). In the easy generation condition, the first key word was provided (e.g., "24 = hours in a d"). Whenever someone failed to generate the solution, it was provided.

When the problems were presented again 1 week later, without extra cues (e.g., "24 = h in a d"), several important findings emerged. People who had solved the problems initially showed far better memory than both those who had only read the completed riddles and those who had been given the solutions after failing to produce them (the latter two groups' average memory score was 66 percent). Among prior solvers, those who had produced the complete solution (difficult generation) had near-perfect solution memory (97 percent), better than those who had been given help with the solution (easy generation; 82 percent). The results are again consistent with the proposal that understanding problem structure is a key determinant of solution memory.

These results are provocative. Near-perfect memory for solutions initially produced is very different from many memory observations showing substantial forgetting. The topic requires further study to delineate the circumstances in which such excellent memory will occur. The finding that helping people to find a solution can hurt their memory for the solution raises the question of whether any kind of help will reduce memory. Theoretically, solution help that still allows the problem solver to work through all the important problem relations should not reduce memory. Future research may provide the answers.

Promoting Insightful Problem Solving

Insightful problem solving can occur in any domain and can sometimes lead to tremendous advances in knowledge. Seeing through a problem and arriving at a well-structured solution to a novel situation are behaviors worth promoting. An important question is whether there are ways to increase the occurrence of insightful behavior.

If the focus is on a single problem or a well-defined class of problems, it is clear that people can be trained to produce solutions. Extensive practice in solving problems in a particular domain allows people to develop effective procedures to solve such problems (Anderson, 1987). According to Anderson's theory, the acquired skill (set of procedures) will transfer to tasks that have the same procedural requirements for solution. This theory has been applied to skill acquisition in domains such as computer programming, and procedures are defined rather narrowly. For example, in Anderson's analysis, evaluating a computer program and generating a program use the same declarative knowledge but involve different procedures. Because of the procedural differences, his theory predicts—and Anderson found—little transfer from evaluation to generation.

Anderson's theory implies that developing skill at being insightful would be difficult. Insight problems differ widely in their content; specific solution procedures seem different. At a broad level, all instances of insightful behavior are procedurally identical—that is, restructuring or reorganization of the problem situation leads to solution. The question is whether this general level of procedural similarity would be sufficient to be the basis of skill development. In different terms, the question is how general a level of skill might be developed.

Earlier we described several types of insight problems. It seems reasonable to suppose that problems within a type have more similar solution procedures than the level of similarity for all insight problems. Thus, learning to solve object-use problems, or spatial insight problems, would represent a more limited version of becoming more insightful. There is evidence of such learning. Lung and Dominowski (1985) gave people practice at solving other dot-connecting problems (all requiring lines to be extended beyond the dots) before presenting the nine-dot problem. People who practiced and received strategy instructions were much more successful on the nine-dot problem (60 percent solutions) than control subjects (9 percent). In another study (Jacobs & Dominowski, 1981), people were given seven different object-use problems to try, with the result that the subjects showed modest improvement by the end of the series. In these experiments, people did not become insight experts, but there was some improvement even though the amount of practice was rather limited. We do not yet know what would happen with greatly extended practice.

Developing procedural skills is not the only way to improve problem solving, however. For example, people who are shown a useful method for representing a problem (e.g., a spatial array) will transfer that method to another problem even though the content and specific solution procedures are different (Novick, 1990). Because finding the appropriate problem representation is an integral part of attaining insight, the idea that people could learn to identify or construct better representations holds some promise. To date, representational transfer has been studied only in a narrow context.

A possible basis for broadly applicable skill is *metacognition*, which refers to a person's awareness of his or her own cognitive processes. Metacognition includes the planning, monitoring, and evaluation of solution processes, and improving these functions could help performance in a wide variety of situations.

An emphasis on metacognition has been found to aid problem solving. For example, requiring people to give reasons for their decisions or the steps they try in problem solving focuses their attention on their own solution processes. This technique has been used to improve both current performance and later transfer to other (similar) problems for several different tasks (Ahlum-Heath & DiVesta, 1986; Dominowski, 1990; Gagne & Smith, 1962). Although the tasks that have been studied might involve some restructuring, these studies did not include any insight problems as described here.

Other techniques emphasizing metacognition have aided solutions to insight problems. Maier (1933) found that lecturing about problem solving and reasoning prior to presenting three object-use problems (including the two-string and box-candle problems) resulted in higher solution rates. The lecture stressed such points as abandoning a solution path that failed and looking for new meanings and new combinations within the given information.

Davidson and Sternberg (1984) devised a more elaborate and theoretically based training scheme to facilitate solutions to arithmetic insight problems. The training stressed three processes involved in insightful problem solving: selective encoding, comparison, and combination. *Selective encoding* refers to focusing on only the relevant problem information and disregarding irrelevant information. *Selective comparison* involves relating new information to information previously stored in long-term memory. *Selective combination* occurs when separate pieces of given information are combined to form novel and relevant wholes. The 7 weeks of training (a few hours per week) focused on these processes, using a variety of procedures (e.g., direct instruction, individual and group problem-solving practice), and the training was successful.

Each of these efforts to promote productive thinking has dealt with a particular type of insight problem. Consequently, we do not know whether more general skills applicable to insightful problem solving can be acquired. Nonetheless, the success that has been achieved justifies some optimism and should encourage the investigation of more complex and extensive training.

FUTURE DIRECTIONS

Let us consider what a focus on insight offers us with respect to understanding problem solving. We begin with the observation that problems are most obviously situations in which some goal is desired but the way to achieve that goal is unclear. There can be no doubt that people sometimes already know what to do to achieve the desired goal; they might have been trained to execute the required procedure, or they might have previously acquired the insight necessary for generating the solution. However, there are also situations in which people do not already know what to do, and this is where acquiring insight becomes relevant.

The situation of particular interest is that in which people have difficulty solving a problem for which they possess all the knowledge necessary for producing a solution. Insightful problem solving involves productive thinking—that is, the person must go beyond past experience and overcome misleading situational influences to formulate a novel approach to a problem. Making this change in problem representation is the essence of restructuring. Note that the change, if it occurs, is inevitably from the familiar, the interpretation promoted by the problem presentation, to a more subtle, more novel representation of the problem.

Failures to solve can occur for various reasons including lack of relevant knowledge, inadequate retrieval of information from long-term memory, or weak monitoring of solution efforts. We should also consider that people fail to solve problems because they fixate on familiar and obvious interpretations of the problem situation.

We need to know more about sources of difficulty for various kinds of problems. We need especially to identify the problem features that encourage inaccurate problem interpretations. We must find ways to distinguish between failures stemming from inadequate knowledge and failures due to fixation on inappropriate approaches to problem solving. We must learn the extent to which, and by what means, people can learn to go beyond the obvious and more often arrive at insightful solutions to problems. The pursuit of answers to these and other questions stimulated by the concept of insightful problem solving seems eminently worthwhile.

REFERENCES

Adamson, R.E. (1952). Functional fixedness as related to problem solving: A repetition of three experiments. *Journal of Experimental Psychology, 44,* 288–291.

Ahlum-Heath, M.E., & DiVesta, F.J. (1986). The effect of conscious controlled verbalization of a cognitive strategy on transfer in problem solving. *Memory & Cognition, 14,* 281–285.

Anderson, J.R. (1987). Skill acquisition: Compilation of weak-method problem solutions. *Psychological Review, 94,* 192–210.

Bourne, L.E., Jr., Dominowski, R.L., Loftus, E.F., & Healy, A.F. (1986). *Cognitive processes* (2nd ed.). Englewood Cliffs, NJ: Prentice-Hall.

Buyer, L.S., & Dominowski, R.L. (1989). Retention of solutions: It's better to give than to receive. *American Journal of Psychology, 102,* 353–363.

Dallob, P.I., & Dominowski, R.L. (1992, April). *Erroneous solutions to verbal insight problems: Fixation or insufficient monitoring?* Paper presented at the meeting of the Western Psychological Association, Portland, OR.

Davidson, J.E., & Sternberg, R.J. (1984). The role of insight in intellectual giftedness. *Gifted Child Quarterly, 28,* 58–64.

DiVesta, F.J., & Walls, R.T. (1967). Transfer of object-function in problem solving. *American Educational Research Journal, 62,* 596–602.

Dominowski, R.L. (1969). The effect of pronunciation practice on anagram difficulty. *Psychonomic Science, 16,* 99–100.

Dominowski, R.L. (1981). Comment on "An examination of the alleged role of 'fixation' in the solution of several 'insight' problems." *Journal of Experimental Psychology: General, 110,* 193–198.

Dominowski, R.L. (1990). Problem solving and metacognition. In K.J. Gilhooly, M.T.G. Keane, R.H. Logie, & G. Erdos (Eds.), *Lines of thinking* (Vol. 2). New York: Wiley.

Dominowski, R.L., & Buyer, L.S. (1985, September). *Retention of problem solutions.* Paper presented to the British Psychological Society—Cognitive Psychology Section.

Dominowski, R.L., & Jenrick, R. (1972). Effects of hints and interpolated activity on solution of an insight problem. *Psychonomic Science, 26,* 335–338.

Duncker, K. (1945). On problem-solving. *Psychological Monographs, 58,* whole no. 270.

Ekstrand, B.R., & Dominowski, R.L. (1968). Solving words as anagrams: II. A clarification. *Journal of Experimental Psychology, 77,* 552–558.

Ellen, P., & Pate, J.L. (1986). Is insight merely response chaining? A reply to Epstein. *Psychological Record, 36,* 155–160.

Gagne, R.M., & Smith, E.C., Jr. (1962). A study of the effects of verbalizations on problem solving. *Journal of Experimental Psychology, 63,* 12–18.

Glucksberg, S., & Weisberg, R. (1966). Verbal behavior and problem solving: Some effects of labeling in a functional fixedness problem. *Journal of Experimental Psychology, 71,* 659–664.

Greeno, J.G. (1977). Process of understanding in problem solving. In N.J. Castellan, D.B. Pisoni, & G.R. Potts (Eds.), *Cognitive theory.* Hillsdale, NJ: Erlbaum.

Jacobs, M.K., & Dominowski, R.L. (1981). Learning to solve insight problems. *Bulletin of the Psychonomic Society, 17,* 171–174.

Jacoby, L.L. (1978). On interpreting the effects of repetition: Solving a problem versus remembering a solution. *Journal of Verbal Learning and Verbal Behavior, 17,* 649–667.

Kohler, W. (1925). *The mentality of apes.* New York: Liveright.

Kohler, W. (1947). *Gestalt psychology.* New York: Liveright.

Lung, C.T., & Dominowski, R.L. (1985). Effects of strategy instructions and practice on nine-dot problem solving. *Journal of Experimental Psychology: Learning, Memory, and Cognition, 11,* 804–811.

Maier, N.R.F. (1933). An aspect of human reasoning. *British Journal of Psychology, 24,* 144–155.

Maier, N.R.F. (1940). The behavior mechanisms concerned with problem solving. *Psychological Review, 47,* 43–53.

Maier, N.R.F., & Burke, R.J. (1967). Influence of timing of hints on their effectiveness. *Psychological Reports, 20,* 3–8.

Maier, N.R.F., & Casselman, G.C. (1970). Locating the difficulty in insight problems: Individual and sex differences. *Psychological Reports, 26,* 103–117.

Metcalfe, J. (1986). Feeling of knowing in memory and problem solving. *Journal of Experimental Psychology: Learning, Memory, and Cognition, 12,* 288–294.

Metcalfe, J., & Wiebe, D. (1987). Intuition in insight and noninsight problem solving. *Memory & Cognition, 15,* 238–246.

Newell, A., Shaw, J.C., & Simon, H.A. (1958). Elements of a theory of human problem solving. *Psychological Review, 65,* 151–166.

Novick, L.R. (1990). Representational transfer in problem solving. *Psychological Science, 1,* 128–132.

Ohlsson, S. (1984). Restructuring revisited: I. Summary and critique of the Gestalt theory of problem solving. *Scandinavian Journal of Psychology, 25,* 65–78.

Polich, J.M., & Schwartz, S.H. (1974). The effect of problem size on representation in deductive problem solving. *Memory & Cognition, 2,* 683–686.

Scheerer, M. (1963). Problem-solving. *Scientific American, 208,* 118–128.

Slamecka, N.J., & Fevreiski, J. (1983). The generation effect when generation fails. *Journal of Verbal Learning and Verbal Behavior, 22,* 153–163.

Smith, S.M., & Blankenship, S.E. (1991). Incubation and the persistence of fixation in problem solving. *American Journal of Psychology, 104,* 61–87.

Van de Geer, J.P. (1957). *A psychological study of problem solving.* Haarlem: Uitgeverig De Toorts.

Weisberg, R.W. (1992). Metacognition and insight during problem solving: Comment on Metcalfe. *Journal of Experimental Psychology: Learning, Memory, and Cognition, 18,* 426–431.

Weisberg, R.W., & Alba, J.W. (1981). An examination of the alleged role of "fixation" in the solution of several "insight" problems. *Journal of Experimental Psychology: General, 110,* 169–192.

Wertheimer, M. (1982). *Productive thinking.* Chicago: University of Chicago Press. (Original work published 1945).

II The Puzzle-Problem Approach

3 Demystification of Cognitive Insight: Opportunistic Assimilation and the Prepared-Mind Perspective

Colleen M. Seifert, David E. Meyer,
Natalie Davidson, Andrea L. Patalano,
and Ilan Yaniv

Insight may occur in many diverse forms, ranging from the relatively mundane to the immensely profound. On the mundane level, there are examples such as the following (modified from Mosler, 1977):

Two men who were walking through a desert stopped when they saw an unusual thing. They had discovered a third man lying on a stretch of sand, and he was dead. They noticed the dead man had carried a small pack with fresh food and water still in it. The dead man also had a larger pack on his back, and on his index finger was a large ring. The two men pondered the cause of the third man's death, but they could not explain it, and so they proceeded onward.

Later, while going along, one of the original two men accidently dropped a handkerchief that he had taken from his pocket to wipe his brow. Then, he suddenly realized how the third man probably died. Overhead, the third man's parachute had broken, and he had fallen precipitously to earth.

Similarly, but on a more profound level, there are examples such as Isaac Newton's legendary discovery of the universal law of gravitation. As the legend goes, Newton went for a trip one autumn in the English countryside. During his sojourn there, he happened to notice an apple fall from a tree. On seeing this, it suddenly occurred to him that, in essence, the moon is like an apple being pulled toward Earth, after which Newton proceeded to formulate his gravitational law and deduce its many physical consequences.

The diversity of such examples, spanning Newton's apple and the man who fell to earth, raises many intriguing questions. What exactly is the nature of insight? Through what type(s) of mental process is insight achieved? How have Newton and other special individuals like him attained it? Must minds such as Newton's remain forever shrouded in mystery, or can they be studied scientifically and described in meaningful detail? Do they have any similarity to those of lesser mortals? Are lesser mortals, because of their limitations, precluded from attaining true insight? May we, despite our own limitations, reach further insights into insight? These and related questions are addressed in this chapter.

In pursuing the hoped-for answers, some prerequisite steps are essential. First, like other scholars before us (e.g., Bowers, Regehr, Balthazard & Parker, 1990), we must state what we mean by the term *insight*. Second, we must determine where we stand along various dimensions that together form a taxonomic framework of alternative perspectives on insight. With these steps completed, our own perspective may then be clearly seen and compared to those of others.

DEFINITION OF INSIGHT

The definition of insight that we adopt here has been endorsed by an old and respected source, *Webster's New World Dictionary* (Guralnik, 1984). According to it, *insight* is "seeing and understanding the inner nature of things clearly, especially by intuition." Moreover, in this context, *intuition* is "the immediate knowing of something without the conscious use of reasoning," *knowing* is "having a range of information," and *reasoning* is "thinking logically and analytically."

Virtues of the Present Definition

Although expressed in ordinary language, such terminology appeals to us for several reasons. If we take *Webster's* at its word, then insight can conceivably occur across a wide variety of domains involving many different types of information, including both factual (declarative) knowledge about the world and procedural knowledge about how to perform mental and physical tasks of one sort or another (Anderson, 1990). For example, recollections of past episodes in our lives might yield insights into our current behavior, encounters with novel events might yield insights into nature's universal laws, and rumination over ways to prove a speculative hypothesis might yield insights into useful modes of logical analysis. This breadth of possibility is consistent with our own expectation that mental processes ranging from memory retrieval to comprehension, explanation, induction, planning, and problem solving can all exhibit insightful outcomes. The potentially extensive venues implied by *Webster's* definition also leave open the encouraging prospect that ordinary people as well as reputed geniuses may, on occasion, experience the joys of insight. Under our current rubric, insight can and should be construed as an integral part of general human intelligence (Sternberg, 1985), making it a key topic for cognitive science.

Phenomenological Characteristics of Insight

Webster's definition, with its reference to "immediate knowing" and "seeing clearly" through subconscious nonanalytical processes rather than "conscious reasoning," likewise implicitly affirms several other intriguing phenomenological characteristics that are often associated with insight (e.g., Halpern, 1989; Metcalfe & Weib, 1987; Ohlsson, 1984a, 1984b). Consequently, our mission will entail explaining how these characteristics actually arise. We hope, for example, to explain (1) *suddenness*, wherein insight seems to happen abruptly through a quantum leap of understanding instead of some gradual incremental process; (2) *spontaneity*, wherein insight seems to happen internally of its own accord without the intention or effort of an instigating agent; (3) *unexpectedness*, wherein insight happens by surprise and without warning; and (4) *satisfaction*, whereby insight elegantly fulfills a previously unresolved need, culminating in a triumphant "Aha!" experience.

On the other hand, however, our current definition does not require that insight involve every characteristic that previous scholars have attributed to it. For example, a process of restructuring, which entails a substantial qualitative reformulation of a problem representation and which classical Gestalt psychologists (Duncker, 1945; Kohler, 1956; Wertheimer, 1959) considered the *sine qua non* of insight, may be optional rather than obligatory here. Instead, we will proceed on an assumption that restructuring constitutes one potential basis of insight, but that insight can (and does) stem as well from the addition of missing pieces to a formerly incomplete yet appropriate mental representation.

Although some cognitive theorists (e.g., Ellen, 1982; Keane, 1989; Ohlsson, 1984a, 1984b) might question this assumption, it may let us deal with many more cases of apparent insight than would otherwise be possible.

ALTERNATIVE PERSPECTIVES ON INSIGHT

Given our current working definition and assumptions, we may examine various detailed alternative perspectives on the nature of insight. For present purposes, three taxonomic dimensions will be used to classify and assess these perspectives. The first dimension concerns whether or not insight actually exists as a distinct, significant cognitive phenomenon. A second dimension concerns whether this phenomenon is scientifically researchable and understandable. Thirdly, another dimension concerns whether insight is mediated through normal mental processes possessed by a diversity of ordinary people. Depending on where an observer of insight stands along each dimension, his or her views can differ markedly.

In what follows, we consider several specific cases, which we call the *business-as-usual perspective*, the *Wizard Merlin perspective*, and the *prepared-mind perspective*. After a survey of them, our own perspective will be outlined more fully and related to these preceding ones.

The Business-as-Usual Perspective

From the perspective of business as usual, insight per se is viewed as either relatively unimportant or even nonexistent as a distinct cognitive phenomenon associated with reasoning, planning, problem solving, and so forth. Adherents to the business-as-usual perspective disavow using the term *insight* (Weisberg & Alba, 1981a, 1981b). To the extent that they acknowledge insight's existence at all, they attribute it to normal mental processes such as memory search, hypothesis testing, and trial-and-error solution attempts based on past experience. Because such processes are open to investigation through standard experimental psychology techniques (Lachman, Lachman & Butterfield, 1979), *business as usual* implies that the phenomenon of insight is certainly researchable

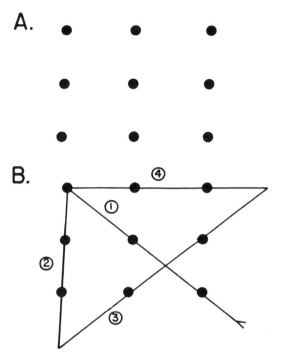

Figure 3.1
The nine-dot problem. Example of an insight problem that supposedly requires restructuring of a mental problem representation. (A) The problem
as it appears in its initial presentation. (B) The required solution, which
involves using a pencil to draw four successive lines that connect the
dots without lifting the pencil from the paper. (Reprinted with permission from Weisberg and Alba, 1981a.)

and understandable, insofar as one chooses to acknowledge its
existence at all.

The business-as-usual perspective merits serious consideration
on the basis of research by investigators such as Weisberg and
Alba (1981a, 1981b, 1982; also see Weisberg, 1992). In these investigator's experiments, test subjects (college students) were asked
to solve the nine-dot problem (figure 3.1), which requires that a
pencil be used to connect nine dots in a rectangular array on a
sheet of paper by drawing four successive lines without lifting
the pencil from the paper. Typically, this is considered an insight
problem, the solution of which depends on intuitively seeing that

the correct lines must extend outside the periphery of the dots' rectangular array. What Weisberg and Alba (1981a) found, however, was that subjects seldom solved the nine-dot problem through a quantum leap of insight springing from this realization. Even when subjects received explicit hints that gave the allegedly necessary insight away, they still often needed many more tries at drawing the lines before reaching a successful solution, and progress toward success appeared to occur only gradually.

From these and other related results, Weisberg and Alba concluded that even in attempts to solve prototypical insight problems, business as usual may provide the best view of what actually happens in people's minds. More specifically, these investigators argued that "spontaneous reorganization of experience does not occur during problem solving" (Weisberg & Alba, 1982, p. 326), and "the terms 'fixation' and 'insight' are not useful in describing the processes involved in the solution of these problems...." (Weisberg & Alba, 1981a, p. 169). Instead, they proposed that:

[S]olution behavior ... can be understood in a straightforward manner: People apply their knowledge to new problems, and if their knowledge is not directly useful, they try to produce something new that will solve the problem through a straightforward extension of what they know. No exotic processes, such as hidden insight, are involved. (Weisberg & Alba, 1981a, p. 189)

Basically, this viewpoint argues that presentation of a problem serves as a cue to retrieve relevant information from memory. Any information that is retrieved then serves as the basis for solution attempts. In this way, it is assumed that problem solving begins with relevant past experience.... A truly novel solution can evolve [through repeated mismatch-driven memory searches] as the problem solver tries to make old knowledge fit the new situation. (Weisberg & Alba, 1981a, p. 171)

If this is so, then problem solving would have much the same appearance as conventional trial-and-error learning, hypothesis testing, and so forth, of which ordinary people and other mammals are usually capable.

In this regard, Weisberg and Alba are not alone. The business-as-usual perspective has also been espoused by a number of other researchers (e.g., Saugstad & Raaheim, 1957; Weaver & Madden, 1949) because of apparent failures to observe spontaneous insightful problem solving in laboratory situations. Some theoreticians who formulate computational models of problem solving have likewise tended toward business as usual by accounting for Gestalt restructuring through standard information-processing mechanisms (e.g., Ohlsson, 1984a, 1984b; Kaplan & Simon, 1990; Keane, 1989). Under their models, the restructuring of a problematic mental representation stems from retrieval processes that search semantic memory for relevant concepts. Difficulties associated with reaching a successful solution are then attributed to a failure in accessing the right solution plans from memory. For example, in his modeling, Keane (1989) has assumed that memory contains all the explicit plans needed to solve given problems; with this assumption, restructuring of a problem would be difficult only because of uncertainties about exactly when to restructure and how to search for a different representation.

The perspective offered by business as usual should not be oversold, however. Contrary to results from the experiments mentioned earlier (viz. Saugstad & Raaheim, 1957; Weaver & Madden, 1949; Weisberg & Alba, 1981a), some laboratory studies of problem solving have revealed apparent intuitive quantum leaps of insight on the part of people who had no prior expectations of impending successful solutions (e.g., Metcalfe & Weib, 1987, Dominowski, 1981). Moreover, many notable observers of insightful performance, having witnessed and contemplated extreme forms of it on a firsthand basis, would strongly dispute whether matters of the mind are always so straightforward and amenable to analyses in terms of memory search, computer metaphors, and other such theoretical formalisms. Doubts of this latter sort appear, among other places, in the book *Logic of Scientific Discovery* by the famous philosopher of science, Karl Popper (1968; cited in Bowers et al., 1990, p. 94), who warned, "There is no such thing as a logical method of having new ideas, or a logical reconstruction of this process. My view may be expressed by saying that every discovery contains 'an irrational element,' or 'a creative intuition.'"

The Wizard Merlin Perspective

Reflecting and magnifying Popper's (1968) personal view, there is the Wizard Merlin perspective on insight. From the vantage point of those who hold it, true insight does indeed occur, and the resulting products may be awesomely spectacular. In the spirit of its namesake, the mythical wizard Merlin, this perspective also embodies a claim that true insight stems from seemingly supernatural mental powers, which are possessed by only a few most gifted individuals, whose minds are neither capable of being mimicked nor open to scientific explanation.

The basis for the Wizard Merlin perspective comes from cases such as that of Richard Feynman, the renowned American physicist who is reputed to have been an intellectual magician and scientific genius of the highest caliber (Gleick, 1992). Starting in his early twenties at the Manhattan Project, which built the first atomic bomb, and continuing throughout the rest of his life, Feynman made myriad insightful contributions to our understanding of the atom's structure and component particles. Among his favorite forms of visualization were so-called Feynman diagrams (figure 3.2), which depict fundamental interactions among electrons and electromagnetic radiation. Using such representational devices, Feynman's research provided penetrating insights into nuclear fission, quantum electrodynamics, superfluidity, and radioactive decay (e.g., Feynman, 1985). Feynman was also instrumental in identifying the crucial component (an excessively cold, shrunken, brittle rubber O-ring) whose failure caused the spectacular destruction of the space shuttle *Challenger* in January 1986.

Because of Feynman's many achievements and the apparent ease with which he attained them, other scientists and mathematicians—outstanding researchers in their own right—marveled at his virtuosity and perpetuated accounts of it, some amusing and others more reverent. On the amusing side, we have the following anecdote, which also involves the Nobel laureate and occasional Feynman collaborator, Murray Gell-Mann (Gleick, 1992, p. 315):

A physicist studying quantum field theory with Murray Gell-Mann at the California Institute of Technology in the 1950's, before standard texts have become available, discovers unpublished lecture notes by Richard Feynman.... He asks Gell-Mann about them. Gell-Mann says, "No, Dick's methods are not the same as the methods used here." The student asks, "Well, what are Feynman's methods?" Gell-Mann leans coyly against the blackboard and says, "Dick's method is this. You write down

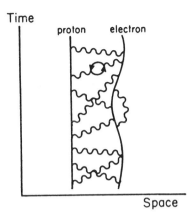

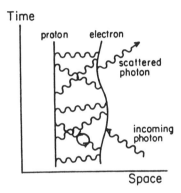

Figure 3.2
A Feynman diagram of the type used by Richard Feynman to depict and
analyze interactions between elementary charged particles and quantum
fields of electromagnetic radiation. (Reprinted with permission from
Feynman, R.P., *QED*. Copyright © 1985 by Princeton University Press.)

the problem. You think very hard." (Gell-Mann shuts his eyes and presses
his knuckles periodically to his forehead.) "Then you write down the
answer."

A further compelling expression of the awe in which Feynman
was held by his contemporaries came from Mark Kac, another
eminent Feynman collaborator. In Kac's words (Gleick, 1992,
pp. 10–11):

There are two kinds of geniuses, the "ordinary" and the "magicians." An
ordinary genius is a fellow that you and I would be just as good as, if we

were only many times better. There is no mystery as to how his mind works. Once we understand what they [sic] have done, we feel certain that we, too, could have done it. It is different with magicians. They are, to use mathematical jargon, in the orthogonal complement of where we are and the working of their minds is for all intents and purposes incomprehensible. Even after we understand what they have done, the process by which they have done it is completely dark. They seldom, if ever, have students because they cannot be emulated and it must be terribly frustrating for a brilliant young mind to cope with the mysterious ways in which the magician's mind works. Richard Feynman is a magician of the highest caliber.

Coming from such esteemed sources, these homages to Feynman bear both good and bad tidings to us. On the positive side, their conviction attests strongly to the seeming reality of insight as a distinct, unique, and impressive mental feat worthy of further investigation; they do not make insight out to be just business as usual. Were the Wizard Merlin perspective accurate, it could likewise account for why some experimental psychologists (e.g., Weisberg & Alba, 1981a) have encountered difficulty in observing quantum leaps of insight by mere college students during problem-solving attempts; maybe only geniuses such as Feynman, with a bent toward Feynman diagrams (see figure 3.2), have what it takes to solve nine-dot problems insightfully! On the negative side, however, this prospect would bode ill for our analyzing and thoroughly understanding the mental processes that mediate true insight. If we accept the Wizard Merlin perspective at face value, then perhaps the best we can do here as cognitive scientists is to catalogue some further cases of inspired genius and then admire them in perpetual awe.

The Prepared-Mind Perspective

Nonetheless, despite the preceding mixed prognosis, some adventurous scholars have forged ahead with attempts to explore the sources of insight in both acknowledged geniuses and ordinary people. As a result, a third point of view, which we call the *prepared-mind perspective* (Posner, 1973), has come into focus. According to it, true insight may indeed occur on some occasions, just as the Wizard Merlin perspective claims. However, also somewhat attuned with business as usual, the prepared-mind perspective does not necessarily attribute cases of insight to enigmatic superhuman mental powers. Rather, on the assumption that insight is a researchable cognitive phenomenon, the latter viewpoint strives toward determining how insight may emerge from a combination of information-processing phases whose joint interactions enable subconscious quantum leaps during the generation of new mental products.

An early example of this endeavor appeared in *The Art of Thought* by Graham Wallas (1926). Working from introspective reports of some prominent creative individuals, Wallas outlined four major phases of information processing that may mediate innovative problem solving and creativity. These phases consist of a synergistic combination of (1) *mental preparation*, (2) *incubation*, (3) *illumination*, and (4) *verification*. At the start of this sequence, the initial preparation phase supposedly entails confronting an important problematic situation, conceptualizing the problem's core aspects, and making exerted tentative unsuccessful attempts to reach a satisfactory resolution. Next, the incubation phase consists of putting the problem aside and thinking instead about other matters for an extended period of time. Then, at some point during incubation, there is an abrupt shift to the illumination phase, wherein a penetrating flash of insight about an appropriate satisfying resolution to the original problematic situation occurs unexpectedly. Given the attained insight, the final verification phase culminates with working out the details of the resolution or determining that it applies successfully.

A compelling, ubiquitously cited illustration of these information-processing phases may be found in the memoirs of the great French mathematician, Henri Poincaré, who offered the following anecdote about his own creative processes (Poincaré, 1913; cited in Mayer, 1992, p. 49):

For fifteen days I strove to prove that there could not be any functions like those I have since called Fuchsian functions. I was then very ignorant; every day I seated myself at my work table, stayed an hour or two, tried a great number of combinations and reached no results. One evening, contrary to my custom, I drank black coffee and could not sleep. Ideas rose in crowds; I felt them collide until pairs interlocked, so to speak, making a stable combination. By the next morning I had established the existence of a class of Fuchsian functions, those which come from the hypergeometric series; I had only to write out the results which took but a few hours.

Just at this time I left Caen, where I was then living, to go on a geologic excursion under the auspices of the school of mines. The changes of travel made me forget my mathematical work. Having reached Countances, we entered an omnibus to go some place or other. At the moment when I put my foot on the step the idea came to me, without anything in my former thoughts seeming to have paved the way for it, that the transformations I had used to define the Fuchsian functions were identical with those of non-Euclidean geometry.... On my return to Caen, for "conscience" sake I verified the result at my leisure.

Moreover, this sort of experience does not appear unique to Poincaré. Numerous compendiums of introspective reports by other innovative mathematicians, scientists, artists, and musicians who have achieved creative insights all subjectively document the occurrence of intense mental preparation, subsequent long-term subconscious incubation, and abrupt unanticipated illumination as crucial precursors to desirable new cognitive products (e.g., Ghiselin, 1952; Koestler, 1964). Personal self-help experts (e.g., Anderson, 1980; Hayes, 1989) have likewise suggested that these precursors may contribute, albeit in less spectacular fashion, to the lives of ordinary people. Consequently, Wallas's (1926) componential analysis of the creative process has been widely disseminated as the received wisdom in popular cognitive psychology textbooks (e.g., Anderson, 1990; Glass & Holyoak, 1986; Halpern, 1989; Hayes, 1978; Lindsay & Norman, 1977; Mayer, 1992; Posner, 1973; Solso, 1988).

Although obviously incomplete, this wisdom may have some further significance as well for us. In particular, Wallas's (1926) analysis points toward at least two obvious places where we might find some wellsprings of insight. One of these is the initial preparation phase, and the other is the intermediate incubation phase, which together supposedly culminate with illumination. If we could determine exactly what mental processes transpire during them, before an insightful outcome emerges, then perhaps we would discover much, if not all, of what there is to know about the nature of insight.

PAST STUDIES OF THE PREPARATION PHASE

Unfortunately, when we pursue this train of thought further and examine past studies of the initial preparation phase in problem solving, the results prove rather disappointing. What we mainly find is why many people *fail* to experience immediate flashes of insight on a regular basis. Normal problem-solving attempts seem to suffer from at least two initial roadblocks. First, people often neglect to exploit information that they have previously stored in memory and that is at least indirectly relevant to solving a given problem. The tendency toward such neglect is particularly evident among novices for whom the problem comes from a domain with which they are not already familiar. A second major roadblock is that when people do apply previously memorized information in an attempt to solve new problems, they often use the information inappropriately. In effect, this then makes the problem even more difficult than it might otherwise have been. Thorough accounts of both these roadblocks to creativity appear in many cognitive psychology textbooks (e.g., Anderson, 1990; Glass & Holyoak, 1986; Halpern, 1989; Hayes, 1978; Lindsay & Norman, 1977; Mayer, 1992; Posner, 1973; Solso, 1988).

Failure to Apply Relevant Prior Information

A well-known demonstration of the first roadblock—failure to apply relevant prior information—has been provided by Gick and Holyoak (1980). In their study, test subjects were asked to give insightful solutions for puzzles such as Duncker's (1945) radiation problem. This problem requires devising a method through which a tumor deep inside a patient's body can be destroyed by a source of radiation without causing any serious damage to surrounding healthy tissue. The most appropriate solution, whose discovery does not typically come easily, involves arranging the radiation such that small amounts of it are directed simultaneously at the tumor along each of many different pathways, summating at the tumor's central site but not creating excessive exposure to the healthy tissue that each pathway traverses.

Before assessing the extent to which their subjects would discover this solution, Gick and Holyoak had some of the subjects read short stories whose content described other situations that were structurally analogous to the forthcoming problem and solution. For example, one of these stories told of a fictitious militaristic attack-and-dispersion situation (Gick & Holyoak, 1980, p. 311):

A fortress was located in the center of a country. Many roads radiated out from the fortress. A general wanted to capture the fortress with his army. He wanted to prevent mines on the roads from destroying his army and neighboring villages. As a result, the entire army could not attack the fortress along one road. However, the entire army was needed to capture the fortress. So an attack by one small group would not succeed. The general therefore divided his army into several small groups. He positioned the small groups at the heads of different roads. The small groups simultaneously converged on the fortress. In this way, the army captured the fortress.

Clearly, this attack-and-dispersion story is relevant to solving Duncker's radiation problem; both of them concern situations in which a central object of attack (i.e., fortress or tumor) can and should be approached by dividing a source of power (i.e., troops or radiation) and directing it along multiple pathways. Under a variety of conditions, however, Gick and Holyoak (1980, 1983) found that presenting such stories to subjects beforehand did not substantially enhance their later success at problem solving compared to control subjects who received no stories. Other investigators have, on multiple occasions, obtained a similar disappointing lack of analogical transfer in the solution of insight problems, even when one might have expected the relevance of certain prior information to seem blatantly obvious (e.g., Perfetto, Bransford, & Franks, 1983; Weisberg, Dicamillo, & Phillips, 1978). The implication, then, is that people may lack easy automatic access to such information during their solution attempts, thereby impeding progress toward insight.

Inappropriate Use of Stored Information

Progress toward insight may also be impeded by the second roadblock, whereby seemingly relevant stored information is accessed but used inappropriately during problem-solving attempts. In this regard, the phenomena of *functional fixedness* and *Einstellung* (problem-solving set) noted by the classical Gestalt psychologists are prime cases (e.g., Duncker, 1945; Luchins, 1942). For example, a good illustration of incipient functional fixedness appears in figure 3.3, which shows the so-called two-string problem that

Figure 3.3
Maier's two-string problem. The insightful solution involves tying the pair of pliers on the floor to one of the strings and then swinging the string like a pendulum so it approaches the other string and both may be grasped simultaneously and tied together. (Reprinted with permission from Anderson, 1990, p. 247.)

Maier (1931) presented to subjects for solving. Here the subjects must tie together the ends of two strings suspended vertically from a ceiling, even though the strings are widely separated and cannot be grasped simultaneously at the outset. Rather, an insightful solution requires using some other available object (e.g., a jar, pliers, or chair on the floor) as an aid.

Among the solutions that Maier (1931) envisioned as being especially insightful, one involved a pair of pliers. This solution required four steps: (1) attaching the pliers to the end of one string, thus treating them as a weight; (2) swinging the string with the attached pliers back and forth like a pendulum, bringing it closer to the other stationary string; (3) catching the swinging string while holding the stationary one; and (4) tying the two strings together. Like the solution to Duncker's radiation problem, however, this solution to the two-string problem did not come easily for subjects. Instead, it seems that they may have been biased toward viewing the pliers as a type of tool for grasping and pinching objects, not as a weight for making a swinging pendulum. If so, then their prior stored knowledge about pliers could actually have hindered them, and they might have been better off if they had never heard of pliers before (Glucksberg & Danks, 1968; Glucksberg & Weisberg, 1966)!

Countervailing Benefits from Prior Knowledge

Of course, specific prior knowledge does not always hinder subsequent problem-solving activity. As mentioned previously, people who are experts at dealing with particular domains may benefit from their prior knowledge in solving problems there. For example, a prototypical case of benefits due to expertise has been reported by Chase and Simon (1973; also see de Groot, 1965), who found that chess masters are superior to chess novices at remembering meaningful arrangements of pieces on a chessboard. The structure of the masters' stored knowledge about chess positions presumably facilitates their ability to select good moves.

Such benefits may likewise accrue to novice problem solvers under at least some circumstances. In particular, during follow-ups to the work of Gick and Holyoak (1980, 1983) on analogical problem solving, some other investigators have found that if one problem is preceded by prior relevant information framed as another analogous problem, rather than as a mere set of declarative facts, then people may transfer the prior information much more readily to the subsequent problem (Adams, Kasserman, Yearwood, Perfetto, Bransford & Franks, 1988; Lockhart, Lamon & Gick, 1988; Needham & Begg, 1991). This suggests that insight might ultimately stem from special types of memory organization used in storing information from problematic contexts. As will become more apparent later, our own theoretical ideas and empirical data reinforce this latter prospect.

Some additional evidence that foreshadows our ideas comes from studies in which experimenters have interrupted subjects during problem solving. Their results suggest two related conclusions. First, people who spend more time on their initial solution attempts before an interruption are more likely to achieve ultimate successful solutions when they later return to the problems (e.g., Silveira, 1971; cited in Posner, 1973, pp. 172–173). Second, under at least some circumstances, people exhibit greater recall of problems on which they have been interrupted than of problems on which they have reached a successful solution (Baddeley, 1963, 1976; Seifert & Patalano, 1991; Zeigarnik, 1927).

Yet the ultimate significance of such results for understanding the nature of insight remains to be determined. On the one hand, the results may simply reflect the fact that stored information tends to stay in a more activated state when initially processed for a longer time. If so, then this would suggest nothing unique about insight per se, given what is known already about human memory in general and its dependence on the duration of exposures to new information (Baddeley, 1976). On the other hand, enhanced recall as a function of problem-solving interruption, and increased solution probability as a function of problem-exposure duration, could also stem from special memory structures and processes dedicated to attaining insightful solutions after initial failures (Hammond & Seifert, 1993; Meyer, Yaniv & Davidson, 1988; Patalano, Seifert & Hammond, 1993; Yaniv & Meyer, 1987; Yaniv, Meyer & Davidson, 1993). Further research on the preparation phase of problem solving is therefore needed to test and discriminate among these various possibilities.

PAST STUDIES OF THE INCUBATION PHASE

Some open questions and potential answers about the nature of insight have also emerged from past studies of Wallas's (1926) proposed incubation phase in problem solving. In evaluating them, it is important to recognize that research on incubation is inherently difficult. To conduct such research properly, an experimenter must first engage test subjects in solving a hard problem, have them initially fail but maintain their interest in the problem, then control what happens during a subsequent incubation phase, and be present later if, by chance, illumination shines forth, so that unobservable mental states surrounding eventual insights are

accurately and discriminatingly recorded. Together, these requirements constitute a large order that has seldom, if ever, been completely filled. Nevertheless, a modicum of progress has been made
toward delineating and testing alternative hypotheses about mental processes that may occur during incubation and eventuate in
insight (e.g., Cook, 1937; Dominowski & Jenrick, 1972; Ericksen,
1942; Fulgosi & Guilford, 1968; Murray & Denny, 1969; Olton &
Johnson, 1976; Patrick, 1986; C. Patrick, 1935, 1937; Silveira,
1971; Smith & Blankenship, 1989; Weisberg & Suls, 1973).

Hypotheses about Incubation Effects

Among the hypotheses considered most extensively are four possibilities (for a review, see Anderson, 1990; Glass & Holyoak, 1986;
Posner, 1973). The first, and least interesting, of these is the
conscious-work hypothesis. As this hypothesis would have it, the
incubation phase simply provides time during which intermittent
covert conscious work on a problem takes place after an initial
preparation phase, thus setting the stage for rapid observable progress toward solution when the problem is later overtly reconfronted. A second mundane possibility is the *fatigue-dissipation
hypothesis.* According to it, the incubation phase allows people
to recover from debilitating mental fatigue caused by the intensity of the initial preparation phase, thereby increasing the likelihood of subsequent successful solution when the problem is later
reconfronted in a refreshed state. Related to the fatigue hypothesis, but more interesting from a cognitive standpoint, is the
selective-forgetting hypothesis. This third possibility assumes
that after the initial preparation phase, the incubation phase
allows stymied problem solvers to forget inappropriate solution
strategies that distracted them initially but that leave relatively
weak residual memory traces. Fourth, and most mysteriously,
there is the *subconscious random-recombination hypothesis,* according to which an incubation phase after intense preparation
allows various bits of relevant information stored in long-term
memory to be recombined subconsciously with one another
through a random process that ultimately yields a fortuitous
insightful synthesis of ideas. The recombination process might,

for example, involve a gradual spread of activation among the elements of associative memory networks (Bowers et al., 1990; Yaniv & Meyer, 1987).

In assessing these various possibilities, a mix of the subconscious random-recombination and conscious-work hypotheses seems most favored by the introspective reports of some creative individuals. For example, Poincaré, the French mathematician, provided the following conjectures about what happens during incubation (Poincaré, 1913, cited in Anderson, 1975, p. 288; also see Ghiselin, 1952, p. 41):

Permit me a rough comparison. Figure the future elements of our combinations as something like the hooked atoms of Epicurus. During the complete repose of the mind, these atoms are motionless, they are, so to speak, hooked to the wall; so this complete rest may be indefinitely prolonged without the atoms meeting, and consequently without any combination between them. On the other hand, during a period of apparent rest and unconscious work, certain of them are detached from the wall and put in motion. They flash in every direction through the space ... where they are enclosed, as would be, for example, a swarm of gnats or, if you prefer a more learned comparison, the molecules of gas in the kinematic theory of gases. Then their mutual impacts may produce new combinations.

Laboratory Studies of Mental Incubation

In contrast, systematic laboratory studies of incubation in problem solving cast some doubt on the validity of such introspections. When experimenters have subjected the mental processes associated with incubation to close controlled scrutiny, two different types of conclusion have emerged instead; either the beneficial effects of incubation on solution activities have been difficult to detect and limited to subsets of subjects (e.g., Cook, 1937; Ericksen, 1942; Murray & Denny; 1969; Dreistadt, 1969; Olton, 1979; Olton & Johnson, 1976) or they have appeared to stem primarily from fatigue dissipation and selective forgetting rather than from a more exotic process of subconscious random recombination of ideas (e.g., Silveira, 1971; Smith & Blankenship, 1989).

An oft-cited illustration of the latter outcome may be found in the study by Silveira (1971). She used the so-called four-chain problem, which goes as follows (Posner, 1973, p. 172):

A man had four chains, each three links long. He wanted to join the four chains into a single closed chain. Having a link opened cost two cents and having a link closed cost three cents. The man had his chains joined into a closed chain for fifteen cents. How did he do it?

After presenting this problem to her test subjects, Silveira (1971) let a control group of them work on it continuously for a half hour, and she observed what proportion of this group solved the problem. Also, the study included four other experimental groups, each of which was interrupted at some point during the initial problem-solving attempt and then brought back subsequently to resume it following an intervening incubation phase. The experimental groups differed from one another and the control group in terms of how much time they spent working on the problem initially (either brief or long preparation) and in terms of how much time they had to incubate before resumption (either a half hour or 4 hours).

Silveira's results showed that the probability of eventually solving the four-chain problem was highest (.85) for the experimental group who had both long preparation and long incubation, intermediate (.64) for the group who had long preparation but short incubation, and less for the other groups. In particular, only about half of the control group who had no incubation phase successfully solved the problem. However, the combination of long preparation and incubation phases did not appear to yield new insights of the sort implied by the subconscious random-recombination hypothesis and Poincaré's speculations about it. Instead, the subjects who prepared and incubated the most in Silveira's (1971) study may have achieved a relatively high solution rate through a different route. They tended to be more focused and persistent in resuming their solution attempts with a promising direction of thought that they had already evolved during the initial preparation phase. This is most consistent with selective forgetting and fatigue dissipation.

Various conclusions might be reached on the basis of this and other past studies of the incubation phase: Perhaps new insights from incubation seldom, if ever, occur. Perhaps mental processes during incubation do not involve residual spreading activation, subconscious random recombination, and other exotic activity that could yield new insights. Alternatively, past studies may not have been conducted well enough to reveal such processes; maybe the problems were not sufficiently motivating, the amounts of preparation and incubation were too little, and the subjects were too normal to exhibit true insightful incubation effects.

EXPANSION OF THE PREPARED-MIND PERSPECTIVE

Whatever the merits of the latter conclusions, we believe that the prepared-mind perspective has much to recommend it but that its focus should be expanded to highlight other possible sources of insight and other possible mechanisms of facilitative mental preparation and incubation. In particular, the hypotheses outlined previously regarding incubation effects seem too narrow. They focus exclusively on internal processes that are assumed to occur inside the problem solver during incubation, without any further outside stimulation from the physical environment after initial preparation. Under the selective-forgetting and subconscious random-recombination hypotheses, for example, incubation would enable progress toward successful solution of a prior problem even if the problem solver were placed in a sensory-deprivation chamber. The potential key role that external events could play as part of the incubation phase is completely ignored by these hypotheses. Nevertheless, it seems plausible to expect that insight would occur more naturally through ongoing incidental interaction with a rich surrounding physical environment.

As Louis Pasteur put it (Posner, 1973, p. 148), "Chance favors the prepared mind." What he presumably meant by this is not that random self-generated recombinations of ideas occur most often to people whose minds are prepared, but rather that prepared minds can and do take advantage of fortuitous encounters with relevant external objects and events. The virtues of mental preparation and opportunistic processing of lucky new experiences have likewise begun to be echoed by cognitive scientists and the artificial intelligencia (e.g., Hammond & Seifert, 1993; Hammond, Seifert & Gray, 1991; Hayes-Roth & Hayes-Roth, 1979; Laird, Rosenbloom & Newell, 1987; Patalano, Seifert & Hammond, 1993; Schank, 1982; VanLehn, 1988).

Relevant Notions from Cognitive Science

Among the notions advocated recently in cognitive science, several are especially relevant to us here. VanLehn (1988) has suggested that significant learning is most likely to occur and to yield lasting benefits at points where an individual reaches an impasse in information processing and then receives new information about how to overcome the impasse. VanLehn's (1988) term for this occurrence is *impasse-driven learning*. He found that it may happen, for example, during instruction on solving arithmetic problems. We assume that impasse-driven learning can contribute to many other types of problem solving as well.

To account for the occurrence of impasse-driven learning not just at the time of an initial impasse but also at future times, Patalano, Seifert, and Hammond (1993) suggested that people engage in *predictive encoding*, a memory strategy whereby information about an impasse is represented and stored in terms of characteristics (e.g., physical and conceptual features) that helpful future stimulus cues may have. On the basis of predictive encoding, these cues, when encountered in the future, can then be related directly back to the impasse and used to resolve it (Hammond, Converse, Marks & Seifert, 1993). This retroactive facilitative access can also be promoted through *failure indices*, which mark information in memory associated with the original occurrence of an impasse (Hammond, Seifert & Gray, 1991; Meyer, Yaniv & Davidson, 1988; Schank, 1982; Yaniv, Meyer & Davidson, 1993).

The Opportunistic-Assimilation Hypothesis

With the preceding notions in mind, we want to promote an additional explicit hypothesis about how insight may stem from the mental preparation and incubation phases of problem solving and other potentially creative activities (Hammond, Seifert & Gray, 1991; Meyer, Yaniv & Davidson, 1988; Patalano, Seifert & Hammond, 1993; Yaniv, Meyer & Davidson, 1993). Our rubric for this is the *opportunistic-assimilation hypothesis*.

Importance of Impasses
According to the opportunistic-assimilation hypothesis, initial information-processing encounters with problematic situations

that end in an impasse (e.g., failure to solve a problem on the first try) leave failure indices in long-term memory. We assume that these special memory traces (the details of which will be described more fully later) explicitly mark the fact that an impasse has occurred. They may then serve as signposts that guide subsequent retrieval processes back to stored aspects of the problematic situation (Schank, 1982).

Under our opportunistic-assimilation hypothesis, an impasse reached during the initial preparation phase of problem solving can set the future stage in other complementary ways. For example, proceeding until impasse helps ensure that all originally available information gets considered and used in the best way possible at the time. This maximizes the degree to which the tentative partial representation of a problem will have an appropriate stable form, like a nearly completed jigsaw puzzle, ready to receive other crucial missing pieces or to be rearranged in an efficient systematic manner after a subsequent incubation phase.

Role of Incubation
Next, regarding the incubation phase, we further assume that a person who has experienced a problem and reached an impasse puts the problem aside and goes about his or her other business. During this subsequent period, numerous encounters with various environmental stimuli may occur and be processed, but no further conscious or subconscious work on the original problem would take place. Nevertheless, according to our opportunistic-assimilation hypothesis, the course of daily events may eventually lead to a fortuitous encounter with an external object or event that is especially relevant to solving the original problem. If so, then as this stimulus and the cues therein are processed through normal ongoing perception and comprehension, they will contact the failure indices that commemorate the original problem.

Under our hypothesis, contact with the "red flags" provided by these special memory traces triggers a process through which the new stimulus is used in an attempt to resolve the old problem. The resulting attempt may involve simply assimilating the new stimulus into the prior memory representation of the problem, like adding a missing piece to a jigsaw puzzle while keeping the previously placed pieces in their former positions. Alternatively, both some assimilation and restructuring might occur, as when the positions of some puzzle pieces are changed to accommodate a new one. Either way, we propose that the end result is a primary source of the insight experience.

Past Precedents Regarding Opportunistic Assimilation
Of course, our proposal and its expansion of the prepared-mind perspective is not entirely new. As mentioned earlier, the possibility that insight may stem from chance encounters with external objects or events, which then interact with previously prepared mental structures, was explicitly articulated much earlier by Pasteur (cited in Posner, 1973, p. 148). This potential source of insight has been acknowledged in a few cognitive psychology textbooks (e.g., Anderson, 1975; Posner, 1973). For the most part, however, textbook authors have either ignored the opportunistic-assimilation hypothesis entirely or given it rather short shrift (e.g., see Glass & Holyoak, 1986; Solso, 1988).

Virtues of Opportunistic Assimilation

Despite its lack of past prominence, the opportunistic-assimilation hypothesis has numerous appealing virtues. For example, it lets us neatly synthesize some of the main themes that characterize the prepared-mind and business-as-usual perspectives on the nature of insight. Furthermore, even the Wizard Merlin perspective may join this desirable synthesis.

Synthesis of Alternative Perspectives
The impasse-driven storage of failure indices at the end of initial preparation, followed by later opportunistic assimilation through ongoing comprehension processes, are consistent with some key claims that advocates of business as usual have made (e.g., Weisberg & Alba, 1981a, 1981b). In particular, it is known already that impasses can drive learning under a variety of circumstances (VanLehn, 1988), failure indices can mediate retroactive access to information about prior failures (Hammond, Seifert & Gray, 1991; Meyer, Yaniv & Davidson, 1988; Schank, 1982; Yaniv, Meyer & Davidson, 1993), and beneficial opportunism can occur when relevant new stimulus situations are encountered (Hayes-Roth & Hayes-Roth, 1979; Meyer, Yaniv & Davidson, 1988; Patalano, Seifert &

Hammond, 1993; Yaniv, Meyer & Davidson, 1993). The application of these notions to the nature of insight then, in essence, retains a large measure of business as usual.

Yet at the same time, this application does not entirely disavow the mental powers that the Wizard Merlin perspective attributes to great masters of insight. Under our present hypothesis, truly masterful insights can come from an interplay among predictive encoding, storage of failure indices, opportunistic assimilation, and the sagacity of the initial memory representation that an intellectual magician forms for a problematic situation (see Lockhart et al., 1988). Although both ordinary people and these magicians may experience the joys of insight, the frequency and depth of the joy might differ, depending on the richness and profundity of the prior preparation phase. Thus, we may have some more helpful clues about where to look—namely, at the details of the initial problem representation—to better understand how intellectual magicians achieve their feats.

Explanation of Phenomenological Characteristics
A second related virtue of the opportunistic-assimilation hypothesis and our expansion of the prepared-mind perspective is that they easily explain why insight seems to have so many intriguing phenomenological characteristics. As outlined earlier in this chapter, among these characteristics are nonanalyticity, subconsciousness, suddenness, spontaneity, unexpectedness, and satisfaction. Each of these mystical properties arises quite naturally in our view, from more "normal" processes.

To be specific, suppose that a problem solver has stored a stable, partial mental representation of an unsolved problem, and he or she later accidentally encounters a crucial missing piece of information that completes it. Then this would cause a sudden change in the prospects for solution. The change may seem spontaneous because the problem solver was not expecting or intending it to happen at the particular moment, and the use of the new information will not necessarily be conscious, because normal perception and comprehension processes work automatically (Lachman et al., 1979), leaving the problem solver unable to explain the resulting solution path. The delay of the solution until the present encounter encourages the feeling that it is intuitive and that it could not have been deduced from prior preparation alone. Also, the satisfying nature of the insight experience is explained by the triumphant filling of a gap in the initial mental representation of the problem. In fact, the sense of elation that accompanies the ultimate "Aha!" experience could serve an important function; it might facilitate the opportunistic assimilation process by increasing physiological arousal and promoting stronger memory consolidation (Baddeley, 1976).

Support from Laboratory Research
The preceding account of why insight has certain phenomenological characteristics gains additional support from the results of previous laboratory research on problem solving. In his influential studies with the two-string problem (see figure 3.3), Maier (1931) included a condition under which he let subjects spend several minutes trying to solve the problem of their own accord. Many failed during this initial phase. Next, some of Maier's subjects received a subtle hint about how the problem could and should be solved. The hint was given by an experimenter who casually brushed against one of the hanging strings, setting it briefly and unobtrusively into motion. Subsequently, within a short period of time, a large fraction of the stymied subjects successfully achieved the appropriate pendulum solution, tying the available pair of pliers to one of the strings and swinging it over near the other string, where both of them could then be grasped simultaneously and tied together. However, many of the subjects who achieved success had no idea about how they arrived at the appropriate solution; they claimed to be completely unaware of the hint. This is exactly what we would expect if opportunistic assimilation of relevant new information occurs through rapid, automatic, subconscious processes of normal perception and comprehension.

That opportunistic assimilation is mediated by prior predictive encoding and storage of failure indices, which result from an initial encounter with a problem, also gains support from some previous laboratory research. In one study, for example, Lockhart and colleagues (1988) gave subjects descriptions of problematic situations that had to be explained. These descriptions consisted of scenarios such as: "A man who lived in a small town married 20 women of the same town. All are still living and he never divorced a single one of them. Yet he broke no law. How could this be?" Before trying to provide the explanation, the subjects received other relevant information expressed in either a simple declarative or temporarily puzzling form. The prior information consisted of statements such as, "It made the clergyman happy to marry several people each week" (declarative form) or "The man married several people each week because it made him happy" (puzzling form), which was then followed by the word *clergyman*.

Lockhart and colleagues' data (1988) showed that subsequent explanations of the problematic descriptions were markedly facilitated by receipt of prior information in a puzzling form, whereas prior information in a simple declarative form had much less benefit. This is exactly what we would expect if the puzzling form of the prior information caused predictive encoding to occur and failure indices to be stored, thus promoting beneficial access when the subsequent problematic descriptions were presented. In essence, the predictive encoding and failure indices proposed here enable what others have called *transfer-appropriate processing* (Adams et al., 1988; Needham & Begg, 1991; Weisberg & Suls, 1973).

Consistency with Anecdotal Cases
The opportunistic-assimilation hypothesis is likewise consistent with a broad sample of anecdotal cases involving alleged occurrences of insight, ranging from the mundane to the spectacular. As mentioned previously, two such cases are those involving the man who fell to earth and Newton's apple. In each of them, insight occurred through an encounter with an unexpected but relevant new external event after an initial problem-solving impasse had been reached. First, there was the stimulus provided by the desert wanderer's accidental dropping of his handkerchief, which triggered the insight that the man who fell to earth had met his demise through a broken parachute. Second, there was the stimulus provided by the falling apple in the English countryside, which inspired Newton to associate the earth's pull with the motions of heavenly bodies, yielding his universal law of gravitation.

Continuing along such lines, we should mention some other noteworthy cases. Interestingly, one of the first main observations that led classical Gestalt psychologists to focus on insight in problem solving involved an apparent instance of opportunistic assimilation (Kaplan & Simon, 1990). The case concerns Sultan, a chimpanzee observed extensively by Köhler (1956). During his studies of Sultan, Köhler placed the chimp in a cage, outside of which were some bananas on the floor. Sultan would have liked to eat one of them immediately, but they were too far from the cage for the chimp to reach them directly. Inside the cage, there were two separate sticks, which Sultan had previously learned to use for manipulating objects. However, neither of the sticks was long enough to reach one of the bananas. In other words, Sultan had a problem. Therefore, he stopped attending to the bananas and went about his other business for the moment, after which the following events occurred, as recounted by Köhler (1956, p. 127; cited in Kaplan & Simon, 1990):

Sultan first of all squats indifferently on the box, which has been left standing a little back from the railings; then he gets up, picks up the two sticks, sits down again on the box and plays carelessly with them. While doing this, it happens that he finds himself holding one stick in either hand in such a way that they lie in a straight line; he pushes the thinner one a little way into the opening of the thicker, jumps up and is already on the run toward the railings, to which he has up till now half turned his back, and begins to draw a banana toward him with the double stick.

At the risk of overanthropomorphizing Sultan's behavior or underestimating his imaginative powers, we would suggest that this anecdote illustrates another prime instance of opportunistic assimilation after an initial problematic impasse. What Sultan seems to have done here is enter an incubation phase that ended with him noticing the chance conjunction of the two sticks, after which he related their contiguity back to his prior problem with reaching a banana, made the necessary additional connection, and proceeded insightfully to use the conjoined sticks for solving his problem. Given our opportunistic-assimilation hypothesis and expansion of the prepared-mind perspective, we would therefore agree with Köhler (1956) that Sultan's behavior indeed manifested significant insight. We would also emphasize that although the insight was clearly real, it did not require the powers of an intellectual magician, consistent with some of the theories of advocates of business as usual (e.g., Weisberg & Alba, 1981a).

In the same spirit, albeit at a more profound level, numerous significant cases of insight on the basis of predictive encoding and opportunistic assimilation can be extracted from the anecdotal reports of famous scientists, mathematicians, artists, and writers (Ghiselin, 1952; Koestler, 1964). Such reports go back at least as far as the time of Archimedes, whose laws of hydrodynamics were reputedly inspired through insights reached while he was taking a casual bath and watching the surrounding water rise, which culminated in his exclamation, "Eureka!" Complementing this example, other more contemporary instances include two major biological innovations: Alexander Fleming's discovery of penicillin, which stemmed from his accidentally noticing an absence of bacterial growth on the bottom of a dish; and the discovery of DNA's structure by James Watson and Francis Crick, who are rumored to have first gained insight about the double helix while sliding down the railing of a spiral staircase and daydreaming of the Nobel prize. (The reply to Watson's asking Crick about exactly where their insight had come from was purportedly, "Elementary, my dear Watson, elementary"; cf. Conan Doyle, 1981).

Relation to Feynman and the Wizard Merlin Perspective

Indeed, even our prototypical intellectual magician, Richard Feynman, whose exploits were chronicled earlier, appears to have gotten some of his best insights through the route of predictive encoding, failure indices, fortuitous stimulus encounters, and opportunisitic assimilation. One particular episode recounted by him stands out in this regard (Gleick, 1992). Feynman's problem here was to formulate a successful theory of beta decay (transformation of neutrons into protons and electrons) and other elementary particle interactions governed by the fundamental weak force of nature. After filling himself for months with preliminary relevant information, and after striving mightily without success, he took a summer vacation to Brazil, where he went regularly to play the bongos and sit on Ipanema Beach. On returning home to the California Institute of Technology, he began interacting again with colleagues about the weak force, which led to the following Feynman recount (quoted in Crease & Mann, 1986, pp. 213–214):

Finally they get all this stuff into me, and they say, "The situation is so mixed up that even some of the things they've established for years are being questioned—such as the beta decay of the neutron is S and T [a specific type of particle interaction]. Murray [Gell-Mann] says it might even be V and A [another specific type of particle interaction], it's so messed up." I jump up from the stool and say, "Then I understand EVVVVVERY-THING!" They thought I was joking. But the thing I had trouble with at the Rochester meeting [a previous conference]—the neutron and proton disintegration: Everything fit *but* that, and if it was V and A instead of S and T, that would fit too. Therefore, I had the whole theory! ... I went on and checked some other things, which fit, and new things fit, new things fit and I was very excited.... I had this new equation for beta decay.... It was the first time, and the only time, in my career that I knew a law of nature that nobody else knew.

Gratifyingly, this quote bodes well for our prospects of developing a general, scientifically testable, cognitive theory of insight that applies to a broad range of individuals. Contrary to previous intimations about Feynman's source of insights (Gleick, 1992, pp. 311–329), it seems that he did not experience insight solely from writing down a problem, closing his eyes, thinking hard, pressing his forehead repeatedly, and then writing down the solution. Instead, we find here that even reputed intellectual magicians, whose spectacular mental feats constitute the focus of the Wizard Merlin perspective on insight, are, by their own admission, major benefactors of predictive encoding and opportunistic assimilation, as our expansion of the prepared-mind perspective would have it. If we take Feynman at his word, then of all his innovations, the best one stemmed from a fortuitous encounter with a relevant but unexpected new event in the environment; someone casually mentioned to him that the V-A rather than S-T particle interaction might be primary, and he proceeded from there on the basis of extensive prior preparation.

STUDIES OF IMPASSES AND OPPORTUNISTIC ASSIMILATION

Of course, one could ask for more support from studies with controlled laboratory methods rather than just anecdotal observation. A worthwhile focus of such studies would appear to be impasse-driven predictive encoding and opportunistic assimilation, given that individuals who have diverse mental abilities, ranging from chimpanzees (e.g., Sultan) through normal college students to intellectual magicians (e.g., Feynman), all apparently reach insight at least partly through these processes. In this section, we therefore describe briefly some results of two representative experiments conducted in our laboratories to investigate these processes further. Our experiments test several specific related predictions that follow from the opportunistic-assimilation hypothesis and the prepared-mind perspective.

For present purposes, we will focus on two such predictions. The first is that ultimate successful solution of an initially unsolved problem will be much more likely if stymied problem solvers are exposed surreptitiously to relevant new information during a subsequent incubation phase. A second prediction tested here is that problem solvers will be much more likely to recall their encounter with a prior problem if they have reached an initial impasse on it than if their solution attempt is interrupted without an impasse being reached.

Experiment 1: Answering Problematic Factual Questions

Our first experiment was designed specifically to test the prediction that exposing problem solvers to relevant new information after an initial failed solution attempt will best promote ultimate successful solutions (for more details, see Meyer, Yaniv & Davidson, 1988; Yaniv, 1988; Yaniv, Meyer & Davidson, 1993).

Method
In pursuit of this objective, we adopted and extended an experimental method developed previously by Yaniv and Meyer (1987). The method involved three phases of testing, which roughly paralleled three of the problem-solving phases that Wallas (1926) has proposed.

During experiment 1's first phase, test subjects (undergraduate college students) were presented with general-information questions such as, "What is a nautical instrument used in measuring angular distances, especially the altitude of the sun, moon, and stars at sea?" These questions came from a set whose answers were presumably known but used infrequently by most of the subjects, as determined through a prior pilot study.

For each question presented in phase 1, the subjects tried to provide the correct answer. They were allowed as much time as they desired to do so. Sometimes they actually succeeded. If so, then we had them rate their confidence that their answer was correct, using a five-point scale. On other occasions (approximately 33 percent of the time), however, the subjects failed in their attempts to provide answers, and they gave up because the presented questions were difficult enough to pose a problematic memory-retrieval situation. When the subjects abandoned their attempts to answer a question, we asked them to rate their "feeling of knowing" about the correct answer before proceeding to the next question.

Following presentation of the general-information questions and solicitation of the correct answers, there was a second phase, during which the subjects were shown a sequence of visual letter strings on a display screen. The letter strings included a variety of words and nonwords (e.g., *spending, dascribe, sextant, trinsfer, asteroid, umbrella*, and so forth). For each string of letters displayed, the subject had to decide whether it was an English word or nonword, indicating the decision quickly and accurately by pressing either a "yes" or "no" button. Thus, the second phase consisted of a *lexical-decision task* (Meyer & Schvaneveldt, 1971).

The subjects were not told that the lexical-decision task of phase 2 had any specific relationship to the prior problematic question-answering task of phase 1; rather, phase 2 was, in essence, a subsequent incubation phase. Nonetheless, among the stimuli displayed, there were *target words* that would have been correct answers to some of the prior general-information questions on which the subjects initially failed. The lexical-decision task therefore provided an opportunity for incidental exposures and assimilation of the solutions to some previous problematic impasses. Also included among the stimuli were *control words* that provided additional distraction and served subsequent informative comparison purposes. For both the control and target words, as well as the nonwords, we measured the subjects' reaction times and accuracy in making their lexical decisions.

After phases 1 and 2 of the experiment, which were conducted in the same test session, the subjects took the rest of the day off.

This allowed an additional period of incubation. Then, on the next day, they returned again for more testing in a third phase.

Phase 3 involved more general-information questions, for each of which the subjects tried to provide the correct answer, as in the first phase. Among the phase 3 questions were some that had been presented during phase 1 and other questions not seen previously in the experiment (e.g., "What do you call one of the thousands of small planets between Mars and Jupiter with diameters from a fraction of a mile to nearly 500 miles?"). The old and new questions had another important property. For some of them, both old and new, the target words that constituted their answers had been exposed previously in the lexical-decision task. For other phase 3 questions, both old and new, their answers were target words not exposed earlier in the lexical-decision task. Thus, our experimental design incorporated two crossed independent variables: question type (old or new), and target-word type (previously exposed or unexposed). For each possible combination of these variables, we measured the probability with which the subjects successfully produced the correct answers to the phase 3 questions.

Rationale
The rationale of this experiment is straightforward. Although our general-information questions were less complex than some of the problems discussed previously, they nevertheless posed a problematic situation for our subjects and led them to occasional initial impasses. Also, because the subjects presumably had stored knowledge relevant to the domain of each question, we would assume that they were, in principle, prepared to assimilate further relevant information after the impasses occurred.

Consequently, our hypotheses about predictive encoding and opportunistic assimilation make some specific predictions about the subjects' performance in phase 3 of the experiment. For example, consider what should happen with old questions presented again during this phase after prior exposure to relevant target words in the intermediate lexical-decision task of phase 2. In this case, we would predict that performance ought to improve significantly compared to what happened in phase 1, because of the beneficial assimilation process mediated by previously stored failure indices. On the other hand, for old questions whose target-word answers were not exposed during the lexical-decision task, we would make a different prediction. The improvement in answering them ought to be much less; in fact, correct answers to them might occur no more frequently than for new phase 3 questions, because in neither of these cases would subjects have a chance to benefit from opportunistic assimilation of the previously exposed correct answers.

At the same time, the method of experiment 1 also provides a potentially strong test of other alternative hypotheses about the source of incubation effects. Suppose incubation facilitates future problem solutions by allowing the strengths of subliminal stored memory traces to grow passively and spontaneously after they are stimulated by an initial unsuccessful problem-solving attempt (e.g., see Bowers et al., 1990). Then even when the target-word answers for questions from phase 1 are not exposed during phase 2, one might still expect performance on these questions to improve during phase 3 because of increased memory-trace strength. By looking for the presence of such improvement, we can test the validity of the latter expectation and the hypothesis from which it stems.

Results

Consistent with these predictions, some results from experiment 1 appear in figure 3.4. Here the top graph shows what happened during phase 3 of question answering on day 2 when approximately a half hour separated the first and second phases of day 1. On the vertical axis is the percentage of cases in which a question was answered correctly in phase 3. On the horizontal axis is the type of question involved (i.e., old ones presented previously in phase 1 or new ones presented for the first time in phase 3). The shading of the vertical bars indicates whether the target-word answers to these questions were exposed or unexposed in the intermediate phase 2 lexical-decision task.

From the top graph, two key results are apparent. First, for old questions, the percentage of correct answers during phase 3 was significantly greater when their target words were exposed previously during phase 2 than when they were not (dark versus light bars on left). In fact, virtually all of this benefit can be attrib-

Separate Phases

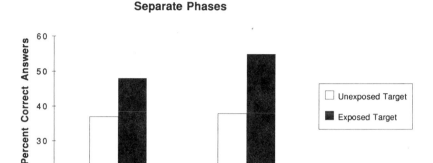

Interleaved Phases

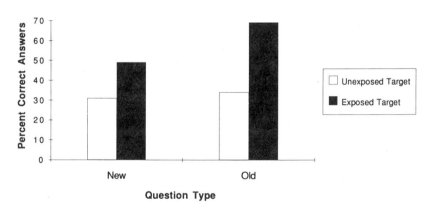

Figure 3.4
Results of experiment 1 with the problematic general-information questions. The vertical axis shows the percentages of general-information questions correctly answered during phase 3 of the experiment. The horizontal axis shows different types of questions that were involved, including old ones whose answers were attempted during phase 1 and new ones not attempted previously. The dark and light bars correspond respectively to cases for which the correct target-word answers were or were not exposed during phase 2, the intermediate lexical-decision task. (For more details, see text; also see Meyer, Yaniv & Davidson, 1988; Yaniv, Meyer & Davidson, 1993.)

uted to cases in phase 3 where the subjects successfully answered old questions on which they had previously failed in phase 1. This is exactly what our opportunistic-assimilation hypothesis would predict; benefits toward resolving a prior problematic situation accrue if and only if an impasse has occurred before and been followed by further incidental relevant information.

A second interesting result in the top graph of figure 3.4 concerns performance on the old versus new questions during phase 3. When the relevant target-word answers were not exposed during the lexical-decision task of phase 2, subjects were no more accurate at answering the old questions than at answering the new ones (right and left light bars). Their further attempts to answer old questions on which they had failed before benefited hardly at all from the intervening incubation phase if the relevant target words were not exposed there. In other words, the subjects manifested no spontaneous improvement on initially failed questions. Once again, this is what we would expect if incubation effects stem primarily from interactions with external cues after an impasse has been reached rather than from a continuation of passive covert conscious or subconscious processing of the sort associated with fatigue dissipation, selective forgetting, and random reorganization in long-term memory.

Further supporting these conclusions, the bottom graph of figure 3.4 shows a pattern of results similar to the top graph except that the interactive effects of question type (old versus new) and target-word type (exposed versus unexposed) are even greater. We obtained this enhancement simply by interleaving phase 1 (initial attempts at question answering) with phase 2 (target-word exposure in the lexical-decision task). Given such interleaving, subjects had to wait less before being exposed to further relevant information after each impasse at question answering. As a result, their traces of prior impasses were presumably stronger at the time of the subsequent beneficial target-word exposures, thereby facilitating opportunistic assimilation.

Yet the latter outcome does not mean that the traces of prior impasses depend solely on temporary residual spreading activation in networks of long-term memory. We found no evidence of any activation in the phase 2 lexical decisions when a relatively long interval separated the exposed target words from the initial question-answering attempts in phase 1. This is consistent with the results of some other investigators (Connor, Balota & Neely, 1992). However, subjects' question-answering accuracy in phase 3 still showed a significant interaction between question type and target-word type under these circumstances (figure 3.4, top graph). It therefore appears that opportunistic assimilation is, as proposed earlier, triggered by reaccessing stored failure indices distinct from and more permanent than residual spreading activation per se (see Meyer, Yaniv & Davidson, 1988; Yaniv, Meyer & Davidson, 1993).

Finally, the importance of failure indices for opportunistic assimilation is likewise demonstrated by another result from our studies. In an extension of the method described here, we replaced the question-answering task of phase 1 with a sentence-verification task (Davidson, 1993). Following this replacement, additional groups of subjects made true-false decisions about sentences of the form, "A sextant is a nautical instrument used in measuring angular distances, especially the altitude of the sun, moon, and stars at sea," which were presented in phase 1. Then, in subsequent phases 2 and 3, our procedure was exactly the same as before; the subjects made a series of lexical decisions about various target and control words, after which they attempted to answer various general-information questions on the next day.

Under these latter conditions, we found no evidence of interactions analogous to those in figure 3.4. Again, this is exactly what our opportunistic-assimilation hypothesis would predict. Because the first phase of our latter method involved no initial impasses (i.e., no failed question-answering attempts in phase 1), we would not expect any stored failure indices to be present in memory at the time of the phase 2 lexical-decision task and, without these, subsequent exposure to relevant new information, as provided by the intermediate target words, would have no future benefit when the problematic questions are later encountered in phase 3 (see Adams et al., 1988; Lockhart et al., 1988; Needham & Begg, 1991).

Conclusions

In summary, the results of experiment 1 support our hypotheses about processes that may underlie insightful performance in problematic situations. We found strong empirical evidence of the important role played by initial impasses, stored failure indices, and opportunistic assimilation of information from subsequent external exposures to relevant information. On the other hand, the present study yielded no evidence of covert passive mechanisms (e.g., spontaneous growth of activation in stored memory traces) that have sometimes been proposed as principal mediators of incubation effects and insight.

Experiment 2: Remembering Failed Solution Attempts

Our second experiment was designed to test another major prediction derived from the opportunistic-assimilation hypothesis (Seifert & Patalano, 1991; Patalano & Seifert, 1993). According to it, people should have especially accessible memories of problems whose initial confrontation ends with an impasse (i.e., failure to reach solution). This prediction follows from two complementary assumptions of the hypothesis: (1) At the time of impasse, indices of the failure are stored in memory, pointing back to it and other associated episodic information; and (2) working on a problem until reaching impasse maximizes the likelihood that all currently available information will be encoded and used to store a stable, albeit partially incomplete and perhaps strained, representation of the problem situation. To the extent that these assumptions hold, a problem solver will have more avenues along which to re-access the problem subsequently than would be the case if initial processing terminates (e.g., is interrupted) prematurely before an impasse is reached. We would therefore predict that, under at least some circumstances, people's probability of recalling prior problems should be greater for failed ones than for successfully completed or merely interrupted ones.

Interestingly, some previous evidence concerning this prediction has been obtained already in a classic experiment by Zeigarnik (1927), who gave subjects a set of various tasks to perform, including arithmetic problems, puzzles, and manual construction activities (e.g., making cardboard boxes). During their performance of half these tasks, the subjects were interrupted before they had finished them, whereas they were allowed to complete the other half of the tasks. After each task was attempted once by the subjects, they next performed a free recall in which they reported as many of the previous tasks as they could. Zeigarnik found that the probability of recall was substantially higher for the interrupted tasks than for the uninterrupted tasks. The positive interruption effect on recall has since become known as the *Zeigarnik effect* (Baddeley, 1976). It is consistent with our prediction that failed problem-solving attempts may be remembered better than successfully completed ones.

However, in subsequent attempts to replicate and extend Zeigarnik's original results, the relatively high probability of recalling interrupted problems has not always been found. For example, after a careful review of the literature, Van Bergen (1968) claimed less than half of the replication attempts successfully obtained the Zeigarnik effect. This disappointing outcome could perhaps be taken as evidence against the effect's robustness and our hypothesis's correctness.

Nevertheless, we suspect there may be principled reasons for the previous frequent failures to replicate the Zeigarnik effect. In particular, many of them may have involved interrupting subjects during their problem-solving attempts *before* they had reached an impasse. If so, then the interruptions may have occurred before subjects had formed stable partial mental representations of the problems and associated them with failure indices. Under these latter circumstances, we would not predict relatively high recall probability for the interrupted problems. On the contrary, our opportunistic-assimilation hypothesis would predict that problem solving interrupted before impasse might well yield poor recall, because the reaccess pathways back to the problem would not yet be in place. Thus, it is not necessarily surprising that past experimenters, insensitive to the importance of reaching impasse, failed in their attempts to replicate the Zeigarnik effect; perhaps they merely interrupted their subjects too soon.

To test this conjecture and to assess the memorability of problem impasses versus problem interruptions, we conducted an analog of Zeigarnik's (1927) original experiment, but we carefully controlled the nature and timing of the circumstances under which problem solving was interrupted (for more details, see Patalano & Seifert, 1993; Seifert & Patalano, 1991).

Method

The experiment involved three different groups of subjects, each of which participated in two successive phases of testing. During phase 1, we gave subjects a series of 20 or more word problems to solve, one by one. Each problem was presented on a separate sheet of paper, and the subjects were supposed to write a solution as quickly and accurately as possible. The problems came from *The Puzzle School* by Mosler (1977) and consisted of various mathematical, logical, and insight puzzles; for example, "What is the largest sum of money in current U.S. coins (but no silver dollars) that a person can have in his pocket without being able to give someone change for a dollar, half-dollar, quarter, dime, or nickel?"

We chose the problems for phase 1 to represent a range of difficulty levels, as determined from a preliminary pilot study. Virtually all of them could be solved within 5 minutes or less by most college students. However, few could be solved within less than 30 seconds, and many caused subjects to experience an intermediate temporary impasse approximately 30 to 60 seconds after a solution attempt started.

At the end of phase 1, the subjects entered the second phase of the experiment. During it, they performed a free-recall task in which they tried to recall all of the problems on which they had worked in phase 1. For each problem recalled, a brief written description of the problem's details was produced. There was no constraint on the order of these descriptions. By examining the content of these reports, we scored the average number of problems that the subjects recalled correctly as a function of the test group in which they participated.

The three different groups of subjects performed under three different problem-solving conditions during phase 1. For one group, the first phase involved a *timed-interruption condition*. Here we let the subjects work on half of the problems until they solved them successfully, which typically took less than a few minutes per problem. During the subjects' attempts to solve the other half of the problems, we interrupted them on each one approximately 30 seconds after the solution attempt had begun, at a point where they seemed well engrossed in their effort but before they had succeeded or reached an impasse. The interrupted and uninterrupted problems were interleaved randomly, so the subjects could not predict exactly whether or when an interruption might occur.

For a second group of subjects, phase 1 involved an *untimed-impasse condition*. The circumstances associated with it were somewhat different from the preceding condition. Here we let subjects work through the series of problems at their own pace for a total of 50 minutes. They were told to work quickly and accurately, and to complete as many problems as possible within this period. For problems that seemed relatively difficult, the subjects were allowed to give up at least temporarily and go on to the next one. They were also encouraged to write down any partial or complete solutions that they produced along the way. This then created a situation in which unfinished problems would likely be left in a state of impasse.

The third group of subjects performed under a *timed-impasse condition*. In this group, the amount of time that the subjects spent on each problem was strictly controlled; it equaled 1 minute per problem. Minute by minute, we gave the subjects one new problem after another. For each one, they were again supposed to write down complete and partial solutions along the way. Because of how the problems varied in terms of their intrinsic difficulty, this procedure helped ensure that the problems for which the subjects did not achieve complete successful solutions would be left in a state of impasse. The timed-impasse condition therefore let us equate how long subjects spent on solved and unsolved problems, while maximizing the chances that impasses were reached for the unsolved problems. Of necessity, such control was not possible in the previous two conditions (i.e., timed interruptions without impasses and untimed impasses), but this third condition helped overcome the inherent confounding associated with them.

Rationale
If our assumptions that underlie the opportunistic-assimilation hypothesis are correct, and if our conjecture about the causes of previous failures to replicate the Zeigarnik effect are correct, then three related results should emerge from experiment 2. In the timed-interruption condition, which does not allow subjects

to reach impasse and store failure indices for interrupted problems, their ultimate free recall should be greater for the solved problems than for the unsolved problems. On the other hand, in the untimed-impasse condition, the recall rate should be higher for the unsolved problems, because subjects are allowed sufficient time to reach impasse and to store stable partial problem representations along with associated failure indices, which then enhance subsequent retrieval. Furthermore, the latter pattern of results should carry over to the timed-impasse condition, because the same beneficial memory storage will be possible there too, even though the time spent on solved and unsolved problems is equated. Our hypothesis predicts that recall performance will not be simply a function of the amount of time spent on a given problem.

Results

Some results of experiment 2 appear in figure 3.5. Here we have plotted the subjects' average percentages of problems recalled in phase 2 (vertical axis) against the condition under which they performed during phase 1 (horizontal axis). The light and dark vertical bars indicate the recall rates for solved and unsolved problems, respectively, in each condition.

As can be seen from figure 3.5, all the results here supported our predictions about circumstances surrounding the Zeigarnik effect. When subjects were interrupted in their problem solution attempts before reaching impasse (timed-interruption condition), the rate of subsequent problem recall in phase 2 was actually greater for solved problems than for unsolved problems (lefthand pair of vertical bars). In contrast, when subjects were allowed to reach impasse in either a self-paced fashion (untimed-impasse condition) or in an experimenter-paced fashion (timed-impasse condition), the recall rate during phase 2 was significantly greater for unsolved problems than for solved problems (middle and righthand pairs of vertical bars). The similarity of results obtained under the untimed-impasse and timed-impasse conditions shows that the latter superiority of recall for unsolved problems is not caused simply by more time being spent on the unsolved problems before an impasse is reached.

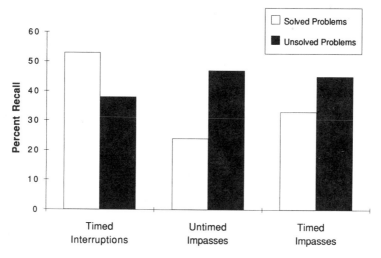

Figure 3.5
Results of experiment 2 with the problem-solving and free-recall tasks. The vertical axis shows the percentages of problems that were correctly recalled after an initial phase of problem-solving attempts. The horizontal axis shows various conditions under which these attempts occurred. The light and dark bars correspond respectively to recall performance for solved and unsolved problems. (For more details, see text; also see Patalano & Seifert, 1993; Seifert & Patalano, 1991.)

Further support of the latter conclusion comes from additional analyses of the results in the untimed-impasse condition, where subjects controlled how much time they spent in trying to solve each problem. After factoring out the times spent on various problems there, and after submitting the recall rates to a multiple-regression analysis with both solution state (solved or unsolved) and solution-attempt duration as independent predictor variables, we still found that the solution state mattered; predicted recall remained higher for problems on which the solution attempts reached impasse.

Conclusions
As we predicted, experiment 2 shows that unsolved problems are more available in memory than are solved problems but only under some specific circumstances. This is consistent with both

Zeigarnik's (1927) results, and subsequent occasional failures to replicate them (Van Bergen, 1968). Most importantly, our research identifies subject-generated impasses and failures in solution attempts as crucial to enhanced memory for past problems. Such memory enhancement apparently stems from the cognitive effort, trace consolidation, and failure indices associated with pursuing solution attempts until impasse is reached. As a result, the greater availability of unsuccessful solutions in memory could significantly promote their later participation in the achievement of ultimate insight.

Interestingly, however, there is one caveat that should be appended to this latter conclusion. In a further extension of the results from experiment 2, we increased the rate at which subjects failed to solve the problems presented under the timed-impasse condition. This involved including more relatively difficult problems. With the latter change, subjects' failure rate increased from roughly 30 percent to well over 50 percent. As a result, the relatively high memorability of the failed solution attempts dropped and became approximately equal to that for the successful attempts. It may be that people have limited capacity or limited motivation for selectively storing, retaining, and retrieving unsolved problems on which impasses have been reached. Perhaps when the human information-processing system becomes overwhelmed with too many problems, its otherwise efficient handling of them deteriorates. Consequently, the attainment of insight may require that the creative individual not be too overburdened with unsolved pressing problematic situations.

Further Implications of the Present Experiments

Taken together, the combined results of experiments 1 and 2 provide an integrated characterization of the processes underlying insight. This is especially gratifying given that the methods used here involved rather different tasks—namely, answering general-information questions on the basis of knowledge stored in long-term memory (experiment 1) and recalling novel word problems (experiment 2). Because of these differences, the ways in which solutions were reached, and the causes of failures when they were not, varied significantly across the two experiments. For example, in experiment 1 with the general-information questions, the subjects' task required activating prior "solutions" (i.e., target-word answers) already stored in memory, and failures presumably resulted from a lack of access to necessary information at the time of the initial solution attempt. On the other hand, in experiment 2 with the novel word problems, subjects had to construct their solutions from scratch rather than retrieving them from memory, and failures at solving the word problems stemmed from an initial inability to finish the construction of a new solution. Nonetheless, as summarized already, the results of the two experiments complement each other nicely and lead to similar conclusions.

Such congruence implies that the inferences drawn from our research are perhaps applicable to a variety of domains involving insight. It also seems, on the basis of what we found, that studies of insight may be best pursued through a variety of empirical methods. The question-answering experiment allowed a controlled test of exposure to external information; presumably, the results from it will generalize to other problem-solving situations. Similarly, the problem-recall experiment showed that later access to failed problems is relatively high, which may likewise have occurred in the question-answering experiment during the subsequent target-word exposure phase. These diverse considerations bode well for future investigations that vary in their details and scope but that all strive toward a unified characterization of insight phenomena.

TOWARD AN INFORMATION-PROCESSING MODEL OF INSIGHT

On the foundation laid in preceding sections, we may now complete this chapter by taking steps toward a more comprehensive model of the mental processes that lead to cognitive insight. As shown already, our opportunistic-assimilation hypothesis and expansion of the prepared-mind perspective account well for the phenomenological characteristics of insight, anecdotal cases, and laboratory data. The present account can therefore help to update and elaborate Wallas's (1926) original analysis. In what follows, we pursue this elaboration to its natural conclusion, outlining a model with several component stages and substages that parallel the preparation, incubation, and illumination phases proposed by Wallas and that fully encompass our own current theoretical views as well.

Substages of the Preparation Phase

The first stage of the present model concerns details of the information processing that takes place in the minds of individuals during the initial preparation phase of problem solving. According to our current views, stage 1 includes four major substages: stage 1a, confrontation with a problem; stage 1b, construal of failure; stage 1c, storage of failure indices in long-term memory; and stage 1d, suspension of initial processing. We assume that in order for preparation to maximize the likelihood of future insightful outcomes, all these substages must be completed before a problem solver moves on to deal with other matters.

Stage 1a: Confrontation with a Problem
Obviously, if ultimate insight is to occur in resolving a difficult problematic situation, the problem first has to be taken seriously and confronted head-on. The would-be problem solver needs sufficient motivation to spend significant amounts of time on an initial careful analysis of the problem situation, pushing ahead as far as possible with it, forming a coherent memory representation of the problem, and using all the available information in a solution attempt. Without these prerequisite investments, there can be little hope of later success. In this respect, we agree with other previous theorists who have stressed the importance of problem analysis and mental representation as part of preparation for insight (e.g., Kaplan & Simon, 1990; Keane, 1989; Ohlsson, 1984b).

Stage 1b: Construal of Failure
A second key substage of preparation in our nascent model is a construal of failure at the end of an initial problem-solving attempt. When an impasse has been reached, it must be deemed such in order that special facilitative memory traces of the impasse (i.e., failure indices) get properly stored. As we have shown through our laboratory studies (Experiments 1 and 2), mere interruption of problem-solving activity by itself promotes neither sub-

sequent enhanced recall nor opportunistic assimilation of relevant new information.

This demonstration implies that under many circumstances, insight in problem solving is unlikely to occur. For example, a problem (1) may not be noticed as such, (2) may be noticed but not attempted, (3) may be attempted but not understood well enough to identify a specific cause of failure, (4) may be understood but interrupted en route to its solution, or (5) may be solved incorrectly but without the problem solver's realizing it. Under the present theoretical analysis, any of these eventualities would fall short of what must happen during preparation to lay the groundwork for later insight.

That serious problem solvers are aware of failure and take account of it is documented by some additional results from our two experiments. In the word-problem study (experiment 2), for example, we collected subjects' confidence ratings after each problem. They were highly correlated with the accuracy of the subjects' solutions (correct, incorrect, or incomplete) and with later free recall. Problems for which subjects had low confidence about their solutions were more likely to be recalled later. Also, in the untimed-impasse condition, where subjects controlled how long they spent on each problem, much more time was spent on problems ultimately left unsolved. Similarly, in the study with answering of general-information questions (experiment 1), subjects spent more time on questions for which the answer was ultimately not recalled, especially when they had a high "feeling of knowing" about it. This may mean that failure is, ironically, most intense when success seems tantalizingly close at hand. It therefore appears that subjects do indeed distinguish their failures from successes, suggesting an awareness on their part that impasses are important.

This then raises a further interesting question: On what basis do problem solvers decide that an initial impasse has been reached and that the preparation phase should be deemed a failure? Although we cannot answer the question for certain, at least two possibilities come to mind, inspired by analysis of stopping rules in other domains of information processing (Meyer, Irwin, Osman & Kounios, 1988). One is that subjects have a preset notion about the maximum amount of time that problems of a particular type should take to solve and, once they have reached this maximum, they declare an impasse. Another possibility is that they declare an impasse when they have exhaustively used, as best possible, all available components of the problem situation but without achieving full success. As indicated by our results concerning feelings of knowing (experiment 1), impasses may be declared even when success seems tantalizingly close at hand.

Stage 1c: Storage of Failure Indices in Memory

Whatever the criterion for declaring an initial impasse, the next substage of our model for the preparation phase of creative problem solving involves storing failure indices in long-term memory, marking the episodic information associated with the problem and the first attempt to solve it. Following proposals by other cognitive scientists (e.g., Hammond et al., 1991), we assume that the failure indices are special markers, distinct from the general heightened activation level that the problem episode may leave (see Anderson, 1990). The purpose of storing the failure indices is, of course, to help guide the problem solver back to the problem when relevant new information is later encountered externally during subsequent ongoing perception and comprehension.

We assume that the failure indices associated with an initial problem-solving impasse may remain present and useful in long-term memory for hours, days, weeks, months, and even years if the impasse has great significance for the stymied problem solver. This may, for example, have been so with Albert Einstein, the inventor of the theory of relativity, who during the last half of his life made an exerted long-time effort to unify the laws of gravitation and electromagnetism but without success (Crease & Mann, 1986). Although our own experiments extended over just a 24-hour period, they too provide some evidence for the endurance of problem failure indices. In experiment 1 on answering general-information questions, these indices lasted significantly longer than the residual memory activation induced by processing the questions initially, as revealed by a comparison of subsequent effects on lexical-decision reaction times versus the probabilities of ultimate correct answers.

Another key characteristic of the stored failure indices for a problem-solving impasse is that they may be integrated with other general knowledge in long-term memory. Our study with the question-answering task suggests this possibility because information presented there within a separate context (the lexical-decision task) was nevertheless recognized and used to overcome prior retrieval failures. If the stored failure indices were separate from the rest of memory, then exposure to relevant information in other contexts would seem less likely to resurrect them. That traces of failures may be accessed across various tasks is especially interesting, given previous pervasive findings of little or no information transfer between different task domains. Perhaps stored failure indices have a unique status for promoting such transfer (see Adams et al., 1988; Lockhart et al., 1988; Needham & Begg, 1991).

Stage 1d: Suspension of Initial Processing

With potentially beneficial failure indices stored away, the last substage of the initial preparation phase may ensue. In our model, we assume that stage 1d simply involves a suspension of information processing for the problem at hand, after which the problem solver may go about his or her other business. This then leads to the next phase, incubation, and its various substages that precede insight.

Substages of the Incubation Phase

According to our current views, stage 2 includes three major substages: stage 2a, intermediate incubation during other activities; stage 2b, exposure to new information; and stage 2c, retrieval of failure indices. We assume that as precursors to future insightful outcomes, all these substages must be completed, just as are those of stage 1.

Stage 2a: Intermediate Incubation

The present model makes some interesting specific claims about what happens during intermediate incubation while the problem solver engages in other activities. Under our assumptions, the sheer passage of time has no bearing per se on whether the problem solver ultimately will achieve illumination and insight. We do not attribute insight to spontaneous subconscious processes that could conceivably occur as part of the incubation phase. As mentioned already, the opportunistic-assimilation hypothesis discounts the roles played by processes that involve growth of sub-liminal memory-trace activation (Bowers et al., 1990), selective forgetting of inappropriate memory traces (Silveira, 1971), and covert random reorganization of knowledge structures. Rather, in our view, the main contribution of the incubation phase is simply to provide the problem solver with incidental exposures to various external stimuli, some of which may be relevant for resolving prior problematic impasses. If the present model is correct, until such exposures occur by chance, the problem solver, in essence, would do no further work on a problem.

Although these are somewhat extreme claims, there is evidence from our research to support them. In particular, Experiment 1 on answering general-information questions revealed no evidence of spontaneous growth in memory-trace activation during an intermediate incubation phase. The incubation phase was beneficial only when it provided exposures to relevant new information—namely, the target-word answers for previously failed questions. This outcome has some potentially significant implications for ways in which insightful problem solving might be facilitated. If our conjectures are correct, then taking regular extended breaks from working on hard problems is well advised but will be most effective if the breaks involve other stimulating activities. Shifting back and forth among tasks, including recreational and unstructured ones, may increase the chances that a stymied problem solver will be exposed to relevant new information. Staying in an old environment, on the other hand, is less likely to provide occasions for such exposures.

At the same time, however, we would not want to dismiss entirely the importance of internal self-driven processes as a part of incubation. Internal processing could conceivably generate new problem-relevant information that promotes insightful solutions, supplementing external encounters with such information. For example, this might happen during the course of dreaming, which in essence simulates external events and stimulus encounters. If an internal dream-based incubation mechanism does exist, its products—just like externally obtained information—could interact beneficially with failure indices stored in long-term memory, thereby leading to insight. The line between illusion, hallucination, and reality may be a thin one.

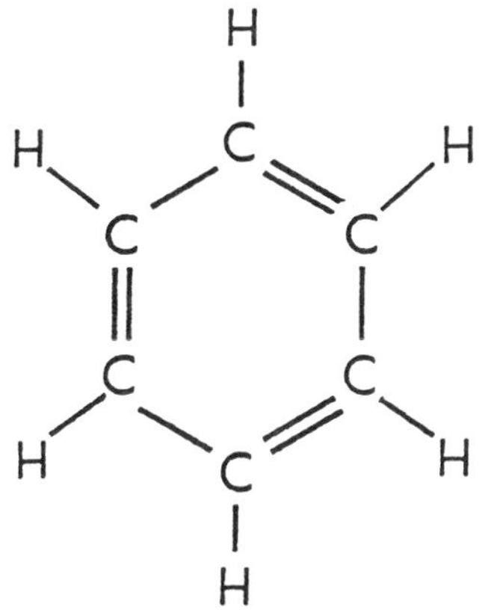

Figure 3.6
The benzene ring discovered by Kekulé through opportunistic assimilation of self-generated perceptual stimulation while dreaming. (See text for further details.)

To be specific, consider the following anecdote, which concerns how the ringlike molecular structure of the organic compound benzene was discovered by the chemist Kekulé (Koestler, 1964, p. 118; cited in Glass & Holyoak, 1986, p. 413):

I turned my chair to the fire and doze.... Again the atoms were gamboling before my eyes.... My mental eye ... could now distinguish larger structures, of manifold conformation; long rows, sometimes more closely fitted together; all twining and twisting in snakelike motion. But look! ... One of the snakes had seized hold of its own tail, and the form whirled mockingly before my eyes. As if by a flash of lightening I awoke.

Apparently what happened here was that Kekulé stimulated himself with new perceptual information through dreaming. His image of the snake seizing its own tail, which closely parallels the actual structure of the benzene ring (figure 3.6), led to opportunistic assimilation and the eventual proposal of the benzene ring.

Stage 2b: External Exposure to New Information
Be this as it may, the present model still maintains that external exposure to new information from the environment is a principal source of insight. We assume that such exposures, and the opportunities for having them, are what make an intervening

incubation phase especially helpful. Our assumption is strongly supported by both the anecdotal cases considered previously and by the laboratory experiments reported here. In the question-answering task of experiment 1, for example, we found that a single subsequent exposure of a target-word answer after an initial question-answering failure was sufficient to increase substantially the probability of a later successful answer (see figure 3.5).

This outcome raises some further interesting questions about exactly which kinds of new information may promote insight. For new information to be helpful, what sorts of relationships must it have to an original problematic situation and the memory representation formed thereof? In answer to this question, there is at least one more discovery we have made: External stimulus cues that are related to the goals of a problem solver's pending solution plans are more likely to remind him or her of those plans than are other types of cue (Patalano, Seifert & Hammond, 1993). Even if the goal-related cues are relatively abstract, they may still be beneficial (e.g., seeing a piece of gum can effectively remind a problem solver about the goal of rehanging a wall poster, just as can seeing a metal tack). Thus, future researchers may wish to focus more closely on how different possible relationships between new information and past solution failures can contribute to insight.

Stage 2c: Retrieval of Failure Indices

Under the present model, the incubation phase would culminate when an exposure to relevant new information triggers the access of failure indices associated with a prior problem-solving impasse. We assume that this triggering takes place during the course of normal perception and comprehension processes that the problem solver uses in dealing with all incoming stimuli. Hence, the final steps on the road to insight may well be subconscious, as perception and comprehension processes usually are. People do not typically become aware of how they perceive or comprehend the environment; all they consciously know is that the products of these processes often seem natural.

Again, our assumptions are consistent with results from previous research. In experiment 1, for example, the lexical-decision task given to subjects during the intermediate incubation phase presumably required some of the same retrieval and comprehension processes used in understanding ordinary language (Meyer & Schvaneveldt, 1971). As we would predict, these processes were sufficient for the failure indices associated with prior unanswered questions to be accessed, and they facilitated opportunistic assimilation of the target-word exposures provided by the lexical-decision task.

Substages of the Illumination Phase

The third stage of the present model concerns details of the processing that takes place during the illumination phase of problem solving, after relevant new information has been encountered in the external environment and previously stored failure indices have been accessed. According to our current views, stage 3 includes two major substages: stage 3a, information interpretation and assimilation, and stage 3b, *insight*! We assume that in order for an encounter with new information to have its full beneficial effect, both of these substages must follow the incubation phase and bring it to final fruition.

Stage 3a: Interpretation and Assimilation

On an encounter with relevant new information, stage 3a begins when contact is made with previously stored failure indices. At this point, normal progress on automatic perception and comprehension processes, which lead incidentally to access of the failure indices, may be interrupted in the same way as high-priority external inputs cause temporary suspension of information processing by time-shared computer-operating systems. After such interruption, our opportunistic-assimilation hypothesis claims that other special problem-solving processes take control to interpret the newly encountered information in light of its potential relevance for past problems. This would presumably involve assessing how the new information fits with, and perhaps overcomes, the particular block(s) that caused earlier solution attempt(s) to be construed as failures. If the latter assessment reveals that the new information can help make progress on the problem and perhaps yield an immediate solution, then under the present model, the new information would be assimilated into the original mental representation of the problem. Also, if need be, problem restructuring (i.e., accommodation of the new information) could occur at this point (see Kaplan & Simon, 1990; Keane, 1989; Ohlsson, 1984a, 1984b).

The steps associated with implementing the assumed interpretation and assimilation processes are crucial ones. They may require lots of attention on the part of the problem solver and induce a significant increase of his or her physiological arousal level (e.g., increases of heart rate, blood pressure, breathing, and neural activity). Increased arousal and the heightened emotions that accompany it can help to focus attention on resolving a previously failed problem and on learning from the opportunity presented by the current exposure to relevant new information (Baddeley, 1976). In effect, the accompanying emotional experience provides an explicit flag that an important event is at hand and that extra effort should be exerted immediately to gain the most benefit from it. Moreover, the increased arousal could amplify the positive reinforcing affect that the problem solver experiences, making it more likely that he or she will seek additional future insights. As we have seen already in the introspective reports by Richard Feynman and others, stage 3a—the act of interpreting and assimilating long-needed and highly important information—can be extremely exciting and gratifying.

Stage 3b: Insight
With the present model, insight comes finally at the end of the illumination phase, stage 3b. It yields two major products: (1) an improved representation of an important previously unsolved problem, which now likely contains the essence of a correct solution; and (2) the delightful "Aha!" experience colored by an increased physiological arousal level with positive affective overtones, which further facilitates opportunistic assimilation and long-term memory consolidation.

Conclusions

In summary, the present model incorporates some normal mental processes and so partly adheres to the business-as-usual perspective on the nature of insight. At the same time, our theoretical assumptions highlight two relatively special mechanisms that instantiate the prepared-mind perspective and that help explain how intellectual magicians perform their insightful tricks without recourse to supernatural mental powers. One special mechanism proposed here relies on failure indices in long-term memory to mark problem-solving impasses. These indices are clearly crucial for intelligent problem solvers who want to achieve their goals but are nonetheless human and therefore subject to disappointments in their initial solution attempts. A second special mechanism proposed here relies on opportunistic assimilation to benefit from encounters with relevant new information, once a prior problem has been reaccessed through the stored failure indices. Because such opportunism gets only occasional chances to take control, it must wait in the wings against a backdrop of ongoing normal processes.

Although our own theoretical ideas may not seem entirely complete yet, we hope that whatever limitations they have at present will at least enable the storage of further helpful failure indices in the minds of this book's readers. We likewise hope that readers' future encounters with other relevant information-processing concepts will trigger subsequent insightful opportunistic assimilation. If so, then perhaps someday all of us will come to understand EVVVVVERYTHING there is to know about the nature of insight!

ACKNOWLEDGMENTS

Support for preparation of this chapter was provided in part by grants from the United States Office of Naval Research. The authors thank Susan Chipman and R.J. Sternberg for helpful comments and encouragement.

REFERENCES

Adams, L.T., Kasserman, J.E., Yearwood, A.A., Perfetto, G.A., Bransford, J.D., & Franks, J.J. (1988). Memory access: The effects of fact-oriented versus problem-oriented acquisition. *Memory & Cognition, 16,* 167–175.

Anderson, B.F. (1975). *Cognitive psychology: The study of knowing, learning, and thinking.* New York: Academic Press.

Anderson, B.F. (1980). *The complete thinker.* Englewood Cliffs, NJ: Prentice Hall.

Anderson, J.R. (1990). *Cognitive psychology and its implications.* San Francisco: Freeman.

Baddeley, A.D. (1963). A Zeigarnik-like effect in the recall of anagram solutions. *Quarterly Journal of Experimental Psychology, 15,* 63–64.

Baddeley, A.D. (1976). *The psychology of memory.* New York: Basic Books.

Bowers, K.S., Regehr, G., Balthazard, C., & Parker, K. (1990). Intuition in the context of discovery. *Cognitive Psychology, 22,* 72–110.

Chase, W.G., & Simon, H.A. (1973). The mind's eye in chess. In W.G. Chase (Ed.), *Visual information processing.* New York: Academic Press.

Conan Doyle, A. (1981). *The adventures of Sherlock Holmes.* Norwalk, CT: Easton Press.

Connor, L.T., Balota, D.A., & Neely, J.H. (1992). On the relation between feeling of knowing and lexical decision: Persistent subthreshold activation or topic familiarity? *Journal of Experimental Psychology: Human Learning and Memory, 18,* 544–554.

Cook, T.W. (1937). Massed and distributed practice in puzzle solving. *Psychological Review, 41,* 330–335.

Crease, R.P., & Mann, C.C. (1986). *The second creation. Makers of the revolution in 20th-century physics.* New York: Macmillan.

Davidson, N. (1993, in preparation). *Opportunistic assimilation of incidental retrieval cues based on declarative vs. interrogative knowledge representations in long-term memory.* Unpublished doctoral dissertation, University of Michigan, Ann Arbor.

De Groot, A.D. (1965). *Thought and choice in chess.* The Hague: Mouton.

Dominowski, R.L. (1981). Comment on "An examination of the alleged role of 'fixation' in the solution of several 'insight' problems. *Journal of Experimental Psychology: General, 110,* 193–198.

Dominowski, R.L., & Jenrick, R. (1972). Effects of hints and interpolated activity on solution of an insight problem. *Psychonomic Science, 26,* 335–337.

Dreistadt, R. (1969). The use of analogies and incubation in obtaining insight in creative problem solving. *Journal of Psychology, 71,* 159–175.

Duncker, K. (1945). On problem solving. *Psychological Monographs, 58*(5), whole no. 270.

Ellen, P. (1982). Direction, past experience, and hints in creative problem solving: Reply to Weisberg and Alba. *Journal of Experimental Psychology: General, 111,* 316–325.

Ericksen, S.C. (1942). Variability of attack in massed and spaced practice. *Journal of Experimental Psychology, 31,* 339–345.

Feynman, R.P. (1985). *QED. The strange theory of light and matter.* Princeton, NJ: Princeton University Press.

Fulgosi, A., & Guilford, J.P. (1968). Short-term incubation in divergent production. *American Journal of Psychology, 7,* 1016–1023.

Ghiselin, B. (1952). *The creative process.* Berkeley, CA: University of California Press.

Gick, M., & Holyoak, K.J. (1980). Analogical problem solving. *Cognitive Psychology, 12,* 306–355.

Gick, M., & Holyoak, K.J. (1983). Schema induction and analogical transfer. *Cognitive Psychology, 15,* 1–38.

Glass, A.L., & Holyoak, K.J. (1986). *Cognition.* New York: Random House.

Gleick, J. (1992). *Genius: The life and science of Richard Feynman.* New York: Pantheon Books.

Glucksberg, S., & Danks, J. (1968). Effects of discriminative labels and of nonsense labels upon availability of novel function. *Journal of Verbal Learning and Verbal Behavior, 7,* 72–76.

Glucksberg, S., & Weisberg, R.W. (1966). Verbal behavior and problem solving: Some effects of labeling in a functional fixedness problem. *Journal of Experimental Psychology, 71,* 659–664.

Guralnik, D.B. (Ed.). (1984). *Webster's new world dictionary of the American language.* New York: Simon & Schuster.

Halpern, D.F. (1989). *Thought and knowledge* (2nd ed.). Hillsdale, NJ: Erlbaum.

Hammond, K.J., Converse, T.M., Marks, M., & Seifert, C.M. (1993). Opportunism and learning. *Journal of Machine Learning, 10,* 279–310.

Hammond, K.J., & Seifert, C.M. (1993). A cognitive science approach to case-based planning. In S. Chipman & A.L. Meyrowitz (Eds.), *Foundations of knowledge acquisition: Cognitive models of complex learning* (pp. 245–267). Norwell, MA: Kluwer Academic Publications.

Hammond, K.J., Seifert, C.M., & Gray, K.C. (1991). Functionality in analogical transfer: A hard match is good to find. *Journal of the Learning Sciences, 1,* 111–152.

Hayes, J.R. (1978). *Cognitive psychology. Thinking and creating.* Homewood, IL: Dorsey Press.

Hayes, J.R. (1989). *The complete problem solver* (2nd ed.). Hillsdale, NJ: Erlbaum.

Hayes-Roth, B., & Hayes-Roth, F. (1979). A cognitive model of planning. *Cognitive Science, 3,* 275–310.

Kaplan, C.A., & Simon, H.A. (1990). In search of insight. *Cognitive Psychology, 22,* 374–419.

Keane, M. (1989). Modelling problem solving in Gestalt 'insight' problems. *Irish Journal of Psychology, 10*, 201–215.

Koestler, A. (1964). *The act of creation*. New York: Macmillan.

Köhler, W. (1956). *The mentality of apes*. (2nd ed.). New York: Harcourt, Brace.

Lachman, R., Lachman, J.L., & Butterfield, E.C. (1979). *Cognitive psychology and information processing: An introduction*. Hillsdale, NJ: Erlbaum.

Laird, J.E., Rosenbloom, P.S., & Newell, A. (1987). SOAR: An architecture for general intelligence. *Artificial Intelligence, 33*, 1–64.

Lindsay, P.H., & Norman, D.A. (1977). *Human information processing* (2nd ed.). New York: Academic Press.

Lockhart, R., Lamon, M., & Gick, M.L. (1988). Conceptual transfer in simple insight problems. *Memory & Cognition, 16*, 36–44.

Luchins, A. (1942). Mechanization in problem solving. *Psychological Monographs, 54* (248).

Maier, N.R. (1931). Reasoning in humans: II. The solution of a problem and its appearance in consciousness. *Journal of Comparative and Physiological Psychology, 12*, 181–194.

Mayer, R. (1992). *Thinking, problem solving, cognition* (2nd ed.). New York: Freeman.

Metcalfe, J., & Weib, D. (1987). Inituition in insight and noninsight problem solving. *Memory & Cognition, 15*, 238–246.

Meyer, D.E., Irwin, D.E., Osman, A.M., & Kounios, J. (1988). The dynamics of cognition and action: Mental processes inferred from speed-accuracy decomposition. *Psychological Review, 95*, 183–237.

Meyer, D.E., & Schvaneveldt, R.W. (1971). Facilitation in recognizing pairs of words: Evidence of a dependence between retrieval operations. *Journal of Experimental Psychology, 90*, 227–234.

Meyer, D.E., Yaniv, I., & Davidson, N. (1988, November). *Spreading activation and memory marking: Mechanisms for metacognition and mental incubation*. Paper presented at the meeting of the Psychonomic Society, Chicago, IL.

Mosler, G. (1977). *The puzzle school*. New York: Abelard-Schuman.

Murray, H.G., & Denny, J.P. (1969). Interaction of ability level and interpolated activity (opportunity for incubation) in human problem solving. *Psychological Reports, 24*, 271–276.

Needham, D.R., & Begg, I.M. (1991). Problem-oriented training promotes spontaneous analogical transfer: Memory-oriented training promotes memory for training. *Memory & Cognition, 19*, 543–557.

Ohlsson, S. (1984a). Restructuring revisited: I. Summary and critique of the Gestalt theory of problem solving. *Scandinavian Journal of Psychology, 25*, 65–78.

Ohlsson, S. (1984b). Restructuring revisited: II. An information processing theory of restructuring and insight. *Scandinavian Journal of Psychology, 25*, 117–129.

Olton, R.M. (1979). Experimental studies of incubation: Searching for the elusive. *Journal of Creative Behavior, 13*, 9–22.

Olton, R.M., & Johnson, D.M. (1976). Mechanisms of incubation in creative problem solving. *American Journal of Psychology, 89*, 617–630.

Patalano, A.J., & Seifert, C.M. (In press). Memory for impasses in problem solving. *Memory and Cognition.*

Patalano, A.J., Seifert, C.M., & Hammond, K. J. (1993). Predictive encoding: Planning for opportunities. In *Proceedings of the Fifteenth Annual Conference of the Cognitive Science Society.* Hillsdale, NJ: Lawrence Erlbaum.

Patrick, A.S. (1986). The role of ability in creative "incubation." *Personality and Individual Differences, 7*, 169–174.

Patrick, C. (1935). Creative thought in poets. *Archives of Psychology, 26*, 1–74.

Patrick, C. (1937). Creative thought in artists. *Journal of Psychology, 5*, 35–73.

Perfetto, G.A., Bransford, J.D., & Franks, J.J. (1983). Constraints on access in a problem solving context. *Memory and Cognition, 11*, 24–31.

Poincaré, H. (1913). Mathematical creation. In *The foundations of science* (G.H. Halstead, Trans.) New York: Science Press.

Popper, K. (1968). *Logic of scientific discovery.* New York: Harper & Row.

Posner, M.I. (1973). *Cognition: An introduction.* Glenview, IL: Scott, Foresman.

Saugstad, P., & Raaheim, K. (1957). Problem solving and the availability of functions. *Acta Psychologica, 13*, 263–278.

Schank, R. (1982). *Dynamic memory: A theory of learning in computers and people.* Cambridge, England: Cambridge University Press.

Seifert, C.M., & Patalano, A.J. (1991). Memory for interrupted tasks: The Zeigarnik effect revisited. In *Proceedings of the Thirteenth Annual Conference of the Cognitive Science Society.* Hillsdale, NJ: Erlbaum.

Silveira, J.M. (1971). *Incubation: The effect of interruption timing and length on problem solution and quality of problem processing.* Unpublished doctoral dissertation, University of Oregon, Eugene.

Smith, S.M., & Blankenship, S.E. (1989). Incubation effects. *Bulletin of the Psychonomic Society, 27*, 311–314.

Solso, R. (1988). *Cognitive psychology.* Boston: Allyn & Bacon.

Sternberg, R.J. (1985). *Beyond IQ: A triarchic theory of human intelligence.* Cambridge, England: Cambridge University Press.

Van Bergen, A. (1968). *Task interruption.* Amsterdam: North Holland.

VanLehn, K. (1988). Toward a theory of impasse-driven learning. In H. Mandl & A. Lesgold (Eds.), *Learning: Issues for intelligent tutor systems* (pp. 19–41). New York: Springer-Verlag.

Wallas, G. (1926). *The art of thought.* New York: Harcourt Brace Jovanovich.

Weaver, H., & Madden, E. (1949). "Direction" in problem solving. *Journal of Psychology, 27,* 331–345.

Weisberg, R.W. (1992). Metacognition and insight during problem solving: Comment on Metcalfe. *Journal of Experimental Psychology: Human Learning, Memory, and Cognition, 18,* 426–431.

Weisberg, R.W., & Alba, J.W. (1981a). An examination of the alleged role of "fixation" in the solution of several "insight" problems. *Journal of Experimental Psychology: General, 110,* 169–192.

Weisberg, R.W., & Alba, J.W. (1981b). Gestalt theory, insight and past experience: Reply to Dominowski. *Journal of Experimental Psychology: General, 110,* 199–203.

Weisberg, R.W., & Alba, J.W. (1982). Problem solving is not like perception: More on Gestalt theory. *Journal of Experimental Psychology: General, 111,* 326–330.

Weisberg, R., DiCamillo, M., & Phillips, D. (1978). Transferring old associations to new situations: A nonautomatic process. *Journal of Verbal Learning and Verbal Behavior, 17*(2), 219–228.

Weisberg, R., & Suls, J.M. (1973). An information processing model of Duncker's candle problem. *Cognitive Psychology, 4,* 255–276.

Wertheimer, M. (1959). *Productive thinking.* New York: Harper & Row.

Yaniv, I. (1988). *Sensitization and accessibility of information during memory incubation.* Unpublished doctoral dissertation, University of Michigan, Ann Arbor.

Yaniv, I., & Meyer, D.E. (1987). Activation and metacognition of inaccessible stored information: Potential bases of incubation effects in problem solving. *Journal of Experimental Psychology: Learning, Memory, and Cognition, 13,* 187–205.

Yaniv, I., Meyer, D.E., & Davidson, N. (1993, submitted for publication). *Dynamic memory processes in retrieving answers to questions: Recall failures, judgments of knowing, and acquisition of information.*

Zeigarnik, B. (1927). Über das Behalten von erledigten und unerledigten Handlungen. *Psychologisches Forschung, 9,* 1–85.

4   The Suddenness of Insight

Janet E. Davidson

When solving certain problems, some people feel they suddenly know the answers, even though they often cannot explain how these answers were found (Metcalfe, 1986b; Poincaré, 1913/1952; Wallas, 1926). This "Aha!" experience forms the basis of several definitions of insight (Duncker, 1945; Kohler, 1956; Maier, 1930). According to these definitions, many of the world's greatest contributions have derived from insightful problem solving, as opposed to more routine and less subjectively sudden forms of problem solving (Gruber, 1979; Nickles, 1978). If major discoveries do stem from sudden realizations, then it is important to understand the conditions under which these realizations occur. Unfortunately, little is known about the mental mechanisms underlying insightful discoveries, and even less is known about individual differences in the ability to make these discoveries.

This chapter has two general goals. One is to explore the nature of insightful problem solving. The other is to examine the relation between insight abilities and intelligent behavior. In considering these goals, the chapter will present a descriptive theory of insight that takes into account the processes that accompany sudden realizations during problem solving and the role that intelligence plays in the use of these processes. First, however, let us set the stage by reviewing two conventional views of the nature of insight.

CONVENTIONAL VIEWS OF INSIGHT

Conventional approaches to insight fall into two basic groups, the special-process view and the nothing-special view.

The Special-Process View

The special-process view is most often associated with the Gestalt psychologists (e.g., Duncker, 1945; Koffka, 1935; Maier, 1930; Wertheimer, 1959), who believed that insight is a process that differs qualitatively from other kinds of mental processes. Included in this view are the ideas that insight (1) results from a sudden restructuring of a problem that is accompanied by the sensation of flashes of inspiration or unconscious leaps in thinking; (2) occurs during greatly accelerated mental processing; and (3) is due to a short-circuiting of normal reasoning processes (see Perkins, 1981). In other words, the special abilities needed to solve insight problems are believed to differ from the abilities required on intelligence tests and tests of conventional problem-solving ability, which have well-defined mental representations, well-defined goal states, and well-defined allowable operators (Atwood & Polsen, 1976; Burke & Maier, 1965; Greeno, 1974, 1978; Thomas, 1974).

Empirical support has been provided for the special-process view. Metcalfe (1986a) found that although feelings of knowing an answer are predictive of memory performance, they do not predict performance on insight problems. In addition, high feelings of confidence (so-called warmth) that one is converging on the solution to an insight problem seem to be negatively predictive of correct solution to insight problems but positively predictive of correct solution to more standard problems (Metcalfe, 1986b; Metcalfe & Weibe, 1987). In other words, subjects who felt they were gradually getting closer to solving insight problems tended to arrive at incorrect solutions, whereas subjects who felt they were far from solving the insight problems and then suddenly felt they knew the answers tended to give correct solutions. Metcalfe concludes that insight problems are correctly solved by a subjectively catastrophic process rather than by cumulative processes. This view fits the Gestalt notion that insight involves a sudden realization of a problem's solution.

Although the special-process view is intuitively appealing, it has at least three problematic aspects. First, it does not pin down what insight is. Defining *insight* as an "unconscious leap in thinking" or a "short-circuiting of normal reasoning" leaves us with a black box of unknown contents. Even if the special-process view were correct, just what insight is would still need to be identified. Second, the bulk of evidence in support of this view is anecdotal rather than experimental and, for each piece of anecdotal evidence to support the view, there is at least one corresponding piece of evidence to refute it (Perkins, 1981). Finally, the special-process view is probably not specific enough to permit direct empirical testing. As a result, the view is not falsifiable as it now stands.

The Nothing-Special View

In contrast to the special-process view, the nothing-special view proposes that insight is merely an extension of ordinary processes of perceiving, recognizing, learning, and conceiving (Perkins, 1981; Weisberg, 1986). Insights, according to the nothing-special view, are merely significant products of ordinary processes, which means that insight problems are not really insight problems at all. Instead, such problems are alleged to measure mostly the recognition of problem-specific prior knowledge (Weisberg & Alba, 1981).

Arguments for the nothing-special view are essentially arguments by default: Because insight processes have not been identified, they have no independent existence. After repeated failures to identify a construct empirically, one can easily be tempted to ascribe the failure to the nonexistence of the construct. However, some research (Davidson & Sterberg, 1984; Sternberg & Davidson, 1982) indicates that a main reason psychologists have had so much difficulty in isolating insight is that it involves at least three processes rather than a single one. What are these processes involved in insightful thinking?

THEORY OF SELECTION IN INSIGHT

According to the three-process theory (Davidson, 1986; Davidson & Sternberg, 1986), insight comprises selective encoding, selective combination, and selective comparison. Insightful thinking occurs when these processes are successfully applied in situations where the individual does not have a routine set of procedures for solving a problem. Each of the processes will be discussed in turn.

Selective Encoding

Selective encoding occurs when a person suddenly sees in a stimulus, or set of stimuli, one or more features that previously have not been obvious. Significant problems generally present an individual with large amounts of information, only some of which is relevant to problem solution. Selective encoding can contribute to insight by restructuring one's mental representation so that information that was originally viewed as being irrelevant is now seen as relevant for problem solution. Also, information that was originally seen as relevant may now be viewed as irrelevant.

Ignaz Semmelweis's discovery of the importance of asepsis is a famous example of selective-encoding insight in science. While on the staff of the general hospital in Vienna, Semmelweis noticed that more women on the poor ward were dying from infection during childbirth than were women on the rich ward. He encoded that doctors washed their hands less frequently while on the poor ward and he realized the relevance that this had for spreading puerperal fever. Unfortunately, Semmelweis committed suicide before others recognized the relevance of his discovery.

Selective Combination

Selective combination occurs when one suddenly puts together elements of a problem situation in a way that previously has not been obvious to the individual. In significant problems, even when the relevant features have been encoded, it often is difficult to find a procedure to combine them appropriately. Darwin's formulation of the theory of evolution seems to have involved selective-combination insight. Darwin had all the facts for a long time: What he finally discovered was how to put them together to form a coherent theory.

Selective Comparison

Selective comparison occurs when one suddenly discovers a nonobvious relationship between new information and information acquired in the past. It is here that analogies, metaphors, and models are used to solve problems. The person having an insight suddenly realizes that new information is similar to old information in certain ways (and dissimilar to it in other ways), and then uses this information better to understand the newly acquired information.

Archimedes' theory of specific gravity is a famous example of a selective-comparison insight. While trying to determine whether silver had been put into King Hiero's crown, Archimedes stepped into a bath. He noticed that the amount of water that was displaced was equal to the volume of his body that was under water. By drawing an analogy between his bath and the problem with the crown, Archimedes suddenly knew how to determine the purity of the crown. He could compute the crown's volume by placing it in water and measuring the amount of displaced water. The crown could then be weighed against an equal volume of gold.

How These Processes Lead to Insight

In sum, these three processes form the basis for a theory of insightful thinking. To the extent that there is a commonality in the three processes, it appears to be in the importance of selection and relevance. In encoding, one is selecting only some of the often numerous possible elements that constitute the problem situation; the key is to select the relevant elements. In combination, an individual is selecting one of many possible ways in which elements of information can be combined or integrated; the key is to select a relevant way of combining the elements in a given situation. In comparison, an individual is selecting one (or more) of numerous possible old elements of information to which to relate new information. There are any number of relations that might be drawn; the key is to select the relevant comparison or comparisons to make for one's purposes.

Not every instance of selective encoding, selective combination, or selective comparison is an insight. To be referred to as *insightful*, the processes must not occur to most people immediately on presentation of the problem. The processes must seem to occur abruptly when they do occur and, once they have occurred, must result in a change in the solver's mental representation of the problem. In contrast, noninsightful encodings, combinations, and comparisons can occur immediately for most people, can occur gradually over extended time periods, and do not necessarily lead to a change in mental representations. It should be emphasized that the proposed theory is process-oriented rather than problem-oriented. One individual may solve a problem correctly by having an insight, whereas another individual may solve the same problem correctly without having an insight. The difference between these two individuals lies in the nature of the processes rather than in the outcome.

Predicting Differences in Intelligent Behavior

The three-process theory of insightful problem solving also makes predictions about individual differences in intelligent behavior. According to the theory, intelligence is, in part, a function of the insight processes. Highly intelligent individuals are more likely to apply spontaneously the three insight processes than are individuals with average or below-average intelligence.

Intelligence, intelligence quotient (IQ), and insight are closely intertwined concepts that should be clarified. *Intelligence* has been defined in many ways (Sternberg & Detterman, 1986) but, for present purposes, it will be defined as "the ability to comprehend information, solve problems, and make decisions in a variety of situations" (see Sternberg, 1985). *IQ* is a measurement of a part of intelligence, particularly that part which applies to the comprehension, knowledge retrieval, problem solving, and decision making required in academic, and primarily abstract, kinds of tasks. Although some investigators have considered IQ to be an operational definition of intelligence (Boring, 1923), this view is uncommon among recent theorists of intelligence (see definitions in Sternberg & Detterman, 1986), most of whom regard conventional intelligence tests as measuring abilities that span only a narrow range of the full set of abilities that constitutes intelligence. It will be argued here that *insight* is also a part of intelligence—namely, that part which is applied to the solution of problems that are ill-structured and nonroutine. IQ and insight both involve the processes of selective encoding, selective combination, and selective comparison (Sternberg, 1985). In the case of

IQ, these three processes are used in familiar ways: The problem solver knows the procedures that are applicable for solving the types of problems found on IQ tests and, consequently, the selection of information is fairly routine. In the case of insight, the problem solver does not have a familiar representation and set of procedures that can be used on the problem (Greeno & Berger, 1987). A new representation and new operators are constructed through the processes of selective encoding, selective combination, and selective comparison.

Research Testing the Three-Process Theory

The three-process theory of insight provided a good account of the data from experiments that involved testing both adults and children on problems requiring various mixtures of the three kinds of insights (Davidson, 1986; Davidson & Sternberg, 1986; Sternberg & Davidson, 1982). Consider some examples of the problems that were used in these studies:

1. One day you decide to visit the zoo. While there, you see a group of giraffes and ostriches. Altogether they have 30 eyes and 44 legs. How many animals are there?

2. George wants to cook three steaks as quickly as possible. Unfortunately, his grill holds only two steaks and each steak takes 2 minutes per side to cook. What is the shortest amount of time in which George can cook his three steaks?

3. Heather and Lynn have three household tasks to perform.
a. Their floor must be vacuumed. They have only one vacuum and the task takes 30 minutes.
b. The lawn must be mowed. They have only one mower and this task also takes 30 minutes.
c. Their baby sister must be fed and bathed. This too takes 30 minutes.
How should Heather and Lynn divide the work so as to finish all three tasks in the shonest amount of time?

Of these particular problems, the first emphasizes selective encoding. The major key is realizing the relevance of the 30 eyes; giraffes and ostriches have the same number of eyes but not the same number of legs. This problem can be solved by simply dividing the number of eyes by two. The second example emphasizes selective combination; if the pieces of information are put together correctly, the problem solver discovers that the steaks can be cooked in 6 minutes. Although the third example also requires selective combination, it is used here as an illustration of how selective comparison was measured. In some cases, subjects were taught how to solve sample problems, such as the steak problem used in the second example, that were similar to a few complex problems in the test booklet. Usually subjects could solve the test problems only if they saw a connection between these items and the related samples. For example, if the problem solver saw a relation between the second and third problems just listed, then he or she would realize that Heather and Lynn need to divide one of the tasks.

In experiments conducted with adults and children, subjects were given sets of problems that were similar to the examples just discussed. Some of the results from this research were as follows:

• Some adults and children have considerable difficulty knowing when to apply the three insight processes; others do not have this difficulty (Davidson, 1986; Davidson & Sternberg, 1986).

• The ability to apply the insight processes is fairly highly correlated with scores on a general intelligence test ($\simeq .6$) (Davidson, 1986; Davidson & Sternberg, 1986; Sterberg & Davidson, 1982).

• High-IQ individuals are slower, not faster, than lower-IQ individuals in analyzing the problems and applying the insights (Davidson & Sternberg, 1986; Sternberg & Davidson, 1982).

• Insight can be trained on the basis of the three processes, and the training effects are both transferable and durable (Davidson & Sternberg, 1986; Sternberg & Davidson, 1989).

There are limitations to these findings on insight abilities and their role in individual differences in intelligence. First, the kinds of problems studied were somewhat narrow in nature. Second, although the theory claims that insight occurs when selective encoding, selective combination, and selective comparison are used in subjectively sudden, nonobvious ways, it is not clear what this means or what conditions prompt the nonobvious and sudden use of these processes.

Extending the Three-Process Theory of Insight

The three-process theory, as previously outlined, is mainly a descriptive theory of insight; little is known about what subjects are actually doing or experiencing when they solve the problems. Previous research testing the theory raises at least as many questions as it answers. Two questions, in particular, will be considered in some detail in this chapter.

First, why do highly intelligent subjects take longer than less intelligent participants to solve the problems? Although the higher-IQ participants perform better than the lower-IQ participants, this slower reaction time is somewhat unusual for intelligence research; usually, faster is considered to be smarter. In an experiment using problems similar to those used by Davidson and Sternberg (1984, 1986), Metcalfe (1986b) found that participants took longer to solve insight problems correctly than incorrectly. In addition, she found that low feelings of confidence (coolness) during problem solving predicted correct responses and high feelings of confidence (warmth) predicted incorrect responses.

A second question of interest is concerned with why the higher-IQ participants spontaneously apply the three types of insight processes, whereas the lower-IQ participants do not. Cuing of the three types of insights shows that the lower-IQ participants can use relevant information, combine information, and apply related old information if this information has been selected for them (Davidson, 1986). Why do they not select, or focus on, this information when the problems are given in uncued form?

One potential reason for the differences in performance and for the differences in the time spent solving the insight problems has to do with differences in participants' abilities to become unfixated on an incorrect solution. A property of many insight problems is that, on the surface, they appear to be routine, and this assumption on the part of the problem solver may bring him or her to an obvious, but incorrect, solution. It seems possible that participants, regardless of their intellectual level, will initially go down such garden paths on some problems. However, the higher-IQ participants might be better able to monitor their performance and would, therefore, know when they are following the wrong paths to solution. Sternberg (1985; Sternberg & Weil, 1980) and others (Markman, 1977, 1979; Flavell, 1981) have found that participants' abilities to keep track of how they are doing on analogies and tests of comprehension are related to intelligence and age: Less intelligent participants and very young children do not seem to keep track of what they have done, what they are currently doing, and what they still need to do.

When solving the insight problems, the lower-IQ problem solvers sometimes do not realize when they are following the wrong paths to solution. Even when they do realize that they are approaching the problem incorrectly, they are unable to break this fixation and approach the problem in a new way. Perhaps the reason that the lower-IQ participants perform better on the cued insight problems than on the uncued problems is because the cued problems have already been restructured for them. In contrast, the higher-IQ problem solvers seem to realize when they are taking wrong paths to problem solutions, and they are better able to switch to new paths when the old ones fail to work. It seems possible that these participants do not benefit much from problem cuing because they already know how to start over and restructure the problems, using selective encoding, selective combination, and selective comparison, to reach the correct solutions. The longer times spent by the higher-IQ participants on the uncued problems, in contrast to the lower-IQ participants, could reflect additional time invested in solution monitoring, searching for relevant information, and problem restructuring.

The importance of spontaneous restructuring to insightful problem solving was originally suggested by the Gestalt psychologists (Maier, 1930; Wertheimer, 1959). Insight, according to the Gestalt view, occurs when the problem solver suddenly sees the problem in a new way. This new perception is often thought to be accompanied by a novel solution and a feeling of "Aha!" The Gestaltists believed that people's inability to produce an insightful solution to a problem often is due to their fixation on past experience. For example, Duncker (1945) gave subjects three cardboard boxes, candles, matches, and thumbtacks. The task was to mount a candle vertically on a wall so that it could serve as a lamp (see figure 1.6). The solution is to melt wax onto the top of a box, stick the candle into the wax, and tack the box to the wall. Subjects who were given boxes filled with the tacks, matches, and candles had a harder time solving the problem than the subjects who received the same supplies outside the boxes. According to Duncker, seeing a box serve the function of a container made it difficult for subjects then to view the box as a platform. In other words, fixation keeps individuals from changing their problem-solving sets, even when old procedures are not relevant to the present situations. Studies conducted by Luchins (1942; Luchins & Luchins, 1950), Duncker (1945), and others (Adamson, 1952; Adamson & Taylor, 1954; Birch & Rabinowitz, 1951) illustrate how fixation on past experience can interfere with insightful problem solving. However, these studies have been criticized for not being representative of problem-solving situations, and other research has been conducted to show that past experience does facilitate problem solving (Maier, 1945; Raaheim, 1965; Weisberg & Alba, 1981).

NEW TEST OF THE THREE-PROCESS THEORY

In our work reported in this chapter, it is hypothesized that (1) insightful problem solving, in contrast to more conventional types of problem solving, requires people to become unfixated from the original way they have represented a problem and then to restructure the problem; (2) the ability to restructure a problem is related to individual differences in intelligence; and (3) selective encoding, selective combination, and selective comparison are used in problem restructuring. There are three general goals for this work. One is to gain a better understanding of what is involved in insightful problem solving and how it differs from other types of problem solving. The second is to learn more about the relation between insight abilities and intelligent behavior. The third is related to the other two goals: It involves a more extensive testing of the three-process theory of insight (Davidson, 1986; Davidson & Sternberg, 1986), to determine whether the theory is plausible and whether it needs to be expanded or modified.

In an attempt to reach these goals, the current study merged the Davidson and Sternberg approach to studying insight (Davidson & Sternberg, 1984, 1986; Davidson, 1986) with Metcalfe's feelings-of-warmth approach (Metcalfe, 1986b). The Davidson and Sternberg approach examined processes and individual differences in insightful problem solving but made no link to the time course, or subjective suddenness, of the insights. Metcalfe's approach examined the time course of insight by having subjects periodically rate how close they felt to solving insight problems. However, Metcalfe's work made no link to processes or individual differences involved in insightful problem solving. Merging these two approaches made it possible to compare subjects' abilities to apply the three insight processes with subjects' assessments of how close they felt to the problems' solutions.

In addition to merging the two approaches, this work extends previous research through the use of a wider range of problems. Although a process-oriented, rather than a problem-oriented, view of insight is being taken, some problems should be more likely to promote the use of insight processes and subjective feelings of suddenness than will other, more routine, problems. Typically, research on insight has not compared subjects' performance on familiar, well-defined problems with their performance on the novel types of problems that are usually believed to lead to insights. Thus, the use of routine, well-defined problems provides a test of discriminant validity for previous views on insight.

Adult subjects of high or average intellectual ability were given problems that varied in their emphasis on selective encoding, selective combination, selective comparison, and standard problem-solving routines. The problems were given with and without cues pointing to solution-relevant information. In addition, Metcalfe's (1986b) measurement of subjects' feelings of warmth that they were nearing solution was used.

Predictions

Several predictions were made. First, it was predicted that highly intelligent individuals would perform better on the uncued insight problems and show more patterns of sudden increases in warmth ratings (insight patterns) than would less intelligent individuals. Second, if cuing the processes helps structure novel problems in an appropriate manner for subjects, then the feelings of warmth should show more incremental patterns than in the uncued condition, where the subjects have to search for relevant information and restructure the problems themselves. (In fact, warmth judgments are named after the searching game wherein one person hides an object and directs others by telling them they are getting warmer [i.e., closer to the object] or colder [i.e., farther away from it] [see Simon, Newell & Shaw, 1979].) Also, subjects of average ability should benefit more from the cues than high-ability subjects because the more intelligent subjects will spontaneously select the relevant information in the problems. Finally, according to the proposed theory, the insight processes should not be used on problems that are familiar and straightforward to the subject. Thus, we should observe nonincremental patterns of warmth ratings for problems solved insightfully and incremental patterns of warmth ratings for problems not requiring insight.

Method

Subjects
The subjects were 48 adults from the New Haven area who were recruited via an advertisement in a local newspaper. Three additional subjects were eliminated from the study because they had difficulty reading the problems and writing answers. All subjects were native speakers of English, and they were paid $5 per hour for their participation.

Materials
Subjects received two booklets, each containing 24 problems. Problems in one of the booklets were presented in cued form, whereas problems in the other were presented without cues. The problems in each were equally divided with respect to their emphasis on selective encoding, selective combination, selective comparison, and routine processes. These problems were selected on the basis of ratings provided by three Yale University undergraduates. The three raters were given definitions for selective encoding, selective combination, selective comparison, and routine problem solving (similar to the ones reported earlier in this chapter) and were asked to determine which process, or processes, seemed to be required to solve each problem in a large set of problems. Forty-eight problems on which the raters were in total agreement were chosen for use in this study.

When the selective-encoding problems were cued, the solution-relevant parts were underlined. When the selective-combination problems were cued, a diagram or a list of steps appeared directly below the problem to help subjects combine information. When the selective-comparison problems were cued, subjects were told specifically which problems were related to the worked-out examples presented at the beginning of the booklet. When the noninsight problems were cued, a diagram of the situation or a statement of the goal appeared directly below the problem.

The items that were used were similar to those used in previous research on problem solving (Davidson, 1986; Greeno, 1978; Metcalfe, 1986b). In addition, half of the subjects received booklets in which there was, at the bottom of each problem, a section delineating 20 warmth ratings. The rating scale to be used was illustrated above each of these sections. A recording of tones spaced 15 seconds apart was used to signal subjects that it was time to write down a rating. The other half of the subjects received booklets that did not contain sections for warmth ratings. A standardized test of mental ability also was administered after the problem-solving task.

Design
The independent variables were (1) intellectual ability (between subjects); (2) presence or absence of cuing (within subjects); (3) type of problem—selective encoding, selective combination, selective comparison, or noninsight (within subjects); and (4) warmth ratings (between subjects). The dependent variables were the numbers of each type of problem correctly solved in the cued and uncued conditions and the warmth ratings for each type of problem in the cued and uncued conditions.

Procedure
Subjects received the two test booklets in a counterbalanced order: Half the subjects received the cued problems followed by the uncued problems, and half received them in the opposite order. Which booklet was cued was also counterbalanced. When the cued booklet was administered, subjects were asked to make use of the cues (underlining, diagrams, explicit instructions) that were given for each problem. In both the cued and uncued condi-

tions, subjects were shown how to solve two sample problems before they began solving the test problems. Subjects were told to show all their work while they solved the problems in both test booklets and to mark any problems that were familiar to them.

For half the subjects, Metcalfe's (1986b) method of collecting warmth ratings was used. While these subjects were working on the problems, a tone was played every 15 seconds. The tone was a signal for subjects to write down, in a space provided in the test booklet, a warmth rating on a scale from 1 to 10, where *1* meant they were "cold" (far from the correct solution), *10* meant they were certain they knew the correct solution, and intermediate ratings indicated intermediate closeness. After a rating of 10 had been given, subjects wrote down the answer. The maximum amount of time allowed for each problem was 5 minutes. If subjects completed a problem before the time limit, their corresponding warmth rating was always 10. Subjects practiced giving warmth ratings before testing began.

It seemed possible that being interrupted every 15 seconds while working on the problems might influence subjects' problem-solving performance. To examine this possibility, the other half of the subjects received the same problems but were not asked to give warmth ratings. All testing was done individually or in groups of two.

Results

The analyses of the results are divided into three sections: descriptive statistics and correlations for performance on the problems and scores on the mental abilities test, problem-solving performance, and warmth ratings.

Descriptive Statistics and Correlations

Performance on the uncued and cued problems was compared for subjects in the warmth-ratings condition and subjects in the no-ratings condition. Proportions correct were 55 percent for uncued problems and 66 percent for cued problems when warmth ratings were given and 57 percent for uncued problems and 61 percent for cued problems when warmth ratings were not given. The difference in performance between the two groups of subjects was not significant: Therefore, results from the two groups were combined in all further analyses except for those focusing specifically on the warmth ratings. Performance was consistent across problems.

The subjects in this study represented a wide range of mental abilities. The mean IQ was 119, with a standard deviation of 22.70 and a range from 70 to 148. For further analyses on the relation between problem performance and intelligence, subjects were separated on the basis of their IQ scores into two groups containing 24 subjects each. The mean IQ for the high-ability group was 137, with a standard deviation of 6.02 and a range of scores from 128 to 148. The mean IQ for the average-ability group was 101, with a standard deviation of 18.23 and a range from 70 to 126. It should be noted that the average-ability group includes individuals with scores well above the prototypical average score of 100. The inclusion of these subjects in the average-ability group provides a rigorous test of differences in problem-solving ability between the highly intelligent group and the group of average intelligence.

As predicted, scores on the mental ability test were highly related to performance on the problem-solving task. The correlation between IQ scores and performance on the uncued problems was .65. The correlation between IQ and performance on the cued problems was .60. Correlations between IQ and performance on each type of problem (selective encoding, selective combination, selective comparison, and noninsight) are listed in table 4.1. IQ was most highly correlated with performance on the noninsight problems and least highly correlated with performance on the selective-encoding problems. This is not surprising, because the

Table 4.1
Correlations of performance on the four types of problems

Problem type	Encoding	Combination	Comparison	Noninsight
Combination	52*	—	—	—
Comparison	64*	55*	—	—
Noninsight	41*	60*	43*	—
IQ	49*	52*	61*	69*

*p < .01.

noninsight problems are similar to some of the problems found on IQ tests, whereas the selective-encoding items are not. Also of interest was the pattern of correlations between scores on the different types of uncued problems. As shown in table 4.1, intercorrelations were significant for all four types ($p < .01$). However, the lowest correlations were between scores on the noninsight problems and both scores on the selective-encoding problems and scores on the selective-comparison problems. Scores on the noninsight problems were more highly correlated with performance on the selective-combination problems.

Problem-Solving Performance and Intelligence

There were several predictions regarding performance on the problems. First, it was predicted that the highly intelligent subjects would perform better on the problems than would the less intelligent subjects. Second, it was predicted that performance on the cued problems would be superior to performance on the uncued problems. Finally, it was predicted that there would be a significant interaction between intellectual level and cuing, with the subjects of average intelligence profiting more from the cuing than the highly intelligent subjects. These predictions were confirmed. Table 4.2 shows the means and ranges of performance on cued and uncued selective-encoding, selective-combination, selective-comparison, and noninsight problems for high-ability and average-ability subjects. In general, it was found that the highly intelligent subjects performed better on all types of problems than the average-ability subjects. Performance on cued problems was better than performance on uncued problems. There was

Table 4.2
Mean performance by intellectual level and problem type

Problem type	High ability		Average ability	
	Uncued	Cued	Uncued	Cued
Encoding	4.16	4.26	2.34	3.44
Combination	3.84	4.12	1.93	3.04
Comparison	4.01	4.19	2.11	3.28
Noninsight	4.02	4.00	3.15	3.95

Table 4.3
Percentage of problems showing a change in strategies

Problem type	Uncued		Cued	
	Correct	Incorrect	Correct	Incorrect
Encoding	.66	.12	.11	.15
Combination	.62	.23	.12	.13
Comparison	.51	.18	.22	.20
Noninsight	.21	.22	.19	.17

also a significant interaction between intelligence and cuing ($F[1, 46] = 4.55, p < .05$). The average-ability subjects benefited more from the cues than did the high-ability subjects.

The written protocols given for each problem were analyzed to determine whether subjects began a problem using one strategy and then switched to another strategy. A switch in strategy was operationally defined as crossing out previous work and starting over using new information. As shown in table 4.3, subjects who correctly solved uncued encoding, combination, and comparison problems switched strategies more frequently than subjects who solved these problems incorrectly. This was not the case on the noninsight problems; subjects rarely changed strategies on these problems, and frequency of switching was not related to accuracy.

To summarize, the analyses of insightful problem-solving performance replicate previous research (Davidson, 1986), even though a different experimental design and a wider range of problems were used. Highly intelligent subjects spontaneously applied the processes of selective encoding. selective combination, and selective comparison; their performance changed very little when these processes were cued. In contrast, subjects of average intelligence did not seem to apply these insight processes spontaneously on these types of problems. However, their problem-solving performance improved when critical features of the problems were noted for them.

The highly intelligent subjects were also better than the subjects of average intelligence at solving problems that did not seem to require insight. As with the other types of problems, the subjects of average ability benefited from the cuing of noninsight problems, but the highly intelligent subjects did not.

It was also found that subjects who solved the insight problems correctly were more likely to switch strategies than were subjects who solved the problems incorrectly. In other words, these problems were restructured before they were correctly solved. Very little restructuring occurred while subjects were solving the noninsight problems and problem restructuring was not related to accuracy.

Warmth Ratings

The analyses of the warmth ratings were based on the procedures used by Metcalfe (1986b). The first analysis examined warmth ratings for correct and incorrect responses on the problems. Subjects for whom answering at least three warmth ratings preceded at least one correct answer and at least one incorrect answer were included in the analysis. There were 22 such subjects. Figure 4.1 shows the pattern of warmth ratings that these subjects gave on the last three intervals before solution for cued and uncued selective-encoding, selective-combination, selective-comparison, and noninsight problems that were solved correctly and incorrectly.

In the uncued condition, lower warmth ratings were given for correctly solved than for incorrectly solved encoding problems, and selective-comparison problems. This was not the case for the uncued selective-combination problems and noninsight problems; for these problems, warmth ratings did not vary as a function of accuracy.

When warmth ratings for all the intervals were analyzed, the ratings were significantly higher for incorrectly than for correctly solved uncued selective-combination problems. However, there was no significant difference in the size of the warmth ratings for the uncued noninsight problems when all the intervals were examined. In the cued condition, no differences were found between the warmth ratings on correctly and incorrectly solved problems for any of the four problem types. The mean warmth ratings for all intervals before solution are shown in table 4.4.

What the analyses of warmth ratings reveal is that on uncued selective-encoding, -combination, and -comparison problems, subjects have lower overall warmth ratings on correctly solved problems than on incorrectly solved ones. In contrast, the correctly solved uncued noninsight problems show warmth ratings nearly

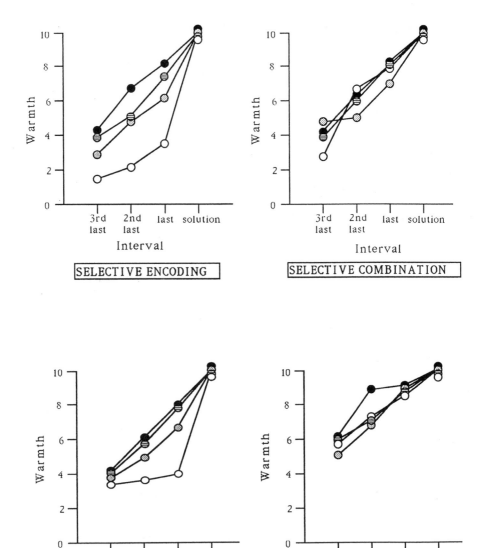

Figure 4.1
Warmth ratings for the last three intervals before solution for correct and incorrect responses. Open circles, correct response, uncued condition; stippled circles, incorrect response, uncued condition; solid circles, correct response, cued condition; hatched circles, incorrect response, cued condition.

Table 4.4
Mean warmth ratings for all intervals before solution for correct and
incorrect responses

Problem type	Uncued		Cued	
	Correct	Incorrect	Correct	Incorrect
Encoding	1.54	3.12	4.45	4.04
Combination	2.16	3.54	3.70	3.35
Comparison	2.27	3.76	4.55	3.69
Noninsight	4.06	3.80	4.49	4.31

equivalent to the incorrectly solved problems. In addition, correctly solved cued problems do not differ significantly from incorrectly solved cued problems for any of the four problem types. In
sum, high feelings of warmth predict failure to solve the uncued
insight problems but do not predict failure on uncued noninsight
problems or on cued problems of all four types.

One other result is noteworthy. Highly intelligent subjects gave
lower warmth ratings on the uncued insight problems than did
subjects of average intellectual ability. This difference is believed
to be due to the fact that the average-ability subjects solved more
of the problems incorrectly and had high feelings of warmth for
their incorrect solutions. Consistent with this account is the fact
that high-ability subjects gave higher warmth ratings on the uncued noninsight problems than did the subjects of average ability.

Warmth rating sequences that showed no more than a 1-point
increase from the first to the last rating before solution were said
to demonstrate an insight pattern of warmth ratings. Protocols
were included that had two or more such ratings. Warmth rating
sequences that showed at least a 5-point difference between the
first and the last warmth rating before solution were said to have
an incremental pattern. Table 4.5 shows the proportion of uncued
correctly and incorrectly solved problems wherein one of these
patterns was demonstrated. A difference-in-proportions test for
the correctly and incorrectly solved encoding and comparison
problems revealed that the correctly solved problems of these
types were more likely to show the insight pattern than were the
incorrectly solved problems. Correctly solved noninsight problems were more likely to show an incremental pattern than were

Table 4.5
Proportion of uncued problems showing an insight or an incremental pattern of warmth ratings

	Insight pattern		Incremental pattern	
Problem type	Correct	Incorrect	Correct	Incorrect
Encoding	.69	.11	.04	.44
Combination	.35	.32	.43	.57
Comparison	.48	.20	.08	.41
Noninsight	.12	.25	.61	.28

Table 4.6
Proportion of cued problems showing an insight or an incremental pattern of warmth ratings

	Insight pattern		Incremental pattern	
Problem type	Correct	Incorrect	Correct	Incorrect
Encoding	.23	.18	.41	.14
Combination	.18	.08	.59	.11
Comparison	.20	.17	.66	.19
Noninsight	.13	.10	.54	.25

the incorrectly solved problems. The difference in proportions between the correctly and incorrectly solved combination problems demonstrating an insight pattern was not significant.

Table 4.6 shows the proportion of correctly and incorrectly solved cued problems that exhibited either type of pattern. A difference-in-proportions test for the correctly and incorrectly solved problems demonstrated that correctly solved problems of all types were more likely to show an incremental pattern.

What these analyses reveal is that correctly solved uncued selective-encoding and selective-comparison problems tend to show an insight pattern (an abrupt increase in ratings before solution). Correctly solved uncued noninsight problems and incorrectly solved cued problems of all four types show an incremental pattern. The solved uncued selective-combination problems demonstrate neither an insight nor an incremental pattern.

Discussion

Insight has been defined, in the past, as a "sudden realization of a problem's solution" (Duncker, 1945; Kaplan & Simon, 1988; Kohler, 1956, 1969; Worthy, 1975). In the study we conducted, it was found that low feelings of closeness to a solution (low feelings of warmth) predicted successful solution of certain types of problems that previously have been classified as insight problems (Davidson, 1986; Davidson & Sternberg, 1986; Metcalfe, 1986b; Weisberg, 1986; Worthy, 1975). These types of problems were ones that emphasized the processes of selective encoding, selective combination and selective comparison. In contrast, feelings of warmth did not predict the solution of problems that did not involve the three processes. These types of problems were ones that had well-defined goals and procedures (Atwood & Polsen, 1976; Greeno, 1974).

In addition, most of the selective-encoding and selective-comparison problems that were correctly solved showed an insight pattern in the corresponding warmth ratings—no more than a 1-point increase in warmth ratings until the rating suddenly jumped to 10 when a solution was reached. In other words, the subjects who correctly solved these problems showed signs of suddenly realizing the solution. Most of the noninsight problems that were correctly solved showed an incremental pattern in warmth ratings—at least a 5-point difference between the first and last warmth rating (see figure 4.1). Because these problems have well-defined goals and procedures, individuals are less likely to have sudden realizations about how to reach a solution.

The results for the selective-combination problems were mixed. Although the correctly solved problems had lower overall warmth ratings than the incorrectly solved problems, these ratings fell between an insight pattern and an incremental pattern; the ratings showed an abrupt increase followed by a pattern of small increments. Insight (or a sudden realization about how to get the solution) seems to be a necessary, but not sufficient, condition for solving many selective-combination problems. Once they have an insight about how to reach a solution, problem solvers must still work out the details. This finding is in agreement with the view that verification follows illumination (Wallas, 1926).

When individuals are provided with information about what is relevant in a problem situation, their subjective feelings of sudden realization decrease. Cues about relevant encodings, combinations, and comparisons lead to incremental patterns, rather than insight patterns, in feelings of warmth. It appears that sudden realizations occur only when one successfully searches for relevant information on one's own. If this information is made obvious to the individual, then search does not have to take place, therefore precluding the "Aha!" experience.

Conclusions

What does this work tell us about the relation between insight and intelligence? The results showed that highly intelligent individuals are more likely than less intelligent individuals spontaneously to select and apply relevant information, to combine and integrate relevant information, and to select and apply relevant examples when solving insight problems. Individuals of average intelligence can make the applications if the information is selected for them; however, they seem to have difficulty finding the information on their own. A related finding was that highly intelligent individuals are more likely than less intelligent individuals to have sudden realizations about a problem's solution. It seems likely that high-ability people are better able to search for information that will help them solve a problem. For example, they might be more successful at looking for relevant facts within a problem, relevant ways of combining facts, and relevant knowledge in long-term memory. As mentioned earlier, sudden realization occurs when the appropriate information is found. In addition to individual differences in the ability to use the three insight processes to constrain problem-solving search, there are other abilities and processes related to intelligence that can influence insight. The two that seem most relevant are general problem-solving processes and transfer of learning.

General Problem-Solving Processes in Insight
Although so-called insight problems involve at least one of the three insight processes, they are never soluble solely by these processes. Typically, they involve a broad range of general problem-

solving processes. Indeed, the insight processes may be used in the service of the more general ones. For example, a difficulty in many insight problems is defining the nature of the problem—that is, figuring out exactly what is being asked. Problem definition is a problem-solving process (Sternberg, 1985) that must occur before a correct solution can be reached. Problem definition may be accomplished, in part, through the insight processes, but inadequate or incomplete problem definition can also inhibit application of the insight processes. If a problem is defined as being routine when it is not, then the problem solver will not search for relevant information to use in solving the problem. For example, consider one of the problems used in the current study:

A car in Philadelphia starts toward New York at 40 miles per hour. Fifteen minutes later, a car in New York starts toward Philadelphia, 90 miles away, at 55 miles per hour. Which car is nearest Philadelphia when they meet?

This problem has a simple solution: The cars are equally close to Philadelphia when they meet. However, only 38 percent of the subjects answered it correctly. Most subjects defined the problem as a rate-distance problem and failed to encode the relevance of the statement "when they meet." Instead, they invoked a set of general processes used in solving verbal-mathematical problems.

Another general process is solution monitoring—assessing, as one is solving a problem, whether the solution one has reached is making sense. In the current study, subjects were given the following problem:

Barbara asked me to bring her a pair of socks from her bedroom. Unfortunately, the bedroom is dark and the light is not working. I know there are black socks and brown socks in the drawer, mixed in the ratio of 4 to 5. What is the minimum number of socks I will have to take out to make sure that I have two socks of the same color?

Many participants began solving this problem by using the ratio information. However, some subjects realized that their answers, such as "20" or "4/5," did not make sense. They then returned to the problem and started over, perhaps realizing then that three socks guarantee a pair regardless of the ratio.

In sum, general problem-solving processes are interactive with, although not identical to, insight processes. The general processes can be viewed as generating the insight processes, which in turn feed back into the general ones.

Transfer of Learning

Selective comparison can be thought of as transfer of learning; one is applying old knowledge to a new situation. Unfortunately, transfer is one of the less well understood phenomena in the literature on learning and problem solving. It is usually not easy to predict when transfer will be achieved. However, several variables are predictive of transfer. For example, more intellectually able subjects are more likely to show transfer from one situation to another (Sternberg, 1985). We also know that more similar structures enhance the likelihood of two problems being recognized as isomorphic (Holyoak, 1984). In addition, to the extent that the surface structures of two problems are similar, people are likely to see relations between them. Unfortunately, they may see analogies that are false: The surface structures of two problems may be close, despite differences in deep structures that render the problems nonanalogous (Gentner & Gentner, 1983).

It has been found that highly intelligent children and adults can transfer their knowledge of certain problems they have learned to problems that are similar in deep structure (Davidson, 1986; Davidson & Sternberg, 1986). Subjects of average intelligence are less likely to make this selective comparison. However, it is not known whether insight will occur if the surface structures of two problems are too similar or if the deep structures of the problems are too complex. Research needs to be conducted using a variety of problems, including the problems used in previous studies where transfer was not found (Gick & Holyoak, 1983).

EVALUATING THE THREE-PROCESS THEORY OF INSIGHT

One goal of this research was to provide a more extensive test of the three-process theory of insight (Davidson, 1986; Davidson & Sternberg, 1983). In general, the theory was supported and previous research was replicated (Davidson, 1986). Selective encoding, selective combination, and selective comparison were found to play an important role in the solution of insight problems and in individual differences in intelligent behavior. Highly intelligent individuals spontaneously applied the three insight processes when solving insight problems, whereas individuals of average intelligence did not. It was also found that high-ability subjects take longer to solve insight problems than do average-ability subjects. This finding supports previous research showing that insightful problem solving is not always faster problem solving (Davidson & Sternberg, 1986; Gruber, 1978; Metcalfe, 1986b). Often a great deal of preparation time must occur before one can experience insight (Gruber, 1979; Wallas, 1926).

By merging the Davidson and Sterberg approach to studying insight (Davidson & Sterberg, 1984, 1986) with Metcalfe's feelings-of-warmth approach (Metcalfe, 1986b), it was found that subjects experienced subjective feelings of realization when they correctly solved insight problems. This finding helps confirm the proposed view that insight occurs when one sees relevant information that has not been obvious previously. Dramatic increases in feelings of warmth were found on problems that tapped the three insight processes but were not found on problems that were more routine. Results also indicated that selective combination might involve routine procedures as well as insight. It seems very likely that selective combination, selective encoding, and selective comparison might be necessary, but not sufficient, components of insightful problem solving. Future research should examine other possible components.

Preliminary results indicate that inability to apply the different insight processes might reflect different sources of problem difficulty. There are at least two ways that an insight problem can be difficult for subjects (Kaplan & Davidson, 1993). One way has to do with stereotype. In this case, the problem solver becomes fixated on a certain path to solution. In fact, many insight problems are designed to lead people down such paths. Errors on the selective-encoding problems, in particular, showed that subjects often followed an incorrect path without realizing it. Misleading information in the problem kept them from selecting the relevant information.

The other main source of problem difficulty involves inability to generate any new paths to solution. If a problem is sufficiently novel or complex, the solver may not know where to begin. For example, one of the problems used in the current study asked subjects to cut a hole in a 3 × 5-inch index card of sufficient size to put one's head through. If subjects did not have the insight to cut a spiral out of the card, they often did not generate any strategies for solving the problem. Highly intelligent subjects seem to be better able than less intelligent subjects to avoid both of these types of problem difficulty.

It should be emphasized that there are limitations to these findings on insight abilities and their role in individual differences in intelligence. One major limitation has to do with the vagueness of the theory. Future in-depth work needs to be conducted on how subjects approach different types of problems, how they begin searching for solutions, and how they mentally represent and restructure problems. This information might then make it possible to concretize and rigorously test the proposed theory. Obviously, the problem of insight is not yet solved. Merging approaches, however, provides a strong foundation on which to build.

REFERENCES

Adamson, R.E. (1952). Functional fixedness as related to problem solving: A repetition of three experiments. *Journal of Experimental Psychology*, 44, 288–291.

Adamson, R.E., & Taylor, D.W. (1954). Functional fixedness as related to elapsed time and set. *Journal of Experimental Psychology*, 47, 122–216.

Atwood, M.E., & Polsen, P.G. (1976). A process model for water jug problems. *Cognitive Psychology*, 8, 191–216

Birch, H.G., & Rabinowitz, H. S. (1951). The negative effect of previous experience on productive thinking. *Journal of Experimental Psychology*, 41, 121–125.

Boring, E.G. (1923). Intelligence as the tests test it. *New Republic*, 6, 35–37.

Burke, R.J., & Maier, N.R.F. (1965). Attempts to predict success on an insight problem. *Psychological Reports*, 17, 303–310.

Davidson, J.E. (1986). Insight and intellectual giftedness. In R.J. Sternberg & J.E. Davidson (Eds.), *Conceptions of giftedness*. New York: Cambridge University Press.

Davidson, J.E., & Sternberg, R.J. (1984). The role of insight in intellectual giftedness. *Gifted Child Quarterly*, 28, 58–64.

Davidson, J.E., & Sternberg, R.J. (1986). What is insight? *Educational Horizons*, 64, 177–179.

Duncker, K. (1945). On problem solving. *Psychological Monographs*, 58(5), whole no. 270.

Flavell, J.H. (1981). Cognitive monitoring. In W.P. Dickson (Ed.), *Children's oral communication skills*. New York: Academic Press.

Gentner, D., & Gentner, D.R. (1983). Flowing waters or teeming crowds: Mental models of electricity. In D. Gentner & A. Stevens (Eds.), *Mental models*. Hillsdale, NJ Erlbaum.

Gick, M.L., & Holyoak, K.J. (1983). Schema induction and analogical transfer. *Cognitive Psychology*, 1–38.

Greeno, J.G. (1974). Hobbits and orcs: Acquisitions of a sequential concept. *Cognitive Psychology*, 6, 270–292.

Greeno, J.G. (1978). Natures of problem solving abilities. In W.K. Estes (Ed.), *Handbook of learning and cognitive processes* (Vol. 5). Hillsdale, NJ: Erlbaum.

Greeno, J.G., & Berger, D. (1987). *A model of functional knowledge and insight* (Tech. Rep. No. GK-1). Office of Naval Research.

Gruber, H.E. (1979). On the relation between "Aha experiences" and the construction of ideas. *History of Science*, 19, 41–59.

Holyoak, K.J. (1984). Analogical thinking and human intelligence. In R.J. Sternberg (Ed.), *Advances in the psychology of human intelligence* (Vol 2, pp. 199–230). Hillsdale, NJ: Erlbaum.

Kaplan, C.A., & Davidson, J.E. (1993, submitted for publication). *Incubation effects in problem solving*.

Kaplan, C.A., & Simon, H A. (1988). *In search of insight* (Tech. Rep. No. AIP-55). Pittsburgh: Carnegie-Mellon University.

Koffka, K. (1935). *Principles of gestalt psychology*. London: Routledge & Kegan Paul.

Kohler, W. (1956). *The mentality of apes* (2nd ed.). New York: Harcourt Brace.

Kohler, W. (1969). *The task of Gestalt psychology*. Princeton, NJ: Princeton University Press.

Luchins, A.S. (194Z). Mechanization in problem solving. *Psychological Monographs*, 54:6, No. 248.

Luchins, A.S., & Luchins, E.S. (1950). New experimental attempts at preventing mechanization in problem solving. *Journal of General Psychology*, 42, 279–297.

Maier, N.R.F. (1930). Reasoning in humans: I. On direction. *Journal of Comparative Psychology*, 12, 115–143.

Maier, N.R.F. (1945). Reasoning in humans: III. The mechanisms of equivalent stimuli and of reasoning. *Journal of Experimental Psychology*, 35, 349–360.

Markman, E.M. (1977). Realizing that you don't understand: A preliminary investigation. *Child Development, 48,* 986–992.

Markman, E.M. (1979). Realizing that you don't understand: Elementary school children's awareness of inconsistencies. *Child Development, 50,* 643–655.

Metcalfe, J. (1986a). Feeling of knowing in memory and problem solving. *Journal of Experimental Psychology: Learning, Memory, and Cognition, 12,* 288–294.

Metcalfe, J. (1986b). Premonitions of insight predict impending error. *Journal of Experimental Psychology: Learning, Memory, and Cognition, 12,* 623–634.

Metcalfe, J. & Weibe, D. (1987). Intuition in insight and noninsight problem solving. *Memory & Cognition, 15,* 238–246.

Newell, A., Shaw, J.C., & Simon, H.A. (1962). The process of creative thinking. In H.E. Gruber, G. Terrell & M. Wertheimer (Eds.), *Contemporary approaches to creative thinking.* New York: Atherton Press.

Nickles, T. (1978). *Scientific discovery: Case studies.* Dordrecht: Reidel.

Perkins, D. (1981). *The mind's best work.* Cambridge, MA: Harvard University Press.

Poincaré, H. (1952). Mathemetical creation. G.B. Halsted (Trans.), Reprinted in G. Ghiselin (Ed.), *The creative process.* New York: New American Library. (Reprinted from *The foundations of science* [G.B. Halsted, Trans.], New York: Science Press, 1913.)

Raaheim, K. (1965). Problem solving and past experience. In P.H. Mussen (Ed.), European research in cognitive development. *Monograph Supplement of the Society for Research on Child Development, 30,* No. 2

Simon, H.A., Newell, A., & Shaw, J.C. (1979). The process of creative thinking. In H.A. Simon (Ed.), *Models of thought* (pp. 144–174). New Haven: Yale University Press.

Sternberg, R.J. (1985). *Beyond IQ.* Cambridge, England: Cambridge University Press.

Sternberg, R.J., & Davidson, J.E. (1982). The mind of the puzzler. *Psychology Today, 16,* 37–44.

Sternberg, R.J., & Davidson, J.E. (1983). Insight in the gifted. *Educational Psychologist, 18,* 51–57.

Sternberg, R.J. & Davidson, J.E. (1989). A four-prong model for intellectual skills development. *Journal of Research and Development in Education, 22,* 22–28.

Sternberg, R.J., & Detterman, D.K. (Eds.). (1986). *What is intelligence? Contemporary viewpoints on its nature and definition.* Norwood, NJ: Ablex.

Sternberg, R.J., & Weil, E.M. (1980). An aptitude-strategy interaction in linear syllogistic reasoning. *Journal of Educational Psychology, 72,* 226–234.

Thomas, J.C., Jr. (1974). An analysis of behavior in the hobbits-orcs problem. *Cognitive Psychology, 6,* 257–269.

Wallas, G. (1926). *The art of thought.* New York: Harcourt Brace Jovanovich.

Weisberg, R.W. (1986) *Creativity: Genius and other myths.* New York: Freeman.

Weisberg, R.W., & Alba, J.W. (1981). An examination of the alleged role of "fixation" in the solution of "insight" problems. *Journal of Experimental Psychology: General, 110,* 169–192.

Wertheimer, M. (1959). *Productive thinking.* New York: Harper & Row.

Worthy, M. (1975). *Aha!: A puzzle approach to creative thinking.* Chicago: Nelson Hall.

5 Prolegomena to Theories of Insight in Problem Solving: A Taxonomy of Problems

Robert W. Weisberg

The concept of insight, introduced into the study of problem solving by the Gestalt psychologists some 75 years ago, has played an important yet controversial role in psychological theorizing. Over those 75 years, we have not learned very much about insight, however, because it is still the center of controversy. For instance, during the last decade a number of investigators have suggested that it is unnecessary to invoke a special construct called *insight* in theories of problem solving (e.g., Langley & Jones, 1988; Perkins, 1981; Weisberg & Alba, 1981a, 1981b, 1982), whereas others have concluded that insight is useful in understanding problem solving (e.g., Dominowski, 1981; Ellen, 1982; Metcalfe & Wiebe, 1987). These diametrically opposed conclusions, which have sometimes arisen from the study of the same problems, lead one to believe that there are still fundamental conceptual problems in this area.

I believe that two related deficiencies have prevented real progress in understanding insight and its role in problem solving. First, we do not yet have a system of classifying problems into those in which insight occurs versus those in which it does not. However, only if we can isolate problems in which insight occurs will we be able to set on a firm base our theories of the mechanisms underlying insight (see also Metcalfe & Wiebe, 1987). Second, formulation of such a taxonomic system requires that we agree on a definition of insight. Often, problems used in studies of insight are not chosen on any formal basis but simply because they have been used in earlier investigations. Sometimes stimulus materials are described as "insight-type" problems, with no further explication of the defining characteristics.

To study any phenomenon scientifically, one must first define the concept of interest and provide a taxonomic classification of experimental situations. However, as the discussion in this chapter will show, these requirements have not always been met in the study of insight in problem solving. This chapter is intended to initiate discussion that will put the study of insight on a firm footing.

First the history of the concept of insight, as proposed by the Gestalt psychologists, is outlined to provide a context for use of the Gestalt definition as the basis for developing theories. Then a taxonomy of problem classification, based on that definition of insight, is proposed and applied to problems from the literature on insight problem solving.[1] Finally, I extend the problem-based analysis that arises from the taxonomy and examine implications for theories of insight.

A number of important findings are elucidated in this chapter:

1. It is possible to use the Gestalt definition of insight to classify problems.

2. The results of the taxonomic classification indicate that a significant proportion of the problems used heretofore in investigations of insight are not actually solved through insight in the classical sense. Hence, it is necessary, and should be possible, to focus research in this area on those problems relevant to understanding insight.

3. An examination of problems classified as insight problems indicates that they are heterogeneous: In some of them, the solution can occur only through insight (so-called pure insight problems), whereas in others, the insightful solution can be brought about either through insight or in other ways (so-called hybrid insight problems). The existence of hybrid insight problems has important implications for studies of insight: Even if one studies insight problems, the data obtained may not be relevant to theories of insight. Again, it should be possible to focus research more precisely on problems that can advance our understanding of the mechanisms underlying insight.

4. Examination of a broad range of problems classified as insight problems also indicates that, when insight occurs, it occurs in different ways for different problems. This heterogeneity in mechanisms of solution indicates that insight may not be a unitary

phenomenon, which sets limits on theories that purport to explain insight in terms of a single set of mechanisms.

5. Finally, the facts that insight in the classical sense does not occur in a significant proportion of problems studied by psychologists, and that a significant proportion of insight problems are hybrid (i.e., can be solved with or without insight), raise questions about the generality and ultimate importance of the concept.

INSIGHT IN PROBLEM SOLVING

The Gestalt psychologists (e.g., Kohler, 1969; Wertheimer, 1982) proposed insight as a mechanism in thinking in response to Thorndike's (1911) conclusion that all behavior was based on trial and error (see Scheerer [1963] and Weisberg [1980] for discussion). Thorndike demonstrated that cats placed in "puzzle boxes" (cages with complicated mechanisms for opening the door) could learn to escape only through laborious trial and error and that any efficiency in behavior was the result of extensive learning in the situation. In contrast to Thorndike's claim, the Gestalt psychologists proposed that, under certain circumstances, organisms could achieve insight into a problem—that is, through analysis of the problem, the thinker could achieve solution, even though there had not been extensive experience in the problem situation. A classic example of this was the response given by one of the children studied by Wertheimer (1982, p. 49) to the problem of determining the area of a parallelogram. The child had already been shown how to calculate the area of a rectangle, by counting the number of small squares that fit inside it (figure 5.1).

Given the parallelogram problem, after she had been shown briefly how to get at the area of the rectangle, she said, "I certainly don't know how to do *that.*" Then after a moment of silence: "This is *no good here,*" pointing to the region at the left end; "and *no good here,*" pointing to the region at the right. "It's troublesome, here and here." Hesitatingly she said: "I could make it right here ... but ... " Suddenly she cried out, "May I have a pair of scissors? What is bad there is just what is needed here. It fits." She took the scissors, cut the figure vertically, and placed the left end at the right.

This example was important to Wertheimer because, although the child obviously knew how to use scissors, she had never been

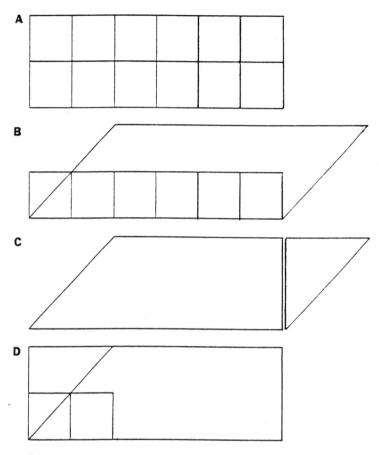

Figure 5.1
An insightful solution to Wertheimer's parallelogram problem. (Reprinted by permission from Weisberg, 1986.)

taught to cut a parallelogram to construct a rectangle in order to calculate area. Even though she did not have the specific knowledge postulated by Thorndike (1911), she was able, through analysis of the exact difficulty that faced her, to go beyond her past experience and create something new.

Productive versus Reproduction Thinking

In the Gestalt conception of thinking, emphasis was placed on this ability to go beyond past experience and produce something new in response to the demands of a problem, which was called *productive* thinking. This was contrasted with *reproductive* thinking, which was the application of some previously acquired knowledge to a problem and which was seen in the behavior of Thorndike's cats. Productive thinking, which depended on past experience in only the most general way, came about when thinkers analyzed deeply and "on their own terms" the requirements of the problem and what was available to bring them about.

Indeed, in the Gestalt view, a reliance on past experience could actually interfere with effective problem solving, because situations that demand productive thinking require that the thinker change perspective and view the problem in a new way. The initial perspective, or the initial structuring of the situation, based on past experience and reproductive thinking, would have to be abandoned and the situation restructured before progress could take place. This restructuring was assumed to form the basis for insight into the problem (Ohlsson, 1984a). (Henceforth, when I use the term *insight*, it will refer to "insight brought about through restructuring of the problem situation," as in the original Gestalt conception.)

The Gestalt perspective became crystallized in an article by Scheerer (1963) *in Scientific American*, in which he claimed that insight as the result of restructuring was the *sine qua non* of problem solving and that undue reliance on past experience (which he called "fixation" on past experience) was its archenemy. This emphasis on fixation as a negative influence on thinking is necessary because, in Gestalt theory, restructuring is the default option: That is, because no special knowledge is needed, an open-minded problem solver will solve the problem, so in order to explain why problem solution does *not* occur, an additional process (i.e., fixation) must be postulated.

In this view, if we could just approach problems free from our preconceptions, we would be able to solve them productively. The assumption is that all the information needed to solve the problem is available within it (or is available in the problem–plus–problem solver equation) and what must change is the way in which the problem is organized, which will result in this information being used to create the appropriate approach to the problem. Scheerer (1963) described a number of problems in which a seem-

ingly simple solution often was not given because, in his interpretation, the thinker was fixated on applying past experience to
the solution process. The Gestalt conception of problem solving
as restructuring has had widespread influence, as evidenced by
the advice to try to look at the problem from a different perspective that has become standard in books and seminars designed to
increase problem-solving performance (e.g., Adams,1979; Amabile,
1989; Bransford & Stein, 1984; Levine, 1988).

However, as noted earlier, controversy concerning the concept
of insight has recently resurfaced in several different arenas.
Perkins (1981) examined the fake coin problem (see problem 5, appendix B) and concluded that insight in that problem could be
explained without postulating any mechanisms other than ordinary cognitive processes such as reasoning and understanding.
However, Metcalfe (1986b), using the same problem, presented
evidence that she interpreted to mean that insight in the Gestalt
sense was important in its solution. Thus, an impasse of sorts has
been reached, with seemingly contradictory conclusions being
drawn from data on the same problem.

A similar situation has developed with reference to the familiar
nine-dot problem (see problem 13, appendix B), for which Scheerer
(1963) claimed that fixation on the shape of the square matrix of
dots resulted in the subjects' inability to find the solution, which
requires that lines be drawn outside the square. However, Weisberg and Alba (1981a; see also Burnham & Davis, 1969) instructed
subjects that the solution to the problem depended on their lines
going outside the square, thereby restructuring the problem for
the subjects. This resulted in their drawing lines outside the
square, but it did not significantly facilitate solution, which con-
tradicts the Gestalt view. In response to these data, several researchers have argued in support of the Gestalt view, on both
empirical and philosophical grounds (e.g., Dominowski, 1981;
Ellen, 1982; Lung & Dominowski, 1985; Metcalfe, 1986a, 1986b;
Metcalfe & Wiebe, 1987; Ohlsson, 1984a; see Weisberg [1992,
1993] for further discussion). Again, investigators are drawing
opposite conclusions from data on the same problem.

Such a state of affairs leads one to believe that the issues involved are not solely empirical ones. These researchers may not
be using the term insight in the same way in their various inves-

tigations. Furthermore, different investigators sometimes study different problems, and it is not necessarily true that insight is involved in all of them. As will be elucidated shortly, lack of agreement on the definition of *insight* has resulted in researchers sometimes studying so-called insight problems that are not solved through restructuring.

Defining Insight

I propose, as a first step in analyzing insight and the processes that underlie its occurrence, that we return to the definition proposed many years ago by the Gestalt psychologists and use it explicitly as the basis for classification of problems. Insight occurs when a problem is solved through restructuring: That is, if we compare the initial solution attempt(s) with the insightful solution, they must be the result of different analyses of the problem.

Another way to discuss restructuring, which allows more precise specification of the phenomenon, is as a change in the thinker's representation of the problem (Ohlsson, 1984b), which consists of (1) the objects in the problem (e.g., the patient, tumor, and rays in problem 14, appendix B); (2) the relations among the objects (e.g., the tumor is inside the patient, the patient's body completely surrounds it, and the rays are outside); (3) the operators that the thinker has available to apply to the objects (e.g., the rays can be aimed at the tumor, and the intensity of the rays can be varied); and (4) the goal or solution to be attained (e.g., the tumor is to be destroyed using the rays). We can ask whether any of these are changed as the thinker works on the problem. This definition can provide the basis for a taxonomy of problems, since any problem not solved through restructuring is, *ipso facto*, irrelevant to the study of insight.

A TAXONOMY OF PROBLEMS BASED ON RESTRUCTURING AND INSIGHT

The first step in classifying problems is to place insight within the broader context of different ways in which problems can be solved. Problem solving sometimes requires little more than that the thinker perform already known routines, merely modifying them to fit a new situation. For example, there is only minimal novelty involved for a mathematically knowledgeable individual carrying out long division, even when the numbers used in the calculations have not been used before. In such a case, problem solution proceeds more or less in a straight line; one could say that solution is based on *continuity* in thinking, as one's knowledge is extended to cope with the new situation.

However, solving a problem does not always proceed directly from problem presentation to solution generation; the initial approach taken by the problem solver may be ineffective, and he or she may have to switch to a new approach before progress can be made. This could be called *discontinuity* in thinking. Some discontinuities, but not all, are the result of restructuring, because theoretically, at least, a thinker could switch from one possible solution to another without reanalyzing the problem, just as one can switch from one path to another in a maze without reanalyzing the problem, because all the paths are available from the beginning.

Thus, to classify a problem as being solved through restructuring, the problem solver must carry out multiple solution attempts, and the correct solution must be the result of a problem representation different from that which was the basis for the initial solution(s). This means that whether a given problem is solved through restructuring depends in part on the way the problem solver approaches it: If a person produces the "insightful" solution as his or her first solution to the problem, then for that subject the problem in question is not solved through insight because there is not even a discontinuity in thinking, much less a restructuring. Assuming that restructuring occurs in some problems, the question of interest for theories of insight then becomes how the change in problem representation occurs.

Continuity versus Discontinuity

The first question to be asked when examining a problem is whether it involves discontinuity in thinking of any sort (see question 1, appendix A). This can be determined through analysis of the structure of the problem, in conjunction with data concerning how subjects attempt to solve it, such as problem-solving protocols. An arithmetically knowledgeable subject carrying out long division should demonstrate no discontinuity: He or she should immediately begin to solve the problem and should continue in one direction.

As an example of a problem that involves discontinuity, we can consider subjects working on a difficult anagram: They should propose incorrect solutions before producing the correct one (i.e., one should see discontinuities in thinking). The radiation problem (problem 14, appendix B) is another example of a problem usually solved after a discontinuity in thinking, as are the farm problem (problem 10, appendix B) and the fake coin problem (problem 5, appendix B).

Discontinuity versus Restructuring
Based on the first step in classification, then, the long division problem would be put aside, and the anagram, radiation, farm, and fake coin problems would be analyzed further. The second classification question (question 2, appendix A) is whether the discontinuity in thinking is brought about through restructuring. An anagram is solved through discontinuity but without insight in the Gestalt sense, because anagram solutions, both correct and incorrect, are produced through the use of cues derived from the anagram (Fink & Weisberg, 1981). Switching among cues changes the solution that is produced, resulting in discontinuity, but no insight occurs because the representation of the problem is not changed: A string of letters is broken into groups, and these serve as cues for retrieval of possible solutions.

In the radiation problem, in contrast, the discontinuity is brought about through restructuring because solution necessitates a switch from using a single beam of rays to adding together two or more weak ones. The representation of the problem clearly is changed. The farm problem also can involve restructuring, as the subject goes from trying to divide the shape in arbitrary ways to trying to use the overall shape as a guide.

The fake coin problem, on the other hand, is problematic as regards the role of restructuring in its solution; it has been referred to in the literature as an insight problem (e.g., Perkins, 1981, p. 45; Metcalfe, 1986b), and it seems to be solved suddenly in at least some cases, in an "Aha!" experience. Based on the

Gestalt notion of restructuring as the basis for insight, however, this clearly is *not* an insight problem: The thinker solves the problem by considering various reasons why the curator might behave as he does, until the date is considered, which leads to the solution. The date is simply one element among several that are considered; in all cases, that element serves as the basis for a reasoning process, but the representation of the problem does not change.

The occurrence of an "Aha!" experience in the fake coin problem thus is insufficient evidence to conclude that insight has occurred, and it may not even be necessary. It is possible, for example, for a problem to be solved through a change in the representation without the occurrence of an "Aha!" reaction. The subjective "Aha!" experience may, in this context, reflect nothing more than that the solution occurs so quickly that the thinker is aroused by its suddenness (see Perkins [1981] for further discussion). This raises the interesting possibility that the "Aha!" experience, a characteristic that has been used without question as an intuitive basis for classifying insight problems (see, for example, Gardner, 1978), may not, in fact, be a criterion.

It is true that solution of the fake coin problem requires that the significance of BC in the date become clear to the problem solver, which could be described by saying that he or she must achieve insight into the significance of BC. However, in this case one is not using insight in the classical technical sense of restructuring. When one achieves insight (meaning, in this case, "understanding") into the significance of BC, one does so by reasoning through the full implications of a piece of information that was already available in the problem, which does not entail restructuring in the Gestalt sense.

Different Types of Insight Problems

On the basis of the first two questions in appendix A, we now have two problems—the radiation and farm problems—that are solved through restructuring. They are not, however, solved in the same way. In the radiation problem, restructuring is necessary for solution, because a subject who begins with a representation of a single source of rays could not achieve the simultaneous convergence solution without thinking explicitly about multiple sources of rays. In the farm problem, a subject could divide the farm into various shapes (perhaps through trial and error), eventually coming upon the correct solution, and might never realize that the shapes are identical to the overall shape of the farm. In this case, the solution would be simply one of many possibilities considered for dividing the shape, and none of these would require changes in the problem representation, so no restructuring would occur, even though the problem were solved. On the other hand, a subject faced with the farm problem might, after several unsuccessful attempts, reason as follows: "I am going to try to divide the piece into parts with the same shape as the whole piece; this might be the key to the problem." This is an example of a solution through restructuring (although the reason for the subject's decision to approach the problem in this way would be unknown).

Thus, that a problem can be solved through insight does not require that it must be. Accordingly, once a problem has been classified as an insight problem, one more question must be asked (question 3, appendix A): Can the solution be brought about only through insight? If so, then the problem is a pure insight problem, the results of which are directly relevant to theories of insight (question 5, appendix A). If the insightful solution to the problem can be brought about with or without insight, it is a hybrid insight problem. Before the results from such a problem can be used to test theories of insight, one must ascertain, in the case of each subject, whether the solution was brought about through restructuring, which requires that we use empirical measures sensitive enough to determine whether restructuring occurred.

Analysis will vary depending on whether pure or hybrid insight problems are used. For example, if one were studying the radiation problem (a pure insight problem), one could use solution time to test a prediction derived from some theory of restructuring. On the other hand, if one were studying the farm problem (a hybrid insight problem), solution time alone would be insufficient because this criterion does not allow us to determine whether the solution occurred through restructuring. If the solution came about without restructuring (e.g., through trial and error), then solution time would be irrelevant to tests of theories of restructuring. A hybrid insight problem thus requires that another step be

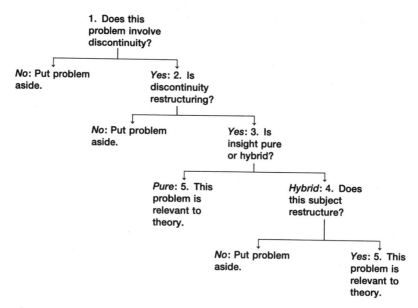

Figure 5.2
Summary of the taxonomic procedure.

carried out (question 4, appendix A) before we can test theories
(question 5 appendix A). The taxonomic procedure is summarized
in figure 5.2, which makes clear the several decisions involved in
classification and the relations among them.

In conclusion, the analysis of a sampling of problems using the
taxonomy in appendix A has resulted in one problem being classified as involving only continuity (long division), three problems
being classified as involving discontinuity but not insight (anagrams, a maze, and the fake coin problem), one classified as a
pure insight problem (radiation), and one classified as hybrid (the
farm problem). Based on these (admittedly nonrandomly selected)
examples, it seems possible to apply the taxonomy in a straightforward manner. Assuming that the taxonomy proves broadly applicable, it will provide a set of problems that could form the data
base for rigorous tests of theories of the psychological mechanisms through which restructuring occurs, which is the final step
in understanding insight. As the first step in providing such a data
base, the taxonomy was applied to a larger sample of problems.

APPLYING THE TAXONOMY: INSIGHT IN SOLVING INSIGHT PROBLEMS?

Appendix B presents the sample of problems, drawn from the literature on insight, on which the taxonomic exercise was carried out. The problems are grouped on the basis of shared subject matter. They were chosen to provide a reasonably wide, although by no means exhaustive, sampling. Included are several of the most well-known problems, which have been in the literature since at least the second generation of Gestalt psychologists (e.g., the radiation and Candle problems [Duncker, 1945] and the two-string and hat-rack problems [Maier, 1930, 1931, 1933]), as well as others that have been used in studies of problem solving. For each problem, recent sources are provided, as is a summary of the typical solutions, including, most importantly, the discontinuity solution. This information is drawn from the literature or surmised from the structure of the problem when no data were available.

Appendixes C and D present the results of the classification. Appendix C presents the results of the first sweep through the sample of problems (i.e., application of question 1, appendix A), a listing of so-called insight problems that are not solved through restructuring. The criterion of restructuring was applied strictly in analyzing the problems, because it was deemed better to err on the side of conservatism and to reject any problem that was questionable. Appendix C summarizes for each problem the basis for the negative conclusion concerning restructuring in the discontinuity solution. Appendix D presents insight problems (i.e., those that are classified positively on the basis of question 2, appendix A) and summarizes for each the basis for the restructuring as well as the type of insight (pure versus hybrid).

Insight Problems in which No Insight Occurs

Appendix C reveals a number of surprises, as several problems that have been included in studies of insight problem solving turn out, on close examination, not to be solved through insight.

Brainteasers and Riddles

All the solutions to the fake coin problem, as discussed earlier, are the result of analysis of elements of the coin or the situation. In this interpretation, consideration of the date is no different from consideration, say, of the metal (e.g., was bronze invented at that time?) or of anything else in the problem, and for none of these does a change occur in the representation of the problem.

The runaway sheep problem is intriguing because subjects overlook the fact that the answer is given to them in the problem itself. Instead, they carry out a calculation that is incorrect as well as unnecessary. However, the fact that subjects misread the problem does not mean that restructuring must occur for them to solve it. This problem takes advantage of the fact that when humans read text, they use their expectations in interpreting it and do not read the words one at a time. Therefore, to solve this problem, one must simply read it in an extraordinary manner (i.e., with careful consideration of each word, taking nothing for granted); based on such an interpretation, no restructuring occurs. This problem catches subjects off guard because it violates one of what Grice (1989) called the *conversational maxims*, implicit rules that we use to govern conversation. The problem violates the maxim of quality: Do not ask about what you already know. The reason that subjects interpret the problem as requiring subtraction is because that is the only way that it makes sense. If one knows that all but nine escape, then asking how many remain is absurd. Subjects may therefore overlook the correct interpretation of the words in the problem because no normal person would ever phrase a problem that way.

Mathematical Problems

The expensive wine and the oil and vinegar problems are difficult, but that, per se, does not mean insight is required for the solution. In the case of the wine, subjects must look carefully at the problem as they attempt a formal or informal algebraic analysis, and those who are not careful will not solve the problem (Sternberg & Davidson, 1982). However, no change in problem representation occurs.

In the oil and vinegar problem, the difficulty may lie in devising any sort of algebraic analysis, or the equivalent, that can even be applied to the problem. Here the problem is particularly opaque but, again, insight does not seem to be involved in the solution. In neither of these cases is the representation of the problem changed as the subject works on it; rather, the difficulty comes from devising or applying a method to the problem.

This initial investigation has revealed several instances of misclassified problems, including one (the fake coin) that has been used in several recent investigations of insight in problem solving and that has provided data applied in the theoretical analysis of insight. Clearly, care should be taken before using data from problems not yet analyzed using the taxonomy.

Problems in which Restructuring Can Occur

Appendix E presents problems classified as being solvable through restructuring, as well as the basis for the restructuring. As we have seen, however, the fact that the solution *can* come about as the result of restructuring does not mean that it *must*, and so each problem in appendix E is classified also as to whether it is pure or hybrid.

Brainteasers and Riddles

Restructuring in the brainteasers and riddles hinges on interpreting the language in the problem. In the animals in pens, basketball, Charlie, hole in card, and lazy policeman problems, the restructuring hinges on interpretation of a noun, and the difficulty arises because the required interpretation is unlikely in ordinary discourse. In the checker games and marrying man problems, the solution hinges on a phrase that turns out to be interpretable in more than one way and, again, the required interpretation is extremely unlikely in ordinary discourse. These problems are all pure insight problems; it does not seem possible to produce the correct solution without restructuring the situation as outlined.[2]

Geometrical Problems

Interpretation of the matchsticks and radiation problems is straightforward: In each case, there is one element in the representation of the problem that must be changed in order to produce the solution. However, for the remaining geometrical problems, interpretation is more complicated because they are all hybrid problems and so the question of whether they are solved through insight in any specific case is an empirical one.

In addition to the farm problem, discussed earlier, a subject could solve the necklace problem either with or without restructuring. After trying unsuccessfully to connect the 4 three-link pieces, one to the next, the subject might then deduce from the problem instructions that only three links can be opened, which could lead to setting aside 1 three-link piece to be manipulated. However, it is also possible that the subject could discover the solution in the course of trying out various combinations, without explicitly setting aside 1 three-link piece to be opened.

As Metcalfe (1986b) presents the triangle of coins problem (see problem 16, appendix B), restructuring occurs when the subject breaks the triangle into the central rosette and three rotating coins. In that analysis, the problem representation would undergo change, from an undifferentiated set of pennies in the shape of a triangle, to one of two parts, a constant section and three movable pieces. However, it is possible that subjects could choose to move coins without deep analysis and solve the problem without ever analyzing it as consisting of constant plus movable components.

The nine-dot problem, the most frequently discussed of all insight problems, raises similar problems of analysis. The classic interpretation of the problem's difficulty was that thinkers were fixated on the square shape of the dot pattern and so were unable to restructure the problem (Scheerer, 1963). However, though a subject were to draw lines only within the square formed by the dots, he or she may not be doing so because the dots are perceived as a square. There is circularity in this reasoning, since there is no evidence, other than drawing the lines, that the subjects are constrained or affected in any way by the shape of the square as a square; subjects might stay within the square simply because they are trying to cover as many dots as possible with each line.

Furthermore, a subject could switch from lines inside the square to outside without further analysis (i.e., without insight): All that is needed is that the subject realize he or she is repeating lines, which could lead to new lines being drawn without restructuring in any strong sense, because the representation of the problem does not change. Hence, this is a hybrid problem.

Manipulative Problems

In the candle problem, use of the box as a shelf or candle holder has been taken as evidence that restructuring has occurred. In my interpretation of this problem, the restructuring occurs in the representation of the goal: The subject switches from trying to attach the candle to the wall to making a shelf or holder for the candle (Weisberg & Suls, 1973). This analysis differs from the one offered by the Gestalt psychologists, in which the solution involving use of the tack box was considered the result of a restructuring in which the subject's perception of the box changed from a container to a shelf (Duncker, 1945). However, there is no evidence, other than the change in the behavior itself, of a change in perception. (See the preceding discussion of the nine-dot problem.) The fact that the box is not used initially, as subjects try to use the fasteners or wax-glue to attach the candle to the wall, says nothing about how subjects perceive the box (Weisberg & Suls, 1973).

Furthermore, the use of the box as a holder or shelf for the candle does not require a change in the representation of the problem: The box is still described as a physical object of a given composition and dimensions. Glucksberg and Weisberg (1966) demonstrated that simply pointing out the box to subjects, which in itself would not change the representation of the box, is enough to trigger box solutions.

In the hat-rack problem, subjects begin by building structures on the floor, but a sturdy structure requires that a long board be made from the two short ones and that this be wedged between floor and ceiling. Restructuring in this case may be twofold: making two boards into one and adding the ceiling to the problem representation.

In an early analysis of the two-string problem, Maier (1931) noted that the specific solution produced depends on how the subject analyzes the problem of grasping the out-of-reach string. If the string being held is perceived as being too short to allow the second string to be reached, then the subject will attempt to lengthen the in-hand string. If the problem solver's arm is analyzed as not long enough to reach the second string, then a ruler or stick will be used to extend the arm and "hook" the second string. If the problem is analyzed as getting the in-hand string to stay put while the other string is retrieved, then the subject will anchor the first string by tying it to a chair that has been placed between the two strings, and so forth. Finally, if the subject analyzes the problem as getting the out-of-reach string to come to the center, a pendulum will be constructed. Thus, the restructuring of this problem hinges on a change in the subject's analysis of the goal of grasping the second string.

Maier also called the pendulum solution *productive* because it requires a deviation from past experience since, when one ordinarily wants to get something, one goes to get it. In the pendulum solution, on the other hand, the string is made to come to the problem solver. However, one could argue that the pendulum solution is no more deviant from past experience than are the other solutions, since we have all had occasion to get something by having it come to us (e.g., catching a ball; waiting for a child to toddle our way; waiting for a bus). We also ask people to bring things to us. Similarly, one could claim that all the solutions discussed by Maier require a deviation from past experience, as none of them has been used in exactly this way in the past.

Mathematical Problems

The horse-trading, socks, and water lilies problems all are pure insight problems. In the horse-trading problem, most subjects analyze the interaction as one large transaction and thereby produce the wrong solution. In the socks problem, most subjects do not know enough statistics to deal with the situation and so are stumped. The solution can come about if the subject changes operators and tries to imagine what would happen if one were to take socks out of the drawer one at a time. After one has drawn two socks, one may or may not have a pair, but after three socks have been chosen, one must have a pair of one color or the other.

In the water lilies problem, all unsophisticated subjects initially approach the problem as one involving a linearly increasing quantity and simply divide the total time in half. However, since the lilies increase exponentially in area, this approach is incorrect, and the subject must change to another representation. Such a switch in representation can occur when the subject tries to imagine what happens as the pond fills up and he or she works backward from the last day rather than carrying out a formal analysis of the problem.

CONCLUSIONS AND IMPLICATIONS

The proposed taxonomy is potentially useful. It has been found to be applicable to a relatively large number of problems from the literature, and classifications were possible with a minimum of ad hoc analyses. Owing to limitations of space, many problems were not considered, but the sample in appendix B is broad enough to be encouraging as regards the potential breadth of the taxonomy.

Questions of Validity

These preliminary results indicate that the proposed taxonomy may have some validity, but the classifications in appendixes C and D are my own; others might have classified the same problems in other ways. The validity of the taxonomy could be established by several methods. One initial test will be whether other investigators agree with the classification presented in appendixes C and D. On a more formal level, independent judges could be taught the taxonomy and could then be tested on a sample of problems. These judges might be researchers in the area or undergraduates. It may also be possible to develop a mechanical procedure (i.e., a computer program) that would apply the taxonomy to candidate problems.

In addition, if the classification produced by the taxonomy is valid, it should have further empirical consequences. If, for example, two problems are classified differently—one as noninsight and the other as insight—then we should be able to find differences in how they are solved that parallel the difference in classification. For the latter problem, most importantly, we should be able to find evidence for discontinuity and restructuring in its solution.

The former problem may reveal evidence of discontinuity but not restructuring. Problem-solving protocols might provide data relevant to this issue.

The taxonomy also permits a finer analysis of problems than simply whether they are solved through restructuring. As was shown in appendix D, there may be differences in how the restructuring is brought about in different problems. If that analysis is valid, then one should find subclasses of insight problems that are solved similarly, which leads to the expectation that there may be positive transfer from one insight problem to another within these subclasses. For example, there might be positive transfer from solving the socks problem to the water lilies, and vice versa, because both require that the problem solver drop a formal mode of solution and concentrate on the changes over time in the events described in the problem. Because the horse-trading problem, although an insight problem, is not restructured in that way, there should be less transfer between it and either of the other two problems.

Insight Problems without Insight

One particularly important finding from this preliminary survey was that a significant proportion of problems studied in the past as insight problems are not, in fact, solved through insight in the classical sense (see appendix C). This result forces us to examine more closely the entire literature in this area, and it also raises the opposite question: Might there be any problems, previously assumed to be solved without restructuring that, on closer examination, prove to be solved through insight? Ohlsson (1984a) briefly notes that the towers of Hanoi, typically taken to be a noninsight problem, can be solved through restructuring. If so, we should be looking carefully at the broad range of situations studied by psychologists interested in problem solving, to define the borders more precisely.

Insight Solutions with and without Restructuring

A second important finding was that a number of the problems classified as insight problems can be solved with or without restructuring (hybrid insight problems). This raises an important methodological issue for research on insight, because the solution of such a problem, per se, is not sufficient evidence to conclude that restructuring occurred, as there is no way of determining which mode of solution was employed. To conclude that a hybrid problem was solved through insight, we must use an empirical measure that is sufficiently sensitive to differentiate between insight versus noninsight modes of solution. The development of theories of insight will thus require that multiple analyses, including a taxonomic analysis, be made on each problem we study before the data from any problem can be used to test theories of insight. The basis for the difference between pure and hybrid insight problems is not immediately apparent yet, but this distinction, if valid, bears further examination.

Changes in Representation without Insight

In the discussion thus far, I have assumed that the only change in problem representation that can occur during problem solving is restructuring (i.e., a change that produces insight), but that is not so. Problem representations can change in many ways, and it therefore becomes necessary to specify when a change in problem representation is a restructuring and when it is not. For example, in the radiation problem, if the subject learns that the patient has blue eyes, that would constitute a change in the representation of the problem, but it would not be a restructuring.

It is necessary here to differentiate between *superficial* and *structural* changes in problem representation (a similar distinction has been made in the domain of analogical transfer in problem solving; see Reeves & Weisberg [in press]). A structural change allows new types of solutions to be proposed or in some way constrains the solutions that can be proposed, whereas a superficial change has neither of those effects.

It should be possible to determine on theoretical grounds, independently of behavior, whether a given change in the problem representation is structural or superficial. For example, referring again to the radiation problem, given that we know that the simultaneous convergence solution requires multiple sources of rays, then any change in the problem representation that makes apparent the availability of multiple x-ray sources or that increases the probability that a subject would think of multiple sources would be a structural change. Because specifying the eye color of the patient does not influence the occurrence of the simultaneous convergence solution, it is a superficial change.

Comparison with Other Taxonomies

A number of other investigators, including Greeno (1978), Metcalfe and Wiebe (1987), and Sternberg and Davidson (1982; Davidson & Sternberg, 1984, 1986, summer), have proposed taxonomies for classifying problems. Metcalfe and Wiebe (1987) proposed an empirical classification, based on subjects' feelings of "warmth" as they approached the solution, a measure related to the child's game wherein it is indicated whether a person is warmer or colder as he or she approaches or moves away from a hidden object. Metcalfe and Wiebe asked subjects, as they worked on a problem, to report periodically how warm they felt they were getting (i.e., how close they thought they were to solution). A problem solved by insight was defined as one in which subjects' feelings of warmth did not increase as the solution was approached; the subjects reported no inkling that they were nearing the solution until they suddenly produced it.

Although the Gestalt conception of restructuring does lead one to believe that insight problems should be solved suddenly, there are difficulties with Metcalfe and Wiebe's (1987) proposed taxonomy based on feelings of warmth. First, using only an empirically based classification makes classifying problems a post hoc process, because one cannot tell whether a problem is an insight problem without first collecting data. This means that the classification system has no theoretical grounding. Second, feelings-of-warmth data cannot be used both as the basis for problem classification and as support for that classification. Without an independent basis for problem classification, use of warmth data becomes circular. In my view, any classification system should be theoretically motivated, with empirical results from converging operations serving to support the theory. In addition, some problems that clearly do not fit the Gestalt conception of insight are classified as insight problems on the basis of feelings of warmth (e.g., anagrams and the fake coin problem; see appendix D). These difficulties, as well as others (see Weisberg [1992] for further discussion), lead one to search for an alternative set of criteria for classifying problems.

Greeno (1978) proposed a taxonomy of problems based on the types of skills assumed to be required for solution. The categories Greeno proposes are (1) problems of inducing structure, typified by an analogy problem on an IQ test (i.e., A : B :: C : ?); (2) problems of transformation, typified by the towers of Hanoi problem; and (3) problems of arrangement, typified by an anagram. Greeno's analysis is independent of the question of insight; that is, within each of his categories, one can ask whether a problem is solved on the basis of restructuring. Therefore, the present taxonomy may be orthogonal to Greeno's.

Sternberg and Davidson (1982; Davidson & Sternberg, 1984, 1986, summer) have proposed that the traditional notion of insight comprises three separate processes. These investigators do not specifically discuss restructuring, in the Gestalt sense, as a criterion for the occurrence of insight, although the following quote indicates that their use of the term is founded on the Gestalt conception:

Insight is the stock in trade of the scientific thinker.... Traditionally, the process or set of processes underlying scientific discoveries has been referred to as *insight*. Many of us recognize our own insights when, in trying to solve a problem, we have an *aha* experience. Suddenly, what seemed to be a murky mess is crystal clear, and we are able to see a solution to a formerly elusive problem. (Davidson & Sternberg, 1986, summer, p. 177)

According to Sternberg and Davidson, some insights are the result of *selective encoding*, which occurs when a thinker encodes only relevant information from a problem that contains both relevant and irrelevant information. An example would be the checker games problem (problem 4, appendix B), in which faulty encoding leads one to assume that the men are playing checkers with each other. The second type of insight is the result of *selective combination*: A problem solver puts together problem elements that are not obviously related. (For example: "With a 7-minute hourglass and an 11-minute hourglass, what is the simplest way to time the boiling of an egg for 15 minutes?") The third type of insight results from *selective comparison*: One discovers a nonobvious relationship between new and old information. In the hat-rack problem (problem 23, appendix B), for example, knowledge of pole lamps might be used as the basis for construction of a hat rack wedged between floor and ceiling.

Sternberg and Davidson do not specify criteria for classifying problems into the various categories, which remains a weakness in their proposal, and they present no independent evidence that the problems in question are actually solved in the ways that they postulate. They also provide no information concerning the bases for these various abilities; that is, they do not discuss in detail why one individual can encode just the right information from a problem while another person focuses on the wrong thing. Most importantly, Sternberg and Davidson use the term *insight* more broadly than it has been used traditionally and, as a result, they classify as insight problems some that do not require restructuring for solution, such as the egg-timing problem presented earlier. Thus, Sternberg and Davidson's taxonomy may not be compatible with the one proposed here or with the Gestalt conception of insight. A potentially important aspect of their conception, however, is their assumption that underlying insight is more than a single process, which is supported by one finding from the present analysis: the heterogeneity of restructuring.

Heterogeneity of Restructuring: Implications for Theories

The taxonomic analysis has uncovered many different ways in which restructuring occurs in insight problems (see appendix D). In some cases it hinges on linguistic factors, such as the interpretation of a noun or a phrase. In other cases, restructuring is based on something entirely different, such as changing the number of sources of rays in the radiation problem or switching from two-dimensional to three-dimensional geometrical figures in the matchsticks problem. The most impressive aspect of these various restructurings is their heterogeneity, which would seem to raise problems for the development of single-process theories of restructuring.

Ohlsson (1984b), for example, has recently developed a theory that attempts to account for restructuring using search of semantic memory within an information-processing framework. He assumes that unsuccessful attempts at solving a problem trigger searches through semantic memory to find a new way of representing the objects and thereby a new way of approaching the problem. This search can result in discovery of a new mode of representation and in restructuring of the situation.

Ohlsson (1984b) illustrates by considering a subject faced with the two-string problem, who decides to use a wrench as a weight to turn one of the hanging strings into a pendulum. To explain the novel use of this wrench, Ohlsson assumes that after trying unsuccessfully to solve the problem, the subject searches memory, starting from the objects available. The presence of a wrench will lead to the category *physical object*, as the wrench is a member of that category. From *physical object*, one can retrieve the concepts of clock and pendulum, because a clock is also a member of the category of physical objects and a pendulum is part of a clock. When the subject searches memory and retrieves *clock* and *pendulum*, these ideas, coupled with the wrench that initiated the search, can result in the subject's suddenly deciding to construct a pendulum, by tying the wrench, as a weight, to the string.

Putting aside questions about whether the restructuring in the two-string problem actually occurs in this way (under Maier's analysis [1931], discussed previously, it does not), and whether search through memory could produce just the configuration of ideas postulated by Ohlsson (1984b), it is interesting to consider whether this view of restructuring could be extended to the socks or the necklace problem, in which search, per se, seems not to be relevant. That is, in the socks problem, restructuring does not come about through search of semantic memory for other objects linked to the principle objects in the problem (i.e., the socks) and which somehow provide a different analysis of them. Similarly, in the necklace problem, the restructuring does not hinge on a search through semantic memory. Thus, if Ohlsson's analysis of the two-string problem is headed in the right direction, it may be only one of several theories that ultimately will be needed to account for restructuring in all its forms, including, presumably, those of which we are presently ignorant because only a handful of problems has been analyzed.

This leads to one final point, which is that we know very little about how restructuring is brought about in insight problems. As this chapter has made clear, much of our research has been concerned with problems not solved through restructuring. Second, research conducted to study insight problems has not provided data helpful in constructing theories of how insight occurs. For example, there have been many studies of the radiation problem over the last 10 years but, in all these studies, the problem was used as the target in studies of analogical transfer (e.g., Gick & Holyoak, 1983; Spencer & Weisberg, 1986), so the development of insight was not examined. Duncker (1945) conducted studies of solution of the problem, but his data were presented relatively informally, and the solution tree that he offered as a summary of his results indicates that the experimenter may have played a too-active role in subjects' work.

Sternberg and Davidson (1982; Davidson & Sternberg, 1984) examined performance on several insight problems, but they were interested primarily in the correlations between solutions of the various problems and measures of IQ, stemming from predictions of their tripartite theory of insight. This method leads to some potentially important conclusions, but the data are not the sort needed to build process theories of problem solving.

Metcalfe (1986a, 1986b; Metcalfe & Wiebe, 1987) also carried out several studies using a number of insight problems. However, since she was interested mainly in obtaining subjects' judgments of how close they were to solution, she too did not study the problems in a way that could lend support to theorizing about the basis for insight.

An important conclusion that can be derived from this chapter is that a moratorium should be placed on theorizing about the mechanisms underlying restructuring and insight until we have available data from problems that we agree are relevant to the study of insight. Only then can we hope to make progress in theory construction.

ACKNOWLEDGMENTS

Thanks are due to Nora Newcombe, Robert Sternberg, and Janet Davidson for comments on earlier versions of this chapter.

NOTES

1. In this chapter, I am not advocating the truth of the Gestalt conception of insight. Rather, it is my belief that *any* theory of the mechanisms underlying insight must rest on an agreed-on conceptualization of the

issues involved, and the historical precedence of the Gestalt view of insight makes it a reasonable place to begin to reshape our conceptualization. In addition, a number of modern researchers have advocated the Gestalt view or close approximations to it (e.g., Dominowski, 1981; Metcalfe, 1986a; Metcalfe & Wiebe, 1987) so it is more than a historical curiosity. Recent critical investigations of insight (e.g., Perkins, 1981; Sternberg & Davidson, 1982; Weisberg & Alba, 1981a,b) are also reactions, explicitly or implicitly, to the Gestalt view. The taxonomy of problems presented in this chapter is neutral vis-à-vis theory except in the weak sense that, if no situations were found in which insight occurred, then any theories that contained such a construct would become irrelevant.

2. For several of these problems, it can be argued that the interpretation based on restructuring is more than infrequent in ordinary usage: It is, in actuality, impossible (Weisberg, 1992). For example, in my dialect, saying that one has "solved" the animals in pens problem by building four concentric pens, with all the animals in the middle one, violates the meaning of the phrase *four pens*. In my interpretation, such a structure is one pen with four fences. Similarly, the checker games problem is not solved by saying that the two men do not play the five games with each other, because when I hear "Two men play five games of checkers...," it cannot mean anything *but* that they played against each other. If these speculations are supported by the interpretations of others, then it may mean that some so-called insight problems will not be useful as research instruments, either because they may not be solved very frequently due to their violation of linguistic rules or because, when they are solved, it may be attributable to an abnormal process as the subject must make decisions about whether the experimenter would violate rules of English.

APPENDIX A:
TAXONOMY OF PROBLEMS

1. Does the problem involve discontinuity in thinking? Determine whether the initial solution is different from the final one.

If *yes*, the problem involves discontinuity; go to question 2. *Examples:* Solving a maze by searching through alternate paths; solving anagrams by trying out possible combinations; fake coin problem (see problem 5, appendix B); radiation problem (see problem 14, appendix B); farm problem (see problem 10, appendix B).

If *no*, the problem involves only continuity of thinking, and so it is not relevant to the study of insight. *Example:* Mathematically knowledgeable subject solving a problem in long division.

2. Does discontinuity come about through restructuring and insight? Compare the initial incorrect solution(s) with the correct one to determine whether a change in analysis of the problem underlies the switch in solution.

If *yes*, the problem involves restructuring and insight; go to question 3. *Examples:* Solving the radiation problem by changing a single source of rays to multiple sources; solving the farm problem by trying to make the small pieces the same shape as the whole piece.

If *no*, the problem does not require restructuring and insight. *Examples:* Solving a maze by searching through alternate paths that are available in the problem; solving anagrams by trying out possible combinations available in the problem; solving the fake coin problem by examining elements in the problem as presented.

3. Is restructuring the only way the solution can come about? Consider possible ways of producing the solution to determine whether restructuring is necessary in all of them.

If *yes*, the problem is a pure insight problem; go to question 5. *Example:* The radiation problem, for which it is not possible to produce the solution without changing the problem representation from a single to multiple sources of rays.

If *no*, the problem is a hybrid insight problem; go to question 4. *Examples:* Solving the farm problem by deciding to make the small shapes the same as the big one versus solving the problem by trial and error without realizing that solution shapes are the same as the large shape; solving the necklace problem by deciding that one of the three-link pieces must be used versus solving the problem without explicitly deciding to break apart a single three-link piece.

4. Is restructuring used by this specific subject to solve this problem? Consider this subject's performance on this problem, using a sufficiently sensitive measure to determine whether restructuring occurs.

If *yes*, the subject's performance on this problem is relevant to theories of insight; go to question 5.

If *no*, the problem is not an insight problem for this subject and so is not relevant to theories of insight. Do not consider the result further.

5. How was the restructuring brought about? This is an empirical question, answered through experiment. It is relevant to testing theories.

APPENDIX B:
SELECTION OF PROBLEMS USED FOR CLASSIFICATION

Brainteasers and Riddles

1. Animals in pens: Describe how you can put 27 animals into four pens so that there is an odd number of animals in each pen.
Source: Metcalfe (1986a)

Initial solutions: Attempt to divide animals in various combinations among four separate pens.

Discontinuity solution: Make four concentric pens and put all 27 animals in the center pen.

2. Basketball: Our basketball team won 72–49, and yet not one man on the team scored as much as a single point. How is that possible?

Source: Gardner (1978)

Initial solutions: Try to interpret the language in the problem to figure out how men could have done it: For example, does "... and yet not one man ... scored as much as a single point" mean "each man scored *more* than a single point?"

Discontinuity solution: Our team is made up of women.

3. Charlie: Dan comes home from work and finds Charlie lying dead on the floor. Also on the floor are some broken glass and some water. Tom is in the room too. Dan takes one look around and immediately knows how Charlie died. How did Charlie die?

Source: Weisberg (1988)

Initial solutions: Various murder scenarios involving two humans (i.e., Tom shot or stabbed Charlie).

Discontinuity solution: Charlie, Dan's pet fish, died of lack of oxygen when Tom, Dan's cat, knocked over the fishbowl, causing it to shatter and spill its contents.

4. Checker games: Two men play five checker games and each wins an even number of games, with no ties. How is that possible?

Source: Sternberg and Davidson (1982)

Initial solutions: Try to determine combinations of games.

Discontinuity solution: The men did not play against each other.

5. Fake coin: A stranger approached a museum curator and offered him an ancient bronze coin. The coin had an authentic appearance and was marked with the date 544 BC. The curator had happily made acquisitions from suspicious sources before, but this time he promptly called the police and had the stranger arrested. Why?

Sources: Metcalfe (1986b); Perkins (1981)

Initial solutions: Consider the elements of the coin to determine what might have been faked. Was bronze invented then? Was the language on the coin wrong?

Discontinuity solution: How could the coin have been dated BC? It must have been fake.

6. Hole in card: How could you cut a hole in a 3 × 5–inch index card that was large enough to fit over your head?

Sources: Metcalfe (1986a, 1986b)

Initial solution: Try to determine a hole shape that would work.

Discontinuity solution: First cut the card into a spiral; then cut a slit in the spiral.

7. Marrying man: A man in a town married 20 women in the town. He and the women are still alive, and he has had no divorces. He is not a bigamist and is not a Mormon and yet he broke no law. How is that possible?

Source: Gardner (1978)

Initial solution: He is from a culture where that is possible.

Discontinuity solution: The man is the minister who married the women to their husbands.

8. Lazy policeman: A woman did not have her driver's license with her. She failed to stop at a railroad crossing, then ignored a one-way traffic sign and traveled three blocks in the wrong direction down the one-way street. All this was observed by a policeman, yet he made no effort to arrest the woman. Why?

Source: Gardner (1978)

Initial solutions: He was lazy. Alternatively, she was his wife so he did nothing.

Discontinuity solution: The woman was walking.

9. Runaway sheep: A farmer has 17 sheep in a pen. All but 9 escape. How many are left?

Source: Sternberg and Davidson (1982)

Initial solution: $17 - 9 = 8$.

Discontinuity solution: If all but 9 *escape, then the farmer has 9 left.*

Geometrical Problems

10. Farm: How can you divide this piece of land (described by the solid lines in figure 5.3) into four equally shaped pieces?

Source: Metcalfe (1986a)

Initial solutions: Cut the farm up in various ways.
Discontinuity solution: See figure 5.3.

11. Matchsticks: Using six matches, make four equilateral triangles, with one complete match making up the side of each triangle.

Sources: Scheerer (1963); Weisberg and Alba (1981a)

Initial solutions: Two-dimensional patterns.

Discontinuity solution: Tetrahedron (a triangular-based pyramid).

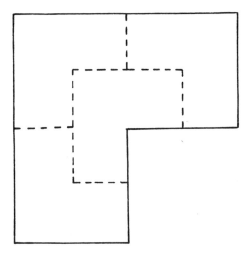

Figure 5.3
Solution to the farm problem.

12. Necklace: A woman has four pieces of chain. Each piece is made up of three links. She wants to join the pieces into a single closed ring of chain. To open a link costs 2 cents and to close a link costs 3 cents. She has only 15 cents. How does she do it?

Sources: Metcalfe (1986a); Wickelgren (1974)

Initial solutions: Attach one chain to the next.

Discontinuity solution: Break up a single three-link piece and use its links to attach the others.

13. Nine dot: Without lifting your pencil from the paper, connect the nine dots (figure 5.4A) by drawing four straight lines.

Sources: Maier (1930); Scheerer (1963); Weisberg and Alba (1981a)

Initial solutions: Connect dot to dot within the square.

Discontinuity solution: See figure 5.4B; lines extend outside the square.

14. Radiation: Suppose you are a doctor faced with a patient who has a malignant tumor in his or her stomach. It is impossible to operate on · the patient but, unless the tumor is destroyed, the patient will die. There is a kind of ray that, if directed at the tumor at a sufficiently high intensity, will destroy the tumor. Unfortunately, at this intensity the healthy tissue through which the ray passes on the way to the tumor will also be destroyed. At lower intensities, the ray is harmless to the healthy tissue, but it will not affect the tumor either. What type of procedure might be used to destroy the tumor with such rays and at the same time avoid destroying the healthy tissue?

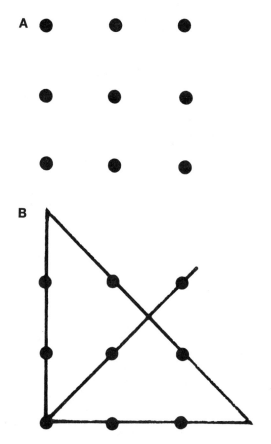

Figure 5.4
The nine-dot problem and its solution.

Sources: Duncker (1945); Gick and Holyoak (1983)

Initial solutions: Use the esophagus or medicine or other such treatment modalities?

Discontinuity solution: Cross two weak bundles of x-rays just at the tumor, so that at only that point is there a sufficiently high intensity to kill the tumor.

15. Trees: How can you plant ten trees in five rows with four trees in each row?

Source: Metcalfe (1986a); Sternberg and Davidson (1982)

Initial solutions: Rectangular matrixes.

Discontinuity solution: See figure 5.5.

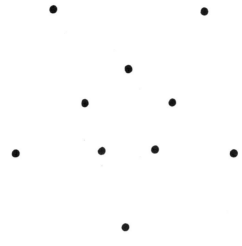

Figure 5.5
Solution to the trees problem.

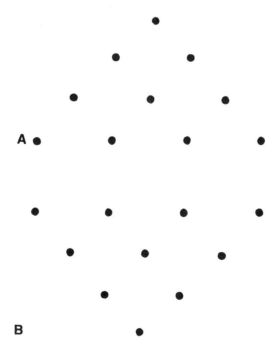

Figure 5.6
The triangle of coins problem and its solution.

16. Triangle of coins: The triangle (figure 5.6A) points to the top of the page. How can you move only three coins and make the triangle point to the bottom of the page?

Source: Metcalfe (1986b)

Initial solutions: Trial and error.

Discontinuity solution: Coins to be moved are at the top, bottom left, and bottom right (see figure 5.6B).

MANIPULATIVE PROBLEMS

17. Candle: Attach a candle to a door so that it can burn properly. Among available objects are a book of matches and a box of tacks.

Sources: Duncker (1945); Glucksberg and Weisberg (1966); Weisberg and Suls (1973)

Initial solutions: Use tacks or hot wax as glue to secure the candle in place.

Discontinuity solution: Use the box from the tacks as a candle holder or shelf.

18. Hat rack: Using two boards, 3 to 4 feet long, and a C-clamp, make a garment rack strong enough to hold a hat and coat.

Source: Maier (1933)

Initial solutions: Structures on floor, with boards joined by clamp in T-shape or X-shape.

Discontinuity solution: Put two boards together as one, securing them with the C-clamp; wedge the new board between the floor and ceiling and hang the garment on the clamp.

19. Two string: Two strings are hanging from the ceiling, far enough apart so that it is impossible to grasp the second string while holding the first. Among the items in the room are a chair and a table on which lay the following objects: a screwdriver and a piece of string.

Source: Maier (1931)

Initial solutions: See text (pages 173–174) for discussion.

Discontinuity solution: See text (pages 173–174) for discussion.

Mathematical Problems

20. Expensive wine: A bottle of wine costs $10. The wine was worth $9 more than the bottle. How much was the wine worth?

Source: Sternberg and Davidson (1982)

Initial solution: $9 and $1.

Discontinuity solution: $9.50 and $.50.

21. Horse trading: A man bought a horse for $60 and sold it later for $70. Then he bought it back for $80 and sold it for $90. How much did he make in the horse-trading business?

Source: Metcalfe (1986a)

Initial solution: Made $10 in total (made $10 on initial sale; lost $10 when he bought it back; made $10 on final sale).

Discontinuity solution: Made $20 ($10 profit on each sale).

22. Oil and vinegar: A small bowl of oil and a small bowl of vinegar are placed side by side. You take a spoonful of the oil and stir it casually into the vinegar. You then take a spoonful of this mixture and put it back in the bowl of oil. Which of the two bowls is more contaminated?

Source: Metcalfe (1986a)

Initial solutions: One or the other is more contaminated.

Discontinuity solution: They are equally contaminated.

23. Socks: If you have black socks and brown socks in your drawer, mixed in the ratio of 4:5, how many socks will you have to take out to be sure of having a pair the same color?

Source: Sternberg and Davidson (1982)

Initial solution: Try to use probability formulas.

Discontinuity solution: By withdrawing three socks, you have a pair, either black or brown.

24. Water lilies: Water lilies double in area every 24 hours. At the beginning of the summer, there is one water lily on a lake. It takes 60 days for the lake to become completely covered with water lilies. On what day is the lake half covered?

Source: Sternberg and Davidson (1982)

Initial solution: Divide 60 by 2; answer is day 30.

Discontinuity solution: On day 59.

APPENDIX C:
INSIGHT PROBLEMS THAT DO NOT INVOLVE RESTRUCTURING

Problem
(see appendix B)   **Why discontinuity is not insight**

Riddles and Brainteasers

5. Fake coin   Discontinuity comes about through consideration of elements available in the problem as presented; no restructuring.

9. Runaway sheep   Correct solution requires careful reading of the prob-
                    lem, not restructuring of the elements.

Mathematical Problems

20. Expensive wine   Solution depends on careful reading of the problem
                      and ability to formulate a solution formula, not on
                      restructuring of the elements.

22. Oil and vinegar   Method for constructing the solution is not appar-
                       ent; no restructuring occurs.

APPENDIX D:
INSIGHT PROBLEMS

Problem (see appendix B)	Basis for restructuring	Type of insight
Brainteasers and Riddles		
1. Animals in pens	Loosen definition of *pen.*	Pure
2. Basketball	*Player* can refer to men or women.	Pure
3. Charlie	Human names can refer to animals.	Pure
4. Checker games	"Two men play five checker games ..." can mean "play games with others."	Pure
6. Hole in card	*Hole* can mean *slit.*	Pure
7. Marrying man	"A man married 20 women" can mean "he got married to them" or "he presided over the marriage ceremony."	Pure
8. Lazy policeman	*Woman* can refer to a pedestrian.	Pure
Geometrical Problems		
10. Farm	Use shape of the large piece as the basis for the shape of the small pieces.	Hybrid
11. Matchsticks	Change from two-dimensional to three-dimensional structures.	Pure
12. Necklace	Break up a single three-link part rather than several parts and use it to connect others.	Hybrid
13. Nine dots	Draw lines outside the square formed by the dots.	Hybrid

14. Radiation	Change from a single to multiple sources of rays.	Pure
15. Trees	Change from a square matrix to other shapes.	Hybrid
16. Triangle of coins	Change from an undifferentiated set of coins to a central rosette and three movable coins.	Hybrid

Manipulative Problems

17. Candle	Change the goal from attaching the candle to the wall to making a shelf or holder for the candle.	Pure
18. Hat rack	Move from a structure *on* the floor to a structure wedged *between* the floor and ceiling.	Pure
19. Two string	Change the representation of the goal, from extending the length of one string, "hooking" one string, or anchoring one string in the center, to making the second string swing to the center (i.e., make a pendulum).	Pure

Mathematical Problems

21. Horse trading	Divide the transaction into two separate transactions.	Pure
23. Socks	Solution depends on a change in the method of approaching the problem, from formal (mathematical; statistical) analysis to consideration of what happens when socks are removed from a drawer.	Pure
24. Water lilies	Change from a formal (mathematical) analysis to consideration of what happens from one day to the next; work backward from the last day.	Pure

REFERENCES

Adams, J. (1979). *Conceptual blockbusting* (2nd ed.). New York: Norton.
Amabile, T. (1989). *Growing up creative. Nurturing a lifetime of creativity.* New York: Crown.

Bransford, J.D., & Stein, B.S. (1984). *The IDEAL problem solver.* New York: Freeman.

Burnham, C.A., & Davis, K.G. (1969). The 9-dot problem: Beyond perceptual organization. *Psychonomic Science, 17,* 321–323.

Davidson, J.E., & Sternberg, R.J. (1984). The role of insight in intellectual giftedness. *Gifted Child Quarterly, 28,* 58–64.

Davidson, J.E., & Sternberg, R.J. (1986, summer). What is insight? *Educational Horizons,* 177–179.

Dominowski, R.L. (1981). Comment on "An examination of the alleged role of 'fixation' in the solution of several 'insight' problems." *Journal of Experimental Psychology: General, 110,* 193–198.

Duncker, K. (1945). On problem-solving. *Psychological Monographs, 58*(5), whole no. 270.

Ellen, P. (1982). Direction, past experience, and hints in creative problem solving: Reply to Weisberg and Alba. *Journal of Experimental Psychology: General, 111,* 316–325.

Fink, T.E., & Weisberg, R.W. (1981). The role of phonemic information in the solution of anagrams. *Memory & Cognition, 9,* 402–410.

Gardner, M. (1978). *Aha! Insight.* New York: Freeman.

Gick, M.L., & Holyoak, K. (1983). Schema induction and analogical transfer. *Cognitive Psychology, 15,* 1–38.

Glucksberg, S., & Weisberg, R.W. (1966). Verbal behavior and problem solving: Some effects of labeling in a functional fixedness problem. *Journal of Experimental Psychology, 71,* 659–664.

Greeno, J.G. (1978). Natures of problem solving abilities. In W.K. Estes (Ed.), *Handbook of learning and cognitive processes: Vol. 5. Human information processing* (pp. 239–270). Hillsdale, NJ: Erlbaum.

Grice, P. (1989). *Studies in the ways of words.* Cambridge, MA: Harvard University Press.

Kohler, W. (1969). *The task of Gestalt psychology.* Princeton, NJ: Princeton University Press.

Langley, P., & Jones, R. (1988). A computational model of scientific insight. In R. Sternberg (Ed.), *The nature of creativity. Contemporary psychological perspectives* (pp. 177–201). New York: Cambridge University Press.

Levine, M. (1988). *Effective problem solving.* New York: Prentice Hall.

Lung, C.-T., & Dominowski, R.L. (1985). Effects of strategy instructions and practice on nine-dot problem solving. *Journal of Experimental Psychology: Learning, Memory, and Cognition, 11,* 804–811.

Maier, N.R.F. (1930). Reasoning in humans: I. On direction. *Journal of Comparative Psychology, 10,* 115–143.

Maier, N.R.F. (1931). Reasoning in humans: II. The solution of a problem and its appearance in consciousness. *Journal of Comparative Psychology,* 12, 181–194.

Maier, N.R.F. (1933). An aspect of human reasoning. *British Journal of Psychology, 12,* 144–155.

Metcalfe, J. (1986a). Feeling of knowing in memory and problem solving. *Journal of Experimental Psychology: Learning, Memory, and Cognition, 12,* 288–294.

Metcalfe, J. (1986b). Premonitions of insight predict impending error. *Journal of Experimental Psychology: Learning, Memory, and Cognition, 12,* 623–634.

Metcalfe, J., & Wiebe, D. (1987). Intuition in insight and noninsight problem solving. *Memory & Cognition, 15,* 238–246.

Ohlsson, S. (1984a). Restructuring revisited: I. Summary and critique of the Gestalt theory of problem solving. *Scandinavian Journal of Psychology, 25,* 65–78.

Ohlsson, S. (1984b). Restructuring revisited: II. An information processing theory of restructuring and insight. *Scandinavian Journal of Psychology, 25,* 117–129.

Perkins, D. (1981). *The mind's best work.* Cambridge, MA: Harvard University Press.

Reeves, L.M., & Weisberg, R.W. (in press). Models of analogical transfer in problem solving. *Psychological Bulletin.*

Scheerer, M. (1963). Problem-solving. *Scientific American, 208,* 118–128.

Spencer, R.M., & Weisberg, R.W. (1986). Context-dependent effects on analogical transfer. *Memory & Cognition, 14,* 442–449.

Sternberg, R.J., & Davidson, J.E. (1982). The mind of the puzzler. *Psychology Today, 16,* 37–44.

Thorndike, E.L. (1911). *Animal intelligence.* New York: Macmillan.

Weisberg, R. (1980). *Memory, thought, and behavior.* New York: Oxford University Press.

Weisberg, R.W. (1986). *Creativity: Genius and other myths.* New York: Freeman.

Weisberg, R.W. (1988). Problem solving and creativity. In R. Sternberg (Ed.), *The nature of creativity. Contemporary psychological perspectives* (pp. 148–176). New York: Cambridge University Press.

Weisberg, R.W. (1992). Metacognition and insight during problem solving: Comment on Metcalfe. *Journal of Experimental Psychology: Learning, Memory, and Cognition, 18,* 426–431.

Weisberg, R.W. (1993). *Creativity: Beyond the myth of genius.* New York: Freeman.

Weisberg, R.W., & Alba, J.W. (1981a). An examination of the alleged role of "fixation" in the solution of several "insight" problems. *Journal of Experimental Psychology: General, 110*, 169–192.

Weisberg, R.W. & Alba, J.W. (1981b). Gestalt theory, insight, and past experience: Reply to Dominowski. *Journal of Experimental Psychology: General, 110*, 199–203.

Weisberg, R.W., & Alba, J.W. (1982). Problem solving is not like perception: More on Gestalt theory. *Journal of Experimental Psychology: General, 111*, 326–330.

Weisberg, R., & Suls, J.M. (1973). An information-processing model of Duncker's candle problem. *Cognitive Psychology, 4*, 255–276.

Wertheimer, M. (1982). *Productive thinking* (enlarged ed.). Chicago: University of Chicago Press.

Wickelgren, W. (1974). *How to solve problems*. New York: Freeman.

6 Cognitive and Affective Components of Insight

Mary L. Gick and Robert S. Lockhart

Before we begin our discussion of insight, we invite you to read the following joke and to try to solve the subsequent riddle and problem.

- The trouble with political jokes is that they often get elected (Long & Graesser, 1988, p. 39).

- A man who lived in a small town married 20 different women of the same town. All are still living and he never divorced a single one of them, yet he broke no law! Can you explain (Gardner, 1978)?

- You are given a checkerboard and 32 dominoes (figure 6.1). Each domino covers exactly two adjacent squares on the board. Thus, the 32 dominoes can cover all 64 squares of the checkerboard. Now suppose two squares are cut off at diagonally opposite corners of the board. If possible, show how you would place 31 dominoes on the board so that all of the 62 remaining squares are covered. If you think it is impossible, give a proof of why.

(A hint to help solve this checkerboard problem is to consider the color of the squares of the board; Kaplan & Simon, 1990.)

We suggest that insight is not a singular concept but has the three component properties, which are common, to a greater or lesser degree, in the processing of these three examples (together with the hint for the problem). First, there is a period where there is a failure to solve the problem or a lack of understanding. In reading the riddle, for example, there is a feeling of miscomprehension (how can a man marry more than one woman without breaking the law?!) until we consider the concept of clergyman or are given it as a hint.

In attempting to solve the checkerboard problem, there may be an initial feeling that the problem is possible because the numbers

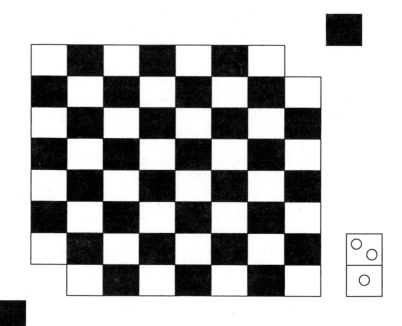

Figure 6.1
The standard mutilated checkerboard problem. (From *How to solve problems* [p. 29] by W. Wickelgren, 1974, New York: W.H. Freeman. Copyright 1974 by W.H. Freeman and Co. Adapted by permission.)

match (64 squares and 32 dominoes, 62 squares and 31 dominoes), yet preliminary attempts to match dominoes to squares simply do not work. This initial state of lack of understanding may be intermittent or continuous, long or brief, depending on both the problem at hand and whether one has to figure out the solution alone or with the help of hints. We have obviously short-circuited this stage in the case of the checkerboard problem by presenting the hint immediately after the problem. (The solution is that the covering is impossible for the following reasons: A domino always covers one black and one white square. Two black squares have been removed. Therefore, 30 dominoes can cover 60 squares—30 black and 30 white—but there will be 2 white squares left over that cannot be covered by the remaining domino.)

The second property of insight is a transition to a solution state, at least part of which does not involve conscious step-by-step reasoning. The third property is a distinctive, accompanying affective response involving suddenness and surprise. In addition, the tone of the affective response may be one of delight, but it might be humor or the groan response common with jokes or a feeling of chagrin and "Why didn't I think of that before?" or "I've been duped!"

In the next section of this chapter, we elaborate our general view of insight. Specifically, we argue that the component properties of insight are a result of certain constraints on the problem-solving process.

INSIGHT AND THE PROCESS OF PROBLEM SOLVING

The Problem-Solving Process

Because our view of insight primarily derives from contemporary research in problem solving, we begin this section with a brief discussion of the problem-solving process, in terms of information-processing theory. Two important processes exist. The first is the generation of a representation of the problem, or the problem solver's understanding of problem elements and operations that can be used to solve the problem. The second is a search for a solution within the constraints of the representation (see Gick [1986] and Newell & Simon [1972] for a more detailed discussion of the problem-solving process). If the implementation of a solution succeeds, then the problem-solving process stops; if it fails, then the problem solver might go back and try to formulate a new representation for the problem that may be more effective, might keep searching within the same representation for a different solution to implement, or might get stuck and give up.

In the mutilated checkerboard problem, for example, before the color hint is given, many people adopt a covering representation for the problem, in which the numbers of dominoes and squares, and their geometrical arrangement, are represented (Kaplan & Simon, 1990). The solutions that are implemented involve attempts to cover the board with dominoes in different arrangements. These covering attempts fail, however, and the problem solver might attempt to construct a new representation of the problem (e.g., seeing whether an analogy to the game of checkers might help [Kaplan & Simon, 1990]), keep trying in vain with the same covering representation, or give up in frustration (Gick & McGarry, 1992). Once the hint is given to consider the color of squares of the board, the problem solver can switch to a parity representation, in which the fact that the domino covers two squares of alternating color (i.e., black and white) is included, and the solution can be generated rapidly by counting squares of different colors (Kaplan & Simon, 1990).

The central difficulty of the mutilated checkerboard problem is in constructing the appropriate representation (Kaplan & Simon, 1990). In contrast, the difficulty of other problems lies not in the representation stages but in the process of applying procedures appropriate to the representation. For example, performing a mental arithmetic task of dividing 9256 by 893 may be cumbersome because of the task of holding information in working memory while completing the division, but the representation of the problem is straightforward. Indeed, a *schema*, or cluster of knowledge associated with a type of problem (e.g., the goal, constraints, and typical solution procedures [Gick, 1986]) might be activated that would lead automatically to setting up the long division process with dividend, divisor, and the rules of arithmetic that follow.

The distinction between representational and procedural aspects of problem solving is discussed in Lockhart, Lamon, and Gick (1988) in distinguishing between *sagacity*, or appropriate conception of problem elements, and *learning*, or application of the consequences of the conception (James, 1890). In our present framework of insight, we further elaborate on this distinction, and we propose that there are three possible points of difficulty in the problem-solving process. One is *accessing* an existing representation that will effectively solve the problem. The second is *constructing* a new representation from existing elements, when no solution-generating representation exists. The third possible dimension of difficulty is *applying* the representation to obtain the solution. We suggest that these are neither all-or-none nor mutually exclusive categories but rather relative dimensions of difficulty, in that as sources of difficulty they may exist to varying degrees for different problems and for different problem solvers.

Insight and Constraints on the Problem-Solving Process

Our central argument is that the three properties of insight—a period of incomprehension, followed by transition to a solution state, which is accompanied by an affective response—result when there is difficulty with either of the processes of access or construction of a representation of a problem, in combination with a perceived clear application of the representation. Thus, not all problems are candidates for insight. For example, solving the mutilated checkerboard problem might involve insight, but the mental arithmetic problem will not, as only the checkerboard problem presents difficulty with the representational stage of problem solving.

Insight and the Problem Solver

Our analysis presumes that the solver is skilled in arithmetic and unskilled in problems such as the checkerboard problem. In other words, whether insight occurs depends not only on the type of problem being solved but also on the skill of the problem solver, as representation of problems is partly based on the expertise of the solver (e.g., Chi, Feltovich, & Glaser, 1981; Gick, 1986; Novick, 1988). One person's insightful problem solving may be another's routine problem solving, owing to differences in knowledge representations. For example, insight may occur when viewing another problem solver's solution if one would not have thought of that solution or did not have access to the solution process (Hayes, 1978).

Conversely, insight may not occur for expert problem solvers who have no difficulty with the representational stages of certain problems. For example, it is possible that mathematicians may have no trouble with the parity representation of the checkerboard problem (Gick & McGarry, 1992; Kaplan & Simon, 1990) because for them it is one of a class of tiling problems in combinatorial geometry where parity is naturally represented (Gardner, 1978). In this case, insight would not be experienced.

In addition, note that we qualify the third dimension, a clear application of the representation, as *perceived*. It is possible that a problem solver might reject the correct representation because its application is not perceived to solve the problem (for examples, see under the heading, Insight and Dimensions of Difficulty in Problem Solving).

Insight and the Affective Component

We propose that the affective response—the "Aha!"—accompanying the transition to a solution state consists of two components. The first aspect of surprise or unexpectedness is a result of the fact that the representation that will solve the problem is different from the initial representations attempted. The second aspect of suddenness derives from the fact that the correct representation leads to easy application and solution and, therefore, the solution seems to appear suddenly.

The surprise aspect of the affective response may vary as a function of the degree of incongruity or dissimilarity between the original representation(s) focused on and the new representation(s) (accessed or newly constructed) that solves the problem. Incongruity resolution figures prominently in some theories of jokes (see Long & Graesser [1988] for further discussion of the incongruity resolution theory), in that the joke sets up an expectation that does not fit with what is generated by the punch line of the joke, and humor is found in the resolution of the incongruity. In fact, hearing a joke may be similar to reading an insight problem, working on it a bit, and then receiving the solution (or a hint that quickly leads to solution). There is an incongruity between the initial representation set up to solve the problem and the one that leads to the solution. (Later we discuss jokes further).

In addition, the nature of the surprise response may vary between positive (delight) and negative (chagrin). As we shall illustrate with examples later, the quality of the surprise may vary as a function of whether the new representation was possessed all along but not accessed (as in the case of simple verbal riddles such as the clergyman) or whether it has to be newly constructed (as in the case of the checkerboard problem).

It is important to note here that we do not mean to imply that the representation itself is achieved suddenly. Achieving the appropriate representation may take a lot of work if one is solving the insight problem alone, especially without hints. However, the consequences of the representation, once achieved, are perceived with a subjective immediacy, leading to the suddenness response.

Finally, although the suddenness element of insight—the "Aha!" response—is the one to have received the most attention and concern, we believe that there are other affective components to problem solving in general and to insightful problem solving in particular. For example, in problem finding—deciding to study a problem in the first place (Getzels & Csikszentmihalyi, 1976)— the affective component may play a big role in motivating the problem solver, in the sense of something being wrong or a curiosity piqued or a feeling of *not* knowing! When construction of a problem representation is difficult in insightful problem solving, it also may have accompanying affective responses. For example, reaching an impasse while attempting the mutilated checkerboard problem (i.e., continually failing to solve it [Gick, 1990]) may result in feelings of being stuck and frustrated or irritated. We discuss the possible role of the affective response resulting from impasses in the final section of this chapter.

INSIGHT AND DIMENSIONS OF DIFFICULTY IN PROBLEM SOLVING

Conceptual Access of Representation

Those problems that provide the simplest and perhaps the purest example of insight have two salient features. One is that their source of difficulty is entirely one of gaining access to an existing representation. The other is that, once accessed, the solution becomes available to the problem solver almost immediately and without effort.

One such problem that has been studied in some detail (Wason 1960, 1977) is as follows: Subjects are asked to discover a rule, known only to the experimenter, that generates sequences of numbers. They may discover the rule by generating sequences of numbers themselves and then asking the experimenter whether this sequence conforms to the rule. At any point, they may state their current rule and find out whether it is the correct one. At the beginning, subjects are told that one example of numbers that conforms to the rule is the sequence 2, 4, 6. Although the rule to be discovered is an extremely simple one embodying a concept well-known to all subjects, typical undergraduates find this problem extremely difficult, many failing to solve it even after 30 minutes or more of concerted effort. Wason's rule was simply "any increasing sequence of numbers." The source of the difficulty is that subjects' strategies for generating and revising their hypotheses lead many never to access this rule. Once accessed, however, the rule's simplicity ensures that its validity is immediately apparent. One can imagine the rush of insight (not to mention other emotions) that one subject experienced on being told the correct rule. This subject, after 50 minutes of conjecturing, testing, and revising in an effort to discover the rule, arrived at the following rule before finally giving up: "The rule is that either the first number equals the second minus two, and the third is random but greater than the second, or the third number equals the second minus two, and the first is random but less than the second" (Wason 1977, p. 313).

Consider next the clergyman riddle given previously. As with all verbal riddles this problem relies on ambiguity and exploits the fact that one particular meaning tends to be dominant. In this example, it is the ambiguity of the verb to marry. Without a disambiguating context, most people would assume that expressions of the form "the man married the woman" are to be understood in the sense of a man getting married, not of his performing a marriage ceremony. Acceptance of this dominant interpretation generates the internal contradiction that constitutes the riddle. The riddle is resolved only when this initial meaning is replaced by the second, nondominant one. Note that, assuming normal cultural experience on the part of the reader, both meanings are potentially available from the outset so that a sentence beginning "[t]he clergyman married ..." would evoke the secondary meaning at the outset.

Let us consider the affective responses in solving problems in which conceptual access is the sole difficulty. First, we consider the suddenness response. In examples such as verbal riddles, suddenness is best understood in terms of the phenomenon of automatization. This phenomenon, extensively studied by experimental psychologists, refers to the rapid and effortless execution of a skill made possible through extensive practice. Learning to type and play the piano are examples of skills that commence as sequences of actions which are painfully slow and effortful but that, with large amounts of practice, become rapid, fluent, and effortless. The form of automatization relevant to verbal riddles is the skill of reading or, in case of listening, of speech comprehension. The literate adult has had such extensive practice at reading and listening that the comprehension of everyday words has all the characteristics of automatization. The extraction of meaning is typically rapid, fluent, and effortless. Indeed, it is so automatized that comprehension of common words cannot be suppressed even when it is in the reader's interest to do so. This fact is dramatically illustrated in the so-called Stroop effect.

The Stroop effect is easily demonstrated, the only equipment needed being a sheet of paper and some colored pens or pencils. To experience the effect, print in a column, color names such as *red*, *blue*, and *green*, but print each in a color different from the color that the word denotes. For example, print *red* using a green pen, *blue* using a green pen, and so on. To make the list quite long, the color names can be repeated at suitable intervals. Beginning at the top of the list, the task is to name as rapidly as possible the colors in which each of the words is printed. To do this you must ignore the word's meaning and attend only to the color itself. Herein lies the difficulty. To appreciate the extent to which the word's meaning is interfering with your naming of colors, try the following. On a second sheet of paper draw, again in a column, a series of small colored rectangles using the same colors used to print the words. Now repeat the task of naming each color; you will find this version of the task trivially easy by comparison.

The difficulty in ignoring a dominant word meaning is probably the major reason why even intelligent, verbally skilled subjects such as college undergraduates find simple riddles such as the clergyman riddle fairly difficult to solve. In a typical experiment, undergraduates solve only approximately one of three such riddles. Interestingly, if they do solve them at all, they do so fairly quickly (within 1 minute), and allowing the subject more time produces rapidly diminishing returns. For example, in Lockhart and colleagues' (1988) second experiment, subjects were given up to 4 minutes to solve each riddle, but 84 percent of all solutions were produced in the first minute, and only 3 percent were produced in the last 2 minutes of the 4-minute interval (see Lockhart et al. [1988] for further discussion of these results).

It is this same inevitability and fluency in the extraction of meaning that underlies the suddenness of insight if and when the correct meaning is accessed. Thus, verbal riddles constitute relatively pure examples of insight in that they exploit a situation in which more than one meaning is available but only one of these meanings is accessed, one that leads to an internal contradiction. The phenomenon of automatization explains why this misleading meaning is difficult to ignore and why, if and when an alternative meaning is accessed, a subject's awareness that this meaning provides a solution to the riddle is rapid and effortless.

The problem of access and the phenomenon of automatization are important contributors to the surprise response that accompanies discovering or being told the solution to these simple riddles. Our observations of affective reactions are based only on anecdotal reports from subjects, but the reactions are consistently expressions of chagrin and self-reproach that stem from the sense of having possessed the "obvious" solution all along. Some subjects express a sense of having been tricked, intentionally misled, or even cheated by the problem.

The difficulty in ignoring a dominant word meaning also contributes to the affective component associated with these simple insight problems. Unlike many unsolved problems that simply leave us with a sense of frustration, problems such as riddles have the added quality of repeatedly confronting the problem solver, as the riddle is read and reread, with a manifestly false interpretation from which there seems to be no escape. (Some researchers have referred to this process as *fixation*; see Dominowski [1981] and Weisberg & Alba [1981] for further discussion of fixation.) Thus, when the solution is obtained, there is not only the satisfaction of having solved the problem but also the sense of having escaped the tyranny of automaticity; the change is not merely from no solution to solution, but from an insistent and compelling false solution to correct solution.

This analysis suggests a simple three-step procedure for generating riddles:

Step 1. Select an ambiguous word or expression.

Step 2. Embed the word in a context that will lead to the automatic accessing of just one of these meanings. Often this requirement is satisfied by a neutral context which simply ensures that a dominant meaning will be accessed, whereas it is a secondary meaning that is required for the solution.

Step 3. Provide a context for which this meaning generates an internal contradiction or an impossible state of affairs.

Armed with this algorithm, it is possible to generate riddles in sanity-threatening profusion. Here is a worked example:

Step 1. The word *lake* means "an inland body of water." However, such water has an ambiguous status: It may be either liquid or frozen.

Step 2. The liquid state of lake water is a dominant interpretation (even in Canada), so that a simple sentence such as "John threw the stone far out into the lake" will lead to the automatic accessing of this liquid-state meaning.

Step 3. A contradictory state of affairs (given this meaning) can be generated by making the following claim: "The stone rested on the surface of the lake for 3 months, after which it sank to the bottom some 10 meters below."

With a small amount of literary embellishment, these two sentences constitute an acceptable riddle that is guaranteed to yield an "Aha!" experience for those who solve it.

A more humorous riddle based on this same ambiguity can be found in Gardner (1978). Again, once the nondominant concept of *ice* or *frozen* is accessed, the resolution of the riddle (that the river was frozen) is effortless and virtually immediate.

The Reverend Sol Loony announced that on a certain day, at a certain time, he would perform a miracle. He would walk for twenty minutes on the surface of the Hudson River without sinking into the water. A big crowd gathered to witness the event. The Reverend Sol Loony did exactly what he said he would. How did he manage it? (Gardner, 1978, p. 96)

Riddles, as the last example suggests, have an element of humor and obvious entertainment value. Indeed, many jokes and cartoons use a version of the riddle algorithm, and the humor or entertainment value of such jokes rests heavily on the reader or listener experiencing insight, in the sense that what is involved in "getting" the joke is the correction of a dominant but inappropriate initial interpretation. Consider two of the most enduring, if not funniest, jokes: Why did the chicken cross the road? Who is buried in Grant's tomb?

Note that although commonly considered jokes, these questions could also be considered riddles. Their principle is a simple one: Each question is cast in a form that suggests an answer which demands information the listener cannot possibly possess, information external to, and in addition to, the information contained in the question itself. This explains the initially perplexed response from the naive listener. The trick, of course, is that each question *can* be answered using only the information contained within the question. Thus, as with riddles, the difficulty stems from an inappropriate representation leading to a failure to access available knowledge.

In the world of syndicated cartoons, one of the great exponents of the insight cartoon is undoubtedly Gary Larson. One cartoon depicts a scene in the cockpit of a plane looking from behind the pilot and copilot. The pilots are looking through the front window at a mass of billowing clouds. Through a gap in the clouds can be seen the figure of a mountain goat. One suitably naive-looking pilot says to the other, "Say ... what's a mountain goat doing way up here in a cloud bank?" Once again the critical component of this cartoon is insight: An initial or dominant interpretation (and that of the naive pilot) generates a question to which there is no apparent answer. Accessing an alternative meaning leads to a rapid inference that provides an answer to the question: It is the plane that is seriously off course, not the goat.

Successful jokes and cartoons depend not only on an initial period of unresolved puzzlement but also on the listener or reader being able ultimately "to get" the joke. The phrase *to get* in this context means that the recipient of the joke possesses the relevant concept and can apply it with facility. For example, the joke given at the beginning of this chapter is easy to get because the initial puzzlement can be eliminated by easily accessing an alternate meaning of the word *joke* once the word *elected* is presented. Many insight jokes preserve much of their humor even when accessing the concept requires some hints from the joke teller or when the listener is given the complete answer. What seems to be essential is that the listener be able to apply the revealed concept with a high degree of automaticity but without further explanation. Jokes that require a detailed explanation as to how and why the new concept serves to resolve an incongruity are usually not considered funny.

Interestingly, some jokes are still funny even on being repeated, and some riddles are still not solved immediately even when they have been heard before and the solution is "known." We suspect that this is because the riddle and joke still have the capability to invoke a dominant but incorrect representation. As we saw in our discussion of the Stroop phenomenon, it is often the case that the activation of a dominant meaning is outside the reader's voluntary control. To the extent that this is so, a reader can reexperience the sense of incongruity, followed by its resolution through a changed representation.

Construction of Novel Representation

Next we consider insight that occurs with problems that require the construction of a new representation before they can be solved. We suggest that if this construction is fairly difficult but, *once constructed*, has a perceived clarity of application, then insight will ensue.

Some standard laboratory insight problems are good examples of this type of situation. Consider first the mutilated checkerboard problem given at the beginning of the chapter. Few subjects produce the correct parity solution to the checkerboard problem without hints (Kaplan & Simon, 1990) or prior analogous problems (Gick & McGarry, 1992). Instead of working within the parity representation, most subjects adopt other representations, which only lead to repeated, frustrating failure to solve the problem. However, some elements of the parity solution are available to subjects when they are working in other representations. For example, while counting dominoes and squares in a covering representation, some subjects occasionally remark that the dominoes can cover all the squares "except these two white ones over here" (Kaplan & Simon, 1990). In addition, some subjects note the parity feature of alternating color of the squares but do not use it in their solution attempts if they are trying to prove that a covering of dominoes and squares is possible. Hence, the strategy of counting squares and the problem element of color of the squares may be separately available to subjects, but their combined use in counting squares of different colors is not. Subjects must construct the novel parity representation, involving both the fact that dominoes cover squares of different colors and the strategy of counting squares of different colors, in order to solve the problem. Once subjects have constructed a parity representation, production of the solution is rapid, typically less than 1 minute (Kaplan & Simon, 1990). Hence, the primary difficulty with this problem is in construction of the representation and not its use.

Another laboratory insight problem in which construction of a representation is a source of difficulty is Duncker's (1945) radiation problem, which involves finding a way to destroy an inoperable stomach tumor with rays. If the rays are applied at high intensity, they will destroy the tumor but will also damage healthy tissue surrounding the tumor. On the other hand, if the rays are applied at low intensity, although they will not destroy the surrounding healthy tissue, neither will they destroy the stomach tumor. Only 10 percent or so of introductory psychology students produce the convergence solution (send many low-intensity rays simultaneously from different directions around the tumor, thereby destroying it but not the healthy tissue) without hints or prior analogous problems (e.g., Gick & Holyoak, 1980, 1983). Typical attempted solutions involve using elements of this convergence solution, however. For example, some solutions involve using low-intensity rays repeatedly or trying a single ray at different time intervals from different directions surrounding the tumor. To generate this solution, subjects must construct a new representation of the rays that incorporates these existing elements together—different rays converging from different directions simultaneously. The consequences of this new representation of the rays usually are perceived immediately. If several low-intensity rays are used from different directions simultaneously, they will have a summative intensity at the tumor without destroying the healthy tissue.

Considering examples outside the laboratory, certain aspects of creative writing (e.g., poetry, construction of metaphors, generating analogies to insight problems and riddles) may also share the features of difficulty in constructing a novel representation yet perceived clarity of the representation once constructed.

The contrast between the ease with which the correct solution is generated once the correct representation is constructed and the difficulty of the failed solutions that precede the correct solution leads to affective responses similar to the simple verbal riddles discussed previously. Again, our comments are based on observations of subjects (and our own responses to solving these kind of problems). For example, in the checkerboard problem, subjects repeatedly reread the problem, looking for clues, but continually fail to integrate the important verbal information that the dominoes cover adjacent squares with the picture that adjacent squares are always black and white. Subjects thus persistently and frustratingly fail to solve the problem (Gick & McGarry, 1992). When they finally arrive at the solution (through hints, self-discovery, or analogy), there is a sense (similar to that experienced with riddles) that the solution was simple and always there, if only they could have seen it. Sometimes there is a feeling of self-reproach and chagrin or of being misled by the problem. (Subjects who have difficulty seeing clearly how the solution follows from the representation are discussed later.) Other subjects laugh ruefully in response to the correct solution. Just as understanding jokes can be viewed as a sort of problem-solving exercise, the solution to some insight problems may be construed as funny.

Interestingly, despite our previous comments that prior mathematical knowledge might help in solving the checkerboard problem (e.g., because of familiarity with the concept of parity), prior knowledge is not always an asset in solving insight problems. Kaplan and Simon (1990) discuss the case of one subject with mathematical knowledge who spent 18 hours and filled 61 pages developing fruitless mathematical representations (e.g., equations involving the number of squares) of the checkerboard problem!

Procedural Application of Representation

Regardless of whether solving a problem entails accessing an already available representation or constructing a novel one, insight will be experienced only to the extent that the relevant consequences of that representation are drawn rapidly and effortlessly. Thus, even if part of the difficulty in solving a problem involves achieving an appropriate representation, there will be no "Aha!" experience if, following this achievement, there remains significant processing to be performed before the implications of the representation can be drawn and evaluated.

A well-documented example of this point is to be found in the nine-dot problem. The challenge is to join nine dots, arranged to form a square, by drawing just four straight lines without lifting pencil from paper. It is difficult because most subjects mistakenly suppose that their lines must not extend beyond the implied border of the square and, under this assumption, no solution is possible. This problem has traditionally been offered as an example of an insight problem on the grounds that the major step in obtaining a solution is that of correcting or restructuring a faulty representation. However, as Weisberg and Alba (1981) have shown, providing subjects with the hint that a solution may go beyond the borders of the square does not yield an immediate solution because, even with the hint, it is by no means obvious where the lines should be drawn. In fact, Weisberg and Alba found that after receiving the hint, more than 75 percent of subjects still were unable to solve the problem. The corrected representation is a necessary but by no means sufficient condition to generate a fast solution. Subjects might be surprised when given the hint to go outside the boundary of the dots, but suddenness of the solution will not result and no insight will occur. Of course, if subjects are presented with the solution, then insight may occur because the solution procedure will seem clear.

The frequently seen matchstick problems fall into the same class. In one of these problems, six matchsticks must be arranged to form four equilateral triangles, all sides being equal to the length of the match. This problem is difficult because the solution requires that the triangles be constructed in three dimensions rather than two, but again this realization does not produce an immediate solution; some nontrivial processing remains to be done. The solution consists of using three of the matches to form an equilateral triangle as the base of a pyramid; each of the remaining three matches is placed standing at each corner of this base, sloping inward so as to converge at the apex, thus yielding four triangles in total: the base plus the three sides of the pyramid.

Although many subjects succeed in solving the radiation and checkerboard problems when given hints or analogies (e.g., Gick & Holyoak, 1980, 1983; Gick & McGarry, 1992), some subjects fail to do so. Moreover, a few (often irate) subjects insist that the checkerboard problem never stated that the domino covered adjacent squares, even though it is explicitly there in the verbal statement! Similarly, a few subjects who are instructed to employ an analogous story that uses convergence as a method of problem solving (e.g., destroying a fire, attacking a fortress; Gick & Holyoak, 1980; 1983) to help solve the radiation problem insist that there is no evidence that rays work in a summative fashion, and so they reject the experimenter's solution. For these subjects, we would argue that the solution obviously does not immediately follow the correct representation and there is no suddenness or insight, although there may be (negatively loaded) surprise caused by the difference between the experimenter's correct solution and subjects' attempted solutions. We suspect that these negative reactions are caused both by failure to see the implications of the representation easily and by the feeling of being tricked (see Weisberg & Suls [1973] for further discussion of subjects' and experimenters' expectations in problem solving).

Although these examples are the stuff of puzzle books, experimental psychologists' laboratory studies, and manuals of creative thinking, they capture many of the important features of scientific discovery. As Weisberg (1986) has argued, in scientific discovery the "Aha!" experience is the exception rather than the rule. Although Weisberg makes this point by emphasizing the gradual trial-and-error nature of the construction of representations, it is also the case that in the history of science most major theoretical breakthroughs involve a process of evaluating a conjectured representation that is not rapid, fluent, or effortless. Kepler's work on the orbit of Mars is a classic example. The representational breakthrough was to replace the circle with the oviform and then the ellipse, but the difficulties did not end with this representational shift. The transition from the initial conjecture of the ellipse to its final confirmation was anything but effortless and was not helped by an arithmetic blunder that occurred during some of the necessary calculations (Hanson, 1958, pp. 73ff). A somewhat similar account can be given of the discovery of the structure of DNA (Watson, 1968), of Darwin's development of the theory of evolution, and many other major discoveries.

For at least two reasons, it is a mistake to suppose that the concept of insight has no relevance to scientific discovery. First, although it is a major misunderstanding of the creative process to suppose that the discovery of complex theories happens in a single "Aha!" experience, it *is* the case that such an experience may be a reasonable description of critical subelements in the development of a theory. For example, Watson (1968, p. 123) gives the following description of part of the final stage of formulating the structure of DNA: "Suddenly I became aware that an adenine-thymine pair held together by two hydrogen bonds was identical in shape to a guanine-cytosine pair held together by at least two hydrogen bonds." This sudden awareness does not correspond to a transition from total puzzlement to total understanding about the overall structure of DNA but, as an important step in the progression toward the final solution, it appears to have the essential properties of insight as we have described it.

Second, even in cases for which evaluating a theory is too complex a process for the implications to be known immediately, expert scientists often seem to have a strong intuitive sense that a newly conjectured representation will work, although formal evaluation may remain a long way off. The term *intuition* may seem a dubious explanation, but such implicit knowledge is a common feature of expertise. Poincaré's celebrated flash of insight into the nature of Fuchsian functions provides a good example. Having had the idea that the transformations he had used to define Fuchsian functions were identical to those of non-Euclidean geometry, Poincaré (1913, p. 388) goes on to say, "I did not verify the idea; I should not have had time ... *but I felt a perfect certainty* [italics added]. On my return to Caen, for conscience sake, I verified the result at my leisure." Such immediate certainty is a good example of what Ohlsson (1984, p. 124) has described as bringing "the goal state within the horizon of the mental lookahead," and it obviously presupposes a high level of expertise (in Poincaré's case, mathematical expertise). The response of a less expert mathematician to Poincaré's conjecture probably would be, "Perhaps, but I need to check it out."

There is something of the same intuitive sense of success, along with the hesitancy that comes from a lack of explicit verification, in Watson's (1986, pp. 125–126) description of the final stages of the discovery of the structure of DNA:

> Upon his arrival, Francis [Crick] did not get more than halfway through the door before I let loose that the answer to everything was in our hand.... However we both knew we would not be home until a complete model was built in which all the stereochemical contacts were satisfactory.... I felt slightly queasy when at lunch Francis winged into the Eagle to tell everyone within hearing distance that we had found the secret of life.

COMPARISON TO OTHER VIEWS

Much of the debate about insight (e.g., Dominowski, 1981; Weisberg & Alba, 1981) has focused on whether insight is a special psychological process and on the phenomenon of suddenness. In some theories of insight (e.g., Weisberg, 1988), it is argued that insight is neither fast nor sudden, neither exotic nor mysterious, but instead is based on past experience, as is other problem solving. We agree that insight is neither mysterious nor exotic and, like problem solving, it is influenced by past knowledge. However, although we do not believe that insight is a special process, we do believe it is real and can be explained within the constructs of psychological theory in problem solving. In particular, as we will argue in more depth later, when access or construction of a representation is difficult, it may be slow and is based on trial and error. It involves search, and there are individual differences in search strategies of problem solvers. However, our argument is that once an appropriate representation that will solve the problem is accessed or constructed, the accompanying affective response involves surprise and suddenness because of the change in representation and its perceived clarity of application. In this sense, then, the cognitive components of insight are not necessarily sudden, but the accompanying affective components do have the quality of suddenness and surprise. We believe that separating the work required to achieve a representation from the consequences once that representation is achieved may help resolve the problem of suddenness versus gradualness in insight[1] (see Lockhart et al. [1988] for further discussion of this point).

Our view of insight shares some features with that of Ohlsson (1984, p. 124), in which insight is reached when the solution is in the "horizon of mental lookahead." In other words, the solver may not have the solution yet but knows it can be found after a suitable representation has been found. Therefore, the procedural steps of the solution must be fairly clear at the time of access or construction of the new representation.

Our framework also shares some common features with that of Dominowski (1981), in which there are two aspects to insight. One is that some piece of information is needed (analogous to our cognitive component of a representation), and the second is that there is awareness of the approach being good, or an understanding (roughly corresponding to our affective component).

Certainly, our concept of insight is most consistent with that of Kaplan and Simon (1990), who define insight as a subjective "Aha!" experience of surprise that results from a change of representation in problem solving. Using the mutilated checkerboard problem as a vehicle, Kaplan and Simon's work has focused on how a change of representation might be attained, and we address this important question in the last section of the chapter.

Our view also is supported by the work of Metcalfe (1986a, 1986b; Metcalfe & Wiebe, 1987). In Metcalfe's experiments, subjects could not predict the success of their solutions in insight problems (i.e., those problems presumed to require insightful processing), whereas they could in routine algebra problems and trivia questions. Up until the moment of solution, subjects did not know that they would be able to solve the insight problems. This finding is consistent with our claim that the difficulty with insight problems is in representation and, once accessed (or constructed), application of the representation is straightforward. In addition, Metcalfe's work supports our claim of a distinctive affective response that accompanies the solution. Because subjects could not predict that they would solve the problem, yet the solution was rapid once the correct representation was found, the element of surprise and suddenness in attaining the solution is real (see also Holyoak, 1990).

In sum, we agree with Metcalfe that solving insight problems may involve different sources of difficulty and different patterns of awareness from those used to solve algebra problems. However, we are not entirely happy with the distinction made by Metcalfe (1986a) between memory and problem solving. Because subjects could predict their responses to trivia questions (e.g., "Who was Tarzan's girlfriend?" [Metcalfe, 1986a]) but not to insight problems, Metcalfe argued that insight is different from memory. We believe that insight may involve memory, depending on whether the difficulty in the insight problems is in accessing an existing representation or in constructing a novel representation. If the difficulty is one of access, as is the case with many of the insight problems that Metcalfe used, then this difficulty involves memory, but of a different sort from that involved in the trivia questions. First, the target of the memory retrieval is different in the two situations. In the case of trivia questions, the target is a concrete fact (e.g., the girlfriend is Jane). In insight problem solving, the target of the memory retrieval process is a concept. As an example of conceptual access needed for an insight problem, consider the pen problem (Metcalfe, 1986a), which requires the problem solver to place 27 animals into four pens with the restriction that each pen contain an odd number of animals. To solve this problem, the concept of concentric circles must be accessed, in which inner pens are contained within outer pens. Using this sense of the word *contain*, the total number of animals contained in a pen is the sum of the animals in one radial section plus animals in the sections contained within that radial section. For example, 3 animals in the innermost pen and 10 in the next outer radial section yields a total of 13 animals contained in that latter pen; 6 animals in the next radial section and 8 in the outer section yields 19 and 27 animals, respectively.

Second, and probably of greater importance, is the difference between the trivia and insight tasks in terms of their cue-target relationships. For trivia items, the cue-target relationship is between an explicit question and a previously learned answer and results in an explicit search through memory for the answer, using the question as a source of cues. With insight problems, the solution is achieved through the initial (and usually faulty) representation of a problem (e.g., the pens do not overlap), which serves as an implicit cue to access a concept, not previously learned as a solution to the problem, that will serve to change the problem solver's representation of the problem and lead to solution (e.g., concentric circles). Moreover, as is the case with the pen problem, the concept that will solve the problem may have been learned in a very different context from the problem (e.g., concentric circles may have been learned in geometry class).

Thus, the source of difficulty in solving some insight problems (including many of those used by Metcalfe) is one of conceptual access and, in this sense, is a memory phenomenon involving capacity of problem content to cue the appropriate concept. For insight problems that have as their source of difficulty the construction of a novel representation rather than the accessing of an existing one, memory and insight problem solving are more distinct, as Metcalfe has suggested, because the difficulty in achieving the insight does not involve a difficulty of memory access.

ACHIEVING A CHANGE IN REPRESENTATION

Our hypothesis about insight is that there is difficulty with the access or construction of the correct representation of a problem (i.e., one that will solve the problem) but not with applying procedures appropriate to the representation. We turn our attention now to the processes by which the correct representation of a problem is accessed or constructed, when initial attempts to solve the problem lead to incorrect representations. There are two important mechanisms: the role of hints and heuristic strategies used by subjects.

The Role of Hints

Hints have been used by experimenters to make insight problems easier for subjects to solve. In addition, hints can serve as dependent measures (e.g., number or type of hints needed) to indicate progress toward a particular solution (e.g., Burke, 1972; Burke, Maier & Hoffman, 1965; Duncker, 1945; Gick & Holyoak, 1980, 1983; Kaplan & Simon, 1990; Maier, 1931). Although hints have been used frequently, little research has been done directly on the types of hints and the way in which they work. In general, hints seem to inform the subject, at a metalevel, that they must use a different representation (see Burke [1972], Kaplan & Simon [1990], and Maier [1931] for further discussion) and may actually provide some of its content. For example, the specific color hint given at the beginning of the chapter informs subjects of the relevance of the color of the squares and often leads to a switch to a parity representation in the checkerboard problem (Kaplan & Simon, 1990).

Other hints are less specific. For example, general hints used by Kaplan and Simon (e.g., "The problem is impossible;" "There is a trick way that does not involve trying to cover the board") result in termination of the exhaustive covering approach to the problem and an attempt to find an alternative representation without benefit of any direct clues about parity. Similarly, hints to use the prior problem, given in analogical problem solving, essentially tell subjects *where* the solution is but not *what* it is. For example, a hint to use a story ("The General," which involves a general attacking a fortress with an army without destroying surrounding villages [Gick & Holyoak, 1983]) to help solve the radiation problem does not explicitly give the subjects the convergence solution.

We suggest that hints can be further divided into explicit hints of the kind we have just described, in which the problem solver is actually told that the information is a hint, and implicit hints that are not explicitly defined as hints but function similarly. For example, the classic example is Maier's (1931) casually brushing the string in the two-string problem, an implicit hint to think of pendulums. In the two-string problem, the subject must tie together the ends of two strings hanging from the ceiling. The difficulty is that the length and spacing of the strings is such that hanging on to one string places the second string out of reach. The solution is to tie a weight on the end of one string, swing it as a pendulum, and then catch it while holding on to the other string. Similarly, a diagram included with both "The General" and the radiation problem is an implicit hint to use the story while solving the problem (Gick, 1985). Clearly, when solving problems outside the laboratory and when no experimenter is present to give explicit hints, implicit hints are all that are available.

Interestingly, both explicit and implicit hints do not always seem to be helpful. If they are inconsistent with the approach taken by subjects, they may be rejected or ignored (Burke et al., 1965; Kaplan & Simon, 1990). For example, subjects given an explicit hint to "use the diagram" to help them solve the radiation problem (when the diagram was presented with both "The General" and the problem) did not perform better than subjects given the diagram without any hint to use it (Gick, 1989). It is possible that if subjects did not see the relevance of the story or diagram anyway, then the hint was useless. In that case, hints may be more effective at the beginning of problem solving, before subjects adopt a wrong representation (Burke et al., 1965).

Heuristics for Achieving a Change in Representation

Casual observation suggests that there are individual differences in insight problem solving, both in terms of success at it and of liking it. Some people hate games and puzzles and do terribly on them, whereas others thrive on them and see them as challenging forms of recreation. What factors might influence success at insight problem solving? Because our analysis hinges on difficulties in problem representation, we turn next to a consideration of strategies for switching problem representations.

In general, the use of problem-solving heuristics or short-cut strategies that are important in finding a solution to a problem (e.g., means-ends analysis [Newell & Simon, 1972]) are also operative in constructing a new representation. That is, in the same way that we do not always examine all possible solutions to a problem when trying to solve it (e.g., solving an anagram such as *grasu*), we search for a new representation by using search strategies that do not require examining all possible representations.

Wickelgren (1974) suggests that when all attempts to solve a problem fail (as they usually do, if one has the wrong representation) and we are stuck in a loop, then a useful heuristic for getting out of loops is to examine the failed attempts and determine whether there is anything common to them that might suggest an unwarranted assumption is being made. Recent work by Kaplan and Simon (1990) empirically verifies the validity of this heuristic strategy, which they called *noticing invariants*, or properties of the problem situation that do not change during solution attempts (e.g., in the checkerboard problem, the two squares left after a covering attempt are always the same color; the position of the removed squares). These invariants serve as possible candidates for new problem representations that involve them.

Although all subjects in Kaplan and Simon's (1990) study noticed some relevant invariants of the problem, there were interesting individual differences. For example, "fast" subjects who solved the problem quickly generated more invariants early in problem solving than "slow" subjects who arrived at the correct solution later. Moreover, fast subjects noticed more perceptual invariants (e.g., color) early on than did slow subjects (see Kaplan & Simon [1990] for further discussion of the noticing invariants and other less commonly used heuristics of representation change).

In our own research, we have evidence that the heuristic of noticing invariants of failed solutions may work between problems as well as within a problem. For example, approximately half the subjects exposed to failed covering attempts to the dinner party problem given in figure 6.2 (either by direct presentation of failed solutions or by being asked to solve the dinner party problem themselves), who were then presented with its correct parity solution, were able to generate the parity solution when later solving the analogous checkerboard problem (Gick & McGarry, 1992). In contrast, if subjects were given only the correct solution to the dinner party problem without first being exposed to failed covering attempts, then transfer of the parity solution from the dinner party problem to the checkerboard problem did not occur without a hint to use the dinner party problem. Noticing a similarity between invariant properties of failed solutions of both the dinner party and checkerboard problems (e.g., there are always two men left out; there are always two squares left out) provides a mechanism for problem solving by analogy to occur. For instance, failed solutions to the checkerboard problem may be incorporated into its representation and used as implicit cues in searching for other problems with similar representations. Once accessed via this search process, the correct parity representation and solution that had been provided to the dinner party problem following the failed attempts can be transformed and applied to the checkerboard problem (Gick & McGarry, 1992).

Thirty-six people are at a dinner party, as illustrated schematically below. The 36 people are seated at 18 tables. Each table only seats two people who are sitting immediately next to each other either in a horizontal or vertical direction. If two people leave, as illustrated by the arrows in the diagram below, can 17 tables be arranged to seat the other 34 people? The people are not allowed to move. Explain your reasoning.

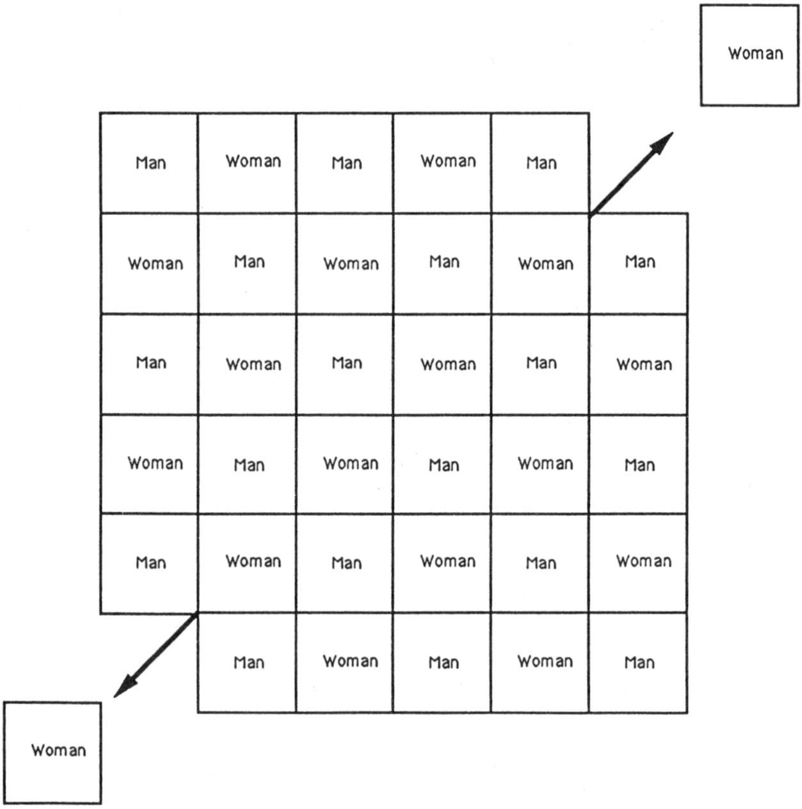

Figure 6.2
The dinner party problem. (Adapted from M.L. Gick and S.J. McGarry [1992], Learning from mistakes: Inducing analogous solution failures to a source problem produces later successes in analogical transfer. *Journal of Experimental Psychology: Learning, Memory and Cognition, 18,* p. 630. Copyright 1992 by the American Psychological Association.)

The heuristic of noticing invariants may apply similarly to the affective component of problem solving. For example, before being given the solution to the dinner party problem, subjects often reach an impasse (i.e., get stuck, give up) (Gick, 1990; Gick & McGarry, 1992). Reaching an impasse might result in subjects feeling frustrated and irritated. Later, when attempting the checkerboard problem by using covering attempts that all will fail, subjects may be reminded of similar feelings experienced while solving the dinner party problem, which can cue its representation and correct parity solution.

The heuristic of noticing cognitive and affective similarities between problem-solving episodes, as a way of providing access to problem representations, may operate similarly in simple verbal riddles. For example, subjects who first read the statement, "The man married several people each week because it made him happy. Clue: clergyman," before attempting to solve the clergyman riddle given at the beginning of this chapter are more likely to solve it than subjects who are given the preliminary statement, "The clergyman married several people each week because it made him happy." Only subjects who are given the former two-part statement may be reminded of similar failures in expectation and similar feelings of miscomprehension and puzzlement (how can a man marry more than one person?) (Lockhart et al., 1988). Subjects who are given the latter statement are less likely to solve the riddle because they have no similar failure expectations by which to link the two episodes (Lockhart et al., 1988). The importance of failures in expectation, and explanations constructed to account for them, in contributing to new knowledge representations have been discussed extensively by Schank (1986).

CONCLUSIONS AND IMPLICATIONS

We have argued that insight is not mysterious but is a set of real psychological processes that have both cognitive and affective components. In particular, we have suggested that the sources of difficulty in problem solving can vary along three dimensions: accessing an existing representation, constructing a novel representation and, finally, applying a representation once it has been accessed or constructed. At the heart of insight is a high degree of difficulty associated with either or both of the first two dimensions, in concert with a trivial degree of difficulty with the third. The combined effect of these cognitive dimensions of insight yields affective responses of surprise and suddenness. The tone of the affective response may range from delight to chagrin. Although surprise and suddenness—the "Aha!" response—is considered the hallmark of insight, there are other affective components of problem solving in general, and insight problem solving in particular, such as frustration or perplexity when an impasse is reached.

The processes involved in insight share features with those involved in understanding jokes. Typical jokes set up representations of concepts that must be revised before the joke can be understood. Application of the revised concept must be fairly automatic; otherwise the joke is not funny if too much explanation is required.

There are several potential areas of fruitful research that follow from our view of insight. One is further examination, following Kaplan and Simon's (1990) work, of how subjects change representations in problem solving, both with and without aid from an experimenter. For example, although much anecdotal evidence exists suggesting the importance of implicit hints or cues—objects or ideas that helped creative thinkers and gave them insight (e.g., Kekule and the snakes [Weisberg, 1988])—more laboratory research is needed to determine how these implicit hints work and, perhaps more importantly, why they sometimes do not work. The principles governing the use of hints in problem solving may be similar to those governing the effectiveness of retrieval cues in memory tasks (e.g., similarity of context). Thus, an understanding of hints would help further our knowledge not only of insight and problem solving but also of memory operations of cuing and reminding (e.g., Ross, 1984).

We know that the heuristic strategy of noticing similarities among failed attempts at solving problems is used by people who are successful at solving insight problems. An interesting empirical question for future research is whether instructions to use this strategy would help people who are unsuccessful at solving insight problems.

Our comments about the affective components of problem solving are based primarily on introspection and observation of our subjects. Further work needs to be done on the affective aspects of problem solving. In particular, we believe that it is time to switch from the emphasis on the "Aha!" response in insight problems to other kinds of affective responses in insight and other types of problem solving. For example, how does reaching an impasse affect problem solving and learning? Does it always serve as a useful reminder of previous impasses, as we have argued here, in that we can learn from our mistakes? (See also Gick & McGarry [1992] for further discussions of this point, and Johnson & Seifert [1992] for the role of failures in planning tasks.) Other areas of study might involve the role of play and following hunches in problem solving (Gardner, 1978).

Finally, we have suggested an analogy between understanding jokes and insight, yet little is understood about humor in general (see Long & Graesser [1988] for further discussion of this point). It is possible that an understanding of the cognitive and affective components of humor will contribute to our understanding of insight, and vice versa.

ACKNOWLEDGMENT

Preparation of this chapter was supported by grants A1212 and A0355 from the Natural Sciences and Engineering Research Council of Canada to Mary Gick and Robert S. Lockhart, respectively.

NOTE

1. Interestingly, although our chapter does not address the kind of intellectual and emotional insight occurring in the therapeutic context, discussion does occur in that literature as to whether therapeutic insight is gradual or occurs in a flash. The point is sometimes made (e.g., Wachtel, 1977) that, except in the movies, insight does not occur in a blinding flash but instead happens more gradually.

REFERENCES

Burke, R.J. (1972). What do we know about hints in individual problem solving? Some conclusions. *The Journal of General Psychology, 86,* 253–265.

Burke, R.J., Maier, N.R.F., & Hoffman, L.R. (1965). Some functions of hints in individual problem-solving. *American Journal of Psychology, 79,* 389–399.

Chi, M.T.H., Feltovich, P.J., & Glaser, R. (1981). Categorization and representation of physics problems by experts and novices. *Cognitive Science, 5,* 121–152.

Dominowski, R.L. (1981). Comment on "An examination of the alleged role of 'fixation' in the solution of several 'insight' problems by Weisberg and Alba". *Journal of Experimental Psychology: General, 110,* 199–203.

Duncker, K. (1945). On problem solving. *Psychological Monographs, 58*(5), whole no. 270.

Gardner, M. (1978). *Aha! Insight.* New York: Freeman.

Getzels, J., & Csikszentmihalyi, M. (1976). *The creative vision: A longitudinal study of problem finding in art.* New York: Wiley.

Gick, M.L. (1985). The effect of a diagram retrieval cue on spontaneous analogical transfer. *Canadian Journal of Psychology, 39,* 460–466.

Gick, M.L. (1986). Problem-solving strategies. *Educational Psychologist, 21,* 99–120.

Gick, M.L. (1989). Two functions of diagrams in problem solving by analogy. In H. Mandl & J.R. Levin (Eds.), *Knowledge acquisition from text and pictures* (pp. 215–231). Amsterdam: North-Holland (Elsevier Science Publishers).

Gick, M.L. (1990). Transfer in insight problems: The effects of different types of similarity. In K.J. Gilhooly, M.T.G. Keane, R.H. Logie & G. Erdos (Eds.), *Lines of thinking* (Vol. 1, pp. 251–265). Chichester, England: Wiley.

Gick, M.L., & Holyoak, K.J. (1980). Analogical problem solving. *Cognitive Psychology, 12,* 306–355.

Gick, M.L., & Holyoak, K.J. (1983). Schema induction and analogical transfer. *Cognitive Psychology, 15,* 1–38.

Gick, M.L., & McGarry, S.J. (1992). Learning from mistakes: Inducing analogous solution failures to a source problem produces later successes in analogical transfer. *Journal of Experimental Psychology: Learning, Memory and Cognition, 18,* 623–639.

Hanson, N.R. (1958). *Patterns of discovery.* New York: Cambridge University Press.

Hayes, J.R. (1978). *Cognitive Psychology. Thinking and creating.* Homewood, IL: Dorsey Press.

Holyoak, K.J. (1990). Problem solving. In D.N. Osherson & E.E. Smith (Eds.), *Thinking: An invitation to cognitive science* (Vol. 3, pp. 117–146). Cambridge: MIT Press.

James, W. (1890). *The principles of psychology*, Volume 2. New York: Dover.

Johnson, H., & Seifert, C. (1992). The role of predictive features in retrieving analogical cues. *Journal of Memory and Language, 31*, 648–667.

Kaplan, C.A., & Simon, H.A. (1990). In search of insight. *Cognitive Psychology, 22*, 374–419.

Lockhart, R.S., Lamon, M., & Gick, M. (1988). Conceptual transfer in simple insight problems. *Memory & Cognition, 16*, 36–44.

Long, D.L., & Graesser, A.C. (1988). Wit and humor in discourse processing. *Discourse Processes, 11*, 35–60.

Maier, N.R.F. (1931). Reasoning in humans: II. The solution of a problem and its appearance in consciousness. *Journal of Comparative Psychology, 12*, 181–194.

Metcalfe, J. (1986a). Feeling of knowing in memory and problem solving. *Journal of Experimental Psychology: Learning, Memory, and Cognition, 12*, 288–294.

Metcalfe, J. (1986b). Premonitions of insight predict impending error. *Journal of Experimental Psychology: Learning, Memory, and Cognition, 12*, 623–634.

Metcalfe, J., & Wiebe, D. (1987). Intuition in insight and non-insight problem solving. *Memory & Cognition, 15*, 238–246.

Newell, A., & Simon, H.A. (1972). *Human problem solving*. Englewood, NJ: Prentice Hall.

Novick, L.R. (1988). Analogical transfer, problem similarity, and expertise. *Journal of Experimental Psychology: Learning, Memory, and Cognition, 14*, 510–520.

Ohlsson, S. (1984). Restructuring revisited: II. An information processing theory of restructuring and insight. *Scandinavian Journal of Psychology, 25*, 117–129.

Poincaré, H. (1913). Mathematical creation. In *The Foundations of Science* (G.B. Halsted, Trans.). New York: Science Press.

Ross, B.H. (1984). Remindings and their effects in learning a cognitive skill. *Cognitive Psychology, 16*, 371–416.

Schank, R.C. (1986). *Explanation Patterns. Understanding mechanically and creatively*. Hillsdale, NJ: Erlbaum.

Wachtel, P.L. (1977). *Psychoanalysis and behavior therapy*. New York: Basic Books.

Wason, P.C. (1960). On the failure to eliminate hypotheses in a conceptual task. *Quarterly Journal of Experimental Psychology, 12*, 129–140.

Wason, P.C. (1977). "On the failure to eliminate hypotheses ..."—a second look. In P.N. Johnson-Laird & P.C. Wason (Eds.), *Thinking: Readings in cognitive science* (pp. 307–314). New York: Cambridge University Press.

Watson, J.D. (1968). *The double helix.* New York: Signet Books.

Weisberg, R.W. (1986). *Creativity: Genius and other myths.* New York: Freeman.

Weisberg, R.W. (1988). Problem solving and creativity. In R.J. Sternberg (Ed.), *The nature of creativity* (pp. 148–176). New York: Cambridge University Press.

Weisberg, R.W., & Alba, J.W. (1981). An examination of the alleged role of "fixation" in the solution of several "insight" problems. *Journal of Experimental Psychology: General, 110,* 169–192.

Weisberg, R.W., & Suls, J.M. (1973). An information-processing model of Duncker's candle problem. *Cognitive Psychology, 4,* 255–276.

Wickelgren, W. (1974). *How to solve problems.* New York: Freeman.

7 Getting Into and Out of Mental Ruts: A Theory of Fixation, Incubation, and Insight

Steven M. Smith

SPINNING YOUR WHEELS

When my partner, Stan, saw Roger's truck slip into the mud on the construction site where we were working, he laughed, slapped his knee, and guffawed, "Now, *that* is what you call spinning your wheels!" Roger alternately spun his wheels forward and backward, digging his truck quickly into a rut up to the axle. Stan didn't let up on Roger the whole time we were towing him out of the rut, but he stopped laughing a few minutes later when it was our truck that slipped into the mud. I mentioned something about Roger getting his revenge, but Stan just shook his head and told me to get a 50-pound sack of quicklime from the back of our truck. We spread the lime on the mud in front of and behind the tires. "Time for a break," Stan announced, and although I didn't understand why at the time, I wasn't about to argue about taking a break. After the break, Stan started up the truck and put it slowly in gear. I expected him to sink quickly up to the axle but, to my surprise, the quicklime had made a new crust on top of the mud, providing just enough traction for the tires to grip, and he drove straight out.

In this case, getting out of a trap was not accomplished by trying harder and sticking to the job; spinning his wheels faster only got Roger deeper into the rut. What was needed was time to allow conditions to become more favorable for getting out of the trap. Analogously, in our thinking, we sometimes start spinning our mental wheels; that is, we work harder and harder at a frustrating problem, but succeed only in getting deeper into a mental rut. In these cases, allowing time for mental conditions to become more favorable for getting out of a mental trap can facilitate discovery of insight into a problem's solution. In this chapter, I will explain what insight has to do with mental ruts, and I will suggest some ways for climbing back out of such ruts.

Although there are many ideas about how insight can be achieved, most approaches are *constructive*, describing, for example, how an insight can be incrementally assembled from parts, how prior knowledge can be transferred or mapped from another domain, or how unconscious sensitivity to a problem helps us notice relevant ideas when they occur. My approach, however, focuses not so much on how insight is constructed but rather on what prevents insight experiences from occurring. Probabilistically speaking, ideas are more likely to pop unexpectedly into mind once we stop ourselves from blocking those thoughts. Although there may be many causes of insight, it is my contention that incubation improves the chances that insight experiences will occur by facilitating escape from the mental ruts that block insight. Furthermore, I propose that patterns of fixation, incubation, and insight in problem solving resemble certain memory phenomena and can be explained, in part, in terms of a theory of memory interference and recovery.

INCREMENTAL PROGRESS VERSUS RESTRUCTURING IN INSIGHT

Experimental psychological research on insight was conducted by Gestalt psychologists, including Köhler (1925), Maier (1931), and Duncker (1945). They characterized insight as a sudden shift in the problem's *gestalt*, or a spontaneous restructuring of the problem's mental representation. This sudden restructuring was supposedly similar to the perceptual restructuring that can occur, for example, when shifting back and forth between alternate interpretations of certain optical illusions.

In the early 1980s, Robert Weisberg and his colleagues revived the subject of insight in order to debunk what Weisberg (1986) referred to as the "myth of insight." Weisberg's characterization of the Gestalt position stated that (1) subjects can fixate (or get stuck) on unwarranted assumptions about a problem because of past experience; (2) this fixation prevents insight; (3) if the source of fixation is removed, insight will occur quickly; and (4) remembering one's past experience is not a central factor in solving insight problems.

Weisberg (1986) proposed that past experience *is* very important for solving problems, although one's retrieved knowledge can be used and combined in novel ways. He also stated that removing mental blocks does not result in a rapid restructuring that leads to successful problem solving (e.g., Weisberg & Alba, 1981), showing that certain so-called insight problems could not be rapidly solved merely because subjects were informed explicitly about blocks that had been traditionally assumed to prevent solutions. He has concluded that insight problems are solved via an incremental accumulation of knowledge relevant to the solution.

In the late 1980s, however, Janet Metcalfe offered important new evidence in support of the restructuring position. Metcalfe (1986a,b; Metcalfe & Wiebe, 1987) examined metacognitions (awareness of one's thinking) as a way of assessing insight and noninsight processes. In her studies, she found that subjects were unable to predict their eventual success on insight problems, whereas they could predict success on memory tasks and noninsight problems. Metcalfe concluded that subjects' lack of partial knowledge of solutions showed that solutions to insight problems do not involve a gradual accrual of remembered knowledge relevant to the problem. If information were remembered gradually during work on insight problems, then subjects should be aware of that partial knowledge, just as they are during work on noninsight problems. The alternative explanation involves a radical transformation in the problem's gestalt (i.e., the conceptualization or mental representation of the problem).

Metcalfe also tested metacognitions of impending solutions during problem solving, asking subjects at 10-second intervals for subjective warmth ratings whereby *warmer* meant "closer to a solution." This on-line metacognitive monitoring technique shows that warmth ratings increase in a gradual, incremental pattern prior to solution of noninsight problems. With insight problems, however, subjective warmth ratings sharply increased only seconds prior to solving a problem. Furthermore, when subjects worked on insight problems, it was found that gradually increasing patterns of warmth ratings were more likely to herald an impending failure rather than an impending solution.

Do solutions of insight problems occur as a rapid restructuring of the problem's gestalt, with ideas breaking suddenly and unexpectedly into awareness? I believe that understanding the role of mental blocks can bring us closer to answering this question.

A PROPOSED VIEW OF INSIGHT

Definitions

To begin, I propose that a distinction be drawn among the terms *insight, insight experience,* and *insight problem. Insight* I define as "an understanding." Insight can refer, for example, to understanding a mechanism, an analogy, an inductive principle, or a reconceptualization. By this definition, insight can be acquired in a variety of ways, including an incremental acquisition of knowledge or via a sudden realization of an idea. The mode of acquiring insight may be independent of its subsequent use: An insightful discovery that dawned suddenly and unexpectedly in the mind of a creative genius can usually be explained to others in increments, as evidenced by the teaching of the brilliant insights of Darwin, Pasteur, or Einstein to college students.

The *insight experience* is the sudden emergence of an idea into conscious awareness, the "Aha!" experience. This is the phenomenon that seems to have been the focus of Gestalt psychologists and studies that have emphasized metacognition (Metcalfe, 1986a, 1986b; Metcalfe & Wiebe, 1987). Metcalfe and Wiebe (1987) defined insight in terms of the metacognitions immediately preceding the moment when a solution is reached. According to this view, abrupt increases in warmth ratings define insight, whereas incremental increases in warmth indicate noninsight problem solving.

It is important to note that insight experiences need not result in profound earth-shattering ideas, such as the theory of evolution, or the idea of special relativity in physics. According to this definition, the essential elements of insight experiences are that ideas are sudden and unexpected, not that they are profound or important.

An *insight problem*, in contrast to a noninsight problem, is one for which the solution is more likely to be reached via an insight experience. The solution to a noninsight problem is less often realized in a flash but is usually constructed incrementally. Because it is expressed relatively and probabilistically, this definition leaves room for the variability in problem solving caused by individual differences and situational factors. Not every solution to an insight problem need be generated by an insight experience, and noninsight problems might be solved via an insight experience. The definition states that the population of solutions for insight problems is more likely than that of solutions for noninsight problems to result from insight experiences.

There are at least two important reasons for identifying insight problems. One is that experimental studies of insight experiences must have a means of eliciting the phenomenon of interest. A second is that examination of insight problems may reveal something important about the nature of insight experiences.

The abruptness and unexpectedness of insight experiences resembles other "mind-popping" phenomena in which a memory or idea emerges suddenly into awareness (Mandler, 1992). Mandler's examples of mind-popping include reminiscence in recall (i.e., remembering something one had not recalled on a previous attempt), incubation in problem solving, and recall of dreams. These are all situations in which conscious constructions arise independently of conscious intentions. Another example is the "pop-up" memory—that is, a retrieval block that is resolved without deliberately searching memory (Reason & Lucas, 1984). Although insight experiences have historically been described as resembling perception, it is apparent that insight experiences also resemble certain types of remembering, particularly those memories that burst suddenly and unexpectedly into consciousness.

Insight experiences often entail an abrupt and unanticipated resolution or transcendence of blocks. Whether resolution of blocks is definitional to insight experiences is open to debate and empirical testing. What I propose is that block resolution is a common feature of insight experiences.

Restructuring is "structuring again," an alteration of a cognitive representation. In contrast, forming an original cognitive structure to represent a problem does not necessarily involve destruction or alteration of another. Ideas on restructuring typically focus on the new cognitive structure, the one on which a final solution is ultimately based, not the original cognitive structures that resulted in failed attempts. The cognitive structures representing initial solution attempts have in common the fact that they do not produce satisfactory problem solutions; if they did lead to solutions, restructuring would not be necessary to achieve insight.

A structure for solving a problem can be thought of as a plan, one that uses a set of operations, and it envisions the type of solution that will be produced by the plan. Plans may vary in their specificity, but even vague plans can be used to attain an expected type of goal. I propose that the cognitive structure revealed in an insight experience is one that did not fit an earlier plan. Noninsight problem solving, in contrast, proceeds within a plan.

If initial plans lead to a solution, or serve as the basis for a solution, then they require no restructuring. Inappropriate plans, however, may hinder discovery of a solution, inadvertently causing a block. Therefore, restructuring involves transcendence of blocks, or revision of plans. It is not necessary actually to have instituted and rejected plans for them to constitute blocks; blocks can be said to occur as long as the inappropriate plans compete or interfere with the cognitive structure that represents a satisfactory solution.

The approach to insight that I have described here is consistent with Metcalfe's results that relate metacognitive warmth ratings to success and failure on insight and noninsight problems (1986a, 1986b; Metcalfe & Wiebe, 1987). If an appropriate gestalt of a problem is initially blocked, then one cannot know how near an appropriate solution is. If the appropriate gestalt is blocked because one is engaged in an inappropriate approach, then incremental feelings of increasing warmth would be based on work completed toward an incorrect solution, which is demonstrated by Metcalfe's (1986b) finding that high warmth ratings tend to indicate impending failures on an insight problem. The variety of blocks that can impede insight I refer to as cases of *fixation*, which I define as "a counterproductive use or undesirable effect of prior knowledge."

Fixation

The primary thesis of this chapter is that fixation blocks insight experiences from occurring. Traditionally, the term *fixation* has been used to refer to an inappropriate adherence to an approach to solving a problem, but I have expanded the definition somewhat to encompass other situations, including remembering and generating creative ideas in more open-ended tasks. Classic demonstrations of fixation in problem solving include Maier's (1931) two-string problem and Luchins and Luchins's (1959) water-jar problem, both of which have been described in detail elsewhere (see chapter 1). Rather than reiterate these cases, I will present more recent examples of blocks in memory and problem solving from my own research.

Fixation in Memory
In terms of research in human memory, the basic concept of interference, or response competition, is most typically used to explain how one piece of learning can negatively affect the use of another learned response. As simplified in figure 7.1, given the stimulus, the probability (p) of retrieving the target response is perfect $(p = 1.00)$ when the target is the only associated response (figure 7.1A). The probability of retrieving the target response decreases if there is another competing response associated with the stimulus, because there is some chance that the competing response

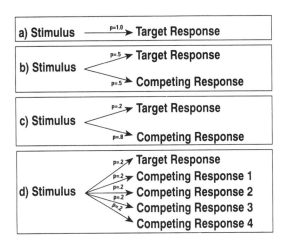

Figure 7.1
Interference as response competition. The probability of retrieving the target response decreases as the number and strength of competing associations increases.

will be retrieved instead of the target (figure 7.1B). This is how response competition operates in this simplified model of interference. Furthermore, the stronger the association between the stimulus and a competitor (figure 7.1C), and the more competing responses there are (figure 7.1D), the less chance there is that the target will be retrieved when the stimulus is used to cue memory.

For example, if the only chemical company you knew was Dow Chemical, then it would be fairly easy to retrieve the name of the company when asked who it is that manufactures napalm. If, however, you also knew other chemical companies, such as DuPont and Monsanto, the chance of retrieving Dow would be decreased, because there would be some possibility of retrieving DuPont or Monsanto instead.

Interference effects can be momentarily increased if you retrieve the interfering competitors. Extending the previous example, once the names Dow, DuPont, and Monsanto are primed, it becomes more difficult to think of the name of the chemical company responsible for the toxic gas leak that killed thousands in Bhopal, India, in 1985. (*Hint*: It was *not* Dow, DuPont, or Monsanto.) Similarly, priming the words *compass*, *astrolabe*, and *protractor* may make it more difficult to remember the correct word for the navigational instrument used for measuring the angle from the horizon to a heavenly object. Such momentary memory blocks are referred to as *tip-of-the-tongue* (TOT) states when the blocks are accompanied by subjective feelings that retrieval of targets seems imminent. This subjective sense of *imminence* goes beyond the more commonly studied feeling that one knows the answer to a question; imminence refers to feeling that after only brief moments the answer will burst into consciousness.

In fact, successful recall is *not* necessarily imminent, even though it may seem to be at the time when one experiences a TOT state. My experimental studies (Smith, 1991) show that few TOTs are resolved (i.e., few correct targets are finally retrieved) if subjects work continuously on retrieving targets, particularly when competitors (e.g., Dow, DuPont, Monsanto) are shown to the subjects in TOT states. I am repeatedly reminded of this fact whenever I experience a TOT state while I am speaking before a crowd of people. If I interrupt my talk to concentrate on remembering a momentarily blocked word or name, I am inevitably frus-

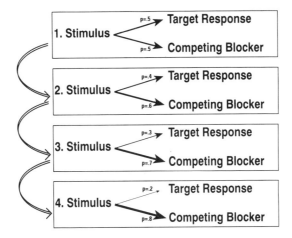

Figure 7.2
The mental rut. Accessing the target becomes increasingly difficult each time the competing blocker is retrieved and incremented in strength.

trated in my attempts to recall the target. This is particularly problematic when a competing word or name keeps intruding. (*Note*: If you are suffering from a TOT experience, the correct chemical company name in the Bhopal, India, case will be given later in this chapter.)

This pattern, in which a block worsens because attempted memory retrievals strengthen the block, describes a *mental rut.* Each time a retrieval attempt is made, the competing blocker is retrieved instead of the correct target, and the blocker becomes temporarily more strongly associated with the stimulus being used to cue memory. The developing strength of fixation is depicted in figure 7.2. This model of fixation can be generalized to other situations beyond memory retrieval, as will be shown later.

Fixation in Problem Solving
Fixation in problem solving can be demonstrated in the problem depicted in figure 7.3. The problems are rebuses, picture word puzzles that suggest common phrases. The phrase depicted is the solution to a rebus. For example, the solution to the example rebus shown in figure 7.3 is *just between you and me*, a common phrase indicated by the word *just* between the words *you* and

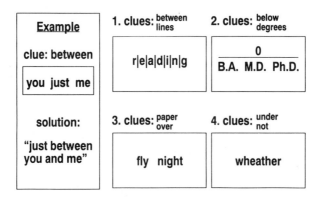

Figure 7.3
Rebus problems. The solution to each problem is a common phrase suggested by the words inside the box. Potential hints are shown above each problem.

me. Now try the other four problems in figure 7.3. Included with each problem is a clue that might give you a hint about the solution. Work the problems from easiest (1) to most difficult (4) for the best effect.

From the first two problems you might learn that the clues are very useful and that the solution often involves the relative positions of the letters and words. The solution to the first is *reading between the lines* and involves the positional element *between*. The solution to the second problem is *three degrees below zero*, this time using the positional element *below*. The third problem might temporarily stump you if you had just completed the first two, because the clues are intentionally misleading, suggesting the phrases *fly paper* and *overnight*, neither of which is the correct solution, *fly by night*. The clues are likewise misleading for the fourth problem and, worse yet, it does not use a positional phrase as in the previous problems. Thus, as illustrated in figure 7.4, work on the earlier problems can cause fixation at different levels. In this case, the search for a solution can be diverted away from the correct target (*ill spell of weather*) at the last step by priming an incorrect piece of information (e.g., the phrases *whether or not* and *under the weather*) or at an earlier step by priming the wrong approach to the problem (e.g., positional solutions). Fixation can conceivably act at any stage of problem solv-

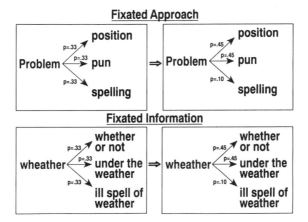

Figure 7.4
Two levels of fixation. Inappropriate approaches to a problem, as well as inappropriate information, can block target approaches and target information if the blocks are temporarily strengthened.

ing, affecting, for example, one's representation of the problem or the knowledge domain in which one analogically searches for ideas.

In problem-solving situations contrived for laboratory research, fixation in a variety of forms has been clearly demonstrated (e.g., Luchins & Luchins, 1959; Maier, 1931; Smith & Blankenship, 1989, 1991). It seems fair to ask whether fixation would have a similar constraining effect on ideas in more realistic tasks, such as the process of creative engineering design. Therefore, with David Jansson, a mechanical engineer, I studied what we referred to as *design fixation*, which we defined as "a counterproductive effect of prior experience on the generation of creative designs aimed at solving a realistic problem" (Jansson & Smith, 1991). Some of the creative design tasks, for example, asked design engineers to generate ideas for a bicycle rack, a measuring cup for the blind, a disposable spillproof coffee cup, and a biomechanical device for taking readings inside of the intestine. In each experiment, all the engineers received the same problem, but half, in addition, were shown an example design. All the experiments showed that the creative designs conformed to the examples when they were given, as compared to the designs of those who

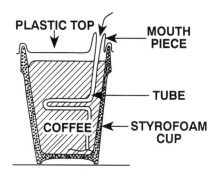

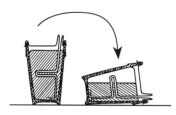

Figure 7.5
Disposable spillproof coffee cup example shown to subjects to induce design fixation. (Reprinted with permission from D.G. Jansson and S.M. Smith [1991], Design fixation. *Design Studies*, *12*[1], 3–11.)

had seen no examples. This conformity occurred even for detrimental features of the examples and even when engineers were explicitly told to avoid those negative features. For example, when designers were shown the sketch in figure 7.5 as an example of a disposable spillproof coffee cup, they were instructed not to use straws or mouthpieces in their designs (mouthpieces prevent cooling while sipping the coffee and can cause scalding). Nonetheless, 56 percent of the designs by these subjects did include a straw or mouthpiece, compared to 11 percent of the designs of those who had not seen the example. Clearly, fixation can occur in creative engineering design, a perfectly realistic task in which insights are needed. This mental rut apparently is difficult to prevent by simply telling people to avoid it.

How, then, does one overcome fixation to achieve insight? My current answer to this question is probabilistic rather than deterministic: That is, I contend that incubation, or getting away from a fixated problem, can increase the chances of avoiding the block and achieving insight.

Incubation

Not much of a traveler, I was curious when I found a retractable cord that would stretch across the tub and latch to the opposite wall in the hotel room where I once was staying. I could have asked anybody what its function was (and I have found out since then that nearly everyone knows), but I took on the problem as a challenge. My best guess at first was that it was a safety device for grabbing onto if one were to slip in the shower. Later I realized that the line was too flimsy for this purpose and would be more a hazard than a safety feature. Then I guessed that it might prevent the shower curtain from attacking me and enveloping my body the moment the shower was on, but I soon found out that the line prevented no such attacks. Daunted and unsatisfied, I put the problem aside. Months later, at another hotel, I saw another of these lines across the tub, but there was no shower nor was there any evidence that there had ever been a shower curtain. Baffled at first at this new twist, it suddenly dawned on me that the line was for hanging out hand-washed clothing to drip dry over the tub and had nothing at all to do with showering.

When initial work on a problem reaches an impasse, we may put the matter momentarily aside. Sometimes, when involved in some unrelated activity during the break or on returning to the problem after the break, a solution will suddenly burst into awareness. This phenomenon, as illustrated by my clothesline realization, is known as *incubation* or, more accurately, an *incubation effect*. Incubation effects are labeled as such only when the time away from the problem leads to *illumination*, another term for an insight experience. The example of my clothesline experience is not a particularly profound or important realization, but it fits my earlier definition of an insight experience because the idea burst suddenly and unexpectedly upon me.

Incubation effects also occur commonly when trying to recall a word or a name. In cases in which we cannot recall a name during a conversation, on an examination, or while giving a talk, the solution is not to continue trying to recall the name but rather to put the matter aside momentarily, because the name is likely to pop into mind later. Inconveniently, retrieval of the errant word or name tends to occur once it is already too late to be useful.

The term *incubation* suggests a biological metaphor, implying that the cognitive pattern resembles a process similar to biological maturation. When an egg is laid, the opaque shell prevents us from seeing the development proceeding within, much as the unconscious proceedings of the mind may be invisible to introspection. According to this metaphor, development of an insightful idea occurs via invisible unconscious processes. The fully mature idea then pops rapidly into awareness once the unconscious development is complete.

The term sometimes used for the idea that insights are created unconsciously while the conscious mind is otherwise occupied is the *unconscious work hypothesis*. Like the little elves that would cobble beautiful shoes only while the cobbler was sleeping, unconscious mental forces are imagined to work away at insights only when the conscious mind temporarily retreats. This is a compelling explanation because when incubation results in insight, it seems that work must have been needed for such a wonderful idea but there is no awareness of the work that went into the insight. Because we can do so many complicated things without much apparent conscious attention (e.g., ride a bicycle, use a fork, tie shoelaces), it may make sense that unconscious processes can create insights as well.

If information critical for an insight experience is not accessible during one's initial work on a problem, but it is accessible later, after time away from the problem, then we can try to explain the change in accessibility in terms of a memory model. This pattern of increasing accessibility of critical information over time is illustrated in figure 7.6. The unconscious work hypothesis, as described earlier, suggests that forces of which we are unaware act during incubation intervals to increase the accessibility of information critical to an insight experience. A slow-spreading activation mechanism, as proposed by Yaniv and Meyer (1987), could support such a pattern of increasing accessibility over time. If information critical to an insight is not retrieved during initial work on a problem, but is partially activated by those initial attempts,

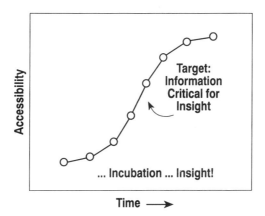

Figure 7.6
Pattern of increasing accessibility of critical target information underlying incubation effects.

then the critical material is "sensitized." Subsequent encounters with stimuli related to the critical information then become more likely to elicit retrieval of that information, thus leading quickly to an insight into the solution of a problem.

Another memory theory, however, provides a different explanation of how incubation can increase the accessibility of critical information. This theory is based on a classic interference pattern of spontaneous recovery (e.g., Barnes & Underwood, 1959; Mensink & Raaijmakers, 1989), and is graphically described in figure 7.7. The pattern of interference begins at the left side of the figure with competition among responses, much the same as described earlier in the discussion of fixation and memory. A well-learned response, labeled *A*, is initially blocked by a more recently learned response, *B*. An interesting finding concerns the time course of this interference effect. Response A recovers spontaneously, or at least without any conscious effort, becoming increasingly accessible over time as response B weakens, in effect losing its power to block response A. This pattern shows an incubation effect for response A; an initially blocked memory is more likely to be accessed due to time away from the block.

The same pattern of shifting accessibility explains why TOT experiences are more easily resolved by taking time away from

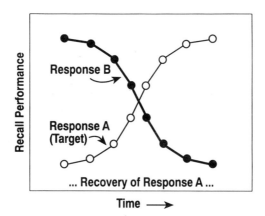

Figure 7.7
Classic pattern of retroactive interference and recovery of original response A. Response A, initially blocked by stronger response B, recovers and increases in accessibility over time as B loses strength.

memory retrieval attempts. Continuing to search for the correct target word or name may serve only to deepen the mental rut, strengthening the retrieval block, as shown at the left of figure 7.7. Taking time away from attempts to retrieve the target allows competing blockers time to lose strength, so that the correct target will be relatively more accessible.

Analogously, this pattern of interference and recovery describes fixation, incubation, and insight in problem solving, as shown in figure 7.8. Here fixation is analogous to the initial memory retrieval block shown in figure 7.7, with critical target information blocked by competing approaches, problem representations, or specific pieces of information. This state of fixation can arise, for example, from a mental rut, as described earlier; continuing to use an inappropriate solution or problem-solving approach can strengthen the competing material. Once the problem is put aside, the strengthening of the fixation ceases and the accessibility of the blocking material instead begins to decrease, as shown in figure 7.8. Incubation time—the time away from the problem—therefore allows the target information to increase in relative accessibility, and this increase in accessibility improves the chances that an insightful solution will be realized.

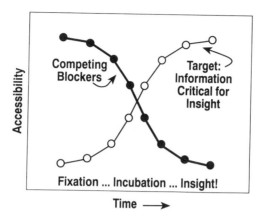

Figure 7.8

Fixation, incubation, and insight as a pattern of changing accessibilities. Initial fixation is caused by competing blockers. After an incubation interval, critical information becomes more accessible, and the chances of an insight experience increase as blockers lose their strength.

Experimental Evidence of Incubation Effects

From a scientific point of view, methods for observing incubation effects and insight experiences in controlled situations are highly desirable if we expect to learn about these phenomena. The usefulness of insight problems, for example, is that they can be used in the laboratory to induce and study insight experiences. Are there also reliable methods for inducing and studying incubation effects?

Incubation effects are common in everyday life, and writers have referred to them at least as early as Wallas (1926), who described incubation as one of the fundamental stages of problem solving. One might think that the experimental psychology research literature would be replete with studies of incubation effects and that by now there would be standard laboratory and classroom methods for producing and observing the phenomenon. However, this is not so. In investigations of incubation, no effects were found by Dominowski and Jenrick (1972), Olton and Johnson (1976), Gall and Mendelsohn (1967), and Gick and Holyoak (1980). Dreistadt (1969) and Fulgosi and Guilford (1968) reported incubation effects, but Olton and Johnson (1976) failed to replicate both findings. Murray and Denny (1969) reported a single effect, restricted to high-ability subjects, yet Patrick's (1986) one finding of an effect occurred only among low-ability subjects. Neither study has been reproduced in a published report. In fact, only a few published articles have ever reported replicated experimental evidence of incubation in the laboratory. The sparseness of experimental evidence has been noted repeatedly in literature on the subject (Kaplan & Simon, 1990; Olton & Johnson, 1976; Smith & Blankenship, 1989, 1991). Is the scarcity of replicable incubation effects attributable to incubation being a rare and enigmatic phenomenon? My observations lead me to believe otherwise.

Consider this: When someone expediently solves a problem, the situation is not relevant to incubation. If someone cannot ever solve a particular problem, incubation will not help. The only situation relevant to incubation is one in which, at the moment, someone has failed to solve a tractable problem. Clearly, incubation can occur only in situations in which problem solving reaches a temporary impasse. Why would people come to an impasse while working on a tractable problem? One possibility is that they are blocked from the knowledge necessary for solving the problem. Thus, I have proposed that incubation effects can be observed if tractable problems are initially blocked, and my experimental studies have supported this hypothesis.

For example, Smith and Blankenship (1989) examined fixation and incubation using rebus problems, such as the four problems shown earlier in figure 7.3. The critical rebus problems in that study were accompanied initially by misleading clues and then were retested either immediately after the initial work on the problem or after a delay. On the retest, subjects first attempted to solve the problem and then tried to recall the misleading clue that had initially been shown with the problem. Figure 7.9 shows both problem-solving performance and recall of the misleading clues as a function of the delay of the retest. In four experiments, retesting produced greater improvement with longer delays, repeated evidence of incubation effects. The improvements in problem solving with longer delays were accompanied by poorer memory of the misleading clues. This pattern of results looks very similar to the theoretical patterns of interference and recov-

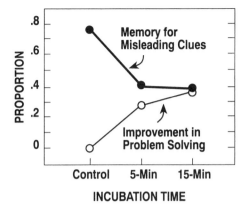

Figure 7.9
Improvement on initially failed problems and memory for misleading clues as a function of incubation time. Longer incubation produced more problem-solving improvement and poorer memory of misleading clues. (Adapted with permission from S.M. Smith and S.E. Blankenship [1989], Incubation effects. *Bulletin of the Psychonomic Society, 27,* 311–314.)

ery described earlier (see figures 7.7 and 7.8). The misleading cues acted as competing blockers, initially strong and gradually becoming less accessible over time. The information critical for solving the rebus problems, initially blocked, recovered with incubation time, thereby improving the chances of success.

This method of first inducing fixation and then retesting after varying delays has now proven useful for observing incubation effects in several studies of both problem solving and memory. Three experiments demonstrated the same patterns of fixation and incubation using remote associates test (RAT) problems (Smith & Blankenship, 1991). For RAT problems, one must think of a word that in combination with each of three test words makes a two-word phrase or compound word. For example, the solution to the RAT problem *"apple/family/house"* is *tree*, because the solution can make the phrases *apple tree, family tree,* and *tree house.* The word *green* is a misleading clue, because it can make a two-word phrase from two of the test words (*green apple* and *greenhouse*), but it does not make a phrase with the third test word, *family.* In those experiments, misleading clues were effective at causing initial fixation and subsequent incubation effects, whether the clues accompanied the initial presentation of the problems or had been studied on a list before subjects were given the problems. This indicates that fixation was caused by memory of the blockers rather than by some type of distraction.

Further evidence linking fixation and incubation to memory phenomena comes from studies of reminiscence and TOT memory blocks. Whereas incubation typically means solving a problem on a retest after failing on a first attempt, *reminiscence* refers to recalling successfully material that one had failed to recall on an earlier attempt. For example, if you were given a second recall test after you had already tried to recall a long list of pictures, you might come up with a few items from the list that you had not recalled on the first test. Smith and Vela (1991) found that such reminiscence effects were greater if an incubation interval was given between the first test and the retest. Similarly, Smith (1991) found that incubation intervals increased the chances of resolving TOT retrieval failures, such as the Union Carbide example given earlier in this chapter. These incubation effects in memory paradigms appear to reflect the same patterns seen in problem-solving studies, that a time interval inserted between an initial failed test and a retest facilitates resolution of the failure.

GETTING OUT OF MENTAL RUTS

If we are to understand how to escape from mental ruts, it is worthwhile to consider briefly a theoretical explanation of the recovery that causes incubation in memory and problem solving. Simply put, theoretical models of recovery emphasize the importance of one's internal cognitive context, which has an effect on what is retrieved from memory during the course of remembering and solving problems. Whereas a problem undertaken in one mental context may lead to a mental rut, another context may lead to an insightful solution. If the initial context in which a problem is attempted leads to fixation, then an incubation interval may allow time for one's mental context to change to one that will yield a solution. Even if it contains no special information that serves as a useful clue to insight, the context can facilitate insight if it is at least not associated with fixated material. If we accept this contextual explanation of incubation, then it would appear that contextual change, rather than time, per se, is needed to escape from mental ruts. Therefore, time away from a fixated problem will encourage insight all the more if you move away from fixated contexts.

Although this contextual explanation of incubation and insight is speculative, there are well-known historical cases of insight occurring in contexts outside the typical workplace. For example, initial efforts at solving important problems resulted in temporary impasses when Archimedes was working on his famous displacement problem, when Kekulé was at work on the structure of the benzene molecule, and when Poincaré worked on what would eventually result in his discovery related to Fuchsian functions in mathematics. The legendary insights in these cases occurred away from the discoverers' regular work contexts—while Archimedes was taking a bath, while Kekulé dozed before the fire, and while Poincaré was stepping onto a bus.

In the beginning of this chapter, we read about a truck that slipped into the mud; the physical rut simply worsened when the truck driver spun his wheels, persisting with a counterproductive strategy that the driver initially believed would get him out of the rut. A more effective strategy was allowing time for conditions to become more favorable for getting out of the mud trap. In the mental domain as well, taking time off and changing contexts can allow mental conditions to become more favorable for escaping a fixated mental rut. Hence, incubation, and perhaps context change, can improve the chances of having insight experiences.

ACKNOWLEDGMENTS

This work was supported by National Institute of Mental Health grant R01 MH4473001, awarded to Steven Smith. I would like to thank Janet Metcalfe for valuable comments and discussions on the subject of insight and Ron Finke for comments on an earlier version of this chapter.

REFERENCES

Barnes, J.M., & Underwood, B.J. (1959). "Fate" of first-list associations in transfer theory. *Journal of Experimental Psychology, 58,* 97–105.

Dominowski, R.L., & Jenrick, R. (1972). Effects of hints and interpolated activity on solution of an insight problem. *Psychonomic Science, 26,* 335–337.

Dreistadt, R. (1969). The use of analogies and incubation in obtaining insights in creative problem solving. *Journal of Psychology, 71,* 159–175.

Duncker, K. (1945). On problem solving. *Psychological Monographs, 58*(5), whole no. 270.

Fulgosi, A., & Guilford, J.P. (1968). Short-term induction of divergent production. *American Journal of Psychology, 81,* 241–246.

Gall, M., & Mendelsohn, G.A. (1967). Effects of facilitating techniques and subject/experimenter interactions on creative problem solving. *Journal of Personality and Social Psychology, 5,* 211–216.

Gick, M.L., & Holyoak, K.J. (1980). Analogical problem solving. *Cognitive Psychology, 12,* 306–355.

Jansson, D.G., & Smith, S.M. (1991). Design fixation. *Design Studies, 12*(1), 3–11.

Kaplan, C., & Simon, H.A. (1990). In search of insight. *Cognitive Psychology, 22,* 374–419.

Köhler, W. (1925). *The mentality of apes.* New York: Liveright.

Luchins, A.S., & Luchins, E.H. (1959). *Rigidity of behavior.* Eugene, OR: University of Oregon Press.

Maier, N.R.F. (1931). Reasoning in humans: II. The solution of a problem and its appearance in consciousness. *Journal of Comparative Psychology, 12,* 181–194.

Mandler, G. (1992, July). *On remembering without really trying: Hypermnesia, incubation, and mind-popping.* Paper presented at the Attention and Performance Symposium XV, Erice, Sicily.

Mensink, G., & Raaijmakers, J.G.W. (1989). A model for interference and forgetting. *Psychological Review, 95,* 434–455.

Metcalfe, J. (1986a). Feeling of knowing in memory and problem solving. *Journal of Experimental Psychology: Learning, Memory, and Cognition, 12,* 288–294.

Metcalfe, J. (1986b). Premonitions of insight predict impending error. *Journal of Experimental Psychology: Learning, Memory, and Cognition, 12,* 623–634.

Metcalfe, J., & Wiebe, D. (1987). Intuition in insight and non-insight problem solving. *Memory & Cognition, 15,* 238–246.

Murray, H.G., & Denny, J.P. (1969). Interaction of ability level and interpolated activity (opportunity for incubation) in human problem solving. *Psychological Reports, 24,* 271–276.

Olton, R.M., & Johnson, D.M. (1976). Mechanisms of incubation in creative problem solving. *American Journal of Psychology, 89,* 617–630.

Patrick, A.S. (1986). The role of ability in creative "incubation." *Personality and Individual Differences, 7,* 169–174.

Reason, J.T., & Lucas, D. (1984). Using cognitive diaries to investigate naturally occurring memory blocks. In J. Harris & P.E. Morris (Eds.), *Everyday memory, actions, and absent mindedness* (pp. 53–70). London: Academic Press.

Smith, S.M. (1991, November). *Tip-of-the-tongue states and blockers with imaginary animals as targets.* Paper presented at the annual meeting of the Psychonomic Society, San Francisco, CA.

Smith, S.M., & Blankenship, S.E. (1989). Incubation effects. *Bulletin of the Psychonomic Society, 27,* 311–314.

Smith, S.M., & Blankenship, S.E. (1991). Incubation and the persistence of fixation in problem solving. *American Journal of Psychology, 104,* 61–87.

Smith, S.M., & Vela, E. (1991). Incubated reminiscence effects. *Memory & Cognition, 19*(2), 168–176.

Wallas, G. (1926). *The art of thought.* New York: Harcourt.

Weisberg, R.W. (1986). *Creativity: Genius and other myths.* New York: Freeman.

Weisberg, R.W., & Alba, J.W. (1981). An examination of the alleged role of "fixation" in the solution of several "insight" problems. *Journal of Experimental Psychology: General, 110,* 169–192.

Yaniv, I., & Meyer, D.E. (1987). Activation and metacognition of inaccessible stored information: Potential bases for incubation effects in problem solving. *Journal of Experimental Psychology: Learning, Memory, and Cognition, 13,* 187–205.

III The Invention-based Approach

8 Creative Insight and Preinventive Forms

Ronald A. Finke

One of my teachers once told me, "If you can't have wisdom, at least have data," to which I would now add, "If you don't have data, at least have insight."

Insight is what distinguishes the enlightened from the benighted, the inspiring from the denigrating, the magical from the mediocre. It is the essential process by which we come to make surprising discoveries and realizations, both about real-world issues and problems and about ourselves.

INSIGHT AND CREATIVE COGNITION

This chapter will consider insight from the standpoint of *creative cognition*. In this approach, one applies the methods of cognitive science to the general problem of trying to understand the basic mental processes underlying creative thinking (Finke, Ward & Smith, 1992). Creative cognition combines the scientific method with the opportunity to engage in creative exploration and discovery. This helps to demystify creativity but without trivializing or sterilizing it, as can often happen when highly contrived or artificial experimental procedures are used (e.g., see Neisser, 1976).

In this chapter, I make a general distinction between divergent and convergent insight. These terms reflect the classic distinction between divergent and convergent thinking (Guilford, 1956; Mednick, 1962). *Divergent thinking* refers to thinking that flows outward from a concept, making contact with other ideas and possibilities that one might not ordinarily consider. It leads to the discovery of remote associations and insights into unusual uses for common things, such as realizing that a pair of scissors can be used as a weapon, a hole punch, or a weight for a pendulum (Maier, 1931). *Convergent thinking*, on the other hand, refers to thinking that focuses on a single idea or possibility, given a collection of facts. Some examples of convergent thinking are realizing that someone is guilty of a crime after taking into account all of the evidence, or discovering that a particular route is the best possible way to get from point A to point B, considering the traffic, the speed limits, and the road conditions.

A corresponding distinction can be made between convergent and divergent insight. In *convergent insight*, one discovers a creative structure or solution that makes sense out of apparently disconnected facts. This is exemplified in classic insight problems, where conventional approaches will not work (Gardner, 1978; Metcalfe & Wiebe, 1987; Weisberg & Alba, 1981). Convergent insight is particularly useful in solving mysteries, where one must collect relevant clues and then discover a coherent explanation for them. The use of convergent insight to solve various types of problems is addressed in other chapters in this book (e.g., see chapter 7) and will not be considered further here.

Divergent insight, in contrast, occurs when one begins with a structure and seeks to find novel uses for it or novel implications of it. As shown by studies on problem finding, artists often generate interesting structures without specific goals in mind, simply to explore the possibilities those structures afford (Getzels & Csikszentmihalyi, 1976; Perkins, 1981). One takes a function-follows-form approach rather than a form-follows-function approach (Finke, 1990). Divergent insight can be likened to the explorer who follows a path to see what might be discovered rather than to confirm what is already known or suspected. In divergent insight, one tries to find the meaning in the structure rather than to structure that which is meaningful. In this chapter, divergent insight will be explored within the framework of creative cognition by using the technique of generating and interpreting preinventive forms.

PREINVENTIVE FORMS

Divergent Insight Using Preinventive Forms

The studies I will describe are taken from Finke (1990). They were designed to investigate the use of mental synthesis in discovering creative inventions and concepts and were based on methods initially developed by Finke and Slayton (1988).

Figure 8.1
Set of object parts in experiments on generating and interpreting preinventive forms. The following names were used to designate each of the parts, from left to right and top to bottom: sphere, half-sphere, cube, cone, cylinder, rectangular block, wire, tube, bracket, flat square, hook, cross, wheels, ring, and handle. (Reprinted with permission from R.A. Finke [1990], *Creative imagery: Discoveries and inventions in visualization*. Hillsdale, NJ: Erlbaum.)

258   The Invention-based Approach

At the beginning of each experiment, subjects were shown the 15 object parts displayed in figure 8.1, which were given simple labels such as *sphere*, *half-sphere*, and *cube*. At the start of each trial, three of these parts were chosen randomly and named. The subjects were instructed to use all three parts to imagine an interesting-looking object, one that might be useful in some general way. The parts could be combined in virtually any manner; they could vary in size, position, orientation, or material, with the constraint that the basic shape of the parts could not be altered, except for the wire and the tube, which were both bendable. Sometimes the same part would be named more than once, in which case the subject would have to use that part the designated number of times. The subjects were also told to try to avoid making their forms correspond to any specific familiar type of object.

Examples of these preinventive forms are shown in figure 8.2. The subjects had little difficulty completing them within a 1-minute time period. They then drew their forms on a response sheet, whereupon they were given the name of a general object category, which was chosen at random and selected from one of the eight possibilities shown in table 8.1. The subjects' task was to try to interpret their preinventive forms as a practical object or device within that category, and they were given 1 minute to do so. For instance, if the category was *furniture*, the subject would try to interpret his or her preinventive form as a chair, a table, or some other type of furniture. Subjects were never told to try to be creative but simply to think of some practical way that the form could be used within that category. They were then asked to provide a description of the object and how it functioned.

The resulting inventions were rated by judges for their apparent originality and practicality, using a 5-point scale. These ratings were then used to classify the forms into one of three categories. If a form received high ratings on both originality and practicality, it was classified as a creative invention. If the form received high ratings on practicality but not originality, it was classified as a practical invention. If the form did not receive high ratings on either dimension, it was classified as an impractical invention. Details of the rating and classification procedure are reported in Finke (1990).

On the average, the subjects were able to interpret their preinventive forms as a creative invention in approximately one out of

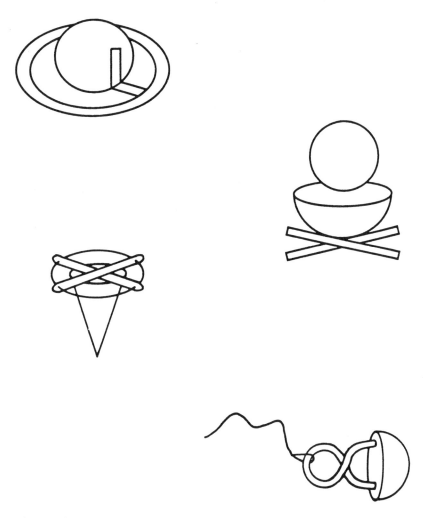

Figure 8.2
Examples of preinventive forms, constructed by mentally combining three of the parts shown in figure 8.1. (Reprinted with permission from R.A. Finke [1990], *Creative imagery: Discoveries and inventions in visualization*. Hillsdale, NJ: Erlbaum.)

Table 8.1
Allowable object categories in preinventive form studies

Category	Examples
Furniture	Chairs, tables, lamps
Personal items	Jewelry, glasses
Transportation	Cars, boats
Scientific instruments	Measuring devices
Appliances	Washing machines, toasters
Tools and utensils	Screwdrivers, spoons
Weapons	Guns, missles
Toys and games	Baseball bats, dolls

Source: Reprinted with permission from R.A. Finke (1990), *Creative imagery: Discoveries and inventions in visualization*. Hillsdale, NJ: Erlbaum.

every six trials. Of the 360 trials in the experiment, there were a total of 120 practical inventions and 65 creative inventions. This was remarkable, given the time constraints for interpreting the forms, the lack of any prior training or practice, and the fact that the subjects were not preselected in any way.

The likelihood of discovering a creative invention was reduced, however, when the subjects were allowed to choose the object category or its parts, or when the category was specified before the preinventive forms were constructed. These findings imply that divergent insight is enhanced when one is forced to explore a structure in unusual or unexpected ways. In addition, the subjects were more likely to make a creative discovery when they were using preinventive forms that they themselves had generated rather than forms that other subjects had provided. This latter finding indicates that divergent insight involves more than simply coming up with creative interpretations of arbitrary shapes and forms.

Some examples of creative inventions that were reported in these experiments are presented in figures 8.3 through 8.5. Displayed here are a *contact lens remover*, a scientific instrument called a *tension wind vane*, and a personal item called a *universal reacher*. These and other inventions that were inspired by the preinventive forms are all the more striking given the severe time limitations that were imposed. When subjects are given extended

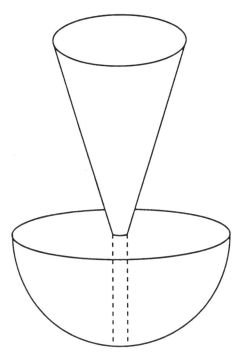

Figure 8.3
The contact lens remover, constructed using the half-sphere, cone, and tube. One places the rubber cone against the contact lens, covers the back of the tube with a finger, lifts the contact off the eye, and then removes the contact from the cone by releasing the finger from the tube. (Reprinted with permission from R.A. Finke [1990], *Creative imagery: Discoveries and inventions in visualization.* Hillsdale, NJ: Erlbaum.)

time to explore their preinventive forms, a creative invention of some sort can be discovered on virtually every trial (Finke, 1990).

Divergent Insight and Suspending Expertise

These studies call attention to the importance of suspending expertise in creative exploration (Johnson-Laird, 1988b). If one has strong expectations about how something should turn out, as when one already knows the type of invention that is required or the type of problem that needs to be solved, one tends to constrain the structure of the forms and the direction of creative explora-

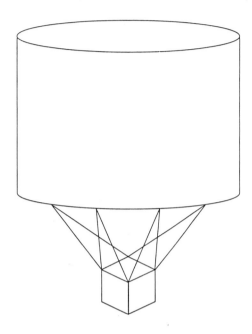

Figure 8.4
The tension wind vane, constructed using the cube, wire, and cylinder.
The cylinder acts as a large sail; as the wind presses against it, slight
changes in its position are recorded by measuring changes in the tension
of the supporting wires. This enables one to make sensitive measures of
wind speed and direction. (Reprinted with permission from R.A. Finke
[1990], *Creative imagery: Discoveries and inventions in visualization.*
Hillsdale, NJ: Erlbaum.)

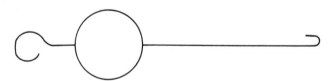

Figure 8.5
The universal reacher, constructed using the hook, sphere, and wire. The
wire is drawn out of the sphere and can be shaped and bent to retrieve
things that fall into hard-to-reach places, while the hook allows the
device to be secured so that both hands can be used to guide the wire.
(Reprinted with permission from R.A. Finke [1990], *Creative imagery:
Discoveries and inventions in visualization.* Hillsdale, NJ: Erlbaum.)

tion. Not knowing these constraints, at least initially, helps one to generate preinventive forms that have a more natural, universal structure. The forms can then be explored not to confirm one's expectations but to allow divergent insights to emerge.

Practical Development and Refinement of Inventions

It should be noted that objects that were classified as inventions in these studies do not necessarily represent the final form that an actual, working invention would take. Indeed, invention prototypes usually need to undergo extensive refinement, testing, and modification (Finke et al., 1992). Rather, these preinventive forms represented the essential idea or concept behind the invention.

Readers can attempt to use these methods to generate and explore their own preinventive forms. Randomly pick out three of the parts shown in figure 8.1 and construct a preinventive form using all three of the parts. Then select one of the object categories in table 8.1, again at random, and try to interpret your form as a new invention within that category. Once you discover a creative invention, you can then refine your design as needed.

Divergent Exploration along Multiple Paths

In showing these inventions to others, I have found that people often think that the inventions were designed with the particular functions indicated by their labels in mind. For instance, in looking at the contact lens remover in figure 8.3, one might have the impression that the form was designed specifically to be this type of object. However, this is an illusion, which I have called the *illusion of intentionality* (Finke, 1990). Had other categories been selected, the same preinventive form would have been interpreted in completely different ways, which, in retrospect, might have seemed just as intentional.

The illusion of intentionality has been explored by having subjects interpret a single form as a different invention within each of the eight object categories. This can be accomplished without difficulty, given sufficient time to interpret the forms. Figure 8.6 presents one of my own attempts to span the categories in this manner, by interpreting a single form in multiple ways. Preinven-

Figure 8.6
Multiple interpretations of a single preinventive form, spanning the eight object categories as follows, from left to right and top to bottom: lawn lounger (furniture); global earrings (personal items); water weigher (scientific instruments); portable agitator (appliances); water sled (transportation); rotating masher (tools and utensils); ring spinner (toys and games); and slasher basher (weapons). (Reprinted with permission from R.A. Finke [1990], *Creative imagery: Discoveries and inventions in visualization.* Hillsdale, NJ: Erlbaum.)

Table 8.2
Allowable subject categories in conceptual interpretation studies

Category	Examples
Architecture	Concepts in building design
Physics and astronomy	Models of the atom, universe
Biology	Methods of animal survival
Medicine	Mechanisms of infection
Psychology	Theories of personality
Literature	Writing styles, techniques
Music	Composition, instrumentation
Political science	Forms of government

Source: Reprinted with permission from R.A. Finke (1990), *Creative imagery: Discoveries and inventions in visualization.* Hillsdale, NJ: Erlbaum.

tive forms can lead to many divergent insights, depending on the particular interpretive paths one chooses to follow.

Conceptual Interpretations of Preinventive Forms

In addition to literal interpretations as concrete objects and inventions, preinventive forms can also be interpreted in more figurative, metaphorical ways, leading to new conceptual insights. This has been shown in variations on the previous studies. After generating preinventive forms, subjects were given a conceptual category, selected at random from those listed in table 8.2. Their task was now to interpret their forms as representing an abstract concept or idea that pertained to that category. For example, if the category were *medicine*, they would try to interpret their forms as a metaphor for how to cure an illness or prevent a disease. It was emphasized that these were to be abstract interpretations. The concepts were then rated on the dimensions of originality and sensibility (where practicality was no longer appropriate, as a creative idea could be sensible without having any obvious practical implications). These ratings were then used to classify the concepts into the categories *creative concepts*, *sensible concepts*, and *nonsensible concepts*.

As might be expected, this task was more difficult than that in which the forms had been interpreted as inventions. On the average, using the same time restrictions as before, creative concepts

Figure 8.7
The concept of conceptual distancing, represented using the cylinder and
two half-spheres. The idea is that people who think or believe in similar
ways often distance themselves in a relationship. (Reprinted with permission from R.A. Finke [1990], *Creative imagery: Discoveries and inventions in visualization*. Hillsdale, NJ: Erlbaum.)

were discovered on 8 percent of the trials. As with the creative
inventions, when subjects were allowed to choose the categories,
the creativity of their interpretations was reduced, in which case
they now had the freedom to find more conventional ways of interpreting the forms.

Some examples of creative concepts in these experiments are
presented in the next two figures. *Conceptual distancing*, an idea
in psychology, is shown in figure 8.7, and *viral cancellation*, an
idea in medicine, is shown in figure 8.8. These represent the
kinds of metaphorical insights that one can discover when exploring preinventive forms.

These discoveries are reminiscent of classic examples of creative insight that supposedly occurred as a result of metaphors
that appeared in dreams. The chemist Kekulé, for example, is reported to have had a dream in which he envisioned snakes coiled
into circles, biting their own tails, which gave him the key insight
into the structure of the benzene molecule and which provided
the foundation for modern organic chemistry (Miller, 1984; Shepard, 1978). I believe the creative process underlying these discoveries is similar to that underlying the creative, metaphorical
interpretation of preinventive forms.

In such cases, however, one needs to take into account the illusion of intentionality. Preinventive forms lend themselves naturally to divergent insight; they can be interpreted in many
meaningful ways, each of which might seem intended or inevita-
ble. How a preinventive form ends up being interpreted can depend on particular needs and concerns, but this does not mean

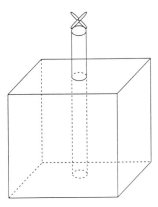

Figure 8.8
The concept of viral cancellation, represented using the tube, cross, and cube. The idea is that two viruses attempting to invade a cell may cancel one another, curing or preventing the disease. (Reprinted with permission from R.A. Finke [1990], *Creative imagery: Discoveries and inventions in visualization*. Hillsdale, NJ: Erlbaum.)

that the form was structured with those considerations in mind. In the case of Kekulé, his coiled snakes might have been interpreted in many other ways besides benzene molecules. If he had been primarily interested in architecture, for example, they might have led him to important insights about how to design a building.

This emphasizes the key distinction between divergent and convergent insight: In convergent insight, one seeks a particular structure that solves a problem or mystery, whereas in divergent insight, one begins with an interesting structure and seeks novel interpretations of it in order to explore new, creative possibilities. Both are important in creativity; one is diagnostic and explanatory, the other playful and exploratory.

THE GENEPLORE MODEL

I next consider the major cognitive processes, structures, properties, and constraints that underlie the use of preinventive forms in divergent insight. This discussion is based on the Geneplore model of creative cognition proposed by Finke, Ward, and Smith (1992).

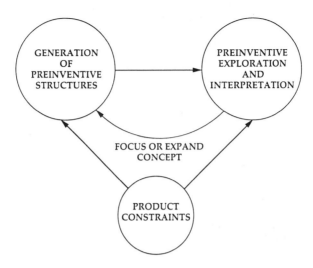

Figure 8.9
The basic structure of the Geneplore model. In the generative phase, one constructs mental representations called *preinventive structures*. In the exploratory phase, one explores various interpretations of these structures, leading to creative insights and discoveries. The resulting concepts can then be focused or expanded according to task requirements or individual needs, by modifying the preinventive structures and repeating the cycle. Constraints on the final product can be imposed during either the generative or the exploratory phase. (Reprinted with permission from R.A. Finke, T.B. Ward, and S.M. Smith [1992], *Creative cognition: Theory, research and applications.* Cambridge: MIT Press.)

The basic structure of the Geneplore model is shown in figure 8.9. Briefly, this model proposes that creative thinking involves two distinct processing stages. In the *generative* stage, mental representations called *preinventive structures* are generated for the purpose of creative exploration, of which preinventive forms are one example. They have various properties, to be considered shortly, that promote creative insight and discovery. In the *exploratory* phase, the structures are explored to discover the creative, interpretive possibilities they afford. These discoveries, in turn, can lead to modifications of the existing structures or the generation of entirely new structures, where the cycle can then be repeated.

Constraints on the structures or their interpretations can be imposed at any time, depending on task demands and individual needs. The optimal time to impose these constraints is regarded as an empirical question that can be answered in creative cognition experiments. As shown in the preinventive form studies, for example, people are more likely to discover creative inventions when constraints on the interpretive categories are imposed only after the forms are generated. There are cases, however, in which it would be necessary to impose such constraints before the forms are generated, as when it is essential to include a particular feature in a design or when a particular function must be satisfied.

Table 8.3 presents the major types of generative and exploratory processes, preinventive structures and their properties, and product constraints. Each of these will be described in some detail in the following sections.

Generative Processes

The most basic generative processes consist of retrieving existing forms or structures from memory and forming associations among them. Various object parts or features could be retrieved and associated in novel ways, leading to new insights for how to design a better product. Alternatively, various words could be recalled and associated to form interesting word combinations, such as *computer mower*, leading to creative verbal or semantic possibilities. These simple associations form the basis of many popular techniques for enhancing creativity, such as *morphological synthesis* (e.g., Allen, 1962).

Mental synthesis and *mental transformation*, which are more complex generative processes, were highlighted in the preinventive form studies. Recall that subjects in these studies were given various object parts and were instructed to imagine assembling them to make a single object. They could combine the parts in any way they wished, transforming their size, position, or orientation in order to do so. As these studies showed, mental synthesis and transformation allow for considerable flexibility in creating new structures, whose novelty and intricacy often result in surprising discoveries. These generative processes are not restricted to preinventive forms and inventions but can be used to generate more abstract and global structures, such as conceptual combinations (Hampton, 1987) and mental models (Johnson-Laird, 1983).

Table 8.3
Examples of cognitive processes, structures, properties, and constraints in the Geneplore model

Generative processes
Retrieval
Association
Synthesis
Transformation
Analogical transfer
Categorical reduction

Preinventive structures
Visual patterns
Object forms
Mental blends
Category exemplars
Mental models
Verbal combinations

Preinventive properties
Novelty
Ambiguity
Meaningfulness
Emergence
Incongruity
Divergence

Exploratory processes
Attribute finding
Conceptual interpretation
Functional inference
Contextual shifting
Hypothesis testing
Searching for limitations

Product constraints
Product type
Category
Features
Functions
Components
Resources

Source: Reprinted with permission from R.A. Finke, T.B. Ward, and S.M. Smith (1992), *Creative cognition: Theory, research, and applications.* Cambridge: MIT Press.

Another generative process is *analogical transfer*, which refers to taking a relationship or set of relationships from one context and transferring it to another. The resulting preinventive structures are then analogous to those that are already familiar, leading to possible creative insights in the new context. For instance, early models for the structure of the atom were generated by transferring established models of the solar system. The relation between the atomic nucleus and its electrons was assumed to be analogous to that between the sun and its orbiting planets. Analogical transfer has been used extensively in the creativity training technique known as *synectics* (Gordon, 1961).

Finally, in the generative process known as *categorical reduction*, one takes a familiar object or structure and then mentally reduces it to more primitive categorical descriptions. For instance, one might take a chair and regard it not in the familiar way, as a piece of furniture, but as a more basic form having various geometrical properties. The result is that one often ends up with a structure that is less loaded categorically and is more likely to be interpreted in creative ways (Finke, Ward & Smith, 1992).

Most of these generative processes have already been studied extensively in traditional areas of cognitive psychology. There is an enormous body of literature, for example, on associative memory and its functions (e.g., Anderson & Bower, 1973; McClelland & Rumelhart, 1986; Mandler, 1980). There have been many recent studies on mental synthesis and transformation, which have helped to reveal their roles in mental imagery, visual comparison, and spatial cognition (Finke, 1989; Finke, Pinker & Farah, 1989; Pinker, 1984; Shepard & Cooper, 1982). Research on analogical transfer has become a major focus in the area of human problem solving (Gentner, 1989; Gick & Holyoak, 1980; Novick, 1988).

Creative cognition not only makes contact with these traditional areas; it also suggests new ways in which they can be extended and developed in creative directions. For example, conventional theories of how mental images are formed, scanned, and interpreted, or of how conceptual categories are constructed and used, could be expanded in light of new findings on the creative aspects of these generative processes.

Preinventive Structures

In addition to preinventive object forms, there are many other types of preinventive structures that are considered in the Geneplore model. Perhaps the simplest are visual patterns and designs that are created by imagining combinations of lines, circles, squares, and other two-dimensional figures, resulting in creative symbols and logos (Finke et al., 1989). These can often be used creatively in advertising and marketing.

Another type of preinventive structure is the *mental blend*, which refers collectively to conceptual combinations, metaphors, and blended mental images. For example, one could imagine combining a bicycle with a surfboard, or the concept of democracy with that of evolution. These mental blends often yield emergent properties and creative discoveries that would not have been anticipated from either of the components alone (Finke et al., 1992; Murphy, 1988).

Preinventive structures called *category exemplars* are created when one generates possible members of unusual or hypothetical categories. These category examplars often have features in common with members of more familiar categories, but they can also have emergent features that lead to creative insights. For example, if asked to imagine an alien creature that lives on a planet very different from Earth, subjects generate creatures that have many features in common with familiar earth animals but that also display a variety of novel features and combinations of features (Ward, 1991).

Larger-scale preinventive structures called *mental models* can also be generated, which represent mechanical and physical systems as well as global, conceptual systems (Gentner & Stevens, 1983; Johnson-Laird, 1983). For instance, one might generate a mental model for how a particular machine works, how the universe was formed, or how a certain piece of music might have been composed. These models can then be tested and refined, leading to additional insights and discoveries.

Finally, preinventive structures can consist of various types of verbal combinations that suggest interesting or novel relations among words or phrases. These combinations are frequently seen in the familiar word play of creative writers, and they have many poetic and other literary applications. Verbal combinations are encouraged in modern "free-writing" techniques, in which one freely generates verbal structures that come to mind and then explores their possible implications (e.g., Elbow, 1981).

Preinventive Properties

What are the properties of preinventive structures that promote creative exploration and that increase the likelihood that a creative insight will emerge? First, and probably most important, the structures should be *novel*. Although it is certainly possible to take a common form or structure and find creative interpretations of it (e.g., Finke et al., 1989), one is more likely to discover a new insight if the structures are relatively uncommon initially.

Second, the structures should be fairly *ambiguous*, lending themselves to a variety of possible interpretations. Like classic ambiguous figures in perception (Attneave, 1971; Shepard, 1990), preinventive structures should have sufficient ambiguity that they allow for multiple paths of exploration and discovery.

Third, there should be an underlying sense of *meaningfulness* about the structures; they should convey the feeling that they have some deeper significance that is yet to be discovered. This is why preinventive structures are often less useful when assembled in arbitrary or haphazard ways (Finke, 1990), as is sometimes recommended in popular creativity techniques (e.g., Adams, 1974).

Fourth, preinventive structures should have *emergent features* that were not explicitly present in or implied by any of their components. This increases the prospects for genuine discovery during the exploratory phase. It also helps to address the criticism that there is nothing truly special about insight, that people are simply retrieving and applying knowledge they already possess Perkins, 1981; Weisberg, 1986).

A fifth property that contributes to creative insight is *incongruity*. Typically, whenever the parts of a preinventive structure appear to conflict, one is motivated to find ways to remove those inconsistencies. This often results in the discovery of deeper relations and implications, and helps to account for the important role that paradox seems to play in the creative process (Koestler, 1964).

The sixth property is *divergence*, which refers to the capacity for the same structure to have different uses within a variety of different contexts. It is especially relevant to divergent insight. Divergence differs from ambiguity in that a structure could have a single, obvious description or interpretation but be useful in many different ways. For instance, a brick is not a very ambiguous form, but it can have many possible uses—as a building block, a paperweight, or a projectile. This property was illustrated in the spanning-the-categories task that was described previously (see figure 8.6).

This is not intended to be a complete list, nor is it implied that these properties are independent. For example, a structure that has a high degree of incongruity is also likely to be quite novel. Rather, it is suggested that these are the main properties one would want to keep in mind when generating preinventive forms. As a rule, they would increase the likelihood of achieving divergent insights and making creative discoveries.

Exploratory Processes

The Geneplore model also considers various types of exploratory processes that can be used when attempting to interpret a preinventive structure. The first, *attribute finding*, refers to the systematic search for emergent features. For example, a person might start out by generating a preinventive form using mental synthesis and then search for unusual or unexpected features in the resulting structure. Attribute finding can also be used to explore emergent properties in conceptual combinations and metaphors.

Conceptual interpretation refers to the process of taking a preinventive structure and finding a metaphorical or theoretical interpretation of it. This process was illustrated in the studies in which subjects were to interpret their preinventive forms as representing abstract ideas in general subject categories such as medicine and literature. More generally, conceptual interpretation can be viewed as applying one's world knowledge to the task of creative exploration.

Functional inference refers to the process of exploring the potential uses or functions of a preinventive structure. This exploratory process is most commonly used when trying to discover new inventions and practical devices, but it is also important in evaluating and testing mental models. Often, the process is facilitated by imagining oneself using the structure or becoming personally involved in it.

In the next exploratory process, *contextual shifting*, one considers a preinventive structure in a new or different context as a way of gaining new insights into its possible uses or interpretations. Contextual shifting is especially helpful when trying to overcome mental blocks to creative thinking. For instance, if one were stuck while trying to interpret a preinventive form as a new kind of tool, one could imagine using the tool in different rooms of one's house, with different types of appliances, or under unusual circumstances, such as when having to fix a broken ladder.

Preinventive structures can also be explored for their possible value in testing hypotheses or solving problems. For example, a person who is stuck on a math problem might generate preinventive structures that could conceivably be related to the problem and then explore whether any of those structures might suggest a solution. In this way, creative solutions to the problem might be found when more direct methods fail.

Yet another exploratory process is *searching for limitations*. In addition to providing insights into creative possibilities and solutions, preinventive structures can provide insights into which ideas or approaches will not work. These discoveries can then restrict future searches and can focus creative exploration in more promising directions. For example, a mental model for an economic system could be explored to discover why it fails, uncovering those features that should be removed and revealing those that need to be included.

In the preinventive form studies, subjects reported using many of these exploratory processes. For example, they often imagined inspecting their forms for interesting or unusual attributes, manipulating the forms in playful ways to discover what functions they might have, placing the forms in different contexts, and regarding the forms as visual metaphors (Finke, 1990). Subjects also tended to become deeply involved in their imaginative explorations, in much the same way that one might become involved in a daydream or a novel (Hilgard, 1977).

Many of the creative discoveries that result from these exploratory processes are genuinely surprising and elicit the classic feeling of sudden insight. Nevertheless, I believe that most of these
processes are highly structured and deliberate. For example, if a
person were trying to interpret a preinventive form as a piece of
furniture, the person might intentionally imagine placing the
form in various rooms of his or her house, having people try to
sit on it, putting various appliances on top of it, and so on, until
new insights emerged. Whereas the insights themselves might be
surprising (Metcalfe, 1986), the exploratory processes from which
they are derived would be under the strategic control of the individual. Although some investigators have argued that insights
sometimes do arise after periods of incubation, during which one
avoids thinking about an issue or problem (e.g., Smith & Vela,
1991; see also chapter 7), I suspect that the majority of creative
discoveries are the result of purposeful explorations.

Product Constraints

Lastly, the Geneplore model considers various types of constraints
that could be imposed on the resulting creative products. These
constraints might be imposed during either the generative or exploratory phase. First, the particular type of product or product category could be constrained. One might require, for example, that
the preinventive structure turn out to be a new type of clock or piece
of furniture. Second, the particular features or functions that the product must display could be constrained: The product might have to
be a certain size or shape, or travel at a certain speed. Third, there
might be constraints on the particular components that are available or on how much money one can spend. As mentioned previously, using the methods of creative cognition, the optimal time
for imposing these various constraints could be determined empirically.

PRACTICAL IMPLICATIONS

Let us consider just a few of the many practical implications of
the methods of creative cognition in stimulating divergent insight and creative discovery.

Product Development

First, the technique of generating and then interpreting preinventive forms has important implications for current efforts to find new ways to develop creative products. Inventions that result from explorations of these forms may have greater intrinsic fascination and appeal, qualities that would very likely enhance the marketability of the resulting products. In fact, when people are shown examples of creative inventions in the preinventive form experiments, they often comment that they would be very interested in owning such a product. This appeal is often lacking in products that are novel only by virtue of having unusual or gimicky features.

Scientific and Conceptual Advances

The methods of creative cognition are also useful for trying to explore new conceptual possibilities in various scientific fields. For instance, preinventive forms could be used as catalysts for creative insights in physics, chemistry, or medicine, where analytical methods alone might be insufficient. A physicist, for example, might try to interpret preinventive forms as representing potentially new concepts in atomic theory or relativity. A medical researcher could explore possible interpretations of a preinventive form to discover new ideas for how to treat a disease.

Creativity Training in the Sciences

At the present time, creativity is seldom emphasized in training people to become scientists or researchers. This is unfortunate, given the many cases in which creative insights resulted from *Gedanken*, or "thought" experiments, in which one envisions a hypothetical, often paradoxical situation and considers its consequences. Techniques for generating preinventive forms and for exploring their creative possibilities might therefore facilitate creative thinking in scientific training.

Creative Artificial Intelligence

The studies reported here also suggest new ways for enhancing creative processes in computers, and may lead to the development of new, more creative forms of artificial intelligence (e.g., see Boden, 1991; Johnson-Laird, 1988a). One practical approach would be to first develop computer programs for generating preinventive forms, taking into account their various properties. These computer-generated forms could then be used to assist creative discovery. With further advances in artificial intelligence, computers could then take over more and more of the exploratory processes. Eventually, heuristics could be developed that would permit computers to identify the most promising creative paths for particular fields of research or topics of interest.

REFERENCES

Adams, J.L. (1974). *Conceptual blockbusting.* Stanford, CA: Stanford Alumni Association.

Allen, M.S. (1962). *Morphological creativity.* Englewood Cliffs, NJ: Prentice Hall.

Anderson, J.R., & Bower, G.H. (1973). *Human associative memory.* New York: Wiley.

Attneave, F. (1971). Multistability in perception. *Scientific American, 225,* 62–71.

Boden, M. (1991). *The creative mind: Myths and mechanisms.* New York: Basic Books.

Elbow, P. (1981). *Writing without teachers.* London: Oxford University Press.

Finke, R.A. (1989). *Principles of mental imagery.* Cambridge: MIT Press.

Finke, R.A. (1990). *Creative imagery: Discoveries and inventions in visualization.* Hillsdale, NJ: Erlbaum.

Finke, R.A., Pinker, S., & Farah, M.J. (1989). Reinterpreting visual patterns in mental imagery. *Cognitive Science, 13,* 51–78.

Finke, R.A., & Slayton, K. (1988). Explorations of creative visual synthesis in mental imagery. *Memory & Cognition, 16,* 252–257.

Finke, R.A., Ward, T.B., & Smith, S.M. (1992). *Creative cognition: Theory, research, and applications.* Cambridge: MIT Press.

Gardner, M. (1978). *Aha! Insight.* New York: Freeman.

Gentner, D. (1989). The mechanisms of analogical learning. In S. Vosniadou & A. Ortony (Eds.), *Similarity and analogical reasoning.* Cambridge, England: Cambridge University Press.

Gentner, D., & Stevens, A.L. (1983). *Mental models.* Hillsdale, NJ: Erlbaum.

Getzels, J.W., & Csikszentmihalyi, M. (1976). *The creative vision: A longitudinal study of problem finding in art.* New York: Wiley.

Gick, M.L., & Holyoak, K.J. (1980). Analogical problem solving. *Cognitive Psychology, 12,* 306–355.

Gordon, W. (1961). *Synectics: The development of creative capacity.* New York: Harper & Row.

Guilford, J.P. (1956). The structure of intellect. *Psychological Bulletin, 53,* 267–293.

Hampton, J.A. (1987). Inheritance of attributes in natural concept conjunctions. *Memory & Cognition, 15,* 55–71.

Hilgard, E.R. (1977). *Divided consciousness: Multiple controls in human thought and action.* New York: Wiley-Interscience.

Johnson-Laird, P.N. (1983). *Mental models: Towards a cognitive science of language, inference, and consciousness.* Cambridge, England: Cambridge University Press.

Johnson-Laird, P.N. (1988a). *The computer and the mind: An introduction to cognitive science.* Cambridge: Harvard University Press.

Johnson-Laird, P.N. (1988b). Freedom and constraint in creativity. In R.J. Sternberg (Ed.), *The nature of creativity: Contemporary psychological perspectives* (pp. 202–249). Cambridge, England: Cambridge University Press.

Koestler, A. (1964). *The act of creation.* New York: Macmillan.

Maier, N.R.F. (1931). Reasoning in humans: II. The solution of a problem and its appearance in consciousness. *Journal of Comparative Psychology, 12,* 181–194.

Mandler, G. (1980). Recognizing: The judgment of previous occurrence. *Psychological Review, 87,* 252–271.

McClelland, J.L., & Rumelhart, D.E. (1986). *Parallel distributed processing: Explorations in the microstructure of cognition.* Cambridge: MIT Press.

Mednick, S.A. (1962). The associative basis of the creative process. *Psychological Review, 69,* 220–232.

Metcalfe, J. (1986). Feelings of knowing in memory and problem solving. *Journal of Experimental Psychology: Learning, Memory, and Cognition, 12,* 288–294.

Metcalfe, J., & Wiebe, D. (1987). Intuition in insight and non-insight problem solving. *Memory & Cognition, 12*, 623– 634.

Miller, A.I. (1984). *Imagery in scientific thought.* Cambridge: MIT Press.

Murphy, G.L. (1988). Comprehending complex concepts. *Cognitive Science, 12*, 529–562.

Neisser, U. (1976). *Cognition and reality.* San Francisco: Freeman.

Novick, L. (1988). Analogical transfer, problem similarity, and expertise. *Journal of Experimental Psychology: Learning, Memory, and Cognition, 14*, 510–520.

Perkins, D.N. (1981). *The mind's best work.* Cambridge: Harvard University Press.

Pinker, S. (1984). Visual cognition: An introduction. *Cognition, 18*, 1–63.

Shepard, R.N. (1978). Externalization of mental images and the act of creation. In B.S. Randhawa & W.E. Coffman (Eds.), *Visual learning, thinking, and communication* (pp. 133–189). New York: Academic Press.

Shepard, R.N. (1990). *Mind sights.* New York: Freeman.

Shepard, R.N., & Cooper, L.A. (1982). *Mental images and their transformations.* Cambridge: MIT Press.

Smith, S.M., & Vela, E. (1991). Incubated reminiscence effects. *Memory & Cognition, 19*, 168–176.

Ward, T.M. (1991, November). *Structured imagination: The role of conceptual structure in exemplar generation.* Paper presented at the annual meeting of the Psychonomic Society, San Francisco, CA.

Weisberg, R.W. (1986). *Creativity, genius, and other myths.* New York: Freeman.

Weisberg, R.W., & Alba, J.W. (1981). An examination of the alleged role of "fixation" in the solution of several "insight" problems. *Journal of Experimental Psychology: General, 110*, 169–192.

9 Constraints on Thinking in Insight and Invention

Matthew I. Isaak and Marcel Adam Just

At long last, your midmorning coffee break arrives. Soon after ingesting a doughnut of indifferent texture, you find yourself in the photocopying room with an armful of documents to copy. The machine processes the first ten copies swimmingly; thankfully, you close your eyes for a split second and sip your coffee. Your brief reverie is then shattered by loud noises emanating from the copier. Glancing at the control panel, you find that a jam has occurred in something cryptically termed the *feeder path*. Knowing that the copier service personnel are unlikely to arrive in the foreseeable future, you attempt to fix the machine yourself. After you skim and ultimately disregard the telegraphic instructions and generic line drawings appearing in the copier's manual, you carefully lift the machine's hood and attempt to trace the paper's odyssey through a labyrinth of rollers, belts, and trays. After initially lifting a roller or two, you catch on, discovering how to retrieve the tangled paper. You congratulate yourself as you lock the copier's hood into place and smile, thinking that the only insight that escaped you is how to get the toner smudges off your dry-clean-only shirt before the workday ends.

That evening, you settle into your favorite armchair to watch the latest new release from your neighborhood video outlet. Glancing at the VCR, though, you discover that the videocassette is in the player but has been ejected. Although you can eject a videocassette from your chair using your remote control unit, you cannot insert an ejected cassette into play position using your remote control. You wish they'd invent a VCR system whose remote control incorporates such a feature.

Mechanical problem solving often is very challenging. As in the case of the malfunctioning photocopier, the solution to a mechanical problem is frequently opaque. The solution exists, but neither its nature nor the means to achieve it may be known. If the problem is solved, though, insight frequently is experienced. Alternatively, the solution to a mechanical problem may not exist yet, as in the case of the user-hostile VCR remote control. Invention is required to generate novel solutions to such problems.

Both laypersons and professionals experience insight and perform acts of invention while solving mechanical problems. Mechanical insight is experienced not only by the hapless novice confronted by, say, a malfunctioning photocopier but also by mechanical experts such as mechanics, machine operators, and repair persons who must daily assemble, operate, and repair mechanical devices. Mechanical insight is a workaday component of such experts' professional challenges. Similarly, while corporate America employs numerous research and development specialists in the service of technological and mechanical invention, our VCR example demonstrates that almost everyone regularly identifies problems requiring novel solutions, which is one step in mechanical invention. Mechanical insight and invention are neither magical nor rare phenomena but instead occur in the everyday problem solving of both experts and novices.

INSIGHT AND INVENTION AS PROBLEM-SOLVING PHENOMENA

In this chapter, we construe insight and invention as problem-solving phenomena. During problem solving, subjects attempt to reach some goal: A secretary, for example, might wish to retrieve crumpled paper from a jammed photocopier. A problem's goal, however, is not immediately attainable. Rather, subjects must decompose the problem into several subgoals. A secretary may have to expose the crumpled paper before it can be reached. Exposing the paper thus becomes a subgoal in the service of the overall goal of retrieving the paper. Operators are used to achieve subgoals, transforming a problem progressively from its initial state, through intermediate states, to its goal state. A secretary might use the lift-roller operator to expose tangled copier paper.

Subjects' choice of operators to move between problem states is typically constrained rather than unlimited. Constraints limit the space of legal intermediate states or operators during problem solving. Consider, for example, cryptarithmetic problems, such as

DONALD + GERALD = ROBERT (Bartlett, 1958). In cryptarithmetic problems, each of the ten digits has a unique alphabetic equivalent. Subjects are given one correspondence, such as $D = 5$, and then are asked to find the values of the remaining letters. These problems include the explicit constraint that different letters cannot stand for the same digit. This unique correspondence constraint prohibits subjects from using, for example, an operator in which A corresponds to 5 when the $D = 5$ correspondence is given. The unique correspondence constraint thus reduces the number of alternative values that subjects may consider at each point during their solution of the problem.

Cryptarithmetic problems are standard problems in which subjects use well-defined operators to move progressively toward the goal. During the course of solving such problems, subjects typically feel incrementally closer to the goal (Metcalfe, 1986; Metcalfe & Wiebe, 1987). Other standard problems include textbook algebra exercises. There is, however, a class of problems, termed insight problems, in which subjects initially use operators that fail to move them toward the goal. While solving insight problems, subjects feel no closer to the solution until they actually reach it (Metcalfe, 1986; Metcalfe & Wiebe, 1987). When the solution is reached, however, subjects usually experience a sudden flash of illumination (Hadamard, 1945; Metcalfe, 1986; Metcalfe & Wiebe, 1987).

Like cryptarithmetic problems, insight problems often include explicit operator selection constraints in their instructions. An often-studied insight problem, the nine-dot problem (see problem 3 in appendix A), requires subjects to join each of nine dots arranged in a 3×3 array with four connected straight lines. These instructions include the explicit operator constraints that lines may not be curved, the pencil should not leave the paper during drawing, and no more than four lines may be used.

One of our major proposals is that insight problems often contain information that leads subjects incorrectly to accept additional operator constraints not mandated by the problem. These additional constraints prevent subjects from using the operators necessary to solve the problem. For example, subjects solving the nine-dot problem generally represent the array as a bounded square. Subjects therefore draw the square perimeter, joining the array's outer dots and leaving the center dot unconnected (Weis-

Table 9.1
Insight problems and the unwarranted operator constraint(s) that must be released in each

Problem	Reference	Operator constraints requiring release
1. Two strings	Maier, 1931	Use chair to reach and secure strings
2. Candle	Duncker, 1945	Box functions as a container
3. Nine dots	Weisberg & Alba, 1981	Contain lines within a square perimeter; use only nondiagonal lines
4. Pigpen	Fixx, 1972	Squares sit on sides; each pig's pen is square, not diamond
5. Necklace	Wickelgren, 1974	Keep chains intact; perform same action on each chain
6. Water lilies	Sternberg & Davidson, 1983	Work forward: sum from zero
7. Matchsticks	Scheerer, 1963	Arrange matches in two dimensions
8. Radiation	Gick & Holyoak, 1980	Ray is indivisible
9. Horse and rider	Scheerer, Goldstein, & Boring, 1941	Keep horses intact
10. Glasses and knives	DeBono, 1967	Use all knives; length of side of supporting platform equals the length of a knife
11. Moneylender	DeBono, 1967	Path is irrelevant
12. Prisoner and rope	Metcalfe & Wiebe, 1987	Segment rope horizontally
13. Pyramid and dollar bill	Unpublished source	Dollar bill cannot be destroyed
14. Triangle of coins	Freedman, 1978	Interchange top and bottom portions of pyramid as whole units
15. Hat rack	Maier, 1945	Floor and ceiling are irrelevant
16. Ten dollars	Gleitman, 1991	Keep track of only recipient's money
17. All your pets	Seifert & Patalano, 1991	There is more than one of each type of pet
18. Thirty-dollar room	Freedman, 1978	Goal is to account for $30.00
19. Phone numbers	Kendall & Thomas, 1962	Do not change prefix values
20. Decimal point	Seifert & Patalano, 1991	Use equivalence operators
21. Ratchet device	Carpenter & Just, 1992	Output motion alternates with alternating input motions

berg & Alba, 1981). The bounded-square representation includes the additional constraints that the lines should be nondiagonal and that they should not extend beyond the array's perimeter (see table 9.1). These constraints therefore preclude the use of operators involving diagonal lines and lines extending beyond the array's perimeter. The problem's solution, shown in appendix A, in fact requires both diagonal and extending lines. We will examine how insight problems lead subjects to overconstrain their choice of operators and why subjects have difficulty releasing operator constraints when solving insight problems. Several insight problems and a mechanical insight problem from our own laboratory illustrate our discussion.

Our second major proposal concerns invention. Invention occurs when a novel device is developed to fulfill some need or perform some task. We propose that invention comprises three phases, which may be distinguished in part by the constraint operations appropriate to each. The three phases of invention are (1) design space limitation, in which the inventor narrows the space of potential novel solutions to a problem; (2) design generation, in which the inventor develops candidate novel solutions; and (3) design analysis, in which the inventor evaluates and revises candidate solutions. We argue that successful invention depends on imposing constraints on the nature of the invention during design space limitation and design analysis and on releasing or reformulating constraints during design generation. Design generation thus taps processes similar to those implicated in insight, and invention and insight may be distinguished primarily by the presence of an analytical component in invention. The traditional emphasis on generative processes and the consequent neglect of analytical processes in creativity may thus contribute to the confusion between insight and invention in the literature (e.g., Hadamard, 1945). Our discussion of invention is illustrated by historical examples of mechanical invention.

INSIGHT: RELEASING UNWARRANTED CONSTRAINTS

The example of the nine-dot problem demonstrates that subjects solving insight problems can impose unwarranted operator selection constraints. These constraints prevent them from using the operators required to solve the problem. Other insight problems similarly lead subjects to adopt representations that incorporate maladaptive operator constraints. In the necklace problem (Wickelgren, 1974), for example, 4 chains, each containing 3 links, must be joined to form a necklace containing 12 links (see problem 5 in appendix A). It costs 2 cents to open a link and 3 cents to close a link. The total cost of making the necklace must be no more than 15 cents. The problem's instructions, therefore, explicitly constrain the total cost of the necklace. The correct solution entails opening each of the three links in one of the four chains at a cost of 6 cents, then using the links to join each of the remaining chains at an additional cost of 9 cents. Most subjects, however, attempt to open the terminal links of each chain and then attach the chains directly to one another, incurring a total cost of 40 cents. Subjects attempting to solve the necklace problem in this way additionally constrain their operators such that they perform the same actions on each of the four chains. This constraint is not mandated by the problem's task environment but instead arises through the operation of some Gestalt-like principle of similarity or action symmetry in which equivalent actions are performed on identical objects such as the four chains. To solve the necklace problem, subjects must first release the constraint that each chain be treated identically. They must then determine that one chain may serve as the source of links that may be inserted between each of the remaining chains to form the complete necklace.

The matchsticks problem (Scheerer, 1963) also leads subjects to impose an unwarranted operator constraint (see problem 7 in appendix A). This problem requires subjects to form four equilateral triangles from six matches. Each side of each triangle must be equal to the length of one match Here, subjects constrain the orientations of the matches to two dimensions (see table 9.1). This constraint is not specified in the problem's instructions but instead arises because people tend not to represent spontaneously in their imaginations the third dimension (Hinton, 1979). To solve the matchsticks problem, subjects must release the constraint limiting their arrangements of the matches to two dimensions and then construct a three-dimensional pyramid (see appendix A, problem 7).

A mechanical problem in which subjects' initial representations often overconstrain their choice of operators is the ratchet device problem (see problem 21, appendix A). In our laboratory, subjects view a drawing, computer display, or three-dimensional model of the device and are asked to describe the motion of the gear wheel (on the left of the device) as the handle (on the bottom right of the device) is moved back and forth. While the gear wheel rotates counterclockwise both when the handle moves to the left and when it moves to the right, most subjects respond that the gear wheel alternates between clockwise and counterclockwise rotations as the handle moves back and forth. When subjects are permitted to manipulate the handle, they discover their mistake and often experience insight as they attempt to explain the gear wheel's constant counterclockwise motion.

It seems plausible that subjects encountering the ratchet device problem first adopt a representation in which the handle is seen as a pump. The action of the recipient of a pump's operation is usually alternating. When a water pump is operated, for example, water evacuates when the pump is moved in one direction but not when it is moved in the other direction. Similarly, when a syringe is depressed, liquid is ejected from a needle. When a syringe is pulled up, however, the needle draws in liquid. Subjects using a handle-as-pump representation, therefore, expect alternating actions on the ratchet device's handle to produce alternating motions of the gear wheel. This constraint discourages their use of operators that test the influence of device components intervening between the handle and the gear wheel itself, such as the short bar and the gear wheel's teeth. Next we examine why subjects initially adopt representations that include unwarranted operator constraints. We then examine how subjects later release such constraints in order to solve insight problems.

Initial Representation Selection

Subjects apply and maintain inappropriate operator selection constraints when solving insight problems because (1) such constraints facilitate the solution of everyday problems with task environments similar to those of the insight problems; (2) the features cuing the operators excluded by such constraints are not salient; (3) subjects lack the knowledge necessary to identify the operators excluded by such constraints; and (4) operations on the problem inform subjects of neither the nature of the constraints they are imposing nor the ways such constraints may be released. Each of these reasons for applying and maintaining inappropriate operator constraints will be discussed.

Subjects solving insight problems often adopt inappropriate constraints because the problems resemble everyday situations in which the same constraints are not inappropriate but, in fact, facilitate the problem's solution. In Maier's (1931) two-string problem, for example, a string suspended from the ceiling must be brought sufficiently close to a second suspended string to tie the strings together (see appendix A, problem 1). The correct solution entails attaching the pair of pliers to the first string, allowing the string to act as a pendulum. The string may then be swung sufficiently close to the second string to allow the two to be tied together. Most subjects, however, place the chair midway between the strings, tie the first string to the chair, then attempt to tie the second string to the first string. Subjects constrain their operators to those involving the chair (see table 9.1) because they have more often used chairs than strings to bring or keep objects within reach. After all, chairs serve as stepladders, shelves, anchors, and doorstops more frequently than strings serve as pendulums.

The candle problem (Duncker, 1945; see problem 2, appendix A) requires subjects to use a thumbtack box as a platform to support a candle on a door. Here, subjects constrain the box to function as a container (see table 9.1). They are therefore unable to select operators in which the box functions as a platform. Subjects attempting the candle problem have probably more often used a small box as a container than as a platform in the successful solution of workaday problems.

Finally, the nine-dot problem resembles connect-the-dots exercises found in children's puzzle books. Subjects therefore use the same representation when they solve the nine-dot problem as they did when they solved connect-the-dots exercises. Many of the dots in a connect-the-dots puzzle form the perimeter of the depicted object. Analogously, subjects solving the nine-dot problem neglect to consider operators in which lines are extended beyond the array's perimeter.

Phenomena such as fixation (Weisberg & Alba, 1981) and functional fixedness (Glucksberg, 1962) capture subjects' tendency to apply constraints to insight problems that are logically superfluous but successful during everyday problem solving. *Fixation* occurs when subjects maintain constraints that hinder their achievement of an insight problem's solution. Subjects solving the nine-dot problem, for example, maintain the perimeter constraint, delaying their solution of the problem (Weisberg & Alba, 1981). *Functional fixedness* occurs when subjects attribute conventional functions to objects in a problem whose solution requires them to generate novel object functions. In the candle problem, for example, subjects represent the small box as a container rather than as a platform (Duncker, 1945). This prevents the subjects' use of an operator in which the box is tacked to the wall. Similarly, subjects solving the two-string problem initially represent the pliers in terms of their usual grasping function rather than their novel pendulum function. An operator in which the pliers are fastened to the string as a pendulum's bob is thus ruled out.

In some problems, subjects may be unable to identify alternative operators because they lack the knowledge to do so. They are consigned to search impoverished representations that frequently overconstrain their choice of operators. In the ratchet device problem, for example, the gear wheel's motion is determined by such details as the presence of the short bar between the device's handle and the lower arm, the asymmetry of the gear wheel's teeth, and the discrepant orientations of the teeth along the device's upper and lower bars. Subjects with low or average mechanical knowledge probably generate a representation in which the handle is seen as a pump. This representation is impoverished in that it does not incorporate components of the device that intervene between the input motion of the handle and the output motion of the gear wheel. Such impoverishment is clearly seen in the drawings subjects make of the device immediately after viewing it (Carpenter & Just, 1992). "Low-mechanical" subjects therefore simply predict that the motion of the gear wheel alternates with alternations in the motion of the handle. Accordingly, subjects scoring poorly on a test of mechanical comprehension generally failed to notice the ratchet device's critical features (Carpenter & Just, 1992). They therefore answered correctly fewer questions about the ratchet device's motion than did higher-scoring subjects and were less likely to solve the ratchet device problem simply by inspecting it than were higher-scoring subjects.

"High-mechanical" subjects adopt a representation in which the handle is seen as a motion propagator. This representation incorporates the knowledge that components intervening between the device's input motion and its output motion, such as the short bar or the gear wheel's teeth, may critically influence the device's output motion. Subjects searching this representation are therefore more likely to complete a vigilant kinematic trace as they track the device's motion from input, through each successive mechanical joint, all the way to output. Thus, high-mechanical subjects more often notice the device's crucial motion determinants and more often solve the problem correctly than do low-mechanical subjects searching a handle-as-pump representation.

Subjects have trouble releasing maladaptive operator constraints. This is because the problem features that could cue alternative representations without such constraints are unfamiliar or not perceptually salient. These alternative representations are, in essence, supported by inadequate retrieval cues (Weisberg & Alba, 1981; Yaniv & Meyer, 1987). In the matchsticks problem, the initial match array is two-dimensional. The array contains no features, such as depth cues, that could cue the third dimension required for the solution. Likewise, the pliers in the two-string problem are visually less salient than the chair. The nine-dot problem's square gestalt deters subjects from considering the space outside the grid's perimeter. In addition, the strict gridlike arrangement of the dots makes the crucial diagonals difficult to see. Finally, the asymmetry of the gear wheel's teeth is a less visually striking feature of the ratchet device than are the gear wheel itself and the handle.

Subjects may also continue to apply inappropriate operator constraints to an insight problem because they cannot determine the contribution of particular operators to its solution. Therefore, subjects cannot determine that their current operators will fail to yield the solution. Moreover, they cannot tell that operators excluded by their constraints could produce the solution. Subjects are unable to gauge the utility of particular operators when solving insight problems because operations on insight problems either completely fail or fully succeed and because the solution typically results from a conjunction of operators rather than a single operator. In the two-string problem, for example, subjects must first set or imagine a string swinging and then attach pliers to the string to serve as a pendulum's bob. Simply setting the string swinging will not yield a partial solution to the two-string problem. Subjects therefore cannot determine the contribution of the swing-string operator to the problem's solution. Similarly, in the nine-dot problem, subjects must both draw diagonal lines and extend lines beyond the grid's perimeter. Diagonal lines alone will not produce the problem's solution. Again, therefore, subjects cannot gauge the utility of the draw-diagonal-lines operator in solving the nine-dot problem. Because subjects cannot estimate the contribution of individual operators to an insight problem's solution, and because each operator combination completely fails until the correct combination is tried, subjects must test operator combinations virtually by trial and error. The impossibility of tests that permit the progressive attainment of an insight problem's solution might account for the fact that subjects feel no closer to the solution until they discover it in a sudden flash of illumination (Metcalfe & Wiebe, 1987).

Releasing Operator Constraints

If subjects are to solve insight problems, they eventually must release unwarranted operator constraints. This can occur when problem features that cue alternative operators become salient or when subjects deploy conscious strategies to generate alternative operators.

Experimental manipulations can highlight problem features that cue alternative operators, thereby facilitating subjects' attainment of an insightful solution (Kaplan & Simon, 1990). Maier's (1931) subjects solved the two-string problem more quickly when the experimenter subtly brushed one of the strings, causing it to swing. This manipulation may have increased the salience of the string's ability to swing, provoking subjects to discard the constraints that had limited their operators to the chair. Once subjects focused their operators on the string, they needed only to hypothesize that the pliers could act as a pendulum's bob. Similarly, the space outside the nine-dot square might be highlighted if the nine dots comprising the nine-dot problem were printed in blue on a page filled with evenly spaced red dots. The surrounding red dots would attenuate the problem's boxlike gestalt. Subjects would thus be less reluctant to extend lines beyond the perimeter of the blue dots. In the matchsticks problem, subjects might release the two-dimensional constraint more readily if depth cues, such as linear perspective or interposition, were present in the initial two-dimensional match array. Finally, directing subjects' attention to ratchet device components intervening between the handle and the gear wheel, such as the short bar and the gear wheel's teeth, should lessen the subjects' tendency to constrain their operators to the handle and the gear wheel itself, facilitating solution of the problem.

Problem features allowing the identification of the correct operators can also acquire salience if an incubation period is imposed between problem-solving attempts. When subjects initially encounter insight problems, the crucial problem features are insufficiently activated to allow the use of the correct operators. In the two-string problem, for example, the chair is more salient at first than the seemingly inconsequential pliers. In the ratchet device, the handle and the gear wheel are highly salient, whereas the short bar and the teeth on the gear wheel are far less salient. During the incubation period, subjects do not attempt to solve the insight problem at hand; however, activation can spread among the elements of the problem and between subjects' representations of external stimuli and problem elements. Activation spreading from external stimuli may sufficiently increase the activation of critical problem features to allow selection of the appropriate operators (Yaniv & Meyer, 1987). For example, an encounter during the incubation period with a toolbox might increase the subsequent salience of the pliers in the two-string problem, increasing the likelihood that the problem will be solved.

Both problem-specific and domain knowledge can help subjects release unwarranted operator constraints. Knowledge of the shape of earlier dot-problem solutions can facilitate subjects' solution of new dot problems (Weisberg & Alba, 1981). The shape of the earlier solutions alerts subjects to the fact that they need not contain their lines within the perimeter formed by the outer dots. They therefore can use more successful operators when faced with a new dot problem. Increasing subjects' domain knowledge may help them identify the correct operators in problems drawn from rich domains, such as the ratchet device. Accordingly, Carpenter and Just (1992) found that subjects scoring poorly on a test of mechanical comprehension did not trace the device's kinematic chain and therefore did not notice critical motion determinants such as the asymmetry of the gear wheel's teeth. High-scoring subjects, by contrast, used the kinematic-trace operator and encoded its critical motion determinants.

Training can also provoke subjects to release or even avoid imposing exclusionary operator constraints. Few subjects solved a problem in which they had to use a screwdriver blade as a wire in an electric circuit (Glucksberg & Danks, 1968). Subjects more often solved the problem after they had practiced classifying objects such as paper clips and crayons according to their conducting properties (Teborg, 1968; cited by Anderson, 1985). Weisberg and Alba (1981) trained subjects to solve dot problems whose solutions violated their tendency to contain lines within a boundary. Such training facilitated their solution of other constraint-violating dot problems. This was true, however, only if the actual shapes of the dot-to-dot solutions on previous dot problems matched or closely resembled the shapes of the solutions on the new problems.

Strategies and heuristics can permit the prolific generation of alternative representations or operators, increasing the probability that subjects will discover the correct operators to solve an insight problem (Kaplan & Simon, 1990). First, attending to facts that remain invariant across solution attempts can cue alternative operators (Kaplan & Simon, 1990). As mentioned previously, subjects solving the matchsticks problem usually constrain their arrangements of the matches to two dimensions. Across two-dimensional solution attempts, subjects will find that there is at least one less match than is required to complete the triangles. When subjects notice this invariant fact, they may be compelled to release the two-dimensional constraint and extend matches into the third dimension. Once subjects use the extend-matches operator, they find that a simple pyramid will solve the problem.

Second, analogy can serve to generate potential operators during the solution of insight problems. In fact, subjects may first use the wrong operators in many insight problems because they make incorrect analogies. In the two-string problem, subjects analogize between the chair and an anchor or weight rather than between the string and a pendulum's shaft and between the pliers and a pendulum's bob. In the nine-dot problem, subjects analogize between the dot array and a box; they therefore try solutions contained within the box. Analogizing between the dot array and a kite might help subjects attend to the array's diagonals and release the nondiagonal line constraint. Finally, as stated earlier, subjects facing the ratchet device problem seem to analogize between the device's handle and a pump's handle. If subjects were encouraged to generate further analogies for the device's handle, they might generate an analogy in which the handle is seen as a crank. Repeated actions on a crank typically produce continuations, rather than alternations, in the output motion. Viewing the handle as a crank might lead subjects to expect the gear wheel to continue rotating in the same direction as the handle is manipulated, allowing them to solve the problem.

Most subjects in our laboratory failed to solve the ratchet device problem through inspection. Construing the handle as a pump did not allow subjects to use operators involving components of the device such as the short bar and the gear wheel's teeth. These subjects were then allowed to manipulate the handle and were asked to explain the gear wheel's constant counterclockwise motion. Their explanations hint at the operators they might have used to solve the problem through inspection. Typically, these subjects began tracing the device's kinematic chain, the same strategy used by high-mechanical subjects who solved the problem through inspection (Carpenter & Just, 1992). The kinematic-trace operator is successful because it assigns clear roles to critical motion determinants such as the asymmetry of the gear wheel's teeth. Interestingly, whereas low-mechanical and mid-mechanical subjects could eventually select the kinematic-trace operator, they often cited critical motion determinants near the device's handle, such as the short bar between the handle and the lower arm, but rarely mentioned critical determinants on or near the gear wheel, such as the asymmetry of the gear wheel's teeth. The ability to select an operator, therefore, does not imply the ability to apply it effectively.

We have argued that solving insight problems requires the release of unwarranted operator constraints. These constraints preclude the selection of the operators that yield the solution. Unwarranted constraints are imposed because the operators specified by such constraints are salient and often successful during the solution of everyday problems with task environments similar to those of insight problems. Subjects then maintain such constraints because the features cuing excluded operators are not salient, because they lack the knowledge necessary to select alternative operators, and because operations on insight problems do not help subjects identify and release their operator constraints. Unwarranted operator constraints may be released when particular problem features are highlighted, when subjects acquire additional domain or problem knowledge, or when subjects try strategies such as analogical play to generate alternative operators or representations.

Our suggestion that insight requires the elimination of unnecessary operator constraints enriches both Gestalt, traditional problem solving and popular accounts of insight. The Gestalt psychologists claimed that insight arises when the elements of a visuospatial problem assume new meanings as the problem is reorganized (Ellen, 1982). The new meanings ascribed to the problem's elements make its solution apparent. The Gestaltists, however, did not adequately define how problem elements acquire meanings or how problem reorganization occurs. We argue that problem elements assume meanings when operators are applied to them. If operators are not applied to a problem element, it is meaningless. Subjects first encountering the two-string problem, for example, probably do not attend to the pliers. They apply no operators to the pliers, and so the pliers are meaningless. Our constraint-release view of insight suggests that subjects adopt constraints that prevent them from applying certain operators. The problem elements to which those operators may be applied are thus rendered meaningless. When they release such constraints, subjects may use previously neglected operators, bringing new elements into prominence and facilitating the problem's solution. Problem-solving theorists suggest that insight results when subjects restructure (Weisberg & Alba, 1981) or re-represent the problem (Kaplan & Simon, 1990) in a way that lends itself to the solution. We suggest that operator constraints are an important component of problem representations and that constraint release may be one way in which problems can be re-represented. Finally, many popular accounts of insightful problem solving (e.g., Adams, 1974) include the notion that insight arises when so-called conceptual blocks are eliminated. Conceptual blocks are similar to the operator selection constraints we have described (Mayer, 1983). However, labeling something as a *block* denotes only that it is an impediment and indicates little about its nature nor about a means to eliminate it. By contrast, if a conceptual block is viewed as a consequence of an unwarranted constraint, then a potential means of eliminating it is to reexamine the legitimacy of the constraints and then to release any unwarranted ones. In other words, operators that examine and modify constraints may be a critical ingredient of insight.

INVENTION: CONSTRAINT OPERATIONS DURING THE GENERATION AND ANALYSIS OF NOVEL SOLUTIONS

Invention refers to the generation of novel devices to perform tasks or fulfill needs. The cotton gin, for example, was developed to clean short-staple cotton (Weisberg, 1993), whereas the airplane represented an entirely novel solution to our species' inability to fly. Because its products are both novel and valuable, invention is a form of creativity. Our account of invention uses as its point of departure existing theory of creativity but goes further to propose how constraint operations may be involved in each phase of the creative process.

Generative versus Analytical Problem Solving

Creativity theorists suggest that creativity entails both generative and analytical processes. For example, Osborn (1963), the originator of brainstorming, proposed that creative problem solving progressed through three stages: (1) problem formulation, (2) idea finding, and (3) idea evaluation. During idea finding, the solver generates as many ideas as possible, whereas during idea evaluation, the solver analyzes the merits and disadvantages of each idea. Wallach (1967) similarly suggested that creativity in both scientific and artistic domains involves two phases: the generation of conceptual possibilities and the analysis of the implications of these possibilities. Anderson (1985) also states that creativity involves both the generation and the judgment of possible solutions to problems. In addition, Finke, Ward, and Smith's (1992) model of creative cognition contains a generative phase and an exploratory phase. In the generative phase, mental representations promoting creative discovery are constructed, whereas in the exploratory phase, the representations are interpreted and analyzed. Finally, Klahr and Dunbar (1988; Dunbar & Klahr, 1989) claim that scientists search two spaces in pursuit of discovery: the hypothesis space and the experiment space. Scientific hypotheses are generated in the hypothesis space and tested, or analyzed, in the experiment space.

Creativity theorists have emphasized the generative processes during creativity because these processes are those that first produce novel solutions and because analytical processes do not by themselves distinguish creativity from more pedestrian problem-solving exercises, such as solving algebra equations. Guilford (1959), for example, suggests that creativity is maximized through the fluent and flexible generation of original ideas. Brainstorming techniques, such as the rapid, uncritical generation of as many ideas as possible (Osborn, 1963), were similarly intended mainly to stimulate idea generation. Products that are valuable as well as novel, however, can arise only if the generated ideas are evaluated effectively. Successful invention, therefore, requires both generative and analytical facilities.

Generative and analytical problem solving have very different goals and are thus facilitated by different heuristics. The goal of generative problem solving is to produce original solutions. Successful generation therefore requires the rapid production of many different ideas, with little immediate regard for their plausibility (Osborn, 1963). Few constraints should be placed on the nature of the ideas generated, and the solver should be prepared to loosen, eliminate, or reformulate any implicitly held constraints on the problem's solution. To this end, a playful, unrestrained attitude toward idea generation is helpful, as is a tolerant or permissive attitude toward implausibility (Wallach, 1967; Wiesner, 1967). In one study of college students who were generating poetry, students who expected to be evaluated on their work were less creative than students who did not expect to be evaluated on their work (Amabile, 1983). The evaluation expectancy increased the stringency with which students judged flaws in their own work during the generation phase. The untimely imposition of constraints on their work during the generation phase decreased students' creativity.

The goal of analytical problem solving is to evaluate the generated ideas according to criteria for their validity. Constraints on the problem's solution must be established and used in such evaluation, rather than released as in generative problem solving. The solver must be sensitive to potential solutions that do not meet the required constraints (Wallach, 1967; Wiesner, 1967), as such solutions may be novel, but not valuable.

Tasks that require both generation and analysis, such as invention, thus require iterations between the imposition and release of constraints and, concomitantly, between permissive and rigorous attitudes toward implausibility or error (Wallach, 1967). Simply increasing the number of potential solutions generated and the open-mindedness with which they are generated will not ensure success, as is implied by definitions of creativity such as Guilford's (1959). Rather, successful creativity depends on increasing both the facility with which solutions are generated and the acuity with which they are analyzed. The need for both types of processes was assessed in a study in which subjects were taught three different ways to generate creative story titles (Stratton & Brown, 1972). One group was trained to generate as many different titles as possible. A second group was trained to evaluate critically the titles it generated but was not trained in fluent generation. Finally, a third group was trained both to generate a large number of titles and to evaluate those titles carefully. Independent judges rated the quality of the titles produced by the third group more highly than the quality of the titles produced by the other two groups. Successful creativity thus requires both fluent, unconstrained generation and rigorous criticism of the generated items.

The Three Phases of Invention

Invention entails three main phases: (1) design space limitation, (2) design generation, and (3) design analysis, mirroring the brainstorming stages of problem formulation, idea finding, and idea evaluation, respectively. During the first phase, design space limitation, the inventor identifies the problem to be solved and defines the general range of possible solutions to a problem. During the second phase, design generation, the inventor specifies candidate solutions to the problem within the range of possible solutions defined in phase 1. Finally, during the third phase, design analysis, the inventor chooses and perfects one of the candidate solutions to yield a final product design. Design analysis frequently necessitates one or more returns to the generation phase as initial candidate solutions prove unsuitable. Inventors therefore alternate between design generation and design analysis rather than moving simply and sequentially from design generation to design analysis. Finke and colleagues' (1992) model of creative cognition is similarly reiterative: Exploratory processes may provoke successive returns to the generative phase as creative products are modified and refined.

Successful invention depends on operations on constraints on the intended invention. As suggested earlier, the appropriate constraint operations, in turn, depend on whether the inventor is limiting the design space, generating designs, or analyzing designs. During design space limitation, the inventor must impose, maintain, and adhere to external constraints on the nature of the invention. These external constraints arise from the problem the invention is intended to solve and from external sources, such as economic and technological limitations, and perhaps from ethical and aesthetic considerations. During design generation, the inventor often must recognize and release or reformulate implicitly held constraints on the nature of the invention. Insight is therefore often implicated in design generation in that it, too, entails calling constraints into question. For example, the inventor might implicitly constrain the form of the invention to adapt to the form of a product fulfilling a related function. Only by releasing such constraints can a novel product arise. Heuristics such as analogy and combinatory play can help the inventor generate alternative forms for the invention that do not conform to these constraints. Finally, during design analysis, the inventor must again refer to constraints on the invention to evaluate and improve the design's performance. Novel solutions must be evaluated to determine whether they are also valuable solutions.

Design Space Limitation
During design space limitation, inventors narrow the space they must search to generate novel solutions to a problem. The deliberate imposition of and adherence to a variety of constraints can help specify potential forms and functions of the intended invention, obviating the need to search large regions of the design space and expediting the design generation process.

Finke's (1990) experiments demonstrate the contribution of design space constraints to creative invention. Subjects were shown a set of 15 object parts, including simple geometrical shapes such as spheres as well as more specialized parts such as hooks and handles (see chapter 8 for more details). The experimenter then named three object parts and told subjects to imagine combining those parts to invent a practical object or device. The inventions could belong to any of eight categories, such as *furniture, toys and games*, and *weapons*. When the experimenter specified the category to which subjects' inventions were supposed to belong as well as the parts the subjects had to use in their inventions, a greater proportion of subjects' inventions were rated as creative than when the invention category was unconstrained. Limiting the design space before generation thus increases the probability of creative invention, perhaps because design space limitations afford the inventor a preliminary sketch of the possible forms and functions of the intended invention.

The most obvious constraint on the nature of the invention is the problem the invention is intended to solve. Before John Harrison invented the marine chronometer in the eighteenth century, navigators were unable to determine the precise location of their ships on the sea. A marine chronometer is a clocklike device permitting the calculation of longitude. Navigators were therefore unable to ascertain the distance from their destination or deviation from their intended course. Such uncertainty was particularly treacherous for ships out of sight of land and battling with high winds and restless oceans. Although navigators could use a sextant to determine their latitude with relative accuracy, their longitude could not be ascertained without good lunar tables or accurate timepieces such as the marine chronometer. The invention of the marine chronometer, therefore, was intended to fulfill navigators' need for an accurate method of determining a vessel's longitude (Smiles, 1884).

Cotton growing is profitable only if the seeds can be cleaned from the bolls efficiently. Before Eli Whitney invented the cotton gin in 1793, cotton growers in the American South were unable to clean short-staple cotton except by hand (Weisberg, 1993). Manual cotton cleaning is extremely slow and unprofitable. Although gins existed to clean long-staple cotton, plantation owners wished to plant the faster-growing and more profitable short-staple variety. Whitney's cotton gin was thus a novel solution to an economic need.

The recognition of the problem to be solved by the invention directs inventors to search general regions of the design space. If inventors recognize that navigators are unable to determine their longitude accurately, they will attempt to search a space of possible instruments that can be used aboard a ship to ascertain one's geographical position. Precise and well-elaborated statements of the goal of the invention constrain design space search more effectively than do vague statements of the problem to be solved by the invention. Proposing that humans cannot fly because their bodies cannot provide the requisite lift and thrust directs inventors to seek ways in which artificial lift and thrust may be provided to humans. By contrast, simply stating that humans cannot fly does little to direct the search for potential design forms and functions.

Imaginative problem finding is occasionally assumed to constitute the magic of creativity and invention (see, for example, Mansfield & Busse, 1981). Smilansky and Halberstadt (1986), moreover, suggest that problem finding processes may better characterize creativity and invention than might such oft-cited divergent thinking processes as considering alternative-solution search paths and combining problem or domain elements in novel or unusual ways. Finally, Smilansky (1984) found that eleventh and twelfth graders found the creation of Raven Progressive Matrices problems to be more difficult than the solution of existing matrix problems and that a low correlation existed between the ability to solve matrix problems and the ability to design them. He concluded that problem creation or problem finding is more diffi-cult than problem solving, perhaps accounting for the rarity of in-vention, and that problem-finding processes are distinct from problem-solving processes.

In contemporary corporate invention milieux, however, the prob-lems to be solved may be fairly clearly specified, obviating the need for a protracted search of the space of potential problems. In addition, in invention, new problems likely emerge rather natu-rally as inventors reiterate through design generation and design analysis. Product tests whose results do not support current de-signs suggest new designs and thus new problems to pursue. In fact, exploiting problematic or surprising results during experi-ments or tests is one heuristic for identifying new problems (Kulkarni & Simon, 1988). Problems are therefore not synthesized from thin air by some deliberate alchemy but rather arise fre-quently as inventors return to design generation after preliminary design analyses.

Even when inventors have clearly specified the goal of the in-vention, there are many potential designs for the invention. For example, airplane inventors may consider designs to provide lift and thrust in which wings flap, as in orinthopters; in which wings do not flap, as in contemporary airplanes; or in which wings are absent and humans wear rocket-propelled jet-packs. Devices such as orinthopters, airplanes, and jet-packs, moreover, typically consist of a number of components. An airplane, for example, consists of wings, rudders, elevators, fuselage, power plant, propellers, and so forth. Not only can the design of each component vary along several dimensions, but the various compo-nents can be arranged in different ways. An inventor may choose to design, say, a steam-powered triplane design with a forward ele-vator, rear rudder, open fuselage, and twin propellers (Bradshaw, 1992). Clearly, the space of potential designs remains large.

Inventors can limit the design space by imposing additional constraints on the nature of the invention. The intended application of the invention, the defects in the invention's precursors, and technological limitations offer further constraints to reduce the search space. First, the way the invention's application was previously handled might well serve to constrain search in the design space. For example, a ship's longitude usually was determined by a log before the marine chronometer was developed (Smiles, 1884). Because a log typically recorded the time and because the marine chronometer was intended to improve on the log, the search for a longitude measurement device was limited to instruments measuring the time, such as the marine chronometer.

Second, if an invention is intentionally sought, its precursor probably has shortcomings. As noted, for example, the cotton gin's predecessors were limited to cleaning long-staple cotton. The specification of the defects in the existing device can also constrain search in the design space. Prior to the development of the marine chronometer, the processes involved in keeping a ship's log, such as calculating and combining allowances for drift and leeway and adjusting these allowances according to the ship's trim, were subject to much estimation and uncertainty. As a result, ships were frequently 100 or 200 miles off their intended course, particularly during rough weather (Smiles, 1884). Designs that required a device to compute drift, leeway, or trim were thus eliminated from the design space searched during the development of the marine chronometer.

Finally, technological constraints can limit the range of possible designs for the invention under consideration. During the seventeenth century, for example, Halley, Newton, and Flamsteed, then the Astronomer-Royal, attempted to perfect a method for determining a ship's longitude by astronomical observation; their efforts, however, were thwarted due to the rudimentary state of astronomical instruments at the time (Smiles, 1884). Consequently, designs for a device to determine a ship's longitude could not rely on the direct calculation of the movement of astronomical bodies.

Design Generation
After limiting the design space, inventors must generate designs for the invention. The designs inventors initially generate are often constrained by implicit analogies to nature or to existing products. Design analysis processes such as considering the appropriateness of the implicit analogies, comparing the designs to

the constraints they must satisfy, and performing design tests typically reveal the inadequacy of these first-pass designs. During further design generation, inventors must release and reformulate constraints on the nature of the invention, just as subjects solving insight problems must release their initial operator selection constraints. Deliberate analogical and combinatory play can help the inventor generate alternative designs, facilitating the elimination and reformulation of unnecessary constraints on the nature of the invention.

Initial invention constraints: Implicit analogies　Before developing invention designs, inventors likely first identify the intended function of the invention. When the inventor then generates initial invention designs, he or she often constrains the form of the invention through implicit analogies to components of nature or existing products whose function matches or approximates that of the intended invention. For example, early airplane inventors frequently imitated the form of animals capable of flight, modeling their flying craft after albatrosses, bats, and various insects such as beetles (Bradshaw, 1992). Similarly. architects have made structural innovations through analogies to our actions toward objects and to the forces, tensions, and interactions within our skeletomuscular system (Mainstone, 1973). Such analogies seem a plausible basis for invention in the mechanical realm as well. For example, joysticks, such as those found on many video games, may well have evolved through an analogy to human ball-and-socket joints, such as the shoulder joint.

The development of the cotton gin, the streetcar, and the marine chronometer exemplify invention through initial analogies to existing products. Whitney's cotton gin was based on earlier gins designed to clean long-staple cotton, which in turn owe their development to the *charka*, a device used for centuries to clean cotton in India (Weisberg, 1993). Early streetcars featured running boards rather than a central aisle, from which conductors collected fares (Lorenz, 1974). Running boards were a design feature imported from preceding horse-drawn carriages. Similarly, after John Harrison determined that the marine chronometer would perform a time-keeping function to calculate a ship's longitude, he first patterned the chronometer after pendulum clocks

(Smiles, 1884), a common timekeeping device of that era. Finally, in an experimental setting, Jansson and Smith (1991) found that engineers who designed products after viewing examples of other products with similar functions included in their own designs unnecessary features of the sample products. This happened even when the engineers were instructed specifically not to borrow features from the sample products.

Invention analogies, such as that between a bird and an airplane, may be viewed as bundles of constraints on function-form correspondences. For example, the bird-airplane analogy contains the constraints that the airplane functions of lift and thrust be realized in wing forms, just as they are in birds. Additionally, the bird-airplane analogy contains the constraint that an airplane's lift be realized in the flapping of the wings, again as in birds. The form-function constraints contained within initial invention analogies generally must be unpacked, released, and reformulated as invention proceeds.

Reformulating invention constraints: Analogical and combinatory play   Analyzing a proposed design often reveals some untenable function-form correspondences. For example, airplane designs in which wings provided both lift and thrust proved unworkable. A return to deliberate analogical and combinatory play can produce new designs with reconstituted function-form constraint packages. In at least some of these new designs, unworkable function-form constraints will be absent, increasing the probability of successful invention.

When design analysis reveals that the initial invention analogy contains untenable function-form correspondence constraints, the conscious generation of alternative analogies, metaphors, and similes (Wiesner, 1967) for the invention can yield new and perhaps more feasible function-form constraint bundles. For example, the pendulum clock metaphor for the marine chronometer contains the constraint that the chronometer's movement mechanism be realized in a pendulum. This function-form constraint proved unworkable, as the accuracy of pendulums was adversely affected by the motion of a ship at sea. The generation of alternative timepiece metaphors for the chronometer, such as hourglasses, sundials, watches, and so forth, could yield a constraint package without the inappropriate pendulum constraint. Indeed, the eventual chronometer was encased and used springs as a movement mechanism, rather like a watch. The elimination or reformulation of function-form correspondence constraints afforded by analogical play might account for the beneficial role analogy has been shown to play in technological advances (Gordon, 1974) and in creative or inventive problem solving generally (Krueger, 1976; Necka, 1985).

Analogical play is a specific heuristic facilitating the integration of diverse elements of experience and knowledge. The more general heuristic of combining discrepant ideas and experiences is termed *combinatory play*. Like analogical play, combinatory play permits the generation of alternative function-form correspondence constraint bundles, some of which may not contain untenable constraints on the realization of an invention's intended functions.

Both the intuitive notions of creativity held by nonpsychologists and the explicit theories of creativity proposed by psychologists support the notion that creative or inventive solutions may arise from the integration of diverse experiences or ideas. Analogous ideas about creativity are held by college undergraduates and by college professors in disciplines in which creativity is not explicitly studied (Sternberg, 1989). One of the four dimensions comprising the undergraduates' implicit theory of creativity was integration and intellectuality, in which creative individuals better recognize the similarities and differences between diverse ideas and things, better form connections between diverse ideas and things, and better combine ideas in novel ways than do noncreative persons. Philosophy professors' implicit theories of creativity included the notions that creative persons toy imaginatively with idea combinations, generate insights regarding the connections between seemingly unrelated ideas, and form useful analogies between ideas. Similarly, physics professors' implicit theories of creativity stated that creative persons search for unity, find order in chaos, and perceive physical and other patterns that escape noncreative individuals. Both the explicit theories of creativity held by creativity researchers and the implicit theories of creativity held by individuals who do not study creativity thus focus on integrating ideas, objects, or experiences.

In the creativity literature, Wallach and Kogan (1965) claimed that creativity involves the production of numerous and unusual associations between ideas. In the problem-solving literature, the integration of experiences or ideas is again seen to facilitate the generation of novel solutions (Ellen, 1982; Yaniv & Meyer, 1987). Whereas knowledge or experience may provide subjects with the means to attack a problem, only the integration of ideas or experiences can lead to inventive solutions. Indeed, instructing or provoking subjects to combine elements of their experience may stimulate invention. Finke (1990) found that subjects engaging in combinatory play with mental images of geometrical shapes such as spheres, cylinders, and disks invented various devices comprising the shapes, such as hamburger makers. Reports in the popular press indicate that workers at 3M, the Minneapolis corporation responsible for Scotch tape, Post-it Notes, and the like, are also encouraged to organize and reorganize disparate objects in the pursuit of innovation.

Imaginal systems probably underlie the ability to integrate diverse elements of experience and knowledge in the service of creative problem solving. An imaginal counterpart to invention's recursive generate-and-analyze cycle may occur in which diverse images are first concatenated in imaginary designs. The resultant designs may then be subjected to imaginal analyses, the results of which, in turn, spur further imaginal design generation. The imaginal generate-and-analyze cycle could include both visual and enactive imagery, which comprises kinesthetic, proprioceptive, and somatosensory representations as well as visual imagery of one's actions with or manipulations of objects (Krueger, 1976). Mainstone (1973) similarly suggests that well-developed kinesthetic, proprioceptive, and somatosensory imagery may facilitate structural invention in architecture. It seems plausible that such representations would also aid mechanical invention, as the motion of, say, some mechanical joints is analogous to the movements of our skeletal joints. The imaginal generate-and-analyze cycle allows inventors to generate numerous alternative designs rapidly and to subject such designs quickly to a large number of tests. The advantage gained by the increase in the number of designs that can be previewed imaginally, as well as the increase in the speed with which they can be tested, likely offsets the transience and poor fidelity of mental imagery.

Design Analysis
After generating a design, the inventor must analyze both the design itself and the analogy on which it is based. The results of these analyses fuel subsequent design generation. Assessing an analogy entails analyzing the tenability of the function-form correspondence constraints it implies. Analyzing a design entails imposing constraints on the invention's function, subjecting the invention to product tests, and comparing the invention's performance during the tests to the constraints imposed earlier.

Analyzing analogies   It may seem intuitive, when designing an invention with a particular function, to make an analogy to the form of a natural phenomenon fulfilling a similar function. The mechanical or technological replication of a natural function-form correspondence, however, is far from trivial. In general, the relationship between a natural form and its functions cannot be realized directly as a mechanical or technological artifact. A natural form, for example, might perform multiple functions that inventors may have to dissociate. For example, a bird's wing provides both lift and thrust. Whereas these functions are dissociated in modern planes, whose fixed wings provide lift alone, early airplane developers created orinthopters, with flapping wings (Weisberg, 1993). This design for a flying craft failed. The difficulty of capturing nature's function-form correspondences in mechanical inventions implies that invention entails not only the generation of analogies but also their analysis.

Analyzing analogies involves unpacking the function-form correspondences they imply, enumerating the implications of such correspondences for the design of the intended invention, and determining whether and how such correspondences may be realized in the invention. Birds, for example, tilt their wings slightly to maintain lateral control (Weisberg, 1993). The Wright brothers therefore designed airplanes with wing tips that could be raised or lowered by a system of wires in an attempt to realize the lateral control function. The wire system added excessive weight to the airplane, however. The brothers then devised designs in which wing tips were warped somewhat. Again, it was difficult to vary as desired the degree of lateral control offered by these designs. Contemporary airplanes use small wing flaps that can be raised or lowered as required.

Analyzing designs: Imposing constraints   Design analysis entails imposing constraints on the function of the invention, evaluating how well the current design meets these constraints, and revising the design so that it better satisfies these constraints. Here, we focus primarily on the establishment of functional constraints for an invention.

John Harrison imposed the following constraints on the function of the marine chronometer: Its accuracy could not be compromised by the sometimes violent motion of a ship at sea, the variations in temperature and humidity in different regions of the globe, the varying effects of gravity at different latitudes and, finally, the temperature of the chronometer itself or that of its lubricating oil (Smiles, 1884). These constraints imply that the chronometer's movement mechanism should be encased, like that of a present-day watch, rather than free, like that of a pendulum. Indeed, a precursor of the marine chronometer, Harrison's compensating pendulum, proved an unserviceable determinant of a ship's longitude because its accuracy was unduly compromised by a ship's sudden rocking motions. Harrison thus replaced the pendulum with two pairs of wound springs for his chronometer's movement mechanism. The vibration of balances near the springs afforded greater stability and timekeeping regularity than did a pendulum's swing. Each pair of springs vibrated two balances in the same plane but in opposite directions. If the motion of one balance was amplified by the tossing of the ship, the vibration of the other balance would be simultaneously lessened. The net vibration thus remained almost constant despite the ship's motions.

Unfortunately, the resulting spring chronometer failed to satisfy the second of the above constraints: The chronometer tended to run fast in hotter weather and slower in cooler weather. Temperature variations affected the springs' elasticity, in turn influencing the rate at which the balances vibrated. Harrison thus perfected his thermometer curb, composed of two thin plates of brass and steel riveted together. Because brass both expands more in heat and contracts more in cold than does steel, the curb became convex on the brass side in hot weather and convex on the steel side in cold weather. While one end of the curb was fixed, the other end was free to bend and unbend as the curb's convexity changed and was connected to the chronometer's springs through pins. The curb's bending and unbending thus shortened and lengthened the chronometer's springs, compensating for the effects of temperature on the springs themselves. The final marine chronometer therefore satisfied all four of the required constraints on its functioning and represented the culmination of a process in which successive precursors, such as the compensating pendulum and the spring chronometer, satisfied an increasing number of the requisite constraints. The development of the marine chronometer also illustrates the iterative nature of invention, in which designs are developed, then checked against the requisite constraints, revised or revamped to improve their functioning, and then tested again.

CONCLUSIONS

Insight and invention frequently are treated as related creative problem-solving phenomena. Indeed, many writers (e.g., Hadamard, 1945) often use *insight* to mean *invention*. In this chapter, we clarified the similarities and differences between insight and invention by analyzing each in terms of constraint operations. Problem solvers use constraints to limit the representations they search or to narrow the field of operators they use during problem solving. Insight problems cue subjects to overconstrain their choice of operators. Subjects must release operator constraints to solve insight problems. Highlighting problem features and providing additional domain or problem-specific knowledge can help subjects release operator constraints. In addition, analogical play can help subjects generate alternative problem representations without maladaptive operator constraints.

Whereas insight depends on releasing constraints, invention requires reiterative cycles of constraint release and imposition. The appropriate constraint operations must be applied during each of the three phases of invention: design space limitation, design generation, and design analysis. During design space limitation, inventors narrow the space of potential novel solutions to a problem. Here, inventors must impose and adhere to constraints on the invention to guide their search through the space of solutions. Invention constraints may derive from the specification of the problem to be solved and from economic and technological limitations. During design generation, inventors develop one or more candidate novel solutions. In this phase, inventors often must release or reformulate implicit constraints on the solution's form. These constraints frequently arise through analogies to natural phenomena or to existing products. Because insight also entails constraint release, insight may be implicated during design generation. The confusion between insight and invention often found in the literature may be due to the emphasis usually accorded to generative processes during the analysis of creative behaviors such as invention. Constraint release in both insight and invention can be facilitated by combinatory and analogical play. Finally, during design analysis, inventors evaluate the adequacy of candidate solutions and revise them if necessary. Here, as in design space limitation, inventors must again impose and adhere to constraints. Constraints during design analysis often stem from the invention's functional requirements.

Our discussion of insight and invention may illuminate the nature of these two psychological processes so that we can better understand what occurs in the minds of inventors and problem solvers with insight. But our construal of these phenomena might also lead to better invention and insight, even in amateur thinkers. The new view that we offer treats constraint release and imposition as powerful mental tools—not new tools, but tools that everyone uses intuitively all the time. What might distinguish the best problem solvers and inventors is their conscious and strategic use of operations on constraints. With enough examples, guidance, and patience, this kind of strategic control of thought is available to everyone.

ACKNOWLEDGMENTS

We would like to thank Patricia Carpenter for her comments on earlier drafts of this chapter.

This work was supported in part by grant N00014-92-J-1209 from the Office of Naval Research, Research Scientist Development Award MH 00662 from the National Institute of Mental Health, and graduate fellowship from the Natural Sciences and Engineering Research Council of Canada.

APPENDIX A:
INSIGHT PROBLEMS AND THEIR SOLUTIONS

1. Two strings

Problem: Consider the room below. How may the two strings be tied together? You may use any of the objects in the room.

Solution: Attach the pliers (visible in front of the jar on the floor) to one of the strings. A pendulum is thus formed, and the string may be swung sufficiently close to the other string to tie the two strings together.

Source: Maier (1931)

2. Candle

Problem: You have a candle, some matches, and a box of tacks. Support the candle on the wall.

Solution: Empty the tackbox. Tack the box to the wall. Set the candle on the platform formed by the box.

Source: Duncker (1945)

3. Nine dots

Problem: Draw four straight lines without lifting your pencil from the paper so that each of the nine dots in A is crossed by a line.

Solution: Shown in B.

Source: Weisberg and Alba (1981)

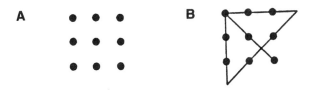

4. Pigpen

Problem: Nine pigs are kept in a square pen, as shown in A. Build two more square enclosures that would put each pig in a pen by itself.

Solution: Shown in B.

Source: Fixx (1972)

A

B

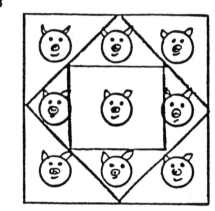

5. Necklace

Problem: You are given four separate pieces of chain that are each three links long, as shown in A. It costs 2 cents to open a link and 3 cents to close a link. All links are closed at the beginning of the problem. Your goal is to connect all 12 links into a single circle as shown in B. The total cost must be no more than 15 cents.

Solution: Destroy one of the chains by opening all three links, at a cost of 6 cents. Use one link to connect two remaining chains. Then use another link to connect the last chain to these. Finally, use the third link to join the ends of the resulting chain. The total connection cost is 9 cents, yielding a 15-cent necklace including the cost of destroying the first chain.

Source: Wickelgren (1974)

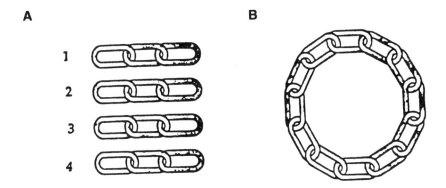

6. Water lilies

Problem: Water lilies on a certain lake double in area every 24 hours. On the first day of summer, there is one water lily on the lake. On the sixtieth day, the lake is all covered. On what day is the lake half-covered?

Solution: Day 59.

Source: Sternberg and Davidson (1983)

7. Matchsticks

Problem: Assemble six matches (A) to form four equilateral triangles, each side of which is equal to the length of one match.

Solution: Construct a three-dimensional pyramid as in B.

Source: Scheerer (1963)

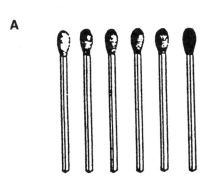

B

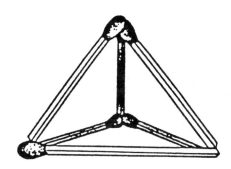

8. Radiation

Problem: A patient has an inoperable stomach tumor. There are certain rays that can destroy this tumor if their intensity is great enough. At this intensity, however, the rays will also destroy the healthy tissue surrounding the tumor (e.g., the stomach walls, the abdominal muscles, and so on). How can one destroy the tumor without damaging the healthy tissue through which the rays must travel on their way?

Solution: Several weak rays can be sent from various points outside so that they will meet at the tumor site. There, the radiation of the rays will be intense, for all the effects will summate at this point but, because they are individually weak, the rays will not damage the healthy tissue surrounding the tumor.

Source: Gick and Holyoak (1980)

9. Horse and rider

Problem: In panel 1, place B on A in such a way that the riders are properly astride their horses.

Solution: The solution is shown in panel 2. A has been rotated 90 degrees so that the two old nags are in the vertical position. The head of each vertical horse is thus joined horizontally with the hindquarters of the other. Finally, B has been superimposed over the middle of A.

Source: Scheerer, Goldstein, and Boring (1941)

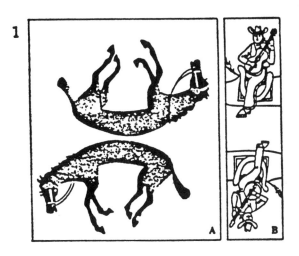

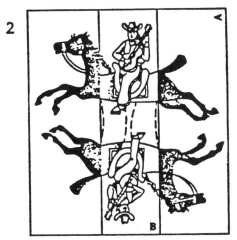

10. Glasses and knives

Problem: Place three upright glasses (shown in A) on a table so that each forms the corner point of a triangle of equal sides and so that the distance between any two glasses is slightly longer than one of the knives. Using the knives, construct a platform on top of the glasses that is strong enough to support the fourth glass, which should be filled with water. No part of any knife may touch the table.

Solution: Shown in B.

Source: DeBono (1967)

A

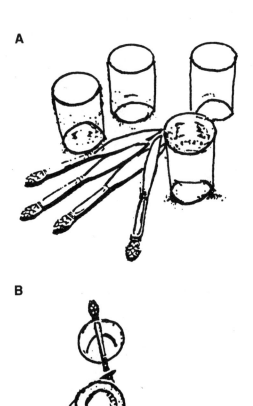

B

11. Moneylender

Problem: An old moneylender offered to cancel a merchant's debt and keep him from going to prison if the merchant would give the money-lender his lovely daughter. Horrified yet desperate, the merchant and his daughter agreed to let fate decide. The moneylender said he would put a black pebble and a white pebble in a bag and the girl would draw one. The white pebble would cancel the debt and leave her free. The black one would make her the moneylender's, although the debt would be canceled. If she refused to pick, her father would go to prison. From the pebble-strewn path they were standing on, the moneylender picked two pebbles and quickly put them in the bag, but the girl saw he had picked up two black ones. What should the girl do?

Solution: When the girl put her hand in the bag to draw out the fateful pebble, she fumbled and dropped it, where it was immediately lost among the others in the path. "Well," she said, "you can tell which one I picked by looking at the one that's left." The girl's quick thinking saved her father and herself.

Source: DeBono (1967)

12. Prisoner and rope

Problem: A prisoner was attempting to escape from a tower. He found in his cell a rope that was half long enough to permit him to reach the ground safely. He divided the rope in half, tied the two parts together, and escaped. How could he have done this?

Solution: He cut the rope in half vertically.

Source: Metcalfe and Wiebe (1987)

13. Pyramid and dollar bill

Problem: A giant inverted steel pyramid is perfectly balanced on its point. Any movement of the pyramid will cause it to topple over. Underneath the pyramid is a $100 bill. How would you remove the bill without disturbing the pyramid?

Solution: Simply slide the bill from under the pyramid. No one said the bill had to remain intact.

Source: Unpublished

14. Triangle of coins

Problem: Moving only three coins, rearrange the ten coins shown in A to make a pyramid with the point at the top.

Solution: Move the coins at each end of the top line to the ends of the line second from the bottom, and then move the very bottom coin to the top of the diagram, as in B.

Source: Frudman (1978)

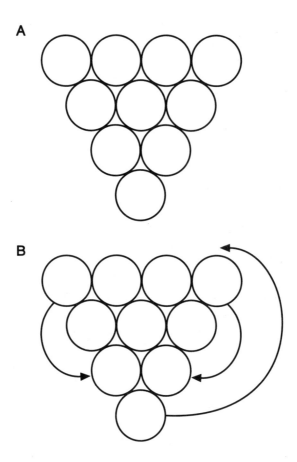

15. Hat rack

Problem: Using two long boards and a C-clamp, build a structure sufficiently stable to support an overcoat and hat. The opening of the clamp is wide enough so that both sticks can be inserted and held together securely when the clamp is tightened.

Solution: Clamp the two boards together and wedge them between the floor and ceiling. The clamp handle serves as the hook for the coat and hat.

Source: Maier (1945)

16. Ten dollars

Problem: Joe and Frank have the same amount of money. How much must Joe give Frank so that Frank has $10 more than Joe?

Solution: $5.

Source: Gleitman (1991)

17. All your pets

Problem: How many pets do you have if all of them are birds except two, all of them are cats except two, and all of them are dogs except two?

Solution: Three (one bird, one cat, and one dog).

Source: Seifert and Patalano (1991)

18. Thirty-dollar room

Problem: Three guests go to a hotel and are told that a room costs $30. Each one gives the room clerk $10. After they are in their room, the clerk discovers that the correct price of the room is $25, so she gives $5 to the bellhop to return to the guests. The bellhop goes to the room, gives each of the guests $1, and keeps $2 for himself. That means each guest has paid $9 for a total of $27, and the bellhop has $2, for a grand total of $29. What happened to the other dollar from the original $30?

Solution: The problem is not to account for $30 but rather simply to account for $27. The calculations have been confused by sometimes adding and sometimes subtracting. Each guest paid $10 originally but got back $1, so all you have to account for is $27. The hotel has $25 of that and the bellhop the other $2. The bellhop's money is not added to the $27; it is subtracted.

Source: Freedman (1978)

19. Phone numbers

Problem: Jane's phone number is ANThill 4729, but I can never remember it. However, I hit on a simple mnemonic: I simply dial the word *AN-THRAX*, the letter *H* being on the same button as the number 4, and so forth. This is a useful mnemonic that might be extended. Can you find a word for my home number, TABernacle 2463, and my office number, VINcent 8225? A telephone's alphanumerical equivalents are as follows: 2 = ABC, 3 = DEF, 4 = GHI, 5 = JKL, 6 = MN, 7 = PRS, 8 = TUV, and 9 = WXY.

Solution: TABernacle 2463 may be written as *VACCINE*, and VINcent 8225 may be written as *TINTACK*.

Source: Kendall and Thomas (1962)

20. Decimal point

Problem: What one mathematical symbol can be placed between a 2 and a 3 to express a number greater than 2 and less than 3?

Solution: A decimal point.

Source: Seifert and Patalano (1991)

21. Ratchet device

Problem: Consider the device shown below. Describe the motion of the gear wheel on the left of the device as the handle on the right of the device is moved alternately to the left and to the right.

Solution: The gear wheel continues a constant counterclockwise motion as the handle is moved alternately to the left and to the right.

Source: Carpenter and Just (1992)

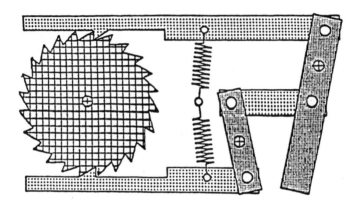

REFERENCES

Adams, J.L. (1974). *Conceptual blockbusting.* San Francisco: Freeman.

Amabile, T.M. (1983). *The social psychology of creativity.* New York: Springer-Verlag.

Anderson, J.R. (1985). *Cognitive psychology and its implications* (2nd ed.). New York: Freeman.

Bartlett, F.C. (1958). *Thinking.* London: Allen & Unwin.

Bradshaw, G.L. (1992). *Heuristics and strategies in the invention of the airplane.* Unpublished manuscript, University of Illinois, Urbana.

Carpenter, P.A., & Just, M.A. (1992). *Understanding mechanical systems through computer animation and kinematic imagery* (Technical Report No. ONR92-1). Pittsburgh: Carnegie Mellon University, Department of Psychology.

DeBono, E. (1967). *The five-day course in thinking.* New York: Basic Books.

Dunbar, K., & Klahr, D. (1989). Developmental differences in scientific discovery processes. In D. Klahr & K. Kotovsky (Eds.), *Complex information processing: The impact of Herbert A. Simon* (pp. 109–143). Hillsdale, NJ: Erlbaum.

Duncker, K. (1945). On problem solving. *Psychological Monographs,* *58*(5), whole no. 270.

Ellen, P. (1982). Direction, past experience and hints in creative problem solving: Reply to Weisberg and Alba. *Journal of Experimental Psychology: General, 111,* 316–325.

Finke, R.A. (1990). *Creative imagery: Discoveries and inventions in visualization.* Hillsdale, NJ: Erlbaum.

Finke, R.A., Ward, T.B., & Smith, S.M. (1992). *Creative cognition: Theory, research, and applications.* Cambridge: MIT Press.

Fixx, J.F. (1972). *More games for the super-intelligent.* New York: Warner Books.

Freedman, J.L. (1978). *Introductory psychology.* Reading, MA: Addison-Wesley.

Gardner, M. (1978) *Aha! Insight.* New York: Freeman.

Gick, M.L., & Holyoak, K.J. (1980). Analogical problem solving. *Cognitive Psychology, 12,* 306–355.

Gleitman, H. (1991). *Psychology* (3rd ed.). New York: Norton.

Glucksberg, S. (1962). The influence of strength of drive on functional fixedness and perceptual recognition. *Journal of Experimental Psychology, 63,* 36–41.

Glucksberg, S., & Danks, J.H. (1968). Effects of discriminative labels and of nonsense labels upon availability of novel function. *Journal of Verbal Learning and Verbal Behavior, 7,* 72–76.

Gordon, W.J. (1974). Some source material in discovery-by-analogy. *Journal of Creative Behavior, 8,* 239–257.

Guilford, J.P. (1959). The three faces of intellect. *American Psychologist, 14,* 469–479.

Hadamard, J. (1945). *The psychology of invention in the mathematical field.* New York: Dover.

Hinton, G. (1979). Some descriptions of the effects of structural descriptions in mental imagery. *Cognitive Science, 3,* 231–250.

Jansson, D.G., & Smith, S.M. (1991). Design fixation. *Design Studies, 12,* 3–11.

Kaplan, C.A., & Simon, H.A. (1990). In search of insight. *Cognitive Psychology, 22,* 374–419.

Kendall, P.M.H., & Thomas, G.M. (1962). *Mathematical puzzles for the connoisseur.* New York: Thomas Y. Crowell.

Klahr, D., & Dunbar, K. (1988). Dual space search during scientific reasoning. *Cognitive Science, 12,* 1–48.

Krueger, T.H. (1976). *Visual imagery in problem-solving and scientific creativity.* Derby, CT: Seal Press.

Kulkarni, D., & Simon, H.A. (1988). The processes of scientific discovery: The strategy of experimentation. *Cognitive Science, 12,* 139–175.

Lorenz, K. (1974). Analogy as a source of knowledge. *Science, 185,* 229–234.

Maier, N.R.F. (1931). Reasoning in humans: II. The solution of a problem and its appearance in consciousness. *Journal of Comparative Psychology, 12,* 181–194.

Maier, N.R.F. (1945). Reasoning in humans: III. The mechanisms of equivalent stimuli and reasoning. *Journal of Experimental Psychology, 35,* 349–360.

Mainstone, R.J. (1973). Intuition and the springs of structural invention. In J. Bryan & R. Sauer (Eds.), *Structures explicit and implicit* (pp. 41–68). Philadelphia: University of Pennsylvania.

Mansfield, R.S. & Busse, T.V. (1981). *The psychology of creativity and discovery: Scientists and their work.* Chicago: Nelson-Hall.

Mayer, R.E. (1983). *Thinking, problem solving, cognition.* New York: Freeman.

Metcalfe, J. (1986). Feeling of knowing in memory and problem solving. *Journal of Experimental Psychology: Learning, Memory, and Cognition, 12,* 288–294.

Metcalfe, J., & Wiebe, D. (1987). Intuition in insight and noninsight problem solving. *Memory & Cognition, 15,* 238–246.

Necka, E. (1985). The use of analogy in creative problem solving. *Polish Psychological Bulletin, 16,* 245–255.

Osborn A.F. (1963). *Applied imagination.* New York: Scribners.

Scheerer, M. (1963). Problem solving. *Scientific American, 208,* 118–128.

Scheerer, M., Goldstein, K., & Boring, E.G. (1941). A demonstration of insight: The horse-rider puzzle. *American Journal of Psychology, 54,* 437–438.

Seifert, C.M., & Patalano, A.L. (1991). Memory for incomplete tasks: A re-examination of the Zeigarnik effect. In *Proceedings of the Thirteenth Annual Conference of the Cognitive Science Society* (pp. 114–119). Hillsdale, NJ: Erlbaum.

Smilansky, J. (1984). Problem solving and the quality of invention: An empirical investigation. *Journal of Educational Psychology, 76,* 377–384.

Smilansky, J., & Halberstadt, N. (1986). Inventors versus problem solvers: An empirical investigation. *Journal of Creative Behavior, 20,* 183–201.

Smiles, S. (1884). *Men of invention and industry.* London: John Murray.

Sternberg, R.J. (1989). Intelligence, wisdom, and creativity: Their natures and interrelationships. In R.L. Linn (Ed.), *Intelligence: Measurement, theory, and public policy* (pp. 119–146). Urbana, IL: University of Illinois Press.

Sternberg, R.J., & Davidson, J.E. (1983). Insight in the gifted. *Educational Psychologist, 18,* 51–57.

Stratton, R.P., & Brown, R. (1972). Improving creative thinking by training in the production and judgment of solutions on a verbal problem. *Journal of Educational Psychology, 63,* 390–397.

Teborg, R.H. (1968). *Dissipation of functional fixedness by means of conceptual grouping tasks.* Unpublished doctoral dissertation, Michigan State University, East Lansing, MI.

Wallach, M.A. (1967). Creativity and the expression of possibilities. In J. Kagan (Ed.), *Creativity and learning* (pp. 36–57). Boston: Houghton Mifflin.

Wallach, M.A., & Kogan, N. (1965). *Modes of thinking in young children: A study of the creativity-intelligence distinction.* New York: Holt, Rinehart & Winston.

Weisberg, R.W. (1993). *Creativity: Beyond the myth of genius.* New York: Freeman.

Weisberg, R.W., & Alba, J.W. (1981). An examination of the alleged role of "fixation" in the solution of several "insight" problems. *Journal of Experimental Psychology: General, 110,* 169–192.

Wickelgren, W.A. (1974). *How to solve problems.* San Francisco: Freeman.

Wiesner, J.B. (1967). Education for creativity in the sciences. In J. Kagan (Ed.), *Creativity and learning* (pp. 92–102). Boston: Houghton Mifflin.

Yaniv, I., & Meyer, D.E. (1987). Activation and metacognition of inaccessible stored information: Potential bases for incubation effects in problem solving. *Journal of Experimental Psychology: Learning, Memory, and Cognition, 13,* 187–205.

IV The Great-Minds Approach

10 Creative Insight: The Social Dimension of a Solitary Moment

Mihaly Csikszentmihalyi and Keith Sawyer

There appears to be a general tendency, in all cultures and historical periods, to differentiate between mental processes that are routine, shallow, and trivial on the one hand, and those that are unusual, profound, and important on the other. In the English language, the word that best denotes the second type of mental process is *insight*, derived from the Old Dutch for "seeing inside." We classify as insightful ideas that seem to get to the core of an issue and people who are prone to have such ideas. Like other words referring to mental processes that are relatively rare and valued—such as *wisdom* or *intuition*—insight is likely to have been selected and preserved in the vocabulary because of its adaptive significance (Csikszentmihalyi & Rathunde, 1990). In other words, a culture that in principle cannot differentiate between more profound and more superficial aspects of an issue because it lacks the concept of insight is likely to have more trouble coping with its material and ideational environment.

An insight is typically said to occur when an individual is exposed to some new information that results in a new way of looking at a known problem or phenomenon in such a way that its essential features are grasped. The term *insight* often is accompanied by a modifier (e.g., *fresh insight, new insight*, or *powerful insight*). Usually we think of some cause that results in insight: For example, "researchers yield new insights on Japan," or "this new metaphor provides fresh and powerful insights." Insight seems to involve (1) an existing state of mind or set of mental structures relevant to the topic and (2) a moment of realization, consequent to new information or a sudden new way of looking at old information, resulting in (3) a quick restructuring of the mental model, which is subjectively perceived as providing a new understanding. These criteria imply that it is impossible to have an insight about a topic unless the person experiencing the insight has had some prior exposure to the issue.

Although the term *insight* can be used to describe moments that we all seem to have from time to time, in this chapter we propose that insight is best studied through mental processes that result in creative products. Whereas examples of insight in everyday life tend to be elusive and debatable, they are both more public and more convincing when they occur to scientists whose work results in Nobel prizes or to artists and writers who enhance our lives with their creative endeavors. In what follows, we discuss the phenomenon of creative insight as reported in a series of interviews with creative individuals from various fields. The moment of insight emerges, in these interviews, as a central aspect of creativity. We suggest that what we learn about insight in the context of the creative process will help us understand insight more generally.

GENERAL OBSERVATIONS ABOUT CREATIVE INSIGHT

Recent studies of scientific creativity (Simonton, 1988a; Gruber & Davis, 1988) and artistic creativity (Getzels & Csikszentmihalyi, 1976; Martindale, 1990) have focused on mental processes or models of the creative process, following in the cognitivist tradition of psychology established in the early sixties. Counter to this dominant mode, a few researchers have attempted to understand the social and cultural influences and environments in which creativity is manifested (Campbell, 1960; Csikszentmihalyi, 1988, 1990a; Harrington, 1990; John-Steiner, 1992; Woodman & Schoenfeldt, 1989). As John-Steiner (1992) points out, these two approaches—the first intrapsychic, the second interpersonal—have not yet been successfully integrated. In this chapter, we hope to begin such an integration by showing the relationship between insight, clearly an intrapsychic process, and the social milieu in which it occurs.

Most studies of creative insight have been conducted by psychologists and therefore tend to focus on the cognitive processes during and leading up to the moment of insight. The tendency has been to assume that this moment occurs when the person is alone; hence, insight has been studied mainly as a cognitive process that occurs in isolation. As the peak experience in creative lives, the moment of insight has fascinated creative individuals and their biographers alike. Consequently, many creativity researchers have focused on the moment of creative insight and attempted to analyze it as a purely intrapsychic cognitive process. In this chapter we will present a different perspective, by expanding out from this moment in time and embedding it within the other relevant stages of the creative process. When we look at the complete "life span" of a creative insight in our subjects' experience, the moment of insight appears as but one short flash in a complex, time-consuming, fundamentally social process. It is true that the individuals we interviewed generally report their insights as occurring in solitary moments: during a walk, while taking a shower, or while lying in bed just after waking. However, these reports usually are embedded within a more complex narrative, a story that describes the effort preceding and following the insight, and the overall sense of these complete narratives stresses the salience of social, interactional factors. It seems that the solitary nature of the moment of insight may have blinded us to the social dimension of the entire creative process.

When we reviewed our interviews, we discovered a common narrative structure in descriptions of creative insight. (For other collections of personal narratives of moments of insight, see Shrady [1972] and Ghiselin [1952].) Respondents described moments of creative insight as being contextualized within a four-stage process. The first stage consists of the hard work and research preceding the moment of insight; the second stage is a period of idle time alone; the third stage is the moment of insight itself; and the fourth stage is the hard work and elaboration required to develop and bring the idea to fruition. Most of these eminent people paraphrased the saying: "Creativity is 99 percent perspiration and 1 percent inspiration."

The periods of hard work that precede and follow a creative insight are fundamentally social, deeply rooted in interaction with colleagues and in the individual's internalized understanding of the culturally constituted domain. The balance of hard work and idle time can also be viewed as a balance between social interaction and individual isolation. The social interaction within which the creative insight is nestled is coincident with this "99 percent perspiration." Thus, the traditional models of creativity, which involve stages and which focus on psychological processes, inadequately represent this social, interactional aspect of the process of creative insight.

Multistage Models of Creative Insight

In the early part of this century, Henri Poincaré (1913, p. 389) described his own process of creative mathematical thought using three stages: "This appearance of sudden illumination [is] a manifest sign of long, unconscious prior work.... [This unconscious work] is possible, and of a certainty it is only fruitful, if it is on the one hand preceded and on the other hand followed by a period of conscious work." Hadamard (1949) proposed a four-stage model of creative insight in which *preparation* is followed by an *incubation* stage, during which the subconscious repeatedly attempts new combinations of mental elements until one becomes stable and coherent enough to emerge into consciousness. This results in *illumination*, the subjective experience of insight. The final stage is *verification*, or conscious evaluation of the insight.

Following these early formulations, many contemporary approaches have been based on two- or three-stage models of creative insight. The two-stage models refer to a first stage of *ideation*, a time-consuming, perhaps subconscious, generation of new ideas or combinations, and a second stage, in which certain privileged *combinations emerge into consciousness* (Epstein, 1990; Milgram, 1990). This second stage is subjectively perceived as the moment of insight. The three-stage models (Feldman, 1988; Langley & Jones, 1988; Ohlsson, 1984; Perkins, 1988; Simon, 1977; Simonton, 1988a) include these two stages but suggest a third and final stage of *evaluation* or *elaboration*, in which the creative insight is developed consciously, with the active use of external sources and prior knowledge, into a communicable symbolic product, whether an artwork or a scientific publication. (See Runco [1990] for a more thorough review of three-stage models.)

Campbell (1960) often is cited as the inspiration for contemporary three-stage models of creativity. He used the evolutionary paradigm to explain the growth of knowledge in general, developing what he called an "evolutionary epistemology," of which creativity is a special case. In his scheme, changes in "ways of knowing" start with (1) a variation stage, during which a large number of novel responses are generated, followed by (2) a selection stage, in which the best-adapted variations are chosen from all the options, and finally (3) a retention stage, during which the selected variants are added to the pool of responses for transmission to the next generation.

Simonton (1988a) developed a theory of scientific creativity based on Campbell's framework. (Perkins [1988] and Martindale [1990] also base their three-stage models on Campbell's evolutionary metaphor.) For Simonton, the variation stage involved the chance permutations of mental elements. He defined these mental elements as "the fundamental units that can be manipulated in some manner" by the creative process (Simonton, 1988b). Some of these chance permutations will be more stable than others, and these configurations will emerge into consciousness, resulting in an experience of insight. At this point, Simonton's theory states, the individual must engage in conscious work to transform the chance configuration into a communication configuration, a symbolic form of the insight that allows communication of the insight, such as a journal article or painting.

Although there are subtle variations in the definitions of these stages of creative insight among different researchers, we propose the following unifying framework: The first stage, *preparation*, which is stimulated by external pressures or by intrinsic motivation, involves focused conscious work, such as studying or analyzing data. These rational thought processes provide the raw material on which the subconscious can begin working. The second stage, which can last a very short time or go on for years, is the stage of *incubation*. The theorists previously cited disagree about just what occurs in the subconscious; Hadamard (1949) argued that active, guided processing is taking place, whereas most current researchers believe that chance combinations of thought processes below the threshold of awareness provide an adequate explanation (Langley & Jones, 1988; Simonton, 1988a, 1988b). The third stage, *insight*, occurs when the subconscious combines or selects an idea which, for reasons that remain poorly understood, emerges into consciousness, resulting in an "Aha!" experience. This insight will be useless unless it is *evaluated* by the conscious mind and *elaborated* for presentation to others. Some researchers have used concepts such as implicit theories of creativity or metacognition to characterize how individuals engage in this fourth evaluative phase (Runco, 1990; Sternberg, 1988).

Social Process Models of Creativity

Stage models such as those just reviewed have been widely used by psychologists as frameworks for analyzing creativity. These models have focused on psychological stages of the individual's creative process, without attempting to represent social influences. How does the individual integrate his or her insights with an ongoing domain of scientific or artistic activity? To what extent is the preparation stage dependent on the symbolic domain or on the social group within which the individual works? Creative individuals rarely work in a vacuum, isolated from the social systems that constitute their domain of activity. The evaluation and elaboration stage also implies a social dimension: How can an insight be evaluated unless the individual makes use of an internalized model of the domain (e.g., by using the formal mathematical procedures endorsed by the culture) and without an intimate familiarity with experts in the field who help select and define what is worthwhile? How can an idea be elaborated if not within the context of a specific domain of endeavor and with an awareness of the social processes required to communicate the idea through the field?

In our interviews, we found that creative individuals had a strong subjective awareness of external social or discipline influences at each creative stage. When asked to describe a moment of creative insight, they typically provided extended narratives that described not just a single moment but a complex, multi-stage process, with frequent discussions of interpersonal contact, strategic or political considerations, and awareness of the paradigm, of what questions were interesting as defined by the discipline. This was particularly salient in the preparation stage and in the evaluation and elaboration stage. Although the moment of creative insight usually occurs in isolation, it is surrounded and contextualized within an ongoing experience that is fundamentally social, and the insight would be meaningless out of that context. Therefore, to better understand the interviews, we needed to incorporate perspectives that explored the ways that social factors influenced the stages of the creative process. We turned to social process models of creativity, recently proposed by several researchers, in an attempt to incorporate social system influences on the creative process.

Harrington (1990) argued for an ecological approach to creativity and compared the influence of the biological ecosystem on the organism to the influence of social environments on the creative individual. Using this metaphor, creativity is described as a psychosocial process that places demands on both individuals and their social contexts, or ecosystems. Extending the ecological metaphor, Harrington discussed the importance of "organism-environment fit" in the creative process and how creative individuals can be active shapers of their environments.

The interactionist model of creativity derived from the symbolic interactionist school within sociology. Woodman and Schoenfeldt (1989) developed this approach to explain how individual differences in creativity might be derived from exogenous factors. The interactionist model explored the combination and interrelation of psychological and environmental factors in human behavior. Woodman and Schoenfeldt proposed the primary components of contextual influences (culture and group, task constraints), social influences (social facilitation, rewards and punishments, role modeling), cognitive style (ideational fluency, problem-solving style), personality traits (autonomy, intuition), and antecedent conditions (past history, socialization, biographical variables). However, their presentation did not attempt to characterize the processes of creativity suggested by stage models.

The systems view developed by Csikszentmihalyi (Csikszentmihalyi, 1988; Csikszentmihalyi, 1990a) proposed that creativity could not be operationalized at the psychological level alone. Like the ecological and the interactionist models, Csikszentmihalyi argued that individual creativity must be defined with respect to a system that includes not only the individual but also social and cultural factors which influence the creative process and help to constitute creativity. He separated these influences into the *field*, the group of gatekeepers who are entitled to select a novel idea or product for inclusion in the domain, and the *domain*,

consisting of the symbolic system of rules and procedures that define permissible behavior within its boundaries (hence the domain
of baseball, chess, or algebra or, more narrowly, a Kuhnian paradigm). The creative process involves the generation of a novel
creative product by the individual, the evaluation of the product
by the field, and the retention of selected products by addition to
the domain. Thus, the creative process involves a recurring circle
from person to field to domain and back to the person, paralleling
the evolutionary pattern of variation (person), selection (field), and
retention (domain).

AN INTERPSYCHIC MODEL OF CREATIVE INSIGHT

The majority of our interviews included descriptions of the creative process that were consistent with the stage models. However, we noticed that these stagelike narrative descriptions tended
to group into two distinct types not formerly discussed in the
literature. These types varied in terms of the length of time involved in the overall creative process. Some individuals described working for several years on a problem before the flash of
insight hit, whereas others spoke of working for a few hours in the
morning and having the insight in the afternoon. Most creative
individuals experience both types of creative process. For example, Darwin's journey on the *Beagle* involved a daily ritual of observing the natural environment, taking notes, and reflecting on
similarities and differences among animals and plants. Each day's
work resulted in new observations about these relationships.
However, the culmination of these many small insights into the
theory of natural selection was a lengthy process, taking years if
one includes not only the journey but the knowledge acquired by
Darwin before boarding the ship. In our interviews, this variation
in time scale applies not only to preparation but also to the phase
of evaluation and elaboration: In some cases, the evaluation occurred in a matter of minutes, whereas in others it took months
or even longer to elaborate or confirm the insight.

These two types of description of creative insight seem so different that they actually may represent two types of creative insight,
resting at two extremes of a continuum. Although the creative
process most likely involves a continuous range of time spans, in

this chapter we will examine these extremes. To distinguish between these two ideal types, it might be useful to adopt the distinction developed by Getzels (1964) between presented problem solving and discovered problem finding. (See also Getzels and Csikszentmihalyi [1976]. For a recent review of this literature, see Hoover [1990].) The short time-frame process tends to occur when a problem is known and preexisting in the domain and all that needs to be found is a solution to it. We will refer to this as a *presented problem-solving process.* The long time-frame process tends to occur when the nature of the problem to be solved is less clear; in fact, the problem itself may not be formulated until the moment of insight. Great creative breakthroughs, paradigmatic shifts, belong to this category. We will refer to this as a *discovered problem-finding process* (figure 10.1).

In both problem-solving and problem-finding narratives, the importance of social interaction is salient. Our interviews suggest that the four-stage perspective must be extended from the intrapsychic to the interpsychic level. If 99 percent of the activity takes place in stages that are predominantly social—the preparation, evaluation, and elaboration stages—then the interpersonal aspect of the process must be seriously considered and, in fact, may be more significant than the intrapsychic aspects of creativity. The isolation that seems to accompany the incubation stage preceding the moment of insight may have obscured the observation that this part of the process serves to juxtapose and integrate information that derives from the domain and from the field and is hence interpsychic in origin.

To link the intrapsychic and interpsychic levels, we suggest postulating a conscious-subconscious interaction that parallels the interpsychic-intrapsychic dimension. Although conscious attention is limited in capacity and must be managed and directed constantly by the individual (James, 1890; Broadbent, 1958; Kahneman, 1973; Hasher & Zacks, 1979; Eysenck, 1982; Csikszentmihalyi, 1978, 1990b), several research traditions have suggested that subconscious mental processing may have a much greater capacity. Researchers from Freud to current cognitive scientists have argued that conscious awareness is the tip of the iceberg, with a significant amount of mental processing occurring beneath the surface. Recent society-of-mind theories have suggested that the

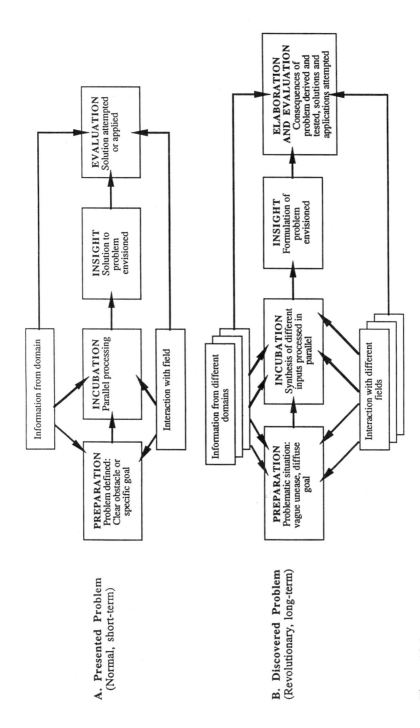

Figure 10.1
The role of insight in the creative process.

subjective sense of a unified self is illusory and that the ego rests at the top of a complex network of progressively less complex, subconscious entities (Minsky, 1985; Ornstein, 1986). Such theories hypothesize that each of these subconscious entities acts as an independent mental processing unit, almost like a pseudoconsciousness, and these entities compete for a turn in consciousness. This competitive interaction results in the ego, or the experience of reflective self-awareness, as an emergent phenomenon (Dennett, 1991).

If conscious attention is serial and limited, whereas the subconscious capacity of the mind is parallel and multiple, how can the individual coordinate them? If it is to result in a public product, everything that is in the subconscious must at some point pass through conscious awareness. All activities of daily life—not only creative insight—must involve a strategic balance of the strengths and weaknesses of the two: conscious awareness, which can be directed but is sequential (one at a time), and the subconscious, which cannot be directed but is parallel and has a much greater capacity. The paradox for the creative individual is somehow to direct this undirectable subconscious process so that useful insights result. In fact, many of our respondents claim that they have developed the ability to do just that: to control without controlling, indirectly to direct the subconscious mind.

Preparation

The preparation stage of the creative process involves many components. Essentially, it requires concentrating attention on a problematic issue—a need, a desire, a challenge, or a specific problem that requires solution—long enough to master and understand its parameters. Issues of motivation, cognition, and socialization all are involved. Hence, it can be said that Leonardo da Vinci prepared himself for his insights into the workings of nature—how the wind blows, how water flows, how birds fly—by an early interest in human anatomy, in mechanics, and in the structural composition of leaves and branches. Likewise, Darwin prepared himself for his insights into evolution through a childhood interest in collecting insects, the reading of geology, and the painstaking observations he made during the voyage of the *Beagle*. Curiosity, interest, access to information, and some impulse that sets questioning in motion are all part of the preparatory phase of the creative process.

The difference between presented problems and discovered problems at this stage of the process is that the former confront the person with a relatively clearly formulated problem within a normal scientific paradigmatic tradition (Kuhn, 1962), whereas the latter confronts the person with a general sense of intellectual or existential unease outside a paradigmatic context. For instance, to increase the profitability of a firm by firing 20 percent of the employees is a presented problem. The questions of who should be fired, when they should be fired, and how to fire them still need to be solved, but the problem itself is not in question. However, one can reject this perception of the problem and ask, "How can the profitability of the firm be increased?" This reformulation would lead to less of a presented problem-solving and more of a discovered problem-finding process. As this example suggests, a process of problem discovery usually yields a presented problem as an outcome. In other words, the problem-finding question, "How can profits be increased?" might yield the answer, "By firing 20 percent of the employees," resulting in a presented problem to be solved.

Incubation

Given the importance of unconscious work in reaching creative insights, a key component of the process must be the filtering mechanism that determines which information will be passed from conscious awareness to the subconscious. The social influences of the domain and the field appear to act as the primary controlling mechanisms of the creative individual's subconscious. Through acculturation and apprenticeship in a given domain, the individual internalizes that domain's built-in assumptions and rules, much as Kuhn's paradigm constrains the thinking of individuals in a scientific field.

This internalized interpsychic, fundamentally social filtering mechanism may rest just beneath conscious awareness or perhaps on the boundary between conscious and subconscious processing.[1] Although the subconscious network cannot be manipulated directly by consciousness, the conscious creation and development of this filter (through education, mentoring or apprenticeship, or reading texts) can influence the subconscious network indirectly. This conscious manipulation takes place during the preparation stage and, in our interviews, the social dimension of this stage is crucial and includes apprenticeship, mentoring, solitary study, and interaction with fellow students.

One major difference between presented and discovered processes at the incubation stage appears to be the diversity of inputs that the latter includes. Revolutionary creative insights seem to be based on the random convergence of ideas from different domains, usually facilitated by interaction with individuals from different fields. For example, Linus Pauling explains the origins of his insights into the mathematical representation of chemical bonds, which earned him a Nobel prize in chemistry, in terms of his original interest in the composition of matter inherited from his pharmacist father plus the chance exposure to the first wave of quantum mechanics at Cal Tech.[2] In his case, incubation consisted in the combination of elements from the domains of quantum physics and chemistry, at the very least. Practically every respondent we interviewed seems to have combined information from more than one domain prior to the occurrence of a major insight.

The preceding discussion suggests a three-level mental model of the preparation and incubation stages of the creative process. This model is applicable to both presented problem-solving and discovered problem-finding creativity; however, because of the longer time frame, the model suggests that problem-finding creativity will make greater use of the subconscious and will combine information derived from more different sources.

Level 1: Conscious Attention (Serial Processing)
Certain stimuli or problematic issues are invested with attention. Choices are made in terms of the three components of the system model: the person, field, and domain. In other words, genetically programmed predilections, learned motives, socialized interests, and cultural values all enter into determining which stimuli or issues will be invested with attention. Only a few chunks of infor-

mation can be attended to at any one time; thus, this level is characterized by serial, directed-attention processing.

Level 2: Semiconscious Filters
A semiconscious filter determines what information is passed to the subconscious. This filter also is structured following the systems model: It is an internal mental image of the field-domain-person trichotomy, and it selects which information is viewed as relevant. Personality traits, such as curiosity, interest, intrinsic motivation, and flexibility, are also important at this level.

Level 3: Subconscious Processing Entities, or the Society of Mind
The distributed, parallel nature of this network of subconscious processing entities allows multiple chunks of information to be viewed simultaneously. Connections between ideas can be tested, perhaps in a subconscious generate-and-test fashion. Of the theorists discussed earlier, only Hadamard (1949) proposed a model in which this incubation stage is distinct from the preparation stage. We suggest that a Hadamard-like incubation takes place but in a parallel fashion: Rather than a Freudian unitary subconscious working on the problem, many smaller entities are interacting randomly and perhaps collectively working on many problems.

The Three Levels Functioning Synchronously
These three levels, in particular the semiconscious filters and the subconscious network, are developed and internalized through professional socialization. Once the individual is socialized into a field, the basic flow of information storage during the preparation stage is from conscious awareness, through the filter, into the subconscious network. This is, in effect, a mapping from diachrony to synchrony: Whereas ideas can be addressed only one at a time in consciousness, once they have passed to the subconscious, ideas that entered awareness in a serial fashion may be considered in parallel.

Insight

The two types of creative insight, presented and discovered, correspond to the well-known distinction first suggested by Thomas

Kuhn (1962) between normal science and revolutionary science (although we are, of course, speaking not only of scientific fields but of all fields of creative activity). So-called normal science consists of working within an accepted tradition, incrementally advancing the field with experiments and discoveries. In contrast, revolutionary science involves the creation of a completely new field, a new domain of activity. It is not simply an incremental advance but instead is a discontinuous leap to a new perspective, what Kuhn calls a new "paradigm." Our model suggests that creative revolutions involve the three-level subconscious process just described, resulting in a discovered problem-finding insight, whereas normal science can proceed as presented problem solving and may remain largely conscious. The small insights that seem to be a frequent part of everyday life are more like problem solving, whereas the revolutionary insights that change the course of history will be problem-finding insights.

Within our three-level model, insight is a type of information retrieval, the reverse of the information storage flow in the preparation stage. This reverse process begins in the subconscious: A particular combination or pattern that has emerged (randomly, undirected) from the subconscious network is strong enough to surface into consciousness. This is similar to Simonton's (1988a) description of how a stable chance configuration gets into conscious awareness. It is also reminiscent of Simon's (1977) suggestion that insight occurs through selective forgetting, a type of mental erosion during which good ideas remain whereas the bad ones simply erode away with time. Our theory suggests a more active subconscious process than Simon's. As similarities between ideas or configurations in different domains are recognized in the subconscious—such as that between geological and biological changes in the case of Darwin, or between subatomic quantum relationships and chemical bonds in Pauling's case—a new configuration combining the two emerges and filters into consciousness. Although in the popular conception, insight results from a specific stimulus (such as the apple that fell on Newton's head), we have not found descriptions of this sort in our interviews. The insights are always described as welling up from the subconscious, but there is never a mention of a specific external stimulus. Perhaps there is, nonetheless, a sort of internal stimulus, a subconscious event that causes a final, critical shift in the subconscious network, like the final shout that releases the avalanche.

Evaluation and Elaboration

In our four-stage model of creative insight, the evaluation and elaboration stage represents a reverse filtering of the insight, from the subconscious network into consciousness. Like the preparation stage, this process also is intricately bound up with the internalized social model of the field and domain. The ensuing elaboration of the insight is palpably social, as individuals develop their artistic or mechanical creation or communicate verbally with colleagues in an attempt to transfer their insight into an exogenous, interpsychic social object.

Figure 10.1 describes a simple linear process. In reality, most creative ideas, especially of a discovered kind, are the result of multiple cycles of preparation, incubation, insight, and elaboration, with many feedback loops, the end result of which is a solution that may be either final or temporary, in which case the cycle may repeat itself again and again. A good example of the complexity of this process appears in Gruber's (1981) work on Darwin, which illustrates how the development of the evolutionary paradigm was the result of a lifetime spent elaborating the implications of an insight that was itself the result of a protracted series of partial understandings.

NARRATIVES OF CREATIVE INSIGHT

To illustrate concrete instances of creative insight, and especially the social contribution to their emergence, we will use data from our ongoing interview study. This study involves structured videotaped interviews of approximately 2 hours' duration with a sample of creative individuals. The respondents who are chosen meet the following criteria: (1) They are persons who have made a creative contribution to the natural sciences, the social sciences, the arts and humanities, or business or politics. (2) They are generally older than 60 years. (3) They are still involved actively either in the domain in which they had achieved fame or in a new domain. Currently, 60 interviews have been completed, and we anticipate a total sample of 100.

This chapter will draw on the content of nine interviews that have undergone preliminary analysis. The nine respondents will be identified as follows:

• Respondent A: environmental activist, organizer of special-interest groups, author of several books (female)

• Respondent B: physicist, holder of two Nobel prizes (male)

• Respondent C: banker, chief executive officer of one of the wealthiest and most influential financial conglomerates in the nation (male)

• Respondent D: mathematician and physicist (male)

• Respondent E: economist, poet, environmentalist (male)

• Respondent F: literary critic, author, rhetorician (male)

• Respondent G: ceramicist of international reputation (female)

• Respondent H: sculptor (female)

• Respondent I: physicist (male)

We will use representative quotations relevant to both presented and discovered processes and from each stage of these processes. The quotations were chosen to highlight the role of social factors at each stage.

Presented Problem Solving

As noted previously, respondents' narratives of moments of creative insight tended to fall into two types: those that seem more everyday and occur within four-stage cycles of short duration and those that are more exceptional, with a four-stage duration of up to several years. The former we have referred to as *presented problem-solving insights*. They involve relatively short incubation periods and a single domain and field, with a fourth stage of evaluation rather than elaboration. The problem-solving insights are more consistent with the popular uses of the term *insight*, which one finds in newspaper articles or in everyday conversation.

Several subjects described problem-solving insights. For example, the political activist, respondent A, described her daily routine as a period of work followed by "off time":

In the morning, that's when I really like intellectual activity, very very finely focused intellectual activities. That's when I write, working at my desk, talking on the phone, and then after lunch is always a time where I like to slack off; maybe snooze for 15 minutes, maybe take a bike ride.... I mean, who knows? When you might suddenly have a terrific "Aha!" idea, I don't know! Mostly it happens to me when I'm gardening..., or doing something steadying with my hands.... I develop a lot of my ideas in dialogue.

In the problem-solving narratives, the stages of preparation and evaluation occur within a day or two of the moment of creative insight. The incubation stage occurs over a period of a few hours, usually on a daily basis, and often in the morning. The evaluation stage occurs immediately after the insight enters consciousness: Because the individual is in a problem-solving mode, it is relatively easy to determine quickly whether the insight is appropriate to the given problem.

The following four sections address each of the four stages in turn, using quotations that are representative of the range of comments on that stage.

Preparation

In problem-solving narratives, some individuals focused on preparation as hard work on a problem which is more specific to that problem than to the domain at large. Others focused on hard work rather than domain influences.

Several of our interview subjects stated that to have creative ideas, you should attempt to have a large quantity of ideas and select from these the good ones. This is consistent with theories of ideational fluency (Milgram, 1990) and Simonton's (1988a) argument that creativity is proportional to productivity. A businessman told us, "Quantity is very important ... I only look for quantity of ideas, and finally the quality will come out." A chemist suggested that "you have a lot of ideas, and throw away the bad ones." Respondent C makes long lists of ideas and then is constantly reviewing the list to rank the ideas.

Respondent D described how collaboration is a key social aspect of the preparation stage, by using the metaphor of the open door:

Science is a very gregarious business; it's essentially the difference between having this door open and having it shut. If I'm doing science, I have the door open. That's kind of symbolic, but it's true. You want to be all the time talking with people ... it's only by interacting with other people in the building that you get anything interesting done; it's essentially a communal enterprise.

Many of the nonscientists also spoke of the importance of collaboration. Respondent C's first impulse when a problem presents itself is to pick up the phone: "When I'm trying to get my mind around something new, I seek out people and talk to them." This is not restricted to a new problem: It is also part of respondent C's daily schedule: "I very much network the world; I travel; there [is] ... probably a group of 40 people, maybe, that I stay in touch with."

Incubation

As we hypothesized earlier, the incubation phase seems to be less of a factor in presented problem solving than it is in discovered problem finding. Nonetheless, many of the individuals we interviewed structured their day to include a period of solitary idle time that follows a period of hard work. The idle time may be in the afternoon, after a hard morning of preparation; or it may be in the morning, based on preparation from the night before. Respondent C schedules this time in the morning:

[Starting at 5:30 AM] I typically try to work either at home or at the office, and that's when I do a good bit of my thinking, and priority setting ... Typically get to the office about 6:30. I try to keep reasonably quiet time until 9:30 or 10. Then you get involved in lots of [interpersonal] transactions ... I do my best work when I have some alone time.

A surprising number of the individuals we interviewed told us that they carefully structure their workday to include a similar period of idle time. Many of them told us that without this solitary, quiet time, they would never have their most important ideas. This daily idle time seems to be a period during which a problem-solving incubation stage may be at work. Several respondents keep their mind idle by engaging in repetitive physical activity on a daily basis. Respondent A compared the repetitive aspect of physical activities to a Zen practice:

Generally, the really high ideas come to me when I'm gardening, or while I'm doing something steadying with my hands. You know, most people have chores, something quite repetitive.... The repetitive physical activities are really like a Zen practice, like the Zen monks sweeping the temple garden. And it's in that motion that you're in tune with the whole universe.

Insight

Almost without exception, our respondents told us that the daily problem-solving insights come to them during this idle time. This is consistent with the model we presented earlier, which suggests that insights will occur after a period of incubation. The banker, respondent C, carries a notepad with him everywhere he goes, and when he has an insight, he begins to write to himself: "It often happens when I'm sitting around a hotel room; I'm on a trip and nothing's going on. I sit and think. Or I'm sitting on a beach ... and I find myself writing myself notes." Respondent D described his daily insights as coming while performing repetitive physical activity: "You don't know how it comes into your head. You're shaving, taking a walk." The economist, respondent E, has his insights during idle time either outdoors or in the bath:

We have this little cabin ... a beautiful little place ... I do a lot of writing out there.... Ideas often come to me in the bathtub. We have a little ritual in the morning; [my wife] takes a short bath, and then I have a 40-minute bath and do some exercise.

Although most respondents described insights as occurring during a solitary idle time, several described how insights can be sparked by interaction. Respondent A emphasized the importance of dialogue in generating ideas:

I develop lots of my ideas in dialogue. It's very exciting to have another mind that is considering the same set of phenomena with as much interest as one is. It's very exciting, the sparks, and dynamic interaction, and very much newer things, new ways of looking at things, that come out of those conversations.

However, respondent D warned us not to be misled by this solitary moment: "That's something you do alone, but not for weeks alone, a few hours, and then you talk to somebody in the hall. So it's solitary but only in small chunks." Even in the most solitary, private moment—the moment of insight itself—many creative individuals are aware of the deeply social nature of their creative process.

Evaluation

Many respondents discussed the act of rapidly evaluating an insight as it enters consciousness. They described the evaluation stage as the point at which the large number of ideas generated would be filtered and selected. This evaluation occurs spontaneously and is phrased in terms of whether the insight is both interesting and relevant. The literary critic, respondent F, described a recursive, social process of evaluation rather than an instant judgment:

In all matters which entail evaluation, I think what we have to do is come to our own clear first impressions ... you enter into it as fully as you can, and you form a judgment, conscious or unconscious, expressed or not, and you talk to somebody, and they say you missed something, and you go back a second time, and sometimes you have a revelation the second time.

Respondent F had perhaps the most elaborate theory of how social interaction influences the evaluation stage of creativity, having coined his own term for collective creativity—*coduction*:

In my last book I coined the term *coduction* for what we do when we evaluate literary works, and I think it might be extended to the kind of ... recursive and ... essentially sloppy, process. I wanted to have a term that had an air of respectability about it, with that *duction* part, and the *co* emphasized the fact that it has to be done communally, in the sense that you try out ideas, you listen to what other people have said, you then change your mind, come back, and do it again.

Respondent G, the ceramicist, described the stages of insight and evaluation in terms of playfulness and discipline: "I was playful in creating these things in my work—but I was completely disciplined in working in factories, working with my clients ... It has to be produced, it has to be produced at a price, it has to be produced to the liking of the foreman." Her concept of evaluation is fundamentally social.

Respondent C always involves people in the process of evaluation: "I'm a big talker. I will talk people through my ideas, bounce ideas off people."

Discovered Problem Finding

The second type of creative insight, *problem finding*, often is what researchers focus on when they study famous scientists or artists. These are the revolutionary insights that pave the way for pathbreaking new work or that integrate two fields which had never crossed paths. Because the psychological and social processes involved are much more elaborate than with problem-solving creativity, we will devote the bulk of our analysis to this type of insight.

In an extended narrative relating his groundbreaking work in quantum electrodynamics, the physicist, respondent D, described how he came to reconcile the approaches of two famous physicists, Feynman and Schwinger. Feynman had recently begun to use idiosyncratic diagrams to solve problems more quickly and as accurately as the complex equations of Schwinger. While Schwinger's equations had been rigorously proved and were accepted by physicists, Feynman's method was somewhat suspect, because no one had been able to integrate it with mainstream physics. Respondent D told us:

The biggest event of my life, from a scientific point of view ... this is what made me famous ... I spent 6 months working very hard, to understand both of them [Feynman and Schwinger] clearly; that meant simply hard hard work of calculating. I would sit down for days and days with large stacks of paper ... and at the end of 6 months, I went off on a vacation, took the Greyhound bus to California, spent a couple of weeks just bumming around in California ... after 2 weeks in California, where I wasn't doing any work, just sightseeing, I got on the Greyhound bus to come back to Princeton and suddenly, in the middle of the night, when we were going through Kansas, the whole thing sort of suddenly became crystal clear, so that was sort of the big revelation for me, the eureka experience or whatever you like to call it, that suddenly the whole picture became clear ... and the result was a theory that actually was useful. So that was the way it happened, sort of the big creative moment of my life. It wasn't, I don't think, particularly unusual; that's the way it happens. You have to do 6 months of very hard work first and get all the components bumping around in your head, and then you have to be idle for a couple of weeks, and then—ping—it suddenly falls into place.... Then I had to spend another 6 months afterward working out the details and writing it up and so forth.... That was my passport into the world of science.

The moment of creative insight occurs during an idle period just after a long period of hard work and must be followed by another long period of hard work. The following four sections address each of the stages in turn, using quotations that are representative of the range of comments on that stage.

Preparation

Almost all respondents emphasized the importance of the preparation stage to the subsequent creative insight. In narratives about problem-finding on a long time scale, preparation was discussed in terms of apprenticeship to a field, learning the basic rules and principles of the domain. Many respondents described this type of preparation, particularly the social and collaborative aspects. Of those who discussed this, all but one were physical or social scientists. The single nonscientist was the sculptor, respondent H, who described the importance of keeping current with other artists' work: "There is no one who goes to museums and looks at objects and looks at artworks and looks at sculpture and looks at paintings more than do artists." A chemist summarized the approach of the scientists: "Study the more fundamental sciences ... learn in the university the more fundamental subjects that are harder to study by oneself."

In addition to the preparation involved in learning a domain, preparation can also take the form of constant daily work in a domain, over a long period of time. Respondent H described the work preceding creative inspiration: "Before you can do such a spontaneous thing, you must have done hundreds of them ... that doesn't come without work." Respondent D described this work as a struggle: "You have to describe it as a sort of struggle.... I have always to force myself to write ... it's awfully hard to get started ... you may work very hard for a week producing the first page.... Without that preliminary forcing and pushing probably nothing would ever happen." On several occasions, respondent C described the importance of preparation as a sort of "domain awareness": "I happen to read broadly, and I very consciously build a very broad spectrum of activities, because I enjoy it. I'm innately curious, but I also think that the real key, at the most senior levels of companies, is to have a perspective."

Respondent G described the primary importance of social factors in her life. She began to make pottery through a series of historical accidents; she had been pursuing a career as a painter. She says, "There was always something happening at the time of my life that influenced where I was going or where I lived—so you can't take my life as a life that was based on my decision alone. It had also to do with the fact that I was curious to see the world." She says you must "first decide what life you want and then fit in your profession." Despite a career distinguished by constant innovation, she continually emphasizes the importance of cultural tradition: "Tradition is your home in designing ... you can only work in your own tradition. Everything I did in my whole life, no matter how different it was, was always based on traditional expectations." She also talked about the culturally constructed notion of aesthetic value: "In pottery, anything that is attractive ... has to have an aspect of obviousness.... This aspect of obviousness has something to do with a common culture ... everybody wants to be different ... this doesn't work." Although the artist's daily work schedule involves more isolation than the scientist's, it is still guided by internalized social norms.

Incubation

Most of the narratives related to problem-finding insight described it as occurring during an extended period of idle time, such as a vacation or sabbatical, in contrast to the daily idle time scheduled in by many respondents who described problem-solving insights. Once again, we see the problem-solving process expanded in time in the problem-finding process. Most respondents had rich, well-developed metacognitive theories of the importance of "off time." Respondent D began his interview by emphasizing the importance of being idle: "I'm fooling around not doing anything, which probably means this is a creative period.... I think that people who keep themselves busy all the time are generally not creative, so I'm not ashamed of being idle."

Respondent E described three sabbaticals, each 1 year long, which he views as the three most creative periods of his life: "These 3 years away were very creative, getting away from the humdrum, getting into a new environment: Stanford, Jamaica, Japan."

Respondents D, H, and I all made interesting observations about their own internal processes of incubation. They believe that the creative process requires an incubation period during which a subconscious idea is continually developed:

The creative process is very largely unconscious.... Somewhere in your mind, there is a great variety of things, disconnected fragments of ideas and thoughts and symbols and so forth. The creative process is somehow just shaking and sorting these until somehow a combination fits together and makes sense. (respondent D)

You have these ideas, and then you work on them. As you work on them, you get new ideas.... One makes the other one come out; it's as though creatures come out. If you don't work on it, they hide in there.... Something has begun to work, and you continue it, you feel the singing inside you. (respondent H)

I would say that scientific intuition is more sort of half-conscious knowledge, where you can see connections between things where a connection is not obvious, almost unconsciously, almost like a dream. (respondent I)

In discussions of the incubation phase, we have found that artists feel the need for solitude more strongly than scientists. The sculptor, respondent H, referred to Thomas Mann in describing the necessity of a period of solitary, hard work:

There are many times when you go down to your studio and nothing comes ... it might be weeks ... and suddenly, you don't know how ... but you've been working on things, and you suddenly say, "Oh, hey, I want to do one thing." So what that means to me is you don't leave that studio ... and suddenly you say, "Oh, I have this idea."

However, even this respondent emphasized the importance of visiting museums and feedback from other artists while creating, and she stressed the importance of daily discussion with her husband, an active collaborator.

Insight
Almost every respondent described moments of discovered problem-finding insight. The descriptions of the moment of creative insight were the richest, most elaborate portions of the narrative. Based on the narratives, these insights always occur during a period of incubation, such as a vacation, a sabbatical, or a long trip. Respondent C remarked that the major creative insights of his career always come while he is on vacation, often while on the

beach. An example was his well-known "memo from the beach," which outlined the structure of the first consumer banking enterprise, in 1974:

I was on a vacation, and I started out saying, "I'm sitting on a beach thinking about the business," and it went on for 30 pages. And it turned out to be the blueprint. I didn't sit down and say, "I'm gonna write a blueprint;" I said, "I'm sitting on the beach thinking," and I sort of thought through the business in a systematic way ... and I shared it with my colleagues.

A more recent insight, leading to a corporate reorganization in the 1980s, occurred while he sat on a bench in Florence: "In September I had been kind of tired ... and I had gone to Italy for a week, just gotten away.... I'd get up early in the morning, and I'd wander around, and I sat on a park bench, between 7 in the morning and noon.... I had a notebook, and I wrote myself long essays on what was going on and what I was worried about." These essays turned out to contain more than 80 percent of the content of a 2-year reorganization plan.

Respondent F described the creative insight as almost peripheral to the social importance of the endeavor: "The feeling is an epiphenomenon of the importance of the experience itself—I guess a sense of trying to save the world, working with people. Everything I've mentioned has been communal, except reading." As noted earlier, even reading, although solitary, involves an interaction with the domain of activity, a form of communication with other individuals in the field. Respondent F described his first important insight as a confluence of personal and social factors: "If I were coming up through the department now, I probably wouldn't have thought of that.... It was a combination of the way of analysis then and the way I was then.... When you look back 25 years later, [your insight] is much less original than you thought, and more a product of the time."

Several creativity researchers have described a polarity between two types or styles of creativity, which we can refer to as *analytical creativity* and *intuitive creativity* (following Simonton, 1988a).[3] Martindale (1990) refers to the two poles respectively as *conceptual* and *primordial* creativity. Perhaps the most appropriate dimension to characterize the narratives just cited would be Freud's distinction between *primary-process cognition* and *secondary-process cognition.* Many of the insights we have described represent periods in which primary-process cognition is dominant. In contrast, descriptions of the preparation stage (and of the entire presented problem-solving process) tend to indicate that secondary-process cognition is dominant.

Elaboration

The problem-finding narratives of insight included a fourth stage of elaboration, in contrast to the evaluation that follows a problem-solving insight. Elaboration of the problem-finding insight includes developing it into a complete solution and communicating it to other individuals in the field. Respondent D emphasized the importance of the subsequent elaboration to the insight itself: "For this shaking and sorting process [of creative insight] to work, there has to be an outlet. Something to write or compose ... and I write for a particular person, audience, and not just for myself." Respondent H repeatedly emphasized the hard work that follows an insight, which she calls a *germ*:

You have a few good ideas, your head begins to swim for a few minutes, you get excited, you have a "moment," and you make your model, and then for weeks and months afterwards, you just work on it.... It's like being a mason, or being a carpenter half the time. That germ of an idea doesn't make a sculpture that stands up.... So the next stage is the hard work.

This respondent proceeded to describe the period of communication with the field that follows this hard work: "To show, you must know galleries ... you must get it out in the open; you can't keep it in the studio."

Respondent A emphasized the importance of implementing and communicating insights; she conceives of her role in life as "altering the cultural DNA" by introducing her ideas into the larger culture:

What I am very interested in and very concerned with is to get my ideas out there, so I get very excited when my ideas are understood and published.... [After you have the idea for a new organization], how do you compress the idea into logic, and into a program of behaviors, which will allow that organization to act powerfully as a new piece of DNA that you're splicing into the dominant culture, that will replicate?

As noted previously, it is respondent D's contention that "it's only by interacting with other people in the building that you get anything interesting done; it's essentially a communal enterprise." In developing the first application of quantum mechanics to chemistry, respondent B described a period of elaboration following his insight; this resulted in a series of papers that, by communicating the insight to chemists, advanced the field of chemistry and resulted in his receipt of the Nobel prize. The banker, respondent C, also emphasized the importance of elaboration by characterizing his work as involving two types of activities: making decisions and getting things done. This pair corresponds to the balance between the solitude of insight and the need for social interaction to elaborate the insight, to make it useful.

Of all subjects, only respondent E claimed to have insights that did not need further elaboration. His writing habits involve speaking in written prose style into a Dictaphone for later transcription, which allows him to generate complete books in a matter of days. He rarely edits the material afterward, describing the process thus: "The last 9 days I was there [in California], I dictated the book a chapter a day and revised it very little actually. I'd been thinking about it for over a year, and it just came through. It was like having this intellectual orgasm, it just comes [laughs]."

Discussion

The narratives of creative insight summarized in the preceding sections are not inconsistent with current psychological theories of the creative process. However, there are several ways in which these narratives diverge from the standard models. First, we have identified two variants of the four stages: (1) discovered problem finding, characterized by a narrative structure of long preparation, long incubation, insight, and elaboration, and (2) presented problem solving, characterized by a narrative structure of hard work, short incubation, insight, and evaluation. Contemporary stage theories of creativity have not explored this distinction.

Second, previous models tend to focus on psychological processes, neglecting the influence of the domain, the paradigm containing prior research results and defining what types of work are appropriate, and the field, the group of researchers and administrators who make up the discipline. In both problem-solving and problem-finding narratives, interactions with members of the field are described at the stages of both preparation and evaluation or elaboration, and involvement with the culturally constituted domain is discussed with reference to preparation, incubation, and evaluation or elaboration. These interviews provide support for our proposed psychological model, in which internalized representations of the concerns of the field and the problems of the domain are involved in the moment of insight itself.

Third, several of the subjects described a creative process in which hard work and insight were coincident processes; rather than one big insight, many smaller ones continuously occurred during the stage of hard work. Respondent F described a creative process that is spread out:

[My creative periods] tend to be sort of spread out rather than moments of actually clear illumination. I've had a few, where at a specific moment in time, I said, "Now *that's* what I'm looking for," and "Now I know," but generally speaking, it's a matter of hard work and steady progress rather than moments of total transformation and clarity.

Processes of creativity such as these are difficult to accommodate within the four-stage model. Perhaps for these individuals, the stages occur on such a short time scale that they are practically simultaneous.

In a fourth variant of the model, several respondents describe a dialectic process alternating between work and idle time, in which the elaboration following one insight or period of idling also functions as the preparation for the next. The sculptor, respondent H, described the process as a dialectic, continually switching between hard work and insight: "You have these ideas, and then you work on them. And as you work on them you get new ideas. Because one complements the other, one makes the other one come out."

Evaluating the psychological models against the narrative material from these interviews results in an expanded, richer perspective on the stages of the creative process. These models are helpful in understanding the narratives, but they need to be expanded to account for the influence of social factors noted in the interviews. Our interviews also suggest that theoretical issues surrounding the distinction between problem solving and problem finding need to be addressed. Finally, variants of the four-stage model in which the stages seem to blend together, or in which work and idle time alternate in a dialectic pattern, need to be more fully elaborated.

CONCLUSION

What do these results suggest about understanding the process of insight, at least as it takes place in the context of creative processes? We believe the following conclusions can be drawn:

• Insight is part of an extended mental process. It is based on a previous period of conscious preparation, requires a period of incubation during which information is processed in parallel at a subconscious level, and is followed by a period of conscious evaluation and elaboration.

• The length of this process depends on whether the insight is embedded in a presented problem-solving process or in a discovered problem-finding process. Problem solving may cycle in a period as short as a few hours, whereas problem finding may take a year or more.

• At every stage, the process that comes before and after the insight is heavily dependent on social interaction. This takes the form of face-to-face encounters and of immersion in the symbolic system of one or more domains.

• Problem-finding insights are characterized by the synthesis of information derived from more than one symbolic domain. These domains may be as far apart as DNA chemistry is from social norms or as close as two neighboring branches of mathematics.

• To achieve such a problem-finding synthesis, the following prerequisites must be met: (1) thorough knowledge of one or more symbolic domains; (2) thorough immersion in a field that practices the domain; (3) focus of attention on a problematic area of the domain; (4) ability to internalize information relevant to the problematic area; (5) ability to let the relevant information interact with information from other domains at a subconscious level where parallel processing takes place; (6) ability to recognize a new configuration emerging from this interaction that helps resolve the problematic situation; and (7) evaluation and elaboration of the insight in ways that are understandable and valuable to the field.

From these considerations, it follows that problem-finding insights are unlikely to occur under the following conditions:

• The absence of a strong interest, curiosity, or intrinsic motivation that drives the person to commit attention to a problematic area in a domain. *A person who is not intrinsically motivated has no incentive to push beyond generally accepted boundaries of knowledge.*

• The absence of a thorough grounding in at least one symbolic domain, presumably as apprentice to an expert, and not having experienced the colleagueship of other expert apprentices. *Creative insights typically involve the integration of perspectives from more than one domain.*

• The absence of interaction with other individuals who are experts in the domain or in potentially relevant other domains. *At every stage of the process, the stimulation and feedback of peers is necessary to select and evaluate potential insights.*

• A schedule in which a person is always busy, goal-directed, involved in conscious, rational problem-solving. *Incubation is facilitated by periods of idling, leisure, and involvement in activities such as walking, gardening, driving* (i.e., activities that require some attention but are automated enough to permit subconscious processes to work just below the threshold of awareness).

• A person's lack of the opportunity or inclination to test the insight and to develop its implications. *A person must be particularly in touch with the field at the stage of evaluation and elaboration; otherwise, the insight is likely to have no effect beyond the individual.*

The narrative data analyzed in this chapter also have many implications for current creativity theory. The influence of social factors at each stage of the creative process needs further attention. Individual differences in the experience of the creative process—such as the dialectic process between hard work and insight, or continuous periods that combine work, insight, and elaboration—could result in a fuller, more accurate theory of creative insight.

If the creative process occurs in both long and short time frames, as both a social and a psychological process, then the relationship between the two should be explored. The pragmatists, including James (1890), Dewey (1938), and Mead (1934), suggested that mental processes were a reflection of social processes. The psychological model we have presented is an elaboration of this position, with the creative individual having internalized the domain of activity. If it is not simply a coincidence that creative processes on these time scales display a similar staged processual pattern, then it would be interesting to explore why and how these parallels exist. Perhaps the psychology of creativity is, in fact, the social process of creativity, absorbed and internalized by those individuals whom we call *creative*.

Although we have chosen to focus on a subset of our respondents in this chapter, the entire sample of creative individuals spoke at length on the subject of creativity. Their descriptions of their own careers and working styles were articulate and complete and are consistent with the accounts reported here. The material in these interviews is interesting as narrative data and as autobiographical descriptions that the respondents use to help structure their experience. For these individuals, interactive social factors are perceived as fundamental to their creativity, and these factors are salient in our interviews. The narratives are examples of how individuals can develop rich, elaborate stories about the events that bring them fame, success and, most important, satisfaction in life.

ACKNOWLEDGMENT

This research was supported by a grant from the Spencer Foundation.

NOTES

1. Note the parallels with Mead's (1934) "generalized other" and with Vygotsky's (1978) descriptions of how social interactions are internalized to become cognitive processes. Our proposal is consistent with Vygotsky and Mead, particularly the latter's claim that each distinct social sphere of individual activity will result in a distinct "other."

2. This anecdote, and those that follow, are based on interviews collected for our ongoing project, Creativity in Later Life, sponsored by the Spencer Foundation.

3. See Martindale (1990, pp. 56–57) for a quick review of theories that include such a dichotomy, starting with Nietzsche's well-known distinction between Apollonian and Dionysian creativity.

REFERENCES

Barron, F. (1988). Putting creativity to work. In R.J. Sternberg (Ed.), *The nature of creativity* (pp. 76–98). Cambridge, England: Cambridge University Press.

Broadbent, D.E. (1958). *Perception and communication.* New York: Pergamon Press.

Campbell, D.T. (1960). Blind variation and selective retention in scientific discovery. *Psychological Review, 67,* 380–400.

Csikszentmihalyi, M. (1978). Attention and the holistic approach to behavior. In K.S. Pope & J.S. Singer (Eds.), *The stream of consciousness* (pp. 335–358). New York: Plenum.

Csikszentmihalyi, M. (1988). Society, culture, and person: A systems view of creativity. In R.J. Sternberg (Ed.), *The nature of creativity* (pp. 325–339). Cambridge, England: Cambridge University Press.

Csikszentmihalyi, M. (1990a). The domain of creativity. In M.A. Runco & R.S. Albert (Eds.), *Theories of creativity* (pp. 190–212). Newbury Park, CA: Sage Publications.

Csikszentmihalyi, M. (1990b). *Flow: The psychology of optimal experience.* New York: HarperCollins.

Csikszentmihalyi, M., & Rathunde, K. (1990). Wisdom: an evolutionary interpretation. In R.J. Sternberg (Ed.), *The nature of wisdom.* New York: Cambridge University Press.

Dennett, D.C. (1991). *Consciousness explained.* Boston: Little, Brown.

Dewey, J. (1938). *Experience and education.* New York: Macmillan.

Epstein, R. (1990). Generativity theory and creativity. In M.A. Runco & R.S. Albert (Eds.), *Theories of creativity* (pp. 116–140). Newbury Park, CA: Sage Publications.

Eysenck, M.W. (1982). *Attention and arousal.* Berlin: Springer-Verlag.

Feldman, D.H. (1988). Creativity: dreams, insights, and transformations. In R.J. Sternberg (Ed.), *The nature of creativity* (pp. 271–297). Cambridge, England: Cambridge University Press.

Getzels, J.W. (1964). Creative thinking, problem-solving, and instruction. In E.R. Hilgard (Ed.), *Theories of learning and instruction* (sixty-third yearbook of the National Society for the Study of Education, pp. 240–267). Chicago: University of Chicago Press.

Getzels, J.W., and Csikszentmihalyi, M. (1976). *The creative vision.* New York: Wiley.

Ghiselin, B. (1952). *The creative process.* New York: Mentor.

Gruber, H.E. (1981). *Darwin on man: A study of scientific creativity.* Chicago: University of Chicago Press. (Original work published 1974)

Gruber, H.E., & Davis, S.N. (1988). Inching our way up Mount Olympus: The evolving-system approach to creative thinking. In R.J. Sternberg (Ed.), *The nature of creativity* (pp. 243–270). Cambridge, England: Cambridge University Press.

Hadamard, J. (1949). *The psychology of invention in the mathematical field.* Princeton, NJ: Princeton University Press.

Harrington, D.M. (1990). The ecology of human creativity: A psychological perspective. In M.A. Runco & R.S. Albert (Eds.), *Theories of creativity* (pp. 143–169). Newbury Park, CA: Sage Publications.

Hasher, L., and Zacks, R.T. (1979). Automatic and effortful processes in memory. *Journal of Experimental Psychology, 108,* 356–388.

Hoover, S.M. (1990). Problem finding/solving in science: Moving toward theory. *Creativity Research Journal, 3*(4), 330–332.

James, W. (1890). *Principles of psychology* (Vol. 1). New York: Henry Holt.

John-Steiner, V. (1992). Creative lives, creative tensions. *Creativity Research Journal, 5*(1), 99–108.

Kahneman, D. (1973). *Attention and effort.* Englewood Cliffs, NJ: Prentice Hall.

Kuhn, T. (1962). *The structure of scientific revolutions.* Chicago: University of Chicago Press.

Langley, P., & Jones, R. (1988). A computational model of scientific insight. In R.J Sternberg (Ed.), *The nature of creativity* (pp. 177–201). Cambridge, England: Cambridge University Press.

Martindale, C. (1990). *The clockwork muse: The predictability of artistic change.* New York: Basic Books.

Mead, G.H. (1934). *Mind, self, and society.* Chicago: University of Chicago Press.

Milgram, R.M. (1990). Creativity: An idea whose time has come and gone? In M.A. Runco & R.S. Albert (Eds.), *Theories of creativity* (pp. 215–233). Newbury Park, CA: Sage Publications.

Minsky, M. (1985). *The society of mind.* New York: Simon and Schuster.

Ohlsson, S. (1984). Restructuring revisited: An information processing theory of restructuring and insight. *Scandinavian Journal of Psychology*, 25, 117–129.

Ornstein, R. (1986). *Multimind.* Boston: Houghton Mifflin.

Perkins, D.N. (1988). The possibility of invention. In R.J. Sternberg (Ed.), *The nature of creativity* (pp. 362–385). Cambridge, England: Cambridge University Press.

Poincaré, H. (1913). *The foundations of science.* New York: The Science Press.

Runco, R.A. (1990). Implicit theories and ideational creativity. In M.A. Runco & R.S. Albert (Eds.), *Theories of creativity* (pp. 234–252). Newbury Park, CA: Sage Publications.

Shrady, M. (1972). *Moments of insight.* New York: Harper & Row.

Simon, H.A. (1977). *Boston studies in the philosophy of science: Vol. 54. Models of discovery.* Boston: Reidel.

Simonton, D.K. (1988a). *Scientific genius: A psychology of science.* Cambridge, England: Cambridge University Press.

Simonton, D.K. (1988b). Creativity, leadership, and chance. In R.J. Sternberg (Ed.), *The nature of creativity* (pp. 386–426). Cambridge, England: Cambridge University Press.

Sternberg, R.J. (1988). A three-facet model of creativity. In R.J. Sternberg (Ed.), *The nature of creativity* (pp. 125–147). Cambridge, England: Cambridge University Press.

Torrance, E.P. (1988). The nature of creativity as manifest in its testing. In R.J. Sternberg (Ed.), *The nature of creativity* (pp. 43–75). Cambridge, England: Cambridge University Press.

Vygotsky, L.S. (1978). *Mind in society: The development of higher psychological processes.* Cambridge: Harvard University Press.

Woodman, R.W., & Schoenfeldt, L.F. (1989). Individual differences in creativity: An interactionist perspective. In J.A. Glover, R.R. Ronning, & C.R. Reynolds (Eds.), *Handbook of creativity.* New York: Plenum.

11 How Scientists Really Reason: Scientific Reasoning in Real-World Laboratories

Kevin Dunbar

How do scientists think and reason? What are the psychological processes involved in scientific reasoning and discovery? These questions have been the focus of a large body of research by cognitive scientists, historians, philosophers, sociologists, and psychologists in the past 40 years and are among the main concerns of this book. Many different approaches have been taken to answering these questions, all with their own vices and virtues. In this chapter, I will discuss two novel approaches that I have been using in my research to investigate the cognitive processes involved in scientific reasoning and discovery. These approaches are making possible the formulation of new models and theories of the cognitive and social mechanisms functioning in scientific discovery.

The first approach involves taking a discovery from a real scientific domain, generating a task that is analogous to what the scientists had to do, giving this task to subjects, and determining whether and how subjects make the discovery (Dunbar, 1989; 1993; Dunbar & Schunn, 1990). Because this approach is based on a real scientific domain rather than an arbitrary task that has a tenuous relationship to real science, it is possible to capture important components of scientific reasoning and discovery.

The second approach is one of investigating real scientists working on their own research. This entailed actually spending extensive periods of time in real scientific laboratories. Data were collected over a 1-year period in four leading molecular biology laboratories. I followed all aspects of particular scientific research projects, including planning the research, executing the experiments, evaluating the experimental results, attending laboratory staff meetings and public talks, planning further experiments, and writing journal articles. Some of the research projects resulted in important scientific discoveries, and some did not. This provides a totally novel database from which to address fundamental questions concerning the cognitive processes involved in scientific discovery.

Using terms borrowed from biological research, I will refer to my work on simulated scientific discoveries as *in vitro* research and my work on scientists' reasoning in real-world contexts as *in vivo* research. I will argue that just as in biological research it is necessary to conduct both in vitro and in vivo research to understand a biological process fully, it is likewise necessary to employ both methodologies in cognitive research to understand fully the cognitive processes involved in scientific reasoning and discovery.

IN VITRO RESEARCH; SIMULATING THE DISCOVERY OF GENETIC CONTROL

In 1965, Jacques Monod and François Jacob were awarded the Nobel prize for discovering that there are regulator genes that control the activity of other genes (see Judson 1979 for an account of their discovery). They discovered this by investigating the utilization of energy sources, such as glucose, in *Escherichia coli. E. coli* need glucose to live, and their most common source of glucose is lactose. When lactose is present, *E. coli* secrete beta-galactosidase enzymes that break down lactose into glucose. Beta-galactosidase is secreted only when lactose is present. Jacob and Monod discovered that a set of regulator genes inhibit the genes that produce beta-galactosidase until the enzyme is needed. These investigators proposed that there are two genes, I and O, regulating the activity of the beta-galactosidase-producing genes and that the production of the enzyme is controlled by an inhibitory regulation mechanism. As can be seen in figure 11.1, when no lactose is present, the I gene produces an inhibitor that binds to the O gene, which prevents the beta-galactosidase genes from producing the enzyme. In the presence of lactose, however, the inhibitor secreted by the I gene binds to the lactose rather than to the O gene. When this happens, the beta-galactosidase genes are no longer inhibited and, consequently, they produce beta-galactosidase. When all the lactose is used, the inhibitor again binds to the O gene, and production of beta-galactosidase stops. Monod and Jacob made

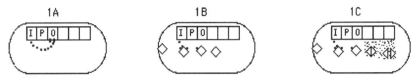

Figure 11.1
The cycle of inhibitory regulation of genes in *E. coli*. In A, the *E. coli* is in an inhibited state: The I gene sends an inhibitor to the O gene, and the inhibitor binds to the O gene; this blocks production of beta-galactosidase from the three beta-galactosidase-producing genes (the three unlabeled genes) In B, lactose (*diamonds*) enters the *E. coli*. The inhibitor binds to the lactose and not the O gene. In C, the beta-galactosidase-producing genes are no longer inhibited, and the beta genes produce beta-galactosidase (*small dots*). The beta-galactosidase cleaves the lactose into glucose, which can then be utilized as an energy source. When all the lactose has been used up, the inhibitor binds to the O gene, and the beta-galactosidase genes are inhibited from producing beta-galactosidase, as in A.

this discovery using various mutations of the I, O, and beta-galactosidase genes. Significantly, they initially believed that genetic control was due to genes switching on, or activating, other genes. It was only after extensive research that they discovered the mechanism of control was inhibition. Not only was this discovery relevant to production of beta-galactosidase, but it also was a general model of genetic control that transformed biological research.

The work of Monod and Jacob provides a problem that can be adapted to the cognitive laboratory. A simulated molecular genetics laboratory was designed that made it possible for subjects to propose and test hypotheses about genetic regulation by conducting experiments using various types of mutants. Two studies were conducted in which subjects were asked to discover how genes control other genes (see Dunbar [1993] for details of these studies). In both studies, subjects were taught about activation using one set of genes, putting the subjects in a knowledge state similar to the one that Monod and Jacob were in prior to their discovery of inhibitory genetic control. Subjects were then asked to discover how another set of genes—the I, P, and O genes—is controlled. The I and O genes function as inhibitors.

In study 1, subjects had to discover that the I and O genes were inhibitors. Given that subjects were taught about activation, as predicted, they all began with one type of hypothesis: That is, the genes are activators that switch on enzyme production. However, subjects found no evidence consistent with an activation hypothesis; rather, all experimental results were inconsistent with an activation hypothesis. At this point, the subjects employed one of two strategies for dealing with the inconsistent evidence. One was to proceed with the goal of finding activation. None of the subjects who used this strategy succeeded at discovering how the genes are controlled. In contrast, subjects who used a second strategy, setting a new goal of attempting to explain the cause of the inconsistent findings, were able to generate a new hypothesis (i.e., that the I and O genes inhibit beta-galactosidase production). Thus, the results of this first study indicated that all subjects initially set a goal of finding evidence consistent with their initial hypothesis and this goal blocked the setting of other goals, such as discovering the cause of unexpected findings.

In study 2, the hypothesis that maintaining one goal blocks the setting of other goals was tested. In this study, the genetic mechanism was changed so that one gene worked as an activator and the other two genes as inhibitors. In this situation, it was predicted that subjects would first set out to achieve their goal of discovering activation and then, after having achieved this goal, they would set a new goal of accounting for the findings that were inconsistent with an activation hypothesis. Once this new goal was set, subjects would be able to generate an inhibitory hypothesis. This was exactly what happened: Twice as many subjects proposed inhibition as in study 1, and more subjects reached the correct conclusion. These findings supported the hypothesis that subjects' goals determine when and how inconsistent evidence is used.

The results of these studies shed new light on a number of aspects of scientific reasoning: All subjects used inconsistent evidence to modify their hypotheses. However, subjects' use of inconsistent evidence was contingent on their current goal. Thus, the goal that subjects set was pivotal to making a discovery. When subjects maintained their initial goal, they did not make a discovery. When subjects changed their goal to one of exploring the cause of unexpected or inconsistent findings, they then made the discovery.

The results of these studies indicate that it is possible to discover important components of scientific reasoning by bringing a real scientific discovery into a cognitive laboratory. Although these types of experiments are generating new insights, it is not yet possible to determine the effects of the social context of science on the discovery process or whether the scientific reasoning strategies used by nonscientists are also used by scientists and vice versa. To achieve a more complete understanding of the specific factors that underlie scientific reasoning and discovery, other research methods are needed.

IN VIVO RESEARCH: REAL-WORLD STUDY OF SCIENTISTS' REASONING

Whereas research on individual subjects has produced many rich and important theories of reasoning in general and some of the components of scientific reasoning in particular, there are several distinct problems with making generalizations about the way in which scientists reason from experiments on individual subjects. First, science takes place in a social context: Generally, groups of scientists work on a problem in a laboratory rather than one scientist working alone. Thus far, cognitive psychologists have tended to investigate scientific reasoning in individuals and have ignored the social context of science. Second, psychologists have used tasks that are not real scientific problems (e.g., discovering an arbitrary rule [Klayman & Ha, 1987, Mynatt, Doherty, & Tweney, 1978]). Third, the subjects that psychologists use generally are nonscientists (e.g., Klahr & Dunbar, 1988). Clearly, scientists working on real scientific problems need to be studied as well. Unfortunately, when scientists have been studied, they have been assigned the same simple and arbitrary tasks that nonscientists are given (e.g., Mahoney & DeMonbruen, 1977). Fourth, subjects in psychology laboratory experiments work on problems that may last for as little as 10 minutes and involve no extensive knowledge of a scientific topic (e.g., Klayman & Ha, 1987). In scientific research, a particular problem may take months, years, or decades to solve, and the scientists have extensive knowledge of a domain.

A number of cognitive researchers have noted the limitations of the types of studies just cited and have turned to historical data on particular scientific discoveries to provide a richer account of the discovery process. Using historical data, researchers have analyzed historical accounts of scientific discoveries to uncover the mechanisms involved in scientific reasoning. For example, Nersessian (1992) and others (e.g., Gooding, 1992; Holmes, 1985; Tweney, 1985) have conducted detailed analyses of diaries and notebooks that make it possible to infer some of the cognitive processes involved in particular scientific discoveries. This approach has yielded rich and important accounts of some of the psychological components of a particular discovery. However, this method also has its drawbacks, the main limitation being that only indirect and selective access to the cognitive processes underlying scientists' discoveries can be obtained.

Another historical method for determining the psychological processes involved in scientific discovery is to interview scientists who have made such a discovery (e.g., Giere, 1988; Karp, 1989; Mitroff, 1974). There are a number of cognitive accounts by researchers who have used this method to detail particular discoveries. For example, Karp (1989) performed a series of extensive interviews with the scientist who discovered a new mechanism of genetic control and built a computational model of the cognitive processes that were involved in the discovery. Although this is clearly a useful approach, retrospective reports are notoriously unreliable (cf. Ericsson & Simon, 1982; Nisbett & Wilson, 1977). Furthermore, research from my laboratory has shown that subjects often are unaware of what leads them to make a discovery (Dunbar & Schunn, 1990). Dunbar and Schunn (1990) found that solving one problem improved performance on an analogically similar problem, yet the subjects did not mention, either during problem solving or in retrospective reports, using any information from the first problem to solve the second problem.

A third approach to uncovering important aspects of scientific research has been the contemporary sociological approach. A number of sociologists investigating scientists working in laboratories have used ethnomethodological approaches, or interviews with the scientists (e.g., Fujimura, 1987; Knorr-Cetina, 1983; Latour & Woolgar, 1986; Mulkay & Gilbert, 1983). This approach focuses on science as it is conducted, rather than the retrospective accounts that some historical approaches have used. Whereas these studies have uncovered important components of the day-to-day workings of scientific laboratories, they have not been concerned with uncovering the cognitive processes used by scientists in their day-to-day research. These sociological researchers have stressed the importance of the social context of science, demonstrating that it has an effect on all aspects of the scientific process. However, exactly how the social context affects the scientist's knowledge remains unexplained.

To summarize, the research from my laboratory and that of other investigators suggests that a number of basic cognitive heuristics and operations form the foundation of scientific reasoning. However, no cognitive scientists have actually investigated real scientists conducting their day-to-day research: That is, there have been no systematic cognitive investigations of how scientists reason *while* conducting their research. Although the standard cognitive and historical analyses have provided rich and important accounts of the psychological processes involved in particular discoveries, there are many crucial aspects of the scientific discovery process to which access cannot be gained using these methodologies. In particular, the on-line cognitive processes and the social interactions involved in a specific discovery are not directly accessible. This suggests that alternate methodologies need to be adopted.

HOW SCIENTISTS REALLY THINK

Let us now look at a study in which I collected data on the reasoning processes and discovery heuristics that scientists used in four of the world's leading molecular biology laboratories at a major US university. The overall goals of this research were (1) to determine what types of reasoning heuristics scientists use to propose experiments, generate hypotheses, and evaluate results; (2) to determine how scientists represent their knowledge of the research projects on which they are working; (3) to uncover the cognitive processes that lead to changes in scientists' representation of their research (that is, to investigate the mechanisms involved in conceptual change and insight); (4) to discover the cognitive mechanisms that groups of scientists—rather than an individual scientist—use to formulate experiments and hypotheses; (5) to discover whether the social context of scientific work can counteract the well-known faulty heuristics that individuals have been shown to use when reasoning scientifically; and (6) to discover whether and what the mechanisms are for the social context to influence conceptual change.

METHOD

Selection of Laboratories

Six laboratories were identified on the basis of the quality of their publications, the type of research they were conducting, and the fact that each laboratory had previously made discoveries that the scientific community regarded as being significant. In addition, the laboratories were of different sizes, and the directors of the laboratories had differing amounts of research experience.[1]

All six laboratories allowed me to investigate them. Of these, four laboratories were judged to be most suitable and were subsequently investigated. These four laboratories varied along two dimensions. First, the laboratories were involved with either developmental biology or pathogens (disease-causing viruses and bacteria). Second, the laboratories were focused at either the cellular or the molecular level (table 11.1). By selecting laboratories in this manner, it was possible to identify which aspects of the research are general, and therefore used by all four laboratories, and which strategies are specific to a particular field, such as developmental biology or molecular biology.

Table 11.1
Research areas of the four laboratories investigated*

	Cell biology	Molecular biology
Developmental biology	Lab A	Lab B
Pathogens	Labs B and C	Lab D

* Owing to the sensitive nature of the research conducted, the identity of the particular laboratories is confidential.

For the purposes of maintaining confidentiality, the names of the scientists will not be revealed. Likewise, the laboratories will be labeled *A*, *B*, *C*, and *D*. All the scientists requested anonymity and that the results of their experiments not be divulged. To maintain confidentiality of the data I obtained, many scientific details of the discoveries made and research projects investigated are omitted from this chapter. Although the scientists did request anonymity it is important to note that all the scientists allowed me free access to their laboratories and permitted me to interview anyone in the laboratory, attend any meeting, read and keep copies of their grant proposals, attend their talks and lectures, and read drafts of their papers. Thus, I had complete access to the day-to-day activities of the laboratories. In addition, the laboratory members were so cooperative that they frequently phoned me to attend impromptu meetings and discussions within the laboratory or to witness what they believed were interesting events occurring in the lab.

Laboratory A

Laboratory A is run by a senior researcher with 300 publications to his credit. He has won numerous awards, has taught students who are now leading researchers in the field, and has made a number of extremely important findings that have revolutionized his field. The laboratory is staffed by 22 postdoctoral fellows, 5 graduate students, and 4 technicians. The director suggested following a number of research projects that he thought might lead to interesting discoveries, and of these I selected four. Two of the four research projects were successful and led to scientific discoveries. Importantly, neither the scientists involved nor I realized that a discovery was about to be made when I began documenting their research. It was only after a few months of observing the research projects that the discoveries were made. Thus, I had collected data before, during, and after a discovery was made. One researcher discovered a new gene that controls cell differentiation, and another discovered how certain cells proliferate into certain regions of the body. Importantly, the latter discovery occurred during a laboratory meeting at which I was present and was audiotaping; that is, I have the moment of discovery on tape.[2] One of the other two research projects was unsuccessful, and the fourth did not progress significantly within the 8-month period of observation.

Laboratory B

Laboratory B is run by a senior researcher who has made many important discoveries in molecular biology. He is well published and has trained many now-eminent scientists. His current research program is concerned with determining a general model of how certain genes control traits in a novel type of bacterium. His laboratory staff was composed of three postdoctoral fellows, five graduate students, and one technician. I followed one of the research projects that was being conducted in this laboratory, as it was the only research project that was just starting. Because the project has been beset by a number of problems, the researchers have made little progress.

Laboratory C

Laboratory C is run by an associate professor who, by studying an organism that has very unusual biological properties, has made a number of important discoveries about how DNA and RNA are coded. He has more than 60 publications to his credit, and his work on RNA is regarded as seminal. The laboratory is staffed by four postdoctoral fellows, two graduate students, and one technician. I followed research projects conducted by the four postdoctoral fellows, all of which resulted in significant breakthroughs.

Laboratory D

Laboratory D is run by an assistant professor who is already famous for his work on viral mechanisms. He has invented a number of widely referenced techniques and is regarded as conducting some of the most innovative work on the human immune-deficiency virus (HIV). Four postdoctoral fellows, six graduate students, and two technicians compose the staff. The director's current research program, which employs a number of novel and ingenious techniques, is focused on discovering the mechanism by which certain genes in HIV allow the virus to infiltrate into the host organism. I followed three research projects on HIV activity, all of which are leading to a new model of an important component of HIV activity that has wide-ranging theoretical and practical implications for molecular biology. The director of laboratory D also has invented a new genetic technique that is likely to be one of the most important inventions in the last 10 years in molecular biology and genetics.

Selection of Research Projects for Investigation

Within each laboratory, particular research projects were selected for study on the basis of (1) an interview with the laboratory director about the research that was going on in his laboratory and (2) whether the research projects had just started or were about to begin. The selection of new scientific research projects made it possible to investigate the cognitive components from the outset. Once the projects were selected, I then met with the staff members who were conducting the research. All staff members of the four laboratories were willing to cooperate. In laboratories A, C, and D, four research projects were studied. In laboratory B, only one research project was studied as it was the only project that was beginning.

Data Collection Procedure

A "pre-present-post" design was used in which data were collected prior to a laboratory meeting (pre), during the meeting (present), and after it (post). This design is similar to the pretest-posttest design used in experimental research (cf. Campbell & Stanley, 1963). The pre–lab meeting component consisted of an extensive initial interview in which the researcher provided background information on his research project and the rationale for conducting the research: That is, the researcher stated the theories, hypotheses, predictions, experimental results, current knowledge in the field, rival theories, relation to other research projects in the laboratory, and problems with the research. In addition, 1 or 2 days before a researcher was supposed to give a laboratory presentation about his research, an interview was conducted in which the researcher was asked to state (1) what research his group had done; (2) why the researcher conducted the experiments; (3) the specific research question, goals, experimental design, and predictions, and why he did not conduct other types of possible experiments; (4) what the results were and what problems, if any, occurred in conducting the experiments; (5) what the researcher believed the experimental results meant; and (6) in what directions the research project was going to go next (that is, what experiments would be conducted next).

The present component of the procedure consisted of either videotaping or audiotaping a laboratory meeting. Notes were kept of contextual information not readily apparent in the audiotapes or videotapes. The post-lab meeting component of the procedure consisted of an interview with a researcher 1 or 2 days after the meeting to determine what the researcher was now doing and whether the meeting had changed his plans. The same six sets of questions that were asked in the pre–lab meeting component were again asked in the post–lab meeting component. This made it possible to determine the effects of the laboratory meeting on the researcher's representation of the research and on plans for future experiments. This pre-present-post design was repeated at least three times over an 8-month period for all research projects.

By comparing the data gathered using the pre-present-post design, the effects of the meetings on scientists' reasoning and on their research can be determined. All interviews and laboratory meetings were audiotape recorded, and extensive notes were kept, which make it possible to understand contextually relevant information. During the last 2 months of the research, a number of laboratory meetings were videotaped, which make it possible to get a visual representation of the data and data analysis techniques that the scientists were using, as well as to analyze the social and situational factors not readily apparent in the audiotapes.

Data Analysis

Transcription
All data collected (i.e., audiotapes, videotapes, notes from grants and pink sheets, drafts of papers with comments, and other relevant materials) were transcribed and coded. Transcriptions were made by two independent transcribers with a background in molecular biology.

Coding

After transcription, the data were coded along a set of dimensions derived from Brutlag, Galper, and Milis (1991), Dunbar (1993), Klahr and Dunbar (1988), Stein (1992), and Ericsson and Simon (1984). The coding schemes provide converging evidence on the cognitive operations, mental representations, and social interactions that the scientists used. Once the data were coded, they were entered into a computerized data base (Sanderson, Scott, Johnston, Mainzer, Watanabe, & James, 1993) with relational search capabilities that make it possible to answer specific questions about the scientists' thinking and reasoning.

In order to give a flavor of the types of attributes that are coded, a partial listing is provided here within each category. However, the existing coding schemes are far richer than that which can be discussed here. The three major categories of knowledge that these coding schemes specify are as follows:

• *Coding of the scientists' representation of their research over time:* Brutlag's 1991 scheme (Brutlag, Galper, & Milis, 1991), which provides a list of attributes for molecular biological knowledge and experiments, was used. Developed by a molecular biologist who is building computational models of molecular biological knowledge, this scheme was adapted as a coding device that specifies the features of the scientists' representation of their knowledge. It specifies the attributes of knowledge relevant to understanding DNA metabolism such as the structure of DNA, its strands, nicks, activity, specificity, activity, and temperatures, and the pH values of reactions. The coding scheme integrates these attributes into an overall model of knowledge and experiments, making possible a representation of the molecular biologists' knowledge and how this knowledge changes over time. Another coding scheme was employed for cellular biological knowledge.

• *Coding of group interactions:* A coding scheme derived from work on discourse analysis and conceptual change was used for group interactions. This coding scheme classifies the types of interactions between speakers (e.g., clarification, agreement and elaboration, disagreement, and questioning), the goals of the speaker, and the current representation of the knowledge. It enables one to chart the effects of the interactions on the speakers' current representation of the research project and to identify whether and when social interactions lead to conceptual changes. Using this scheme allows us to identify the specific types of social interactions and the various combinations of factors that must be present for conceptual change to occur. In addition, the coding scheme enables us to make predictions about whether the interaction will lead to a change in the speaker's representation and what the speaker will do.

• *Coding the scientists' cognitive operations:* All data were coded using standard protocol analysis techniques (cf. Ericsson & Simon, 1984) that I have used previously (Dunbar, 1993a; Klahr & Dunbar, 1988; Klahr, Dunbar, & Fay, 1989). First, a task analysis, which determines the current state of knowledge, the goal state, and the series of cognitive operations that the scientists apply to get from their current state of knowledge to their desired state, was conducted for each research project. The second step involved coding the data in terms of the cognitive operations identified in the task analysis. The third step was to formulate a model of how the scientists actually combine these cognitive operations into heuristics that guide their research. This third step necessitates bringing together into one overall scheme the coding of the scientists representation of their research, the coding of the group interactions, and the coding of the scientists' cognitive operations.

OVERALL RESULTS

A select sample of the analyses conducted on the present data are provided here (see Dunbar [1993b, 1993c] and Dunbar & Baker [1993a, 1993b] for the complete analyses). There were numerous intralaboratory and interlaboratory similarities of the mental representations, experimental heuristics, and problem-solving heuristics used by all four laboratories. Indeed, the analyses reveal that the basic components of the scientists' cognitive operations are surprisingly similar and differ largely in the way that these operations are combined. This high degree of regularity in the data makes it possible to apply rigorous data analysis techniques and to draw highly generalizable conclusions about scientific reasoning.

A number of trends have emerged from the data: First, scientists make extensive use of negative evidence to discard their hypotheses. Second, the use of local analogies where knowledge is imported from the same scientific domain is a common mechanism of conceptual change. By contrast, distant analogies were used to highlight salient features of the problem being discussed. Third, the social context of the research produces significant changes in the representation of the problem and modulation of individual reasoning biases. The particular types of social interactions and cognitive states that are present when conceptual change occurs have been identified. Overall, these results reveal that both domain-specific knowledge and the social context of scientific research prevents scientists from making many of the reasoning errors identified in individual subjects in cognitive psychology laboratories.

MECHANISMS UNDERLYING CONCEPTUAL CHANGE AND INSIGHT

The circumstances under which conceptual change and insights occurred will be addressed. Conceptual change and insight occurred in the face of inconsistent experimental findings, as a result of the use of analogy, in the context of group discussions, and as a consequence of surprising findings.

Inconsistent Results and Conceptual Change

Surprisingly, results inconsistent with the scientists' current hypothesis quickly led to the discarding of hypotheses. The discarding of a hypothesis on the basis of inconsistent evidence occurred under very specific circumstances. First, inconsistent evidence tended to be used to change specific features of a hypothesis, whereas the overall type of hypothesis remained the same. For example, a scientist changed his hypothesis from "this particular sequence is necessary to initiate binding of the protein" to "any sequence in this region that has a base-pair mismatch will be bound to by this protein." Note that, in this situation, the conceptual change that occurred was minimal. This type of conceptual change displayed the usual generalization-specialization heuristics that have been identified in previous work on reasoning, such as the findings obtained in my in vitro work on scientific reasoning, discussed earlier in this chapter.

The second use of inconsistent evidence was more interesting: In this case, the evidence was not only inconsistent with the current hypothesis but was also inconsistent with any hypothesis of that type, and the scientist needed to invent a totally new type of hypothesis (or *concept*, or *frame*, depending on one's terminology) to account for the data. This type of conceptual change rarely occurred within an individual. As in laboratory studies of cognition, individual scientists out of a group context usually attributed inconsistent evidence to error of some sort and hoped that the finding would go away. However, when the finding was presented at a laboratory meeting, the other scientists tended to focus on the inconsistency, to dissect it, and either (1) suggested alternate hypotheses or (2) forced the scientist to think of a new hypothesis. This happened at numerous laboratory meetings and was one of the main mechanisms for inducing conceptual change in a scientist when inconsistent evidence occurred. Often, it resulted in the phenomenological experience of insight in which the scientist exclaimed that he or she now knew what was going on in the experiment. As we will see later, the particular mechanics of the interaction are crucial to whether conceptual change did or did not occur.

The way in which inconsistent evidence was treated also varied as a function of experience. Less experienced scientists were more willing to maintain a hypothesis than more experienced scientists. However, while the more experienced scientists showed much less confirmation bias than did the less experienced researchers, they often displayed what we term a *falsification bias*: Often, they discard good data that actually confirm their hypothesis. This falsification bias appears to be the result of much experience with being proved wrong. We are currently simulating this falsification bias in an experiment in our laboratory (Baker & Dunbar, 1993). These findings indicate that a crucial factor in determining whether people will maintain a hypothesis in the face of inconsistent evidence is domain-specific knowledge rather than a reasoning bias per se.

Analogy and Conceptual Change

My colleagues and I are currently coding all the uses of similarity in the corpus. Already coded are all instances in which a scientist notes that something is similar, or different, from something else. We can then look at instances of analogical reasoning. A preliminary analysis of the data indicates that analogies were an important source of knowledge and conceptual change. In three of the four laboratories, analogies were used frequently, numbering from 4 to 22 in any meeting. Three different classes of analogies were employed. First, analogies were sometimes from the same domain, in which the scientist drew an analogy from a previous experiment to the current experiment (*local analogies*). Second, a whole system of relationships from a similar domain might be mapped onto the domain on which the laboratory was working (*regional analogies*). Third, a concept might be mapped from a very different domain to the domain on which the scientists are working (*long-distance analogies*). These different types of analogies are used under different circumstances.[3]

Local Analogies
Local analogies were very frequently used, usually when the experiment on which a researcher was working had problems. The researcher made an analogy to an experiment in a very similar research area or similar research technique or protocol. The actual analogical mapping that occurred was to map the unsuccessful problem with which they were working to another similar experiment that was successful. The scientist would then determine what the difference was between the successful and unsuccessful experiments and substitute the different components from the successful approach into the unsuccessful approach. For example, at one meeting a scientist was having difficulty in purifying a protein and said:

[s]o I had to pursue another method that would solubilize the proteins, but would also stick to the beads, and basically, this is a method by James Digby and it's also, this method is also a similar method found in Maniatis. Basically, the key step is the 8-molar urea step, which just, it just solubilizes everything. But anyway, this is a protocol; it basically

was just followed exactly since this worked for someone else; I figured it might work for me too.

Such use of local analogies does not immediately appear to be a very sophisticated type of reasoning and certainly not the type of reasoning that has been the focus of much cognitive research. However, the use of local analogies is one of the main mechanisms for driving research forward. In the field of molecular biology, at least 60 percent of the experiments have technical problems that need to be resolved, and local analogical reasoning is one of the main methods that scientists use when they experience problems with their experiments. This type of reasoning occurred in virtually every meeting I observed, and often numerous times in a meeting. New knowledge is added to the scientists' representation by making the analogy, and thus the research is moved forward.

Regional Analogies
In regional analogies, the scientists mapped entire systems of relationships from one domain onto another, the two domains being of different classes that belonged to a common superordinate category (e.g., phage viruses and retroviruses were mapped onto each other, and both are members of the superordinate category, *virus*). This type of analogy was not frequent but did occur from time to time. It rarely occurred when scientists were having a problem with an experiment. Instead, this type of analogical reasoning was employed when the scientists were working on elaborating their theory and planning new sets of experiments. For example, one laboratory held a meeting that drew an analogy between one class of virus and another. Although a considerable amount is known about certain types of viruses, little is known about many basic components of retroviruses. Furthermore, because retroviruses are considered very different from other types of viruses, researchers rarely use knowledge of one to inform their research about the other. This laboratory tried to map knowledge from one class of virus onto retroviruses, the goals being to use this knowledge to fill in gaps in their own understanding by drawing sets of 1-to-1 mappings, and to suggest new questions to ask about retroviruses.

Mapping over an entire system of relations proved a very powerful tool. The finding that this was a rarely used type of analogy is consistent with much psychological work on analogy, but the reasons may be very different. In this case, and in the other cases in this study, this type of analogy tended to be used only after the scientists had already started to formulate a model of the entire process that they were investigating. Hence, the scientists had a system of relations and mechanisms in their own domain that they could then map to another domain. Until they had built such a representation of their own domain, it would not have been possible to map over the other domain. My colleagues and I are currently conducting an experiment to test the hypothesis that analogical mapping of sets of relations is most likely to occur, and lead to conceptual change, when subjects have built up a fairly detailed representation of the target domain.

Long-Distance Analogies
Long-distance analogies were used but not frequently. They were never used to solve experimental problems or in model building. Rather, long-distance analogies were used to highlight features of the research that were salient and were usually employed to bring home a point or to educate new staff members of a laboratory. Whereas distant analogies were used to change the representation of knowledge in people, they were not a driving force in making any of the discoveries observed over the year. This use of analogies often led to significant insights on the part of other laboratory staff members, making the exact point clear. The following excerpt from a conversation is one example of a highlighting use of a distant analogy:

Postdoctoral fellow: What goes on in the flagellar pocket is a real big question right now, and there's not much known about it. It's a very specialized domain of the plasma membrane, and it has a very specialized function. What's in the flagellar pocket and what goes on in the flagellar pocket [has], uh, not been studied in any great depth or detail. An interesting question. OK.

Professor: It's sort of semiclosed. It's open to big molecules, like LDL gets in—

Postdoctoral fellow: Things get in, but things don't ... It's like the Hotel California—you can check in, but you can never check out.

It is important to note that this use of long-distance analogies is very different from that proposed by other researchers. Many researchers have argued that many of the analogies that scientists use in their publications or talks were actually causal in making particular discoveries. That is, scientists first make the analogy and then map features of the analogy onto the problem they are investigating and so make the discovery. In the corpus of data we collected, we did not find one instance wherein a long-distance analogy led to any conceptual changes or insights on the part of a researcher. Instead, the long-distance analogies were used to highlight features of a point that a scientist makes. We are now monitoring the publications that the researchers are writing to determine whether long-distance analogies creep into the publications, though they were not present in the discovery. If this proves true, then the suggestion is that at least some of the analogies scientists have used in their publications were not causal in making a discovery but were added when writing up the research. Hence, the importance of long-distance analogies and their causal roles in making discoveries may have been overemphasized by some researchers.

Analogy Use and Social Structure

Whereas use of analogy was common in the laboratories, analogical reasoning did not occur at all in one of the laboratories. Two questions immediately arise here: Did the lack of analogical reasoning have a detrimental effect on conceptual change? Why did this laboratory fail to engage in analogical reasoning? The single laboratory that did not engage in analogical reasoning did not make any real gains in understanding the genes on which the staff was working. Recall that the most common use of analogies in the laboratories was when an experiment did not work. In this situation, scientists drew analogies to other experiments in an attempt to solve their problem. However, in the laboratory that did not make analogies, the scientists used a different strategy when they encountered problems in their research; they manipulated experimental variables such as raising the temperature, varying chemical concentrations, and so forth, to make things work. Thus, a problem that could have been solved by making an analogy to another similar experiment (local analogy) or to another organism (regional analogy) was not made, leaving some problems unsolved, either temporarily or over the long term. Indeed, very similar research problems were encountered in the other laboratories, but they were solved much faster through the use of local and regional analogies. This finding is consistent with the hypothesis that local and regional analogies are a potent source of conceptual change.

Why were the staff members of this one laboratory not making use of analogy? The social structure of the laboratory appears critical to whether analogies will be used. All the staff of this laboratory came from highly similar backgrounds and consequently drew from a similar knowledge base. In the other laboratories, the scientists came from widely differing backgrounds, and these different sources of knowledge were important components in the construction of analogical mappings. When all the members of the laboratory have the same knowledge at their disposal, then when a problem arises, a group of like-minded individuals will not provide more information to make analogies than would a single individual.

The finding that the social structure of the laboratory has an effect on types of reasoning and conceptual change may explain why many experimental studies of reasoning by groups show that groups perform no better than individuals working alone. In these studies, the groups of subjects are generally homogeneous with respect to background and, according to the mechanisms of conceptual change that I am invoking, should not produce conceptual change. My colleagues and I currently are conducting a number of experiments to test this hypothesis. These results go beyond merely stating that social structure is important. They indicate that groups of individuals must have different pools of knowledge, from which to draw to make fruitful analogies. Merely having a group of scientists (rather than a single one) working on a particular problem will not result in the use of analogies.

Analogy Use and Expertise

As the above section on analogy use and social structure indicates, one of the key components in analogical reasoning is the knowledge to which the laboratory staff has access. Not only the knowledge possessed by the group but also that of an individual scientist is important. We have found that the more expert the scientist is, the more analogies the scientist will make, the more similarities that he or she will note and, consequently, the more overall research success he or she will have.

The experts clearly have more knowledge at their disposal, and their knowledge is organized and represented in ways different from those of the less expert scientists. This is evident in the interactions of the scientists with one another. An expert scientist tends to see many of the deep structural features as very obvious and treats them almost as surface features. The novice scientists have great difficulty seeing the deep structural features. Therefore, when making productive analogies, it is much easier for the expert scientist, for whom the deep features are obvious so he or she can readily map these features onto other domains. For the novice scientists, the mappings onto other domains are difficult and nonobvious. Thus, experts make both more analogies and more productive analogies.

Social Context and Conceptual Change

In the preceding sections, we have seen that social factors affect scientists' interpretation of inconsistent information, as well as their ability to formulate and use analogies. The goal of the present analyses of social interactions is not to restate the obvious: that social interactions are important. Instead, our goal is to identify the precise mechanisms by which groups of scientists change one another's representation of knowledge. In our analysis of the laboratory meetings, my colleagues and I have begun to uncover a number of social mechanisms that facilitate conceptual change. To address this issue, we are analyzing sets of instances where conceptual change occurred and did not occur. Specifically, we are investigating whether conceptual change did or did not occur (1) following questions that force the scientist to think about his or her work at a different conceptual level or using a different goal, (2) when the scientist was asked to engage in deductive, causal, or inductive reasoning, (3) when the scientist was asked to give more details of a particular aspect of his or her theory or data, (4) when the scientist's theory or data was challenged by another member of the laboratory group, and (5) following questions from different types of people such as research assistants, graduate students, postdoctoral fellows, professors, or a Nobel prize winner! We are just beginning to obtain answers to these questions from our database, which allows us to identify particular patterns of social interactions as well as prior knowledge states that result in conceptual change.

Analyses of the data reveal that question answering is a potent mechanism of inducing conceptual change in scientists. One question that produced a number of small conceptual changes in all the laboratories and fostered a major scientific discovery in one scientist was of the type that forced the scientist to change from thinking about the research at one level to thinking about it at another level. For example, a scientist may be conducting a series of experiments aimed at discovering the mechanism by which a certain type of lymphocyte binds to a certain type of cell. The scientist is concerned with the experimental details and particular components of the mechanism. Other scientists may ask this researcher a question about how the lymphocyte got there in the first place rather than how it binds. This new question forces the scientist to reorganize his or her knowledge, and on doing so, his or her original question also is answered. Thus, members of a group can induce a scientist to adopt new perspectives and goals that can result in reorganization of knowledge and a scientific discovery. We currently are analyzing a scientific discovery that occurred under this type of questioning (Dunbar & Baker, 1993a, 1993b).

Because there were many cases in which conceptual change did or did not occur during laboratory meetings, we have been able to uncover the mechanisms by which social interactions and cognitive representations interact to produce conceptual change. An analysis of the interactions surrounding the making of discoveries indicates that sequences of specific types of interactions and knowledge states occur. In particular, we have identified that when (1) surprising findings occur, (2) the researcher believes that these findings are not due to error, and (3) other members of the group challenge the researcher's interpretation of the findings, significant conceptual change will occur. The challenges force the scientist to look at the data with different questions and goals, thereby changing the scientist's representation of the findings.

When the researcher believes that the findings are due to error, no amount of challenging or suggestion of other explanations will result in conceptual change.

Another form of questioning is one that triggers a chain of reasoning that can then result in a reconceptualization of a theory, data, or experimental design. Often the question is asked when the speaker has left out some details about which he or she was unsure. The speaker then engages in, for example, deductive reasoning, and often other members of the laboratory will also engage in this reasoning process, resulting in a very different conception of a problem. This frequently occurred when the scientist had a problem with his or her experiment. If analogical mapping did not achieve a solution, the members of the laboratory would attempt to deduce what the source of the problem was and then suggest a solution, thereby changing the representation of the problem. Hence, certain types of social interactions that occur in a laboratory meeting have specific effects on the types of reasoning strategies that scientists use. We are now beginning to identify which combinations of social interactions and cognitive states lead to which types of reasoning.

One of the laboratories engaged in extensive group problem solving whenever a problem arose in the research. Many members of the laboratory reasoned about the research, and often the results of one person's reasoning became the impetus for another person's reasoning. This resulted in rapid reconceptualization of problems and in significant changes in all aspects of the way the research was conducted. Situations in which group problem solving occurs provide a rich example of the way that cognitive and social mechanisms interact. We have found that subgroups focus on particular features of the problem, change these features, and then pass on their part of the solution to another member of the group. The researcher then picks up the proposed solutions and integrates them into his or her conceptual framework, and the group proceeds through another round of problem solving.

On Serendipity

A common event in all research is the presence of surprising results. Often, unusual results are of no interest; other times, surprising results lead to significant discoveries. Scientists frequently attribute to serendipity discoveries based on surprising findings. An example of the view that serendipity is the source of many discoveries appeared in a recent issue of the journal *Science*, where a reporter discussed a particular scientific discovery in the following way: "As with many surprising discoveries, the finding that DNA injection could get the cells of living animals to produce proteins came serendipitously" (*Science*, March 19, 1993, p. 1691). The particular scientists in question discovered that their control condition had a much better effect than any of their experimental conditions. They then focused on the control condition and discovered a new mechanism to introduce foreign DNA into a host. Although many scientists and journalists may regard certain scientific discoveries as serendipitous, the data we have collected indicate that many findings designated as serendipitous are not so. Rather, such findings are the result of careful experimentation and planning designed to expose novel mechanisms.

My colleagues and I have found that experimental results in which the control condition produces unusual results are very common and were the source of many discoveries in our studies. One of the scientific discoveries that we recorded, as well as other discoveries in the laboratories that we have been investigating, occurred when a control condition produced surprising results. Furthermore, during my initial interview with the director of laboratory A, the director said one of the most important strategies he uses in his research is to follow up surprising results. In the laboratory meetings, he employed this strategy numerous times, forcing the other scientists to focus on surprising findings, particularly when they involved the control condition, and consequently to gain new insights into their research.

The standard explanation for using a control condition is that it allows the scientist to determine whether the effect observed with the experimental condition is really due to the experimental manipulation or is due to other factors. A control condition is regarded as a check on the experimental conditions. The finding that, in the laboratories I have investigated, control conditions often generate surprising results leads us to conclude that the manner in which scientists choose control conditions and the way in which the results of controls are interpreted are crucial to understanding scientific discovery and insight. When a scientist selects a control for an experiment, many factors have to be taken into account and researchers often use more than one control. The control conditions serve functions other than checking to see that the experimental effects are real. Even when a scientist correctly predicts that the experimental conditions should produce a particular effect, other (or more important) mechanisms may be involved that the control condition can uncover.

This type of analysis suggests that far from being serendipitous, surprising findings (e.g., in a control condition) make it possible to uncover hidden mechanisms in an orderly manner. The scientist carefully constructs controls that serve the function of both checking the experimental conditions and exposing hidden mechanisms, should they be there. In the data we have collected, the scientist usually is looking for the desired results in the experimental conditions, and to do this the scientist has formulated a rich set of hypotheses and mechanisms that could account for a wide variety of possible findings. When the control conditions produce unusual results, the scientist is already considering a host of potential mechanisms, and thus a surprising finding allows the scientist to focus on the aspects of his or her current conceptual structure that need to be changed or rejected. The surprising finding is genuinely surprising, but the use of controls and an already richly articulated conceptual structure enable the researcher to make sense of the findings and propose novel theories. The manner in which experiments are constructed minimizes the role of serendipity to the extent that when surprising results do occur, the scientist already has a constrained set of active hypotheses and mechanisms that can be used to interpret the findings.

Risk!

One of the most intriguing aspects of this research has been the scientists' assessment of risk in their research. Most of the research scientists engaged in two or more research projects. The scientists tended to work on one high-risk and one low-risk project concurrently. The scientists categorized projects as high-risk if they rated a research project as having a low probability of working out but had the prospect of being an important discovery. They rated a project as low-risk if they could see that the project had a high probability of success. Often the low-risk projects were not regarded as ones that could produce important discoveries. Given that postdoctoral fellows tended to be concerned with getting a job in the near future, they often were reluctant to engage in high-risk projects, as the high-risk projects might not result in any publications, and so fewer job opportunities. The laboratory directors often were much more enthusiastic about high-risk projects as their goals were more long-term than were the goals of the postdoctoral fellows. Furthermore, given that there were many combinations of high-risk and low-risk projects occurring in a laboratory at any one time, the probability of one of these projects working was fairly high. By getting the postdoctoral fellows to conduct combinations of high-risk and low-risk projects, the directors helped ensure that the researchers would at least make a small discovery that would lead to a publication, and facilitate their own more long-term goals. (Dunbar [1993c] provides a detailed account of the role of risk assessment in scientific research.)

How to Make a Discovery

The findings discussed in this chapter have clear implications for the conduct of successful research. The following heuristics have been identified as being potentially important in making discoveries:

1. Members of a research group should have different but overlapping research backgrounds. This will foster group problem solving and analogical reasoning.

2. Analogical reasoning should be engaged in when problems arise in the research. In particular, the scientists should make both local and regional analogies.

3. Researchers should be encouraged to engage in combinations of high-risk and low-risk projects. This increases the probability that each scientist will have achieved a tangible result.

4. Surprising results should be noted. These surprising results can be used to generate new hypotheses and research programs.

5. Opportunities should be provided for the members of the research group to interact and discuss the research, by having overlapping research projects and breaking the laboratory into smaller groups working on similar problems.

CONCLUSION

This chapter has provided an overview of two approaches that I have used to investigate the cognitive processes involved in scientific reasoning and discovery. The first approach—investigating aspects of scientific reasoning—is conducted in the laboratory. Using this approach, the researcher has experimental control over aspects of the discovery process. As in other biological sciences, this in vitro approach makes it possible to isolate aspects of the reasoning process and to tease apart particular mechanisms. For example, the in vitro research I have discussed shows that the goals that subjects set are crucial to understanding scientific reasoning. Previous research using the in vitro approach has also identified important components of scientific reasoning (e.g., Klayman and Ha, 1987; Klahr & Dunbar, 1988).

However, as in other biological sciences, it is also necessary to investigate the processes of interest in their real-world context. Indeed, in this chapter, I have argued that in vivo investigations of the cognitive processes involved in real-world scientific reasoning and conceptual change are also needed, as they reveal novel mechanisms of reasoning that would be impossible to uncover using in vitro methods. For example, by using the in vivo methodology, entirely new insights were uncovered regarding the ways that analogies are used and their role in conceptual change and the mechanisms underlying conceptual change in the social context of science. Further, use of this in vivo approach to cognition demonstrates that it is possible to investigate complex cognitive processes in the real world. In summary, the in vivo approach is vital to achieving a more complete understanding of the specific mechanisms that underlie scientific reasoning and discovery.

The studies discussed in this chapter demonstrate that some of the mechanisms that have been found in the cognitive laboratory can be seen to be at work in the real world and, more importantly, that a new range of mechanisms can be uncovered by investigating real-world scientific contexts. Thus, I advance the claim that both in vivo and in vitro investigations are necessary to understand cognition and conceptual change. As in the biological sciences, the results of in vivo work can be brought into the laboratory and analyzed using in vitro methods. This cross-fertilization of the two approaches ensures that neither approach becomes paradigm-bound.

ACKNOWLEDGMENTS

This research was supported by a grant from the Spencer Foundation, grant number OGP0037356 from the National Sciences and Engineering Council of Canada, and a leave of absence given by the Department of Psychology at McGill University. I would like to thank Laura Ann Petitto for her comments on earlier drafts of this chapter.

NOTES

1. Clearly, to undertake this research I had to have a firm grasp of molecular biology, which I studied for 5 years prior to conducting the studies.

2. I use the term *discovery* in the manner used in cognitive science. Sociologists and historians of science have argued that a finding is not a discovery until the scientists have convinced other scientists that their finding is a discovery. With this view in mind, I continue to investigate these scientists to determine whether and how their findings become accepted as discoveries by the scientific community.

3. It is important to note that we regard these different types of analogies as existing on a continuum rather than as discrete classes of analogy. A more complete account of our findings on analogical reasoning is not yet published (Dunbar, 1993b).

REFERENCES

Baker, L., & Dunbar, K. (1993). [Falsification bias in expert reasoners.] Research in progress.

Brutlag, D.L., Galper, A.R., & Milis, D.H. (1991). Knowledge-based simulation of DNA metabolism: prediction of enzyme action. *CABIOS, 7,* 9–19.

Campbell, D.T., & Stanley, J.C. (1963). *Experimental and quasi-experimental designs for research.* Boston: Houghton Mifflin.

Dunbar, K. (1989). Scientific reasoning strategies in a simulated molecular genetics environment. *Proceedings of the Eleventh Annual Meeting of the Cognitive Science Society.* Hillsdale, NJ: Erlbaum.

Dunbar, K. (1993a). Scientific reasoning strategies for concept discovery in a complex domain. *Cognitive Science, 17,* 397–434.

Dunbar, K. (1993b). [Real-world analogical reasoning.] Manuscript in preparation.

Dunbar, K. (1993c). [Cognitive components of scientific discoveries that are determined by risk management and social constraints.] Manuscript in preparation.

Dunbar, K., & Baker, L. (1993a). [Anatomy of a scientific discovery.] Manuscript in preparation.

Dunbar, K., & Baker, L. (1993b). [Group problem solving: What is it, and when is it successful?] Manuscript in preparation.

Dunbar, K. & Schunn, C.D. (1990). The temporal nature of scientific discovery: The roles of priming and analogy. *Proceedings of the Twelfth Annual Meeting of the Cognitive Science Society.* Hillsdale, NJ: Erlbaum.

Ericsson, K.A., & Simon, H.A. (1984). *Protocol analysis: Verbal reports as data.* Cambridge: MIT Press.

Fujimura, J.H. (1987). Constructing 'do-able' problems in cancer research: Articulating alignment. *Social Studies of Science, 17,* 257–293.

Giere, R.N. (1988). *Explaining science: A cognitive approach.* Chicago: University of Chicago Press.

Gooding, D. (1992). The procedural turn. In R.N. Giere (Ed.), *Minnesota studies in the philosophy of science: Vol. 15. Cognitive models of science.* Minneapolis: University of Minnesota Press.

Holmes, L. (1985). *Lavoisier and the chemistry of life: An exploration of scientific creativity.* Madison: University of Wisconsin Press.

Judson, H.F. (1979). *The eighth day of creation.* New York: Simon and Schuster.

Karp, P.D. (1989). Hypothesis formation as design. In J. Shrager & P. Langley (Eds.), *Computational models of discovery and theory formation* (pp. 275–315). San Francisco: Morgan Kaufmann.

Klahr, D., & Dunbar, K. (1988). Dual space search during scientific reasoning. *Cognitive Science, 12,* 1–48.

Klahr, D., Dunbar, K., & Fay, A.L. (1989). Designing good experiments to test bad hypotheses. In J. Shrager & P. Langley (Eds.), *Computational models of discovery and theory formation* (pp. 355–402). San Francisco: Morgan Kaufmann.

Klayman, J., & Ha, Y. (1987). Confirmation, disconfirmation, and information in hypothesis testing. *Psychological Review, 94,* 211–228.

Knorr-Cetina, K.D. (1983). The ethnographic study of scientific work: Towards a constructivist interpretation of science. In K.D. Knorr-Cetina & M.J. Mulkay (Eds.), *Science observed: Perspectives on the social studies of science.* Newbury Park, CA: Sage Publications.

Latour, B., & Woolgar, S. (1986). *Laboratory life: The construction of scientific facts.* Princeton, NJ: Princeton University Press.

Mahoney, M.J., & DeMonbruen, B.G. (1977). Psychology of the scientist: An analysis of problem solving bias. *Cognitive Therapy and Research, 1,* 229–238.

Mitroff, I.I. (1974). *The subjective side of science.* Amsterdam: Elsevier.

Mulkay, M., & Gilbert, G.N. (1983). Scientist's theory talk. *Canadian Journal of Sociology, 8,* 179–197.

Mynatt, C.R., Doherty, M.E., & Tweney, R.D. (1978). Consequences of confirmation and disconfirmation in a simulated research environment. *Quarterly Journal of Experimental Psychology, 30,* 395–406.

Nersessian, N. (1992). How do scientists think? Capturing the dynamics of conceptual change in science. In R.N. Giere (Ed.), *Minnesota studies in the philosophy of science: Vol. 15. Cognitive models of science.* Minneapolis: University of Minnesota Press.

Nisbett, R.E., & Wilson, T.D. (1977). Telling more than we can know: Verbal reports on mental processes. *Psychological Review, 84,* 231–259.

Sanderson, P.M., Scott, J.J.P., Johnston, T., Mainzer, J., Watanabe, L.M., & James, J.M. (1993). [MacSHAPA and the enterprise of exploratory sequential data analysis.] Manuscript submitted for publication.

Stein, N. (1992). [A taxonomy of discourse processes.] Manuscript in preparation.

Tweney, R.D. (1985). Faraday's discovery of induction: A cognitive approach. In D. Gooding & F. James (Eds.), *Faraday rediscovered.* New York: Stockton Press.

Wason, P.C. (1960). On the failure to eliminate hypotheses in a conceptual task. *Quarterly Journal of Experimental Psychology, 12,* 129–140.

12 Insight and Affect in the History of Science

Howard E. Gruber

This chapter addresses two different meanings of insight—one concerned with problem solving, the other with understanding—and their merging in creative scientific thinking. Some analogies between perception and insight, as well as the distinction between two kinds of saltatory growth (many small steps versus a few great leaps), are discussed. Long delays between reports of insight and the events reported tend to vitiate the accuracy of memory. In the history of science, three kinds of error may enter into accounts of insight: telescoping, rationalization, and decontextualization.

Six scientific discoverers—Archimedes, Kekulé, Poincaré, Einstein, Darwin, and Piaget—will be considered, to illustrate and explore the points just made, to examine different forms of insight, and to open a discussion of the relation between insight and affect. The affects exhibited at moments of insight are seen in relation to the longer stream of affects of which they are a part.

DEFINITIONS OF INSIGHT

Insight has at least two chief meanings, each prevalent in different intellectual communities. Among students of creativity and cognitive psychologists, *insight* refers to that glorious moment when one suddenly "sees" the solution to a problem. The emphasis is on suddenness and surprise, solution and correctness. The issue of correctness is important. Ordinarily, we would not speak of a false insight, although we might speak of a misleading *feeling* of insight. This distinction brings out a more general point: An insight can be construed as a subjective experience with a particular emotional color.

Perhaps surprisingly, some Gestalt psychologists represent an important exception to the idea that cognitive psychologists treat insight under the heading of problem solving. In the concluding chapter of *Gestalt Psychology*, "Insight," Köhler (1947) barely mentions problem solving. For him an insight is a subjective experience, a feeling that things make sense, a *verständlicher Zusammenhang*, which, he writes, "may be expressed in English as understandable relationship" (Köhler, 1947, p. 326). For example, the felt desire to approach an attractive person is experienced as determined by the attributes of the other. In this usage, the term *insight* applies not only to perceptual and other cognitive processes but also to moods and motives experienced as making sense. Something similar could be said of Asch's (1952) extensive treatment of insight.

In contrast, a seminal work by the founder of Gestalt psychology, Max Wertheimer (1945/1959), has as its central theme insightful problem solving, as does his student's celebrated monograph (Duncker, 1945). Thus, the pioneering cognitive behaviorist, Osgood, could plausibly label insight a Gestalt concept, "a mode of problem-solving," and sum up its major attributes as "suddenness ... smoothness ... point in behavior sequence where solution occurs ... novelty" (Osgood, 1953, pp. 610–611).

Among psychoanalysts and other students of personality, *insight* refers to the condition of having knowledge rather than to the moment of attaining it. There is not much difference between the phrases *an insightful remark* and *a perceptive remark*. Nor is there, in these phrases, any implication of sudden access to the insight. Emphasis is on self-knowledge as the aim; intuition is taken for granted as the way.

Wallace (1991, pp. 41–42) has stressed the point that *insight* refers to "a *family* of phenomena occurring in creative work. The family includes problem finding ... problem resolution, synthesis, discovering similarities, analogies, increase in certainty, recognizing error, the *mot juste*, and so on." Although these all may occur as relatively sudden transformations of the cognitive field, she points out that each has an internal microgenesis, and each occurs within the context of a longer developmental sequence.

A full systematic study of insight would delineate the major types of insight, analyze their internal structures, and examine their *raison d'être* or psychological functions, varying from type to type in their cognitive, motivational, and affective aspects. For the present, I consider only the distinction between insight as problem solving and insight as understanding.

In ordinary life, we can accept the disjunction between understanding and problem solving. Sometimes we just experience a meaningful, coherent world in which events make sense. You turn the page *because* you have gotten to the end of it and you want to go on reading. Sometimes things become problematic; you struggle with a problem and perhaps solve it. You recognize the fact that you have solved the problem (insight), and you go on with your life. With any luck, no new problem will arise for awhile.

However, in a life of creative work, such as a scientist's, the worst luck of all would be to encounter no new problems. We seek out problems as a way of testing and expanding our understanding of the world. The two meanings of insight come together: Efforts toward comprehension evoke problems, and so on in a swirling stream. In our study of insight, we need to see how problems requiring insightful solutions grow out of a given understanding and then how solution leads to changes in that understanding. This is a worthy challenge.

In some treatments of insight, the phenomenon is viewed as an isolated event and, moreover, an event that climaxes an isolated process, solving one particular problem. In this chapter, as in my other publications, I have tried to show how insights, whether they are small steps or great leaps, are part of a coherent life. They express the thinker's organizations of affect and purpose as well as his or her organization of knowledge.

Let us consider the famous story of Archimedes. Students of creativity who recount it often make it appear as though the problem of ascertaining the purity of the metal in Hiero's crown was given to Archimedes, he took his bath and made his observations of water displaced by his body, had his flash of insight, and then ran naked through the streets crying "Eureka!" (See, for example, Dampier, 1948.)

What really happened in the bath we do not and may never know, but we do know that Archimedes wrote an important 47-page, highly deductive mathematical treatise on floating bodies. It is more plausible to think of the problem of the density of Hiero's crown as embedded in this enterprise than as an isolated event. Hence, our task is not only to understand the inner structure of each episode of insight but to relate this structure to the creative life of which it is a part.

My colleagues and I (see Wallace & Gruber, 1989) have called this effort the *evolving systems approach*. In this view of creative work, there are three major subsystems: (1) an organization of knowledge, (2) an organization of purpose (the network of enterprise), and (3) an organization of affect. These are taken as loosely coupled, thus permitting the indeterminacy and consequent freedom necessary in any approach to creative work. Because the creative person is considered systemically and holistically, the approach encourages examination of the diverse psychological and psychosocial functions that constitute the individual. The approach leads us to undertake case studies of creative people at work and to do so in such a way that illuminates the developing system as a whole. As each creative person is necessarily a unique configuration, the generalities that our case studies arrive at bear more on method and on what to look at than they do on inductive generalizations about characteristics that creators may share.

The creative person is considered as an *evolving* system. Therefore, in the study of insight, we are especially concerned with the way in which each insight is a move in the development of the creator and of his or her work. By the same token, we are particularly on the lookout for the many moments of insight occurring in a creative life, rather than supposing that the heart of the matter lies in one great creative leap. Thus, insights express and are part of the functioning of the creative system rather than its rupture.

PERCEPTION AND THOUGHT

The use of the term *insight* to denote an aspect of thought reflects a widespread, if not always explicit, belief in the quasiperceptual nature of thought. Perhaps we ought not to speak of a *belief* but rather of a direct experience of the kinship of perceptual and other organized cognitive phenomena. Consider the manifold uses of the phrase *I see*. Written with a period, it carries the weight of *I follow your argument*. But written with an exclamation point—*I see!*—it carries the weight of *Land Ho!*—a discovery.

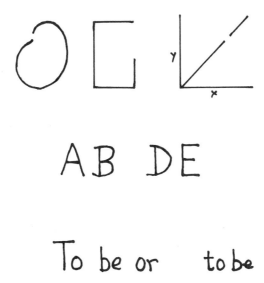

Figure 12.1
A variety of gaps evoking gap-filling behavior.

Cognitive Gap-Filling Behavior

What do the configurations shown in figure 12.1 have in common? Of course, they each contain a gap; they all provoke cognitive gap-filling behavior, as do interrupted events (see Gruber, Fink & Damm, 1957). What is more, there is a *correct* way to fill each gap. Further still, the gap-filling behavior is elicited immediately or almost so.

Correct does not mean that the obvious solution is the only correct one. However, in the examples given we can say that the structure to be completed has evolved to the point where it does elicit one most probable, least problematic, most immediate solution.

Immediate refers both to the rapidity of the solution or gap-filling behavior and to its nonmediated quality. That is, no intermediate process is detectable in conscious experience. Of course, indirect means, such as chronometric experiments, may reveal such intermediate processes. The need to make this remark highlights the fact that when we talk about insight, we have in mind conscious experience. Could there be an unconscious insight?

Filling the gap does not merely complete the figure. The very act of apprehending the structure-with-a-gap transforms and enriches the cognitive situation.

Other Structural Transformations

It must be remembered that the Gestalt psychologists placed great emphasis on structural features of perception and extended this effort to include the quasi-perceptual nature of thought (Wertheimer, 1945–1959). Lewin (1935) pointed out the motivational parallels, and, as he describes their work, his students, Zeigarnik and Ovsiankina, extended the idea of gap-filling behavior to the tensions produced by the interruption of a task. This is an important issue for our present purpose, because all creative work necessarily involves interruptions of various durations (Gruber, 1988).

Consider figure 12.2. For most observers, the subjective contour generated by the converging lines that do not quite meet define an area that is noticeably brighter or more insistent than the merely white paper on which the figure lies. Not to be ignored also is the fact that the subjective contour defines an area that has a phenomenal shape.

I have played with this figure for a long time. One day, while reading Bergson (1912), I was struck by the analogy between the figure and a remark he makes about the relation of metaphors to their targets. A single metaphor is always imperfect, but a set of metaphors all almost converging on the same target do illumi-

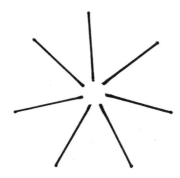

Figure 12.2
A perceptual metaphor for Bergson's (1912) idea of converging metaphors.

nate and define it (Bergson, 1912, pp. 20–21). My experience of analogy was immediate.

We can see already that gaps are not the only structural features that elicit immediate insights. In the Bergson–subjective contour analogy the experience of analogy, for me when I first perceived it, was as immediately and affectively charged as any experience to which I might say, "I see!" Yet "I see!" is not quite the right ejaculation for such analogy-seeing. We might better say, "Look!"

Other phenomena (e.g., good continuation, figure-ground reversals, context effects, and relativistic determination) well-known to perception psychologists also have their direct and fairly obvious analogs in the world of thought.

VARIETIES OF SUDDEN CHANGE

Sudden has one meaning to the evolutionist interested in the appearance and disappearance of species. It has another meaning to the neuroscientist interested in nerve transmission. Somewhere between lie the time scales of the historian of science and the student of creative problem solving.

Often when we think in terms of a growth model of psychological processes, we have in mind gradual, incremental changes that can be described by the equations of infinitesimal calculus. However, growth may take other forms. Recent research on bodily growth in humans suggests that it typically occurs in spurts. In figure 12.3, a smooth curve could obviously be drawn through the data points, but a stepped curve, as shown, fits the data more faithfully (Lampl, Veldhuis, & Johnson, 1992). The crucial decision to make daily measurements of bodily dimensions was based on the investigators' doubt about the notion of smooth, incremental growth. In studies of the growth of ideas, we rarely have data permitting a clear-cut distinction between step functions with small steps and smoothed curves. It should, however, be pointed out that psychologists have known for a long time that learning curves often exhibit a series of plateaus, which amounts to almost the same idea of alternation between periods of stasis and of saltatory growth. Thus, the very same series of events looked at in one perspective seems like a gradual change and in another perspective a sudden leap.

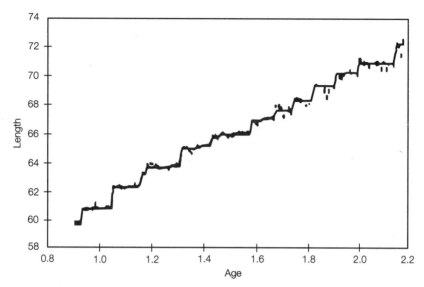

Figure 12.3
A stepped-growth curve illustrating many small "discontinuous, aperiodic, saltatory spurts." Daily length measurements of a male infant from 90 to 218 days of age. (Adapted with permission from M. Lampl, J.D. Veldhuis, and M.L. Johnson [1992], Saltation and stasis: A model of human growth. *Science, 258,* 801–802.)

Wittgenstein (1969, p. 21), in his remarks on certainty, writes: "When we first begin to *believe* anything, what we believe is not a single proposition, it is a whole system of propositions. (Light dawns gradually over the whole.)" He was not writing about insight but about the systemic character of beliefs that make certainty possible. To continue his dawn metaphor, we ought to qualify his remark with the observation that at dawn, although the light grows gradually, our *experience* reflects the effect of thresholds: Things pop out.

SOME INSIGHTS IN THE HISTORY OF SCIENCE

Historical and biographical accounts leave something to be desired as data for psychologists. Accounts of many of the most celebrated cases of insight were written long after the fact, even posthumously. Such delays have led to several kinds of error: telescoping, rationalization, and decontextualization.

Kinds of Error

Telescoping
In the loss of detail due to limitations of memory, intermediate steps drop out and beginnings and ends remain. In the older literature on memory, this was known as the *bowed serial position effect*. Gestalt psychologists interpreted the phenomenon as attributable to the greater perceptual prominence of the two ends of the process (Asch, Hay & Mendoza, 1960). In any event, the consequence for long-term memory is to replace many small intermediate steps by one or two points, suggesting a leap.

Rationalization
Changes in intuition and in affective feeling disappear from memory and are replaced by post hoc rational and empirical accounts. The widespread supposition that Einstein used the Michelson-Morley experiments as an empirical basis for inferring the theory of relativity is an example of this kind. Such rationalizations of historical events fitted in well with the philosophical agenda of those philosophers of science interested in the problem of justification rather than that of discovery.

However, for psychologists and others interested in the context of discovery, nonrational, intuitive processes have loomed large. Scientists such as Poincaré have seized on such nonrational aspects of thought as central and prevalent. As a result, in the psychology of science now prevailing, errors of the first kind predominate.

It should be noted that those problems that arise out of the limitations of memory do not occur in the use of notebooks written on the spot, as in my work with Darwin's notebooks (Gruber, 1974/1981a) or Holmes's work with the notebooks of Lavoisier and Krebs (Holmes, 1989).

Decontextualization
A coherent episode in which a moment (or several) of insight occurs can be thought of as a figural event seen or remembered against a background of several overlapping contexts. The context includes nonfigural aspects of the momentary situation in which the insight occurs, as for Maier's (1931) subjects in his cele-

brated pendulum experiment. The key point was that the experimenter produced a slight movement of the pendulum, which was critical for discovering the solution (deliberately swinging the suspended object so that it could be reached from another vantage point), but the subjects were usually unaware of the initial slight movement (Maier, 1931).

The context also includes the enterprise in which the problem in question is a part (as in Archimedes' case, his prolonged reflections on floating bodies). In addition, it may include the wider intellectual currents that contribute to defining the problem, to dictating the forms of acceptable solutions, and to suggesting the psychological theory that will shape the way in which the insight is recorded and interpreted (as in Poincaré's conversion to intuitionism, discussed later).

Let us turn now to a more concrete examination of some cases of scientific insight.

Archimedes' Bath

The term *Eureka experience* is emblematic of the idea of sudden insight. Supposedly, as already mentioned, Archimedes noticed the rise in water level when he entered his bath and realized that the amount of water displaced would be proportionate to the volume of the object immersed: Hence, a true gold crown would have a smaller volume than one in which silver or other metals had been mixed.

However, no less a psychologist than Galileo (1586/1961) insisted that this story was implausible. First, it would not give a measure of the proportions of gold and silver in the alloy, if any, used in the crown; the result would be far cruder than needed. Second, from his knowledge of Archimedes' other work (especially the treatise on floating bodies), Galileo perceived a solution that would have been readily available to his gifted forerunner: the use of a special balance for measuring density by measuring what *proportion* of its weight in air a body loses in water. Galileo even went on to invent a specialized balance beam that would measure this quantity directly. Galileo believed that Archimedes would have thought like him.

Heath (1897) proposed a somewhat different reconstruction of Archimedes' probable path. Heath drew explicitly on the reasoning in Archimedes's treatise, "On Floating Bodies," and constructed a formalization of Archimedes' thinking as it applied to the problem of Hiero's crown. The most important point, that Galileo (and Heath) saw Archimedes' solution as growing out of long-standing concerns and a highly elaborated point of view, is reflected in more recent studies of Galileo by Drake (1978).

The trouble with the legendary version is its crude empiricism or stimulus-boundness, suggesting that Archimedes actually learned about displacement at the moment of stepping into his bath and thus "saw" the solution. Galileo's more constructivist account need not be read as altogether excluding the influence of the bath experience or the possibility of a flash of insight. As Archimedes thought and wrote about the physics of floating bodies, he may have often seen and thought about the water displaced by his body. If at the moment in question he was midcourse in constructing a new set of ideas and a solution to a new problem (i.e., in the manner Galileo proposed), then the sight of displacement would be assimilated or mapped onto a schema different from before, and thus have different consequences. Even the simple act of submerging an object or oneself in water has many subtleties. Which ones are selected and exploited depends on where the thinker is at the time. For example, the usual shorthand account focuses on the *volume* of water displaced, which would be almost directly visible. However, Galileo and Heath both stress the centrality of the *weight* of the water displaced.

We can accept Galileo's sophisticated caveat without denying the importance of the bath as long as we remember that Archimedes was immersed in thought.

Nonetheless, this founding incident must remain shrouded in doubt. The first record of it we have was written by Vitruvius, nearly three centuries after Archimedes died.

Kekulé's Dreams

Let us turn now to the story of Kekulé's dreams and reveries. No creative person's subjective account of thinking could provide a more dramatic instance of sudden illumination born of strong contact with freely flowing primitive processes of the unconscious mind.

In 1981, I published a reinterpretation of the Kekulé story based on the documents then available to me (Gruber, 1981). My goal was not so much to cast doubt on Kekulé's version but to show how, carefully read, the story really supported the evolving systems approach to creative work (see Gruber, 1989). Recently, however, I read a brief article casting doubt on the whole story (Wotiz & Rudofsky, 1984). I telephoned Professor Wotiz and he informed me that a book is in press exposing the whole story as a case of scientific fraud (Wotiz, 1993). At this writing, I have not yet seen the book, but I have checked my summary of the 1984 article with Professor Wotiz. Here I present both versions: first a somewhat abbreviated version of my own effort in 1981 and second a brief summary of the questions raised by Wotiz and Rudofsky in 1984.

Kekulé's Account of His Reveries

In 1890, Kekulé recollected a thought process that had occurred in 1854:

During my stay in London ... One fine summer evening I was returning on the last omnibus. ... I fell into a reverie [*Träumerei*], and lo, the atoms were gambolling before my eyes! Whenever hitherto, these diminutive beings had appeared to me, they had always been in motion; but up to that time I had never been able to discern the nature of their motion. Now, however, I saw how, frequently, two smaller atoms united to form a pair; how a larger one embraced two smaller ones; how still larger ones kept hold of three or even four of the smaller; whilst the whole kept whirling in a giddy dance. I saw how the larger ones formed a chain, dragging the smaller ones after them, but only at the ends of the chain. ... The cry of the conductor: "Clapham Road," awakened me from my dreaming; but I spent a part of the night in putting on paper at least sketches of these dream forms. This was the origin of *Structurtheorie*. (Kekulé, 1890, cited in Japp, 1898)

Arthur Koestler (1964, p. 170) comments on this passage: "The whirling, giddy vision reminds one of the hallucinations of schizophrenics, as painted or described by them. Kekulé's case is rather exceptional, but nevertheless characteristic in one respect: the sudden abdication of conceptual thought in favor of semi-conscious visual conceits."

The Evolving Systems Approach to Creative Work

And yet it seems to me that a different story can be read in Kekulé's memories, a story of the evolution of a point of view, of protracted purposeful work, and of the growth of a highly specialized mental language or modality of thought. Of course, there were at least two moments, but probably many more, similar to the two accounts Kekulé gave in his autobiographical address. However, these instants did not come out of the blue and, in order for each to do its work, Kekulé had to seize it and make it a part of the project he was pursuing.

Kekulé's recollections were included in an address he gave in 1890, decades after the events described. The second reverie he recounted, leading to the hypothesis of the benzene ring structure, occurred in 1865, eleven years after the first. Let us put aside any questions we have about the fallibility of memory for such subtle events. Here is one of the first minds of the nineteenth century reporting on itself: There must be some important connection between Kekulé's thought processes and his description of them.

Visualization

It should not be thought that Kekulé "saw" the real structure of the benzene ring. He got a very general idea of a ring structure, a hypothesis (as he called it himself), an idea that could be realized in numerous ways, as subsequent controversy showed. Kekulé's description of his thinking suggests that it would be natural for him to perceive more than one of these possibilities, and he did so, using at least three different visualizations between 1865 and 1866.

Hein (1866) has given a clear account of Kekulé's visual thinking. It was, he says, probably strengthened and focused by his early training as an architect. It was not merely a modality of thought but was bound to Kekulé's view that a model should be more than a formal accounting for a set of valences. It should give an idea of *how* "the atoms of a polyatomic molecule are ar-

ranged in space so that all the attractive forces are satisfied." Kekulé's main emphasis was on hexagonal configurations in a plane.
Some writers interpret this to mean that Kekulé thought in terms
of two-dimensional space. A more plausible interpretation is that
he thought of chemical structures in general as lying in three-
dimensional space, within which, of course, some planar configurations are possible.

Kekulé's account suggests that such visions were not unusual
for him but were the way, or one of the ways, he thought. His
dreams or reveries were extensions of his waking thought. In examining more closely Kekulé's account of the 1854 reverie, four
points stand out. First, we notice that the type of imagery he describes was by no means new to him ("Whenever, hitherto ... up
to that time ..."). Kekulé had evolved a special form of imagery in
which he could think directly; he had already had many ideas in
that modality, and now he had a new one.

Second, it is clear from the record of Kekulé's life and from his
recollection of 1854, that he had many occasions to move back
and forth between his personal imagery and other forms of
thought ("I spent part of the night in putting on paper at least
sketches ...").

Third, the way the tale is told strongly suggests that the
thought process was no millisecond flash but a process somewhat
extended in time.

Fourth, as so often happens when thinking goes well, it has a
twin character of objectification and spontaneity. The dramatist's
characters talk to each other in the dramatist's head. Kekulé's
atoms gambol before his eyes. As with any highly practiced
skilled performance, each act plays itself out effortlessly and spontaneously. It seems to happen out there yet remains under the
control of the thinking, acting person. Because they are Kekulé's
thoughts, the imaginary atoms do not become tennis balls in an
imaginary game or even atoms in Brownian motion; rather, they
explore the structural possibilities of chemical knowledge.

Thinking moves from one modality to another, from visual
images to sketches, to words and equations explaining (i.e., con-
veying the same meaning as) the visualizations. The thinker is
pleased to discover that certain structures remain invariant under
these transformations: *These* are his ideas. Dialogue, both internal

and external, is a ubiquitous part of the process. By 1860, *Structurtheorie* had advanced to the point that Kekulé and others organized an international congress to consider ways of determining valences.

We must ask, how does Kekulé knows that he has had a new idea? His illumination, when it occurs, immediately strikes him not only as a solution but as novel. His recognizing the new idea as *new for him* means that he has a mental record of his own previous moves. Similarly, he must have some sense of history. To know what is *new for others*, he must perceive the significance of his own thinking in its historical context.

This was my reading of the Kekulé story in 1981. The 1984 article by Wotiz and Rudofsky, however, casts doubt on all of this: How much credit does Kekulé deserve for the invention of structural chemistry or, indeed, for the idea of the benzene ring? Did Kekulé's dreams occur at all? If they did, were they Kekulé's dreams or did he borrow the picturesque dance of the atoms from someone else? Kekulé himself seems to have suggested that the after-dinner speech in which he first revealed the allegedly decades-old story was concocted for the amusement of his listeners, not to be taken too seriously.

The Critique by Wotiz and Rudofsky

Experience tells us that it takes historians of science years to resolve such questions. Now Professor Wotiz informs me that the sorting has been done and that we are faced with a monumental case of scientific fraud. If so, we must also confront the thought that every case of one person's successful fraud is also a case of another person's gullibility. Many chemists and many students of creativity believed Kekulé's account. In particular, his image of the two snakes biting each other's tails, which suggested the benzene ring structure, was widely cited as illustrating the importance of intuitive and primary-process thinking, even in the scientific domain.

Of course, it does not follow that if the Kekulé myth is a fallacious example of insight, all our thinking about insight is wrong. If Kekulé could construct a plausible scenario, perhaps it was plausible because it was near the mark. On the other hand, we should not scramble too hastily for such cover. The main point of this whole episode may turn out to be a methodological one: Anecdotal evidence, especially as colored and misted over by the passage of time, is weak. The case study method, as developed by my collaborators and myself for the most part avoids the use of isolated anecdotes and relies heavily on tracing thought processes in context as they are reflected in documents such as notebooks and letters produced at or close to the time at which the thought itself took place. Even such material leaves plenty of room for variant interpretations, but at least it reduces the hazards of relying too heavily on second-hand sources and decaying memories.

The Lesson for Students of Insight

Since writing the above account I have had the opportunity to read the book edited by Wotiz and Rudofsky (1993). The various chemists and historians of chemistry whose papers are included by no means agree on the main features of the Kekulé story. What emerges is that all the major issues deserve close study by anyone interested in the psychology of creative work: the complex history of and many participants in nineteenth century structural chemistry; the veracity of Kekulé's account and the reliability of old memories; and the generality and plausibility of Kekulé's self-description as it might pertain to other chemists' thinking.

All in all, I believe we can now accept Kekulé's own version as true, or approximately true. Nevertheless, the way the discussion has unfolded should be chastening to students of insight. The lesson is not to reject anecdotes of insight, but to study them in historical perspective and in this effort to bring to bear one's general knowledge of the creative process. Above all, to be avoided are both the telescoping of great swaths of history into an account of the achievements of one person and the telescoping of one significant figure's protracted work into a single compressed anecdote.

Poincaré's Bus

There is a certain irony in the way students of creativity have used Henri Poincaré's famous moment of insight, taking it out of context and ignoring the mathematician's excellent description of the relationships between microgenetic and macrogenetic processes making up a complex event, extended in time.

Poincaré's essay, "Mathematical Discovery" (1952), is one of the best-known, most widely cited, and often reprinted accounts of what seems to be a Eureka experience. Arieti (1976), for example, gives a succinct but full enough account of the event as a whole but then boils it down to the received, truncated version: "At the moment he put his foot on the step, the idea came to him.... This was the creative moment." (Arieti, 1976, p. 268)

I have asked a number of informed individuals—historians, psychologists, and mathematicians—what they remember about Poincaré's essay. Almost invariably the response comes, "He put his foot on the step of the bus ...," perhaps with some doubt as to whether Poincaré was mounting or dismounting. (He was mounting. Without spoofing, and judging from my own experiences, this may be significant. Starting a trip, or entering a tub, for an intellectually preoccupied person, is like moving into a pleasantly empty time. Dismounting or detubbing is different.) This episode provides an excellent example of the transformation in memory known as *telescoping*: A complex event, extended in time, is compressed into an instantaneous point. This entails a double loss—the disappearance of the inner temporal structure or microgenesis of the momentary event and the neglect of its multiple relations with other processes.

Poincaré on Intuitive Thinking

The key passage in Poincaré's essay is a three-page narrative of mathematical thinking (Poincaré, 1952, pp. 52–54) leading up to his first treatise on Fuchsian functions. This work did not quite spring from nowhere but was anticipated in its point of view and style of thought in Poincaré's first published work in 1878, when the mathematician was 24 years old. It was not until 1908, almost 30 years later, that Poincaré gave the lecture on mathematical discovery that was included in *Science and Method*, published the same year. Until 1900, Poincaré had been the supreme mathematical analyst. At the Second International Congress of Mathematics in 1900, he proclaimed: "We believe that we no longer appeal to intuition in our reasoning ... We may say today that ab-

solute rigour has been attained" (Bell, 1937). However, in the ensuing years he moved rapidly in an intuitionist direction. In this
he was not alone. There were other similar stirrings, but Poincaré
was a princely forerunner of the intuitionist school of mathematical thought. Moreover, in the years just preceding his essay on
mathematical discovery, there had been a series of questionnaires
administered to mathematicians and monographs were published
on the psychology of mathematical thought, generally stressing
the role of dreamwork and intuition. However, none of these reports came from mathematicians of Poincaré's caliber, so his contribution was an important addition (Hadamard, 1945).

Science and Method is one long argument in praise of both psychological and mathematical intuition: "[W]hat the true scientist
alone can see is the link that unites several facts which have a
deep but hidden analogy. The anecdote of Newton's apple is probably not true, but it is symbolic, so we will treat it as if it were
true" (Poincaré, 1952, pp. 27–28). In a critique of bare analytical
logic, aimed especially at Russell, Peano, and Hilbert, Poincaré
(p. 193) concludes: "Logic therefore remains barren, unless it is
fertilized by intuition." He describes a possible relation between
stepwise calculation and penetrating intuition:

[W]hen a somewhat lengthy calculation has conducted us to some simple
and striking result, we are not satisfied until we have shown that we
might have foreseen, if not the whole result, at least its most characteristic features... The reason is that in analogous cases, the lengthy calculation might not be able to be used again, while this is not true of the
reasoning, often semi-intuitive, which might have enabled us to foresee
the result. This reasoning being short, we can see all the parts at a single
glance, so that we perceive immediately what must be changed to adapt it
to ... problems of a similar nature." (Poincaré, 1952, pp. 31–32)

In this discussion, Poincaré proposes a sequence of processes, a
sort of model of mathematical discovery:

Arduous work → Sound conclusion → Naming the result

→ Compression of thought → Further economies

→ Intuitive grasp

A similar flow is described, or perhaps proposed, in a later chapter.
In building an arch, when the edifice has been constructed stone
by stone, the scaffold must be removed. Only then can the form

of the whole be seen: "What good is it to admire the mason's work in the edifices erected by great architects if we cannot understand the general plan of the master? Now pure logic cannot give us this view of the whole; it is to intuition we must look for it" (Poincaré, 1952, p. 126). Impersonal though they are, it seems reasonable to suppose that these remarks allude to Poincaré's own experience as a mathematical masterbuilder.

Poincaré's Account of His Insight: Seven Steps
Now let us turn to Poincaré's frankly autobiographical fragment. Even without understanding the mathematics, there is much to be gained from a close reading of his recollections. The event, as a whole, stretches over an indefinite period of time, evidently several months. It can be divided into seven episodes, and summarized as follows:

1. *Caen*: For a fortnight, Poincaré has been working on a mathematical problem, to prove the *non*existence of the class of functions he later called *Fuchsian*. A sleepless night, occasioned by too much coffee and too much obsession, leads to a first important idea. By morning, he has established the contrary of his original intention. Nothing is said of any sudden illumination. But he does speak of ideas "surging" and "jostling one another," and he does distinguish this phase from the next morning when he devoted a few hours to "verify" the result. He seems to be describing a two-phase sequence of intuitive combinatorial work of discovery followed by some more rigorous process of proof. Although he speaks of the surging ideas sometimes forming a "stable combination," this does not seem to mean the sudden emergence of *solution*. Judging from the whole of Poincaré's essay, his remembered experience, or his impression, is that stable combinations surge up from what he calls the "subliminal ego" only if they are interesting and plausible enough to be presented to consciousness. Whereas many potential ideas are thus excluded, many such plausible combinations arise, only to be discarded.

2. *Caen*: At a time unspecified but soon after the first episode, Poincaré formed a new intention, to represent the functions he had just found in a new way. Quite consciously and deliberately, he adopted the strategy of reasoning backward: "I asked myself

what must be the properties of these series, if they existed, and I succeeded without difficulty in forming the series that I have called *Theta-Fuchsian*" (Poincaré, 1952, p. 53).

3. *Coutances*: Poincaré attended a geological conference 90 km from Caen, where he was living. Here, with no forewarning, he had his celebrated foot-on-the-step-of-the-bus illumination, a perception or recognition of the identity of two mathematical transformations. He waited until his return to Caen to verify this "finding."

4. *Caen and seaside*: Poincaré had begun work on a seemingly unrelated mathematical project. Making no progress, he went away for a few days. "One day, as I was walking on the cliff, the idea came to me, again with the same characteristics of conciseness, suddenness, and immediate certainty ..." (Poincaré, 1952, p. 54). Again he had perceived an identity, previously unnoticed, between two mathematical transformations.

5. *Caen*: Returning to his home and teaching post, Poincaré deduced the consequences of his new finding and set about systematizing and generalizing it. He succeeded easily, with one notable exception. Struggling with this obstacle did help him "better understand the difficulty, which was already something. All this work was perfectly conscious" (Poincaré, 1952, p. 54).

6. *Mont-Valerien and Caen*: Poincaré was in military service near Paris, 200 km from Caen. "... [M]y mind was preoccuppied with very different matters. One day, as I was crossing the street, the solution of the difficulty which had brought me to a standstill came to me all at once. I did not try to fathom it immediately, and it was only after my service was finished that I returned to the question. I had all the elements and had only to assemble and arrange them," (Poincaré, 1952, p. 54). Clearly, the solution that came to him all at once was not a finished product but something that needed further fathoming and reorganizing.

7. *Caen*: Now having all the elements of a definitive treatise, Poincaré (1952, p. 55) composed it "at a single sitting and without any difficulty."

Of these seven episodes, then, three include sudden illuminations—on the bus, on the cliff, and in the street. Another is described as freighted with intuitive thought. The remaining three are characterized as conscious and deliberate work. For Poincaré, one of the hallmarks of his sudden illuminations is the suspension of intentional work on the problem, although this is not necessarily the case for other individuals.

Thus, Poincaré gives a detailed first-order description, not of one great insight but of a continuously working, evolving system of thought that produces important insights from time to time. As I read him, he is probably thinking about mathematics almost all the time. During the period described, he was working not only on the problem of automorphic functions but also on a wide range of mathematical subjects. For Poincaré, mathematics was a language in which he thought. "To Poincaré ... analysis came as naturally as thinking" (Bell, 1937, Vol. 2, p. 597). For him, making plausible or polite mathematical statements was probably similar to a non-mathematician spontaneously uttering well-formed sentences in a language he knows well—No more mysterious than that, and no less!

Einstein said somewhere, "If atoms could talk, I would surely listen." But there are many difficulties in listening to people describe their thinking. We are not required to take such descriptions at face value (Ericsson & Simon, 1984). Subjective reports will inevitably be selected and organized in ways influenced by the subject's theoretical perspectives. Poincaré was functioning both as mathematician and as psychologist when he wrote his essay on mathematical discovery. *Intuition* does not have quite the same meaning in these two universes of discourse. As a recent convert to intuitionism, Poincaré strove to apply his point of view in both domains. We cannot read his recollections as unprocessed memories, for they have gone through this complex and uncertain system of filters. To these difficulties must be added the more mundane facts of forgetting and telescoping that enter into all recollections. Despite these reservations, Poincaré's account and others like it are surely a great mine of knowledge about creative thinking.

There are at least three levels in Poincaré's description: mathematics itself, his own thoughts about mathematics, and his more general reflections on the psychology of thinking. All of these must be considered seriously. If a thinker says, "My thoughts came at random," we do not have to believe there was a Monte Carlo machine in his head. Indeed, we have good enough experimental evidence that it is impossible to have random thoughts. Nevertheless, if the process feels haphazard to the thinker, that means something. The feeling may stem from the felt spontaneity of the process; or it may be difficult to perceive a conventionally acceptable ordering of the ideas; or the ideas that arise may seem irrelevant to the line of thought that later prevailed. We cannot escape the task or the risks of interpretation.

The Importance of Purpose

Poincaré was very careful to emphasize the ways in which the creative process is regulated by the thinker's conscious and enduring purposes. On the one hand, he compares the elementary ideas of a mathematician's thought process to molecules in a gas whose collisions produce new combinations. On the other hand, he says of these elements, "Now our will did not select them at random but in pursuit of a perfectly definite aim. Those it has liberated are not, therefore, chance atoms; they are those from which we may reasonably expect the desired solution" (Poincaré, 1952, p. 61). Finally, whatever is produced by these unconscious processes must be developed in a second period of conscious work. "It never happens that unconscious work supplies *ready-made* the results of a lengthy calculation in which we have only to apply fixed rules.... All that we can hope from these inspirations ... is to obtain points of departure for such calculations...." [The latter] "demand discipline, attention, will, and consequently consciousness" (Poincaré, 1952, pp. 62–63).

Thus, Poincaré's argument, after his intuitionist conversion, was a carefully balanced one. The conscious purposeful person sets up a mental situation with a number of constraints, all promoting the likelihood that thinking will go in a certain direction. Within the context, the subliminal ego operates with a certain absence of discipline that permits the unexpected couplings that must then be exploited in a disciplined way.

Miller (1992) has recently published a more detailed account of Poincaré's thinking, agreeing in most respects with the picture I have given. Miller bases himself on his own discoveries of manuscript material and on other documents previously available only in French (Toulouse, 1910).

Miller emphasizes Poincaré's description of himself as a nonvisualizer and as relying heavily on unconscious thought processes. Although in some of his other writings (1984) Miller has stressed the intuitive nature of much physical thought, it seems quite reasonable that some such thinking could be both intuitive and nonvisual. As for unconscious thought processes, the question might well be posed: How could a visualization be unconscious?

A further question arises from the study of Poincaré: What is the relation between purpose and unconscious thinking? Poincaré emphasizes the idea that he often worked without a clear sense of purpose, or as Miller puts it, Poincaré had his initial great insight about Fuchsian functions as a sudden "illumination with no predetermined parth" (Miller, 1992, p. 399). This self-description dovetails with Poincaré's characterization of Einstein: "Einstein is one of the most original thinkers that I have ever met.... Since he seeks in all directions, one must expect the majority of the paths on which he embarks to be blind alleys" (quoted in Miller, 1992, p. 386).

Having a sense of purpose is in no way incompatible with working with no predetermined path. It seems that Poincaré (and Einstein) worked from first principles and had a sense of what the end product might be. At least two years before his famous insight on the step of the bus Poincaré "suspected that there ought to be certain generalizations of elliptical functions of a single complex variable.... But he did not know exactly what they were or whether these solutions even existed" (Miller, 1992, p. 398). He always had a clear sense of the argument as a whole; when appropriate he could skillfully go beyond the immediate goal, enlarging the question so that he was dealing with the problem at hand in the most general way possible. All these attributes are aspects of purposeful work. Thus, without contradiction, creative work can be purposeful and protracted, playful and intuitive, deeply knowing and yet partially unconscious, just as Poincaré described himself.

Poincaré's reflections on the creative process resemble the evolving systems approach, stressing the idea of creativity as purposeful work with, of course, provision for much spontaneity. Nonetheless, one vital point must be added. Poincaré as psychologist is examining what I would call a single project within a single enterprise. Such episodes are very far from constituting the whole creative process. Poincaré's own narrative shows how indispensable it is for the creator to marshall efforts in an extended series of such episodes, composing an intellectual growth process on another time scale. For this growth to display any sense and order, the intentional episodes must be embedded in a still larger framework of purpose, regulated by an overarching point of view.

Einstein's Phases

Max Wertheimer knew Einstein in Berlin and interviewed him frequently about his thinking. In his account of these interviews, Wertheimer (1945/1959) describes Einstein's development of the theory of relativity as a drama consisting of eight acts from 1895 to 1905, in which year Einstein conceived and published the theory of special relativity. There are several ensuing acts that bring the story up to 1916 and the theory of general relativity. Each act has a complex inner structure. The whole is characterized by prolonged and impassioned efforts to reach understanding and coherence, by depression and despair when progress is blocked, and by a sense that unresolved paradoxes are unbearable. Wertheimer gave special emphasis to the idea of conceptual gaps; sometimes progress consisted in filling a gap, thus altering the whole theoretical structure and revealing new gaps.

Arthur Miller (1975, 1981, 1986), physicist and historian of science, has severely criticized Wertheimer on several counts: Wertheimer stressed the importance of the Michelson-Morley experiment, whereas the best historical evidence is that this played only a secondary role in Einstein's thinking; Wertheimer confused the sequence of events in a few places, in good part because of misunderstandings about physical theory; and, probably most important of all, Wertheimer's account is simplistic, treating Einstein's thinking as though it occurred in isolation.

Miller's (1981, 1986) own account describes two broad phases. In the years leading up to 1905, Einstein slowly interwove philosophical, physical (both experimental and theoretical), and technological materials into a new outlook. Philosophically, especially in his struggle to free himself from the assumption of absolute time, he was particularly indebted to his readings of Mach, Hume, and Kant. In a second phase, in 1905 itself, he developed the theory of special relativity. Thus, Einstein's work was thoroughly embedded in the intellectual currents of his time, and his own progress was part of a broad movement of thought to which, of course, he contributed greatly. An important part of Miller's reconstruction of Einstein's thinking is the idea of the fusion of axiomatization and visualization. Having interwoven the three major strands, Einstein was in a position to decide what axiomatizations might be fruitful, but he was not limited to such largely verbal thinking. For the most part, he thought in terms of kinesthetic feels and visual images.

Although Miller is critical of Wertheimer's application of Gestalt theory, he does not reject that theory altogether. Instead, he argues for a fusion of it with Piagetian constructivism and a more thorough grasp of historical facts. Although Miller does not enumerate a specific series of stages, his treatment suggests a larger number of steps than Wertheimer's and by no means in a linear sequence of straightforward progress. In any event, both authors' accounts are devoid of any suggestion that scientific progress comes through mysterious, gigantesque leaps into the dark.

INSIGHT AND AFFECT

Thus far in this chapter, I have treated insight as both an experience and a problem-solving act or series of acts with cognitive, motivational, and affective characteristics. We have seen how insights occur in the course of protracted, purposeful work, but we have still to account for the emotional aspect of insights.

In contemporary theory, emotion and cognition are widely treated as separate but interacting systems. This is true not only of the evolving systems approach to creative work but of more general psychological theories (Izard, 1984). In some accounts, it appears that the experiencing subject is in an affectless state until some special event occurs that triggers an emotion. On the other hand, in the evolving systems approach, we conceive of the thinking, feeling person as exhibiting a stream of thought, a stream of purpose, and a stream of affect. They are in continual interaction, yet each has its own varying contents, tempos, and rhythms.

Thus, the context for a given moment of insight includes such features of the temporally extended internal milieu as the feelings the subject has been experiencing in the period leading up to the insight. The "same" insight, arising on a platform of despair, is not really the same if instead it emerges out of a stream of pleasurable activity. This way of looking at insight as temporally extended and situated has among its advantages the fact that it expands the data base on which we can draw to understand the subject's affect.

The Feeling Tone of Darwin's Malthusian Moment

A number of investigators have documented the events leading up to Darwin's great moment in which he saw how Malthus's theory of population growth could be used in a theory of evolution through natural selection. In my own work, (Gruber, 1981a) I have stressed how Darwin's notebooks reveal numerous partial insights, on several occasions almost attaining the clarity of the Malthusian moment.

Darwin's notes for September 28, 1838, the fateful day, do not say anything explicit about his feelings, but both the format of the notes and the contents convey an air of excitement. Words are underlined, doubly underlined, and triply underlined. He inserted between the lines and in the margins commentaries on his commentary. There is liberal use of metaphor and emphatic language—for example, the opening and closing sentences of the passage (transcribed in Barrett, Gautrey, Herbert, Kohn & Smith, 1987, pp. 374–376; Kohn [1980] is especially helpful in sorting out the initial entry and the interlinear additions):

We ought to be far from wondering of changes in number of species, from small changes in nature of locality. Even the energetic language of Decandolle does not convey the warring of the species as inference from Malthus....

... One may say there is a force like a hundred thousand wedges trying [to] force every kind of adapted structure into the gaps in the economy of nature, or rather forming gaps, by thrusting out weaker ones.

All this is concentrated into approximately 250 words, covering two pages of a notebook that could be slipped into a largish pocket. Darwin may have had the notebook with him while visiting his brother Erasmus, in whose home he did this reading of Malthus, or he may have waited until his return home, later the same day, but the passage was certainly written soon after the actual insight.

Excited he may have been, but his thinking was not immediately galvanized to exploit the new idea. Instead, he went on with other observations and reflections that were part of his many-sided network of enterprise. The immediately following note concerns interracial crosses among humans. The next day's entry is mainly about observations of the sexual behavior of various primates, especially their curiosity about women.

We can get some idea of the affective context of Darwin's thinking at that time from his correspondence with the geologist Charles Lyell, who was Darwin's chief scientific mentor for at least 10 years. Lyell is the man who had earlier literally danced with delight when Darwin told him about his theory of the formation of coral reefs, a theory supplanting Lyell's own version.

On August 9, 1838, Darwin wrote to Lyell a long letter touching on many topics. He is "full of admiration" for Lyell's new edition of the *Elements of Geology*, and he is the more enthusiastic because Lyell had cited Darwin's *Journal of the Beagle Voyage* (Darwin, 1839; Lyell read it in manuscript) extensively, as well as because of Lyell's "juicy" style. Darwin is just back from a visit to a special geological formation in Scotland. He is ecstatic about "the gorgeous sunset, & all nature looking as happy as I felt." He is "astonished" at his geological observations of the parallel roads of Glen Roy that he had gone to Scotland to study. Now back in London, he thinks Lyell will be "amused at some of the ridiculo-sublime passages" of a certain entomologist, Professor Hope (who had once been one of Darwin's mentors), and he writes, "I am living very quietly, & therefore pleasantly & am crawling on slowly, but steadily with my work" (Darwin, 1986, pp. 95–98).

On September 6, 1838, Lyell replied from Scotland. He is full of interest in Darwin's geologizing and full of praise for Darwin's *Journal*, which Lyell's father is reading with great pleasure, but apprehensive about the reception of the *Elements*. He discusses his schedule of work when in London—2 hours work, 2 hours rest, 2 hours work—but he has sometimes made the mistake of not counting as work the times when, while "resting," he got into an excited discussion "with clever people" at his club, the Athenaeum. He gives Darwin some advice on participating in the affairs of the British Association of Science and closes with some more geological observations (Darwin, 1986, pp. 99–102).

Darwin's reply, dated September 14, 1838, is the nearest in time, among extant documents of any interest, to the Malthus insight of September 28. Like the other letters, it is varied and bubbly. He is "astonished & delighted" at Lyell's "gloriously long letter." He refers to his *Journal*, not yet published, as his "first born child" but as "dead, buried & forgotten" because of various publishing delays. He admires an article about Comte's *Cours de la Philosophie* (Comte, 1830–1835), especially "some fine sentences about the very essence of science being prediction." Finally, he offers Lyell staunch support regarding some geological critiques he has received; the letter reeks with certainty on geological issues where the two men are very much in agreement. Darwin wants Lyell to return to London from Scotland, lest "the Scotch mists will put out some volcanic speculations."

After referring to the vicissitudes of writing and publishing, vis-à-vis his geological work, Darwin says that he is tempted to neglect geology

"by the delightful number of new views, which have been coming in, thickly & steadily, on the classification & affinities & instincts of animals—bearing on the question of species—note book after note book has been filled with facts, which begin to group themselves *clearly* under sub-laws." (Darwin, 1986, pp. 104–108)

From this brief glimpse of a protracted dialogue, we can see the excitement of these two men at practicing science, their utter self-confidence and conviction of their rightness, their roles in a mutual admiration society coupled with their scorn for certain nonmembers of their little band of *cognoscenti*. We can see also their love of nature and their absorption in both theoretical and empirical science, this work being the chief source of pleasure for both of them. Finally, we can see a hint of a change of pace, a movement toward a crescendo, in Darwin's description of "new views ... coming in, thickly & steadily ...." These excerpts convey something of the climate of affect in which Darwin was working and thinking at the time when, visiting his brother, he picked up Malthus's *Essay on Population* (1826) "for amusement." We do not actually know that Darwin experienced *joy* at his moment of insight on September 28, but if the moment did give him a lift, it must have been a real high, because the plateau from which he rose was already a state of elevated happiness.

Piaget's Joy

If there is a certain surprise value in Max Wertheimer's use of many stages rather than one "Gestalt switch" to describe Einstein's thought, it might also come as a surprise that Jean Piaget, the great exponent of slow, protracted intellectual growth, experienced moments of insight and sometimes described children in those terms too. Piaget was aware of his kinship with the Gestalt psychologists but also went to some lengths to clarify the distinction between his approach and theirs. I can only touch on it here but will develop the point more fully in another place (see Gruber, in preparation).

A good example of this dialogue between related approaches is Piaget's discussion of the distinction between the fifth stage of infant development ("tertiary circular reactions" and "discovery of new means through active experimentation") and the sixth stage ("invention of new means through mental combinations"). Piaget (1936/1952, p. 348) writes:

[T]he sudden inventions characteristic of the sixth stage are in reality the product of a long evolution of schemata and not only of an internal maturation of perceptive structures.... This is revealed by the existence of a fifth stage, characterized by experimental groping.... What does this mean if not that the practice of actual experience is necessary in order to acquire the practice of mental experience and that invention does not arise entirely preformed despite appearances?

The inventions Piaget has in mind, looked at from an adult point of view, are very modest indeed—such as grasping the idea that to insert a pencil in a certain hole one may have to reverse it because it is the pointed rather than the blunt end that must enter the hole. The following are Piaget's comments regarding his daughter Jacqueline's attempts to complete this task. Jacqueline is 20 months old and has been having difficulty inserting the point of a pencil in a hole if her father hands it to her with the blunt end toward the hole.

At about the thirtieth attempt, Jacqueline suddenly changes methods. She turns the second pencil over ... and no longer tries a single time to put it in by the wrong end ... one has the impression of a sudden understanding, as of an idea which arises and which, when it has suddenly appeared, definitively imposes itself. (Piaget, 1936/1952, p. 340)

Piaget's key point is that if one has not seen, or if one disregards, the long series of earlier gropings, the sudden insight will appear to come from nowhere. Saying this does not detract from the importance of the sudden insight, but it does put it into a different context—the evolving schema of a pencil. We might add to this that countless such small steps are indeed lost through the incompleteness of most experimental studies, contributing to the error of telescoping discussed earlier. However, here it is the investigator doing the telescoping rather than the creator compressing his or her own past.

In the course of one of many interviews, I asked Piaget about his own experiences of insight. He said that they come to him "while writing. As soon as I have a few pages done there is an internal logic that imposes itself." He gave a very good description of incubation: After he worked for a few hours he would go for a walk, not think about very much, and when he went back to his desk his ideas would be clearer (*plus claires*). Notice that he is not describing a moment of sharp insight or solution to a problem, just a clarification. Wittgenstein's remark, "Light dawns gradually over the whole," seems to fit very well here. From many encounters, I would certainly say that Piaget took pleasure in such moments, but he didn't seem moved to run naked in the streets or even do a jig.

However, he did describe one grander moment: The most beautiful moment in his life, by Piaget's own account, was when he discovered a group of 256 transformations of certain logical structures. He described rhapsodically the joy he felt as he worked this out during a 14-day ocean crossing to Brazil. "It was wonderful, the open air, the sea breezes, but always the calculations, no temptations!" Notice that this "moment" of insight lasted approximately 2 weeks. The rhapsodic feeling as part of his own thought processes was fully foreshadowed in the character of Sebastien, the protagonist (i.e., himself) of Piaget's (1918) novel, *Recherche.*

On the whole, Piaget was more interested in the growth of the child's understanding than in the child's problem solving. Of course, observing the child solve problems is an important window to understanding. Nonetheless, actually observing and analyzing the process of problem solving is a relatively recent interest in Geneva, exemplified especially in the work of Inhelder and her group (Inhelder et al., 1992) and in the work of Leiser and Gilliéron (1990).

In Piaget's description of children thinking, the affect most in evidence is interest and curiosity but, in at least one case that he often recounted, there is a suggestion of joyful triumph. A child, the son of a mathematician friend, was absorbed in arranging and rearranging a collection of blocks in different configurations (e.g., straight line, circle, square), then counting them each time. The number always came out the same. Finally the child cried out, "Once you know, you know forever!"

CONCLUSION

Why is cognitive growth likely to be composed of a series of relatively small steps? Why, even when the goal is very grand, is the path toward it divisible into Poincaré's seven episodes, Einstein's eight steps, and so forth?

Imagine if one's thinking underwent a radical transformation every 24 hours or every week. Life would be painfully chaotic; the sense of personal identity and of personal connection with one's ideas would be lost. Therefore, if insights are to be relatively frequent, they must be of a sort and must occur at such a rate that they can be assimilated into existing mental structures *without destroying them*. Piaget's idea of assimilation and accommodation applies well here. Life, including cognitive life, is and must be continuous.

The need for continuity also helps to account for the seeming disproportion that sometimes exists between the affect felt and the achievement it reflects. One might reasonably suggest that in the bath legend, Archimedes' joy far exceeded the importance of his discovery, but that attitude neglects the transformation of the cognitive field that takes place when the creator is totally engrossed in a problem: *Nothing else exists*. A step taken is only small when seen from outside, by a viewer not similarly engrossed (see Köhler, 1971). The well-trained historian or psychologist has a different perspective from the discoverer. It is our task to situate the creator in a social-cognitive world, though for the creator, that may be a world well lost. We might add that even though it feels so to the creator in the toils, in fact the lost world is not lost but has become background to the problem that is paramount or figural.

Nevertheless, some cognitive changes do feel bigger than others. Even if the path followed consists of small steps, the attainment of numerous partial goals and subgoals, there must be a few last steps by means of which one enters the goal region (Henle, 1956). The creative worker must have some sense of the importance of the task at hand, and some creators deliberately set high, almost unattainable, goals. Do a high level of aspiration, high stakes, and high hopes lead to the heights of happiness? Why not? But not permanently, for an insight that closes one chapter opens the next one. If solutions come, can new problems be far behind?

ACKNOWLEDGMENTS

I thank Doris B. Wallace for her insightful comments on a preliminary draft of this chapter. I am grateful to Roald Hoffmann for his very helpful suggestions.

NOTE

1. The descriptions of Archimedes, Kekulé, and Poincaré are adapted from a previous publication (Gruber, 1981b).

REFERENCES

Arieti, S. (1976). *Creativity: The magic synthesis*. New York: Basic Books.

Asch, S.E. (1952). *Social psychology*. Englewood Cliffs, NJ: Prentice Hall.

Asch, S.E., Ceraso, J., & Heimer, W. (1960). Perceptual conditions of association. *Psychological Monographs, 74*, whole no. 3.

Asch, S.E., Hay, J., & Mendoza, R. (1960). Perceptual organization in serial rote-learning. *American Journal of Psychology, 73*, 177–198.

Barrett, P.H., Gautrey, P.J., Herbert, S., Kohn, D., & Smith, S. (Eds.). (1987). *Charles Darwin's notebooks, 1836–1844.* Ithaca, NY: Cornell University Press.

Bell, E.T. (1937). *Men of mathematics.* Harmondsworth, England: Penguin.

Bergson, H. (1912). *The introduction to a new philosophy.* Boston: John W. Luce.

Comte, A. (1830–1835). *Cours de philosophie positive.* Paris.

Darwin, C. (1839). *Journal of researches into the geology and natural history of the various countries visited by H.M.S. Beagle.* London: Colburn.

Darwin, C. (1986). *Correspondence: Vol. 2. 1837–1843.* Cambridge, England: Cambridge University Press.

Drake, S. (1978). *Galileo at work: His scientific biography.* Chicago: University of Chicago Press.

Duncker, K. (1945). On problem solving. *Psychological Monographs, 58*(5), whole no. 270.

Ericsson, K.A., & Simon, H.A. (1984). *Protocol analysis: Verbal reports as data.* Cambridge, Mass.: MIT Press.

Galileo, G. (1961). La bilancetta [The little balance]. In L. Fermi & G. Bernardini (Eds.), *Galileo and the scientific revolution* (pp. 133–143).

Gruber, H.E. (1981a). *Darwin on man: A psychological study of scientific creativity* (2nd ed.). Chicago: University of Chicago Press. (Original work published 1974)

Gruber, H.E. (1981b). On the relation between "Aha! experiences" and the construction of ideas. *History of science, 19,* 41–59.

Gruber, H.E. (1988). Networks of enterprise in creative scientific work. In B. Gholson, A. Houts, R.A. Neimayer & W. Shadish (Eds.), *Psychology of science and metascience.* Cambridge, England: Cambridge University Press.

Gruber, H.E., Fink, C.D., & Damm, V. (1957). Effects of experience on the perception of causality. *Journal of Experimental Psychology, 53,* 89–93.

Gruber, H.E. (1989). The evolving systems approach to creative work. In D.B. Wallace & H.E. Gruber, *Creative people at work: twelve cognitive case studies* (pp. 3–24). New York: Oxford University Press.

Gruber, H.E. (1993). Piaget: A man thinking. Manuscript in preparation.

Hadamard, J. (1945). *The psychology of invention in the mathematical field.* Princeton, NJ: Princeton University Press.

Heath, T.L. (Ed.). (1897). *The works of Archimedes.* New York: Dover.

Hein, G.E. (1966). Kekulé and the architecture of models. *Kekulé centennial: Advances in chemistry, 61,* 1–12.

Henle, M. (1956). On activity in the goal region. *Psychological Review*, *63*, 299–302.

Holmes, F.L. (1989). Antoine Lavoisier and Hans Krebs: Two styles of scientific creativity. In D.B. Wallace & H.E. Gruber (Eds.), *Creative people at work: twelve cognitive case studies* (pp. 44–68). New York: Oxford University Press.

Inhelder, B., Cellérier, G., Ackerman, E., Blanchet, A., Boder, D., de Caprona, D., Ducret, J.J., & Saada-Robert, M. (1992). *Le Cheminement des Découvertes de l'Enfant*. Lausanne: Delacchaux et Niestlé.

Izard, C.E. (1984). Emotion-cognition relationships and human development. In C.E. Izard, J. Kagan & R.B. Zajonc (Eds.), *Emotions, cognition, and behavior* (pp. 17–37). Cambridge, England: Cambridge University Press.

Japp, F.R. (1898). Kekulé Memorial Lecture, 1897. *Memorial lectures delivered before the Chemical Society, 1893–1900* (p. 100). London: Gurney & Jackson.

Koestler, A. (1964). *The act of creation*. New York: Macmillan.

Köhler, W. (1947). *Gestalt psychology*. New York: Liveright.

Köhler, W. (1971). The obsessions of normal people. In M. Henle (Ed.), *The selected papers of Wolfgang Köhler* (pp. 398–412). (Original work published 1958). New York: Liveright.

Kohn, D. (1980). Theories to work by: Rejected theories, reproduction, and Darwin's path to natural selection. *Studies in the History of Biology*, *4*, 67–170.

Lampl, M., Veldhuis, J.D., & Johnson, M.L. (1992). Saltation and stasis: A model of human growth. *Science*, *258*, 801–802.

Leiser, D., & Gillièron, C. (1990). *Cognitive science and genetic epistemology: A case study of understanding*. New York: Plenum.

Lewin, K. (1935). *A dynamic theory of personality*. New York: McGraw-Hill.

Lyell, C. (1838). *Elements of geology*. London: Murray.

Maier, N.R.F. (1931). Reasoning in humans: II. The solution of a problem and its appearance in consciousness. *Journal of Comparative Psychology*, *12*, 181–194.

Malthus, T.R. (1826). *An essay on the principle of population*. (6th ed., 2 vols). London: Murray.

Miller, A.I. (1975). Albert Einstein and Max Wertheimer: A Gestalt psychologist's view of the genesis of special relativity theory. *History of Science*, *13*, 75–103.

Miller, A.I. (1981). *Albert Einstein's special theory of relativity: Emergence (1905) and early interpretation (1905–1911)*. Reading, MA: Addison-Wesley.

Miller, A.I. (1984). *Imagery in scientific thought: Creating 20th-century physics.* Boston: Birkhauser.

Miller, A.I. (1986). On Einstein's invention of special relativity. In A.I. Miller, *Frontiers of physics: 1900–1911.* Boston: Birkhauser.

Miller, A.I. (1992). Scientific creativity: A comparative study of Henri Poincaré and Albert Einstein. *Creativity Research Journal, 5,* 385–418.

Osgood, C.E. (1953). *Method and theory in experimental psychology.* New York: Oxford University Press.

Piaget, J. (1918). *Recherche.* Lausanne: La Concorde.

Piaget, J. (1952). *The origins of intelligence in children.* New York: International Universities Press. (Original work published 1936)

Piaget, J. (1965). *Sagesse et illusions de la philosophie.* Paris: Presses Universitaires de France.

Poincaré, H. (1952). *Science and method.* New York: Dover. (Original work published 1908)

Toulouse, E. (1910). *Henri Poincaré.* Paris: Flammarion.

Wallace, D.B. (1991). The genesis and microgenesis of sudden insight in the creation of literature. *Creativity Research Journal, 4,* 41–50.

Wertheimer, M. (1959). *Productive Thinking* (enlarged ed.). New York: Harper & Row. (Original edition published 1945)

Wittgenstein, L. (1969). *On certainty.* New York: Harper & Row.

Wotiz, J.H. (Ed.). (1993). *The Kekulé riddle: A challenge for chemistry and psychology.* Boulder, CO: Cache River Press.

Wotiz, J.H., & Rudofsky, S. (1984, August). Kekulé's dreams: Fact or fiction? *Chemistry in Britain,* 720–723.

13 The Inception of Insight

Maria F. Ippolito and Ryan D. Tweney

While it is common to conclude, as did Metcalfe and Wiebe (1987, p. 243), that "insight problems are ... solved by a sudden flash of illumination," a number of researchers have argued that sufficiently rich descriptions vitiate against the notion of insight as instantaneous (Bowers, Regehr, Balthazard & Parker, 1990; Csikszentmihalyi, 1988; Gruber, 1981; Perkins, 1981; Simon, 1981; Westfall, 1980; Windholz, 1984; see also Clement's [1989] discussion of "eurekaism versus accretionism"). The discussion of insight that follows is compatible with the latter view of insight as a complex process rather than the sudden, unpredictable emergence of a model of some aspect of the real world.

Furthermore, our contention is that "because inspiration is always dependent on the mental preparation that went before, it often does fail for the passively expectant ... waiting for the magic flow of ideas" (Flower & Hayes, 1977, p. 451). Therefore, we will devote considerable attention to the portion of the insight process during which mental preparation predominates, to what Kaplan and Simon (1990, p. 390) have characterized as "the less selective search that precedes ... rapid reasoning."

Salthouse (1992, pp. 291–292) has written that: "A common characteristic of expertise in virtually every domain is that high levels of performance are accomplished by overcoming limitations that serve to restrain the performances of most people." Much of this chapter will be devoted to an exploration of the ways in which insightful problem solving overcomes such restraining limitations. In particular, we introduce a novel way to characterize the *inception* of insight, a notion that permits us to contend that insight is a form of expertise and that the hallmarks of the insight process are those that have come to be associated with expert problem solving.

A number of studies have found that the problem solving of experts is characterized by superior memory performance, an enhanced capacity to perceive complex patterns, and a "deep" representation of the problem. The problem-solving efforts of experts also tend to be characterized by the allotment of substantial time to qualitative analysis of the problem as well as by persistent self-monitoring. Finally, one of the most consistent findings of studies of problem solving is that expertise is highly content-specific—that is, that experts tend to excel primarily in their own domains (Glaser & Chi, 1988).

Most studies of expertise (e.g., Chi, Glaser & Farr, 1988; Ericsson & Smith, 1992) have focused on externally defined, conventional domains such as chess (Chase & Simon, 1988) and physics (Chi, Glaser & Rees, 1982; Simon & Simon, 1978). However, we will characterize insight as emerging from a developing expertise in a *self*-defined and *problem*-defined domain because we maintain that insightful discovering is hyperresponsive to the specifics of individual context. (For a closely related discussion of the importance of individual agency in scientific discovery, see Gooding [1990].) Henry James expressed a similar sentiment when he characterized the novelist as a "watcher at the window:"

> The house of fiction has ... not one window, but ... a number of possible windows...; every one of which has been pierced or is still pierceable ... by the need of the individual vision and by the pressure of the individual will...., insuring to the person making use of it an impression distinct from every other. (cited in Allott, 1967, p. 132)

It is only later, as a result of the sharing of discoveries, that the domains in which insightful discovering originated acquire the patina of conventionality. Thus, accounts of insight that fail to consider the mental context or setting of the discovery may leave crucial questions unanswered.

Given that expertise tends to be domain-specific and that the domain of an insight is, in large measure, defined by the individual's mental preparation and the problem being solved, we believe that the study of individual process in context can make a valuable contribution to the understanding of insight. Although we will refer to the pronouncements of a number of notable artists and scientists to illustrate the inception of insight, the focus of this chapter will be on a single individual engaged in the solving of a particular problem.

While this "joining of investigator to setting can be the throw of the dice that Einstein resented so deeply" (Kagan, 1989, p. 216), a throw of the dice, the path of a falling feather (see Tweney, 1989a), or, we contend, the process of insight is only explainable when the setting is carefully examined. Insights emerge from a dynamic blend of context and behavior.

Our story of the insight process centers on an article entitled "On a Peculiar Class of Optical Deceptions," published by the English physicist Michael Faraday in 1831. We will first utilize Faraday's exploration of optical deceptions to illustrate the ways in which the deployment of perceptual processes can affect the self-defined and problem-defined domain in which the insightful discovering unfolds.

PERCEPTUAL REHEARSAL: MAKING THE INVISIBLE VISIBLE

Perceptual rehearsal, the saturation of one or more of the senses with all aspects of the phenomenon of interest to the discoverer, is a means of defeating the inherent biases of our perceptual apparatus and increasing the impact of unexpected sights. More than a century ago, William James (1890b, p. 344) wrote that experts "'see into the situation' ... full of delicately differenced ingredients which their education has little by little brought to their consciousness, but of which the novice gains no clear idea." In like manner, we contend that perceptual rehearsal arranges for the education of the problem solver such that stimuli that are virtually invisible as a result of typical perceptual processing become visible (Tweney, 1992a). Perceptual rehearsal provides the insightful problem solver operating in a self-defined and problem-defined domain with an enhanced ability to perceive patterns germane to the problem to be solved, to be alert, as Einstein was, "to small signals in the large 'noise' of ... [the] experimental situation" (Holton, 1971–1972, p. 96).

Faraday's (1831) account of optical deceptions began with informal descriptions of ordinary phenomena that his audience would

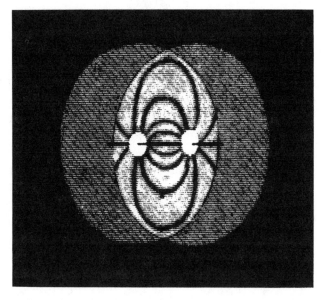

Figure 13.1
Optical deceptions produced by two rotating spoked wheels. (Reprinted
with permission from M. Faraday [1831], on a peculiar class of optical deceptions. *Royal Institution Journal*, 2, 205–223, 333–336.)

have readily recognized—for example, the interplay of sunlight
with shadow in the presence of spinning cogwheels and carriage
wheels. Faraday noted that, depending on the observer's perspective, two overlapping spinning wheels could present a spectral
alteration in visual reality. Under the right conditions of lighting,
one could perceive a variety of illusory figures: bars, curved arcs,
and the like (figure 13.1). The domain-evolving process first involved Faraday's collection of perceptions in the world. Then, to
explore the cause of such appearances, Faraday reconstructed the
visual phenomena he had observed using pasteboard, paper, pins,
sunlight when it was available, and candlelight when it was not
(figure 13.2).

Once he had arranged for small-scale analogs duplicating the
real-world optical phenomena that had triggered his interest, Faraday generated perceptions for the benefit of his mind's eye, "the
meeting point where visual information from the external world
is combined and coordinated with visual representations stored

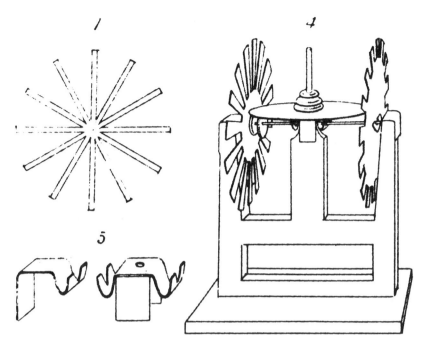

Figure 13.2
Faraday's apparatus for the study of optical deceptions. (Reprinted with permission from M. Faraday [1831], on a peculiar class of optical deceptions. *Royal Institution Journal, 2*, 205–223, 333–336.)

in ... memory" (Chase & Simon, 1988, p. 492). Faraday did not then simply sit back and watch. To explain the perceptual world he had made, Faraday embarked on a series of experiments, manipulating the phenomena to uncover their sources.

Faraday altered the relative velocity and position of the wheels and the direction of spin, as well as the characteristics of the background, the depth and placement of the cogs cut into pasteboard circles, the placement of the light source, and the location of the observer. He extended his activities beyond the mere collection of perceptions, utilizing the apparatus he had constructed to generate perceptions. Thus, Faraday was more than a mere observer of particular aspects of the optical deceptions of interest; he was the choreographer of a rich, dynamic process that led to ever richer perceptual arrays.

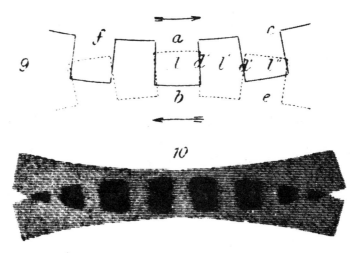

Figure 13.3
A dynamic explanation of the appearances generated by two toothed wheels. (Reprinted with permission from M. Faraday [1831], on a peculiar class of optical deceptions. *Royal Institution Journal*, 2, 205–223, 333–336.)

The generated perceptions provided critical constraints on the dynamic geometrical arguments that Faraday later developed to explain in detail the phantom bars and curved arcs as, for example, in figure 13.3. As the figure suggests, he was able to generate geometrically the seen appearances by moving the shapes of the cogs across each other in the mind's eye, accounting even for some of the quantitative properties of the deceptive appearances.

Note that if insight were merely the result of the quantity of time spent on a problem domain, predicting insight would not be difficult; anyone with an *idee fixe* or the willingness to engage in a sufficient amount of haphazard exploration would achieve a viable product. Although time spent in a domain is probably necessary for an insightful product, it is not sufficient. The level of domain-specific expertise achieved is a product of the quantity *and* quality of preparatory perceptual experience. When Faraday's intent was to demystify an optical deception, he collected perceptions until he had the raw material necessary to reconstruct the deception of interest. Part of Faraday's strategy was actively to enlarge not just the quantity but also the range of his perceptual experience.

Thus, the activity we refer to as *perceptual rehearsal* perturbs the typical process of automatic selection that yields perceptions, thereby expanding the limited ability of the problem solver to contemplate the unexpected. That is, perceptual rehearsal ensures the availability of numerous variations and of alternate perspectives of the stimuli of interest, in effect postponing perceptual conclusions about these stimuli.

Erik Erikson (cited in Briggs, 1990, p. 214) described this aspect of the creative process as analogous to child's play: "The child can throw ... [a] ball to the floor again and again, seeing it roll a hundred times, and never be bored." Similarly, Goodfield (1981), in her report of a research scientist pursuing a genetic discovery, described the excruciating repetitions of apparently mundane perceptual exercises by a vigilant, driven researcher. Newton (cited in Briggs, 1990, p. 60) said, when asked how he was able to make his discoveries, that it was because "I keep the subject constantly before me, and wait until the first dawnings open slowly little and little into the full and clear light." And De Maupassant (1888, cited in Allot, 1967, p. 130) spoke of this process as "looking at everything one wants to describe long enough, and attentively enough ... In order to describe a fire burning or a tree in a field, let us stand in front of that fire and that tree until they no longer look to us like any other fire or any other tree."

One result of perceptual rehearsal is selective encoding, which Sternberg and Davidson (1983) identify as one of the three key processes of insight (see also Davidson & Sternberg, 1984). That is, Faraday's purposeful flooding of his vision with varied and carefully chosen perceptions of the optical phenomena of interest must inevitably have affected his encoding of this class of perceptions.

Perhaps perceptual rehearsal also serves, in part, the purpose of absorbing the processing capacity of short-term memory, making premature closure (Csikszentmihalyi, 1988; Getzels & Csikszentmihalyi, 1976; Kolanczyk, 1989; Nickerson, Perkins & Smith, 1985; Parnes, 1975; Perkins, 1981; Simon, 1981), entrenchment (Sternberg, 1981), or functional fixedness (Duncker, 1945; Keane, 1989) less likely and ensuring the "fresh view of the universe" that Tolstoy (1896, cited in Allott, 1967, p. 131) believed was essential to creativity.

D.H. Lawrence (1925, cited in Allott, 1967, p. 102) wrote that "when the novelist puts his thumb in the scale, to pull down the balance to his predilection, that is immorality." Both Darwin (Kagan, 1989) and Faraday (Cantor, 1991) professed their intention to delay commitment to any one hypothesis. So, too, Beethoven (Wallace, 1989), Kafka, and Wordsworth (Murray, 1978) imposed a waiting period on themselves before they began to write. And in *Productive Thinking*, Wertheimer (1945, p. 240) wrote: "Often the possibility of a shortcut closure is seductive.... Often the impatient desire to find the solution focuses the eye too inclusively." Similarly, Nersessian (1992) has emphasized the role of *increasing* constraint satisfaction during the course of analogical concept formation (see also Reitman, 1965, who makes the same point with respect to musical composition), implying that conclusions arrived at or constraints applied too early in the game may be dysfunctional.

Einstein and Infeld (1938, cited in Hayes, 1989, p. 140) wrote, "The formulation of a problem is often more essential than its solution, which may be merely a matter of mathematical or experimental skill. To raise new questions, new possibilities, to regard old problems from a new angle, requires creative imagination and marks real advance in science."

Getzels and Csikszentmihalyi's (1976) research on so-called problem finding in the arts provides a view of the behaviors of artistic problem solvers during this period of increasing constraint satisfaction. In Getzels and Csikszentmihalyi's study, art students were provided with various materials and videotaped as they each arranged and drew a still life. Amazingly, problem finding that included extended handling and repositioning of the provided items prior to the commencement of drawing, and the periodic reexamination or rearrangement of the still life materials throughout the drawing process, predicted artistic success 7 years later. Those of Getzels and Csikszentmihalyi's subjects who later became successful artists engaged in problem-finding experiments that transcended the standard perceptual identification of the items; their problem finding was focused on the effects of lighting; on the interplay of texture, color, and lines; on, in short, the interaction of these evanescent qualities *across* items.

Faraday (1831) began his study of optical deceptions with simple materials, rearranging velocities, the direction of spin, angles of light and vision, and the background. Later, he devoted considerable time to relational qualities of the spinning wheels, such as their shadows and reflections. Just as the student artist who was superior at problem finding returned to the arranged objects frequently during the drawing process, there was a back-and-forth nature to Faraday's work (Gooding, 1990, see also Tweney, 1992c; Tweney & Hoffner, 1987). Arnheim (1962) has documented an analogous back-and-forth style during Picasso's painting of *Guernica*, and Scardamalia and Bereiter (1992) have similarly identified "composing episodes" in the working of expert writers.

Note that "talent is a long patience" (de Maupassant, 1888, cited in Allott, 1967, p. 130). During perceptual rehearsal, the insight process often appears to be unproductive. Keats (cited in Briggs, 1990, p. 104) referred to the "negative capability" for "being in uncertainties ... without any ... reaching after fact and reason." Simone de Beauvoir (1959, p. 17) spoke of the period prior to symbolic representation when "white ... [is] only rarely totally white; and the blackness ... [is] relieved by lighter touches ... [with] grays and half tones everywhere." For Faraday, this was a stage of the discovery process during which he achieved some successes but also experienced a number of "informative failures" (Gooding, 1990, p. 159).

THE DISTILLATION OF INCEPTIONS

As has been made clear in the preceding discussion of perceptual rehearsal, insight entails more than just the collection of relevant data. "Mere observation does not suffice, if only because mere observation will not permit the elimination of the deceptive part of the appearances" (Tweney, in press). William James (1890a, p. 287) declared of artistic enterprises:

That unity, harmony ... which gives to works of art their superiority over works of nature, is wholly due to *elimination*. Any natural subject will do, if the artist has wit enough to pounce on one feature of it as characteristic, and suppress all merely accidental items which do not harmonize with this.

And "every scientific enterprise must, at least implicitly, factor out the possible 'deceptions' in the evidence of the senses" (Tweney, in press). In the words of de Maupassant (cited in Allott, 1967, p. 71), "[H]aving made ... [the] choice of subject [one] should select from this life, crowded as it is with accidents and trivialities, only those characteristic details that are useful ... all the incidentals ... [one] must reject."

Ultimately, in "the best ... enterprises ... the observer's ability to 'see' the phenomena directly can be dispensed with *even in principle*" (Tweney, in press). The claim in this chapter is that the ability to recreate the workings of selected aspects of the world, independent of sensory receptor input, is critical to insight. Flower and Garbin (1989, p. 152) also discuss the "decoupling of perceptual mechanisms from sensory input"; however, their focus is on these mechanisms when access to the sensory world is denied during altered states of consciousness induced by, for example, dreaming or psychoactive drugs. Our contention is, rather, that reconstructions of selected aspects of the world arise from the intentional rehearsal of selected perceptions and that the emergent reconstructions participate in problem-solving activities which take place within conscious awareness.

In the thought experiment that served as the germ for his theory of relativity, Einstein chased "a point on a light wave" (Miller, 1989, p. 174); upon transcending the physical world, the properties of light became clear to him. Flaubert (cited in Allott, 1967, p. 155) reported that when he "wrote about Emma Bovary's poisoning ... [he] had the taste of arsenic ... strongly in ... [his] mouth," and "the perfection and power of Beethoven's musical imagination" outlived his ability to collect auditory perceptions (Rolland, 1929, p. 268). Faulkner's imaginary Yoknapatawpha County was the product of his youthful perceptual experience in "'that little patch up there in Mississippi'" (Sherwood Anderson, cited in Millgate, 1989, p. 25). Yet, once that county had taken shape, the histories of its inhabitants and places unfolded independently of the extant world of the author. "For Faulkner himself Yoknapatawpha always retained as it grew and changed in his imagination an absolute integrity and reality" (Millgate, 1989, p. 42). Faulkner did not find it necessary to breathe life into the inhabitants of this county from moment to moment. Characters that first appeared in his later works "like all his characters ... had always been there, waiting in what Faulkner liked to call the attic, ready to make another public appearance" (Millgate, 1989, p. 38).

Subsequent to perceptual rehearsal, the mind's eye turns inward and the rehearsed perceptions give way to inceptions. Thomas Hardy (1891, cited in Allott, 1967, p. 74) referred to the novel as "an artificiality distilled from the fruits of closest observation," which phrase aptly defines what we call an *inception*. Inceptions are "the beginning of something;" the word derives from the Latin "to take in" (Morris, 1969, p. 664). Inceptions of the phenomena of interest embody the constraints of the real-world perceptions from which they have been distilled, where *distillation* consists of "separation from ... unrelated or attenuating factors" (Morris, 1969, p. 382). The viability of these reconstructed perceptions (sans their real-world context) depends on emergence from the distillation process of inceptions that operate in ways veridical to reality. Note that our terminological distinction between perceptions and inceptions is meant to suggest that these made entities are both *more than* and *less than* perceptions. Nersessian's (1992, p. 40) account of physicist James Maxwell's creative process implies exactly such entities: "Maxwell generated a ... representation for electromagnetism ... at an intermediate level of abstraction: concrete enough to give substance to the relationships ... and yet abstract enough to generate a novel representation."

Rather than made representations of the real world, inceptions are the made beginnings of an imagined world (to purloin Goodfield's phrasing). Not quite models or images of reality, they are nonetheless more than just perceptions. Inceptions can be observed and rearranged independent of the physical world that spawned them.

Chase and Simon (1988, p. 490) characterized perceptions as "web-like or network-like ... in overall topology." Certain connections hold among the elements of "perceptual structures," and these interconnections are essential to the integrity of perceptions. Inceptions preserve this weblike topology. As Briggs (1990, p. 203) contends, "Vision must lie partly in the spaces *between* thoughts—the spaces of nuance and omnivalence ... 'great spaces filled with vague forms.'" These forms *seem* vague only because certain dynamic, connective information contained in inceptions recedes as a result of translation into symbols; it must to enable us to talk about them. William James (1890a, p. 255) posed this observation in the form of a question more than a century ago: "What is the shadowy scheme of the 'form' of an opera, play, or book, which remains in our mind ... when the actual thing is done? What is our notion of a scientific or philosophical system?" The symbolic representations capture sufficient truth to permit the understanding of an insightful discovery but reproduce only selected aspects of the inceptions that exist in the mind's eye of the discoverer. "Knowledge *about* a thing is knowledge of its relations.... Of most of its relations we are only aware in the penumbral nascent way of a 'fringe' of unarticulated affinities about it" (James, 1890a, p. 259).

In a fine characterization of inceptual processes, the physicist Richard Feynman (Feynman, Leighton & Sands, 1964, pp. 20–9 and 20–10) spoke of his "picture" of electromagnetic fields, denying that Maxwell's equations can be visually represented:

When I start describing the magnetic field moving through space, I speak of E and B fields and wave my arms and you may imagine that I can see them. I'll tell you what I see. I see some kind of vague shadowy, wiggling lines—and there is an E and B written on them somehow, and perhaps some of the lines have arrows on them ... which disappear when I look too closely at it.... When I talk about the electromagnetic field in space, I see some kind of superposition of all the diagrams which I've ever seen drawn about them.

For Feynman, there was no confusion between his symbolic representation of fields via Maxwell's equations and his inceptual representation of fields. Nor was there confusion with the perceptual representation; for Feynman, the perceptual phenomena associated with fields (the image of moving magnets, say) were not confused with the fields themselves. In their studies of expertise, Chi, Glaser, and Rees (1982, p. 18) have similarly found that it is "predominantly the experts who construct an elaborate representation and ... this representation need not correspond directly to a physical representation, but may be more abstract." (See also Scardamalia & Bereiter, 1992, on the "knowledge-transforming" strategies of expert writers.)

Inceptions stand between the perceptual and the symbolic, yet the focus of most inquiries about insight has been on symbolic, rather than inceptual, characterizations of insight. Backward selection has been applied to the problem of insight, but often this heuristic has been utilized only to identify component symbols that describe the insightful product, in large part disregarding the dynamic inceptual process from which the insight emerged. Consider that a number of computer studies of creative problem solving have purported to arrive at the same insightful solutions as the human discoverers on which the computer programs were modeled. Yet the representation of the perceptions that the computer recombines is in the hands of the programmer and is merely symbolic, not inceptual. For example, Chase and Simon (1988, p. 490) stated that "in artificial intelligence studies, perceptual structures are represented as assemblages of description lists, the elementary components of which are propositions asserting that certain relations hold among elements." Thus, all that is vague about the weblike structure is omitted (see Newell, 1990, for discussion of the importance of adding the capacity of perception to computer models, and Tweney, 1992b, for a similar critique). However, is the omitted information an unimportant part of the discovery process or is it merely too vague to be captured by someone viewing the insightful product solely through symbolic mediators? Our contention is that the representation of perceptions in the manner described by Chase and Simon is too willing to accept a given set of elements as if that were all one needed to get a proper account. In Nersessian's (1992, p. 11) apt phrasing: "A different form of representation is needed to accommodate the data of change."

Consumers of scientific and artistic discoveries have, of course, long subsisted on a diet of inceptions converted to signs and symbols by the discoverer. Thus, there is no denial here that a computer can be programmed to understand such discoveries when provided with the appropriate symbols. The question is whether the alteration of computer routines to include the ability for perceptual rehearsal and the consequent formation of inceptions would permit computer models of human thought to extend their activities beyond understanding to discovery. Note that Faraday was not content merely to *read* accounts of the research studies of other scientists. Faraday (Williams, 1965), like Feynman (Briggs, 1990), often duplicated the experiments of others, an indication of the importance placed on gaining firsthand perceptual experience with the discoveries of others.

Hence the story of insight begins with "the sensory world ...,
what the scientist [or artist] makes of that world, and how the resulting made entity [an *inception*, in our present terminology] ...
participates in the larger generalizations that are the end-product"
(Tweney, in press). Requisite to every insightful enterprise,
whether scientific or artistic, is a perspective on reality not
bound by the initial conclusions of the senses.

Whereas perceptual rehearsal and the subsequent distillation of
inceptions may seem an inefficient or wasteful approach in terms
of a single problem, the inceptions that are the products of perceptual rehearsal may contribute not just to extant but to future problem-solving efforts. In Perkins's (1981, p. 114) words: "Focused
evaluation can sensitize a person to considerations that will
become simply noticed later." For both Faulkner and Faraday, inceptual scraps that did not meet the selection criteria were not
discarded but set aside. Some characters that had always been in
Faulkner's "attic" first appeared in his later novels, and Faraday's
carefully indexed diaries provided him with a readily accessible
verbal and pictorial record of his perceptual experiences (Tweney,
1991).

FEELINGS OF KNOWING AS THE SELECTION TOUCHSTONE

The preceding paragraphs have focused on the made world of inceptions and have said little about the process by which inceptions are later selected. There has been a longstanding emphasis
on selection in discussions of creativity. For example, Henry
James (1897, cited in Allott, 1967, p. 76) spoke of "life being all
inclusion, and art being all discrimination and selection." The
mathematician Poincaré said that "discovery is discernment,
selection" (cited in Westcott, 1968, p. 49). Ernest Hemingway was
unsuccessful in completing his short story, "The Killers," until
he got the selection process right. In Hemingway's words: "I
guess I left as much out of 'The Killers' as any story I ever wrote.
Left out the whole city of Chicago" (Hotchner, 1966, p. 164). Faraday, too, wrote of the many "thoughts and theories which have
passed through the mind of a scientific investigator [and] have
been crushed in silence and secrecy" (cited in Koestler, 1964,
p. 213, who also refers to the "similar confessions" of Darwin,

Huxley, Planck, Kepler, and Einstein). Similarly, in their recent studies of the writing process, Scardamalia and Bereiter (1992, p. 172) found that "when ... [expert writers] produce texts, they bring to mind a great deal of information that they later toss out."

Both artists and scientists seek to reveal some aspect of reality; toward that end, they purposefully discard that which clouds or obscures, selecting that which clarifies or unifies. Earlier, perceptual rehearsal was characterized as serving to delay perceptual selection with regard to the phenomena of interest; inceptual selection subsequently takes place independent of the sensory domain. Our contention is that the selection of inceptions is constrained by feelings of knowing.

Feelings of knowing are defined here as an individual's belief, unsubstantiated by factual information, that he or she is capable of proceeding in a way that will lead to the successful solution of the problem at hand, the sense that the right answer is within the reach of the problem solver. Feelings of knowing are, in the words of Joseph Conrad, "the inward voice that decides" (Karl, 1979, p. 454). Underlying the concept of feelings of knowing is the fact that all accounts of insight presume a self. To discover something is to relate the self properly to the object of discovery; insight can be said to occur when this relation is satisfied. Thus, the emotional component of insight is explicable; we say "Aha!" because of the feeling of self-validation. In effect, our cognitive model works, and there is a corresponding increase in self-esteem; nature has just patted us on the back.

Empirical studies of feelings of knowing (Glenberg, Wilkinson & Epstein, 1982; Metcalfe, 1986; Park, Gardner & Thukral, 1988; Perkins, 1981; Pressley & Ghatala, 1988; Yaniv & Meyer, 1987) have attempted to link feelings of knowing to the products of thought, with the expectation that feelings of knowing would predict insights; however, the findings of these studies have been inconsistent. The mixed results yielded by studies of feelings of knowing are not surprising: "Extensive search accomplishes nothing unless the person looks in the right places" (Perkins, 1981, p. 132). The fact that the potential discoverer is engaged in selection implies that he or she knows in advance what constitutes wheat and what constitutes chaff. This "does not mean that the maker knows at some level just what the product will be before making it. On the contrary, products are vaguely and tentatively conceived, groped for, caught at, discovered" (Perkins, 1981, p. 276). However, the discoverer has devised a way of deciding which inceptions to factor out (as either deceptions or as simple irrelevancies).

We suggest that feelings of knowing are the touchstone the individual uses to separate those inceptions that participate in combinatory play from those that are, for the moment, disregarded. This implies that feelings of knowing empower the selection process only; viewed in this manner, feelings of knowing would not necessarily be expected to predict an insight. As implied by the mixed results of the research studies cited, feelings of knowing may also be associated with inappropriate selection criteria. Thus, such feelings do not guarantee either the quality of the inceptions or the thoroughness of the preparatory perceptual rehearsal with regard to a particular problem.

We suspect that feelings of knowing are shaped by accumulated problem-solving experience (just as perceptual processes are influenced by sensory experience), as well as by knowledge of the problem at hand. Sternberg (1989, p. 121) has pointed out that a theory of expertise based largely on accumulated knowledge, in effect, dooms the expert to becoming the inhabitant of a golden cage: "Knowing more about a topic can actually interfere with retrieval of information about the topic." He proposes that domain-general and domain-specific skills are "complementary, with both operating interactively with each other" (Sternberg, 1989, p. 124; see also Ceci, 1989; Siegler, 1989; and Scardamalia's & Bereiter's 1992 characterization of the "dialectical process" employed by expert writers). Weber and Perkins (1989) make a similar point in their discussion of the "power-generality tradeoff." In contrast to the rapid drop in the power of machine intelligence to solve problems as the generality of the usable heuristics increases, the corresponding decline for human intelligence is much gentler. "Humans often find ideas or strategies generated by middle- or even high-generality heuristics quite provocative and powerful" (Weber & Perkins, 1989, p. 51).

What is being suggested here is that the touchstone that empowers the selection of inceptions is formulated based on domain-specific knowledge *and* past problem-solving experience. Each problem-solving experience, in turn, alters the domain-general component of the selection touchstone. Individuals such as Faraday, who go to great lengths to arrange for *diverse* perceptual rehearsal in the domains of the problems of interest to them, not only gather knowledge germane to specific problems but also arrange for a corresponding evolution of their feelings of knowing. Because feelings of knowing are self-affirming by definition, they are only as valid as the entire body of problem-solving experience on which they are based. In other words, knowing (or expertise) is insufficient to formulate a problem domain. The discoverer must rely, in part, on feelings of knowing, perhaps in the form of high-generality heuristics, to select inceptions and thus define the domain of problem solution. "Feeling *and* knowing both contribute to the success of an enterprise" (italics added; Perkins, 1981, p. 115).

CONSTRUCTING A MENTAL MODEL

Einstein (cited in Holton, 1971–1972, p. 103) referred to the mental rearrangement of selected sensory reconstructions (inceptions) as "combinatory play," which he identified as "an essential feature in productive thought—before there is any connection with logical construction in words or other kinds of signs which can be communicated to others." Poincaré (1946, cited in Epstein, 1991, p. 366) spoke of "ideas [that] rose in crowds" and collided "until pairs interlocked ... making a stable combination." Chekhov (1886, cited in Allott, 1967, p. 304) said that "one has to snatch at small details, grouping them in such a manner that after reading them one can obtain the picture on closing one's eyes" (see also "selective combination" in Davidson & Sternberg, 1984, and Sternberg & Davidson, 1983).

Combinatory play has a role in our characterization of the insight process as well. Ideas, skills, and rules participate in combinatory play; however, it is not solely these static elements but also the ways in which ideas, skills, and rules interact that contribute to the process of insightful discovery. The ideas, skills, and rules that form the junctures of interacting inceptions are emergent properties of the created problem domain, analogous to the emergent domain-specific skills evinced by experts (Chi, Glaser & Farr, 1988).

In Faraday's study of optical deceptions, the distillation process generated inceptions that could be manipulated independently of the visual apparatus and the physical world. The selected inceptions, furthermore, embodied the dynamic, interactive qualities and the constructive potential we associate with perceptions. These inceptions empowered combinatory play in the problem domain of the optical deceptions of interest in the same manner that domain-specific knowledge empowers the superior performance of experts.

In 1983, de Kleer and Brown (1988, p. 270) attempted "to develop a model of how one acquires an understanding of mechanics, devices such as physical machines, electronic and hydraulic devices, or reactors." In the pursuit of this goal, they distinguished between envisioning—"an inference process which, given the device's structure, determines its function" (deKleer & Brown, 1988, p. 271)—and troubleshooting. "Troubleshooting is, in many ways, the inverse of envisioning. The troubleshooter needs to move from known function to unknown structure" (de Kleer & Brown, 1988, p. 282). The processes of envisioning and troubleshooting can be extended beyond physical devices to the understanding of physical and psychological processes such as those embodied in optical deceptions.

After aggregating a rich store of perceptions, Faraday then assembled the inceptions critical to the visualization of the optical deceptions. Once Faraday had distilled the structure of these optical deceptions, he constructed a geometrical mental model to envision the interfunctioning of the human eye and the real world, a model that explained how the optical deceptions worked. In later experiments, Faraday utilized what he knew about the functioning of the eye to enhance "the multiplicity of small events during a simultaneous moment of time" (Tweney, 1992c, p. 164) and to reveal previously unknown structure (troubleshooting). Thus, Faraday's science alternated between the external physical world and his internal reality, between envisioning (constructing a mental model) and troubleshooting (testing the workability of the mental model).

This back and forth of envisioning and troubleshooting is an "effort of constructive abstraction" (Tweney, 1990, p. 480) that potentially engenders a "restructuring of the thought-material"

(Duncker, 1945, p. 29). The ideal end point of this stage of scientific discovery—during which the associative combination of selected inceptions, ideas, skills, mechanical representations (cf. Gorman & Carlson, 1990), and rules takes place—is the construction of a viable mental model. Combinatory play utilizes inceptions to generate "images of wide scope ... [which] serve as levels and scaffolds for building the actual creative products" (Briggs, 1990, p. 194).

Mental models have been characterized in a number of ways (see Eysenck & Keane, 1990). Johnson-Laird (1983) characterizes both images and mental models as representations that serve as a kind of high-level programming language in the human brain. Mental models differ from images in that "images correspond to views of models; as a result either of perception or imagination ... [mental models] represent the perceptible features of corresponding real-world objects" (Johnson-Laird, 1983, p. 157). In the sense that mental models are more than just images or perceptions, the Johnson-Laird characterization is compatible with our notion.

Montgomery (1988, p. 86) speaks of insight as having occurred when, via manipulation of the constructed mental model, one has achieved a "structural balance." Although we are in general agreement with Johnson-Laird and with Montgomery, we would like to emphasize the dynamic character of the term *mental model*. The mental models suggested here as the end products of insight are more correctly described as dynamic representations of dynamic systems rather than static replications of real-world objects. This emphasis on the dynamic is intended to convey a conception of mental models as more akin to organisms than to devices that can be reduced to the enumeration of structures or translated into machine language. Henry James (1884, cited in Allott, 1967, p. 234) placed this restriction on the novel as well: "A novel is a living thing, all one and continuous, like every other organism, and in proportion as it lives will it be found, I think, that in each of the parts there is something of each of the other parts."

The construction of mental models may well satisfy the drive toward simplicity or unity believed to underlie insightful discoveries (Briggs, 1990; Perkins, 1981). In Einstein's words, "Man

seeks for himself ... a simplified and lucid image of the world ...
This is what the painter does, and the poet, the speculative philosopher, the natural scientist, each in his own way" (Holton, 1978,
pp. 231–232). In the last year of her life, Virginia Woolf (1941, cited
in Allott, 1967, p. 236) wrote that "if there is one gift more essential to a novelist than another, it is the power of combination—
the single vision."

The goal of the construction of mental models is dynamic workability—that is, the mental model must be *runnable* (cf. Tesla,
cited in Shepard, 1978) and must be able to be visualized across
some nontrivial time interval. In an 1853 letter to his brother,
Flaubert (cited in Allott, 1967, p. 231) wrote:

This novel makes me break out in a cold sweat! ... Each paragraph is good
in itself and there are some pages that are perfect, I feel certain. But ... *it
isn't getting on*. It's a series of well-turned, ordered paragraphs which do
not flow on from each other. I shall have to unscrew them, loosen the
joints, as one does with the masts of a ship when one wants the sails to
take more wind.

This, then, is what we are claiming amounts to insight—the seeing, in the mind, of the dynamic reasons for a perception.

Such seeing can be tracked in Faraday's experiments. Faraday's
diary records for the optical deceptions experiments have not sur-
vived; nonetheless, it is still possible to reconstruct a plausible
way in which inceptions emerged from the rehearsal of the perceptions that became available to him in the course of his observations and experiments. In fact, Faraday (1831, pp. 291–296) was
explicit that, having covered the experimental production and
manipulation of the phenomena in the first part of his paper, he
would now turn to an attempt to explicate the causes. These he
locates, as we noted earlier, in the coacting influences of particular dynamic properties of the geometry of the visual array and in
the characteristics of the observer's visual system:

The eye has the power ... of retaining visual impressions for a sensible
period of time; and in this way, recurring actions, made sufficiently near
to each other, are perceptibly connected, and made to appear as a continued impression ... But during such impressions, the eye, although to the
mind occupied by an object, is still open, for a large proportion of the
time, to receive impressions from other sources; for the original object
looked at is not in the way to act as a screen ... the result is that two or

more objects may seem to exist before the eye at once, being visually superposed. (Faraday, 1831, pp. 296–297)

Note that Faraday's description is inviting the reader to construct an inceptual representation of a process by which a four-component system (object 1, object 2, eye, and mind) operates in a simple repetitive fashion across time. Using a modern, psychologistic symbolism, we might represent this as a flow chart, letting each of the four components participate in a loop such that object 1 continues to drive a representation in the mind component even as it is shaded by object 2 to the eye component (and vice versa). Faraday's goal, though, is to provide more than a symbolic representation; he asks the reader to formulate an inceptual picture using commonly observed phenomena, such as the carriage wheel phenomena with which he began his article. Thus, the persistence of vision in the eye is related to "the luminous circle visible when a lighted coal or taper is whirled round" (Faraday, 1831, p. 296), and the visibility of two objects seen at once in the mind is related to the "schoolboy experiment of seeing both sides of a whirling halfpenny at the same moment" (Faraday, 1831, p. 297).

Having goaded his reader to the level of inceptions, Faraday (1831, p. 297) is now able to use them in the combinatory play that will result in his formal model:

So it is in the appearances particularly referred to in this paper, they are the natural result of two or more impressions upon the eye, really, but not sensibly, distinct from each other. If, whilst the eye is stationary, a series of cogs like those represented by the continuous outline [Faraday here refers to our figure 13.3] pass rapidly before it, they produce a uniform tint to the eye ... If another series of cogs, represented by the dotted outline, and close to the first ... pass with equal velocity in the same direction, it will produce its corresponding tint [and so on, through a consideration of the various possibilities—cogs traveling in opposite direction, with unequal velocities, etc.].

Rhetorically, then, Faraday had led the reader from an inceptual understanding of common phenomena to an inceptual understanding of the rich domain of his experimental results; what remained was to cash this in as a formal model.

To develop a more formal model of the phenomena, Faraday appealed to two sources: the experimental manipulations shared with the reader in the first part of the paper and the reader's understanding of the nature of geometrical relations. If we think of the former as perceptual, then the latter must be symbolic; what stands between is the inceptual. In particular, Faraday (1831) provides a detailed translation of the inceptual model developed on page 297 (and quoted previously) into the formal geometrical terms that constitute the final symbolic result. Thus, on page 298 of his article (Faraday, 1831), he refers to the lettered components of the figure to describe precisely the time and space relationships that define the appearance of spectral figures in the cogwheel experiment; the precise description (which invokes the reader's symbolic knowledge of geometry) is what allowed Faraday to derive quantitative relationships among the variable characteristics of the experimental objects and the details of the observed phenomena. At this point, he had a testable scientific model. We need not follow him through the remaining arguments of further verification and generalization to appreciate this point— that Faraday has given us a microcosm for all creative scientific endeavor.

Faraday demonstrated that the human eye is limited in the speed at which it can collect visual images. Impressions received in rapid succession, such as the alteration of position when a wheel is spinning, are therefore summed through a time-lagged "window." Faraday applied this model to the explanation of a biological issue that had puzzled earlier investigators. When observed under the microscope, certain rotifers (figure 13.4) appear to have spinning wheels at the mouth end—biologically an impossible structure! Faraday argued that the appearance was deceptive, that in fact the "wheels" were cilia vibrating to and fro, the appearance of a wheel being generated by the same visual processes that accounted for the spectral patterns generated by rotating carriage wheels.

Note that the locus of the explanation was not in the physical or biological world but in the perceptual world: Faraday showed how the human eye works, not how cilia worked. Though he offered no experimental proof of the assertion (which others had argued for as well), placing this finding in the context of the deceptions research leads to a minor "Aha" experience: "Of course, that is what they *must* be!"

Figure 13.4
Faraday's illustration of a microscopical "animalcule," actually a rotifer.
(Reprinted with permission from M. Faraday [1831], on a peculiar class of optical deceptions. *Royal Institution Journal*, 2, 205–223, 333–336.)

An insight of this sort often *seems* to entail the sudden emergence of a model of the perceptual dynamics of the world. The automobiles we drive also *seem* to come to life suddenly if we focus on the responsive roar of the engine when we turn the key rather than on the various aspects of automobile construction and maintenance. As we have argued, via Faraday's optical studies and in our introductory comments, an appropriate description vitiates against the notion of insight as instantaneous.

Faraday (1831) did more than solve the riddle of the wheel animalcule and this particular optical deception. In fact, his comparatively minor paper signals a change in the way in which he interpreted visual information collected in the world, and in the laboratory, from that point forward. In the words of the genetic scientist whom Goodfield (1981, p. 116) studied: "I missed them because I was not looking for them. Now I am, and I see them. *But they were there all the time!* And what has changed? Only my thoughts."

Appearances come to have a different meaning for the problem solver after the emergence of a model. Truth, in this account of insight, is constructed from real-world perceptions, not discovered in the real world. The scientific argument of Faraday persuades us precisely because it provides a better model of reality rather than reality itself. All insight is like this. The success of an insight depends on its psychological function in changing the meaning of appearances. "Aha!" says Archimedes, "I now see that when I sink into the tub I displace no more than my own weight in water." For him, the appearance of bathing has changed, as has the appearance of the problem of specific gravity.

Faraday's work on optical deceptions has provided us with some insights about insight by giving us a tangible, though relatively simple, case study of scientific research that we have used to structure our own account. The claim made here is that insight is best seen as the end product of the essential element in creativity, namely *the construction of a mental model that works*. In this regard, we can see that every insight is a successful thought experiment.

CONCLUSIONS

In the context of present-day psychological research on illusions, Faraday's (1831) optical deceptions paper is unremarkable. At best, it occupies a minor place in the broader context of Faraday's own research. Faraday is best remembered, of course, for his work in the physics of electromagnetic fields. His most famous discovery, that of the induction of electrical currents by changing magnetic fields, occurred late in 1831, just months after the publication of the optical deceptions article. As in the optical deception experiments, Faraday had to "stop time" for his account of electromagnetic induction to work. He had to operate within many constraints—mathematical constraints based on least-action notions, a huge body of relevant experimental results (his own and others'), and Faraday's own beliefs that there is no "action-at-a-distance" (Tweney, 1989b). The observer's perceptual dynamics were only a footnote here, albeit an important one.

Faraday's discovery of electromagnetic induction marked the beginning of an intense, nearly continuous series of research efforts on the nature of electricity and magnetism that occupied him until the end of his career. While strongly committed to experimentation as the "test of truth," Faraday's goal throughout his career was the elaboration of a coherent and consistent theory of the interaction of force and matter; his work culminated in the development of the first truly modern field theory (Nersessian, 1984; Tweney, 1992a), an account that relied on lines of force penetrating all space, the denial of a physical ether, and a conception of matter as amounting to centers of force, rather than as hard, impenetrable stuff. Lines of force were central in Faraday's account. As he conceptualized them, the lines of force were immaterial, inaccessible to vision. Although the reality of these lines of force had to be accessed in a manner that bears little overt resemblance to Faraday's approach to unraveling the optical puzzle, the process was again one of the construction of an inceptual world via perceptual rehearsal and the emergence of a mental model from this constructed reality.

We have, then, a model of insight as a process. To apply the model, we should seek evidence of a crucial role for the repetition of key perceptual aspects of the phenomena of interest, the development of inceptions in the mind's eye, the selection of which inceptions to focus on, and the active construction of a workable mental model. Whereas our verbal description of this process may be read as specifying separable stages in the development of an insight, the intention is that at every stage the back-and-forth movement between hand and eye and mind is apparent. Hence, the stages are not monotonically ordered, but instead they interpenetrate one another.

The preceding illustration of the inception of insight centers on a plausible reconstruction of the activity of a scientist engaged in solving a specific research problem, a fit between the terms of our model and the richness of the available records. Our hope is that this framework for the insight process will initiate scrutiny of the "vague forms" in ways that are less vague.

REFERENCES

Allott, M. (Ed.). (1967). *Novelists on the novel*. London, England: Routledge & Kegan Paul.

Arnheim, R. (1962). *Picasso's Guernica: The genesis of a painting*. Berkeley: University of California Press.

Bowers, K.S., Regehr, G., Balthazard, C., & Parker, K. (1990). Intuition in the context of discovery. *Cognitive Psychology, 22*, 72–110.

Briggs, J. (1990). *Fire in the crucible: The self-creation of creativity and genius.* Los Angeles: Jeremy P. Tarcher.

Cantor, G. (1991). *Michael Faraday: Sandemanian and scientist.* New York: St. Martin's Press.

Ceci, S.J. (1989). On domain specificity ... more or less general and specific constraints on cognitive development. *Merrill-Palmer Quarterly, 35*, 131–142.

Chase, W.G., & Simon, H.A. (1988). The mind's eye in chess. In A. Collins & E.E. Smith (Eds.), *Readings in cognitive science: A perspective from psychology and artificial intelligence* (pp. 461–493). San Mateo, CA: Kaufmann.

Chi, M.T.H., Glaser, R., & Farr, M.J. (Eds.). (1988). *The nature of expertise.* Hillsdale, NJ: Erlbaum.

Chi, M.T.H., Glaser, R., & Rees, E. (1982). Expertise in problem solving. In R.J. Sternberg (Ed.), *Advances in the psychology of human intelligence* (pp. 7–73). Hillsdale, NJ: Erlbaum.

Clement, J. (1989). Learning via model construction and criticism: Protocol evidence on the sources of creativity in science. In J.A. Glover, R.R. Ronning & C.R. Reynolds. *Handbook of creativity* (pp. 341–381). New York: Plenum.

Csikszentmihalyi, M. (1988). Motivation and creativity: Toward a synthesis of structural and energistic approaches to cognition. *New Ideas in Psychology, 6*, 159–176.

Davidson, J.E., & Sternberg, R.J. (1984). The role of insight in intellectual giftedness. *Gifted Child Quarterly, 28*, 58–64.

de Beauvoir, S. (1959). *Memoirs of a dutiful daughter* (James Kirkup, Trans.). New York: Harper & Row.

de Kleer, J., & Brown, J.S. (1988). Assumptions and ambiguities in mechanistic mental models. In A. Collins & E.E. Smith (Eds.), *Readings in cognitive science: A perspective from psychology and artificial intelligence* (pp. 270–287). San Mateo, CA: Kaufmann.

Duncker, K. (1945). On problem-solving (Lynne S. Lees, Trans.). *Psychological Monographs, 58*(5).

Epstein, R. (1991). Skinner, creativity, and the problem of spontaneous behavior. *Psychological Science, 2*, 362–370.

Ericsson, K.A., & Smith, J. (Eds.). (1992). *Toward a general theory of expertise: Prospects and limits.* Cambridge, England: Cambridge University Press.

Eysenck, M.W., & Keane, M.T. (1990). *Cognitive psychology: A student's handbook.* Hillsdale, NJ: Erlbaum.

Faraday, M. (1831). On a peculiar class of optical deceptions. *Royal Institution Journal, 2*, 205–223, 334–336.

Feynman, R.P., Leighton, R.B., & Sands, M. (1964). *The Feynman lectures on physics* (Vol. 2). Reading, MA: Addison-Wesley.

Flower, L., & Hayes, J.R. (1977). Problem-solving strategies and the writing process. *College English, 39*, 440–461.

Flower, J.H., & Garbin, C.P. (1989). Creativity and perception. In J.A. Glover, R.R. Ronning, & C.R. Reynolds (Eds.), *Handbook of creativity* (pp. 147–162). New York: Plenum.

Getzels, J., & Csikszentmihalyi, M. (1976). *The creative vision: A longitudinal study of problem finding in art*. New York: Wiley.

Glaser, R., & Chi, M.T.H. (1988). Overview. In M.T.H. Chi, R. Glaser & M.J. Farr (Eds.), *The nature of expertise* (pp. xv–xxviii). Hillsdale, NJ: Erlbaum.

Glenberg, A.M., Wilkinson, A.C., Epstein, W. (1982). The illusion of knowing: Failure in the self-assessment of comprehension. *Memory & Cognition, 10*, 597–602.

Goodfield, J. (1981). *An imagined world: A story of scientific discovery*. New York: Harper & Row.

Gooding, D. (1990). *Experiment and the making of meaning*. Dordrecht, Netherlands: Kluwer Academic Publishers.

Gorman, M.E., & Carlson, W.B. (1990). Interpreting invention as a cognitive process: The case of Alexander Graham Bell, Thomas Edison, and the telephone. *Science, Technology, & Human Values, 15*, 131–164.

Gruber, H.E. (1981). Chance, choice, and creativity. In R.D. Tweney, M.E. Doherty & C.R. Mynatt (Eds.), *On scientific thinking* (pp. 340–344). New York: Columbia University Press.

Hayes, J.R. (1989). *Cognitive processes in creativity*. In J.A. Glover, R.R. Ronning & C.R. Reynolds (Eds.), *Handbook of creativity* (pp. 135–146). New York: Plenum.

Holton, G. (1971–1972). On trying to understand scientific genius. *The American Scholar, 41*, 95–109.

Holton, G. (1978). *The scientific imagination: Case studies*. Cambridge, England: Cambridge University Press.

Hotchner, A.E. (1966). *Papa Hemingway*. New York: Random House.

James, W. (1890a). *The principles of psychology* (Vol. 1). New York: Dover.

James, W. (1890b). The principles of psychology (Vol. 2). New York: Dover.

Johnson-Laird, P.N. (1983). *Mental models*. Cambridge, Harvard University Press.

Kagan, J. (1989). *Unstable ideas: Temperament, cognition, and self* (chapter 6). Cambridge: Harvard University Press.

Kaplan, C.A., & Simon, H.A. (1990). In search of insight. *Cognitive Psychology, 22,* 374–419.

Karl, F.R. (1979). *Joseph Conrad: The three lives.* New York: Farrar, Straus and Giroux.

Keane, M. (1989). Modelling problem solving in Gestalt "insight" problems. *The Irish Journal of Psychology, 10,* 201–215.

Kolanczyk, A. (1989). How to study creative intuition. *Polish Psychological Bulletin, 20,* 57–68.

Koestler, A. (1964). *The act of creation.* New York: Macmillan.

Metcalfe, J. (1986). Feeling of knowing in memory and problem solving. *Journal of Experimental Psychology: Learning, Memory and Cognition, 12,* 288–294.

Metcalfe, J., & Wiebe, D. (1987). Intuition in insight and noninsight problem solving. *Memory & Cognition, 15,* 238–246.

Miller, A.I. (1989). Imagery and intuition in creative scientific thinking: Albert Einstein's invention of the special theory of relativity. In D.B. Wallace & H.E. Gruber (Eds.), *Creative people at work: Twelve cognitive case studies* (pp. 25–43). New York: Oxford University Press.

Millgate, M. (1989). *The achievement of William Faulkner.* New York: Random House.

Montgomery, H. (1988). Mental models and problem solving: Three challenges to a theory of restructuring and insight. *Scandinavian Journal of Psychology, 29,* 85–94.

Morris, W. (Ed.). (1969). *The American heritage dictionary of the English language.* Boston: American Heritage.

Murray, D.M. (1978). Write before writing. *College Composition and Communication, 29,* 375–381.

Nersessian, N. (1984). *Faraday to Einstein: Constructing meaning in scientific theories.* Dordrecht, Netherlands: Martinus Nijhoff.

Nersessian, N. (1992). How do scientists think? Capturing the dynamics of conceptual change in science. In R.N. Giere (Ed.), *Cognitive models of science* (pp. 3–44). Minneapolis: University of Minnesota Press.

Newell, A. (1990). *Unified theories of cognition.* Cambridge: Harvard University Press.

Nickerson, R., Perkins, D., & Smith, E. (1985). *The teaching of thinking.* Hillsdale, NJ: Erlbaum.

Park, C.W., Gardner, M.P., & Thukral, V.K. (1988). Self-perceived knowledge: Some effects on information processing for a choice task. *American Journal of Psychology, 101,* 401–424.

Parnes, S. (1975). Aha! In I. Taylor & J. Getzels, (Eds.), *Perspectives on creativity* (pp. 224–248). Chicago: Aldine.

Perkins, D.N. (1981). *The mind's best work*. Cambridge: Harvard University Press.

Pressley, M., & Ghatala, E.S. (1988). Delusions about performance on multiple-choice comprehension tests. *Reading Research Quarterly, 23,* 454–463.

Reitman, W.R. (1965). *Cognition and thought: An information processing approach*. New York: Wiley.

Rolland, R. (1929). *Beethoven the creator* (Ernest Newman, Trans.). New York: Harper & Brothers.

Salthouse, T.A. (1992). Expertise as the circumvention of human processing limitations. In K.A. Ericsson & J. Smith (Eds.), *Toward a general theory of expertise: Prospects and limits* (pp. 172–194). Cambridge, England: Cambridge University Press.

Scardamalia, M., & Bereiter, C. (1992). Literate expertise. In K.A. Ericsson & J. Smith (Eds.), *Toward a general theory of expertise: Prospects and limits* (pp. 172–194). Cambridge, England: Cambridge University Press.

Shepard, R.N. (1978). Externalization of mental images and the act of creation. In B.S. Randhawa and W.E. Coffman (Eds.), *Visual learning, thinking, and communication* (pp. 133–189). New York: Academic.

Siegler, R.S. (1989). How domain-general and domain-specific knowledge interact to produce strategy choices. *Merrill-Palmer Quarterly, 35,* 1–26.

Simon, H.A. (1981). The psychology of scientific problem solving. In R. Tweney, M. Doherty & C. Mynatt (Eds.), *On scientific thinking* (pp. 48–54). New York: Columbia University Press.

Simon, H.A., & Simon, D.P. (1978). Individual differences in solving physics problems. In R.S. Siegler (Ed.), *Children's thinking: What develops?* (pp. 215–231). Hillsdale, NJ: Erlbaum.

Sternberg, R.J. (1981). Intelligence and nonentrenchment. *Journal of Educational Psychology, 73,* 1–16.

Sternberg, R.J. (1989). Domain-generality versus domain-specificity: The life and impending death of a false dichotomy. *Merrill-Palmer Quarterly, 35,* 115–130.

Sternberg, R.J., & Davidson, J.E. (1983). Insight in the gifted. *Educational Psychologist, 18,* 51–57.

Tweney, R.D. (1989a). A framework for the cognitive psychology of science. In B. Gholson, W.R. Shadish, Jr., R.A. Neimeyer & A.C. Houts (Eds.), *Psychology of science: Contributions to metascience* (pp. 342–366). Cambridge, England: Cambridge University Press.

Tweney, R.D. (1989b). Fields of enterprise: On Michael Faraday's thought. In D.B. Wallace & H.E. Gruber (Eds.), *Creative people at work: Twelve cognitive case studies* (pp. 90–106). New York: Oxford University Press.

Tweney, R.D. (1990). Five questions for computationalists. In J. Shrager & P. Langley (Eds.), *Computational models of scientific discovery and theory formation* (p. 471–484). San Mateo, CA: Morgan Kaufmann.

Tweney, R.D. (1991). Faraday's notebooks: The active organization of creative science. *Physics Education, 26*, 301–306.

Tweney, R.D. (1992a). Inventing the field: Michael Faraday and the creative "engineering" of electromagnetic field theory. In R.J. Weber & D.N. Perkins (Eds.), *Inventive minds: Creativity in technology* (pp. 31–47). New York: Oxford University Press.

Tweney, R.D. (1992b). Serial and parallel processing in scientific discovery. In R.N. Giere (Ed.), *Minnesota studies in the philosophy of science: Vol. 15. Cognitive models of science* (pp. 77–88). Minneapolis: University of Minnesota Press.

Tweney, R.D. (1992c). Stopping time: Faraday and the scientific creation of perceptual order. *Physis, 29*, 149–164.

Tweney, R.D. (in press). Shifting sands: Sight and sound in Faraday's acoustical researches. In D. Gooding (Ed.), *Sensation and cognition: Essays on the changing role of sense experience in the history of science.* Chicago: University of Chicago Press.

Tweney, R.D., & Hoffner, C.E. (1987). Understanding the microstructure of science: An example. *Proceedings of the Ninth Annual Meeting of the Cognitive Science Society* (pp. 677–681). Hillsdale, NJ: Erlbaum.

Wallace, D.B. (1989). Studying the individual: The case study method and other genres. In D.B. Wallace & H.E. Gruber (Eds.), *Creative People at work: Twelve cognitive case studies* (pp. 25–43). New York: Oxford University Press.

Weber, R.J., & Perkins, D.N. (1989). How to invent artifacts and ideas. *New Ideas in Psychology, 7*, 49–72.

Wertheimer, M. (1945). *Productive thinking.* New York: Harper & Brothers.

Westcott, M.R. (1968). *Toward a contemporary psychology of intuition.* New York: Holt, Rinehart & Winston.

Westfall, R.S. (1980). Newton's marvelous years of discovery and their aftermath: Myth versus manuscript. *Isis, 71*, 109–121.

Williams, L.P. (1965). *Michael Faraday: A biography.* New York: Da Capo.

Windholz, G. (1984). Pavlov vs. Kohler: Pavlov's little-known primate research. *Pavlovian Journal of Biological Science, 19*, 23–31.

Yaniv, I., & Meyer, D.E. (1987). Activation and metacognition of inaccessible stored information: Potential bases for incubation effects in problem solving. *Journal of Experimental Psychology: Learning, Memory, and Cognition, 13*, 187–205.

V   The Metaphors-of-Mind Approach

14 Foresight in Insight? A Darwinian Answer

Dean Keith Simonton

"I can remember the very spot on the road, whilst in my carriage, when to my joy the solution occurred to me" (quoted in F. Darwin, 1892/1958, p. 43). So recollected Charles Darwin regarding one of the more momentous insights in the history of science. The solution that came to him marked a keystone to his theory of evolution by natural selection. Nor was Darwin's experience unique. Under various names—hunches, illuminations, inspirations, quantum leaps, acts of intuition, and the like—flashes of insight have received credit for some of the greatest contributions to human culture, whether in the sciences or the arts. Whenever geniuses offer their recollections of the creative processes that guided them to greatness, they often assign insight the primary place in the list of cognitive acknowledgments (e.g., Ghiselin, 1952; Platt & Baker, 1931).

In this chapter, I will argue that Darwin's revolutionary insights into biological evolution have implications beyond just the origin of species. In particular, the Darwinian process also provides a broader model for understanding the origins of insights in the annals of human achievements. The emergence of new ideas in the heads of creative geniuses follows a pattern remarkably close to the appearance of new varieties of life forms on this planet.

INSIGHT

Darwin's theory of evolution underwent many transformations during his lifetime, and his theory has undergone even greater modifications by the hands of others since his death more than a century ago. None of these refinements, complications, and controversies concern us here. Instead, I wish to sketch the *generic* process that defines the gist of the Darwinian perspective on the origin of species. This conceptual core consists of four components (cf. Campbell, 1960, 1965, 1974):

1. There exists some mechanism for producing *variation*. In biological evolution, these variations originate from more than one source. Recombination of genetic material during sexual reproduction provides a steady source of variations, whereas genetic mutations offer another, more sporadic (but also more audacious) source.

2. The production of these variations is at some level *blind*. Neither any cosmic teleology nor some individualistic acumen dictates their generation. In classic Mendelian genetics, for example, the genes are subjected to independent assortment, a purely random procedure that exploits no a priori wisdom about the optimal combination of traits. Mutations, too, appear without any insight into whether the novel traits actually will benefit the organism. Indeed, many mutations are so lethal that the egg cannot develop further after fertilization.

3. These blind variations feed into some relatively stable process of *selection*. Darwin originally stressed the importance of environmental fitness: Those organisms best adapted to a particular ecological niche will be favored in the struggle for survival. Later, he added sexual selection as well: Some characteristics are better at attracting mates. Modern evolutionary theory has introduced still other possibilities, such as developmental constraints. Whatever the specifics, these selection pressures operate so that certain variations enjoy an above-average probability of reproducing their kind.

4. The variations that survive this selective winnowing enter some *retention* procedure. In biological evolution, the best genes are preserved on the chromosomes, to fuel further Mendelian recombination. Owing to this retention process, the most adaptive genetic traits can become more common in the population gene pool, whereas the most deleterious traits become less common and may eventually disappear.

Many distinguished psychologists have recognized that this Darwinian process describes more that just the origin of species. The same process operates in creativity, so well. Thus, William

James (1880, p. 456) proposed:

[T]he new conceptions, emotions, and active tendencies which evolve are originally *produced* in the shape of random images, fancies, accidental outbirths of spontaneous variation in the functional activity of the excessively unstable human brain, which the outer environment simply confirms or refutes, adopts or rejects, preserves or destroys—selects, in short, just as it selects morphological and social variations due to molecular accidents of an analogous sort.

Later, B.F. Skinner (1972) argued that creativity involved a trial-and-error process in which creative behaviors are shaped by the reinforcements dispensed by the environment. Epstein (1990, 1991), one of Skinner's students, has even developed Skinner's ideas into a formal ("generativity") theory that successfully predicts simulated insights in pigeons!

Still, for our present purposes, it is Donald Campbell's 1960 model of creative thought that holds the most promise. He actually called his scheme the *blind variation and selective retention theory*. According to this model, ideas undergo haphazard recombinations in the mind. The resulting blind variations then pass through a selective filter. Only a subset of the ideational combinations are retained for further cognitive processing. Although it sounds simple, the theoretical implications are profound and varied. Over the past few years, in fact, many others have expanded Campbell's basic model into more comprehensive theories of discovery and creativity (e.g., Eysenck, 1993; Kantorovich, 1993; Kantorovich & Ne'eman, 1989; Martindale, 1990; Shrader, 1980; Stein & Lipton, 1989; see also Findlay & Lumsden, 1988).

My modest contribution to this school is the chance configuration theory of creative genius (e.g., Simonton, 1988b, 1988c). According to this system, creativity begins with the chance permutation of mental elements. The latter include ideas, concepts, recollections, emotions, sensations, or any other basic component of mental functioning. Most of these permutations are too unstable to enjoy anything more than an extremely ephemeral existence in the fancy. Nonetheless, from time to time, a specific combination of elements coalesces to form a cohesive whole, or conceptual Gestalt. This so-called chance configuration represents the insight that transfers to more deliberate and elaborate processing at later stages in the creative process.

All this may seem too abstract to offer us much insight into insight. Hence, to make the Darwinian model more convincing, let us look at some concrete illustrations of the proposed process.

Some Illustrations

As noted earlier, creative geniuses often will offer reports on the thought processes behind their discoveries. They will also narrate stories about some of the more objective conditions that contributed to their insights. Both the introspections and the anecdotes lend support to the theory advocated here.

Introspections

Many creators have hinted at the importance of a two-step, variation-selection procedure. Paul Valéry (quoted in Hadamard, 1945, p. 30), the French poet and essayist, may have put it most succinctly: "It takes two to invent anything. The one makes up combinations; the other chooses, recognizes what he wishes and what is important to him in the mass of the things which the former has imparted to him." John Dryden (1664/1926, p. 1) claimed, in his Epistle Dedicatory of "The Rival Ladies," that this play commenced "when it was only a confused mass of thoughts, tumbling over one another in the dark; when the fancy was yet in its first work, moving the sleeping images of things towards the light, there to be distinguished, and then either chosen or rejected by the judgment." Finally, Albert Einstein (quoted in Hadamard, 1945, p. 142) maintained that "combinatory play seems to be the essential feature in productive thought," this "vague play" taking place "before there is any connection with logical construction in words or other kinds of signs which can be communicated to others."

Perhaps the most detailed description of the fundamental process was written by Henri Poincaré, the eminent mathematician. Poincaré's introspections illustrate the Darwinian model of creativity so well that Campbell recently referred to his own theory as *Poincaréan* (Campbell, 1991). In describing the origins of one significant insight, for example, Poincaré (1921, p. 387) noted: "Ideas rose in crowds; I felt them collide until pairs interlocked, so to speak, making a stable combination. By the next morning I had established the existence of a class of Fuchsian functions." He went on to compare these colliding images to "the hooked atoms of Epicurus" that jiggle and bump "like the molecules of gas in the kinematic theory of gases" so "their mutual impacts may produce new combinations" (p. 393). This represents an explicit and vivid statement of how free variations yield chance configurations.

Anecdotes

We could quote many more examples of similar introspective reports (see Campbell, 1960; Simonton, 1988c, chapter 2), but instead let us turn to another phenomenon that, on first glance, may appear unrelated. In 1940, Walter Cannon, the distinguished physiologist, published an excellent essay entitled "The Role of Chance in Discovery." Here he discussed the phenomenon of *serendipity*, which occurs when an individual "chances upon" a major discovery totally by accident. Typically, a researcher is investigating one question in the laboratory when he or she unexpectedly stumbles on another, often utterly related finding. Classic examples in the history of science and technology include animal electricity, laughing-gas anesthesia, electromagnetism, ozone, photography, synthetic coal-tar dyes, dynamite, the phonograph, vaccination, saccharin, x-rays, radioactivity, classical conditioning, penicillin, sulfa drugs, Teflon, and Velcro (see also Austin, 1978; Mach, 1896; Shapiro, 1986).

Moreover, although seldom acknowledged, serendipity occurs in the arts as well as the sciences. For instance, Henry James (1896/1908, p. v), the novelist brother of William James, provided this instance:

It was years ago, I remember, one Christmas Eve when I was dining with friends: a lady beside me made in the course of talk one of those allusions that I have always found myself recognizing on the spot as "germs." The germ, wherever gathered, has ever been for me the germ of a "story," and most of the stories straining to shape under my hand have sprung from a single small seed, a seed as minute and windblown as that casual hint for "The Spoils of Poynton" dropped unwittingly by my neighbour, a mere floating particle in the stream of talk.

Many of James's best stories emerged from "stray suggestions," "wandering words," or "vague echoes" that fill up everyday social exchanges. Consequently, we can speak of serendipity as a truly general process for the origination of new ideas.

The most critical point, however, is that serendipity often represents but one facet of an underlying process that accounts for the free variation procedure as well (Kantorovich, 1993). Those people who make their minds accessible to chaotic combinatory play will also make their senses more open to the influx of fortuitous events in the outside world. Both the retrieval of material from memory and the orientation of attention to environmental stimuli are unrestricted. This intimate connection is evinced in the thinking patterns and working habits of Charles Darwin himself.

[Darwin had a rare] instinct for arresting exceptions: it was as though he were charged with theorizing power ready to flow into any channel on the slightest disturbance, so that no fact, however small, could avoid releasing a stream of theory, and thus the fact became magnified into importance. In this way it naturally happened that many untenable theories occurred to him; but fortunately his richness of imagination was equalled by his power of judging and condemning the thoughts that occurred to him. He was just to his theories, and did not condemn them unheard; and so it happened that he was willing to test what would seem to most people not at all worth testing. These rather wild trials he called "fool's experiments," and enjoyed extremely. (F. Darwin, 1892/1958, p. 101)

Examples such as this one demonstrate Pasteur's famous remark, "Chance favors the prepared mind." Serendipitous insights are not dispensed indiscriminately on all, for only the most creative see their world as a busy and buzzing world of intellectual and aesthetic opportunities.

Some Clarifications

The very idea that great insights might ensue from a chance process often raises a lot of eyebrows. Many would like to believe that the creative genius is more self-possessed, that an individual has more conscious and deliberate control over the thoughts that produce breakthroughs. To quiet potential concerns, I will address two issues—randomness and consciousness.

How Chaotic Is the Insight Process?
Terms such as *chance, blind, haphazard,* and *random* elicit all sorts of surplus meanings that sometimes create more confusion than clarification. This befuddlement often inspires people to dismiss Darwinian models outright, without comprehending what

the models actually maintain. For example, the mechanism behind Darwinian theories is too often confused with the notion of
random search, discussed in the literature on problem solving
(e.g., Eysenck, 1993). According to cognitive psychologists, people
solve problems by defining a search space of givens, goals, and operations, and then deliberately pick their way through this space
using some heuristic (Hayes, 1989; Newell & Simon, 1972). A
heuristic is a rule of thumb or guideline or strategy that enables
the individual to narrow the scope of the search and, in any list
of such heuristics, random search falls right at the bottom. It requires little intelligence and even less foresight; it is extremely
stupid and inefficient. The problem solver simply engages in an
often hopeless trial-and-error process; everything that can be tried
is tried until either the goal is achieved or the individual gives up
in total frustration.

Now there is no doubt that insights sometimes emerge from
just such a procedure. In working out the details of the DNA
model, James Watson had to figure out which nucleic bases
would fit together. The only solution was to sit at a desk with
molecular models and deliberately try out various combinations
until something came out snug. His task was tedious and idio-
tic—and ultimately successful.

Nevertheless, the Darwinian model does not view this episode
as prototypical. Instead, the variations are presumably generated
by a far less orderly, free-associative procedure—what Freudians
might call *primary process thinking*. The products of this
mechanism are unpredictable and uncontrollable, the associative
meanderings freewheeling. William James (1980, p. 456) described
it this way:

Instead of thoughts of concrete things patiently following one another in
a beaten track of habitual suggestion, we have the most abrupt cross-cuts
and transitions from one idea to another, the most rarefied abstractions
and discriminations, the most unheard of combination of elements, the
subtlest associations of analogy; in a word, we seem suddenly introduced
into a seething cauldron of ideas, where everything is fizzling and bob-
bling about in a state of bewildering activity, where partnerships can be
joined or loosened in an instant, treadmill routine is unknown, and the
unexpected seems only law.

Therefore, we are not speaking of a deliberate act of generating
random combinations. In fact, as we will see shortly, the idea-

tional variations usually occur precisely when the mind is not actively grappling with the problem that instigated the whole process.

The concept of randomness causes confusion in yet another way. Frequently, we tend to view chance as a discrete quantity. Either the phenomenon is random or it is not. This is misleading. A continuum connects the utterly capricious with the altogether determined (Simonton, 1993). An illustration may be drawn from the realm of correlational statistics. Suppose we have two variables, a criterion y and a predictor x. To discern how much we can predict y using x, we can calculate the correlation coefficient, r. Clearly, if $r = 1.0$, scores on the predictor variable allow us to predict scores on the criterion variable with perfect precision. Luck does not figure into the equation. At the other extreme, if $r = 0$, x gives us no information whatsoever about y, and any successful prediction of y would demand pure luck. Correlation coefficients between zero and unity thus embody a continuum between unadulterated randomness and unqualified predictability. The higher this decimal fraction is, the better is the opportunity for predicting the correct answer within a given margin of error.

An analogous continuum underlies human problem solving. At one extreme lie problems that can be solved using straightforward *algorithms*. If I ask you to divide 489 by 73 without a calculator, you will apply the rules of long division that you learned in elementary school. Chance will not play a part in your calculation unless it be some trivial mistake. For less well-defined problems, such as those that dominate much experimental research on problem solving, chance plays a bigger role. Chance often will decide how quickly you arrive at the best representation of the problem as well as whether you select the optimal heuristic for reaching the goal. As problems become more novel and complex, the number of potential representations and heuristics proliferate. For the kinds of problems on which historical creators stake their reputations, the possibilities seem endless, and the odds of attaining the solution appear nearly hopeless.

At this point, problem solving becomes more nearly a random process, in the sense that the free-associative procedure must come into play. Only by falling back on this less disciplined resource can the creator arrive at insights that are genuinely profound. As Poincaré (1921, p. 386) remarked,

[The most useful ideational permutations] are those which reveal to us unsuggested kinship between other facts, long known, but wrongly believed to be strangers to one another.... [Hence,] among chosen combinations the most fertile will often be those formed of elements drawn from domains which are far apart. Not that I mean as sufficing for invention the bringing together of objects as disparate as possible; most combinations so formed would be entirely sterile. But certain among them, very rare, are the most fruitful of all.

This passage illustrates the danger hidden in the application of logic and heuristics. Too often, persons fail to make significant insights because they exclude whole domains of elements from entering into the combinative hopper. Yet what appears logically irrelevant may actually provide the missing piece of the puzzle. When Gutenberg was trying to devise a method to mass-produce the Bible, the solution came from a most unexpected quarter— the presses that he saw whip into action during the Rhineland wine harvest!

So commonplace are fantastic syntheses such as these that Arthur Koestler (1964) made them the cornerstone of his theory of humor, discovery, and invention. According to him, the creative process entails *bisociation*. By this term, Koestler means that the creator suddenly sees the congruence between two sets of ideas (or "matrices") that originate in unrelated domains of experience, and probably the only way two irrelevant realms can be brought together is by the crazy confluence of rather haphazard and whimsical trains of association. Thus, the more offbeat is the bisociation, the greater must be the role of chance in generating it, on the average. However, at no time can we draw a sharp line between solutions determined by a secure logic and insights happened upon by an erratic fancy.

Observe that we find a comparable continuity in the variation process that sustains biological evolution. In the first place, because Mendelian recombination applies mostly to genes that have already proved their adaptive value, variations from this source are not completely at the mercy of chance. These biological heuristics may even reflect themselves in the contrast between dominant and submissive traits. Furthermore, owing to the phenomenon of *linkage*, certain genes—those that appear close together on the same chromosome—will not mix freely. In fact, because the likelihood of *crossover* increases with the distance between the loci, the odds of recombination can vary continuously rather than by big steps. At the other extreme, genetic mutations appear so unrestrained that chance must play a far bigger part than is the case in genetic recombination. Even so, constraints may often operate on the scope and frequency of mutations within a population. Once again, we end up with an approximate continuum of processes that produce variations with different degrees of a priori determination.

How Cognizant Are We of the Insight Process?

Some creative individuals may protest: "I don't think that way! I certainly don't spend all my time rambling in autistic reverie! Rather, my thoughts are coherent and directed from start to finish!" For example, Edgar Allan Poe once described the process by which he created *The Raven*. However romantic the product, Poe was emphatic in stating that this popular poem emerged from a rational, systematic procedure. "It is my design to render it manifest that no one point in its composition is referable either to accident or intuition—that the work proceeded, step by step, to its completion with the precision and rigid consequence of a mathematical problem" (Poe, 1846/1884, p. 160).

Let us look at a more contemporary example: Herbert Simon is undoubtedly one of the most brilliant psychologists alive today, and he is one of the few Nobel laureates among us. Nevertheless, Simon stands in the forefront of those cognitive psychologists who believe that insights arise by a process that is intrinsically logical (e.g., H.A. Simon, 1973). So logical is the process that Simon believes that we can already program computers to make scientific discoveries (e.g., Langley, Simon, Bradshaw, & Zythow, 1987). Presumably, Simon would not argue such a thing if he believed that this logic of discovery contradicted his own introspective experiences. Indeed, Simon has used protocols collected during problem-solving sessions to show that straightforward, deliberate, rational, and conscious processes can reproduce discoveries that made history (e.g., Qin & Simon, 1990).

How do we respond to these claims? One solution is simply to dismiss them outright. We might just maintain that human beings are ignorant of the full operation of their own cognitive processes (as in Nisbett & Wilson, 1977). According to this view, Poe and Simon lack cognizance of what actually goes on in their heads. However, this answer may be too glib. After all, if we take this approach we also should dismiss the introspections of William James and Poincaré, on similar grounds (cf. Perkins, 1981).

Another distinguished French mathematician, Jacques Hadamard, offered a path out of this dilemma. He observed that to isolate the most fruitful combinations,

[It is first] necessary to construct the very numerous possible combinations.... It cannot be avoided that this first operation take place, to certain extent, at random, so that the role of chance is hardly doubtful in this first step of mental process. But we see that the intervention of chance occurs inside the unconscious: for most of these combinations—more exactly, all of those which are useless—remain unknown to us. (Hadamard, 1945, p. 28)

There we have it: The blind variations happen mostly in subterranean domains, and we usually witness only the chief results. Hadamard's suggestion contains some grain of truth, yet we must avoid two potential pitfalls in this explanation.

First, we should not expect too much of these unconscious processes. Experimental research suggests that information processing below the thresholds of awareness is far from sophisticated (see Greenwald, 1992, and ensuing commentary). Even if we may wonder how much these findings apply to creative intellects of the highest order, we still cannot expect the unconscious mind to produce polished mathematical proofs or finished novels. In all likelihood, the unconscious mind is simply the repository of some rather primitive cognitive and affective associations that can form linkages that the conscious mind would deem preposterous (cf. Ochse, 1989). Once these intuitive insights emerge, the conscious mind often must do the real work, verifying the hunch, elaborating the details, or providing the logical justifications.

Second, we should not maintain that the free-associative process is invariably inaccessible to awareness. Sometimes it is, and sometimes it is not, depending on several circumstances.

On the one hand, whenever the ideational variations dip into vivid imagery, they can often command more central attention. A classic instance is Kekulé's account of his discovery of the benzene ring: "I fell into a reverie, and lo! the atoms were gambolling before my eyes" (quoted in Findlay, 1948, p. 37). Soon they formed a circle and—Eureka! This example pinpoints a second condition that favors awareness: The creators may be daydreaming or in some alternative way unoccupied with an otherwise distracting activity, so they can sense the fancy's operations. Poincaré's introspections about "ideas arising in crowds" fall into the same class. He could report that experience because he had made the mistake of drinking coffee shortly before going to bed, and the resulting insomnia enabled him to contemplate his intuitive meditations.

On the other hand, under contrasting circumstances, the variational fancy may operate below the threshold of direct awareness. Frequently, the individual may engage in some rather everyday activity that requires only a more or less habitual attention to external stimuli, leaving enough information-processing capacity for less mundane thoughts. One example is taking a walk. Thus, Poincaré (1921, p. 388) could report the following incident:

I turned my attention to the study of some arithmetical questions apparently without much success and without a suspicion of any connection with my preceding researches. Disgusted with my failure, I went to spend a few days at the seaside, and thought of something else. One morning, walking on the bluff, the idea came to me, with ... [characteristic] brevity, suddenness and immediate certainty, that the arithmetical transformations of indeterminate ternary quadratic forms were identical with those of non-Euclidean geometry.

Darwin's own insightful carriage ride is in the same class of episodes, as is the first "Eureka!" experience in recorded history, that of Archimedes in a bathtub. A slightly different perspective, but one that produces the same result, involves our lack of awareness, at times, of what is going on because we are not yet alert enough to support *self*-consciousness, as happens when we lie in a "hypnagogic state." Hadamard (1945, p. 8) may have been alluding to this possibility when he asserted "the sudden and immediate appearance of a solution at the very moment of sudden awakening." We need only assume that the sudden awakening concerned full awareness, after the mind has previously slipped into that nebulous boundary between dream and daydream.

Whatever the complete set of conditions, we must remember that the line between unconsciousness and consciousness is not hard and fast. As in the case of chance, we are dealing with degrees. The core consciousness contains the central focus of attention, where our information-processing machinery is concentrated, but surrounding that core is a peripheral awareness of subliminal stimuli and partially retrieved memories. That periphery fades off into the ill-defined realm of the unconscious according to the magnitude of cognitive activation. Normally, each of us is not fully aware of what is going on at that farthest fringe. One may sense merely a vague feeling that something is going on in the back of one's mind. This mental sensation is not unlike the tip-of-the-tongue phenomenon and feeling-of-knowing states investigated by cognitive psychologists (e.g., Brown & McNeill, 1966). Nevertheless, when the succession of subconscious images chances on a bona fide insight, core consciousness will suddenly change focus and spotlight the discovery. The upshot is the dramatic subjective experience of illumination or inspiration. Consciousness then bears the fruits of the unconscious labors. Poincaré's beach stroll exemplifies this event perfectly.

I do not know whether this answer would appease either Poe or Simon, but I have offered a sketch of a reasonable response. I believe that Poe and Simon have overstated the monopoly of willful and conscious reason. For instance, I invite the reader to scrutinize Poe's 1846 "Philosophy of Composition" for the non sequitur's in this supposed proof (Poe, 1846/1884). At certain critical points in his step-by-step logic, Poe was obliged to make decisions that seem to go well beyond the confines of simple deduction. One case in point was his inspired choice of the single word *Nevermore* as the poem's refrain. I seriously doubt that anyone could now write a computer program that would duplicate Poe's poetic achievement.

As for Simon's explicit quest for an actual discovery program that makes Nobel-prize quality insights, we have insufficient time to delve into all the criticisms that we can inveigh against the very idea (see Csikszentmihalyi, 1988; Sternberg, 1989; Tweney, 1990). Here I will counter only with the opinion of a fellow Nobel laureate, Max Planck (1949, p. 109), who held that the great scientists "must have a vivid intuitive imagination, for new ideas are not generated by deduction, but by an artistically creative imagination." That fancy is necessary to produce variations which advance beyond logical conventions. Although we must always distrust introspective testimonials, Planck's assertion is more compatible with other key features of the insight process, some of which will be discussed next.

FORESIGHT

Thus far we have been discussing insight in the present tense, yet certain circumstances may arise that anticipate the occurrence of insights, and insights themselves should anticipate future events. Our discussion must therefore expand into the future tense, particularly with regard to how to prepare for insight and what to predict from them.

Preparation

According to introspective reports, insights usually come "out of the blue." One of Poincaré's (1921, p. 388) anecdotes is often quoted as an illustration:

I left Caen, where I was then living, to go on a geologic excursion under the auspices of the school of mines. The changes of travel made me forget my mathematical work. Having reached Coutances, we entered an omnibus to go some place or other. At the moment when I put my foot on the step the idea came to me, without anything in my former thoughts seeming to have paved the way for it, that the transformations I had used to define the Fuchsian functions were identical with those of non-Euclidean geometry.

This episode, combined with those cited earlier, led Margaret Boden (1991, p. 14) to declare, "*The bath, the bed and the bus*: this trio summarizes what creative people have told us about how they came by their ideas." The appearance of insights cannot be forecast except to say that big insights normally arise when least expected.

Even so, the absence of predictability does not mean we cannot identify conditions that are most likely to lead to insight. On the contrary, insights do not appear without the groundwork first being laid by the creative individual. This preparation takes two forms, long-term and short-term.

Long-term Preparation

Not everyone has insights; some unfortunates are lucky if they have one solid revelation in their entire life. Others overflow with so many novel ideas that only death turns off the spigot. How can we account for these obvious individual differences in insight generation? Cognitive psychologists have offered one answer: The insightful person must first build up a huge reservoir of discipline-relevant information. Herbert Simon (1986) has even expressed the requirements in quantitative terms. Judging from chess grand masters and other experts, the expertise required for accomplished and consistent problem-solving skills presupposes approximately 50,000 "chunks" or "patterns" of information (e.g., Simon & Chase, 1973; Chase & Simon, 1973).

One way of explaining this number more concretely is to specify how long it takes to acquire this amount of domain-specific information. If one works at mastering some field several hours daily, mastery will be achieved in approximately 10 years. For example, the finest chess players have usually been staring at chess positions for 3 to 13 hours per day for a full decade (Simon & Chase, 1973). Those masters who try to take shortcuts to chess acclaim often find themselves making dumb mistakes in international competition (Holding, 1985, pp. 32–33). A similar pattern emerges for creative achievement. Hayes (1989, pp. 293–299) has studied the careers of 72 top composers in the classical repertoire and found it is rare for any to get a big hit without first devoting 10 years to composition. Even a prodigy such as Mozart did not break this rule; he produced a decade's worth of juvenilia before he began to compose masterpieces (see also Simonton, 1991b).

Nevertheless, we must be careful how we specify this expertise. It is not enough to have spent 10 years accumulating 50,000 chunks of information. That raw data must be structured in a distinctive way. Otherwise, it will not support the unbridled wanderings necessary to generate the ideational variations (Simonton, 1980). Expertise can be intelligent without being imaginative, and it is imagination that is essential. For instance, H.A. Simon (1986) noted that educated persons have vocabularies of approximately 50,000 words. Even so, two individuals with lexicons of equal size may show rather disparate literary abilities. For the more talented person, the words will be richly interconnected in a complex network of denotative and connotative meanings. This allows the discovery of *le mot juste*, the prime precondition for deeply evocative expressions. The less able person may receive the same score on the verbal scholastic aptitude test but exhibit nowhere near the same fluency and originality. That individual's composition will be admirably competent but strangely uninspired.

Ernst Mach, the Austrian physicist, highlighted this crucial difference almost a century ago. After admitting the assets of "a powerfully developed *mechanical* memory, which recalls vividly and faithfully old situations," Mach (1896, p. 167) insisted that "more is required for the development of *inventions*. More extensive chains of images are necessary here, the excitation by mutual contact of widely different trains of ideas, a more powerful, more manifold, and richer connection of the contents of memory." More recently, Derek Price (1963, p. 107), a historian of science, argued that "a scientist of high achievement ... [has] a certain gift of what we may call *mavericity*, the property of making unusual associations in ideas, of doing the unexpected. The scientist tends to be the man who, in doing the word-association test, responds to 'black' not with 'white' but with 'caviar'."

If only such extravagant associative networks can provide the substrate for insights, how can creators ensure that their expertise is organized in the proper fashion? I believe it is the outgrowth of both nature and nurture (Simonton, 1987a). Some happy intellects may be born with a proclivity for mavericity. Both psychiatric and psychometric studies have shown that creative individuals often display thinking patterns and attitudes that parallel those in psychotic populations (e.g., Barron, 1969; Götz & Götz, 1979a, 1979b; Gough, 1976; MacKinnon, 1962). These "thought disorders" may be subclinical, but they suffice to permit some bizarre conceptual tendencies, such as clang associations and overinclusive thinking. At the game time, we have ample evidence that these mental dispositions have a conspicuous genetic origin (Eysenck 1993). For example, creative personalities come from family pedigrees that contribute more than their expected share of psychiatric patients (e.g., Juda, 1949; Karlson, 1970; Richards, Kinney, Lunde, Benet & Merzel, 1988). Creative geniuses may have acquired some additional resources, such as ego strength, that permit them to keep up appearances despite the intrusion of psychopathic thinking tendencies (Barron, 1969). Hence, certain people may be born with a disposition to structure their knowledge in highly entropic associative networks (Eysenck, 1993). Once such people attain the 50,000 chunks, they are all get to burst out with insights.

Apart from any genetic component, environmental influences must play a role as well. Systematic analyses of the biographies of eminent creators reveal that they most often emerge from extremely rich, even chaotic childhoods (Goertzel & Goertzel, 1962; Goertzel, Goertzel & Goertzel, 1978; Roe, 1952; Simonton, 1984a, 1984c, 1992b; Walberg, Rasher & Parkerson, 1980). Their homes afford considerable amounts of intellectual and cultural stimulation. They usually acquire an early taste for omnivorous and voracious reading. Their home life may have been disrupted by broadening experiences, such as parental loss or financial ups and downs. Their educational achievements are sometimes uneven but varied, with a striking tendency away from conformity to a single way of looking at their discipline. They often study under more than one mentor and find inspiration among a diversity of predecessors. They may be either ethnically or professionally marginal, where this marginality enables them to see issues in a totally different light from the majority in their field. These and other antecedents of eminence all influence the developing creator, producing a person who can generate a more heterogeneous array of associative variations.

Short-term Preparation
The preceding section addresses long-term preparation for an entire lifetime of creative insights, yet preparation occurs on a shorters scale as well. The mind must prepare for single insights too. Seldom do creative individuals arrive at a finished solution to a critical problem all at once. Instead, it often takes a preparatory phase of preliminary work, during which the creator explores the possibilities and makes a few futile forays. After frustrated initial attempts at solution, the individual enters a period of incubation, during which other projects and responsibilities consume core attention. Only later will the insight appear in the guise of some illumination.

These constitute the first three steps of the creative process according to the classic treatment by Graham Wallas (1926), who inferred the steps from the introspective reports of historical geniuses such as Hermann von Helmholz. What is of interest here is how these steps fit in the Darwinian picture. To elucidate, we must return to Poincaré (1921, pp. 393–394), who suggested a solution using the imagery of the "hooked atoms" of thought mentioned earlier:

> The role of the preliminary conscious work ... is evidently to mobilize certain of these atoms, to unhook them from the wall and put them in swing. We think we have done no good, because we have moved these elements a thousand different ways in seeking to assemble them, and have found no satisfactory aggregate. But, after this shaking up imposed upon them by our will, these atoms do not return to their primitive rest. They freely continue to dance.... The mobilized atoms are ... not any atoms whatsoever; they are those from which we might reasonably expect the desired solution. Then the mobilized atoms undergo impacts which make them enter into combinations among themselves or with other atoms at rest which they struck against in their course.... However it may be, the only combinations that have a chance of forming are those where at least one of the elements is one of those atoms freely chosen by our will. Now, it is evidently among these that is found what I called the *good combination*.

In the language of cognitive psychology, the preparation phase has a *priming* function. Certain relevant associations must be activated. These activated associations then spread through the complex manifold of the associative network, generating a diversity of combinations (cf. Findlay & Lumsden, 1988).

The preparation period is followed by the incubation period in part because the proper combination may not be immediately forthcoming, even if all the necessary elements have been activated. The atoms may have to jostle about for a considerable time before a subset compound forms a stable configuration. More importantly, not all the mandatory parts of a viable solution may have been activated during the preparation phase. If a component is missing, the variations cannot converge on a solution no matter how long the ideas undergo permutation. Moreover, perhaps the only way the missing piece can become activated is by a rather tenuous and tortuous chain of associations (cf. Mednick, 1962), which may necessitate a reduced level of arousal, because high arousal tends to increase the dominance of high-probability associations at the expense of low-probability associations (Simonton, 1980; Zajonc, 1965). It's no accident, then, that the final insight may arise when the individual is engaged in some relaxing activity, as during Poincaré's beach stroll.

Yet this does not tell the whole story about the incubation phase. Frequently, the missing piece of the puzzle is inaccessible even should the creator walk up and down the coast a million times. The ideas already activated cannot, by themselves, excite into action the critical component. Instead, the mind must be primed by some external stimulus. Though arising unpredictably from the environment, this stimulus sets in motion a new chain of associations that converges with those activated at the preparation phase. The outcome is the long-sought insight. These extraneous inputs, moreover, need not operate in an obvious fashion, but rather subliminal stimuli may often do the trick nicely (see, for example, Maier, 1931).

It is my brief that this need for external, even if subliminal, associative priming is the main business of the incubation period. The hiatus between preparation and illumination is a period of vague searching for the missing associative link. Bombardment by the diversity of surrounding events eventually primes that train of thought that can connect the disparate parts of the desired Koestlerian bisociation. This priming process handily explains four contextual features of insights:

1. Insights frequently occur when the creator gives up on a particular problem and turns to other activities. Even taking a total vacation from professional concerns may expose the incubating mind to the influx of new and potentially fruitful associations.

2. Those individuals who are most prolific in the production of important insights commonly engage in many varied projects simultaneously (e.g., R.J. Simon, 1974; Tweney, 1990). As Poincaré (1921) indicated in the beach-stroll anecdote, the central component of a major synthesis often emerges from cross talk between hitherto unrelated works in progress. This cross talk helps account for why a creative career normally becomes what Howard Gruber (1989) aptly labeled a *network of enterprises*, a cluster of loosely connected projects.

3. Eminence in a creative endeavor is strongly associated with having many professional contacts (Simonton, 1984a, 1992a, 1992b). Whether deliberately or inadvertently, exchanges with rivals, correspondents, colleagues, collaborators, and other associates can prime new associative explorations.

4. Individuals who are most productive of original ideas usually display exceptional intellectual versatility (Raskin, 1936; Simonton, 1976; White, 1931). One manifestation of this versatility is an insatiable curiosity about developments beyond the confines of a particular specialty area. For instance, productive scientists are more likely to keep abreast of advances in fields far removed from their own (e.g., Manis, 1951; R.J. Simon, 1974). These outside interests mean that such intellectuals receive incessant stimulation from material that may excite a novel string of associations. Charles Darwin read the *Essay on Population* for recreation, yet the Malthusian thesis propelled Darwin toward the central insight of his own theory.

What these occasions share is the individual's exposure to stimuli that lie outside the restricted domain of the specific problem at hand. Accordingly, when the preparation period fails to get all the necessary atoms bouncing off one another, these incidental priming effects may loosen those missing atoms and thus catalyze the final insight. To return to the biological analogy, sometimes simple genetic recombination of parental genes is not enough to save a species from extinction. Instead, it may take the miracle of a random mutation to introduce new genetic material that can then produce more adaptive combinations.

Prediction

If what we have said is true, the insight process reflects very little foresight. The best long-term preparation is simply to acquire a rich base of knowledge that can support wild associations and, although short-term preparation for a particular problem can get the ball rolling, the creator may not identify a solution without first entering an incubation period. During this phase, various associative avenues are explored, sometimes at the subtle impetus of external events, with minimal a priori guidance. The mind does no more than generate ideational variations, typically at the fringes of awareness, in the blind hope that everything will coalesce into an answer. And as foresight's final disgrace, the whole process often converges on a solution to the wrong problem, as happens in serendipitous insights.

One would hope that once an insight had sprung out of the chaos, that product would at least bode well for the future, but the connection between insight and final creative success is not nearly so easy. At two levels, the personal and the social, the promise of insights may fail to be fulfilled.

Personal Prognosis
Creativity is a very wasteful business. It spews forth insight after insight, only a tiny fraction of which survive further scrutiny. The great Michael Faraday (quoted in Beveridge, 1957, p. 79) lamented:

[T]he world little knows how many thoughts and theories which have passed through the mind of a scientific investigator have been crushed in silence and secrecy by his own severe criticism and adverse examinations; that in the most successful instances not a tenth of the suggestions, the hopes, the wishes, the preliminatory conclusions have been realised.

Evidently, these false positives appear because they satisfy some crucial criteria without meeting all essential requirements. The insufficiencies are not realized until the tentative insight is placed under the intense light of evaluation.

Poincaré (1921) provided some fascinating introspections on this curious circumstance. He began by affirming that, in general, "the sterile combinations do not even present themselves to the mind of the inventor. Never in the field of his consciousness do combinations appear that are not really useful" (p. 386). He then immediately qualified this generalization by adding "except some that he rejects but which have to some extent the characteristics of useful combinations" (Poincaré, 1921, p. 386). Moreover, often sterile combinations enter awareness because they appeal to a mathematician's "emotional sensibility," especially the sense of "beauty and elegance" (p. 391). Therefore, occasionally "a sudden illumination seizes upon the mind of the mathematician ... that ... does not stand the test of verification; well, we almost always notice that this false idea, had it been true, would have gratified our natural feeling for mathematical elegance" (p. 392).

False insights are particularly likely when the more judgmental side of the mind is turned off; then incomplete syntheses can slip by a more rational evaluation. We get primary process without secondary process. Altered states of consciousness induced by certain drugs can provide a cornucopia of useless revelations. William James (1902, p. 387) gave a classic example in his *Varieties of Religious Experience*:

Nitrous oxide and ether, especially nitrous oxide, when sufficiently diluted with air, stimulate the mystical consciousness in an extraordinary degree. Depth beyond depth of truth seems revealed to the inhaler. This truth fades out, however, or escapes, at the moment of coming to; and if any words remain over in which it seemed to clothe itself, they prove to be the veriest nonsense. Nevertheless, the sense of a profound meaning having been there persists; and I know more than one person who is persuaded that in the nitrous oxide trance we have a genuine metaphysical revelation.

Given the occurrence of these specious inspirations, we must probably be forever cautious about screaming "I have found it!" The legend about the first bathtub revelation tells us that Archimedes ran home stark naked, hollering "Eureka!" to amazed bystanders. Imagine his chagrin if he had arrived home only to discern that his insight merely satisfied his emotional sensibility but was otherwise completely useless!

Social Prophecy

Alas! Even when the insight survives the next stage of the creative process—what Wallas (1926) called *verification*—the creator is not off the hook. This marks but the first level of a hierarchy of linked variation-selection processes. The creative genius presents to the world a vast array of insights, which then are accepted or rejected by contemporaries and posterity. Only a small percentage of a creator's life work will endure these further levels of selection. Consequently, the sole route to assured success is to generate a great profusion of varied insights and thereby maximize the odds that at least something will survive.

Frank Barron (1963, p. 139) phrased it well: "The biography of the inventive genius commonly records a lifetime of original thinking, though only a few ideas survive and are remembered to fame. Voluminous productivity is the rule and not the exception among the individuals who have made some noteworthy contribution." Thomas Edison obtained 1093 patents, many for totally worthless inventions. The futile development of one failed idea alone cost Edison all the money he had earned from the electric light bulb. Pablo Picasso created nearly 20,000 works over the course of his career, far from all claiming the status of master-pieces. Picasso himself admitted that many of his pieces were "fakes." Finally, W.H. Auden warned, because great poets are so prolific, "The chances are that, in the course of his lifetime, the major poet will write more bad poems than the minor" (quoted in Bennet, 1980, p. 15).

Hence, any creative career is a history of hits and misses. Some intellectual or aesthetic insights have an impact on potential ap-preciators, whereas others fall by the wayside and, apparently, the creative genius cannot do anything to escape this hit-or-miss happenstance. This inability is apparent in the *equal-odds rule* (cf. Simonton, 1988a). Suppose we follow the course of a creator's career by tabulating the number of offered works per consecutive interval, such as decades or half decades. Then let us determine the subset of these products that actually could count as suc-cesses, such as those journal articles that receive frequent cita-tions or those paintings that hang in the best museums. We can now calculate a quality ratio, or the proportion of hits to total attempts. How does this ratio change as the creator ages? Does it improve, as the genius gains heuristics that can bypass the chance permutation process, or does the ratio deteriorate as the creator's intellect deteriorates? The answer is neither of these. The quality ratio does not systematically change with age but rather fluctuates randomly throughout one's career. The odds of producing a successful work in any one period of a creator's life are simply a probabilistic function of the total number of insights offered (see, for example, Simonton, 1977, 1985)—in other words, the more shots at the target, the more bull's-eyes.

I believe that the absence of any trend is telling evidence to sup-port the conclusion that insights reflect little foresight. No creator can tell beforehand which of the many works he or she spawns will outlast the sociocultural selection process. Indeed, the biogra-phies of almost every creative genius mention personal favorites that failed to impress others as well as highly popular pieces for which the creators had little regard. Beethoven's Fifth Symphony was not *his* favorite product in that form, and among his piano compositions he had a rather low opinion of both his *Moonlight* Sonata and the bagatelle *Für Elise*. Einstein regretted his pioneering efforts in developing quantum theory, while proclaiming a unified field theory that his colleagues believed was sadly illconceived.

From a Darwinian perspective, episodes such as these should not surprise us. From the moment of conception, parents are absolutely ignorant of their offspring's prospects for survival. Ultimately, because the variation-generation process is blind, it displays no foresight. The The parents can do is beget a large brood in the hope that at least a few of their progeny will inherit the optimal combination to survive and propagate the family genes.

POSTSCRIPT

The implications of the Darwinian viewpoint are far more comprehensive and varied than could be outlined in this chapter. Nonetheless, to whet some appetites, allow me to enumerate but four extensions that warrant detailed discussion:

First, the model helps us accommodate the full range of mental processes involved in creativity (Eysenck, 1993; Kantorovich, 1993; Simonton, 1988c, chap. 2). For example, this perspective offers a special niche for the operation of otherwise bizarre mental imagery, such as homospatial and Janusian thinking (Rothenberg, 1979, 1986, 1987) and imageless thought (Roe, 1952). Such inclusiveness contrasts starkly with the explanations expressed in current cognitive psychology, which tends to stress only those processes that can be easily translated into computational models (Boden, 1991).

Second, a mathematical model derived from this theory predicts how insights are distributed over the course of a career (Simonton, 1984b, 1989). The model accounts for both individual differences and interdisciplinary contrasts in career trajectories, including the location of the first, best, and last major influential insight (Simonton, 1991a, 1991b, 1992a). One curious feature of this application is that it takes Poincaré's metaphor of the "kinematic theory of gases" seriously enough to derive differential equations that are formally similar to chemical reactions. However, instead of predicting the concentration of new compounds over the life of a test tube, the formula predicts the emergence of novel configurations over the career of a creator!

Third, this theory enables us to predict fluctuations in artistic styles. Colin Martindale (1986, 1990) not only has advanced just such an extension but has ingeniously tested its implications by applying computer content analyses to actual literary creations.

Fourth, the variation-selection model explains the circumstances that allow two or more individuals working independently to come up with identical insights (Simonton, 1979, 1987b). This is the phenomenon of multiple discovery and invention (cf. Lamb & Easton, 1984; Merton, 1961). In fact, a stochastic model based on the Darwinian premise can even handle the eventful case when both Darwin and Wallace independently arrived at the same evolutionary theory (Simonton, 1987b)!

REFERENCES

Austin, J.H. (1978). *Chase, chance, and creativity: The lucky art of novelty*. New York: Columbia University Press.

Barron, F.X. (1963). The needs for order and for disorder as motives in creative activity. In C.W. Taylor & F.X. Barron (Eds.), *Scientific creativity: Its recognition and development* (pp. 153–160). New York: Wiley.

Barron, F.X. (1969). *Creative person and creative process*. New York: Holt, Rinehart & Winston.

Bennet, W. (1980, January–February). Providing for posterity. *Harvard Magazine, 82*, 13–16.

Beveridge, W.I.B. (1957). *The art of scientific investigation* (3rd ed.). New York: Vintage.

Boden, M.A. (1991). *The creative mind: Myths & mechanisms*. New York: Basic Books.

Brown, R.W., & McNeill, D. (1966). The "tip of the tongue" phenomenon. *Journal of Verbal Learning and Verbal Behavior, 5*, 325–337.

Campbell, D.T. (1960). Blind variation and selective retention in creative thought as in other knowledge processes. *Psychological Review, 67*, 380–400.

Campbell, D.T. (1965). Variation and selective retention in socio-cultural evolution. In H.R. Barringer, G.I. Blanksten, & R.W. Mack (Eds.), *Social change in developing areas* (pp. 19–49). Cambridge: Schenkman.

Campbell, D.T. (1974). Evolutionary epistemology. In P.A. Schlipp (Ed.), *The philosophy of Karl Popper* (pp. 413–463). La Salle, IL: Open Court.

Campbell, D.T. (1991). Autopoietic evolutionary epistemology and internal selection. *Journal of Social and Biological Structures, 14*, 166–173.

Cannon, W.B. (1940). The role of chance in discovery. *Scientific Monthly, 50*, 204–209.

Chase, W.G., & Simon, H.A. (1973). Perception in chess. *Cognitive Psychology, 4*, 55–81.

Csikszentmihalyi, M. (1988). Motivation and creativity: Toward a synthesis of structural and energistic approaches to cognition. *New Ideas in Psychology, 6*, 159–176.

Darwin, F. (Ed.). (1958). *The autobiography of Charles Darwin and selected letters.* New York: Dover. (Original work published 1892)

Dryden, J. (1926). Epistle dedicatory of "The rival ladies." In W.P. Ker (Ed.), *Essays of John Dryden* (Vol. 1, pp. 1–9). Oxford: Clarendon Press. (Original work published 1664)

Epstein, R. (1990). Generativity theory and creativity. In M. Runco & R. Albert (Eds.), *Theories of creativity* (pp. 116–140). Newbury Park, CA: Sage Publications.

Epstein, R. (1991). Skinner, creativity, and the problem of spontaneous behavior. *Psychological Science, 2*, 362–370.

Eysenck, H.J. (1993). Creativity and personality: Suggestions for a theory. *Psychological Inquiries, 4*, 147–178.

Findlay, A. (1948). *A hundred years of chemistry* (2nd ed.). London: Duckworth.

Findlay, C.S., & Lumsden, C.J. (1988). *The creative mind: Toward an evolutionary theory of discovery and innovation.* San Diego: Academic Press.

Ghiselin, B. (Ed.). (1952). *The creative process: A symposium.* Berkeley: University of California Press.

Goertzel, M.G., Goertzel, V., & Goertzel, T.G. (1978). *300 eminent personalities: A psychosocial analysis of the famous.* San Francisco: Jossey-Bass.

Goertzel, V., & Goertzel, M.G. (1962). *Cradles of eminence.* Boston: Little, Brown.

Götz, K.O., & Götz, K. (1979a). Personality characteristics of professional artists. *Perceptual and Motor Skills, 49*, 327–334.

Götz, K.O., & Götz, K. (1979b). Personality characteristics of successful artists. *Perceptual and Motor Skills, 49*, 919–924.

Gough, H.G. (1976). Studying creativity by means of word association tests. *Journal of Applied Psychology, 61*, 348–353.

Greenwald, A.G. (1992). New Look 3: Unconscious cognition reclaimed. *American Psychologist, 47*, 766–779.

Gruber, H.E. (1989). The evolving systems approach to creative work. In D.B. Wallace & H.E. Gruber (Eds.), *Creative people at work: Twelve cognitive case studies* (pp. 3–24). New York Oxford University Press.

Hadamard, J. (1945). *The psychology of invention in the mathematical field.* Princeton, NJ: Princeton University Press.

Hayes, J.R. (1989). *The complete problem solver* (2nd ed.). Hillsdale, NJ: Erlbaum.

Holding, D.H. (1985). *The Psychology of chess skill.* Hillsdale, NJ: Erlbaum.

James, H. (1908). Preface to "The Spoils of Poynton." In *The novels and tales of Henry James* (Vol. 10, pp. v–xxiv). New York: Scribner's. (Original work published 1896)

James, W. (1880). Great men, great thoughts, and the environment. *Atlantic Monthly, 46,* 441–459.

James, W. (1902). *The varieties of religious experience: A study in human nature.* London: Longmans, Green.

Juda, A. (1949). The relationship between highest mental capacity and psychic abnormalities. *American Journal of Psychiatry, 106,* 296–307.

Kantorovich, A. (1993). *Scientific discovery: Logic and tinkering.* Albany, NY: State University of New York Press.

Kantorovich, A., & Ne'eman, Y. (1989). Serendipity as a source of evolutionary progress in science. *Studies in History and philosophy of Science, 20,* 505–529.

Karlson, J.I. (1970). Genetic association of giftedness and creativity with schizophrenia. *Hereditas, 66,* 177–182.

Koestler, A. (1964). *The act of creation.* New York: Macmillan.

Lamb, D., & Easton, S.M. (1984). *Multiple discovery.* England: Avebury.

Langley, P., Simon, H.A., Bradshaw, G.L., & Zythow, J.M. (1987). *Scientific discovery.* Cambridge: MIT Press.

Mach, E. (1896). On the part played by accident in invention and discovery. *Monist, 6,* 161–175.

MacKinnon, D.W. (1962). The nature and nurture of creative talent. *American Psychologist, 17,* 484–495.

Maier, N.R.F. (1931). Reasoning in humans: II. The solution of a problem and its appearance in consciousness. *Journal of Comparative Psychology, 12, 181–194.*

Manis, J.G. (1951). Some academic influence upon publication productivity. *Social Forces, 29,* 267–272.

Martindale, C. (1986). Aesthetic evolution. *Poetics, 15,* 439–473.

Martindale, C. (1990). *The clockwork muse: The predictability of artistic styles.* New York: Basic Books.

Mednick, S.A. (1962). The associative basis of the creative process. *Psychological Review, 69*, 220–232.

Merton, R.K. (1961). Singletons and multiples in scientific discovery: A chapter in the sociology of science. *Proceedings of the American Philosophical Society, 105*, 470–486.

Newell, A., & Simon, H.A. (1972). *Human problem solving.* Englewood Cliffs, NJ: Prentice Hall.

Nisbett, R.E., & Wilson, T.D. (1977). Telling more than we can know: Verbal reports on mental processes. *Psychological Review, 84*, 231–259.

Ochse, R. (1989). A new look at primary process thinking and its relation to inspiration. *New Ideas in Psychology, 7*, 315–330.

Perkins, D.N. (1981). *The mind's best work.* Cambridge: Harvard University Press.

Planck, M. (1949). *Scientific autobiography and other papers* (F. Gaynor, Trans.). New York: Philosophical Library.

Platt, W., & Baker, R.A. (1931). The relation of the scientific "hunch" to research. *Journal of Chemical Education, 8*, 1969–2002.

Poe, E.A. (1884). The philosophy of composition. In *The works of Edgar Allan Poe* (Vol. 5, pp. 157–174). London: Routledge. (Original work published 1846)

Poincaré, H. (1921). *The foundations of science: Science and hypothesis, the value of science, science and method* (G.B. Halstead, Trans.). New York: Science Press.

Price, D. (1963). *Little science, big science.* New York: Columbia University Press.

Qin, Y., & Simon, H.A. (1990). Laboratory replication of scientific discovery processes. *Cognitive Science, 14*, 281–312.

Raskin, E.A. (1936). Comparison of scientific and literary ability: A biographical study of eminent scientists and men of letters of the nineteenth century. *Journal of Abnormal and Social Psychology, 31*, 20–35.

Richards, R., Kinney, D.K., Lunde, I., Benet, M., & Merzel, A.P.C. (1988). Creativity in manic-depressives, cyclothymes, their normal relatives, and control subjects. *Journal of Abnormal Psychology, 97*, 281–288.

Roe, A. (1952). *The making of a scientist.* New York: Dodd, Mead.

Rothenberg, A. (1979). *The emerging goddess: The creative process in art, science, and other fields.* Chicago: University of Chicago Press.

Rothenberg, A. (1986). Artistic creation as stimulated by superimposed versus combined-composite visual images. *Journal of Personality and Social Psychology, 50*, 370–381.

Rothenberg, A. (1987). Einstein, Bohr, and creative thinking in science. *History of Science, 25*, 147–166.

Shapiro, G. (1986). *A skeleton in the darkroom: Stories of serendipity in science.* San Francisco: Harper & Row.

Shrader, D. (1980). The evolutionary development of science. *Review of Metaphysics, 34,* 273–296.

Simon, H.A. (1973). Does scientific discovery have a logic? *Philosophy of Science, 40,* 471–480.

Simon, H.A. (1986). What we know about the creative process. In R.L. Kuhn (Ed.), *Frontiers in creative and innovative management* (pp. 3–20). Cambridge: Ballinger.

Simon, H.A., & Chase, W.G. (1973). Skill in chess. *American Scientist, 61,* 394–403.

Simon, R.J. (1974). The work habits of eminent scientists. *Sociology of Work and Occupations, 1,* 327–335.

Simonton, D.K. (1976). Biographical determinants of achieved eminence: A multivariate approach to the Cox data. *Journal of Personality and Social Psychology, 33,* 218–226.

Simonton, D.K. (1977). Creative productivity, age, and stress: A biographical time-series analysis of 10 classical composers. *Journal of Personality and Social Psychology, 35,* 791–804.

Simonton, D.K. (1979). Multiple discovery and invention: Zeitgeist, genius, or chance? *Journal of Personality and Social Psychology, 37,* 1603–1616.

Simonton, D.K. (1980). Intuition and analysis: A predictive and explanatory model. *Genetic Psychology Monographs, 102,* 3–60.

Simonton, D.K. (1984a). Artistic creativity and interpersonal relationships across and within generations. *Journal of Personality and Social Psychology, 46,* 1273–1286.

Simonton, D.K. (1984b). Creative productivity and age: A mathematical model based on a two-step cognitive process. *Developmental Review, 4,* 77–111.

Simonton, D.K. (1984c). *Genius, creativity, and leadership: Historiometric inquiries.* Cambridge: Harvard University Press.

Simonton, D.K. (1985). Quality, quantity, and age: The careers of 10 distinguished psychologists. *International Journal of Aging and Human Development, 21,* 241–254.

Simonton, D.K. (1986). Stochastic models of multiple discovery. *Czechoslovak Journal of Physics [B], 36,* 138–141.

Simonton, D.K. (1987a). Developmental antecedents of achieved eminence. *Annals of Child Development, 5,* 131–169.

Simonton, D.K. (1987b). Multiples, chance, genius, creativity, and zeitgeist. In D.N. Jackson & J.P. Rushton (Eds.), *Scientific excellence: Origins and assessment* (pp. 98–128). Newbury Park, CA: Sage Publications.

Simonton, D.K. (1988a). Age and outstanding achievement: What do we know after a century of research? *Psychological Bulletin, 104,* 251–267.

Simonton, D.K. (1988b). Creativity, leadership, and chance. In R.J. Sternberg (Ed.), *The nature of creativity: Contemporary psychological perspectives* (pp. 386–426). New York: Cambridge University Press.

Simonton, D.K. (1988c). *Scientific genius: A psychology of science.* Cambridge, England: Cambridge University Press.

Simonton, D.K. (1989). Age and creative productivity: Nonlinear estimation of an information-processing model. *International Journal of Aging and Human Development, 29,* 23–37.

Simonton, D.K. (1991a). Career landmarks in science: Individual differences and interdisciplinary contrasts. *Developmental Psychology, 27,* 119–130.

Simonton, D.K. (1991b). Emergence and realization of genius: The lives and works of 120 classical composers. *Journal of Personality and Social Psychology, 61,* 829–840.

Simonton, D.K. (1992a). Leaders of American psychology, 1879–1967: Career development, creative output, and professional achievement. *Journal of Personality and Social Psychology, 62,* 5–17.

Simonton, D.K. (1992b). Social context of career success and course for 2,026 scientists and inventors. *Personality and Social Psychology Bulletin, 18,* 452–463.

Simonton, D.K. (1993). Blind variations, chance configurations, and creative genius. *Psychological Inquires, 4,* 225–228.

Skinner, B.F. (1972). *Cumulative record: A selection of papers* (3rd ed.). New York: Appleton-Century-Crofts.

Stein, E., & Lipton, P. (1989). Where guesses come from: Evolutionary epistemology and the anomaly of guided vision. *Biology & Philosophy, 4,* 33–56.

Sternberg, R.J. (1989). Computational models of scientific discovery: Do they compute? [Review of *Scientific discovery: computational explorations of the creative process*]. Contemporary Psychology, 34, 895–897.

Tweney, R.D. (1990). Five questions for computationalists. In J. Shrager & P. Langley (Eds.), *Computational models of scientific discovery and theory information* (pp. 471–484). San Mateo, CA: Kaufmann.

Walberg, H.J., Rasher, S.P., & Parkerson, J. (1980). Childhood and eminence. *Journal of Creative Behavior, 13,* 225–231.

Wallas, G. (1926). *The art of thought.* New York: Harcourt, Brace.

White, R.K. (1931). The versatility of genius. *Journal of Social Psychology, 2,* 460–489.

Zajonc, R.B. (1965). Social facilitation. *Science, 149,* 269–274.

15 Insight in Minds and Genes

David N. Perkins

How long does an insight take? If we look to our own experiences, our memories of those giddy moments when things fall into place, we probably answer "a few seconds" or "a few minutes." If we choose to answer from classic sources, we might remember Darwin in 1838, months into his struggle to find a mechanism for evolution, accidentally reading Malthus on the topic of population pressures and astounded by the conception of natural selection forming in his mind like a backward-running movie of a shattering pane of glass (Darwin, 1911). Alternatively, we might imagine Alexander Fleming in 1928, his attention caught by a spot of mold on a laboratory culture of bacteria, and how the crust of bacteria avoided the region of the mold; therefore, the mold must work against the bacteria—an "antibiotic" (Koestler, 1964).

The brevity of episodes of insight is one of their hallmarks. In contrast to the prestidigitator's "Now you see it, now you don't," insight follows the pattern "Now you don't see it, now you do." This observation does not mean that all the thinking gets done in the course of a minute or two. As will be seen later, a number of factors argue that the brief moments in which an insight builds and emerges should be considered only the tip of the iceberg of the phenomenon of insight. Nonetheless, the brevity, or at least the illusion of brevity, is one of the things to be explained.

One surprising path toward an explanation turns away from the obvious and natural focus on human cognition. When we say insight happens rapidly, inevitably our scale is a human one, bound up with our daily experience. But the human mind is not the only system that makes discoveries. Do other systems that make discoveries sometimes make sudden ones? Do they show analogs of the human phenomenon of insight and, if so, what can we learn about human insight through comparison?

The process of evolution is one such system of special interest here, for it creates. Indeed, it created us, the very creatures who are able to puzzle over such problems. Is there an analog of insight in the process of evolution? If there is, can we understand human insight better by looking at structural features of insight disclosed by comparing human discovery and evolution? Finally, how long does the evolutionary equivalent of insight take?

In a few sentences, those questions define the mission of this chapter—to illuminate human insight by comparing it with phenomena of biological evolution, events on a time scale some 10^{13} coarser, the ratio of a minute to 10 million years. To preview the argument, its principal propositions go something like this:

1. Human insight presents some typical characteristics, including a long search, a precipitating event, and a rapid culmination.

2. These characteristics can be generalized into the concept of *generative breakthrough events*, episodes of sudden innovation that might appear in any creative system, including evolution.

3. Evolution does offer insightlike episodes—that is, episodes with the characteristics of generative breakthrough events. The evolution of birds is one example; the creatures of the Burgess Shale near the dawn of multicellular life provide another.

4. The work of any creative system can be viewed as a process of search through a space of possibilities or a "possibility space."

5. The searches of creative systems commonly occur in possibility spaces with vast, relatively clueless regions, in the midst of which occur small pockets rich with clues, in which rapid progress can be made. Possibility spaces with this structure are called *Klondike spaces.*

6. Typical earmarks of insights (more generally, generative breakthrough events) such as suddenness are consequences of the Klondike topography. The basic phenomenon of insightlike episodes has little to do with intelligence or cognition.

7. Besides analyzing insight, it is worth analyzing insightfulness. The insightfulness of a creative system is its adaptation to the demands of effective search in a Klondike space. More insightful systems make more discoveries.

8. Human cognition not only generates insights but does so in an insightful way: That is, human processes of search often are well adapted to the topographies of Klondike spaces.

9. In contrast, evolution as classically conceived by Darwin lacks this insightfulness. It is a brute-force process.

10. However, modern conceptions of evolution suggest that evolution may be smarter than Darwin imagined. On a vastly greater time scale than human beings, genes in their passages and perturbations from generation to generation may function in an insightful way.

HUMAN INSIGHT: THE CASE OF DARWIN

The history of inquiry offers many tales of sudden insight. One of the best-known and most paradigmatic is Charles Darwin's discovery of the principle of natural selection. The example is doubly apt because it resonates well with the second theme of this chapter, not human insight but the insightlike episodes produced by the process of evolution itself.

In 1838, the young Darwin had returned some 15 months since from his famous 5-year voyage on the *Beagle*, a ship making geological and biological explorations. The flora and fauna Darwin surveyed at the Galapagos Islands and other sites convinced him that evolution was a reality. Nothing else made sense of the subtle variations and especially the *partial* adaptations that he encountered: If organisms were created to match their niches, adaptation would be perfect.

Evolution occurred, but how? Darwin cast about for months for a mechanism. Many of the ideas he conceived and recorded carefully in his notebooks seem strange from the standpoint of today's biological sophistication (Gruber, 1974; Perkins, 1981). Some appear more sensible—for instance, the analogy Darwin constructed between evolution and "artificial selection," the deliberate breeding of horses and other animals for desirable traits—but none quite gave Darwin the mechanism he sought.

The breakthrough came in the fall of 1838, in a moment seemingly away from the puzzle that had been nagging Darwin for more than a year. Darwin (1911, p. 68) captured the episode in his autobiography as follows:

In October 1838 that is, fifteen months after I had begun my systematic enquiry, I happened to read for amusement "Malthus on Population," and being well prepared to appreciate the struggle for existence which everywhere goes on from long-continued observation of the habits of animals and plants, it at once struck me that under these circumstances favorable variations would tend to be preserved, and unfavorable ones to be destroyed.

Darwin's notebooks of 1838 offer a closer scan of his response to his idea. Although he certainly found it of interest, he did not clear the decks to focus on it. Indeed, his notebooks reveal many other notions set down with equal enthusiasm. Darwin turned to other matters for some days and then revisited the idea of natural selection, expanding it and articulating it precisely. Soon it became the mainstay of his explanation for the origin of the species (Gruber, 1974).

Pivotal for paleontology, Darwin's moment of truth was emphatically ordinary as a moment of insight. A dozen other well-known epiphanies have much the same structure—for example, Alexander Fleming's discovery of penicillin, Roentgen's discovery of x-rays, Gutenberg's invention of the printing press, and Archimedes' probably apocryphal eureka experience on devising the principle of displacement of water (Koestler, 1964). We can understand at least the outer dress of insight better by listing its typical features.

1. *An insight follows a long search*: That is, characteristically people invest extended work on a problem before the insight occurs. In simple laboratory problems, this can be a matter of minutes. In Darwin's case, it took some 15 months by his own report (Darwin, 1911, p. 68). The insight may occur while one is actively working on the problem or, as in Darwin's case, while doing something else.

2. *An insight discloses the hidden*: Darwin's notion, simple-seeming in retrospect, did not come easily. Darwin did not publish his discovery for nearly 20 years, during which no other person arrived at the same conception. Alfred Russell Wallace (1905) independently devised the principle of natural selection in 1858, which finally mobilized Darwin to publish the theory jointly with Wallace.

3. *An insight is an achievement of understanding and thereby generative*: To have an insight into something is to understand the something better. Inherently, understanding is generative. It explains numerous specific cases (for instance, particular cases of adaptation) as well as leading to further enquiries.

4. *An insight begins with a precipitating event*: In the case of Darwin, the precipitating event was his reading of Malthus. Remarkably, Wallace (1905) came to the equivalent idea of survival of the fittest 20 years later while reading the same book!

5. *An insight is achieved rapidly, a kind of falling into place*: The autobiographies of both Darwin and Wallace disclose this rabbit-from-the-hat phenomenon (Darwin, 1911; Wallace, 1905).

These five features do not reflect any sort of theory about insight. Rather, they constitute surface observations. They mark five characteristics of episodes of insight highlighted in the literature. Perhaps the most conspicuous omission from the list is *incubation*, a period of inactivity between active work on the problem and achievement of a resolution during which progress is somehow made nonetheless. Writers such as Wallas (1926) and Hadamard (1949) have made much of this stage, but I do not include it here because I believe there is little evidence for it, a point that is argued later in this chapter.

One word of caution is in order. Not every cognition people term *insight* necessarily shows all five hallmarks. For example, sometimes we consider as insight an understanding hard-won through assiduous work over a long period of time, which lacks the fifth characteristic. Sometimes an insight may emerge with no obvious precipitating event, the fourth characteristic. Nonetheless, the five features together capture the prototypical episode of insight and thereby help to bound the phenomenon under investigation.

CREATIVE SYSTEMS

Examinations of scientific and humanistic creativity tend to focus on the human case, Einstein's on the heart of matter, Conrad's on the heart of darkness. However, systems other than the single human mind create. Consider culture as manifested in the social evolution of mores and languages. Rarely does anyone sit down to design a code of behavior or a syntactical construction, yet these structures evolve through the trials and transmissions of society (cf. Dawkins, 1976).

Machines also have been said to create in significant senses. In her recent book, *The Creative Mind*, Margaret Boden (1991) reviews the accomplishments of a number of artificial intelligence systems that produce drawings, mathematical theorems, and other products with some claim to originality.

Common to these cases of solo human, culture, and artificial intelligence is the generation of what might be called *adaptive novelty*. Something is produced—a sonnet, a syntactical construction, a corollary—that, on the one hand, serves some function in its context and, on the other, shows novelty in its context. The novelty may be only relative; many ideas and inventions are discovered and rediscovered. Nonetheless, from the standpoint of understanding the system—human, social, or machine—relative novelty is just as good.

The criterion of adaptive novelty suits a further case, indeed the one most often advanced as an analog of human creativity: the process of evolution (Campbell, 1960, 1974; Perkins, 1981, in press). At least in an analogical sense, evolution invents. It yields adaptive novelty in forms such as holly plants, humpback whales, and human beings. The ingenuity of nature is a classic theme in the writings of the great biologists, Darwin among them.

Let us call the several systems that produce adaptive novelty "creative systems" (Perkins, 1988b, 1992, in press). This opens the way for us to compare and contrast various creative systems, asking how each achieves what it does and articulating any general principles they share. One might object that all the other systems—culture, artificial intelligence, and evolution—fall significantly short of the human case and do not deserve to be labeled *creative*, but how short they fall is debatable. In any case, we gain more by adopting a broad rather than a narrow conception of creativity and investigating how creative systems achieve what they do. Contrasts among creative systems could teach us much about the special genius of each.

However, this chapter focuses not on creativity in general but on insight in particular. Therein lies a problem. In its prototypical meaning, *insight* refers specifically to an achievement of understanding. Darwin came to understand a possible mechanism of evolution through his insight about the "struggle for existence," and Gutenberg came to understand how to secure enough force to press ink into paper by observing a wine press (Koestler, 1964). But the dispersed social processes that generate customs and languages, and the biological processes that create new species, presumably do not understand anything: They are blind. The artificial intelligence programs discussed by Boden (1991) may sometimes be said to understand in limited senses, but here too the label can certainly be challenged.

If insights always involve understanding, we lose the opportunity to compare the human case with creative systems that, although they produce adaptive novelty, do not seem to produce understandings. However, there is a way around this dilemma. We can generalize the concept of insight. We can detach it from understanding specifically and look more broadly to the structural features of an episode of insight that do not depend specifically on understanding. Let us speak of a generative breakthrough event [GBE]. The characteristic profile of an insight can be recast in GBE terms as follows.

1. *A GBE follows a long search*: That is, a search touches on a large number of candidates—several dozens to millions—before the GBE occurs.

2. *A GBE discloses the hidden*: That is, it involves the discovery or generation of something at least rare and often masked by factors that divert the search.

3. *A GBE is generative, leading to a range of further developments*: Here the notion of understanding is dropped, but generativity, a key characteristic of understanding, is preserved.

4. *A GBE begins with a precipitating event.*

5. *A GBE is achieved rapidly, a kind of falling into place*: Rapidly is, of course, a relative term, particularly to the rate of search— that is, the GBE occupies much less total time than the preceding long search.

The source of these five characteristics should be clear. They are straightforward generalizations from the five characteristics of an episode of insight, the only really major adjustment being the third item. There, understanding is dropped as a criterion. However, the idea of generativity is preserved as a more general stand-in.

This generalization makes more apparent something present in the original list of five features: They employ a metaphor of search. The first speaks directly of search, the second of finding, the third of events leading on to other things. Of course, the use of concrete physical language to describe abstract processes is commonplace in human cognition (Lakoff & Johnson, 1980). However, the theme of search is meant more seriously here. Individual human creators, artificial intelligence programs, social processes such as those that develop languages and customs, and the process of evolution all can be said to search in some sense. A later section takes up this metaphor of search and makes it more precise. Meanwhile, with GBEs as a generalized conception of insight, let us turn to considering some candidate insights that unfolded in millions of years rather than tens of seconds.

EVOLUTIONARY INSIGHT

The Case of Birds

The emergence of birds is one of many evolutionary episodes of success snatched from the jaws of defeat. The losing jaws in this case are the dinosaurs, who departed this planet in a massive wave of extinction approximately 65 million years ago. It now is generally recognized that all modern birds descended from the dinosaurs, who therefore live on in aerial form. Some scholars have even proposed that the taxonomy of animals be rewritten to make birds a kind of dinosaur.

Evolution has been at work for nearly 4 billion years of the Earth's $4\frac{1}{2}$ billion–year history (Gould, 1989, pp. 57–58). But evolution's discovery of birds is particularly easy to relate to, both because birds fill our skies and because flight has figured centrally in humankind's hunger to master a greater range of environments. The basic timeline goes something like this:

180 mil. BC   Emergence of the dinosaurs.

170 mil. BC   Emergence of pterosaurs (pterodactyls), flying lizards.

215 mil. BC   Earliest fossil birds, protoavis, already with fully
developed feathers. Bird fossils from this era rare.
Pterosaurs continue to dominate the skies.

150 mil. BC   Archaeopteryx, the other known early fossil bird.
Pterosaurs still thrive.

95 mil. BC   Water birds similar to modern type appear.

65 mil. BC   Extinction of the dinosaurs, pterosaurs, and many
other forms of life.

35 mil. BC   Dramatic radiation of birds since the demise of the
dinosaurs, including flightless birds, many modern
types. Wesson (1991, p. 240) notes that "the profusion of specialized birds left the pterosaurs far
behind."

How well does this ladder of evolution match the features of a
GBE? Let us consider the features one by one.

• *Long search*: Evolution *is* a long search, ongoing all the time.
The process of variation and adaptation operates continuously,
seeking new and viable adaptive forms.

• *Disclosing the hidden*: Certainly, flight represents a radical departure from the initial adaptations of those organisms that have
achieved true wings, all of them initially ground dwellers. According to Wesson (1991, p. 47), winged flight has been "invented"
only five times in the history of the biosphere, by insects, pterosaurs, birds, and two different kinds of bats—fruit-eating and
insect-eating—which apparently evolved flight independently of
one another. Wesson argues that the especially distinctive achievement of birds is feathers, which are complex organs with intricate
interlocking structures that keep them light and stiff. Feathers
serve the purpose of insulation as well as flight. In contrast, fur-
like structures have evolved many times. Batlike wings have
evolved three times (pterosaurs and the two kinds of bats) but
feathered wings only once.

• *Generativity*: Flight yielded the entire range of birds in all their
variety, with adaptations to a wide range of very different ecologi-

cal niches. Gould (1989, pp. 297–298) notes that large ground birds even assumed the roles of major predators, and were at least as successful as marsupials, in South America before it become connected to North America a few million years ago.

• *Precipitating event*: As the chart above indicates, there seem to have been two critical junctures, not one—the development of feathers and at least partial flight approximately 200 million years ago, and the rapid adaptive radiation of birds some 50 million years ago. We can only speculate on the precipitating event of each because the early fossil record of birds is sparse.

As to the first, the precipitating event presumably was the accidental appropriateness of feathers for supporting partial flight, perhaps in the form of hopping and gliding. Preflight feathers may have been insulation for warm-blooded dinosaurs (Gould, 1980). Alternatively, brightly colored feathers along the "arms" of dinosaurs may have served as sexual displays, a pattern still evident in many modern birds (Wesson, 1991, p. 47).

As to the second precipitating event, the natural hypothesis looks to typical evolutionary opportunism: The birds were filling the ecological niches abandoned by the extinct pterosaurs.

• *Achieved rapidly*: Here again the story here has to take into account the two-phase evolution of birds indicated in the chart. Feathers appeared early in the fossil record. The first feathers anatomically have virtually the same structure as the feathers of modern birds (Wesson, 1991, p. 47), which suggests that feathers were rather rapidly achieved. Gould and others, propounding the contemporary view of punctuated equilibrium in evolution, note that many evolutionary adaptations seem to have been achieved rapidly on a geological time scale, rather than through gradual evolution (Gould, 1980, chapters 17–18).

Whereas feathers may have evolved quickly, birds were not a conspicuously successful species early on. Some 150 million years lay between the first birds and the great diversification of birds that in a period of 30 million years or so yielded a range of species similar to that we see today. This, then, was the second geologically sudden event in the development of birds.

The Creatures of the Burgess Shale

The development of birds is a late chapter in the story of the evolution of multicellular life, volume 2 of *Life on Earth.* Volume 1, concerning single-celled life, covers by far the longer period. Curiously, life in minimal form does not seem to be a difficult chemical achievement. Earth is approximately 4.5 billion years old. As far back as 3.75 billion years, there is evidence of life, which might have arisen even earlier; rocks older than this have been so transformed that they would not show signs of life anyway (Gould, 1989, pp. 57–58). Though long, this first volume is not especially dramatic. For almost 2.5 billion years, the only life forms were single cells of simple internal structure. More complex cells eventually developed and held center stage for another 700 million years.

One of the puzzles of the evolutionary record concerns why more complex multicellular forms of life took so long to appear. Apparently, the coordination of activities across cells to create larger organisms was a severe evolutionary challenge, which finally was met some 570 million years ago at the beginning of the Cambrian era, in what is called the Cambrian explosion. In the evolutionary blink of some 50 million years, a variety of complex multicellular life forms appeared in the seas.

Our best snapshot of life in those remote days comes from fossil samples gathered in the Canadian Rockies at the eastern border of British Columbia. The fossil deposits of the Burgess Shale, named after the nearby Burgess Pass by the great naturalist C.D. Walcott, were formed when undersea landslides occurred. These landslides swept tons of silt along with diverse organisms that lived in and above the silt down into lower waters. There, low-oxygen conditions deferred decay while the chemistry of fossilization went to work (Gould, 1989, pp. 64–70). The consequence 530 million years later is rich fossil beds preserving in stone not only the hard shell-like parts of those prehistorical organisms but the soft body parts as well. The summary timeline looks like this:

3.7 bil. BC   Chemical signs of life.

1.4 bil. BC   Complex cells appear.

570 mil. BC   Beginning of the Cambrian era, the Cambrian explosion of diversification of multicellular life.

530 mil. BC   Burgess Shale organisms. More recent findings at other sites suggest that the development of Burgess-like creatures stretches back into the early Cambrian era (Gould, 1989, pp. 224–227).

The fossils of the Burgess Shale have challenged in at least three ways the classic view of evolution. Traditionally, evolution has been seen as a gradual process that advances from more primitive and undifferentiated forms toward more precisely adapted forms, according to the survival of the fittest. First, far from being generic in their biological designs, the creatures of the Burgess Shale show rather subtle and complex adaptations to their ocean environment. They appear much more fine-tuned than one would expect at the dawn of multicellular life.

Second, hardly a few simple types, the Burgess fauna represent a far greater diversity of fundamentally different biological designs than have appeared anytime since. To appreciate this point fully, we need to remind ourselves that biologists organize the world of living things into a hierarchical taxonomy. At the top of this taxonomy sit the five great kingdoms of contemporary biology—animals, plants, fungi, complex single cells, and simple cells (including bacteria). The next division down consists of phyla. Although the exact number is somewhat debated, there are some 20 or 30 contemporary animal phyla, including such major phyla as annelids (worms and some related creatures), arthropods (insects, lobsters, crabs, etc.), mollusks (clams, snails, etc.), and chordates (creatures with backbones and a few others) (Gould, 1989, p. 99).

The Burgess Shale discloses some 15 to 20 animal organisms as different from today's creatures and one another as one would expect of separate phyla. In addition, the shale includes representatives of all the major modern animal phyla. A dilemma for taxonomists is whether actually to recognize each of these creatures as signifying a separate phylum (Gould, 1989, pp. 99, 208–209). Nonetheless, the structural contrast is there. This far-gone era hosted more fundamental structural diversity of animal forms than can now be found on the face of the earth. Far from evolution branching out like a tree from some primal type, it is as though evolution conducted a brainstorm, generating a diverse array and pruning down.

The final paradox of the Burgess Shale is that the obvious survivors were not always the actual survivors. For example, of two phyla of wormlike creatures, one thrives today in immense diversity, whereas the other survives only in a few odd forms. Yet the first of these was much the rarer in the Burgess Shale (Gould, 1989, pp. 292–295). The same has happened many times in evolution. Remember, the dinosaurs held sway for more than 100 million years. They were the only sizable land animals in their day. As Wesson (1991, p. 214) states, "There was no nondinosaur larger than a poodle during the dinosaur reign." Today, all gone. In the Burgess Shale, much of the future lay with some forms of life not at all dominant then. One of them was a rather innocuous creature called *Pikaia* that had the precursor of a backbone, a so-called notochord. *Pikaia* could be the ancestor of all the chordates, including us.

Again, it is worth taking stock of this episode in the history of the Earth's biota. Does the Burgess Shale tell us of another GBE?

• *Long search*: The search behind the Cambrian explosion was the longest, least superficially promising search in the history of life, more than 3 billion years from the earliest signs of life to the beginning of the Cambrian era.

• *Disclosing the hidden*: Several fundamentally different anatomical designs made their appearance in the Cambrian explosion, many indicative of phyla that do not exist today. Indeed, nature rarely produces something as radically distinct as a phylum.

• *Generativity*: The generativity of the Cambrian explosion shows clearly in the diversity of phyla.

• *Precipitating event*: Here there is little basis for speculation. Perhaps the event could have been a billion years earlier.

• *Achieved rapidly*: The Cambrian diversification occurred over a period of 100 million years or so. This is long even on a geological time scale, to be sure, but it must be measured against the preceding 4 billion years and the ensuing 500 million up to the present, during which no new major phyla appeared.

Thus, the creatures of the Burgess Shale offer a second and larger-scale example of the earmarks of a GBE. Of course, these are chosen cases, but many more can be found in the fossil record. As noted earlier, a number of paleontologists have urged that the evidence of the rocks denies the original notion of gradual evolution. Rather, organisms appear to emerge in a punctuate manner, with long periods of little change for a class of organisms interrupted by brief periods of rapid extinction, diversification, shift in dominance, and so on. Such circumstances inherently have most of the features of a GBE.

POSSIBILITY SPACES

The parallels between the GBEs of human insight and those of evolution are intriguing. Does some very general mechanism or factor—so general as to apply to human cognition over a matter of minutes and the work of evolution over millions of years—account for this similarity of structure? To pursue this question, we need some analytical machinery. Let us look to the notion of search through a possibility space.

The idea of possibility spaces (often called *problem spaces*) has played a central and generative role in cognitive science over the past 30 years (Boden, 1991; Ernst & Newell, 1969; Newell & Simon, 1972). To visualize this idea, consider for example the game of chess. The chess player, puzzling over a position, ponders the possibilities; he or she thinks ahead, for example moving a rook forward in the mind's eye, imagining the opponent's response, conceiving a counter to that. In other words, the chess player explores a branching tree of possibilities, finally choosing a move and making it actual.

Beyond the scope of a single move, an entire game of chess can be considered a journey through a vast space of possibilities. Every legal board position is a possible state in this space. Chess players start from the initial standard position. The player playing white ponders the immediate possibilities, chooses one, and moves the piece that makes that possibility real. The opponent responds in the same fashion. Move by move, the configuration of pieces on the board changes. As the players continue their game, they blaze a trail of states through the space of possibilities, each state connecting to the next via one or another player's legal move.

Ideally, it all ends with checkmate by one or another player. Each position that satisfies the conditions for a checkmate is, of course, also a state in the possibility space. All those checkmate positions are called *end states* because, when the play advances to those states, the game is over. The goal of play is to achieve one of these checkmate end states. Another kind of end state, to be avoided if you have a chance of winning, is *stalemate*, which constitutes a tie.

The notion of search through a possibility space has been used as a framework for investigating a number of formal well-defined tasks such as chess play, the proving of theorems in logic, and the solving of cryptarithmetic problems (Newell & Simon, 1972). In such research, the investigators typically develop a computer program that searches through immediate possibilities and chooses moves using some of the same principles that human beings seem to employ. What the computer does is compared to what human subjects do. If the match is good, this is evidence that the computer program constitutes a model of human cognition in that situation.

The concept of search through a possibility space also has been applied to understanding open-ended creativity, less constrained by formal rules. Some of this work involves functioning programs and some simply conceptual analyses. In any case, the focus falls on such creative pursuits as discovering scientific laws, developing inventions, or creating works of art (Boden, 1991; Perkins, 1981, 1992, in press; Langley, Simon, Bradshaw & Zytkow, 1987; Weber & Perkins, 1992).

Consider, for example, the poet at work on a poem. The states in the poet's possibility space might be considered partial poems, the words written down on paper thus far. The poet works with the partial poem of the moment, exploring alternative extensions—perhaps this line or that will do, perhaps this idea or that calls for expression. The poet may jot trial words in the margin. Eventually, the poet adds a word or a line, which is considered a move. It changes the partial poem into another larger partial poem. If the poet deleted something, this would change the current partial poem into another, smaller partial poem. Sometimes moves are more radical—for instance, discarding most of the poem in favor of a single line that represents a new point of departure. Thus, the poet moves through the possibility space of partial poems. When the poet judges the poem to be done, this is an end state.

Another example is an inventor at work designing a particular device. The inventor works with partial inventions, rough and incomplete mental and physical sketches. Each partial invention is a state in the space of possibilities the inventor is searching. The inventor makes moves by adding or subtracting features from the partial invention of the moment. Some moves may be more radical, scrapping an entire partial invention for a different point of departure toward the same goal. When the inventor arrives at a sketch that seems workable and efficient, this is an end state.

Thus far this discussion has illuminated nothing about creative thinking as such. It simply introduces a formalism, showing how such creative pursuits as poetry writing and the development of inventions can be treated as searches through possibility spaces. In the following sections, I will use the concept of possibility spaces to characterize some differences between less and more creative searches and to discuss the place of insights and, more generally, GBEs in all this.

In the meantime, three complications require comment. First, the chess player thinks of more than the configuration of pieces on the board, also entertaining general strategies and tactics. The poet, likewise, pays attention to more than the words on the page, thinking of general messages and moods to express, and the inventor thinks about more than the sketch of the moment. How does an analysis in terms of search through possibility spaces accommodate this?

In their classic writings on problem solving, Newell and Simon (1972) allow for *planning spaces*, conceptual structures more abstract and compressed than those of the base space (the configurations of pieces, the partial poems, the partial inventions). The inquirer can explore a planning space to generate plans and then translate them into concrete moves in the base space. Although not all plans play out well in the base space, the tactic is, in general, a powerful one. Through the notion of planning spaces, and perhaps other ideas in like spirit, the idea of search in a space of possibilities can honor the multilevel character of thinking.

A second complication concerns the end states in search through a possibility space. In cases such as chess play, the end states are set in advance by the strict formal rules. In contrast, in many creative endeavors, the goals and, hence, what count as end states evolve along with the problem. The poet may start out with only the vaguest idea of the shape of the ultimate poem. Part way through, the poet may substantially revise the direction of the work in response to emergent opportunities, as may the inventor. Indeed, Getzels and Csikszentmihalyi (1976) have found such sudden shifts to be a hallmark of what they term *problem finding*, a trait demonstrably related to creative productivity.

Accommodating this feature of creative search requires expanding the notion of search through a possibility space. We must acknowledge that goals (which are criteria for satisfactory end states) may shift as the search proceeds. The overarching aim of the search process becomes to find a state of the search space that satisfies the current state of the evolving goals. Moreover, some searches have no final end states, only temporary ones. Poets may go back to poems and revise them after years have passed. Inventors constantly return to their own and others' inventions and improve them further.

A third complication recognizes that the possibility space may change during the actual course of the search. For instance, in the case of the inventor, someone else may invent something similar to the target device, propose an advancement that obviates the need for the target device, or make a related technical breakthrough that eases the way to the target device. Not only may circumstances change the possibility space but the search process itself might do so. As a result of work in a planning space, possibilities may come to be represented in a new way. For instance, an inventor might decide to represent circuits as a matrix of connections among components rather than as a circuit diagram.

KLONDIKE SPACES AND HOMING SPACES

With the notion of possibility spaces at hand, we must still address how that notion can clarify the nature of insight. A clue comes from a classic parable of cognitive science, Herbert Simon's story of the ant. In *The Sciences of the Artificial*, Simon (1981, p. 63) wrote:

We watch an ant make his laborious way across a wind- and wave-molded beach. He moves ahead, angles to the right to ease his climb up a steep dunelet, detours around a pebble, stops for a moment to exchange information with a compatriot. Thus he makes his weaving, halting way back to his home.

Simon goes on to ask how we should understand the complexity of the ant's path. He suggests that the complexity lies in the terrain, not the ant. The ant is a rather simple mechanism responding to an intricate topography. This suggestion can be extended to the general idea of search in possibility spaces: The possibility spaces of chess play, poetry writing, or other pursuits are complex, whereas the basic mechanisms of human behavior, Simon urges, are rather simple. We need to understand the complexity of the paths people trace as they think, not so much in terms of complex psychological mechanisms as in terms of the topography of the possibility spaces through which they search.

This is a bold statement, perhaps too bold. There is no need here to press a case for Simon's proposition in its fullest form. However, I will argue in the next few pages that the key characteristics of GBEs (including human insights) should be seen as consequences of general features of the topography of the possibility spaces concerned. This argument requires definition of two extreme kinds of topography that a possibility space might have.

Homing Spaces

The first of these is called a *homing space* (Perkins, 1992). The key characteristic of a homing space is its clue-rich character. By definition, in a homing space clues that point the way toward end states—that is, toward the goal—are abundant. By tracking these clues, the search mechanism can home in fairly easily on a resolution to the task at hand.

For example, imagine a good student working on an algebraic word problem involving the setting up and solving of a quadratic equation. The process is not truly algorithmic, but how to proceed is not mysterious. The student begins to set up an equation by translating the givens of the problem. Then the student searches briefly for a solution by factoring. If factoring does not serve, the student adopts an algorithmic method such as the quadratic formula. Note that a not-so-good student will not fare as well. The good student, by definition, can read the clues in the situation and discern reasonable actions to try next. The point is that the clues are there. A typical algebraic word problem is clue-rich for those familiar with that kind of terrain. The path toward the solution is relatively straightforward.

For another example, imagine a fellow writing a letter to protest irregular trash pickups in his neighborhood. The person, in effect, is searching through a space of partial letters to arrive at a complete and satisfactory letter for his purpose. This space of partial

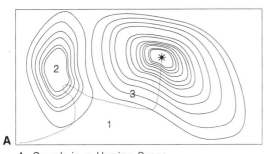

A. Search in a Homing Space
   1. Small clueless regions. 2. Occasional false
   targets. 3. Large clued regions lead to the target.

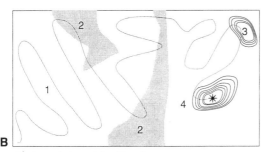

B. Search in a Klondike Space
   1. Large clueless regions. 2. Barrier regions of low promise.
   3. False local Homing region. 4. Local Homing region.

Figure 15.1

letters is full of clues to the person with some experience in letter writing: Is the inside address and conventional greeting in place? Does the letter have a good opening? Does it state its concern promptly and clearly? Does it give evidence of the problem? Does it request the corrective action desired? As the writer starts with the first words of his partial letter, these remind him of other needs. Soon the first draft is done. Some editing may ensue, though probably not radical revision. The writer has homed in on a satisfactory letter with relatively few detours.

As these examples suggest, successful navigation in a homing space is very much a matter of expertise as defined in contemporary cognitive psychology (e.g. Chase & Simon, 1973; Chi, Glaser & Rees, 1983; Ericsson & Smith, 1991). If you are expert enough to know the signs and what to do about them, you can find your way to a solution fairly readily. Homing spaces invite this sort of convergent thinking.

Figure 15.1A illustrates a homing space in abstract form. The contour lines represent the presence of clues that point the way toward end states. An effective search process climbs the contour lines toward an end state. Of course, homing spaces are not entirely benign. One hazard is a trail of false clues leading to a nonsolution, as illustrated in the figure. However, again by definition, in a homing space such false solutions are not plentiful.

Klondike Spaces

A different kind of possibility space topography makes more creative demands. In a *Klondike space*, by definition, no clear path of clues leads to goal states (Perkins, 1992, in press). Imagine, for instance, searching for gold in the Klondike. Pockets of gold occur here and there in the gravel deposits and riverbeds, but just where is hard to say. One needs to cast about, try downstream and over the hill, look for surface signs. Only when one gets close and detects the glitter among the gray pebbles can one home in.

Alternatively, imagine a poet at a difficult juncture, striving for just the right word or phrase. Perhaps much of the poem has come easily, in homing style, but here an expression is needed that the poet cannot easily craft. The poet casts about, tries this and that. Nothing seems right. Finally, a phrase appears promising. The poet modifies it, then modifies it again. Yes, that will do. The poet's initial wide-ranging search shifts to a rapid homing process to refine a promising lead.

These examples illustrate the casting about forced by the lack of clues in a Klondike space. They also illustrate another point: Klondike spaces typically have miniature homing spaces within them: That is, when one gets close enough to an end state in a Klondike space, one begins to see clues that point the way.

It is also allowed, by definition, that Klondike spaces can have low-grade clues, indications of promise that make some regions better bets than others without pointing a clear path to an end state. For instance, in the Klondike metaphor, the miners know something about the kind of topography that at least shows promise. This can be as much of a trap as a help: Sometimes goal states may lie isolated from the point where the search starts by intervening regions of low promise. Then effective search requires large jumps and new starts in fresh regions, rather like miners skipping one valley that shows no signs of gold and going on to try the next.

Figure 15.1B represents a Klondike space in abstract form. The same sorts of contour lines as in figure 10.1A appear here too but in much smaller regions. An effective search process needs to cast about, exploring the space widely in order to hit on clues that then point the way to an end state. Effective search may require a search process that finds its way into whole new regions of the possibility space, again as illustrated in the figure.

Thus, in a Klondike space, a clue-following strategy is not enough. A clue-following strategy only serves when one is close to an end state. The human problem solver at work in a Klondike space needs, in addition to conventional clue-oriented expertise, another kind of expertise. An effective search process in a Klondike space involves casting a wide net, avoiding redundant coverage of the same regions, searching for new regions altogether, and so on. Roughly, a more divergent style of search is required.

INSIGHT IN MINDS AND GENES

The notions of Klondike and homing spaces help us understand GBEs in both evolution and human thinking by locating the origins of the key features of a GBE in the topography of the possibility space searched rather than in the mechanisms of the search process. In particular, search that occurs in a Klondike space tends to show a GBE story line. The GBE story line gets imposed by the structure of the space as follows (also see figure 15.1B).

• *Long search*: Because a Klondike space does not provide good information about where to search next, search processes run long, with modest progress.

• *Finding the hidden*: Goal states are hidden by low frequency, lack of clues, and barrier regions of low promise.

• *Precipitating event*: With good fortune, eventually a search hits on one of the local homing space regions embedded in the Klondike space.

• *Final achievement rapid*: Relatively rapid progress follows as the search mechanism takes advantage of the homing clues.

The one aspect of a GBE not captured by the Klondike model is generativity. A goal state encountered in the Klondike space need not be generative, leading on to diverse other goal states. Correspondingly, in evolution some organisms are very successful in themselves but are not bridges to further diversification. In human affairs, some inventions address their target problems very well but lead to little else. Generativity, in effect, is yet another desideratum beyond viability or functionality. *Generative* solutions in the possibility space would be even more sparsely distributed than solutions in general, and thereby would be all the more subject to the GBE pattern.

This argument shows how search in a Klondike space accounts for the pattern of a GBE. It remains to be argued whether evolution and human thinking conduct searches in Klondike spaces—that is, whether they proceed in possibility spaces with large clueless regions and small isolated regions of promise and payoff.

To evaluate the case of evolution, we need to envision the possibility space of biological organisms. Every state in this space is a possible, but not necessarily viable, organism. Imagine a selection of anatomical and physiological structures cobbled together to constitute a candidate organism. Most of these configurations will not be viable. Indeed, a standard point in evolutionary biology is that most mutants are harmful rather than helpful. Viable forms are rare rather than common, and even more so forms that have great potential to prove generative, radiating outward into a great range of adaptations, as with birds.

In the classic Darwinian model of natural selection, evolution searches by means of the generate-and-test cycle of natural selection. Genetic variation yields new trial organisms that either survive and thrive or die off. The rarity of viable forms argues that this search process occurs in a Klondike space. The GBE structure commonly encountered in evolution emerges more or less inevitably in consequence of the structure of that space.

We also find in evolution episodes of more continuous change as an organism homes in on a particular form. A classic example is the evolution of the horse from a relatively small animal some 55 million years ago to the modern large horse, a series of steps well-documented in fossils (Wesson 1991, p. 40). This is, of course, a homing process, a sign that within the Klondike space of evolution abide homing space regions.

In the human case, the general answer to whether search occurs in Klondike spaces is no. To deal with the problems they face, people rely on an enormous knowledge base about what those problems are like, the expertise that serves us so well in familiar circumstances (e.g., Chase & Simon, 1973; Chi, Glaser & Rees, 1983; Ericsson & Smith, 1991). By drawing on their knowledge resources, people home in rather quickly on adequate resolutions to most problems they face, with a modest amount of search.

One reason that human endeavor has a predominantly homing character is that we human beings make it that way. The character of a search space, whether Klondike or homing or something in between, is not solely determined by the problem at hand. It is the joint consequence of the problem at hand and the knowledge embedded in the search process. For example, a high school algebra problem may be a pure trial-and-error problem for a student who does not know algebra. To that student, it presents a Klondike space. In contrast, for the student familiar with algebraic techniques, it presents a homing space through which the student can smoothly navigate to a solution. General and specialized knowledge of various sorts embedded in the search process helps to make more like a homing space what otherwise might present a pure Klondike challenge.

Despite all that, many problems and opportunities faced by human individuals and humankind in general *do* have a Klondike character. They outstrip the ready reach of the knowledge base accumulated by the individual or society. They also often violate assumptions embedded in that knowledge base, assumptions that, in effect, hide solutions. As already noted, the historical record around Darwin's discovery of the principle of natural selection constitutes an argument that the idea of natural selection is far from obvious. The same can be said for many discoveries that follow the GBE pattern. Thus, we have the many episodes of insight that pepper the history of inquiry.

In summary, evolution, by its very nature, operates in a Klondike space (with some qualifications, as noted in the final section of this chapter) and has many consequent GBEs. In contrast, human thinking operates most of the time in homing spaces, but enough Klondike circumstances arise to generate plenty of GBEs over which to marvel. It should be added that the stark contrast between Klondike and homing spaces overdraws the matter for explanatory purposes. A more subtle account could speak of possibility spaces in which Klondike and homing aspects predominate to varying degrees.

Other Klondike Spaces

An analogy between human insight and evolutionary GBEs has been developed at some length. It is fair to ask whether these are unique examples or whether other processes show a similar GBE pattern. A brief examination of three examplary cases—artificial evolution, perceptual shifts, and humor—will serve to illustrate that indeed the GBE pattern does occur elsewhere, and for similar reasons.

Note that none of these cases involves creativity of a high order, as did Darwin's invention of the theory of natural selection or evolution's "invention" of innumerable subtly adapted organisms. These are examples on a much more modest scale. Indeed, in the case of humor, hearers of a joke deserve hardly any credit for their Klondike search for meaning, as the joke is designed to lead the hearers' cognitions to the preordained insight. Nonetheless, all these cases involve search processes that proceed at some length because resolutions are rare, are not clearly pointed to by clues along the way, and often are masked by other factors. Thus, we see the typical Klondike profile with its GBE.

Artificial Evolution
This refers not to biologists' efforts to create evolution in the laboratory but to a thriving area of computer science. In a number of ways, programmers are seeking to simulate evolutionlike processes in computers. Such a program typically uses a variation of what is called the *genetic algorithm* (Langton, Taylor, Farmer, & Rasmussen, 1992; Levy, 1992, pp. 153–187). The computer begins with a random collection of data structures that often themselves are small programs. A testing process eliminates a percentage that are deemed less fit. A reproduction process copies the remainder to fill out the collection again, also introducing random mutations and sometimes combining parts of one data structure with parts of another, an analog of sexual reproduction. Then the process repeats.

A number of these simulations have shown that the genetic algorithm can produce good results. The data structures improve dramatically over time by whatever criterion is in use, often in ways hard to anticipate. Moreover, two of the programs that simulate organic evolution most closely show the pattern of GBEs highlighted here. As the genetic algorithm runs, long periods of stability appear, punctuated by sudden shifts in the dominant data structures. At a very general level of analysis, the reason for these shifts appears to be the Klondike factor articulated earlier: More viable data structures in the evolutionary world created by the program are statistically rare, and they also often are hidden because they involve a substantial shift from the data configurations that predominate at a given point. Consequently, the search process shows the typical Klondike profile of sudden relatively rapid progress after a period of little change.

Perceptual Shifts
Perceptual shifts are a familiar laboratory phenomenon in perceptual psychology. The classic example is the Necker cube, a drawing of a transparent cube that every few seconds spontaneously seems to shift into a different orientation. Another is the well-

known beauty-crone figure that sometimes looks like a lovely woman, sometimes like an aged crone. In effect, a perceptual shift constitutes an insight into an alternative viewing of the stimulus at hand.

The story behind many such perceptual shifts seems to be this: The perceptual system searches for interpretations of the stimuli put before it as a form in space—for instance, a cube in a certain orientation. Indeed, the work of the perceptual apparatus can be viewed as a search process that tests hypotheses (Gregory, 1970, 1972) or that seeks to optimize certain variables (Attneave, 1982; Perkins, 1982). Even after an initial interpretation is achieved, search continues for alternative interpretations. However, alternative interpretations that make sense are statistically rare. Most stimuli, unlike Rorschach inkblots, do not have alternative, radically different interpretations, and those that do usually have only one or two others. Moreover, the interpretation initially made tends to mask others (Wyatt & Campbell, 1951). This is a Klondike pattern. In keeping with such a pattern, perceptual shifts occur after some time but then rather rapidly.

Humor
The connection between humor and insight has often been noted (e.g., Koestler, 1964; Perkins, 1981). Much humor has the pattern of a long lead-in followed by a moment of insight where the joke comes together and we laugh. Typically, the punch line of a joke lets us see the story-so-far in a new light, restructured in a manner that gives it very different implications. For example, there is the tale of the priest bragging to the rabbi about how well his nephew is doing in the hierarchy of the Catholic Church—first a priest, then a bishop, then a cardinal, and now even being considered for pope. In a proper telling, all this is spun out at some length. At each stage, the rabbi is conspicuously unimpressed. In frustration, the priest finally speaks out, "What do you want—Jesus Christ himself?" The rabbi's reply: "Well ... one of our boys made it."

Here the Klondike plotline seems to go as follows. As we hear a story-based joke, or any narrative for that matter, we engage in a search for meaning. We build a mental model of how the elements fit together. There are not many alternative major understandings of the story, and a good joke keeps clues out of the way until the end so as to avoid giving away the climax. The punch line of the joke is a calculated precipitating event. It triggers a restructuring of the meaning of the story-so-far. In the case of the preceding joke, we discover that becoming pope is not all that impressive when measured by the standard to which the rabbi alludes.

INSIGHTFULNESS IN MINDS AND GENES

I have argued that even the blind search mechanism of Darwinian evolution can produce GBEs. The leap to a resolution characteristic of insight has nothing to do with intelligence. It reflects the topography of the possibility space being searched and occurs in cases when the search process is mindless.

However, we cannot conclude from these arguments that minds have nothing to offer GBEs, that Darwin and others who have achieved notable insights needed no special mental reach. Rather, to give the mind its due, instead of focusing on insights, we should focus on *insightfulness*, by which I mean the extent to which the search process in question is adapted to cope well with search in a Klondike space. Does the search process in question easily get lost, cover old ground, get trapped in regions of marginal promise, or easily miss clues when they do occur? Or does the search process avoid such hazards? None of these contrasts affect the basic hallmarks of a GBE, but they all affect how often GBEs are likely to occur.

In insightfulness rather than insight, we find the real difference between minds and Darwinian evolution. The searches human beings conduct are much better tuned to cope with the hazards of Klondike spaces than is the blind search process of Darwinian natural selection. (Later, I will argue that Darwinian evolution is probably too simple a model of evolution anyway; genes may be more insightful than they seem from the Darwinian perspective.) Let us look at several contrasts between the insightfulness of minds and genes.

• *Knowledge-driven thinking*: Natural selection, as usually conceived, has no memory. The cards of genetic diversity are shuffled, dealt, and fall as they may. As already emphasized, modern psychology has recognized how profoundly people depend on a rich knowledge base. Even when a human inquirer faces a Klondike problem, the knowledge the inquirer has often includes more clues to seek, more guideposts along the way to a solution. The knowledge in effect creates larger homing spaces inside the Klondike space, reducing the time that needs to be invested in divergent search.

• *Generating good bets*: Relatedly, when humans engage in generate-and-test strategies, the items that get generated tend to be so-called good bets. For example, master chess players tend to generate good moves right away, before extended search (Chase & Simon, 1973). Better poets tend to produce better candidate lines when they brainstorm options (Perkins, 1981). In effect, some constraints that the search process might have applied in filtering options after generating them instead get applied more efficiently in guiding the generation of options in the first place (Perkins, 1981, 1988a, 1988b). As classically conceived, nature simply shakes the genes up and takes a chance.

• *Brainstorming*: When human inquirers face impasses, they often deliberately widen the scope of search, brainstorming a number of very different approaches. Variation in natural selection usually is thought of as blind to the pressures of the moment. It introduces the same degree of variation in easy times or hard.

• *Looking for generativity*: Natural selection, as usually conceived, cares only about survival, not generativity. It does not seek out organisms with high potential for further diversification. In contrast, human inquirers often deliberately search for theories and frameworks with generative potential.

• *Pursuing promise*: A basic limitation of natural selection, as usually conceived, is that it operates only through trying out organisms that can actually survive. In natural selection, there is no such thing as a promising first draft. Human creators commonly deal with promising first-draft inventions, theories, poems, and so on, that are not at all viable as they stand. Natural selection would count them all as failures and look elsewhere.

• *Planning*: As mentioned previously, search in a single possibility space does not honor the richness of human cognition. Poets and inventors not only navigate in the possibility spaces of partial poems and partial inventions but think about their enterprise more broadly—where they are going, how they might get there, what might go wrong. They think in possibility spaces of goals and plans as well as the base space of poems or inventions. Natural selection makes no allowance for such planning levels of search.

In these and other ways, human inquirers show a great deal more insightfulness than natural selection: That is, human search is much more finely adapted to the challenges of Klondike spaces that work against achieving GBEs. Not only are people better than evolution at handling Klondike spaces; it seems that people can improve at it. Note that many of the characteristics admit of improvement: One can learn to plan better, commit oneself to looking for generativity, and adopt strategies of brainstorming. Such tricks of the creativity trade, straightforward though they seem, are not common coin. Research on the personalities and thinking characteristics of more versus less creative people shows clearly that workaday thinking often is not very well adapted to Klondike challenges (cf. Perkins, 1981, 1990, 1992).

I will not pause here to make an elaborate case for the notion that people can learn to be at least somewhat more creative (see Perkins, 1984, 1990). Instead, I will emphasize one simple point. As described earlier, most human thinking has a homing character, yet Klondike situations, when we encounter them, have their distinctive demands. Most people simply are not very well prepared to recognize or cope with those peculiar demands, not because they are so difficult to manage but because they call for a style of thinking rather different from the usual homing mode of operation.

OTHER VIEWS OF INSIGHT

The view of insight developed here is unusually abstract. It deliberately reaches beyond the human case to consider other creative systems and resists the conclusion that insight is a distinctively human or even intelligent phenomenon. It looks to very general characteristics of possibility spaces to account for the principal features of insight, and it looks to very general characteristics of search processes to account for insightfulness. How does all this compare with efforts to explain insight that cleave closer to the human case and the details of human cognition? Let us briefly consider several such accounts.

Selective Encoding, Combination, and Comparison

Sternberg and Davidson (Davidson & Sternberg, 1984; Sternberg, 1985) argue that insightful thinking depends on high selectivity in cognitive processing. In particular, they urge the importance of three processes: selective encoding, selective combination, and selective comparison. Selective encoding involves high and appropriate discrimination in encoding the relevant attributes of a situation. Selective combination involves assembling the elements of a situation into situation-relevant wholistic configurations. For instance, Darwin's theory of natural selection is identified as a case of selective combination: The facts with which Darwin worked had been available for some time. Selective comparison involves finding nonobvious links between new and old information, as for instance in constructing an analogy.

Selective processing does not appear to speak specifically to the hallmarks of insight identified earlier. More selective processing presumably would help with all sorts of cognitive activities, not just insight. More selective processing would improve homing searches as much as searches in Klondike spaces.

However, selective processing does help to explain insightfulness, why some people achieve insights that others do not. More selective processing would aid in the detection of clues scattered here and there in a Klondike space. This, in turn, would lead to more precipitating events. More selective processing would also aid in the consequent homing search.

Indexing and Retrieval Mechanisms

Langley and Jones (1988) propose an account of insight that specifically denies the role of search in a possibility space. These authors suggest that initial efforts to solve the problem at hand establish mental structures readily retrieved when a stimulus later proves relevant to the problem. Thus, for instance, Darwin could recognize the potential significance of Malthus's ideas to his dilemma even though he might not have been thinking about evolution at the time.

I agree that something like this happens in many episodes of insight. Indeed, under the label *noticing*, I have proposed a rather similar mechanism (Perkins, 1981), although not at the level of details offered by Langley and Jones. In the present framework of Klondike and homing spaces, the stimulus that triggers a recognition is a precipitating event. Unless this event proves to be a false alarm, what ensues is a homing search that proceeds toward a resolution.

However, let me suggest that the analysis of Langley and Jones (1988) does not actually deny the central role of search through possibility spaces in the sense developed here. Instead, their account makes the point that insights may occur when a person is not consciously searching. Nonetheless, search is search, whether it occurs consciously and deliberately or by way of unconscious recognition mechanisms. Once set up by deliberate effort with a problem, those unconscious mechanisms basically constitute another mechanism of search operative even though the person may not be concentrating on the problem consciously. These mechanisms presumably also do service while the problem solver *is* focusing on the problem.

Problem Restructuring

Ohlsson (1984a, 1984b) argues that insight characteristically involves problem restructuring. In approaching a problem in a conventional way, the thinker may encounter an impasse—that is, he or she can see no way to proceed. This impasse encourages the thinker to reach for a new way to represent the problem. If the thinker succeeds in this quest, the new problem representation may open a ready path to a resolution.

Ohlsson's account seems entirely consistent with the view presented here. As mentioned earlier, a search through a possibility space may include work in an associated planning space that leads to restructuring the nature of possibilities, in effect modifying the possibility space itself. The kind of restructuring Ohlsson describes amounts to work in a planning space that redefines the possibility space. Search then proceeds in a reformulated possibility space with a different and more tractable structure, perhaps indeed more of a homing space. Basically, problem restructuring is one kind of precipitating event accessible to human cognition but presumably not to Darwinian natural selection and other mindless search processes.

Incubation

Not uncommonly, insights occur after some period of time away from the problem. This might happen for many reasons. For instance, the problem solver may recognize problem-relevant clues that happen to come up later or may forget entrapping assumptions during a delay before returning to the problem (Langley & Jones, 1988; Perkins, 1981).

However, some hold that during periods of incubation, reasoning proceeds unconsciously (Hadamard, 1949; Wallas, 1926). The suddenness of insight reflects the abrupt surfacing into consciousness of the gradually developed conclusions. Indeed, the term *incubation* usually connotes something of the sort. This account therefore offers an explanation for the suddenness of insight entirely different from the present Klondike space account.

The resolution, in this case, is to reject incubation as an explanation. There are at least two reasons to do this. First of all, most of the accounts of sudden insight simply do not require an appeal to extended unconscious reasoning. As I argued in *The Mind's Best Work* (Perkins, 1981), noticing and other mechanisms explain them perfectly well. Second, psychologists have sought evidence of incubation in laboratory studies (e.g., Dreisdadt, 1968; Olton, 1979; Olton & Johnson, 1976). Typically, subjects work on a problem for a while, take a break, and then return to the problem. Control subjects work without a break but for the same total length of time. Sometimes the experimenter may provide environmental features to provide clues if the subjects are alert enough to notice them. These studies generally show no impact of the inactive period, although the presence of environmental clues can help. In summary, there is little reason to believe that incubation, in the sense of extended unconscious reasoning, exists.

In Summary

With the exception of incubation, the present view of insight is consistent with several other accounts in the literature. The view elaborated here simply analyzes the phenomena of insight at a greater level of abstraction. Mechanisms such as problem restructuring, noticing the relevance of environmental cues, and selective combination of cues are merely several among many ways in which a precipitating event can occur.

The specificity of these accounts is both an advantage and a limitation. They offer the benefits of more detailed mechanisms but encompass less well the generality of the phenomenon. With the exception of selective processing, another limitation seems to be that they have more to do with insight than with insightfulness. They recount what happens when an insight occurs and the factors that make our minds ready for insights but say less about what makes a search process, in all its aspects, more likely than another to yield insights and why. Note that much of the insightfulness of human search does not concern the breakthrough episode specifically. Such characteristics as brainstorming and looking for generativity have to do with the general management of the search rather than specifically with breakthrough episodes. In other words, insightfulness does not focus solely on moments of insight. Rather, insightfulness has to do with the entire conduct of search in Klondike circumstances. Actual moments of human insight are the tips of a much larger iceberg of insightfulness.

ARE GENES INSIGHTFUL AFTER ALL?

I have argued that the Darwinian process of variation, selection, and preservation appears to offer little room for insightfulness. As classically conceived, the process involves no mechanisms for controlling the manner of search or tapping prior knowledge. Evolution simply flails about, trial and error in its purest form.

If evolution is so uninsightful a process, how does evolution come up with the breakthroughs that it does? The usual answer to this is brute force. Natural selection proceeds over millions and millions of years, and evolution proceeds in a parallel manner, trying out many different variations during the same generation. With its long time scale and parallel processing, natural selection can achieve amazing biological designs through a relatively dumb process.

However, some evolutionists have challenged this picture and the classic mechanism of natural selection itself. They have urged either that more is going on than natural selection or, at least, that natural selection involves helpful complications beyond a simple rolling of the genetic dice each generation. Let us revisit some of the categories of insightfulness mentioned earlier to determine whether insightfulness might be found not just in human thinking but in evolution too.

Knowledge-driven Thinking

In the human genome, up to 99 percent of the genes do not function to direct the development of the organism (Wesson, 1991, p. 229). They are passive or latent. Similar figures apply to other organisms. It has been suggested that these passive genes constitute a repertoire of adaptations that can be invoked from the history of the organism. One phenomenon indicative of this is the rapid response many insect species make to insecticides (Wesson, 1991, pp. 236–237). Some develop heritable resistance within a single harvest season, which suggests the activation of existing latent resources more than a haphazard genetic search for a new solution, a homing rather than a Klondike process.

Generating Good Bets

Human thinkers generate likely candidates for the challenges they face. In laboratory studies, bacteria often adapt in very few generations to feed on substances they normally cannot use at all (Wesson, 1991, p. 234), which suggests that whatever trial variants are generated are good bets to take advantage of the available nutrients. The good bets may come from a latent repertoire, as in knowledge-driven thinking.

Brainstorming

Human thinkers at an impasse sometimes generate a diverse set of possibilities. Likewise, under a variety of stress conditions many organisms can increase the rate of mutation, "brainstorming," as it were, to find a new path (Wesson, 1991, pp. 238–239).

Looking for Generativity

Human inquirers often seek out specifically generative theories and frameworks, ones that lead to other things. In the biological world, high variation is especially advantageous in times of rapid change, with consequent adaptation pressure. In conditions that call for diversification, organisms apparently can become genetically predisposed to vary genetically: change itself becomes an agenda. Experiments in selecting bacteria for variability show that the bacteria increased in variability, preserving variability itself as a trait (Wesson, 1991, p. 211). One organism displaying high variability is a species of cichlid fish. The young of a single brood show major variations in teeth and the structure of the digestive system. Perhaps because of this high variability in the cichlid fish generally, cichlid fish over a period of 1 million years have differentiated into some 300 species, many with very different life-styles, in seven East African lakes (Wesson, 1991, p. 211).

Pursuing Promise

Human inquirers often try out imagined versions or prototypes before the real thing. In the higher organisms capable of considerable learning, something structurally analogous appears to happen in the evolution of behaviors. Often, learning drives evolution (Wesson, 1991, p. 241). For instance, a bird or a mammal might learn some initial adaptations to a new ecological niche, although very imperfectly attuned to it. Then adaptation pressures go to work, making the learned adaptations genetic and adding others.

The initial learning is structurally analogous to the human's pursuit of promise. An animal, within the scope of its lifetime, can try out a new niche—indeed several—and often withdraw unscathed if unsuccessful. If the creature proves somewhat successful, it may occupy the niche, and its progeny and others of its kind follow suit. The longer-term higher-investment process of genetic evolution can proceed. Organisms that do not learn as well cannot take advantage of this trial-run pattern.

Insightful Genes

These examples suggest that evolution may be insightful after all. There is no mystical or teleological intent to this statement; it posits no god or other master planner behind evolution. Rather, evolution may be insightful in the sense defined earlier: The process of evolution may be well adapted, in a number of ways, to search in a Klondike space, much better adapted than the classic Darwinian trial-and-error process would suggest.

Of course, the features of evolution mentioned previously do not always challenge natural selection as the basic underlying mechanism, but they at least point out that natural selection operates within a supportive context, a repertoire of passive genes, creatures that can learn and hence try out new niches in their lifetimes, and so on. Hence, to understand how the mechanism of evolution searches, it simply is not enough to speak of random variation and survival of the fittest, even if that is the core of the process.

By comparing human inquiry to the process of evolution, we get a better fix on those characteristics of search that suit the challenge of Klondike spaces, and we find that many of the phenomena of insight and insightfulness are systemic rather than specific to the human case. We even disclose what is arguably a new case of thinking in a broad sense, the heuristic search process that evolution undertakes. The process of evolution seems to have as much of a claim to thinking as many programs in artificial intelligence research (cf. Boden, 1991).

If so, the case of evolution would provide the *Guiness Book of Records* with the slowest "thinking" process known. Remember the opening question, how long does an insight take? Along the way we have identified some insightlike events in evolution that spanned a few million years. But, of course, the principle of brevity still holds. This is the mere wink of an evolutionary eye.

ACKNOWLEDGMENT

Some of the ideas in this chapter were developed under a grant from the MacArthur Foundation. I thank the foundation for its encouragement and support.

REFERENCES

Attneave, F. (1982). Pragnanz and soap bubble systems: A theoretical explanation. In J. Beck (Ed.), *Representation and organization in perception*. Hillsdale, NJ: Erlbaum.

Boden, M. (1991). *The creative mind: Myths and mechanisms*. New York: Basic Books.

Campbell, D. (1960). Blind variation and selective retention in creative thought as in other knowledge processes. *Psychological Review, 67,* 380–400.

Campbell, D. (1974). Evolutionary epistemology. In P.A. Schilpp (Ed.), *The Philosophy of Karl Popper* (Vol. 14, parts I and II). La Salle, IL: Open Court.

Chase, W.C., & Simon, H.A. (1973). Perception in chess. *Cognitive Psychology, 4,* 55–81.

Chi, M.T.H., Glaser, R., & Rees, E. (1982). Expertise in problem solving. In R.J. Sternberg (Ed.), *Advances in the psychology of human intelligence* (pp. 7–75). Hillsdale, NJ: Erlbaum.

Darwin, C. (1911). *The life and letters of Charles Darwin* (Vol. 1) (Francis Darwin, Ed.). New York: Appleton.

Davidson, J.E., & Sternberg, R.J. (1984). The role of insight in intellectual giftedness. *Gifted Child Quarterly, 28,* 58–64.

Dawkins, R. (1976). *The selfish gene*. New York: Oxford University Press.

Dreisdadt, R. (1968). An analysis of the use of analogies and metaphors in science. *Journal of Psychology, 71,* 159–175.

Ericsson, K.A., & Smith, J. (Eds.). (1991). *Toward a general theory of expertise: Prospects and limits*. Cambridge, England: Cambridge University Press.

Ernst, G.W., & Newell, A. (1969). *GPS: A case study in generality and problem solving*. New York: Academic Press.

Getzels, J., & Csikszentmihalyi, M. (1976). *The creative vision: A longitudinal study of problem finding in art*. New York: Wiley.

Gould, S.J. (1980). *The panda's thumb: More reflections in natural history*. New York: Norton.

Gould, S.J. (1989). *Wonderful life: The Burgess Shale and the nature of history*. New York: Norton.

Gregory, R.L. (1970). *The intelligent eye*. New York: McGraw-Hill.

Gregory, R.L. (1972). A look at biological and machine perception. In B. Meltzer & D. Michie (Eds.), *Machine intelligence 7*. Edinburgh: Edinburgh University Press.

Gruber, H. (1974). *Darwin on man: A psychological study of scientific creativity*. New York: Dutton.

Hadamard, J. (1949). *The psychology of invention in the mathematical field*. Princeton, NJ: Princeton University Press.

Koestler, A. (1964). *The act of creation*. New York: Dell.

Lakoff, G., & Johnson, M. (1980). *Metaphors we live by*. Chicago: University of Chicago Press.

Langley, P., & Jones, R. (1988). A computational model of scientific insight. In R.J. Sternberg (Ed.), *The nature of creativity: Contemporary psychological perspectives* (pp. 177–201). Cambridge, England: Cambridge University Press.

Langley, P., Simon, H.A., Bradshaw, G.L., & Zytkow, J.M. (1987). *Scientific discovery: Computational explorations of the creative processes*. Cambridge: The MIT Press.

Langton, C.G., Taylor, C., Farmer, J.D., & Rasmussen, S. (1992). *Artificial life II*. Redwood City, CA: Addison-Wesley.

Levy, S. (1992). *Artificial Life: The quest for a new creation*. New York: Pantheon.

Newell, A., & Simon, H. (1972). *Human problem solving*. Englewood Cliffs, NJ: Prentice Hall.

Ohlsson, S. (1984a). Restructuring revisited: Summary and critique of the Gestalt theory of problem solving. *Scandinanvian Journal of Psychology, 25*, 65–78.

Ohlsson, S. (1984b). Restructuring revisited: An information processing theory of restructuring and insight. *Scandinavian Journal of Psychology, 25*, 117–129.

Olton, R.M. (1979). Experimental studies of incubation: Searching for the elusive. *Journal of Creative Behavior, 13*(1), 9–22.

Olton, R.M., & Johnson, D.M. (1976). Mechanisms of incubation in creative problem solving. *American Journal of Psychology, 89*(4), 617–630.

Perkins, D.N. (1981). *The mind's best work*. Cambridge: Harvard University Press.

Perkins, D.N. (1982). The perceiver as organizer and geometer. In J. Beck (Ed.), *Representation and organization in perception*. Hillsdale, NJ: Erlbaum.

Perkins, D.N. (1984). Creativity by design. *Educational Leadership, 42*(1), 18–25.

Perkins, D.N. (1988a). Creativity and the quest for mechanism. In R.S. Sternberg & E. Smith (Eds.), *The psychology of human thought* (pp. 309–336). Cambridge, England: Cambridge University Press.

Perkins, D.N. (1988b). The possibility of invention. In R.J. Sternberg (Ed.), *The nature of creativity: Contemporary psychological perspectives* (pp. 362–385). Cambridge, England: Cambridge University Press.

Perkins, D.N. (1990). The nature and nurture of creativity. In B.F. Jones & L. Idol (Eds.), *Dimensions of thinking and cognition instruction*. Hillsdale, NJ: Erlbaum.

Perkins, D.N. (1992). The topography of invention. In R.J. Weber & D.N. Perkins (Eds.), *Inventive minds: Creativity in technology*. New York: Oxford University Press.

Perkins, D.N. (in press). Creativity: Beyond the Darwinian paradigm. In M. Boden (Ed.), *Dimensions of creativity*. Cambridge, MA: MIT Press.

Simon, H.A. (1981). *The sciences of the artificial*. Cambridge: MIT Press.

Sternberg, R.J. (1985). *Beyond I.Q.: A triarchic theory of human intelligence*. New York: Cambridge University Press.

Wallace, A.R. (1905). *My Life* (Vol. 1). New York: Dodd, Mead.

Wallas, G. (1926). *The art of thought*. New York: Harcourt, Brace.

Weber, R.J., & Perkins, D.N. (1992). *Inventive minds: Creativity in technology*. New York: Oxford University Press.

Wesson, R. (1991). *Beyond natural selection*. Cambridge: MIT Press.

Wyatt, D.F., & Campbell, D.T. (1951). On the liability of stereotype or hypothesis. *Journal of Abnormal Social Psychology, 46*, 496–500.

16 An Investment Perspective on Creative Insight

Robert J. Sternberg and Todd I. Lubart

We usually assume that so-called insightful people possess one or more abilities that less insightful people either lack or possess only in limited degree. The insightful person is perhaps better at reorganizing or reformulating problems, at finding shortcuts to problem solving, or at breaking through mental blocks. Clearly, more insightful people are better endowed with certain abilities than are less insightful ones.

Yet such abilities may be the beginning rather than the end of the story. Despite the screening for abilities that occurs before people become scientists, literary scholars, philosophers, or artists, how many truly insightful people do we meet in any pursuit? Is it possible that with all our screenings for ability, we are missing something that is not, strictly speaking, an ability at all?

If we start with the nature of an insight, we start with a thought that seems (subjectively) to come out of nowhere to surprise, to delight, and to represent an unexpected twist in the route to the solution of some problem. In essence, a problem, or a route to problem solution is suddenly reformulated. Whereas the routine problem or solution to a problem may be available to anyone, the insightful solution is available to only a few. If everyone has access to it, it seems to lose its character as an insight or, at least, as a creative insight, because creative insights are distinguished by their novelty as well as their quality and appropriateness.

In this chapter, we argue that creative insight requires a specific attitude in addition to cognitive abilities. This attitude is one of searching for the unexpected, the novel, and even for what others might label as bizarre. The creatively insightful person seeks the paths that others avoid or even fear; he or she is willing to take risks and stray from the conventional. Drawing on concepts from the world of financial investment, we call this attitude for insight a willingness to buy low and sell high. We will use investment concepts throughout this chapter to offer a new perspective on insight, particularly the attitude needed for insight. Previously, we have found the investment metaphor to be useful for examining creativity in general (Sternberg & Lubart, 1991a, 1991b, 1992).

Before we turn to the investment view, however, we want to clarify the relationship between the *attitude* for insight and the cognitive *abilities* for insight. We propose that the buy low–sell high attitude puts an individual in the right frame of mind for using his or her insight-relevant abilities most effectively. Following Davidson and Sternberg (1986), we consider these cognitive abilities to be selective encoding, selective comparison, and selective combination. *Selective encoding* is the noticing of potentially relevant information for a problem from amidst a stream of available information. *Selective comparison* involves the perception of an analogy between old and new information. Finally, *selective combination* refers to the meaningful synthesis of disparate information in a new way. These information-processing skills are discussed in chapter 4.

INVESTMENT AND CREATIVE INSIGHT

The standard advice given to an investor in the financial markets is to buy low and sell high. What could be more obvious? Yet even though everyone knows that one should follow the buy low–sell high strategy, few people do so (Dreman, 1982). Look at the New York Stock Exchange. When the market is low, there is relatively little buying or selling, whereas when the market is high, there is much more activity.

What Almost Everyone Knows and Almost No One Does

Of course, one might attribute this counterproductive trend to only the novices, to the small investors who do not know any better, but this would be incorrect. Even expert managers of mutual funds seem not to heed their own advice. Consider the following story, which elucidates this fact. In June 1967, the editors of *Forbes* magazine threw darts at the New York Times stock market page. The 28 stock listings that the darts pierced became the basis for a simulated stock portfolio, with $1000 invested in each stock. Seventeen years later, the $28,000 portfolio was worth $131,697.61, a 470 percent gain equal to a 9.5 percent annual compounded rate of return. Only a minuscule number of mutual fund portfolios exceeded this rate of return during the same period (Malkiel, 1985).

One might attribute the success of the editors to sheer brazen luck, but the fact is that random selections of stocks via computer perform at nearly the level of the *Forbes* portfolio and surpass the performance of the large majority of mutual funds. Moreover, even mutual funds that do better than average in 1 year have only a 50 percent chance of doing so the next. Very few managed funds consistently perform better than would be expected by chance, and most perform worse (Malkiel, 1985). Whatever these managers may be doing, they are not buying low and selling high.

Why is it that even expert fund managers, who often are paid extraordinary amounts of money for their financial management expertise, do not buy low and sell high? Are they like overweight weight-reduction experts, addicted drug counselors, or divorced marriage therapists? Or is there something else going on here, something subtle that makes it difficult to follow the best advice even if that is what one wishes?

Successful investors have to be bold enough to take risks and ready to act contrary to the behavior of other investors. They may have to take short-term losses for long-term gains. There is no guarantee when or whether one's stocks will increase in value.

However, to be bold is difficult. When a professional fund manager buys out-of-favor stocks, he or she seems even more foolish than an individual amateur investor, who has only his or her own money to lose. The fund manager has the money of thousands or even tens of thousands of people in his or her hands. The pressure to produce favorable results is enormous.

Suppose, though, that the financial instrument bought by the individual investor or fund manager shows a gain, and thus becomes widely recognized as a good investment. Its value will rise rapidly, and it will no longer be possible to buy it at a low share price. The investor who formerly seemed foolish will now seem prescient; she cornered the market when others did not know how. All sorts of people will be clamoring for her financial acumen and advice.

Buy Low, Sell High: A Key to Creative Insight

Buying low and selling high, treated metaphorically, can be viewed as an attitude for approaching a problem or project. In this arena, *buying low* means actively pursuing ideas that are unknown or out of favor but that have growth potential, whereas *selling high* involves moving on to new projects when an idea or product becomes valued and yields a significant return.

For creative insight to occur, a person must be willing to buy low—to entertain unusual, novel, or unpopular ideas for solving a problem at hand. Often, insightful solutions are blocked, we suggest, because the problem solver never allows himself or herself to explore whole regions of the potential solution space. People tend to buy high, pursuing only those potential problem solutions or ideas that are obvious or commonly chosen routes to problem solution. Why do people limit themselves when working on a problem or project? As in financial investment, the key may be the *risks*, which are inherent to buying low.

THE ELEMENT OF RISK

Risk, in general, is defined as "the possibility of loss or injury" (*Webster's Ninth New Collegiate Dictionary*, 1983). In financial investments, it is "the chance that expected security returns will not materialize and, in particular, that the securities you hold will fall in price" (Malkiel, 1985, p. 187). In practical terms, most would agree that risk is the chance of a loss, and losses are indeed possible when one is gambling with either money or ideas.

Two Kinds of Risk

There are two types of risk to be considered: market risk and specific risk. *Market risk* depends on the financial health of a market as a whole. *Specific risk* depends on the trends of a specific security, on top of the vagaries of general market trends. One can invest in indexed mutual funds that are pegged to and so reflect the activity of representative market stocks, hence taking market risk. One can also invest in a specific industry, such as pharmaceuticals and, by so doing, will assume specific risk as well, because pharmaceuticals will perform partly as a result of the market as a whole and partly as a result of what is occurring within that industry.

These risks apply directly to creative insight. Buying low in any domain entails risk, for the field, product, or idea in which one invests may never succeed. Just as not all stocks that are of low value will ever go up, not all ideas or solution paths that are untested will yield creative insights. Indeed, one can expect that a majority will not. Someone who buys low and sells high must be a maverick, ready to take chances and possibly fail.

Market and specific risks come into play for creative insight as well as financial investment. Basically, every project or problem that may yield creative insights involves multiple nested risks. For example, if a person decides to study acquired immunodeficiency syndrome (AIDS), the search for creative insights into the disease involves at least two levels of risk. First, research on the topic in general may not yield any insightful results. Second, there is risk associated with the particular methodology chosen to study AIDS.

To buy low, one must take the risk that what one buys at a low price will later increase in price. When selling high, one also assumes the risk that what one sells at a high price may increase in value still more. It is never certain. It has been found that, on average, return increases with risk but not proportionately to the amount of risk taken (Malkiel, 1985). Still, those who do not take chances will not reap the rewards.

Problem Framing

An important factor that affects risk taking is the way in which a problem is framed. Framing effects arise when alternative outcomes are evaluated in relation to different points of reference (Kahneman & Tversky, 1982). Different framings of a scenario can lead a person to take greater or lesser investment risks. Kahneman and Tversky (1982) have found that most people are risk-aversive when choosing between potential gains but that they are risk-seeking when choosing between potential losses. For example, if someone has a 100 percent chance of winning $80 versus an 85 percent chance of winning $100 but also a 15 percent chance of winning nothing, he or she will probably pick the risk-averse situation and opt for the 100 percent chance of winning $80. In contrast, consider a bet with the odds framed in terms of losses. If a person has a 100 percent chance of losing $80 versus an 85 percent chance of losing $100 and a 15 percent chance of losing nothing, she or he will probably choose the second bet, giving the wagerer the chance of losing nothing at all. Thus, whether one selects the more risky bet depends on whether gains or losses are involved.

How are these findings potentially relevant to the study of creative insight? For the most part, creative insights involve a potential gain, which, according to Tversky and Kahneman (1982), means that people will tend to be risk-aversive. To the extent that we see less creativity than we would like, this risk aversion may be a cause.

People's willingness to take risks for achieving creative insights may depend in part on the way these risks are presented to them. For example, perhaps one is considering drafting an offbeat, original annual report for a superior, thereby risking either praise or condemnation. The individual could try to fill the report with insightful ideas, but these ideas will defy conventional company thinking. Whether one dares to have the insightful ideas in the first place may depend on whether one imagines the outcome in terms of potential gains (praise, a raise, perks) if the report is favorably received or potential losses (disfavor, loss of supervisor's respect) if it is rejected. The same considerations could be applied to decisions such as whether to embark on a long-shot scientific project, to create an avant-garde poem, or to write a nonstandard term paper in school.

Taking Risks

Beyond the effects of problem framing, people generally show an aversion for risk taking, preferring to work with ideas that are already fairly well developed and accepted (Dreman, 1977; Kahneman & Tversky, 1982; MacCrimmon & Wehrung, 1985). To anyone who has withstood the isolation and, often, the ridicule of going against the trends, this aversion for risk taking is not surprising. Approbation and rewards do come to those who break molds, but breaking molds is not for the faint hearted.

Risk aversion may ultimately be traced to a low tolerance for failure. An interesting study by Clifford (1988) shows that failure tolerance declines as children progress through school, perhaps owing to systemic rewards for good grades. Clifford presented fourth, fifth, and sixth graders with math, spelling, and vocabulary problems that were marked as varying in difficulty from a second-grade level to a ninth-grade level. Fourth graders chose problems rated 6 to 8 months below their ability level; fifth graders chose problems meant for the beginning of fourth grade; and sixth graders chose problems rated $1\frac{1}{2}$ years below their difficulty level.

Nonetheless, we believe that at least some people are not content to follow the crowd; they have both the desire and the ability to buy low. In our discussion and examples of creative insight, we want to stress that we are not speaking only of the Copernicuses and Einsteins of the world: Neither financial nor creative success is limited to well-heeled or high-stakes individuals. In the financial world, there are both large-scale and small-scale investors, just as there are in creative investment. We often think of creative insights in terms of those who have achieved fame—for instance, the evolutionary theory of Charles Darwin or the architectural works of Frank Lloyd Wright. However, creative insights are exhibited by more than the rarefied fraction of the population who engage in high-level or public pursuits. They can be found in our daily lives—in cooking, raising children, remodeling or decorating a home. Furthermore, it is not an all-or-none phenomenon. There is a continuum of creative insights, just as there is a continuum of risks and profits across investments.

INVESTMENT STRATEGIES

Assuming one is willing to take some risks, how does one go about actually making an investment of time and energy to yield creative insights? Strategies that are useful in selecting financial investments can also be employed in the creative domain. Our discussion of investment strategies (this section) and investment vehicles (the next section) addresses the issue of *sustaining* creative insights beyond an isolated occurrence. In other words, we are interested in how a person goes about choosing a domain or topic so that multiple insights are possible, leading to a series of creative products. Consider two of the main strategies used to make investment decisions—technical analysis and fundamental analysis—and their implications for sustained creative insights.

Technical Analysis

Technical analysis is the study of past financial trends to predict future market behavior. It derives from the sound psychological principle that the best predictor of future behavior is past behavior of the same kind. By examining trends and especially cycles, technical analysts predict where things are going on the basis of where they have been. A technical analyst sees the market as largely psychological rather than logical because people, in general, and investors, in particular, create markets that repeat past patterns of behavior. Use of technical analysis requires both knowledge and intelligence—the knowledge to know what trends to look for and the intelligence to know how to interpret and extrapolate from them.

Technical analysis can be applied to creative work as well as to financial markets as both can be cyclical. One need not be a fashion designer to know that this is true of neckties, for example, which vary from wide to narrow and back again, conservative to flamboyant patterns and back again, and so on. In the scientific world, much the same thing happens. In psychology, for instance, models of how the mind works were for many years serial, implying that events are mentally processed in succession. Then parallel models were introduced that suggested mental events are processed all at once. Later, it was shown that parallel and serial models seem to be pretty much indistinguishable, in that one can always mimic a parallel model with a serial one, or vice versa, so parallel models were out again. Now, however, they have regained enormous popularity.

The implication for creative insight is that by studying trends in one's field, one can learn to identify problems and solutions of a kind that others will soon see but have not yet seen and thus work toward an insightful solution before others can do so.

Fundamental Analysis

The basic idea of fundamental analysis is that one can best decide where to invest by focusing on the intrinsic properties of an investment vehicle (e.g., a stock)—its company earnings, dividends, growth, management, and so on. The fundamental analyst seeks to determine what a security should be worth in comparison to its current value. If the security's intrinsic value is estimated by the fundamental analyst to be above market value, he buys; if the security is estimated to be overvalued, he sells. Use of fundamental analysis, as with technical analysis, requires knowledge and intelligence. One must know what variables are important in predicting the future success of a security and also have the intelligence to interpret the information about these variables.

Fundamental analysis provides another means for deciding in what areas of creative endeavor to invest one's energy, by looking at available information and research trends. If a field, specialty, problem, or type of solution within a field seems to be underrepresented at a given time, one has a buy signal; if it is overrepresented, one has a sell signal. If a domain lacks young blood or is casting about for leadership, that too may be a signal to jump into the fray.

Of course, the problem in the creative domain, as in the financial domain, is that many people are doing fundamental analysis simultaneously and may come to similar conclusions. For example, as the AIDS epidemic became more and more threatening, a number of researchers saw a new field with potential for creative insight and with little competition for increasingly generous funds. However, the very fact that a number of investigators drew the same conclusion at the same time resulted in more and more researchers competing for the same insights and resources. By the time they all had invested, the vehicle had lost some of its attraction because the rational process of fundamental analysis had led so many to exactly the same conclusion.

INVESTMENT VEHICLES

Once an investor has selected a decision-making strategy, the choice of where to invest one's resources must still be made. The kinds of stocks one may buy are illustrative of the kinds of domains and projects that people can choose to pursue. Some of these investment options may be more conducive to creative insight over the long term than other options.

Selecting the right investment vehicle (field, problem, approach to problem, or type of solution) is a time-consuming process requiring the motivation, intelligence, and knowledge to work hard and effectively at analyzing one's options. The time, however, will be well spent when the investment decision pays off and paves the way for creative insights to occur.

Concept Stocks

Concept stocks represent industries or businesses that are highly favored at a given time. They are exemplars of some concept that is believed to be of key importance, such as biotechnology, computers, or aviation. Those who invest in these stocks often imagine themselves to have virtually no possibility of loss. After all, how could society exist nowadays without new drugs, information processing, or swift air travel? Nonetheless, the typical course of concept stocks includes some extremely good years, followed by some awful ones and, in some cases, good ones again. For example, biotechnology stocks soared until people began to doubt whether any truly usable products would come from the biotechnical research. The stocks then sank, only to go up again when useful products were indeed emerging, such as Genentech's tissue plasminogen activator (TPA), a protein that dissolves blood clots in the arteries after heart attacks. Computer stocks did extremely well for a number of years, until it became apparent that the market had become saturated. Those who were going to buy home computers had already bought them, and there were so many companies producing cheap clones that it was not clear consumers would purchase name brands. The stocks sank. Similarly, aviation is almost certainly a wave of the future, but changes in gasoline prices, consumer willingness to travel, and competition among carriers have had deadly effects, and some airlines have even been forced into bankruptcy. Thus, concept stocks come and go, although at a given time, they appeared to be a sure bet.

Concept stock parallels can be found in areas of creative endeavor. Self-help books were a hot concept during the selfless 1960s as well as the selfish and perhaps narcissistic 1980s. In each decade, self-improvement was a primary goal, and people bought books telling them how to accomplish it. Thus far in the 1990s, however, such books have not been as successful. Books that 10 years ago seemed to be full of fresh new creative insights today often seem pedestrian and repetitive to readers. There may be any number of reasons—a recession, which has cut into the sales of all books; saturation of the market; or a feeling that the effects of such books are minimal, for instance. In psychology, connectionist or neurally inspired network models to simulate human information processing became a concept stock for theorists beginning in the mid-1980s. Connectionism seemed to offer potential for many insights into cognition across a wide range of topics applied to the paradigm. Recently, though, there has been skepticism about the insights that connectionist models have yielded.

Oddly enough, even when one knows the up-and-down history of these fad concepts, it is difficult to convince oneself that today's fad is not the end of the line; one wants to believe that this trend, unlike the others, is here to stay. At one time, it appeared that S. Sternberg's (1969) memory-scanning paradigm would generate new theoretical insights indefinitely, but few paradigms last forever, and this one was not exceptional in this regard. Those who invest all their financial, intellectual, or creative resources in a concept must be ready for the day in which a once-inviolable concept no longer seems sacred or perhaps even worthwhile.

Blue-chip Stocks

Blue-chip stocks are another investment option. They are like concept stocks in that they are securities of well-regarded companies, but blue-chips' value inheres in the company rather than in the concept it represents. For example, the Goodyear Company makes an unexciting product—automobile tires—but it has been successful in that market for a long time, and there is no end in sight for the demand for tires, so it may be a blue chip even if it is in no way a hot concept. Blue chips usually are not at the top of the scale in terms of performance but rather are solid buys that tend to perform at least reasonably well even in harder times.

We do not claim, however, that blue chips represent a haven of permanent safety. For example, IBM was a blue-chip stock for many years, but a government antitrust suit had a price-bashing effect that almost no one anticipated. Now, IBM's stock price reflects these problems. Similarly, AT&T looked safe before it became the object of an antitrust suit, which effectively broke up the company into a greatly shrunken version of its former self. Likewise, each of the three major Detroit automobile manufacturers has been regarded as blue chip in its time, only to see sales and profits sag in the face of unexpected and still undaunted foreign competitors.

For creative insights, certain paradigms, schools of thought, or methodologies can be considered blue chips. In psychology, for example, the priming methodology used to investigate basic human information processing has yielded a steady flow of minor insights. The truly creative insights, the revolutionary ones, we believe stem from a third class of investment vehicles, growth stocks.

Growth Stocks

The term *growth stock* is a generic one for stocks of usually small, fledgling companies that have not yet had an opportunity to prove themselves. Both the potential risk and the potential gain are great. The successes become oft-told tales—of how one could have become a millionaire, with no sweat, by investing in Xerox. The problem, of course, is that for every Xerox there are thousands of companies that do not do nearly as well, many of which fail completely. Nonetheless, growth companies offer a true opportunity for smart investing if one selects well: *This* is the tough job.

The same principles apply in creative endeavors. When new fields and problems arise, as they do almost continually these days, and when new starts emerge in these fields, it is difficult to determine which will be lasting successes and which will soon be yesterday's bright lights and today's flickering ones. Yet, without doubt, much of the most creatively insightful and influential work of the future will come from the newest fields and newest people within those fields.

CAPITAL

In investing, the types of investments made and the particular choices made within those investments depend, in part, on the capital available. A stock such as Berkshire Hathaway is out of range for those who cannot afford its price of more than $20,000 per share. Investments in real estate often involve substantial capital, and many mutual funds require sizable minimum investments.

The concept of capital is also relevant to creatively insightful endeavors. In particular, some theorists have focused on the concept of *human capital* as a determinant of potential and actualized creativity. Let us explore what human capital is as well as its role in creative insight.

Walberg (1988) notes that *capital* is an asset that gives rise to income or, more broadly, utility—including nonmonetary benefits such as tranquility or honor. Human beings, according to Walberg, are themselves capital investments of a society. Rubenson and Runco (1992, p. 134) define *capital* as "productive resources, such as land or tools, that can be used to transform raw materials into desired goods. *Human capital* refers to specific skills and knowledge which enter into the productive process." In their view, part of human capital is the creative potential of the individual.

For creative insight, an individual's assets would include selective encoding, selective comparison, and selective combination skills, plus knowledge on which to draw, and attitudes for buying low and selling high. For creative performance, in general, an individual's capital would include a broader array of personal resources, of which insight skills are one part. Some examples of the other personal resources useful for creativity are intellectual styles favoring ill-defined problems, task-focused motivation, and personality traits such as perseverance to overcome obstacles on a project (Sternberg & Lubart, 1991a, 1991b, 1992).

Expanding on the notion of human capital, Rubenson and Runco (1992) explain why younger people may be greater risk takers and hence more prone to major creative insights and, ultimately, discoveries and inventions (see Lubart & Sternberg, in press). According to these theorists, older creators will, on the average, possess more knowledge of their fields. Drawing on this accumulated knowledge, these older creators will be able to produce minor contributions at lesser cost than younger creators can. Because the proportionate cost of minor contributions is greater for younger innovators, they have less incentive to make them. On the other hand, their relative lack of human capital—specifically, knowledge—lowers the proportionate cost for them of more revolutionary contributions, because such a contribution is likely to reduce the value of existing knowledge. Those who will be adversely affected by this reduction in value will be those with substantial investments in that (outdated) knowledge. With less vested interest in the knowledge base that already exists, younger innovators can feel more free to try to change it than can their seniors.

Thus, knowledge forms an interesting portion of one's human capital. For creative insight, an intermediate level of knowledge may be optimal. With too little knowledge, major insights will not occur because there are not enough raw materials. Conversely, with too much knowledge, major insights will not occur because they would devalue one's current knowledge base. Essentially, people become committed to their knowledge base, which relates to laboratory evidence of conceptual fixedness and diminished insight.

MARKET DEMANDS

How an individual decides to invest his or her human capital depends on another aspect of creative insight, the environment. The value of different sorts of creative insight to society is anything but constant. Sometimes only certain kinds of creative insights are in demand. The social environment is a factor that cannot be ignored when making or evaluating investments, either financial or creative.

There are many social factors that can contribute to the value of creative insights, just as there are social factors that contribute to the value of an investment. Political instability, for example, tends to raise the value of some necessary investments (e.g., precious metals or defense industries) and to lower the value of desirable but nonessential others (e.g., tourism or fashion industries). According to Simonton (1984), political turmoil creates more demand for creative insights because of a greater need to find imaginative solutions to serious problems. However, the resultant demand for creative insight, like that for stocks, may be unequally distributed. Those persons in applied sciences will probably find more demand for their creative services than those in basic sciences or the humanities. Furthermore, thinkers may find that their creative range is perhaps more circumscribed than in boom times. When money is tight, there may be more demand for insightful ideas to cut costs on already existing products or to create less expensive alternatives than for exciting new options.

Ironically, the person seen as the most creatively insightful is not always the one most successful in the marketplace. Rubenson and Runco (1992) have suggested that the demand for creative insight is driven by a marginal utility curve: Up to a certain point, those seeking creative solutions are willing to pay, whether monetarily or otherwise, for these solutions but, after a certain point, the increased yield through additional creativity is not seen as sufficient to justify a further increase in price. When the cost of producing more creative insight barely exceeds the benefit, increased problem-solving efforts will not be rewarded. For example, an advertising agency may hire the second-best job candidate because the agency's leaders do not believe that paying to get the very best talent will necessarily make a considerable difference. The extra revenue produced by the very best individual may not justify the additional cost. In general, different social environments may also have different marginal utility curves for creative insights because these novel ideas will change the status quo, and some environments value conformity more than others (Lubart, 1990; Mann, 1980).

Thus the marketplace for creative insights cannot be ignored, but neither can it be the sole motivator of activity. The impetus toward innovation ultimately has to come from within, not without. The most creatively insightful work is not likely to come from attempts to please one crowd or another. Rather, one needs to think in ways that others simply may not like or understand or to ask questions that others will find impertinent or irreverent. In the words of Garry Trudeau, creator of the controversial and influential Doonesbury political comic strip, on his receipt of an honorary degree at Yale University in 1991:

The impertinent question is the glory and engine of human inquiry. Copernicus asked it and shook the foundations of Renaissance Europe. Darwin asked it and redefined humankind's very sense of itself. Thomas Jefferson asked it and was so invigorated by it that he declared it an inalienable right.... Whether revered or reviled in their lifetimes, history's movers framed their questions in ways that were entirely disrespectful of conventional wisdom.

EVALUATING INVESTMENTS

Evaluation of an investment, like judgment of market demands before investing, is heavily dependent on the environment or marketplace. Thus, in a fundamental sense, evaluation of both financial and creative worth is parallel, because in both cases it is based largely on social consensus. A stock is valuable because other investors collectively desire to possess it. A product is insightful and creative because appropriate judges collectively agree that it is (Amabile, 1982).

Previous accounts of people's conceptions of creativity suggest novelty or statistical rarity, high quality, and appropriateness to problem constraints as the main criteria for judging creative performance (Amabile, 1982; Jackson & Messick, 1965; MacKinnon, 1962; Sternberg, 1985, 1988). We believe that these same dimensions are used for determining whether a problem solution is insightful. Indeed, it is essentially an insight or series of insights that forms the basis of a creative product.

A distinction can be drawn between judgments of creativity, insight, or financial worth made by external observers and judgments by the individual producing the work (or investing in the financial instrument). For example, an individual investor may see value in a stock that the market does not value. In the creative realm, a problem solution may be insightful and creative for the producer but merely repetitive for society in general.

Also the producer has greater knowledge of how the idea or product was generated, which will affect his or her personal judgment. For example, if an idea comes suddenly without any apparent preparation, then it is more likely to be considered an insight than if the idea came by slow methodical work. However, external judges usually are not aware of the process used to generate a problem solution. Therefore, these judges are likely to focus purely on the novelty, quality, and appropriateness of the idea. Conversely, the external judge may have an affective experience of surprise (due to the novelty of the idea) and may ask himself or herself "Why didn't I think of that?" (due to the quality and appropriateness of the idea), but the external judge will not have the eureka experience that is a hallmark of insight for the producer.

Another parallel between the investment and creative realms is the importance of characteristics of the judges, which may echo the cultural and economic environment's trends and mores. Sometimes the value of either a company or a creative product is not initially obvious in a particular context. Long ago, the advent of books was considered a calamity by some. Writing down ideas and stories encouraged laziness in thinking and memory in a way that would undermine intellectual civilization! The original thinker must be prepared for the fact that it can take years before creative value is fully recognized by society at large: Witness also the many artists who gain fame only posthumously.

In addition, there is a potential paradox in judging the value of a creative product, just as in valuing many kinds of financial investments. How much is a rare coin worth? Is it a good long-term investment? The silver or gold in the coin may be worth just a few dollars, yet discriminating buyers with knowledge of the numismatics market may pay hundreds of thousands of dollars for that coin, whereas a novice might not be willing to buy it at any price because she or he does not recognize its value. This can happen in evaluating a fine new idea or a rare antique chair. So who is making the *correct* judgment as to worth?

In an attempt to establish some standards in evaluation, we use consensus techniques. These techniques are not perfect, however. Although one might think that the collective good sense of a group would be better than that of any one individual, there is ample evidence to suggest that sometimes the reverse is true. Irving Janis (1972, p. 3) described a phenomenon he referred to as *groupthink*, "instances of mindless conformity and collective misjudgment of serious risks."

In investing, there have been any number of crazes that have exemplified groupthink. Probably the most often cited is the tulip mania of seventeenth-century Holland. In the early 1600s, tulips were fashionable in Europe. Holland was the chief source of bulbs, and Dutch horticulturists had developed many rare varieties. In 1633, the general public began investing in tulip bulbs, and the prices began to rise. The Semper Augustus variety reached a value of somewhere between $6000 and $8000 (converted from Dutch florins) per pound. One pound of the variety Gheele Croohen sold for $30 one month and $1575 the next. Rumors of foreign orders fanned the flames, and a futures market developed. However, in 1637, dealers began having difficulty finding buyers. In short order, the market collapsed, and the valuable bulbs were suddenly nearly worthless (Dreman, 1977).

Any investment collectible is susceptible to such trends, as can be seen in the sometimes wild gyrations of the art, precious gems, rare coins, and rare stamps markets. The same is true in real estate, stocks, and bonds. There is no supreme judge of a financial investment any more than there is an ultimate judge who can say the true value of a new idea. Nonetheless, despite its relativism, it is the working tradition to use consensus techniques for judging both financial and creative worth. We must hope that those involved in the evaluation of original works will strive to see beyond their own time and place and develop knowledge and appreciation of insight and creativity in themselves so they can better judge it in others.

COSTS

Many of the costs and benefits of economic investments apply equally to investments in creative, insight-driven work. Take one of the most lamented costs, taxes. As people earn more from investments, they pay more in taxes. In graduated tax structures, their proportional contribution increases as well. One not infrequently hears complaints that it simply is not worth the work to earn more because one ends up paying almost all of it back in taxes. To benefit, one needs the knowledge and intelligence to predict costs before the bills come due as well as to know later how to minimize them. One also needs the motivation to find ways of cutting costs.

In creatively insightful work, other kinds of taxes may effectively rob an individual of his or her opportunity for further insights and originality. For example, one may be called on to repay awards and public or professional recognition by later serving on panels that evaluate the award nominations of others. Such committees almost invariably require great amounts of time without proportionate recompense, perhaps of any kind. Similarly, someone whose writing is frequently published may be asked to review work of others and, ultimately, to edit journals, both of which will take time from his or her own writing. Successful individuals in business and education find themselves more and more in demand as mentors, spokespeople, and committee members. Furthermore, as one's reputation increases, the demand increases for speeches or articles that reiterate one's unique contributions for different audiences; the content repetition alone is not conducive to groundbreaking thinking! As a result of all of these time thieves, it is not uncommon for the creatively insightful individual eventually to find himself or herself with almost no time left for creative endeavors. One must learn how to say no to the pileup of demands so as to leave time to continue one's creative work.

Paradoxically, another potential cost of creative endeavor, especially at the early stages of a career, is rejection and even ostracism for attempting to buy low. It was noted how fledgling innovators have less investment in the established order. If, then, they try to overturn that order, those with vested interests rarely come expressing thanks for being shown that they have been wrong for many years or that they have been passing their time on work that will soon be passé. Rather, there may be attempts—not always subtle—to punish the creatively insightful individual for upsetting the applecart. Thus the creatively insightful individual may find himself or herself at odds with the community of investors, having to convince them of the value of his or her innovation when these others have a stake in the status quo. The most insightful discoveries and inventions may even go unheeded because colleagues simply are not ready for or do not want to hear them. Again, a contrary spirit and a willingness to believe in oneself are invaluable at such times.

Lastly, as an individual acquires a more and more valuable portfolio of creative accomplishments, the person faces the same danger as a mature company—namely, that she or he may not be able to muster the resources to deal with a rapidly changing world and will be a bad investment in terms of potential for future human capital gains. Indeed, there is even the possibility that the person will enter creative bankruptcy. Such individuals may make few creative commitments and have trouble meeting what few they have made. Creative bankruptcy can happen at any time in a career. Again, what diminishes is not any insight ability but rather the attitude and spirit of buying low and selling high.

Nonetheless, individuals can recover from such bankruptcies, just as they can from financial ones. Modes of recovery are variable; they may involve changing fields, reeducating oneself, or simply deciding on a fresh angle from which to approach one's work. Creative bankruptcy, like the personal kind, need not be permanent, as long as the motivation to create and succeed remains strong.

BENEFITS

All these cautions about the risks and costs of creative insight, while they must realistically be acknowledged, are perhaps unduly negative. The world is full of people, from the famous to the ordinary, who have developed and capitalized on creative insights in their own lives. These creative individuals receive valuable dividends from their work, just as do financial investors. Personal satisfaction and a sense of fulfillment from having championed one's own ideas against nay-sayers are profits reaped by the creative investor. It is human nature to fight for what it believes in, not to give up in the face of opposition, and to win over doubters. To succeed in this is extremely rewarding.

Just as financial dividends can be reinvested in one's capital and thereby generate more interest, so too do creative accomplishments build on themselves. Good work snowballs into more and perhaps greater work as we gain confidence in ourselves, as others' expectations increase, and as new challenges—contracts, commissions, assignments—are offered. Those whose standards for themselves are high are usually the ones who achieve the most, and innovative success starts a self-perpetuating cycle of creativity.

The sheer fun of working on a project that is important and challenging to us, and potentially beneficial to others, cannot be overlooked either. We test ourselves most when we take stock of our abilities and set our sights on doing the best we can as innovatively as we can. Perhaps it should be reiterated that there is a continuum of creative insight and that it can occur in almost any context. One's best, most insightful contribution may possibly be in designing a new technique for brain surgery but, for most of us, it is more likely to be in landscape design, counseling, accounting, sales, coaching, and so on—anywhere we find ourselves in the course of our days. Living and working more imaginatively is a joy in itself.

The benefits of creative insight to the individual and, potentially, to society almost certainly outweigh the costs; the history of human endeavor attests to this. Those who take the risks are those who make major, lasting contributions for which they are long remembered and even sometimes handsomely rewarded. Nonetheless, not everyone will be an Einstein or a Carnegie. Hence, making it into the history books or striking it rich, while desirable, should not be one's source of motivation. Instead, the impetus for creative insight and change must come from within, for that is also where the rewards will be enjoyed most intensely. Each person must find his or her own place in the spectrum of creative expression in order to reap the highest returns on the investment. Hence, the returns will vary with the person, but all will know the pleasure of having changed the world in some definable way.

THE INVESTMENT METAPHOR: LIMITATIONS AND COMMENTS

We recognize that creative insight and investment are not strictly analogous. Analogies are, by their nature, imprecise. In using metaphors, therefore, it is important to recognize points of dissimilarity as well as similarity; in fact, examining where the metaphor is imprecise often yields more understanding of the concept. The investment metaphor is no exception.

Creators usually must work personally (and hard!) to bring their ideas to fruition. Creatively insightful people need to invest themselves in their projects to yield the value added to the initial idea. Some work may be done by employees, assistants, or disciples, but only after the insightful thinker has laid the intellectual or technical groundwork. On the other hand, financial investors generally do not promote the companies or products in which they have invested. Indeed, to do so vigorously might be seen, at best, as manipulating the market and, at worst, as illegal. To render investment and creativity more strictly analogous, stockholders would need to be able to work for or promote openly the company in which they had invested, to make their investments succeed.

One other caution is necessary regarding our investment metaphor. In our experience, some people find an economic parallel distasteful. Others see financial considerations of any kind as antithetical to creativity. However, such concerns, though understandable, are superficial. We want to show that there are major conceptual points of comparison between financial and creative investments; we are not equating creativity and money. Perhaps this is clearer when one considers that the concept of investment is by no means limited to the financial domain. In a broad sense, people constantly invest time, effort, and intellectual and emotional energy in careers and relationships. Our theory makes only structural, not content, parallels. For consistency, however, we have concentrated on references to financial investment in our investment theory.

Metaphors are to be used as helpful frameworks for comparison and nothing more. They should guide but not control thinking. We find that the investment analogy is useful for discussing creative insight, but we also know that theorists run into trouble when they start taking their own analogies too seriously, essentially becoming controlled by them rather than controlling them.

We believe that buying low and selling high, with its accompanying considerations of market and specific risk, investment strategies, investment vehicles, capital, market demands, skills, costs, and benefits, aptly and accurately parallels the process of effective creative, insightful involvement in a field. No one metaphor can capture a concept fully, however, and so it is helpful to look at a problem from multiple points of view. To this end, chapters 14 and 15 apply concepts from evolutionary theory to understanding insight. We believe that the cognitive approach to insight is also an important one, and we have taken it ourselves in some of our work. However, exclusive reliance on cognitive models may rule out one of the most important factors for creative insight, which is not an ability so much as an attitude toward life.

REFERENCES

Amabile, T.M. (1982). Social psychology of creativity: A consensual assessment technique. *Journal of Personality and Social Psychology, 43,* 997–1013.

Clifford, M.M. (1988). Failure tolerance and academic risk taking in ten- to twelve-year-old students. *British Journal of Educational Psychology, 58*(1), 15–27.

Davidson, J.E., & Sternberg, R.J. (1986). What is insight? *Educational Horizons, 64,* 177–179.

Dreman, D. (1977). *Psychology and the stock market.* New York: Amacon.

Dreman, D. (1982). *The new contrarian investment strategy.* New York: Random House.

Jackson, P., & Messick, S. (1965). The person, the product and the response: Conceptual problems in the assessment of creativity. *Journal of Personality, 33,* 309–329.

Janis, I.L. (1972). *Victims of groupthink.* Boston: Houghton, Mifflin.

Kahneman, D., & Tversky, A. (1982). The psychology of preferences. *Scientific American, 246*(1), 160–178.

Lubart, T.I. (1990). Creativity and cross-cultural variation. *International Journal of Psychology, 25,* 39–59.

Lubart, T.I., & Sternberg, R.J. (in press). Lifespan creativity: An investment theory approach. In C. Adams-Price (Ed.), *Creativity and aging: Theoretical and empirical perspectives.* New York: Springer-Verlag.

MacCrimmon, K.R., & Wehrung, D.A. (1985). A portfolio of risk measures. *Theory and Decision, 19*(1), 1–29.

MacKinnon, D.W. (1962). The nature and nurture of creative talent. *American Psychologist, 17,* 484–495.

Malkiel, B.G. (1985). *A random walk down Wall Street* (4th ed.). New York: Norton.

Mann, L. (1980). Cross-cultural studies of small groups. In H.C. Triandis & R.W. Brislin (Eds.), *Handbook of cross-cultural psychology: Vol. 5. Social psychology* (pp. 155–210). Boston: Allyn and Bacon.

Rubenson, D.L., & Runco, M.A. (1992). The psychoeconomic approach to creativity. *New Ideas in Psychology, 10*(2), 131–147.

Simonton, D.K. (1984). *Genius, creativity, and leadership.* Cambridge: Harvard University Press.

Sternberg, R.J. (1985). *Beyond IQ: A triarchic theory of human intelligence.* New York: Cambridge University Press.

Sternberg, R.J. (Ed.) (1988). *The nature of creativity: Contemporary psychological perspectives.* New York: Cambridge University Press.

Sternberg, R.J., & Lubart, T.I. (1991a). An investment theory of creativity and its development. *Human Development, 34,* 1–31.

Sternberg, R.J., & Lubart, T.I. (1991b, April). Creating creative minds. *Phi Delta Kappan,* 608–614.

Sternberg, R.J., & Lubart, T.I. (1992). Buy low and sell high: An investment approach to creativity. *Current Directions in Psychological Science, 1*(1), 1–5.

Sternberg, S. (1969). Memory-scanning: Mental processes revealed by reaction-time experiments. *American Scientist, 57,* 421–457.

Walberg, H.J. (1988). Creativity and talent as learning. In R.J. Sternberg (Ed.), *The nature of creativity* (pp. 340–361). New York: Cambridge University Press.

Webster's Ninth New Collegiate Dictionary (1983). Springfield, MA: Merriam-Webster.

Epilogue: Putting Insight into Perspective

Jonathan W. Schooler, Marte Fallshore, and
Stephen M. Fiore

Insight invites metaphors. In this book alone, insight elicited comparisons with evolutionary theory, both Darwinian (Simonton, chapter 14) and punctuated equilibrium (Perkins, chapter 15); gold mining (Perkins, chapter 15); spinning wheels in the mud (Smith, chapter 7); perceptual gap filling (Gruber, chapter 12); the noncontinuous growth of babies (Gruber, chapter 12); humor (Gick & Lockhart, chapter 6); investment theory (Sternberg & Lubart, chapter 16); the interpsychic and intrapsychic dimension (Csikszentmihalyi & Sawyer, chapter 10); and the kinematic theory of gases (Poincaré, cited in Simonton, chapter 14, and others). There are many possible reasons for this plethora of metaphors. A positive view would be to observe, as have many in this text, that insight solutions often follow from analogies (e.g., Davidson, chapter 14; Dunbar, chapter 11; Finke, chapter 8; Gick & Lockhart, chapter 6; Isaak & Just, chapter 9; Mayer, chapter 1). Thus, discussants of insight would be remiss not to draw on the device that they argue is of such value. From a more skeptical perspective, the multitude of analogies to insight may result from a fundamental lack of agreement regarding what insight is and how it works (e.g., Weisberg, chapter 5). Somewhere between these two views lies the suggestion that insight requires multiple analogies to illuminate its multifaceted nature. As Gruber observes, "A single metaphor is always imperfect, but a set of metaphors all almost converging on the same target do illuminate and define it" or, to use an analogy, a single metaphor may shine a spotlight whereas many metaphors can light up the stage. Toeing this middle line, we will draw liberally on various metaphors of insight in order to clarify and highlight a number of central issues surrounding insight's definition, mechanisms, and relationship to other types of thought.

THE DEFINITION OF INSIGHT

After reading this book, one may be a bit perplexed about exactly what *insight* means. Although most usages of the term *insight* incorporate the suggestion that it involves the sudden unexpected solution to a problem, many different, sometimes contradictory characterizations of the term appear throughout these chapters. Traditionally speaking, there are two rather different possible usages of the concept of insight. As Smith notes in chapter 7, insight can be used to represent a state of understanding—that is, to gain insight into something. However, insight also can be described as an experience involving "the sudden emergence of an idea into conscious awareness." Although the difference between these two meanings of *insight* appears substantial, they sometimes are treated as if interchangeable. For example, Csikszentmihalyi and Sawyer (chapter 10) discuss insight both with respect to "seeing inside" and "a moment of realization," and their interviews with creative individuals do not always clearly distinguish between these two formulations.

Even when insight is discussed with respect to its more common psychological usage as an *insight experience*, the components of that experience are not always characterized in the same way. For example, Gick and Lockhart (chapter 6) suggest that the sudden affective "Aha!" experience is a defining component of the insight experience, whereas cognitive restructuring (constructing a new problem representation) is a common but not necessary component of insight. In contrast, Weisberg (chapter 5) uses restructuring as the sole defining criterion for insight and suggests that the "Aha!" experience may not be a criterion. Ippolito and Tweney (chapter 13) seem to ignore both the "Aha!" and the restructuring components of insight and instead characterize it as a special form of perception requiring "the ability to recreate the workings of a selected aspect of the physical world, independent of sensory receptor input."

To confuse matters further, a central theme running through a number of chapters is that insight is associated with a disparate set of processes that can be elicited by distinctly different types of problems. Weisberg (chapter 5), for example, posits three types of problems: change in initial representation, change in goal, and language interpretation problems. Dominowski and Dallob (chapter 2) address spatial, verbal, and object use problems, whereas Gick and Lockhart (chapter 6) distinguish between novel representation and conceptual access problems. Davidson (chapter 4) divides insight problems according to whether they require selective encoding, selective comparison, or selective combination, while Mayer (chapter 1) talks about schema completion, visual reorganization, reformulation, mental block, and analogy problems. We should note also that although many researchers propose different types of problems that elicit certain types of insight processes, they also acknowledge that different problem solvers may answer the same problem by drawing on very different processes (e.g., Davidson, chapter 4; Perkins, chapter 15). Indeed, Davidson and Gick and Lockhart (chapter 6) suggest that certain people need not even employ insight processes to solve insight problems correctly.

In addition to the complications associated with multiple types of insight problems, processes, and problem solvers, a number of researchers observe that there is no commonly agreed-on operational definition by which insight problems may be identified (e.g., Dominowski & Dallob, chapter 2; Weisberg, chapter 5). In light of the current absence of a clear theory of what constitutes an insight problem, Weisberg proposes that "a moratorium should be placed on theorizing about the mechanisms underlying restructuring and insight."

To salvage the general concept of insight from these complexities, it is useful to distinguish between the *explanation* of insight and the *event* of insight. If insight is defined with respect to its explanation, then, given the variety of elements that have been postulated to be involved in insight, we might reasonably question whether they all deserve to be classified under the same heading. If, however, insight is defined as an event and, in particular, a transitional event in which the solver moves from an impasse state to a solution state, then it becomes more sensible to consider it as a single construct. To use another metaphor, consider an explosion (the possible parallels between insight and explosionlike conditions have been proposed before; see Metcalfe's

[1986] depiction of insight as a catastrophic process and, in this volume, Perkins's characterization of insight as a generative breakthrough event). Clearly, there are many different and distinct processes that can lead to an explosion. Nevertheless, these processes all are united in that they lead to a sudden violent dispersal that results in the transition to a state very different from that preceding the explosion. Similarly, although many different processes may lead to an insight, these all can be united by the insight event that results in the transition of the solver to a solution state very different from the nonsolution state that preceded the insight.

The characterization of insight as a transition event in which "a problem solver suddenly moves from a state of not knowing how to solve a problem to a state of knowing how to solve it" (Mayer, chapter 1) provides an operational definition that can be measured empirically. Specifically, Metcalfe's (1986) warmth rating paradigm, in which subjects provide frequent estimates of their nearness to a solution (see Davidson, chapter 4, this book) is able reliably to reveal whether a problem-solving procedure leads to a sudden transition to a solution. This approach seems to provide a clear definition for what might otherwise be a murky construct, but Weisberg (chapter 5) raises two criticisms concerning the use of the warmth rating paradigm for operationally defining *insight*. First, Weisberg notes that such a definition allows only post hoc classifications and thus does not provide a theoretical basis on which to define insight. Second, he argues that using the warmth rating paradigm to identify insight results in a circular argument because "warmth data cannot be used both as the basis for a problem classification and support for that classification."

Weisberg's difficulty with the warmth-rating operationalization of insight seems to stem from his desire to connect the definition of the insight event itself with an explanation for that event. Weisberg specifically suggests that the definition of *insight* should be made in the context of a theory or explanation of insight. Though such a goal sounds lofty, a strong case can be made that the operational definition of the insight event should be *independent* of the theories used to explain that event. Again, the metaphor of explosions may be of value. One might have a theory for what leads to certain types of explosions, but ultimately the definition of an explosion is not whether a certain set of theoretically explosive conditions exists but, rather, whether an explosion actually occurs. To mix metaphors (we couldn't resist), the poof is in the pudding. So, too, no matter how sophisticated our theories of insight, we must have a strict operational definition of what constitutes the occurrence of an insight event in order to test those theories. If the insight event occurs in a situation that the theory does not predict, we should modify the theory, *not* the definition of the event; otherwise, the theory will never be falsifiable. In short, we will be able to advance, compare, and select our theories of insight only if we are able to use a definition of *insight* that is not inherently tied to any one particular theoretical perspective and that allows independent verification of insight through empirical means. Problem situations that result in a sudden transition from a nonsolution state to a solution state, as indicated by warmth ratings or other empirical measures, represent a definition of *insight* that fits with the preceding constraints as well as corresponds to our commonly shared understanding of the term.

Although defining *insight* using an atheoretical operationalization helps us find common ground and provides an empirical basis for determining when insights have occurred, such a definition, by its very nature, cannot provide a theoretical understanding of the basis for insight. As Mayer observes, "Providing a name for this process does not substitute for providing an explanation" (chapter 1). Nevertheless, the claim that insight involves the sudden shift from a nonsolution state to a solution state offers a starting point on which explanations of insight can be based. First, the absence of perceived progress to the solution prior to the insight suggests that would-be solvers are at an impasse. Thus, the questions raised by the preceding definition include: What causes the impasses that keep the solver in a nonsolution state prior to the insight? What conditions enable the solver to overcome the impasse? Why does the overcoming of an impasse lead to a sudden solution? To provide a conceptual scaffolding for considering these questions, we first review the frequently made analogies between insight and two basic everyday experiences—perception and searching physical space.

TWO COMMON METAPHORS OF INSIGHT

The Vision Metaphor

Characterization of the experience of insight as comparable to an object suddenly becoming visible permeates both our folk conceptions of insight and psychological insight theories. The term in*sight* itself emphasizes its parallels with vision, and other common language characterizations of insight similarly invoke visual qualities. Insights often are described as "a sudden flash," "a moment of illumination," or "seeing the light." Pictorial representations of insight (e.g., comics) also reflect the visual quality of this experience, using the characterization of a light bulb appearing over someone's head. The analogy of perception guided early Gestalt theorists, who characterized the processes of insight in terms of many of the same principles of good form, such as closure, used to account for perception. The Gestaltists' perceptual characterization of insight remains considerably influential to this day. For example, Ellen (1982) suggests that insight is akin to Gestalt classic figure ground reversals (e.g., the necker cube) and, in this book, Gruber (chapter 12) hypothesizes that a process comparable to perceptual gap filling (equivalent to the Gestalt notion of closure) may play an important role in insight. Other approaches too have emphasized the parallels between insight and vision. For example, Ohlsson (1984) discusses the discovery of insight solutions as occurring when the solution is in "the horizon of mental lookahead." In this text, Ippolito and Tweney (chapter 13) explicitly characterize "insight as a special form of perception" and Simonton (chapter 14) suggests that discoveries are associated with situations in which consciousness is able to "suddenly change focus, and spotlight the discovery."

The Problem Space Metaphor

A second metaphor that is associated with discussions of insight is the notion that thought is equivalent to moving through physical space. As Roediger (1980, p. 232) notes, "In thinking of consciousness, or more broadly, of mind, we usually resort to a metaphor of an actual physical space, with memories and ideas as objects in the space." Psychologists and nonpsychologists alike describe processes related to insight using such phrases as *searching one's mind*, *changing the direction of thought*, *approaching the problem from a different angle*, *thoughts in the back of one's mind*, and *finding the solution*. In the domain of problem solving, the mental space metaphor has been merged with a computer metaphor (e.g., Newell & Simon, 1972), in which the problem solver moves through a problem space from subgoal to subgoal in order to reach the final goal. The movement through the problem space requires the use of operators, which are actions (e.g., multiply, move, etc.) that fulfill certain subgoals, thereby moving the solver to a new problem state. Although the potential range of operators and problem space routes available to problem solvers is virtually infinite, the limited processing capacity of humans substantially constrains the number of operators that are used and the routes that are explored (Newell & Simon, 1972).

The physical space metaphor of thought provides a number of ways to characterize insight problems. From the standpoint of the searcher, as Isaak and Just (chapter 9) suggest, the problem space characterization of insight leads to the possibility that one may define the boundaries of the problem space so as to preclude finding the solution. From the standpoint of the problem, as Perkins (chapter 15) notes, some problems will offer more clues regarding where one is than others. Thus, by Perkins's account, insight problems may be characterized as corresponding to physical spaces, such as those involved in gold mining, in which one has little idea of progress and then suddenly hits the mother lode.

Combining the Vision and Spatial Metaphors

Although frequently discussed independently, the vision and spatial metaphors of thinking complement one another well. To move through a physical space, it helps to be able to see where to go next. Similarly, in problem solving, the movement from one state to the next requires some assessment of what operators are available. Thus we can readily combine the vision and physical space metaphors of problem solving by proposing a two-process model: (1) a pattern recognition process comparable to vision that surveys the possible directions in which to move (i.e., identifies the potentially applicable operators) and (2) a reasoning process that decides between the potential directions (selects a set of operators) and moves forward (executes the operators). With respect to insight, this characterization is particularly useful because it suggests that multiple factors may contribute to an impasse. One may have a fine vantage point yet still fail to see the goal. In such cases, the problem is one of recognition. Alternatively, one may be heading in the wrong direction and need to determine a way to move to a location that affords a better view. In this latter case, the impasse involves both reasoning (finding and following a route to a better view) and recognition (identifying what one sees when the view is improved). With this analogy in mind, we now consider some of the sources of impasses to insight.

THE CAUSES OF IMPASSES

Recognition Failure

Many discussions of the impasses to insight suggest that the difficulty is simply one of perspective: All the information needed to solve the problem is at hand, but one simply is not looking at it from the right angle. In classic Gestalt discussions of the impasses to insight, this type of impasse was compared to figure-ground illusions, in which the perceptual definition of what is figure and what is ground determines what is seen. From the perspective of the visual–physical space analogy, one has a clear view of the goal but simply fails to recognize it. We turn now to a discussion of two sources for such recognition failures—the overemphasis of irrelevant cues and the underemphasis of relevant cues.

The Overemphasis of Irrelevant Cues

One well-documented reason for people's failure to recognize solutions when they are at hand is that the problem solvers focus excessively on particular sources of information and consequently fail to see the big picture. The excessive focus on inappropriate or irrelevant cues is discussed by a number of contributors to this book. According to Isaak and Just, "Insight problems often contain information that lead subjects to incorrectly accept additional operator constraints not mandated by the problem" (chapter 9). To support this claim, Isaak and Just identify the unnecessary problem constraints elicited by a number of classic insight problems. For example, in functional fixedness problems, the solver is distracted by an object's standard function, which results in failure to recognize that the object can be used for other purposes.

Evidence for impasses resulting from excessive emphasis on irrelevant cues comes from other sources as well. For example, Smith (chapter 7) reports that inventors have great difficulty ignoring dysfunctional design elements involved in prior designs. Smith also finds that providing subjects with misleading hints can interfere temporarily with subjects' ability to solve puzzle problems. Finke (chapter 8) reports that the creativity of subjects' visual imagery inventions is reduced when their images are initially constrained to a particular category. Gick and Lockhart (chapter 6) suggest that many puzzle problems are effective because they invoke ambiguous interpretations (i.e., multiple meanings are potentially available) but the dominant interpretation is inappropriate for solving the problem.

To make matters worse, as individuals continue to work on a problem from the wrong perspective, they may increase the salience of the inappropriate problem elements by perseverating on them, further reducing the likelihood of shifting perspective. To use Smith's (chapter 7) analogy, the more they spin their wheels, the deeper the rut. Empirical evidence for this intuitive claim is suggested by Lockhart, Lamon, and Gick (1988), who found that the vast majority of solutions to insight puzzle problems occur in the first minute of problem solving. One reasonable interpretation of this finding is that with increased activation of the wrong perspective, the problem solver becomes less and less able to switch perspectives. Additional evidence for the suggestion that working on a problem from the wrong perspective can interfere with one's ability to recognize alternative interpretations that are seemingly obvious comes from research on the recognition of out-of-focus pictures. Bruner and Potter (1964) observed that exposure to extremely out-of-focus pictures impairs subjects' ability to recognize moderately out-of-focus versions of the same picture. Bruner and Potter (1964) proposed that this suggests that ill-fated attempts to recognize extremely out-of-focus pictures cause subjects to formulate hypotheses and adopt perspectives which then interfere with the subjects' ability to recognize the correct interpretation when it becomes more available.

The Underemphasis of Relevant Cues

Reconsider the previously cited situation of recognizing out-of-focus pictures. The subjects' emphasis on inappropriate perspectives generated while attempting to recognize very out-of-focus pictures interfered with their ability to attend to the relevant information presented in the successively more focused pictures, which would have enabled a correct identification. A number of chapters in this book advance the theme that impasses can result from the inability to recognize the relevance of available cues. For example, Gick and Lockhart (chapter 6) observe that for many insight problems, "the source of difficulty ... is one of conceptual access ... involving capacity of problem content to cue the appropriate concept." Davidson (chapter 4) observes that lower-intelligence subjects' difficulty with insight problems often occurs because they fail to engage in selective comparison—that is, to recognize relationships between certain features of the problem and information acquired in the past. Similarly, a number of researchers report that the manner in which relevant prior information is encoded can determine whether it is retrieved and used to recognize the solution (see Dominowski & Dallob, chapter 2; Lockhart et al., 1988). In these cases, the would-be solvers are in a state in which they "possess all the knowledge necessary for producing a solution" (Dominowski & Dallob). They simply fail to recognize the correspondence between what they are currently encountering and what they already know.

Searching the Wrong Space

Although some impasses may be associated with situations in which the solver fails to see the solution despite being poised to do so, other impasses require the solver to move to a completely different vantage point. Such a situation is equivalent to being lost in Perkins's (chapter 15) ill-defined Klondike space, far away from any useful vein of gold. In such situations, no form of perspective shifting will be sufficient to allow one to see the solution; rather, the would-be-solver must actively move to new vantage points," avoiding redundant coverage of the same regions, searching for new regions altogether" (Perkins, chapter 15). Examples of such situations include the manner in which subjects must solve the mutilated checkerboard problem described by Gick and Lockhart (chapter 6) and Kaplan and Simon (1990). As Gick and Lockhart suggest, the solution of such problems, unlike those that are constrained simply by conceptual access, requires the would-be problem solver to engage in the active construction of a new problem representation. Many impasses to scientific insights may similarly occur because the investigators simply are not in a place to see the solution. Thus, Simonton's observation (see chapter 14) that important scientific discoveries require at least 10 years of intensive learning in a domain suggests that prior to that time, the researcher simply has not moved into a location in the problem space where insightful solutions may be visible.

HOW IMPASSES ARE OVERCOME

The suggestion that the impasses to insight result either from recognition failure or from being in the wrong place implies that techniques for overcoming impasses should facilitate the recognition process or assist the would-be solver in moving to a more suitable vantage point. In fact, considerable evidence is provided in this book that both of these general approaches can facilitate the overcoming of impasses.

Improving Solving Recognition

Techniques for overcoming impasses that result from a failure to recognize the solutions that are seemingly obvious rely on reversing the processes that cause such oversights. Thus, one general approach for reversing such impasses is to find ways of reducing the salience of inappropriate cues, and the other is to increase the salience of appropriate cues.

Deemphasizing Inappropriate Problem Elements
If seeing the solution is hindered as a result of a focus on distracting problem elements, then techniques that reduce the salience of

such elements will increase the likelihood that a more useful perspective is adopted.

Forgetting   The passage of time appears to be one of the best remedies for overcoming the salience of inappropriate cues. If one assumes that the activation of inappropriate problem elements increases as one continues to work on the problem, then a delay during which this activation can decay may increase the likelihood that one may take a more suitable perspective. In effect, a delay gives the person the opportunity to take a fresh look at the problem. The suggestion of forgetting as a mechanism for overcoming impasses dates back to Woodworth (1938) and has been reintroduced by a variety of other theorists (e.g., Anderson, 1981; Simon, 1966). In this book, Smith (chapter 7) describes research demonstrating that the negative effects of misleading hints on various problem-solving activities attenuates with the passage of time and suggests that the passage of time facilitates the overcoming of impasses by helping one "escape from the mental ruts that block insight."

Changing context   A related technique for reducing the salience of inappropriate problem elements may be to consider the problem in a different physical or psychological context. Specifically, a variety of work suggests that reinstating the context of prior situations, either physically (e.g., Smith, Glenberg & Bjork, 1978) or psychologically (e.g., Bower, 1981; Malpass & Devine, 1981), can increase subjects' access to the information associated with that situation. By the same token, shifting physical or psychological contexts may be helpful by reducing the degree to which the reinstatement of inappropriate problem elements occurs. To our knowledge, there have not been any experimental studies of this hypothesis, but anecdotal reports offer considerable evidence. For instance, there is the classic case of Poincaré experiencing his insights while on vacation (producing changes in psychological as well as physical context). Also, Csikszentmihalyi and Sawyer (chapter 10) report that many individuals experienced insights while engaging in everyday routines outside the context of their work, and it is common folk knowledge that insights often occur in the shower. Accordingly, thinking about a problem in a new

physical or psychological context that is not, in itself, too resource demanding may reduce the salience of previously emphasized inappropriate problem elements, thereby providing a fresh
perspective.

Accessing Appropriate Problem Elements

In addition to deemphasizing the inappropriate aspects of a problem, changes in perspective leading to recognition of problem
solutions can also be elicited by the access of problem-relevant
information. In the case of perception, an out-of-focus picture can
be entirely reconfigured simply by introducing a single word describing its content. Similarly, in the case of riddles, the punch
line provides the listener with an instantaneously new view of
the riddle (see Gick & Lockhart, chapter 6). So too, the simple
encounter of a cue in the environment, or the spontaneous surfacing into consciousness of some relevant bit of information,
can trigger the recognition of an insight solution. We will review briefly these two sources of accessing appropriate problem
elements.

Cues in the environment   The value of encountering information
that can suddenly enable one to recognize the solution to a problem is suggested by both historical and experimental discussions
of insight. For example, Seifert, Meyer, Davidson, Patalano, and
Yaniv (chapter 3) describe how the physicist, Richard Feynman,
on hearing a single phrase about the possible nature of neutron
decay, leaped up and exclaimed, "Then I understand EVVVV-
VERYTHING." Like the viewer who has just been given the
name for an out-of-focus picture, or a listener who has just heard
the punch line to a joke, Feynman instantly saw the whole picture. Seifert and coauthors propose a compelling explanation for
how the environment can prompt such sudden revelations. According to these researchers, when faced with a problem that cannot be solved, individuals store memory traces or "failure indices"
of the impasse that "help guide the problem solver back to the
problem when relevant new information is later encountered."
Seifert's group provides evidence for these failure indices from
two diverse paradigms. In a tip-of-the-tongue study, subjects benefited from prior exposure to target items only when those items

corresponded to definitions they had failed to produce in an earlier tip-of-the-tongue test. In a memory-for-problems paradigm, subjects showed superior memory for unsolved problems as compared with solved problems only when they had been allowed to reach an impasse on those problems (the classic Zeigarnik effect). These authors concluded that impasses create special mental markers (failure indices) that keep the mind ever vigilant for the sought-after information. When the critical information is found, the partial picture suddenly becomes complete and the solution is recognized (see also Langley & Jones, 1988, and Perkins's discussion of their work in this book).

Unconscious retrieval   Cues that may prompt the spontaneous recognition of a problem solution may also surface from the unconscious. For example, a number of researchers have speculated that problem solving may initiate the spread of activation to concepts related to the problem elements. With sufficient activation, critical operators may rise above the threshold of awareness and become available to the problem solver. Such unconscious spreading activation mechanisms have been incorporated into a number of theories of insight (e.g., Bowers, Regehr, Balthazard & Parker, 1990; Langley & Jones, 1988; Ohlsson, 1992; Yaniv & Meyer, 1987; see also Isaak & Just in this book). In addition, unconscious search mechanisms are included in a variety of the discussions in this book, although Seifert and coauthors (chapter 3) present evidence refuting this view. Csikszentmihalyi and Sawyer (chapter 10) observe, "The paradox for the creative individual is to somehow 'direct' this undirectable subconscious process so that useful insights result." Perkins (chapter 15) suggests, "Once set up by deliberate effort with a problem, those unconscious mechanisms basically constitute another mechanism of search operative even though the person may not be concentrating on the problem consciously." According to these views, when the products of these unconscious searches are brought into conscious awareness, the solver's perspective on the problem is spontaneously altered and the solution is seen. As Simonton (chapter 14) observes, "When the succession of subconscious images chances upon a bona fide insight, core consciousness will suddenly change focus and spotlight the discovery."

In some situations, access to the critical information that can prompt sudden recognition of a problem solution may result from a combination of environmental cues and unconscious retrieval processes. A number of studies suggest that environmental cues that are not recognized when encountered can nevertheless subsequently facilitate insights. For example, Maier (1931) observed that subjects frequently solved the two-string problem after one of the strings was accidentally brushed by the experimenter, even though the subjects were not explicitly aware of the hint (see Mayer, chapter 1). Dunbar (chapter 11) and Schunn (1990) found that subjects' problem solving benefited from prior exposure to analogically similar problems even though their retrospective reports showed no evidence that the subjects recognized the relevant similarities between the two problems. In recent research in our laboratory (Schooler & Melcher, 1993), we have found that subjects can benefit from one-word hints to puzzle problems, even when they do not recognize the hints as such. These findings suggest that the environment may set into action unconscious retrieval processes that ultimately can bring to consciousness a cue that can prompt recognition of the solution.

Searching for a New Problem Representation

When the difficulty in solving a problem is simply that one lacks the proper perspective then, as indicated earlier, recognition of the solution can be prompted by passive processes involving the apprehension of new information or unconscious memory retrieval. If, however, the problem solver is not poised to recognize the solution, then more active processes must be engaged to overcome the impasse. We now review briefly some of the considerations involved in actively finding a new problem space.

Recognizing that One is Lost

The recognition that one is at an impasse may be an important first step in encouraging individuals to search actively for a new problem space. For example, Dunbar (chapter 11) observed that when researchers accepted that an unexpected finding was valid and concluded that their existing theory was mistaken, significant conceptual advancement frequently followed. Csikszentmihalyi and Sawyer's interviews of creative individuals (see chapter 10) suggest that the most important insights result from problem finding, in which individuals identify a current impasse and then devote significant effort to resolving it.

A common explanation for the ability of recognition of an impasse to facilitate its being overcome is that recognizing an impasse forces the individual to take stock of his or her problem-solving status and to consider ways of fundamentally redefining the problem. For example, Kaplan and Simon (1990) and Gick and Lockhart (chapter 6) suggest that encountering impasses may cause subjects to search for alternative problem spaces by adopting metastrategies such as noticing invariants of their previous failed solution attempts. In chapter 11, Dunbar suggests that the social pressure of conceding an impasse in the context of laboratory meetings forces scientists actively to consider alternative approaches, thereby leading to insights. Dunbar also reports that subjects in a laboratory experiment who conceded that their initial hypothesis was not succeeding in accounting for the data were forced to search for alternative interpretations and were consequently much more likely to move to a new approach that could lead to a solution. Discussions of historical examples of insights similarly suggest that the recognition of an impasse can lead individuals to attempt to search for new problem approaches. For example, Gruber (chapter 12) reports that Einstein's development of the fundamentally new approach to physics grew out of "his struggle to free himself from the assumption of absolute time."

Attributes Associated with the Ability to Find Alternative Approaches

Recognition that one needs to find a new way to approach a problem may be an important first step in the search for a new problem space, but one still needs to determine the alternative direction in which to progress. Unfortunately, the types of problems that elicit this kind of impasse are also the types of problems that provide few cues regarding which way to go (see Perkins, chapter 15). Accordingly, success in actively searching for a viable alternative approach requires would-be solvers to draw on a number of different attributes.

Perseverance   One critical attribute involved in actively find-ing an alternative approach is simple perseverance. As Edison is often quoted as saying (Csikszentmihalyi & Sawyer, chapter 10), "Creativity is 99% perspiration and 1% inspiration." Many of the authors in this book note that finding the correct approach to a problem often involves simply trying out as many approaches as possible. In short, because the direction in which one needs to go is unclear, one may have to search a long time before getting any-where. Consequently, as Simonton (chapter 14) observes, the indi-viduals with the most creative contributions are also the ones who are the most productive: "The more shots at the target, the more bulls-eyes." Csikszentmihalyi and Sawyer (chapter 10) make a similar observation in their interviews of creative indivi-duals. For example, one chemist remarked, " 'You have lots of ideas, and throw away the bad ones' ".

Risk taking   As Simonton (chapter 14) observes, "For the kinds of problems on which historic creators stake their reputations, the possibilities seem endless, and the odds of attaining the solution appear nearly hopeless." Given that the odds for the big dis-coveries are always long shots, as Sternberg and Lubart (Chap-ter 16) note, important insights, like investments, may require a willingness to take risks. As Dunbar (chapter 11) observes, suc-cessful research laboratories often maintain a combination of low-risk and high-risk ventures, thereby enabling them to main-tain some balance.

Playfulness   A third attribute mentioned by a number of authors as necessary for finding alternative approaches to problems is an ability to toy with different options. For example, Finke (chapter 8) reports that creative inventions often result from subjects "manipulating the [preinventive] forms in playful ways." Isaak and Just (chapter 9) suggest that inventors' search for alternative operators for generating designs often requires "deliberate analogi-cal and combinatory play," and Simonton concurs, stating, "Those people who make their minds accessible to the chaotic combinatory play will equally make their senses more open to the influx of fortuitous events in the outside world." Similarly, Ippolito and Tweney (chapter 13) report that Einstein considered combinatory play of selected sensory experiences to be "an essential feature in productive thought."

Broad knowledge   In addition to having knowledge in one's own area of expertise, a number of researchers suggest it is important to have knowledge of a broad variety of areas, thereby enabling one to make connections that others might have missed (see Simonton, chapter 14; Dunbar, chapter 11; Sternberg & Lubart, chapter 16).

The ability to recognize analogies   Finally, and perhaps most importantly, the ability to find alternative problem approaches requires the ability to recognize analogies. As virtually all the contributors to this book observe, analogies represent one of the central sources of insight. From the perspective of the present discussion, the value of analogy is that it may enable the individual to conceptualize better the ill-defined problem space in which he or she is working by relating it to some other problem space that is better defined.

The ability to recognize analogies draws on many of the attributes listed previously. In addition, it seems likely to depend critically on the individual's skill at extracting the basic elements of a problem at a sufficient level of abstraction to enable the recognition of the problem's similarity to domains that superficially appear to have little in common with it (see Lee, 1991).

The Flash of Insight: Overcoming an Impasse and Sudden Solution

Having reviewed the mechanisms underlying the formation and overcoming of the impasses to insight, we now must confront the central question of insight (at least, when it is defined as the sudden shift from an impasse state to a solution state): How is it that the solver moves so suddenly from an impasse to a solution state? We share the view that the sources of the suddenness of insight are closely aligned with those associated with the suddenness of various perceptual processes. Throughout our previous discussion of the causes and techniques for overcoming impasses, we have attempted to draw parallels between the processes of insight and those of perception. As noted, these parallels permeate psychological theories as well as our everyday vocabulary and expressions. Nevertheless, some researchers remain skeptical about the parallels between the suddenness of insight and perception (e.g., Weisberg, 1986). We offer here some new evidence demonstrating these parallels and then explore their possible sources.

Further Evidence for the Perceptual Nature of Insight
We have used throughout our discussion the analogy relating insight to recognizing out-of-focus pictures. Like insights, recognition of out-of-focus pictures can be hampered by mental set (e.g., Bruner & Potter, 1964) and facilitated by a simple cue. Moreover, apprehension of the contents of an out-of-focus picture typically is experienced as a sudden shift from an absence of any sense of what is depicted to a full identification of the picture's contents and configural properties. Given these parallels, we wondered whether insight and recognition of out-of-focus pictures might actually draw on some shared cognitive processes. To test this theory, Schooler, McCleod, Brooks, and Melcher (1993; for discussion, see Schooler & Melcher, in press) conducted an individual-difference study, correlating subjects' performance on eight standard insight problems with their performance on a variety of cognitive measures including vocabulary, Scholastic Aptitude Test math and verbal tests, embedded figures, need for cognition, anagrams, remote associates, categorization speed, mental rotation, noninsight problem solving, and, most importantly, recognizing out-of-focus pictures. Of all these measures, recognizing out-of-focus pictures was the single best predictor of insight performance, with a correlation coefficient of 0.45 ($p < .001$). Thus, it appears that the suddenness of insight and perception may be associated with some shared cognitive processes.

Potential Shared Sources of Suddenness in Perception and Insight
Having, we hope, persuaded the reader that parallels between the suddenness of perception and insight are worthy of consideration, let us now explore what some of the mutual sources of suddenness might be.

Not consciously mediated   As Gruber (chapter 12) notes in drawing his analogy between insight and perceptual gap filling, both visual recognition and sudden insight share a "non-mediated quality.... That is, no intermediate process is detectable in conscious experience." The nonmediated quality of sudden insights is also a component of other researchers' characterizations. For example, Gick and Lockhart (chapter 6) discuss the final recognition of insight solutions as drawing on automatic, nonconscious processes. According to these authors, a "characteristic of insight is a transition to a solution state at least part of which does not involve conscious step-by-step reasoning." Similarly, Simon (1986) suggests that the suddenness of insight is comparable to the nonconsciously mediated process of recognition. Metcalfe's (1986) and Davidson's (chapter 4) results on the low warmth ratings preceding insight solutions further support the notion that subjects are not aware of the processes that induce insights. Additional empirical evidence for the nonmediated quality of many insights is suggested by a recent protocol analysis conducted by Schooler and Melcher (in press). In this study, we found that whereas a variety of elements of subjects' verbal protocols were predictive of noninsight problem-solving success, there was very little in the contents of subjects' insight problem-solving protocols that heralded success, suggesting that the critical processes were not reportable. The precise nature of the nonmediated recognition processes that lead to insight still need to be specified but, given the strong correlation between visual recognition abilities and insight recognition, it seems likely that pattern recognition processes may be involved in each. As our understanding of visual recognition mechanisms has become more highly advanced (e.g., Hopfield, 1982; Marr, 1982), it might be profitable to explore their applicability to the recognition of insight solutions.

Coherence   A second quality that characterizes the suddenness of both visual recognition and insight solutions is the seeming nonambiguity of the recognized product. When an out-of-focus picture is identified, it is with a strong sense of certainty. The experience is "Oh, of course, it is a_____." Similarly with many insight problems, when a solution becomes apparent, it seems clear that it is correct. In both cases, the source of the nonambiguity may result from certain distinctive properties of the situations that elicit sudden recognition. Specifically, the recognition of both insight solutions and out-of-focus pictures frequently share two qualities: First, prior to the solution, there are a number of problem elements that are presented together but lack coherence; second, when the solution is found, distinct coherence in the relationship between the problem elements is perceived. In the case of the out-of-focus picture, suddenly all the disparate shadings and features congeal to produce a single coherent image. Similarly with insight, when the solution is seen, all the parts suddenly seem to fit together. This analysis suggests that suddenness of both insight and visual recognition may be associated with situations for which there exists a potential source of coherence that can unite a seemingly disparate set of elements. Alternatively, rather than replacing a sense of noncoherence, as in the case of recognizing out-of-focus pictures or Feynman's making order out of chaos, insights may be associated with situations in which one coherent pattern can substitute for another. Such coherence substitutions may be comparable to reversible perceptual images such as necker cubes, in which "elements at one moment are seen as one unity; at the next moment, another unity appears with the same elements" (Ellen, 1982, p. 324). Many insight problems and riddles (e.g., Gick & Lockhart, chapter 6) may be associated with situations in which one constructs a coherent representation and then suddenly shifts to an alternative coherent representation.

The Gestalt psychologists referred to this coherence as the *gestalt*, a view that some have criticized owing to the lack of precision with which *gestalt* was defined (e.g., Weisberg & Alba, 1982). We suggest that the notion of gestalt or problem coherence simply be equated with the basic constructs of pattern recognition. In short, our cognitive information-processing systems may be structured to recognize coherent patterns of information in the environment in a manner comparable to that by which the visual system determines invariances in the visual world and uses its knowledge of those invariances to classify what it encounters. This view is supported by the work of Anderson and L. Schooler (1991), which suggests that memory is remarkably attuned to patterns of information in the environment in a manner comparable to that with which perception is sensitive to the invariances in the physical world (see also, Gibson, 1979; Marr, 1982).

RELATING INSIGHT TO OTHER TYPES OF THOUGHT

The question of the relationship of insight to other types of problem solving has been a source of some controversy. At one end of the spectrum is the suggestion that insight processes are outside the purview of cognitive science (e.g., Wertheimer, 1985). At the other end is the suggestion that insight is indistinguishable from other types of problem solving (e.g., Weisberg, 1986). However, the view represented by the majority of contributors to this book is that insight can be characterized within the framework of standard cognitive psychological constructs while at the same time being distinguished from other types of problem solving. Having already reviewed how insight may be conceptualized within the context of standard cognitive constructs, we now turn to how it may be distinguished from other types of problem solving.

Noninsight Problem Solving

A number of researchers have distinguished insight problem solving, which involves a sudden discovery of a solution, from noninsight problem solving, in which the would-be solver engages in a series of incremental arguments, each building on the past and leading gradually to a solution (e.g., Davidson, chapter 4; Metcalfe & Wiebe, 1987). Understanding the reason for this difference between insight and noninsight problem solving may be best accomplished by considering the respective sources of their difficulty. As suggested earlier, the fundamental difficulty for solving insight problems may be recognizing an approach that will lead to the solution. As we have argued, once the approach is recognized, the solution may be immediately apparent (but see discussion under the heading, Hybrid Problem Solving). Thus, the processes involved in insight problem solving are likely to be associated in large part with what we term *approach-recognition*, which entails identifying the possible operators that are available. In contrast, with noninsight problem solving, the correct approach to the problem may be recognized at the outset; however, the difficulty for solving these types of problems may be successfully executing the operators necessary to fulfill that approach. Thus, the processes involved in noninsight problem solving are likely to be associated in large part with what we term *approach-execution,* which involves successfully deciding among and executing the identified operators. In terms of the visual-spatial metaphor, the constraint for insight problem solving is to see where to go, whereas the constraint for noninsight problem solving is to move oneself successfully to the readily perceived destination.

This characterization of the differences between insight and noninsight problem solving suggests that the two types of problem solving should differentially rely on various skills. Insight problem solving should rely relatively more on pattern-recognition processes, whereas noninsight problem solving should rely more on reasoning skills and the ability to maintain a representation of where one is and where one is going. Recent findings in our laboratory support these predictions. In an individual-difference study we found that, although the recognition of out-of-focus pictures is highly correlated with insight problem solving, it is not significantly correlated with noninsight problem solving, which supports the notion that insight problem solving may rely particularly on the ability to recognize an effective approach, given seemingly disparate information. Evidence for the unique demands of noninsight problem solving was provided in our recent protocol analysis. Specifically, we found that, whereas the use of logical arguments was not predictive of successful insight problem solving, it was highly predictive of noninsight problem solving, which supports the notion that noninsight problem solving relies particularly on the ability to reason through a set of arguments. In addition, we found that frequently rereading the problem was negatively correlated with noninsight but not insight problem solving. This suggests that compared to insight problem solving, noninsight problem solving may place greater demands on the solvers' ability to maintain a representation of the problem conditions (where one started) and the goal conditions (where one needs to end up).

Hybrid Problem Solving

Insight problems may tend particularly to tap approach-recognition skills and noninsight problems approach-execution skills, but many problems may tap both types of skills. For example, although Davidson (chapter 4) found that her selective comparison and selective encoding problems behaved like typical insight problems with respect to warmth ratings (i.e., abrupt increase of warmth at the time of solution), her selective combination problems showed characteristics of both insight and noninsight problems. These elicited an initial abrupt increase in warmth ratings followed by a further gradual increase as the solution was approached. Such a pattern of results suggests that selective combination problems elicit the initial constraint of finding the correct problem approach but that once that approach is recognized, a number of operators still must be executed before the solution is found. As Davidson (chapter 4) notes, "Once they have an insight about how to reach a solution, subjects must still work out the details."

The alternation between the approach-recognition skills required for insight and the approach-execution skills required for noninsight problems seems to characterize most real-world types of problem solving. As many authors note, moments of inspiration (or approach-recognition) are typically intermingled with periods of fleshing out the inspiration. For example, Gruber (chapter 12) and Csikszentmihalyi and Sawyer (chapter 10) illustrate how inspirations typically occur within the context of a larger step-by-step analysis of a problem. Isaak and Just (chapter 9) suggest that inventions require the alternation between the generation of possible approaches to the problem and the subsequent analysis of the viability of those approaches. Finke (chapter 8) similarly suggests that invention may involve successive iterations of generation and exploration. In short, many creative endeavors may follow a cyclical process involving viewing the problem to determine where to go, implementing a set of procedures to get to the viewed destination, reviewing the problem from the new vantage point to determine the next step, and so on.

USING THE WRONG PROCESS AT THE WRONG TIME

The notion that creative thought can require alternations between approach-recognition and approach-execution raises the prospect that one might be led to engage in the wrong process at the wrong time. In fact, in a recent series of experiments, Schooler,

Ohlsson, and Brooks (1993) found evidence suggesting that the use of language, while suitable for the problem execution demands of noninsight problems, may lead subjects to fail to apply the nonreportable approach-recognition processes required by insight problems.

Over the past several years, our laboratory staff has been documenting the disruption that can ensue when subjects are asked to verbalize tasks associated with nonreportable processes. For example, in a number of studies, we have found that verbally describing a previously seen face can interfere with subjects' subsequent ability to recognize that face (e.g., Schooler & Engstler-Schooler, 1990; Fallshore & Schooler, submitted). Our interpretation of this result, termed *verbal overshadowing*, is that verbalization may emphasize verbalizable processes at the expense of nonverbalizable ones. Consistent with this view, we have found that verbalization disrupts a wide variety of tasks hypothesized to involve nonreportable processes, including color recognition (Schooler & Engstler-Schooler, 1990), taste judgments (Wilson & Schooler, 1991), aesthetic evaluations (Wilson, Lisle, Schooler, Hodges, Klaaren & Lafleur, 1993), visual imagery (Brandimonte, Hitch & Bishop, 1992; Brandimonte, Schooler & Gabbino, 1993), and implicit learning (Fallshore & Schooler, 1993). In contrast, verbalizalion does not seem to impair tasks that involve more readily verbalizable attributes, including statement-recognition (Schooler & Engstler-Schooler, 1990) and face-recognition situations that elicit consideration of relatively verbalizable individual features as opposed to the relatively nonverbalizable configural properties (Fallshore & Schooler, submitted).

Given that insight problem solving often is associated with nonreportable processes (including processes potentially highly comparable to perceptual recognition), Schooler, Ohlsson, and Brooks (1993) speculated that insight might also be vulnerable to verbalization. To explore this hypothesis, Schooler and colleaques had subjects engage in verbalization (thinking aloud) while solving insight and noninsight problems. Compared to the silent control subjects, subjects who verbalized were substantially less likely to solve the insight problems but exhibited no decrement on the noninsight problems. Schooler and colleagues' interpretation of this finding was that verbalization may have caused subjects to focus on the reportable reasoning process associated with noninsight problem solving, thereby interfering with the nonreportable approach-recognition processes required by insight problems.

CONCLUSION

The notion that verbalization may interfere with insight takes on particularly troubling dimensions in the context of a book on insight. Just as explaining a joke can cause it to lose its humor, discussants of insight may find it challenging to be insightful. Although the basic mechanisms of insight lend themselves to scientific scrutiny, we may still feel, when all is said and done, that something is missing. It seems likely that our understanding of the insight processes discussed in this book (such as forgetting, operator selection, representation construction, and perceptual pattern recognition) ultimately may be sufficient to characterize the basic aspects of insight such that we can program a computer to elicit insightful behavior (see Simon, 1986). However, even that level of explanation may still feel incomplete. Indeed, while we may be able to explain the source of the affective component of insight (for example, as resulting from the discovery of an unexpected coherence between seemingly disparate items), we may never be able to explain the feeling itself. One might approach a description of the feeling of insight through metaphor: For example, insight feels the way a blind person might after suddenly acquiring sight. However, in using metaphor, we must be ever cautious not to confuse the metaphor with the object being discussed. The feeling of insight may be similar to gaining sight, but it is not identical. The process of insight may mimic visual pattern recognition, but they remain distinct. So, too, insights may only resemble the insightful computer outputs to which scientific analyses such as those in this book may someday lead. The inability of any single metaphor to illuminate all of the facets of insight suggests that we should remain ever on the look out for alternative ways of viewing insight.

ACKNOWLEDGMENTS

This work was supported by a grant from the National Institute of Mental Health. We thank Merrill McSpaddenn, Carmi Schooler,

Maryanne Garry, and Earl Hunt for their helpful comments in discussions about this chapter. We also thank Tonya Schooler for her comments on an earlier draft.

REFERENCES

Anderson, J.R. (Ed.). (1981). *Cognitive skills and their acquisition*. Hillsdale, NJ: Erlbaum.

Anderson, J.R., & Schooler, L.J. (1991). Reflections of the environment in memory. *Psychological Science, 2*, 396–408.

Bower, G.H. (1981). Mood and memory. *American Psychologist, 36*, 129–148.

Bowers, K.S., Regehr, G., Balthazard, C., & Parker, K. (1990). Intuition in the context of discovery. Cognitive Psychology, 22, 72–110.

Brandimonte, M.A., Hitch, G.J., & Bishop, D.V.M. (1992). Influence of short-term memory codes on visual image processing: Evidence from image transformation tasks. *Journal of Experimental Psychology: Learning, Memory, and Cognition, 18*, 157–165.

Brandimonte, M.A., Schooler, J.W., & Gabbino, P. (1993, September). *Release from verbal overshadowing*. Paper presented at the European Society for Cognitive Psychology Conference, Copenhagen, Sweden.

Bruner, J., & Potter, M. (1964). Interference in visual recognition. *Science, 144* (24 April), 424–425.

Dunbar, K., & Schunn, C.D. (1990). The temporal nature of scientific discovery: The roles of priming and analogy. *Proceedings of the 12th Annual Meeting of the Cognitive Science Society*. Hillsdale, NJ: Erlbaum.

Ellen, P. (1982). Direction, past experience, and hints in creative problem solving: A reply to Weisberg and Alba. *Journal of Experimental Psychology: General, 111*, 316–325.

Fallshore, M., & Schooler, J.W. (1993). Post-encoding verbalization impairs transfer on artificial grammar tasks. *Proceedings of the 15th Annual Meeting of the Cognitive Science Society*. Hillsdale, NJ: Erlbaum.

Fallshore, M., & Schooler, J.W. *The verbal vulnerability of perceptual expertise*. Manuscript submitted for publication.

Gibson, J.J. (1979). *The ecological approach to visual perception*. Boston: Houghton Mifflin.

Hopfield, J.J. (1982). Neural networks and physical systems with emergent collective computational abilities. *Proceedings of the National Academy of Science, 79*, 2554–2558.

Kaplan, C.A., & Simon, H.A. (1990). In search of insight. *Cognitive Psychology, 22*, 374–419.

Langley, P., & Jones, R. (1988). A computational model of scientific insight. In R.J. Sternberg (Ed.), *The nature of creativity. Contemporary psychological perspectives* (pp. 177–201). Cambridge, England: Cambridge University Press.

Lee, J.S. (1991). *Abstraction and aging: A social psychological analysis.* New York: Springer-Verlag.

Lockhart, R.S., Lamon, M., & Gick, M. (1988). Conceptual transfer in simple insight problems. *Memory & Cognition, 16,* 36–44.

Maier, N.R.F. (1931). Reasoning in humans: II. The solution of a problem and its appearance in consciousness. *Journal of Comparative Psychology, 12,* 181–194.

Malpass, R.S., & Devine, P.G. (1981). Guided memory in eyewitness identification. *Journal of Applied Psychology, 3,* 343–350.

Marr, D. (1982). *Vision.* San Francisco: Freeman.

Metcalfe, J. (1986). Feeling of knowing in memory and problem solving. *Journal of Experimental Psychology: Learning, Memory, and Cognition, 12,* 288–294.

Metcalfe, J., & Wiebe, D. (1987). Intuition in insight and noninsight problem solving. *Memory & Cognition, 15,* 238–246.

Newell, A., & Simon, H.A. (1972). *Human problem solving.* Englewood Cliffs, NJ: Prentice Hall.

Ohlsson, S. (1984). Restructuring revisited: II. An information processing theory of restructuring and insight. *Scandinavian Journal of Psychology, 25,* 117–129.

Ohlsson, S. (1992). Information-processing explanations of insight and related phenomena. In M. Keane & K. Gilhooley (Eds.), *Advances in the psychology of thinking.* London: Harvester-Wheatsheaf.

Roediger, H.L.I. (1980). Memory metaphors in cognitive psychology. *Memory & Cognition, 8,* 231–246.

Schooler, J.W., & Melcher, J. (1993, November). *The ineffability of insight.* Paper presented at the Annual Meeting of the Psychonomic Society. Washington, D.C.

Schooler, J.W., & Engstler-Schooler, T.Y. (1990). Verbal overshadowing of visual memories: Some things are better left unsaid. *Cognitive Psychology, 22,* 36–71.

Schooler, J.W., McCleod, C., Brooks, K., & Melcher, J. (1993). [Individual differences in solving insight and analytical problems]. Unpublished raw data.

Schooler, J.W., & Melcher, J. (in press). The ineffability of insight. In S. Smith, T. Ward, & R. Finke (Eds.), *The creative cognition approach.* Cambridge: MIT Press.

Schooler, J.W., Ohlsson, S., & Brooks, K. (1993). Thoughts beyond words: When language overshadows insight. *Journal of Experimental Psychology: General, 122,* 166–183.

Simon, H.A. (1966). *Scientific discovery and the psychology of problem solving in mind and cosmos: Essays in contemporary science and philosophy.* Pittsburgh, PA: University of Pittsburgh Press.

Simon, H.A. (1986). The information processing explanation of Gestalt phenomena. *Computers in Human Behavior, 2,* 241–255.

Smith, S.M., Glenberg, A., & Bjork, R.A. (1978). Environmental context and human memory. *Memory & Cognition, 6,* 342–353.

Weisberg, R.W. (1986). *Creativity: Genius and other myths. What you, Mozart, Einstein, & Picasso have in common.* New York: Freeman.

Weisberg, R.W., & Alba, J.W. (1982). Problem solving is not like perception: More on Gestalt theory. *Journal of Experimental Psychology: General, 111,* 326–330.

Wertheimer, M. (1985). A Gestalt perspective on computer simulations of cognitive processes. *Computers in Human Behavior, 1,* 19–33.

Wilson, T.D., Lisle, D.J., Schooler, J.W., Hodges, S.D., Klaaren, K.J., & Lafleur, S.J. (1993). Introspecting about reasons can reduce post-choice satisfaction. *Personality and Social Psychology Bulletin, 19,* 331–339.

Wilson, T.D., & Schooler, J.W. (1991). Thinking too much: Introspection can reduce the quality of preferences and decisions. *Journal of Personality and Social Psychology, 60,* 181–192.

Woodworth, R.S. (1938). *Experimental psychology.* New York: Henry Holt.

Yaniv, I., & Meyer, D.E. (1987). Activation and metacognition of inaccessible stored information: Potential bases for incubation effects in problem solving. *Journal of Experimental Psychology: Learning, Memory, and Cognition, 13,* 187–205.

Contributors

Mihaly Csikszentmihalyi
Department of Psychology
University of Chicago
Chicago, Illinois

Pamela Dallob
Department of Psychology
University of
Illinois at Chicago
Chicago, Illinois

Janet E. Davidson
Department of Psychology
Lewis & Clark College
Portland, Oregon

Natalie Davidson
Department of Psychology
University of Michigan
Ann Arbor, Michigan

Roger L. Dominowski
Department of Psychology
University of
Illinois at Chicago
Chicago, Illinois

Kevin Dunbar
Department of Psychology
McGill University
Montreal, Québec

Marte Fallshore
Learning Research and
Development Center
University of Pittsburgh
Pittsburgh, Pennsylvania

Ronald A. Finke
Department of Psychology
Texas A&M University
College Station, Texas

Stephen M. Fiore
Learning Research and
Development Center
University of Pittsburgh
Pittsburgh, Pennsylvania

Mary L. Gick
Department of Psychology
Carleton University
Ottawa, Ontario

Howard E. Gruber
Department of Developmental
and Educational Psychology
Teachers College, Columbia
University
New York, New York

Maria F. Ippolito
Department of Psychology
Bowling Green State University
Bowling Green, Ohio

Matthew I. Isaak
Department of Psychology
Carnegie-Mellon University
Pittsburgh, Pennsylvania

Marcel Adam Just
Department of Psychology
Carnegie-Mellon University
Pittsburgh, Pennsylvania

Robert S. Lockhart
Department of Psychology
University of Toronto
Toronto, Ontario

Todd I. Lubart
Department of Psychology
Yale University
New Haven, Connecticut

Richard E. Mayer
Department of Psychology
University of California
Santa Barbara, California

Janet Metcalfe
Department of Psychology
Dartmouth College
Hanover, New Hampshire

David E. Meyer
Department of Psychology
University of Michigan
Ann Arbor, Michigan

Andrea L. Patalano
Department of Psychology
University of Michigan
Ann Arbor, Michigan

David N. Perkins
Graduate School of Education
Harvard University
Cambridge, Massachusetts

Keith Sawyer
Department of Psychology
University of Chicago
Chicago, Illinois

Jonathan W. Schooler
Learning Research and
Development Center
University of Pittsburgh
Pittsburgh, Pennsylvania

Colleen M. Seifert
Department of Psychology
University of Michigan
Ann Arbor, Michigan

Dean Keith Simonton
Department of Psychology
University of California, Davis
Davis, California

Steven M. Smith
Department of Psychology
Texas A&M University
College Station, Texas

Robert J. Sternberg
Department of Psychology
Yale University
New Haven, Connecticut

Ryan D. Tweney
Department of Psychology
Bowling Green State University
Bowling Green, Ohio

Robert W. Weisberg
Department of Psychology
Temple University
Philadelphia, Pennsylvania

Ilan Yaniv
School of Business
University of Chicago
Chicago, Illinois

Author Index

Subject Index

Accommodation, 427
Acquired immunodeficiency
  syndrome (AIDS), 539
Affect
  insight and, 421–427
  similarities, noticing, 223
Affective components
  insight and, 202–203
  of problem solving, 225
"Aha!" reaction, 166, 213, 214,
  225, 232. *See also* Suddenness of
  insight
AIDS (acquired immunodeficiency
  syndrome), 539
Algorithms, 472
Anagrams, 45–46
Analogical concept formation, increasing constraint satisfaction
  and, 440
Analogical play, 305–308
Analogic transfer, 271
Analogy/analogies, 213
  analyzing, 308–309
  conceptual change and, 381–384
  expertise and, 385–386
  generation of operators, 294
  implicit, 304–305
  recognizing, in finding alternative
  approaches, 576
  selective comparison and, 128–
  129
  social structure and, 384–385
  understanding and, 38
Analytical creativity, 354
Analytical problem solving, 296–
  299

Anecdotes, 469–470
"Animalcule", microscopical, 454–
  455
Animals in pens brainteaser/riddle,
  192
Answering, of problematic factual
  questions, 95–102
Approach-execution skills, 581,
  582
Approach-recognition skills, 580,
  582
Area problems/solutions, 22–23
Artificial evolution, 519
Artificial intelligence, 278, 500,
  501
Artificial selection, 497
Assimilation, 427
  in illumination phase, 117–118
  in incubation phase, 87–88
Associationism, 6
Associationist theory, 12
Associations, 482–483
Attack-and-dispersion situation,
  78
Attitude for insight, 535–536
Attribute finding, 274
Automatization, 205, 206
Awareness, 476

Banana problem, 11
Basketball brainteaser/riddle, 192
Benzene ring discovery, 115
Birds, evolution of, 502–504
Bisociation, 473
Blind variations, 466, 467, 475
Blue-chip stocks, 545–546